SOCIAL WORK PROCESSES

SOCIAL WORK PROCESSES

BEULAH ROBERTS COMPTON
University of Minnesota, Minneapolis

and

BURT GALAWAY
University of Minnesota, Duluth

 1975

The Dorsey Press *Homewood, Illinois 60430*

Irwin-Dorsey Limited Georgetown, Ontario L7G 4B3

First Printing, January 1975
Second Printing, July 1975
Third Printing, September 1975
Fourth Printing, February 1976
Fifth Printing, August 1976
Sixth Printing, November 1976

ISBN 0-256-01676-3
Library of Congress Catalog Card No. 74–18710

Printed in the United States of America

*Dedicated to those
from whom we have learned much—
our families, the clients with whom we have worked,
and the students we have known.*

PREFACE

This book is intended for those who are beginners in the process of learning to be competent social workers. This may include B. A. students, individuals who have entered practice without an undergraduate preparation in college and are now anxious to learn about the work they are doing, or M.S.W. students who are beginning their graduate preparation.

Our purpose in developing this text is to present to the beginning social work student, or to the beginning practitioner, a basic set of concepts and principles from which he or she may be able to develop a foundation of general practice knowledge. It is our belief that what is presented here is both basic enough and realistic enough that, once integrated by the student, it will serve as the foundation for a more elaborate and sophisticated structure of social work competence as the beginner accumulates more experience as both a learner and a practitioner. Our goal is to present a text that describes and analyzes the elements of practice—organized within a problem solving framework—in such a way that the student not only intellectually grasps the nature of social work processes, but also gains some knowledge of the trials and tribulations, joys and satisfactions of social work practice in today's world.

The selection and organization of knowledge in the field of social work is a perennial problem, and probably will continue to plague the profession. We believe that there are at least four large areas of knowledge that the competent social work practitioner will have integrated into his own practice formulations: (1) theories of man and society and their interaction which will help him to answer such questions as how does the individual and his social systems grow, develop, stabilize, change, function and dysfunction, and what is the effect of each upon the other, (2) knowledge of social work as a profession, and something of its history that takes into consideration the societal context within which it has developed and functioned over time, (3) knowledge of social welfare agencies, institutions, delivery systems, or other organized structures within which social work services have, over time, been lodged; and the effect of the structure and function of these delivery systems upon the way problems have been defined and the way social work practice has been shaped, (4) the nature of social work practice itself which includes some historical perspective of the development of the various practice modalities, general concepts, and principles of the practice processes, and a more sophisticated and specialized practice competence. It was our decision, in keeping with our purpose, that we would focus on the nature of the basic social work processes within this fourth area of knowledge, recognizing that this one volume will not "a social worker make."

The text is organized into 13 chapters. Each begins with the authors' development of the notions and concepts to be dealt with in that particular chapter. This material is followed by two or three reprints of the works of other authors that relate to the issues of that chapter. Each chapter ends with a brief annotated bibliography. The first five chapters of the text deal with the basic concepts of all social work processes. The last seven chapters present a specific model of social work practice and the processes that make the model work.

The readings at the end of each chapter are not presumed to be a representative sample of the literature. They were selected to complement the authors' statement so that the book would stand as a text built upon the authors' approach to social work processes. We attempted to select reprints that would contribute to the richness or the sense of complexity of the issues developed in each particular chapter. From the vast amount of material available, our goal was to select examples that would (in combination with the authors' work) give students a realistic, intellectual grasp of the nature of social work processes and that might serve to raise questions for further work or discussion.

We cannot predict the future of the profession, or the knowledge and skill that the future will demand of those who would practice in the name of social work—so we have developed this text to present what we see as the processes of the profession in today's world. It is precisely because we do not know what problems the future will present to the workers of tomorrow that we believe in the problem solving framework for practice. Such a model recognizes the inherent uniqueness of each problem while recognizing the function of knowledge. It is a relatively open framework which not only allows for use of current knowledge but allows for the integration of new knowledge, and, in fact, encourages seeking after the new. It demands the careful consideration of problem definition and goals in such a way that client system and practitioner become partners, and it demands a continual monitoring of service outcomes and client goal achievement. We have tried to present the material, and have selected and organized the readings and bibliographies, to stimulate the beginning of a journey toward professional competence rather than to present an arrived at destination.

We are indebted to so many people who have helped us in our own professional development, challenged our thinking, and supported us in the development of this book that we cannot possibly mention them all. So we must select only a few. First, we must recognize the contributions of our families, the social work professors we have had, the clients and others with whom we have worked professionally, and the students we have known. All of these persons, individually and collectively, have served as a source of learning and stimulation for use.

We wish to thank our colleagues of our two schools of social work who offered many insights and ideas and gave generously of their time in reading and commenting on the manuscript. We especially wish to thank professors Helen Yesner and Annalee Stewart who used the manuscript in their classes during this last year, and thus could give us live and objective feedback from both undergraduate and beginning graduate classes as to its utility.

We want to thank our own students of the last three years who have reacted with both criticism and support to the bits and pieces of the manuscript as they have appeared in their assigned readings, and especially the beginning graduate students of this last year who have read and discussed the completed manuscript with us.

We owe special thanks to the reviewers who commented on the manuscript as it was in process and on the finished document: Rhonda Connaway, School of Social Work, Washington University; Sheldon Gelman, School of Social Work, Pennsylvania State University; Gwendolyn C. Gilbert, School of Social Work, The Ohio State University; H. Wayne Johnson, School of Social Work, University of Iowa; Sylvia Krakow, School of Social Work, Boston University; and Louis Lowy, School of Social Work, Boston University. Their willingness to take time to read and share their thinking about the work resulted in strengthening the manuscript. Those who generously gave us permission to reprint their articles or to quote from their writings deserve acknowledgement and gratitude. Their generosity has contributed greatly to the strength of the text. Without their willingness to share, the book would be quite different. In spite of such generous help from others, we must accept the final, sole responsibility for the content of this text.

Wendy Gaskill as the chief typist, Jan Goodno, Sue Nelson, and Sue Newlin who ably assisted her deserve special recognition and our most heartfelt thanks, not only for typing the manuscript, but for taking care of the myriad of details with cheerfulness, calmness, and efficiency. Alice Chen, a social work teaching assistant, was most efficient in locating fugitive materials, supervising reprint reproduction, and in helping in any way she could. We also wish to acknowledge the contribution of Georgia Ann Guevara, Larry Ray, Pamela Jones and Elsie Fairchild, teaching assistants at the School of Social Work, University of Southern Mississippi, who assisted with the indexing.

This book is the result of our collaborative efforts as fellow faculty members at the University of Minnesota Schools of Social Work. We have found both teaching and writing together to be a fruitful venture in cooperation in the fullest sense of the word. The fact that one name precedes the other in the listing of the two authors does not in any way indicate that one member of the team is a senior author and one member a junior. The listing of the names is simply the result of an accident of the alphabet.

Together we have 15 years of practice experience representing the fields of public assistance, child welfare (with emphasis on foster care and protective services), corrections, day care, and private family agencies. We have held positions ranging from beginning B.A. workers to M.S.W. workers to supervisor to associate executive. Between us we have had 25 years of teaching experience in both class and field. The classroom experience includes continuing education courses and numerous institutes and workshops for employed practitioners, undergraduate teaching in the fields of social work practice and social welfare policy, M.S.W. classes in both general practice and specific practice modalities, and Ph.D. seminars. This book has come from this experience and from our desire to introduce others to a profession that we have found so challenging and stimulating.

December 1974   BEULAH ROBERTS COMPTON
                                                       BURT GALAWAY

CONTRIBUTORS

BARTLETT, HARRIETT, M.   M.A., University of Chicago. Formerly Professor, Simmons College School of Social Work, Boston.

BOLMAN, WILLIAM.   M.D., Harvard Medical School. Currently Professor of Psychiatry, University of Hawaii School of Medicine, Honolulu.

BROWN, ROBERT.   D.S.W., University of Southern California. Currently in private practice at Alhambra Psychiatric Hospital, Rosemead, California.

COMPTON, BEULAH ROBERTS.   Ph.D., University of Chicago. Currently Professor, School of Social Work, University of Minnesota, Minneapolis.

FOX, EVELYN E.   M.S.W., University of Wisconsin, Madison. Currently Social Worker, Development Evaluation Center, Central Wisconsin Colony, Madison.

GARWICK, GEOFFREY.   M.A., Hartford Seminary. Currently Dissemination, Consultation, and Utilization Coordinator, Program Evaluation Resource Center, Minneapolis, Minnesota.

GERMAIN, CAREL B.   D.S.W., Columbia University. Currently Professor of Social Work, Columbia University School of Social Work, New York.

GORDON, WILLIAM E.   ACSW. Ph.D., University of Minnesota. Currently Professor of Research in Social Work, George Warren Brown School of Social Work, Washington University, St. Louis, Missouri.

GROSSER, CHARLES.   D.S.W., Columbia University School of Social Work. Currently Professor, Columbia University School of Social Work, New York.

HALLECK, SEYMOUR.   M.D., University of Chicago. Currently Professor of Psychiatry, University of North Carolina, Chapel Hill.

xi

HANLON, ARCHIE.   D.S.W., University of California, Berkeley. At time of death, Associate Professor, University of Pennsylvania School of Social Work, Philadelphia.

HARTMAN, ANN.   D.S.W., School of Social Work, Columbia University. Currently Associate Professor, School of Social Work, University of Michigan, Ann Arbor.

HOBBS, NICHOLAS.   Ph.D., Ohio State University. Currently Provost, Vanderbilt University, Nashville, Tennessee.

HUDSON, JOE.   Ph.D., University of Minnesota. Currently Director of Planning and Research, Minnesota Department of Corrections, St. Paul.

INBERG, AVIVA, C.   Student, School of Social Work, University of Minnesota, Minneapolis.

JOHNSON, WENDELL.   Ph.D., University of Iowa. At time of death, Professor Emeritus of Speech Pathology and Psychology, University of Iowa, Iowa City.

KADUSHIN, ALFRED.   Ph.D., New York University. Currently Professor of Social Work, University of Wisconsin, Madison.

KIRESUK, THOMAS J.   Ph.D., University of Minnesota. Currently Chief Clinical Psychologist of Hennepin County Mental Health Service (Minneapolis, Minnesota) and Principle Investigator of National Institute of Mental Health Funded Program Evaluation Resource Center.

KRAMER, RALPH M.   D.S.W., University of California, Berkeley. Currently Professor, School of Social Welfare, University of California, Berkeley.

MALUCCIO, ANTHONY N.   M.S.W. and Doctoral Candidate, Columbia University School of Social Work. Currently Associate Professor, University of Connecticut School of Social Work, West Hartford.

MARLOW, WILMA D.   M.S.W., Columbia University School of Social Work. At time of death, Assistant Professor, University of Connecticut School of Social Work, West Hartford.

McPHEETERS, HAROLD.   M.D., University of Louisville. Currently Director, Commission on Mental Illness and Retardation, Southern Regional Education Board, Atlanta, Georgia.

MILLER, HENRY.   D.S.W., Columbia University. Currently Associate Professor, School of Social Welfare, University of California, Berkeley.

NELSON, MARIAN A.   M.S.W., University of Wisconsin, Madison. Currently in private practice, Seattle, Washington.

PATTI, RINO J.   D.S.W., University of Southern California. Currently Associate Professor, University of Washington School of Social Work, Seattle.

PHILLIPS, DORIS.   D.S.W., George Warren Brown School of Social Work of Washington University. Currently engaged in research on the history of day care in the United States.

PURCELL, FRANCIS P.   M.S.W., Denver University. Currently professor of social work, San Francisco State University, San Francisco, California.

REISTROFFER, MARY. M.S.W., Loyola University, Chicago. Currently Associate Professor, Center for Social Service, University of Wisconsin Extension, Milwaukee.

RESNICK, HERMAN. Ph.D., Bryn Mawr College School of Social Work. Currently Associate Professor, School of Social Work, University of Washington, Seattle.

RUTMAN, LEONARD. Ph.D., University of Minnesota. Currently Assistant Professor, School of Social Work, Carleton University, Ottawa, Canada.

RYAN, ROBERT. D.S.W., University of Denver. Currently Associate Professor, School of Social Work, Ohio State University, Columbus.

SALOMON, ELIZABETH. M.S.W., University of California at Berkeley. Currently Caseworker, Child Study Center, Cleveland Metropolitan General Hospital, Cleveland, Ohio.

SCHWARTZ, WILLIAM. Ed.D., Teachers College, Columbia University. Currently Professor of Social Work, Columbia University School of Social Work, New York.

SPECHT, HARRY. Ph.D., Brandeis University. Currently professor, School of Welfare, University of California, Berkeley.

SPITZER, KURT. M.S.W., Wayne State University School of Social Work. Currently Associate Professor, Wayne State University School of Social Work, Detroit, Michigan.

TABER, RICHARD H. M.S.S. (Applied), Case Western Reserve University. Currently Assistant Professor, Southern Connecticut State College, New Haven, Connecticut.

WELSH, BETTY. M.S.W., University of Pittsburgh. Currently Associate Professor, School of Social Work, Wayne State University, Detroit, Michigan.

CONTENTS

INTRODUCTION   1

1. THE FOCUS OF SOCIAL WORK INTERVENTION   5

Focus of social work intervention. The casework, group work, and community organization conceptualization of social work activities. The orientation of this book.

The social worker in the group   *William Schwartz,* 17
A systems approach to the delivery of mental health services
in black ghettos   *Richard H. Taber,* 38

2. SOURCES AND FUNCTIONS OF KNOWLEDGE   50

Definition of terms. Development of knowledge and theory in social work. Function of knowledge in social work practice. General systems theory as a conceptual framework: *The open system. Boundaries. Tension. Feedback and purposive systems. Change and stability.* Potential values of systems theory. Is knowledge necessary? Criteria for the selection of knowledge. Dealing with incomplete knowledge.

Knowledge and value: Their distinction and relationship in
clarifying social work practice   *William E. Gordon,* 74
Social work curriculum   *Council on Social Work Education,* 84
To think about the unthinkable   *Ann Hartman,* 89

3. **VALUES IN SOCIAL WORK PRACTICE**   102

What is meant by social work value? Respect for the dignity and uniqueness of the individual. Client self-determination.

>   Code of ethics   *National Association of Social Workers,* 116
>   Value dilemmas in social casework   *Henry Miller,* 117
>   Humanistic values and social casework   *Elizabeth L. Salomon,* 127

4. **THE SOCIAL WORK RELATIONSHIP**   138

A review of the literature. Social work roles and relationship. Purpose as an element of relationship. Development of relationship. Elements of the relationship: *Concern for the other. Commitment and obligation. Acceptance and expectation. Empathy. Authority and power. Genuineness and congruence. Rational and irrational elements in the helping relationship.* The helping person: *Maturing people. Creativity. Capacity to observe self. Desire to help. Courage. Sensitivity.* Race and the social work relationship.

>   The impact of professional dishonesty on behavior of
>   disturbed adolescents   *Seymour L. Halleck,* 170
>   Being understanding and understood: Or how to find a
>   wandered horse   *Wendell Johnson,* 181

5. **COMMUNICATION AND INTERVIEWING**   192

Communication and interviewing. Barriers to communication. Responsibilities of the worker. Some ideas about technique.

>   Feedback in family interviewing   *Robert A. Brown,* 206
>   The racial factor in the interview   *Alfred Kadushin,* 216

6. **PROBLEM SOLVING: A MODEL FOR SOCIAL
    WORK PRACTICE**   233

Dewey and problem solving. Problem solving and the practitioner's responsibility. The client system and problem solving. Basic assumptions of the model. Presentation of the problem-solving outline. Outline of problem-solving model—short form. Outline of problem-solving model—long form.

>   A problem focused model of practice   *Kurt Spitzer and
>   Betty Welsh,* 253
>   Social study: Past and future   *Carel B. Germain,* 263

7. **THE CONTACT PHASE: PROBLEM IDENTIFICATION,
    INITIAL GOAL SETTING, AND DATA COLLECTION**   275

Getting started. Defining the problem. Goal setting. Preliminary contract. Areas of data collection. Sources and methods of data collection.

Of plums and thistles: The search for diagnosis   *Doris Campbell Phillips,* 292

The house on Sixth Street   *Francis P. Purcell and Harry Specht,* 301

8. **THE CONTRACT PHASE: JOINT ASSESSMENT, GOAL SETTING, AND PLANNING**   312

Definition of the service contract. Joint assessment and decision making. Setting goals. Planning for intervention.

Professional judgment in assessment   *Harriett M. Bartlett,* 320

The case for the contract   *Anthony N. Maluccio and Wilma D. Marlow,* 326

9. **INTERVENTIVE ROLES: IMPLEMENTATION OF THE PLAN**   339

The concept of interventive roles. The social broker role. The enabler role. The advocate role. Roles are not functional specializations.

Social welfare objectives and roles   *Harold L. McPheeters and Robert M. Ryan,* 348

Community development programs serving the urban poor   *Charles F. Grosser,* 351

Sources of gain in psychotherapy   *Nicholas Hobbs,* 360

The social worker as advocate: Champion of social victims   *The Ad Hoc Committee on Advocacy, National Association of Social Workers,* 371

10. **EVALUATION**   382

Continuous client evaluation. Assisting with program evaluation.

Basic goal attainment scaling procedures   *Thomas J. Kiresuk and Geoffrey Garwick,* 388

Family-worker joint goal evaluation   *Beulah Roberts Compton,* 401

Evaluating human services process approach   *Leonard Rutman and Joe Hudson,* 407

11. **THE ENDING PHASE: REFERRAL, TRANSFER, AND TERMINATION**   422

Referral. Transfer. Termination.

The termination process: A neglected dimension in social work   *Evelyn F. Fox, Marian A. Nelson, and William M. Bolman,* 431

12. **THE NATURE OF TEAMWORK**   446

The problem of competition. The problem of professional and agency culture. The problem-solving approach to teamwork. Methods of planning and sharing.

Dynamics of teamwork in the agency, community, and
    neighborhood *Ralph M. Kramer,* 454
On reducing contention between foster family parents and
    child-placing agencies *Mary Reistroffer,* 464

**13. THE SOCIAL WORKER, THE PROFESSION, AND THE
BUREAUCRATIC STRUCTURE**   **472**

The interstitial profession. The bureaucratic organization. Conflicts between the bureaucracy and the professional. Types of bureaucrats. Agency
bureaucracy and the worker. Client, worker, and bureaucracy. Changing
the bureaucracy. The profession as a system.

Casework beyond bureaucracy *Archie Hanlan,* 492
Changing the agency from within *Rino J. Patti and
    Herman Resnick,* 499

14. CONCLUSIONS   **513**

Social work as a problem-solving process. Social work as a client–worker
relationship. Social work as a rational process. The beginning.

A student's view of social work *Aviva C. Inberg,* 516

INDEX   **525**

INTRODUCTION

Climactic changes occurred in social work and social work education during the late 1960s and early 1970s. For the first time since 1939 undergraduate social work education was officially recognized, standards were set, and accreditation of undergraduate programs by the Council on Social Work Education was instituted. Bachelor's degree social workers from accredited programs are afforded full membership rights in the National Association of Social Workers, and, reflecting the increasing social consciousness of youth, large numbers of students are enrolling in proliferating social work courses.

From these students has risen a frequent and reasonable demand to be taught something about how social workers engage in practice and serve as agents of change. What is the nature of social work intervention? What is its purpose? How is it carried out? And what are the processes through which the social worker and the client move? In this book an effort is made to identify, conceptualize, and organize certain common elements of social work practice so that they can be logically and systematically examined by a student exploring the potentials of an exciting profession. This book rests on the assumption that common social work processes can be identified—processes which can be applicable to workers regardless of the setting (corrections, mental health, schools, public welfare, etc.) or the "relational system" (individual, family, small group, community) in which they practice.

As used here, process may be defined as "a series of actions, changes,

1

or functions that bring about an end or result."[1] Thus we will be examining actions the social worker takes in conjunction with clients to bring about planned change. Client, in this context, will take on a generic meaning and refer to those for whom the worker offers professional services, including individuals, families, small groups, and communities.

As a text-reader the book is an effort to combine the advantages of both textbooks and readers. Thirteen extensive chapter introductions provide continuity and integration, and set forth the viewpoints of the authors. Selected readings in each chapter provide additional perspective and introduce the student to part of the related social work literature.

Underlying the author's viewpoint are five further assumptions:

1. As a human service profession, social work shares with other human service professions, as well as with many elements of the society at large, a common set of values concerning the dignity of man, the right to equal opportunity, and the qualities of justice. The different human service professions may, however, operationalize these values differently; the way in which they are operationalized for social work is the particular concern of this book.

2. The goals of social work intervention are the solving of specific, particular problems experienced by individuals, groups, or communities in their attempts to resolve discrepancies in their social existence or to achieve their social goals. The term *problem* is defined in the most basic sense as "a question or group of questions that need to be resolved" and does not necessarily carry implications of fault, blame, or weakness.

3. Self is the basic tool used by the worker in mobilizing resources within the client and the community in order to alter the interaction of the two.

4. The breadth of the social work profession requires that practitioners develop skill and knowledge in a wide range of content areas.

5. The problem-solving focus of social work is best carried out in a partnership arrangement between worker and client. This partnership arrangement holds major implications for the processes of problem formulation, data collection, assessment, planning, and intervention.

Social work practice occurs within the framework of an agency. This book, however, does not focus on agency services. The focus instead is on the actions of the social worker to bring about change, and the book is offered as an aid for learning beginning social work practice skills. These skills require the application of professional knowledge and principles to unique human situations. Because each situation is unique, the application of such knowledge and principles always involves the utilization of an elusive quality—judgment. For professional social

---

[1] *American Heritage Dictionary of the English Language* (Boston: Houghton Mifflin, 1973), p. 1043.

workers, judgment develops with maturity, experience, and continued learning.

Judgment is to be distinguished from intellectual capacity. It might be defined as the ability to make the most effective choice among alternatives which professional knowledge, perception as developed by knowledge and experience, and informed "hunches" present for one's decision. Professional judgment develops through personal maturity and continual learning from one's experiences, from exposure to new knowledge, and from encounters with a wide range of professional problems and relationships. The struggle toward professional judgment and professional skills in acting is a lifelong educational experience in which no one ever fully arrives. The authors certainly do not conceive of themselves as fully developed "knowers," but rather as "seekers after knowledge" who have mastered valuable concepts in their journey. This book is an attempt to share selected knowledge and principles related to basic social work processes. It is a beginning book that should provide students with a coherent framework for beginning practice. Whole books could be, and have been, written about each of its chapters.

This is not a book of rules or an easy do-it-yourself manual. The authors do not believe that the social work student can be supplied with a set of rules to be invariably followed. What is offered is a set of principles, processes in which the principles can be applied, and an opportunity to begin developing skill and judgment in their application. In this sense this book and social work are in the best of the liberal arts tradition—a tradition which requires the disciplined exercise of judgment.

Chapter 1

THE FOCUS OF SOCIAL
WORK INTERVENTION

What do social workers do? Where and how do they intervene? For most of us these are perplexing questions—questions made more perplexing by our lack of contact with social workers and the diffuseness of social work practice. From life experiences most of us have little difficulty identifying the job of the doctor as healing the body—mediating between the physical organism and environmental influences which threaten health. (The doctor's job becomes much less clear and less understood when he moves out of the area of physical illness and into the treatment of alleged mental illness.) Likewise, the lawyer's job as mediator between the individual and the legal institutions which have been developed to insure a reasonably orderly society is usually understood. And few of us, because of our life experiences, have any difficulty identifying the job of the teacher in transmitting the accumulated knowledge of the culture. But what about social workers? What is their job?

William Schwartz, in the article reproduced in this chapter, takes the viewpoint that "every profession has a particular function to perform in society: it has received a certain job assignment for which it is held accountable."[1] To Schwartz the social work job assignment is to "mediate the process through which the individual and his society reach out for each other through a mutual need for self-fulfillment."[2] The Schwartz mediating model rests on the assumption that the interests of the indi-

---

[1] William Schwartz, "The Social Worker in the Group," *The Social Welfare Forum, 1961* (New York: Columbia University Press, 1961), pp. 150–51.

[2] Ibid., pp. 154–55.

vidual and the interests of society are essentially the same, but that in a complex and changing society the individual's desire to belong as a full and productive member and the society's ability to integrate and enrich its people are sometimes blocked. Social work intervention is directed toward these blockages and toward freeing the "individual's impetus toward health, growth, and belonging; and the organized efforts of society to integrate its parts into a productive and dynamic whole."[3]

This first chapter has three objectives:

1. The focus of social work intervention will be further explored in light of Schwartz's mediating model.
2. The organization of social work actions in the traditional format of casework, group work, and community organization will be considered in light of this focus of social work intervention.
3. An alternative view of social work actions will be identified. This view will become the focus for the balance of the book.

FOCUS OF SOCIAL WORK INTERVENTION

Martin Rein suggests that one of the obstacles to the development of a professional social work creed has been difficulty in defining the social work profession.[4] Nevertheless, efforts have been made to define both the target and the nature of social work practice. In 1958 a commission of the National Association of Social Workers published a working definition which defined social work practice as a "constellation of value, purpose, sanction, knowledge, and method."[5] The working definition identified three purposes of social work practice:

1. To assist individuals and groups to identify and resolve or minimize problems arising out of disequilibrium between themselves and the environment.
2. To identify potential areas of disequilibrium between individuals or groups and the environment in order to prevent the occurrence of disequilibrium.
3. In addition to these curative and preventive aims, to seek out, identify, and strengthen the maximum potential in individuals, groups, and communities.[6]

---

[3] Ibid., p. 155.

[4] Martin Rein, "Social Work in Search of a Radical Profession," *Social Work* 15:2 (April 1970), p. 15.

[5] Commission on Social Work Practice, National Association of Social Workers, "Working Definition of Social Work Practice," *Social Work* 3:2 (April 1958), p. 5.

[6] Ibid., p. 6.

Also in 1958 Werner Boehm published a widely used definition of social work:

> Social work seeks to enhance the social functioning of individuals, singularly and in groups, by activities focused upon their social relationships which constitute interaction between man and his environment. These activities can be grouped into three functions: restoration of impaired capacity, provision of individual and social resources, and prevention of social dysfunction.[7]

Both of these definitions clearly place the focus of social work intervention on the interaction or disequilibrium between man and his environment. In this sense both are consistent with Schwartz's mediating approach, inasmuch as they consider social work as in some way intervening or mediating between people and their social environments.

Harriett Bartlett writes of a social work focus on social functioning, which she defines as the "relation between the coping activity of people and the demand from the environment."[8] For Bartlett the concept of social functioning does not refer to the functioning of individuals or groups, which she finds characteristic of earlier definitions, but "attention is now directed primarily to what goes on between people and environment through the exchange between them. This dual focus ties them together. Thus person and situation, people and environment, are encompassed in a single concept, which requires that they be constantly reviewed together."[9]

William Gordon, with whom Bartlett is in agreement, finds that "the central focus of social work traditionally seems to have been on the person in his life situation complex—a simultaneous dual focus on man and environment."[10] From this Gordon notes that

> Emphasis has been on individualizing the person-situation complex in order to achieve the best match between each person and his environment, in which either person-behavior or environmental situation may deviate widely from the typical or normative. We conclude, therefore, that the central target of technical social work practice is *matching* something in person and situation—that is, intervening by whatever methods and means necessary to help people be in situations where

---

[7] Werner W. Boehm, "The Nature of Social Work," *Social Work* 3:2 (April 1958), p. 18.

[8] Harriett M. Bartlett, *The Common Base of Social Work Practice* (New York: National Association of Social Workers, 1970), p. 116.

[9] Ibid., p. 116.

[10] William E. Gordon, "Basic Constructs for an Integrative and Generative Conception of Social Work," in *The General Systems Approach: Contributions toward an Holistic Conception of Social Work,* ed. Gordon Hearn (New York: Council on Social Work Education, 1969), p. 6.

their capabilities are sufficiently matched with the demands of the situations to "make a go of it."[11]

The focus of social work intervention is on the interaction between humans and their environments. In Schwartz's terms social workers mediate; in Gordon's terms social workers match something in environment to something in person; and in Bartlett's terms social workers seek to strike a balance between people's coping ability and environmental demands. Social workers may at times direct change strategies toward individuals, may at times direct change strategies toward the environment, and may at times direct change strategies toward the interaction of individual and environment. But in all cases, these strategies are directed toward changing the nature of the person-situation interaction.

But does changing the nature of the interaction mean changing the individual or changing the environment? This is an old issue in social work which was enunciated at an early date by Porter Lee in his distinction between social work as cause and social work as function.[12] Our contention is that social workers do both and that the debate as to whether the profession should focus primarily on individual change or primarily on environmental change results from a largely incorrect formulation of the focus of social work intervention. The parties to this debate tend to perceive social workers as either focusing on the individual or on the environment and miss the central focus on the interaction of the two. Gisela Konopka has pointed out the inappropriateness of this dichotomous thinking in social work,[13] and Martin Rein notes that both individual and social change approaches can be used to either support or challenge contemporary standards of behavior.[14] Recent research by Merlin A. Taber and Anthony J. Vattano finds no sharp distinction between clinical and social orientations among practicing social workers and suggests that most social workers are able to integrate both functions.[15] Rein's concept of radical casework is particularly well suited to a social work focus on person-situation interaction. For Rein, "a radical casework approach would mean not merely obtaining for

[11] Ibid., pp. 6–7.

[12] Porter R. Lee, "Social Work: Cause or Function," *Proceedings of the National Conference of Social Work, 1929* (Chicago: University of Chicago Press, 1929), pp. 3–20. For a useful discussion of this issue from a historical perspective, see Clarke A. Chambers, "An Historical Perspective on Political Actions vs. Individualized Treatment," in *Perspectives on Social Welfare*, ed. Paul E. Weinberger (New York: Macmillan, 1969), pp. 89–106.

[13] Gisela Konopka, *Edward C. Lindeman and Social Work Philosophy* (Minneapolis: University of Minnesota Press, 1958). See especially chap. 9, "Integration of Value, Method, and Knowledge."

[14] Rein, "Social Work," p. 19.

[15] Merlin A. Taber and Anthony J. Vattano, "Clinical and Social Orientations in Social Work: An Empirical Study," *Social Service Review* 44:1 (March 1970), pp. 34–43.

clients social services to which they are entitled or helping them adjust to the environment, but also trying to deal with the relevant people and institutions in the clients' environment that are contributing to their difficulties."[16]

To recapitulate, the focus of social work activity is directed toward the interaction of man and his environment, in accordance with Schwartz's view of the social worker as a mediator.[17] This process of mediation requires the ability to direct change strategies toward person and environment and the interaction between them. The debate as to whether social workers should be stretcher-bearers or social engineers fails to account for a dual focus on both person and situation. But this raises a central question. Are the actions and practice strategies of social work organized in such a way as to facilitate the focus on the person-situation interaction?

THE CASEWORK, GROUP WORK, AND COMMUNITY ORGANIZATION CONCEPTUALIZATION OF SOCIAL WORK ACTIVITIES

Traditionally, social workers have thought of themselves as case-workers, group workers, or community organizers. Each group in this trinity is assumed to use methods characterized by distinctive skills and change strategies. The primary variable distinguishing these methods, however, is not related to what the social worker does but to the number of persons with whom he interacts. Caseworkers interact with individuals and families. In the implementation of change strategies, group workers interact with members of groups, and community organizers with community representatives.[18]

Schwartz notes the inappropriateness of basing a definition of method on the number of persons with whom the worker interacts and suggests that the terms casework, group work, and community organization refer to the relational system in which the worker implements method. For Schwartz, method is "a systematic process of ordering one's activity in the performance of a function. Method is function in action."[19] Thus method becomes a systematic way in which social workers carry out

[16] Rein, "Social Work," p. 19.

[17] Schwartz, "The Social Worker," pp. 154–55.

[18] One of the difficult tasks for the community organizer is to define community; the community organizer interacts with individuals and groups who allegedly represent some larger entity (the community). For more discussion of this point see Roland Warren, ed., *Perspectives on the American Community* (Chicago: Rand McNally, 1966); Thomas Meenaghan, "What Means 'Community,'" *Social Work* 17:6 (November 1972), pp. 94–98.

[19] Schwartz, "The Social Worker," p. 151.

their function, i.e., the systematic way in which they mediate between the individual and the social environment. Schwartz conceptualizes five essential tasks which constitute the social worker's method:

1. Searching for a common ground between the client's perception of need and social demand.
2. Detecting and challenging obstacles which obscure the common ground.
3. Contributing data to the client.
4. Lending a vision to the client.
5. Defining the requirements and limits of the client-worker system.[20]

Herbert Bisno also considers casework, group work, and community organization a faulty conceptualization of social work method because "the inclusion of a quantitative attribute of the potential transactional unit and the designation of the method (without suggesting the nature of problem or appropriate problem solving technique) has led to an illicit bond between a given method and a given, but arbitrarily restricted and limiting, client system."[21] Bisno is making the same objection as Schwartz: designation of method on the basis of the size of the client system is illogical. Methods, according to Bisno, "are techniques sufficiently generalized to be common to a discipline, practice, or range of disciplines and practice."[22] As an alternative to the casework–group work–community organization model, Bisno conceptualized nine social work methods which may be utilized with any size of client system: adversary, conciliatory, developmental, facilitative-instructional, knowledge development and testing, restorative, regulatory, role-implementing, and rule making.[23]

In addition to the illogic of basing a definition of method on the size of the relational system (Schwartz) or the client transactional system (Bisno), the casework, group work, community organization model has an additional major shortcoming. This approach encourages the dichotomous thinking of changing the individual or changing the environment instead of maintaining the primary focus of social work intervention on the person-situation interaction. Too often, for example, caseworkers are looked upon as changing the individual (i.e., helping individuals adapt to the realities of environment) and community organizers are looked upon as the experts in environmental change. Group workers are divided into both camps, depending largely on the purpose of the

---

[20] Ibid., p. 157.

[21] Herbert Bisno, "A Theoretical Framework for Teaching Social Work Methods and Skills with Particular Reference to Undergraduate Social Welfare Education," *Journal of Education for Social Work* 5:1 (Fall 1969), p. 8.

[22] Ibid., p. 7.

[23] Ibid., pp. 9–12.

group. Some groups are directed toward producing change within their own members (therapy groups, socialization groups, etc.) or toward providing opportunities for meeting normal developmental needs (club groups, etc.); others are directed toward change outside of group members (social action groups, neighborhood organizations, tenant groups, etc.).

Martin Rein notes that the association of social change with community organization and of individual change with social casework may oversimply social work inasmuch as work with individuals can be directed toward changing social standards and work with groups or communities can be and is directed toward helping people adapt to their current situations.[24] We agree with the Rein formulation and think that this distinction has been largely missed in social work—the expectation remains that the community organizer will work to produce community change, the caseworker to produce individual change, and the group worker to do either depending on the nature of the group. This expectation diverts the focus of social work from the person-situation interaction to either the person or the situation depending on the particular method in which the practitioner has been steeped.

A third problem relates to the organization of social work activities into casework, group work, and community organization. This has led to training specialists in each of these methods with very limited effort to prepare people to assess a person-situation interaction except through the colored glasses of their particular methodological orientation. Thus community organizers see problems in terms of community change, group workers in terms of working with groups, and caseworkers in terms of individual intervention. Abraham Kaplan noted this same problem in terms of research methodology and formulated a law of the instrument: "Give a small boy a hammer, and he will find that everything he encounters needs to be pounded. It comes as no particular surprise to discover that a scientist formulates problems in a way which requires for their solution just those techniques in which he himself is especially skilled."[25] In the same way the conceptualization of social work activities in terms of casework, group work, and community organization leads to a tendency to define problems for intervention in terms of the worker's particular methodological frame of reference rather than a careful assessment of the person-situation interaction.

In addition to the casework, group work, and community organization framework, two other conceptualizations of social work activities—the micro-macro approach and the setting of practice approach—require brief discussion.

---

[24] Rein, "Social Work," p. 19.

[25] Abraham Kaplan, *The Conduct of Inquiry: Methodology for Behavioral Science* (San Francisco: Chandler, 1964), p. 23.

Recently considerable attention has been given to efforts to reconceptualize social work strategies in terms of micro-macro approaches. This conceptualization is implied in Helen Harris Perlman's article "Casework Is Dead." Perlman makes an impassioned plea for two kinds of practitioners—those skilled in the delivery of individualized services and those skilled in social change.[26] Micro approaches focus on the individual either as an individual or as a member of a family or a small group and are directed toward assisting him in coping with environmental stress. Macro approaches are directed primarily toward the community or larger social systems and toward producing change in these systems. Werner Boehm discussed the two approaches in terms of intervention in social situation (helping individuals as individuals or in small groups) and intervention in the social resource structure (efforts to bring about more adequate resources for individuals within the community).[27] Micro strategies generally encompass most of casework, family counseling as done in social work, and group work activities directed toward helping individuals in a group setting. Macro strategies encompass community organization policymaking, planning, and group work strategies directed toward change outside of the group members themselves. While the micro-macro formulation has the advantage of logically relating strategies within these two major categories, it suffers from the major limitation of the casework, group work, community organization conceptualization. The focus is on the individual or the situation, with two groups of experts being prepared—one to intervene with the individual and the other with the situation. This continues a basic dichotomy in social work, which detracts from the primary focus on the person-situation interaction.

A closely related issue is prevention versus rehabilitation in social work. Arguments are advanced that social workers may spend too much time dealing with the casualties of modern society instead of attacking root problems in efforts at prevention. This is an unacceptable dichotomy for two reasons. First, to a large extent it is a renewed manifestation of the issue of work with the community versus work with individuals. Prevention is frequently assumed to require social change, with rehabilitation perceived as helping individuals to cope with immediate situations. We consider all social work activity as both preventive and rehabilitative. Helping a mentally ill person is rehabilitative, but it also prevents future distress. Efforts to provide deprived children with adequate nutrition, clothing, and in some cases substitute living arrangements, if effective, are both rehabilitative and preventive. The second objection relates

---

[26] Helen Harris Perlman, "Casework Is Dead," *Social Casework* (January 1967), pp. 22–25.

[27] Werner W. Boehm, "Toward New Models of Social Work Practice," in *Social Work Practice, 1967* (New York: Columbia University Press, 1967), pp. 3–18.

to the matter of timing and client readiness. The social worker, as an agent of the client, does not intervene until the client (individual, family, group, or community) perceives a problem and is ready to engage in a process of problem solving; for the social worker to act otherwise increases the danger of doing to or for rather than with. Once a client decision occurs, the actions of the social worker may be both rehabilitative and preventive. The social worker may at times be called upon to serve as an agent of society (as may occur, for example, in dealing with child abuse or delinquency); in such instances we think it highly unlikely that either prevention or rehabilitation will occur until the client and the worker discover a mutually acceptable area for joint problem solving. Rehabilitation is preventive and prevention may be rehabilitative; ideally neither occurs until a client has perceived a problem, after which client and social worker engage in a mutual problem-solving undertaking.

Another approach has been to conceptualize methods in relation to a particular setting or social problem area. Thus, we might think of social work in relation to mental health services, corrections, economic dependency, etc. The integrating theme is not the relational system, for one can easily think of work with individuals, small groups, and large organizations in relation to any of these problem areas. Emphasis is placed on the unique characteristics of the social problem under consideration. This approach has merit, and certainly many social workers do wish to specialize in particular problem areas by developing advanced knowledge and skills in them. The approach does not, however, provide a useful basis on which to organize a book directed to social work students who are just entering education for professional practice. This book therefore deals with processes of social work practice found in all settings and leaves the specialized setting or problem-related component for further professional education or perhaps later learning at an agency in-service level.

This chapter has established that the traditional conceptualization of social work activity as casework, group work, and community organization has three major weaknesses: (1) This conceptualization of method is based primarily on the size of the client system in which the worker intervenes, rather than on activities utilized by the worker. (2) This formulation tends to encourage the dichotomous approach of changing the individual or changing the situation rather than a focus on the person-situation interaction. (3) The education of specialists in each method has resulted in a tendency to see problems in terms of the methodological skills of workers rather than in terms of complete assessment of the client-situation interaction.

Brief mention was made of the micro-macro conceptualization of practice, which is primarily a refinement of the casework, group work, and community organization formulation and which presents the same short-comings. Similar difficulties are found in the prevention-rehabilitation dichotomy in social work. A practice or social problem basis for organizing social work activity was briefly mentioned and, while this holds potential, it is not a practical basis for the organization of a book for the beginning social work student.

If these approaches do not provide a useful conceptualization of social work activity, what does? Can we organize social work activities and thinking about them in such a way that a focus is clearly maintained on the person-situation interaction, method is defined in relation to worker activity, and the impact of the law of the instrument is reduced?

THE ORIENTATION OF THIS BOOK

Herbert Bisno sets forth a way of thinking about social work activities which may help avoid these difficulties. Bisno suggests that there are basically two levels of skill involved in social work—skills in knowing what method to use (remember that Bisno does not use the term *method* in the traditional sense) and skills in the actual use of method.[28] John Kidneigh advances a similar formulation when he suggests that social workers must possess both the capability of "deciding what to do" and "of doing the decided."[29] Kidneigh, using the tripartite division of powers in government as an analogy, suggests further that social workers must possess skill at resolving problems which arise in the doing of the decided. More important than his reference to this third activity, which will not receive attention here, is Kidneigh's contention that "social work practice in any of its recognized methods, in any of its programs or settings, consists of these functions of deciding why and what to do, doing the decided, and resolving questions which arise in the course of the doing."[30]

The Kidneigh and Bisno divisions of skill provide a helpful guide to refining the more global Schwartz model. Schwartz identifies the mediating function of the profession and conceptualizes five tasks which may be necessary to accomplish the function. Operationalizing the mediating function and the associated tasks will involve processes in both areas suggested by Kidneigh and Bisno—arriving at decisions about how to mediate and implementing those decisions. These social work change processes include actions to define the problem, actions to collect

---

[28] Bisno, "A Theoretical Framework," p. 9.

[29] John C. Kidneigh, "A Note on Organizing Knowledge," *Modes of Professional Education*, Tulane Studies in Social Welfare (New Orleans: School of Social Work. Tulane University, 1969), vol. xi, p. 159.

[30] Ibid., p. 159.

information on which to base decisions, actions to engage the client in goal-setting and decision making, actions to produce change, and actions to evaluate progress.

Using this approach, we can think of a social work generalist as a person who is skillful in the deciding-what-to-do area. Such practitioners will not be limited in their vision by any preferred relational system or prior methodological commitment and will be able to focus their attention on the totality of the person-situation interaction. In the process of deciding-what-to-do the practitioner is free to examine variables in the person, variables in the situation, and variables that relate to the interaction of the two. Abilities at data collection and assessment are essential for such a practitioner in order to both define the problem and arrive at a practical and workable decision as to what needs to be done.

At the second level of doing-the-decided the profession needs to provide its clients with a wide range of interventive strategies. Some strategies may require highly skilled specialists. In some situations the generalist practitioner will possess skills in the necessary interventive strategies, and he may implement the change decision. In other situations the generalist may call in a specialist for assistance. In some instances the specialist may carry most of the responsibility for the implementation of the service plan; in others more of the doing-the-decided will be the responsibility of the generalist, who will work as a team member with the specialist in meeting the objectives of the service plan.

The division of social work processes into the two broad categories of deciding-what-to-do and doing-the-decided represents the focus taken by this book. This contrasts with division according to the size of the relational situation in which the worker functions or the specific social problem with which the worker is attempting to cope. Deciding-what-to-do requires that the social worker and the client engage in processes of problem definition, data collection, and contracting. Doing-the-decided involves the client and the social worker jointly in any of a great number of change strategies. Rather than attempt a cataloging and discussion of the types of change strategies, the authors will conceptualize doing-the-decided in relation to the process of evaluation and to three interventive worker roles available to the client and the worker.

RECAPITULATION

By now you have been introduced to three basic ideas of this book which will be recurring in various forms in subsequent chapters. First, the focus of social work intervention is on the person-situation interaction. A corollary of this approach is that a focus solely on the individual or the situation is inappropriate—the long debate in the social work profession about individual services versus social reform loses sight of the basic focus of the profession. Second, thinking of social work activities in terms of casework, group work, and community organization is not a viable conceptualization; that approach stresses the relational system in which the worker functions rather than the activities of the worker, tends to maintain a focus on the individual or the situation rather than on the interaction of the two, and leads to analyses of client situations and interactions in terms of a worker's interventive skills rather than the needs of the client. Third, this book follows an alternative organization of social work activities into skills and actions needed to decide-what-to-do and skills and actions in doing-the-decided.

A LOOK FORWARD

Let's take a short and a long look forward. Immediately following are articles by William Schwartz and Richard Taber. Schwartz develops the concept of the mediating function of social work which is central to the position of this book. Taber offers an example of the type of social work practice which follows from an acceptance of the mediating function.

In the long view, readers of this book will be introduced to the social work processes of data collection, assessment, contracting, intervention, and evaluation. Because of the importance of teamwork in human services and the fact that social work is practiced in agencies (some of which are highly bureaucratic) a chapter is devoted to an examination of each of these aspects of social work practice. Before moving to the processes (the problem-solving model) by which the focus of social work intervention is implemented, we will give consideration to three very important elements of social work practice—the knowledge base, the value base, and the use of relationship.

The social worker in the group*

William Schwartz

Professions have a way of moving periodically through eras of rediscovery in which an old truth comes alive with the vigor and freshness
of a new idea. Such an occurrence seems to be taking shape in social
work practice as we face the realization that the problems of people
do not lend themselves easily to arbitrary divisions of labor among the
various agencies of social welfare. In fact, this particular truth has been
rediscovered several times, cutting deeply, in each instance, into established forms and calling for new institutional and professional
alignments.

This stubborn fact has precipitated a reexamination of social work's
historic system of designating the functions of agencies by reference
to the number of people involved in the client-worker system at one
time. Thus the casework agency, as we have known it, was one which
derived its distinguishing characteristics from the fact that its workers
talked to people one at a time; the group work agency (later called
the "group service agency") worked with people in small, cohesive
groups; and the community organization agency assumed the function
of leadership with representative bodies and similar associations.

This typology emerged at an early stage of specialization and has
remained relatively stable over the major course of social work history
—not, however, without a certain marked degree of uneasiness throughout. Group workers have struggled for years with the need to "individualize," wondering whether they were "doing casework" when they
dealt with individual problems, and continually raising the issue of
whether individual or group problems should take priority. The agencies
of social casework have been concerned about the reluctance of workers
trained in the one-to-one relationship to carry these skills into committee
work, multiple interviewing, group consultation, and other group constel-
lations. And the community organization workers have been faced continuously with the vital connection between the tasks that people undertake and the uniquely personal ways in which they approach them.

These vague but pervasive concerns have now begun to crystallize
into new conceptions about the appropriate client-worker systems

* Reprinted with permission of the author and Columbia University Press from
National Conference on Social Welfare, *Social Welfare Forum, 1961* (New York:
Columbia University Press, 1961), pp. 146–71.

through which agencies carry out their functions. The rapid development of social work services in the institutional therapeutic settings has created a community model which lends itself poorly to a type of specialization based solely on the number of people with whom the social worker interacts at a given time. In these settings, the caseworkers have been pressed into group service, just as the psychiatrists and the psychologists had before them;[1] and the group workers have found themselves involved in a degree of intensive individualization beyond anything they had ever experienced.

In general practice, the developing emphasis on the family as a unit of service has forced both caseworkers and group workers into new modes of activity. The former have been constrained to understand and work with the dynamics of family interaction; the latter, to replace the comfortable aura of friendly visiting with a more sophisticated and focused approach. In both agency types, the traditional forms have been changing, with caseworkers turning more and more to the group as a unit of service and group workers rekindling their old concern with ways of offering skilled individual guidance for those who need it.[2]

In the area of community organization, the picture is less clear. There seems to be little doubt, however, that its conceptualizers are recognizing another old truth, namely, that the only way to work with communities is to work with people, singly and together, and that skill in the helping process needs to be abstracted and formulated into teachable concepts. The newer theoretical attempts lean heavily toward organizing the experience of community workers into concepts that reflect the language and central concerns of social work method. Genevieve Carter, for example, has addressed herself directly to an analysis of the helping process in community organization, and her concept of "cumulative sequence" is an interesting attempt to relate the order of community change to that of individual growth and development.[3]

Concurrently, the unification of social workers within a single professional association and the efforts of the social work schools to conceptualize the common elements in practice have dramatized the need

---

[1] See, for example, "The Psychiatric Social Worker as Leader of a Group," Report of Committee on Practice, Psychiatric Social Work Section, National Association of Social Workers (New York: the Association, n.d.; mimeographed).

[2] See, for example, *The Use of Group Techniques in the Family Agency: Three Papers from the FSAA Biennial Meeting, Washington, D.C., April 1959* (New York: Family Service Association of America, 1959); "Committee Statement on the Role of the Caseworker in a Group Work Agency" (Chicago: Chicago Area Chapter, National Association of Social Workers, 1958; mimeographed).

[3] Genevieve W. Carter, "Social Work Community Organization Methods and Processes," in Walter A. Friedlander, ed., *Concepts and Methods of Social Work* (Englewood Cliffs, N.J.: Prentice-Hall, 1958), p. 248.

to combine the learnings of workers from the various fields and settings into a functional scheme that can be taught and practiced under the name of "social work." Such a scheme would not eliminate specialization but would certainly redefine it; most important, it could create a new integration within which the component parts could be differentiated on a basis more consistent with the facts of life as they actually exist in the community.

The new conceptual framework would be built on the recognition that the function of a social agency is determined more realistically by the social problem to which it has been assigned than by the specific relational systems through which the social worker translates this function into concrete services. It would accept the fact that there is no known correspondence between a function such as child placement, or family welfare, or recreation, or social planning, and the exclusive use of the one-to-one or the one-to-group structure to carry it out. And it would become increasingly clear that any agency should be capable of creating, in each specific instance, that system of client-worker relationships which is most appropriate to its clients' requirements.

A significant corollary would then emerge quite naturally, namely, that the single variable embodied in the number of people one works with at a time is simply not significant enough to be endowed with the designation of "method." Not significant enough, that is, if we reserve the term "method" to mean a systematic mode of helping which, while it is used differently in different situations, retains throughout certain recognizable and invariant properties through which one may identify the social worker in action. In this light, to describe casework, group work, and community organization as methods simply mistakes the nature of the helping process for the relational system in which it is applied. It seems more accurate to speak of a social work method, practiced in the various systems in which the social worker finds himself or which are established for the purpose of giving service: the family, the small friendship group, the representative body, the one-to-one interview, the hospital ward, the lounge-canteen, the committee, the street club, the special-interest group, and many others. Within this frame of reference, the task of safeguarding the uniqueness of the various so-called methods fades before the real problem of abstracting from all these experiences the common methodological components of the helping process in social work.

This is partly why any serious attempt to define a unique entity called "social group work" begins to turn, under one's very hand, into a description of something larger and more inclusive, of which the worker-group system is simply a special case. Having now, after many years of shifting identification, found a resting place in social work function and the social agency network,[4] group workers can indeed make a significant conceptual contribution to the theoretical problems involved in working with groups. But the context has changed, and the moment has passed, for a definition of "group work method." Rather, we must now search for those common elements in social work practice—the very elements which attracted group workers into the social work fold— from which social workers in all settings can draw the specifics of their own practice. The job can no longer be done most usefully by first defining social group work (or casework or community organization) and then trying to fit the description into the general framework of helping theory. The process is now rather the reverse: by laying the groundwork in a social work methodology, we may begin to analyze and clarify the activities of the social worker as he works with people in groups.

To both of these endeavors—building the common model and describing the special case of the group system—those who have been schooled in the traditions of social group work have a rich store of experience from which to contribute. The task is, of course, rendered doubly difficult by the fact that any worker who attempts it must break the bonds of his own training, since he himself has been reared in the ancient fallacies. But, clumsy though these first efforts must be, it seems inevitable that they will be made, and in increasing number;[5] for they represent an indispensable part of the still larger task of conceptualizing the generic framework of the social work profession as a whole. These larger issues are embodied in the Curriculum Study of the Council on Social Work Education[6] and in the work of the Commission on Social Work Practice of the National Association of Social Workers.[7] The present segment of this over-all task deals only with those activities through which the social worker functions in direct relationship with people of established or potential client status; the focus is on the helping process itself and on the factors which determine its nature and its variations. In what follows, we shall not presume to create a comprehen-

---

[4] For a more detailed account of the developing integration of group work and social work see the writer's "Group Work and the Social Scene" in Alfred J. Kahn, ed., *Issues in American Social Work* (New York: Columbia University Press, 1959), pp. 110–37.

[5] Although not dealing specifically with the method component, an outstanding effort to develop a foundation for a unifying theory in social work has been made by Gordon Hearn, *Theory Building in Social Work* (Toronto: University of Toronto Press, 1958). See also Joseph W. Eaton, "A Scientific Basis for Helping," in Kahn, op. cit., pp. 270–92, and Harriett M. Bartlett, "The Generic-specific Concept in Social Work Education and Practice," ibid., pp. 159–90.

[6] Werner W. Boehm, *Objectives of the Social Work Curriculum of the Future*, The Comprehensive Report of the Curriculum Study, Vol. I (New York: Council on Social Work Education, 1959).

[7] Described by Harriett M. Bartlett, "Toward Clarification and Improvement of Social Work Practice," *Social Work*, III, No. 2 (1958), pp. 3–9.

sive theoretical statement but simply to highlight a few of the essential components around which such a statement will need to turn.

Let us begin, then, with three fairly simple propositions:

1. Every profession has a particular function to perform in society: it has received a certain job assignment for which it is held accountable.
2. This assignment is then elaborated in certain characteristic modes of activity—certain action patterns designed to implement the professional function.
3. These action patterns are further fashioned and developed within the specific systems in which they operate.

These propositions lead to a working definition of method as a systematic process of ordering one's activity in the performance of a function. Method is function in action.

This line of reasoning thus calls for three major lines of inquiry, each of which carries its own theoretical problems. The first line of inquiry is designed to produce an accurate functional statement which formulates as precisely as possible the particular assignment drawn by the social work profession in the society which creates and sustains it. The second inquiry is designed to convert the functional statement into those patterns of activity through which the social work function is implemented. Third line of investigation is directed to seeking out the specific adaptations of the general methodological pattern in the various concrete situations in which the social worker performs his job.

Requirements for a functional statement

The central requirement is to recognize at the outset that the very idea of function implies the existence of an organic whole, a dynamic system, in which the worker performs certain movements in relation to the movements of others. In Parsons's words:

> The very definition of an organic whole is as one within which *the relations determine the properties of its parts.* . . . And in so far as this is true, the concept "part" takes on an abstract, indeed a "fictional" character. For the part of an organic whole is no longer the same, once it is separated factually or conceptually from the whole.[8]

And Lawrence Frank, in describing what he calls "organized complexities," speaks of the need for a field concept describing

> circular, reciprocal relations . . . through which the component members of the field participate in and thereby create the field of the whole,

---

[8] Talcott Parsons, *The Structure of Social Action* (New York: McGraw-Hill Book Co., 1937), p. 32; italics added.

which field in turn regulates and patterns their individual activities. This is a circular, reciprocal relation, not a serial cause and effect, stimulus and response relation.[9]

This model of a dynamic system which surrounds and incorporates the movements of the worker provides specific clues for our statement of social work function. First, it helps us realize that function is itself *an action concept* and that it cannot be understood as a description of what social workers know, or feel, or hope to achieve. To say, as we often do, that the social work function is to "understand behavior," or "be sensitive to need," or "effect changes," is to beg the functional question entirely. Such statements remain fixed at the level of what the worker may need in order to carry out his function, or what he may envision as a result of having performed it well—they say nothing about the function itself. The social worker's philosophy, social aspirations, attitudes toward people, and even his knowledge about them, are not unique to the profession and do not, in themselves, represent its assignment in society. Properly viewed, these qualities are simply prerequisite to the forms of action through which the profession justifies its social position.

Second, the model illustrates the need for the statement to reflect the activity of the social worker *as it affects, and is affected by, the activity of others* within the system. The failure to understand this feature of the helping system has created great difficulties in both the practice and the theory of social work. The inability to see the system as one "within which the relations determine the properties of its parts" has made it possible to imagine that one may deal with human beings by reference to certain discrete characteristics rather than to their movements within the relational system through which they seek help. To "diagnose" the client, to inventory his "needs," and to recapitulate his life history leave undone the task of understanding how these facts, if such they be, may be moving the client as he acts and reacts within the present field. Where the properties of parts are determined by their relations, the search for discrete characteristics is at best "interesting" and at worst produces a situation in which, in Merton's words, "understanding is diminished by an excess of facts." It should be stated that the uneasy attempt to take over the language and the sequence-of-treatment concept of the medical profession has confused and retarded our own attempts to find terms and concepts which would truly describe the helping process in social work. For the helping relationship as we know it is one in which the client possesses the only real and lasting

---

[9] Lawrence K. Frank, "Research for What?" *Journal of Social Issues*, Kurt Lewin Memorial Award Issue, Supplement Series, No. 10 (1957), p. 12.

means to his own ends. The worker is but one resource in a life situation which encompasses many significant relationships. And movement, at any given moment, is based on the movement of the preceding moment, as each new event calls for a reorientation of the worker to a new complex of demands for his skill. Such a process is patently different from one in which the function of the person in difficulty is to supply information and the function of the worker is to create action based upon this information, by which division of labor a "treatment" or a "cure" is effected.

The third clue offered by the organic model is the need to represent the *limited field of influence* in which any part of a dynamic system operates. This involves acceptance of the fact that, within such a system, any single part affects only those with which it interacts; and, further, that it affects even these in a limited way, in accordance with its specific function. This recognition can help to scale down the grandiose, cure-all aspirations of any single profession, and to avoid couching its objectives in the language of absolutes—"achieving individual maturity," "fulfilling human needs," and the like.

Fourth, the model points to the fact that, within a dynamic relational system, the interplay of movements of the various actors is in effect an *interplay of functions*. Thus, as the worker is moved by the question "What am I doing here?" so are the others in the situation moved, consciously and unconsciously, by the same question. The worker-client interaction is one in which each needs and uses the other in order to carry out his own sense of purpose within the relational system.

Our next question must then be: What are the systems within which the social work profession in general, and the social worker in particular, derives and carries out the social work assignment?

First, there is the general system of society itself, within which the profession has been set in motion and assigned to a given sphere of influence consistent with its ability to perform certain necessary tasks.

Second, there is the social agency system, within which the social worker translates agency function into concrete services. The agency situation represents a kind of partialization of the larger social system, from which it draws its own special assignment; and the agency creates, in addition, a unique subculture of its own, out of its own mode of living and working.

Third, there is the specific client-worker relationship—one-to-one or one-to-group—in which the social worker expresses both his general function as a professional and his specific function within the agency complex. The client-worker relationship, viewed from a distance, may thus be seen to be a system within a system within a system.

This is, of course, a simplified version of the relationship of parts to a dynamic whole. It is simplified precisely because we need to choose, from the immensely complex network of relationships in which the social worker finds himself, those which exercise the most significant determining effects upon his movements.[10] We may say that the social worker's movements, within any specific helping relationship, reveal certain constant elements, which he derives from his professional identification, and certain variant elements, which he derives from his agency identification and from the situations in which he operates. The common components of social work function emerge from the social work position within the social scheme; its adaptive components are those which express the specific ways in which the professional function is put to work.

Function: The professional assignment

Let us now venture a proposal for the functional statement itself. We would suggest that the general assignment for the social work profession is to mediate the process through which the individual and his society reach out for each other through a mutual need for self-fulfillment. This presupposes a relationship between the individual and his nurturing group which we would describe as "symbiotic"—each needing the other for its own life and growth, and each reaching out to the other with all the strength it can command at a given moment. The social worker's field of intervention lies at the point where two forces meet: the individual's impetus toward health, growth, and belonging; and the organized efforts of society to integrate its parts into a productive and dynamic whole.

More specifically, the social work assignment emerges from the fact that, in a complex and often disordered society, the individual-social symbiosis grows diffuse and obscure in varying degrees, ranging from the normal developmental problems of children growing into their culture to the severe pathology involved in situations where the symbiotic attachment appears to be all but severed. At all the points along this range, the social work function is to mediate the individual-social transaction as it is worked out in the specific context of those agencies which are designed to bring together individual needs and social resources—the person's urge to belong to society as a full and productive member and society's ability to provide certain specific means for integrating its people and enriching their social contribution. Placed thus, in Bertha Reynolds's old phrase, "between the client and the community," the social worker's job is to represent and to implement the symbiotic striv-

---

[10] The interdependence of dynamic systems and the problems of abstracting one or another for analysis are discussed in Ronald Lippitt, Jeanne Watson, and Bruce Westley, *The Dynamics of Planned Change* (New York: Harcourt, Brace and Co., 1958), pp. 5–11.

ings, even where their essential features are obscured from the individual, from society, or from both.

It should be emphasized that this conception is different from that which places the social worker in a sphere of concern known as "dysfunctioning." While it is true that the profession operates in areas where the individual-social interaction is impaired, these areas are only part of the social work field of action. The problems of symbiotic diffusion are inevitable in any complex society and apply not only to social pathology but to the normal, developmental processes and to the ongoing social effort to order the relationship between needs and resources. The concern with developmental tasks has provided part of the traditional preoccupation of the leisure-time agencies, while the ordering of needs and resources has engaged those agencies concerned with social planning and action.

This is obviously only a brief outline of the symbiotic model; its rationale has been elaborated by Kropotkin,[11] Mead,[12] Sherif,[13] Murphy,[14] Bergson,[15] and many others. For our present purposes, the important points are: the fundamental impetus of people and their groups carries them toward each other; this impetus is often blocked and diverted by a diffusion of the relationship between self- and social-interest; where the impetus can be freed to operate, it constitutes the basic motivation, for both individual and social change, with which the social worker engages himself.

This strategic location of social work as a kind of third force implementing the basic identity of interest between the individual and his group creates its own problems when the social worker falls prey to the very diffusion against which his function is set. It is at these times that we hear the controversies about whether he should be more concerned with social or with individual problems, with "content" or "process," "ends" or "means," and so on. This debate disregards the most essential characteristics of social work: that it stands on the meeting ground between the two; that it is inextricably involved with both; and that it sees no contradictions, even where the dualism looms large in the popular mind. The social work function is based on "the recognition of the fact that the individual's normal growth lands him in essential solidarity with his fellows, while on the other hand the exercise of

[11] P. Kropotkin, *Mutual Aid, a Factor of Evolution* (New York: Alfred A. Knopf, 1925).

[12] George Herbert Mead, *Mind, Self and Society* (Chicago: University of Chicago Press, 1934).

[13] Muzafer Sherif, *The Psychology of Social Norms* (New York: Harper, 1936).

[14] Gardner Murphy, *Human Potentialities* (New York: Basic Books, Inc., 1958).

[15] Henri Bergson, *The Two Sources of Morality and Religion;* tr. R. Ashley Audra and Cloudesley Brereton, with the assistance of W. Horsfall Carter (Garden City, N.Y.: Doubleday, 1954).

his social duties and privileges advances his highest and purest individuality."[16]

Method: The professional tasks

The transition from function to method is essentially a problem in dividing a broad assignment into its component activities. For this purpose, we have chosen the term "task" as an organizing concept around which to gather up the various movements of the worker in any given client-worker system. The implication is that any function can be broken down into a number of tasks necssary to carry it out, and that any specific act performed should come under one or another of these headings. Our emphasis here is on categories of activity rather than on small discrete movements; for the latter may involve us in problems that lie outside the scope of method as we conceive it. While the concern with specific acts is important, the units of activity cannot be so small as to take us either into mechanical prescriptions for worker responses or into problems of personalized style and technique. The tasks are common and are based on a professional method held in common; but many of the helping acts in a given situation are heavily charged with the unique movements and personal artistry of the individual worker.

We envisage the following tasks as those required of the worker as he carries out his social work function within the helping relationship:

1.   The task of searching out the common ground between the client's perception of his own need and the aspects of social demand with which he is faced.

2.   The task of detecting and challenging the obstacles which obscure the common ground and frustrate the efforts of people to identify their own self-interest with that of their "significant others."

3.   The task of contributing data—ideas, facts, value-concepts—which are not available to the client and which may prove useful to him in the attempting to cope with that part of social reality which is involved in the problems on which he is working.

4.   The task of "lending a vision"[17] to the client, in which the worker both reveals himself as one whose own hopes and aspirations are strongly invested in the interaction between people and society and projects a deep feeling for that which represents individual well-being and the social good.

5.   The task of defining the requirements and the limits of the situa-

---

[16] James Mark Baldwin, *The Individual and Society; or, Psychology and Sociology* (Boston: Richard G. Badger, the Gorham Press, 1911), p. 16.

[17] A phrase borrowed from another context. See Norman Kelman. "Goals of Analytic Therapy: a Personal Viewpoint," *American Journal of Psychoanalysis,* XIV (1954), p. 113.

tion in which the client-worker system is set. These rules and boundaries establish the context for the "working contract" which binds the client and the agency to each other and which creates the conditions under which both client and worker assume their respective functions.

The social worker in the group

As we move this methodological pattern into the worker-group situation, the first problem is to specify some of the salient characteristics of the small-group system which help create the social climate within which the worker functions.

First, the group is an enterprise in mutual aid, an alliance of individuals who need each other, in varying degrees, to work on certain common problems. The important fact is that this is a helping system in which the clients need each other as well as the worker. This need to use each other, to create not one but many helping relationships, is a vital ingredient of the group process and constitutes a common need over and above the specific tasks for which the group was formed.

Second, the group is a system of relationships which, in its own unique way, represents a special case of the general relationship between individuals and their society. The present group is, in other words, but one of the many associational forms through which its members interact with social values, social objectives, and social resources. More specifically, the cultural climate of the group is drawn from three major sources: Generalized social attitudes about what is good and bad, right and wrong, worthy and unworthy, permeate the group and form a part of its culture. The agency in which the group is embedded has drawn from the general culture its own characteristic and unique constellation of approved attitudes and behaviors. The group itself, by the nature of its central problem, by the activities in which it engages, and by the particular personalitites it brings together, creates its own conditions for success and failure.

Finally, the group is, as we have indicated, an organic whole: its nature cannot be discerned by analyzing the separate characteristics of each component but by viewing the group organism as a complex of moving, interdependent human beings, each acting out his changing relationship to society in his present interaction with others engaged in a similar enterprise. In this framework the worker is more concerned with what the member does and feels in the present situation than with what the member *is*. Further, the demands of society can be understood more clearly as they present themselves to the group member in the immediate situation than in abstract, holistic terms like "democratic responsibility" or "social maturity." It is, in fact, this very partialized and focused character of the present enterprise that makes helping and being helped possible and manageable. The implications for the worker himself are that his ability to help is expressed in action and that this action is limited, as in any functional system, to certain areas in which he has some control. He acts to help others act, and the emphasis on new ways of moving, of interacting, is more realistic and productive than the concern with total being, with discrete characteristics, a.id with totalistic conceptions of change.

With these observations in mind, let us examine the activities of the social worker in the group, following the pattern of the five major tasks outlined above:

1. As he pursues his search for common ground, the worker's movements are fashioned by four major assumptions about the connections for which he is seeking. The first is that the group member's main access to new ideas, new attitudes, and new skills lies through his ability to discern their usefulness to him and to invest affect in the tasks required to make them his own. The second assumption is that such connections—between individual aspirations and social objects—are always present, no matter how obscure they may seem to the members themselves. To conceive of a situation in which the connections do not exist would be to postulate a group in which the members are completely beyond the call of social demands—a situation in which the group itself would be a futile device since its members could exercise no effect upon each other. The third assumption is that these connections are both specific and partial. A gang of adolescents does not rush eagerly toward the ideal of "democratic values"; youngsters in a Jewish Center do not respond quickly to the generalized notion of "Jewish identification"; hospital patients do not invest themselves equally and evenly in the tasks of rehabilitation. In each of these instances, the attraction between the individual's sense of need and the aspirations of society is present and inherent; but it is partial, elusive, and comes into the open only at certain significant points.

The final assumption is that these connections cannot be established in any permanent sense. From meeting to meeting, almost from moment to moment, the group members meet reality on new ground, with new connections constantly to be discovered as each member works at the job of building a bridge between past and present experience.

The worker's search for common ground is expressed in two major forms of activity. One is his efforts to clarify the function of the group and to protect this focus of work against attempts to evade or subvert it—whether by the agency, the group, or its individual members. The other is represented by consistent efforts to point up for the members those areas in which they feel, however faintly, an interest in the social objects which confront them. The clarification of group function represents an active demand by the helping agent that the agency, the group, and its members begin their working relationship with a clear "contract" and a common understanding of the issue: What are we doing here together? All of this is based on the worker's conviction that the search for common ground begins most auspiciously on a field where the members and their tasks have been, so far as possible, brought face to face. The endeavor to uncover and discover connections between individual goals and social realities is rendered infinitely more difficult when the terms of these realities are themselves shifting and unstable; as, for instance, when the worker "builds character" while pretending to teach basketball, or "improves social relations" when the group has enlisted his skill in clay modeling. Further, these attempts to guard the focus of work do not end when the initial statement has been made and the terms of the agreement reached. His activities in this regard persist as he continues to guard the focus of work or, where change in focus is feasible and permissible, he helps the group to consider such changes openly and realistically.

The second complex of activity through which the worker searches for common ground begins with the worker's efforts to seek out the general lines of subject-object connection. This is a kind of internal process whereby he looks deeply into the characteristics of both subject and object to find the elements of attraction and to alert himself to the possibilities of future engagement. What is the attraction beween the gang member's hostility toward social norms and society's demand for conformity to these norms? Between the Jewish youngster's desire to be like others and the agency's emphasis on Jewish belongingness? Between the shock of diagnosis experienced by patients in an orientation group and the hospital's need for the patients to move smoothly into the necessary procedures, rules, and routines?

These are, in a sense, "diagnostic" attempts, but such preparatory insights cannot effectively be used to impose a series of prefabricated connections on a ready-made series of events. For the most part, this awareness of the general lines of connection is used in three ways: it enables the worker to be more responsive to subtle and convert requests for help; it compels him to focus on the here-and-now, and to see through the members' evasions and denials to the strengths that lie hidden; and it helps him to structure the situation to favor strength rather than weakness.

2. As the search for common ground continues, the helping agent is constantly confronted with another task which, though it is a corollary of the first, is important enough to be considered on its own terms. This task evolves from the fact that the member's access to social reality is constantly impeded by obstacles which are thrown up in the course of the engagement. The existence of these obstacles is usually obscure to the group member himself. His awareness is limited by his incomplete

vision of the common ground and by his own subjectivity, which makes it difficult for him to recognize his own defenses, to distinguish between internal and external deterrents, and to assess his own productivity at any given moment. Thus, a force is needed within the learning group system that will challenge the obstacles as they appear, by calling attention to their existence and asking the group to come to grips with them. This is the second major task of the helping person.

These obstructions stem from many sources and appear in many forms. They originate in past experience and crystallize in the moment-to-moment events of the group situation. They are created by the attitudes of the members, the human image projected by the worker, the nature of the things to be learned, and the function of the agency. The origins of the obstacles are, in fact, so complex and interrelated that it is impossible for the worker to define causation as he approaches them in the context of the group experience.

Fortunately, it is unnecessary for him to do so. What is necessary is that he recognize these phenomena, that he accept them as relevant to his professional responsibilities, and that he offer help with the concrete learning problems they indicate. Whatever its underlying source, each obstacle always takes the form of a very specific struggle between the members and their present tasks: the group has a decision to make, has stressed its importance again and again, but falls into aimless chatting whenever the subject comes up; a member accepts a task with enthusiasm, and repeatedly fails to perform it; a group proceeds, half-heartedly and unsuccessfully, on a course unanimously approved by the members but, in fact, subtly imposed by the worker; another group moves independently, but guiltily, along its "chosen" lines of action.

In these instances, there is an obstruction that lies between the group members and a valued objective, distorting their perception of what is valued and frustrating their efforts to act openly in their own self-interest. There is a path they need to take, and cannot—because its entrance is blocked by taboo. The taboo may be present in the conditions that surround them; often, its complexity is such that it combines several factors. A discussion group may become dull and unproductive because it has built up a fund of resentment against a respected but authoritarian leader. Unable to deal with their need to conform, with the leader's unassailable correctness, or with the general subcultural proscription against self-assertion, the members have no recourse but to express their resistance in listlessness and apathy.

The area of taboo may be painful enough to ward off recognition and remain buried in consciousness as it invisibly directs the actions of the members; or, the group may be aware of its existence but does not dare to enter an unsafe and risky region. Thus, in our example, the members' respect for the leader and their need to be liked by him can be so great that they cannot accept any flaw in him, but can feel only guilt for their own unexplainable lapse of ambition; or they may, on the other hand, feel their resentment against the beloved autocrat but shrink from hurting him or from exposing themselves as rebels.

In either event, the effect is evasion of the obstacle that impedes their path to productivity. Consciously or unconsciously, the members withhold their energies from the task before them. Instead, they devote themselves to movements which reflect no real investment in content, but only their efforts to create the best imitation they can muster.

In the activities designed to carry out the worker's task of dealing with obstacles, he directs himself toward three major forms of endeavor. The first includes those actions in which he reveals the fact that an impediment exists and that this is permissible. His actions here are not "interpretive" in the usual sense; he has no way of "diagnosing" the nature of the difficulty, and no right to ask the members to deal with his causative explanations, even if he were extremely intuitive in this regard. He asks them, simply, to recognize the fact that an obstacle exists, in the form of apathy, evasion, or inconsistency, between them and a desired objective.

The second category includes those movements by which the worker offers support and assistance as the members enter the area of taboo and seek to determine the nature of the impediment. This is to say that the worker helps them to examine the ways in which they are operating against their own interests in this situation. The attempt here is not to exorcise the taboo—that is, eliminates its power for all time—but to help the members identify it and examine its effects. It is important only that they recognize the source of their present frustration and free themselves to determine the direction of their self-interest. In this aspect of the worker's activity, he is asking them to recapture control of their own impetus, and to begin by discountenancing the illusion of work where none exists.

In the third category of activities, the worker moves to keep the function of the group alive lest it be lost in the preoccupation with obstacles. The challenging of obstacles is based on the fact that they come between the member and the social product. When these impediments cease to be regarded as such and become objects of interest in their own right, the analytical process itself becomes an obstacle which needs to be dealt with. This calls for certain movements through which the helping person exercises a kind of "demand for work," an emphasis on performance; he asks the group members to continue with their functional tasks even as they examine the obstacles to their achievement. This is still another way of saying that the examination of obstacles is part of the group function itself and that one does not cease as the other begins.

3.   The third task encompasses those movements in which the helping agent makes a contribution of data in the group situation. The term "data" is used here to denote any ideas, facts, or value-concepts which the members may find useful as they involve themselves within the system. Whether the members' tasks are related to the specific problems of mastering facts and concepts in an established sequence, or to a less tangible complex of attitudes and feelings, the worker has a responsibility to offer what he feels they can utilize from his own store of experience. The worker's grasp of social reality is one of the important attributes that fit him to his function; while his life experiences cannot be transferred intact to other human beings, the products of these experiences can be immensely valuable to those who are moving through their own struggles and stages of mastery.

Thus, nothing can be more destructive to the worker's function than his decision to withhold knowledge on the sole grounds that the member must make his own way. Such withholding is inevitably interpreted by the individual as deprivation, hence rejection; and the result is generally the very opposite of what the worker intends. It is common, for example, to find situations where the group members spend a major part of their energies in straining to find answers which lie hidden in the worker's questions; in this game of educational hide-and-seek, dependency increases as frustration mounts and as the members learn to search for hidden answers rather than to explore the nature of the problem itself.

In providing access to data, the worker is, in effect, providing access to himself. His demand for a culture of work, and for a free sharing of ideas, can best be met if he makes himself available, as he would have them become available to him and to each other. What he knows should be accessible to the members of the group, not after they have tried to proceed "on their own," but in the course of their deliberations so that they may use him in their work. The need to withhold is generally felt by workers whose relationship to the group is too fragile to be sustained in a culture of work. Where the dependence on authority is already great—and not necessarily created by the worker—the reluctance to offer more information to be swallowed whole is a natural one. But the fear of creating dependency must be met in other ways. The worker who finds common ground, is sensitive to the climate in which the subject-object engagement proceeds, and is prepared to challenge the obstacles as they appear, will have no fear that the problem-solving process will been endangered by his assumption of full status as a knowing person in the group system.

As the worker makes his contribution of data, several major considerations guide his movements. The first is his awareness that his offering represents only a fragment of available social experience. If he comes to be regarded as the fountainhead of social reality, he will then have fallen into the error of presenting himself as the object of learning rather than as an accessory to it. Thus, there is an important distinction to be made between lending his knowledge to those who can use it in the performance of their own tasks and projecting himself as a text to be learned. In the first instance, the worker is used in accordance with his function as a mediator of the subject-object relationship; in the second, the worker himself becomes the object.

The second consideration lies in the relationship between the information he shares and the function of the group as this function is understood by the members and by the agency. Often, the worker is tempted to "expose" the group to certain facts and ideas which may, in some future context, be found useful. Such efforts generally serve to confuse rather than enlighten, since there is no frame of reference within which the data assume weight and significance. Where these acts of the worker constitute a series of ideological "plugs," the effect is to breed a vague distrust of the worker's purpose and of his stated desire to assist the group to carry out its own function.

The function of the group may be considered a general frame of reference to be considered by the worker as he selects the data he will share with the members. Even more important as a factor is the specific working context within which he makes his contributions. Again, this assumes the existence of a culture of work, within which the worker's offering is but a single, important ingredient and the worker is but one of many sources of social reality; with his data, as with everything else, the test of utility will inevitably lie in its appropriateness to the demands of the current task. This is the sense in which the old group work injunction that "program is a tool" is important. It is a tool, not of the worker, but of the group and its members; and, like all tools, each fact, idea, or concept must be fashioned to the specific job for which it is to be used.

The final consideration is that, while the worker's own opinions represent important data, they are such only when presented honestly as opinion rather than as fact. There are many occasions where the member is at the mercy of the worker's power to disguise the distinction between the two. The temptation to becloud this distinction is strong, and often unconscious; culture-bound and ego-bound, the worker is himself unclear in many important areas about the difference between reality and his own constructions of it. But the struggle to distinguish between subjective perceptions and external reality is at the heart of all human learning and growing, and the worker who is not engaged in this struggle himself will find it impossible to help others in the same endeavor. As he helps them to evaluate the evidence they derive from other sources—their own experiences, the experience of others, and their collaboration in ideas—so must he submit his own evidence to the process of critical examination. When the worker understands that he is but a single element in the totality of the member's experience, and when he is able to use this truth rather than attempt to conquer it, he has taken the first step toward helping the member to free himself from authority without rejecting it.

4. The responsibility for contributing data is related to the fourth task that expresses the function of the helping agent. This involves those activities through which the worker reveals, frankly and directly, his own hopes and aspirations concerning the outcome of the group experience. Borrowing a phrase used by Norman Kelman in another context, we would designate this task as that of lending a vision to the members of the group.[18]

In these activities, the worker reveals himself as a person whose own aspirations are deeply invested in the interaction between people and society, and who has, through his own struggles, developed a vision of what life can and should be like. In his enthusiasm, his sense of urgency, and his capacity for empathy, the worker demonstrates that his own life experience is involved here, that he has a stake in society, and that he is not here simply to dispense solutions to problems that are beneath him and irrelevant to his own concerns.

More specifically, the worker reveals his emotional involvement in three important ways. The first is his faith in the system itself and in the conditions under which the growing experience takes place. By his movements to safeguard the function of the group, he expresses his respect for the dignity of the group itself and for the reasons which created it. By his refusal to trade identities with either the members or their materials, he demonstrates his faith in the constructive power inherent in the relationship of one to the other.

The second aspect of the worker's personal investment is revealed in his attitude toward the relevant data of the group system. In this respect, the worker's activity reflects something of what the material means to him—its excitement, its depths, and its importance in the human scheme. As the worker shares his own intense involvement with the materials, he projects himself as a living example of their power to attract and intrigue the human mind. It is only in this sense that the helping agent is a salesman; and without the slightest intent to be one but simply by virtue of his position as, so to speak, a pleased consumer. Without this sense of enthusiasm, this vision of immense possibilities, and his status as a model of mastery, the worker's contribution to the subject-object relationship resolves itself into a mechanical questioning

---

[18] Ibid. Dr. Kelman speaks of the necessity to "lend our vision to the patient" as the psychoanalytic process proceeds. Although his meaning here is slightly different from ours, his general intent is similar to the one we mean to convey.

and answering; with it, there can be a challenge, a driving curiosity, and a strong motive for work.

Finally, the worker's affect is a strong component in his relationships with the members of the group. The professional relationship can be described as a flow of affect between worker and member, combining the expectations and perceptions of one with the other, as they work together—each on his own tasks—within the group system. Their inter-action is based on the circumstances which brought them together; and it is in the work itself that their feeling for each other grows. In this light, the worker's efforts to establish relationship go much deeper than the kind of wooing activity in which he seeks to gain the member's acceptance and approval through the exercise of his personal warmth and attractiveness. The human qualities of the worker, however engaging they may be, should not be used to divert, to charm, or to build personal dependency.

The worker, sensitized by his own need to cope with the complexities of living and growing, has a fund of feeling from which to draw his attempts to understand the member's struggles in detail. This under-standing is reflected, not in a generalized "wanting to help," or "giving love," or "accepting them as they are," although these purposes provide an important ideological base from which to operate. Rather, his under-standing is communicated in his ability to empathize with the precise feelings engendered in the learner by the demands of a particular task in a specific situation. The worker's ability to call up parts of his own experience, to communicate his feeling, and to demonstrate an active faith in the productive capacities of the member are important parts of the image of vitality that he projects.

In all, the worker's feeling involvement in the group system demon-strates better than words his conviction that the process of growing is complicated and difficult, but also challenging and rewarding if one is left free to conjure with it and to test one's experience under conditions where one can err without failing completely. The worker lends his vision to the members, not in order to exchange it for theirs, but because his aliveness, his faith in productivity, and his stake in work are inherent in his function as a helping person.

5. The agency, the worker, the group, and its members are related to each other by certain rules and requirements imposed upon them by the terms of their agreement. These requirements emerge first in the conditions under which the group is established, its function identi-fied, and its procedures initiated. Later, the rules are modified, amplified, and reinterpreted as their concrete implications become clearer in the events of group life. These expectations are not limited to those imposed upon the members by the agency, or by the worker; they are reciprocal in that each actor imposes certain restrictions and is bound by others.

Thus, while the group and its members are held to certain policies and procedures, the agency and the worker are also limited by standards such as equal treatment, consistency in approach, the members' concept of fair play, and so forth.

To the extent that the terms of the agreement are specific and unambiguous, the participants are free to pursue their tasks within the system in their own characteristic ways. Where the rules are, or become, obscure and vaguely defined, the major energies of both worker and members become diverted to exploring the boundaries and testing the limits of the group situation. This leads us to the final task of the helping agent, in which he calls upon the participants of the learning group to face the necessities inherent in the conditions of their association. This definition of the requirements begins with the worker's first attempts to identify the specific responsibilities that have been undertaken by the agency, the group, and the worker himself; it continues as he monitors these realities and calls for clarification at those points where they become obscure.

The most important aspect of these requirements is that they emerge from the function of the group and the necessities of work rather than from the personal authority of the helping agent. As such, they are parts of a reality which is imposed by the nature of the setting, the conditions of group life, and the purposes for which the group has been assembled. The worker is often frustrated by his "inability to set limits," when his real difficulty arises from his failure to recognize that his task is to explain a situation rather than to create one. Club members find it a great deal easier to accept situational realities and limitations— dress requirements, bans on smoking, and so on—than those imposed by the worker in his own name for reasons which are ambiguous, or moralistic, or designed to build character. Since people do not join clubs to have their characters built, such taboos are not perceived as interpretations of reality, and in fact are not.

Science and art in the helping process

Because of our emphasis on viewing the social worker in action, we have concentrated our analysis on his movements within the group system rather than on the personal and professional equipment which he brings to the job. Most attempts to identify the foundations of professional skill have resulted in an encyclopedic and somewhat frightening inventory of virtues. There is, after all, no sphere of knowledge, no personal strength, and no field of competence which is irrelevant to the responsibilities of the human relations worker. And yet we know that the tasks of helping are not performed best by paragons but by those who want to help, know what they are trying to do, and have sufficient mastery for themselves and of social realities to offer their strengths in the struggles of others. Thus, the central problem for the helping agent does not lie in his nearness to perfection but in the extent to which he can mobilize the powers he does possess in the service of others. In order to find the common ground, he must use certain specific knowledge about human beings; in order to contribute data, to reveal his own stake in society, to define the rules, and to challenge the obstacles in the learner's path, he must be free to share what he has of sensitivity, science, and personal maturity. Where the worker proceeds from a clear sense of focus and function, his own strengths are tools that he uses in the specific tasks that he is called upon to face. As such, his powers are not pitifully inadequate replicas of a formidable ideal but full-blown strengths which he is free to own and to share.

There is nothing in the conception of a professional methodology which denies or subordinates the uniquely personal and artistic component which each worker brings to his administration of the helping function. On the contrary, the concept of a disciplined uniqueness is inherent in the definition of art itself. In a broad sense, we may view artistic activity as an attempt, by someone innately endowed with extreme sensitivity to the world about him, to express strong personal feelings and aspirations through a disciplined use of his materials. The analogy between the helping agent and the creative artist can be struck at several points. In both, there is an emphasis on feeling, on an empathic quality which is cherished as a tool of the craft; both feel a constant need for fresh insights into the nature of things and for new ways to express their view of the world; in both, there is a strong preoccupation with essences and basic principles; there is a high degree of subjectivity, of self-consciousness, which constitutes a major element in their ability to create new vistas and new perspectives; in both, the creativity is nourished by the continuous search for truth and is, in fact, an expression of this search; and both require an atmosphere in which one is free to explore, to err, to test reality, and to change.

If we add to these the powerful urge of both the artist and the social worker to communicate their view of life and to affect the experience of others through their artistry, then the sense in which the helping art is distinguishable from that of the painter, the musician, or the writer lies only in that which they are impelled to express, the nature of their materials, and the processes through which they move in order to carry out their functions.

A *systems approach to the delivery of mental health services in black ghettos**

Richard H. Taber

In our attempt to develop new and more effective models for the delivery of mental health services to children in a black lower socio-economic community, we have found the concept of the ecological systems approach extremely useful. Using this model, we have explored the ecology of our community in order to define naturally occurring systems of support within the community—systems which, when utilized as a target for special types of intervention, could maximize the impact of our work.

This paper will focus on the rationale for our selection of two small natural groups: a partial social network composed primarily of mothers of highly disorganized families with young children, and a peer sub-system of 14–17-year-old boys. The ecological framework provided significant direction to our attempts to approach and work with these indigenous systems in such a way that members of the natural groups were given mental health services without being required to perceive themselves as patients.

The Rebound Children and Youth Project is jointly sponsored by the Children's Hospital of Philadelphia and the Philadelphia Child Guidance Clinic. It is charged with providing comprehensive health, dental, mental health, and social services to children in the area adjacent to these two institutions.

The community is a black ghetto in which 47% of the families have incomes below $3,000 and "only 38% of the 1,131 children covered in our survey are growing up within an intact family unit" (5). The project enjoys a positive image in the neighborhood because of the involvement of the community in ongoing planning and the sensitive work of indigenous community workers as well as the provision of much-needed pediatric services on a family basis.

We began this project with the view that many children in the black ghetto live with several pervasive mental health problems, primarily

---

* Reprinted from Richard H. Taber, "A Systems Approach to the Delivery of Mental Health Services in Black Ghettos," *American Journal of Orthopsychiatry*, 40:4 (July 1970), pp. 702–9. Copyright 1971 by the American Orthopsychiatric Association, Inc. Reproduced by permission.

poor self-image and the concomitant sense of powerlessness. There are three ways of conceptualizing this problem. One is the individual psychological approach, which would identify early maternal deprivation as a primary cause. This factor can be identified in numerous cases we see clinically. Many children in this population have experienced early separation, abandonment, or maternal depression.

A second is the sociopolitical point of view, which directs attention to the systematic oppression and exploitation of this population by a predominantly white power structure. It also identifies historical and current influences which have undermined the family structure in the black ghetto and points to white racism as the source of black feelings of inferiority.

The ecological systems approach, the third way, directs our attention to the transactions and communications which take place between individual members of the poor black population and the systems within and outside of their neighborhood—that is, what actually goes on between the individual and his family, the individual and the extended family, the individual and the school, the individual and his job, the individual and the welfare agency, etc. Our exploration of these transactions, or "interfaces between systems," shows that most of the transactions which take place are degrading and demoralizing, and are experienced by the ghetto resident as "put downs."

When the problems of poor self-image and sense of powerlessness are approached from the concept of ecological systems, pathology is seen as the outcome of transactions between the individual and his surrounding social systems. Because no one element of these systems can be moved or amplified without affecting other elements, the ecological approach to the delivery of services requires exploration of the ways in which "the symptom, the person, his family and his community interlock" (2).

As an example, to plan effective services for a 15-year-old boy we must explore not only the boy as an individual but also what takes place at the interfaces between the boy, his family, the school, and other formal institutions and at the interface with peers, adults, and other representatives of the larger society. Chances are that his family expects little of him that is positive except that he stay out of trouble. He may often hear that he is expected to turn out to be a no-good bum like his father. At the interface with adults in the neighborhood he meets with open distrust and hostility. If he should wander out of the ghetto into a white area, his blackness, speech, and dress quickly cause him to be labeled as a hoodlum and treated with suspicion. He sees the police or "man" as a source of harassment and abuse rather than protection. If he is still in school he has become used to not being expected to learn (3). He may not know that the curriculum was designed with someone else in mind, but he is certainly aware that his style of life and the style of learning and behavior expected in school do not mesh (8). If he is in contact with a social or recreational agency, chances are that its program is designed to "keep him off the streets" and control his behavior. Competence is not expected from him and cannot be demonstrated by him. However, his peer system, usually a gang, does give him an opportunity to demonstrate competence. He is needed by the gang in its struggle to maintain "rep" and fighting strength. Gang membership offers him structure, a clear set of behavioral norms, a role and opportunity for status—all essential elements in the struggle toward identity. He is, however, then caught up in a system of gang wars and alliances which he has little or no control over, and which limits the availability of role models.

Adults in the ghetto neighborhood have similarly limited opportunities for self-definition as persons of worth and competence. For reasons which have been dealt with elsewhere (6), a mother may not perceive herself as able to control her children's behavior outside of her immediate presence; yet she is expected to do so by a whole series of people representing systems within her neighborhood—her neighbors and relatives, the school, etc.—and outside her neighborhood—the attendance officer, the police, etc. Her transactions with people representing formal social agencies and other social systems are usually experienced as destructive. In the interface with welfare, legal, medical, and other services, she receives attitudinal messages which are critical or punitive or, at best, patronizing. If she goes for therapy or counseling in a traditional psychiatric setting, she must accept another dependency role—that of patient. One of the conditions of receiving such help is usually that she admit to a problem within herself. She may also perceive the therapist's interpretations of her behavior as robbing her of any expertise about herself. What may hurt her most are the verbal and nonverbal attacks she receives from moralistic neighbors.

One source to which she can turn for acceptance and support in dealing with personal and interfamilial crises is her social network of friends, relatives, and neighbors. An important function of the network is to offer her guidance in her contacts with external systems. A friend or relative may accompany her to an appointment. Often after an unsuccessful encounter at an interface, the group will offer sympathy from collective experience and suggestions for avoiding or coping with the system the next time the need arises.

Having identified the existence of these two social groups in our community (the social network and the gang), we began to wonder how to utilize our knowledge so as to intervene in these systems in a way that would maximize their natural mental health functions. Unlike members of an artificial group, members of a natural group have day-to-day contacts and ongoing significance in each others' lives. The effects of therapeutic intervention in them should be able to transcend a one-hour-a-week interview and reverberate through the ongoing system. Also, intervention with natural community groups fits with our point of view that the answer to the problems of ghetto residents must come from the emergence of self-help groups within the community. Sources outside the community will never be willing or able to pour enough resources into the ghetto to solve the problems there. And our recognition of the value of local self-help organization brings us to a point of substantial agreement at the interface between our project and emerging black awareness and black nationalism.

We sought to work with natural systems without requiring that the people perceive themselves as patients. The intervenor sought to define his role as that of advisor, rather than leader or therapist. We felt that this model would prove most effective for the promotion of indigenous leadership and help establish the self-help system on a permanent basis. Through successful task completion, people would have concrete reason to see themselves as worthwhile and competent.

In order to avoid making people patients, we chose to focus attention on transaction and communications at strategic interfaces rather than on individual problems. We find that this focus is more syntonic with the point of view of our target population, because members of the disorganized lower socioeconomic population tend to see behavior as predominantly influenced by external events and circumstances rather than intrapsychic phenomena (5, 8).

One advantage of an approach which does not require that people perceive themselves as patients is that the natural group and the intervenor's involvement are visible. This increases the potential of the group for having an impact on other individuals and systems in the community. And the individual, far from being shamed because he is a patient, feels the pride of being publicly identified as a member of a group which enjoys a positive image in and outside the community.

The "C" Street network

The social network we chose to work with was one of highly disorganized family units which had been observed in the course of an anthropological study of families in the neighborhood (4). The families which formed the core of this network lived on "C" Street, a street which has a reputation in the neighborhood as a center of wild drinking, promiscuous sexual and homosexual behavior, the numbers racket, and gambling.

The approach to the "C" Street network was planned by a project team which included a pediatrician and two indigenous community workers. Our plan was to seek to improve child-rearing practices and parent-child communication by raising the self-esteem and effectiveness of the parents. The indigenous community workers played a key role in introducing the mental health intervenor to members of the network and have played important ongoing roles as linking persons in the interface between network members and the white middle-class social worker.

Our approach to the system was through one couple in the network who in response to a survey question had indicated interest in participating in a discussion group on neighborhood problems. The worker introduced himself as a person interested in working with neighborhood discussion groups. It was agreed that such a group might be most effective if it were limited to people who knew each other well or who were related. Despite the expressions of interest by the network members, it was several weeks before the group began meeting formally. Before the members could trust the intervenor and before they could feel that meeting together might really accomplish something, it was necessary for the social worker to have many contacts with the members in their homes or on the street. In addition to discussions of members' ideas of what could be accomplished by meeting together, these contacts were social in nature, since it was necessary for the members to see the intervenor as a person who was sincerely interested and was not turned off by clutter, roaches, etc.

Initially we wanted to let the network define itself, but we were also committed to including the men of the community in our intervention program. Because of the sex role separation in this group, however, we had limited success in including men in formal group meetings, although the intervenor did have other contacts with the men in the network.

One critical step in the development of this program was that the network members, assisted by the community workers, needed to help the intervenor unlearn some of the anti-organizational principles of group therapy and to recognize the importance of ordered, structured communications. In other words, the group itself had to push "to stop running our mouths and get down to business." Once officers had been elected and rules had been developed for conducting meetings and a dues structure set up, the group became task-oriented. The format was that of an evening meeting in the home of one of the members, the formal business meeting followed by a social time during which refreshments including punch and beer are served. The first main areas of concern were more adequate and safer recreation for the children and improvements in housing. Through group and individual activity, houses were fixed up and the street beautified. Recreation for the children included children's parties an bus trips, planned and executed by the mothers, and the sponsorship of a play-street program.

One of the community workers is now working more closely with the group as the social worker begins to step back. The group plans to run its own play-street program thus summer, as they are convinced that they can do a better job than the community house that ran it last year.

The Nobleteens

The other natural group which we began to intervene with was a subsystem of the local gang. The boys initially contacted were still in school, although far behind; they did not have major police records. The intervenor discussed with them the idea of getting together with other boys to discuss what it's like to grow up black in a ghetto community. They were asked to bring their friends.

Letters and personal reminders were used for the first several weeks. The intervenor was frequently out on the street, available for informal encounters. Unlike the adult network, where almost all our contacts have continued to be in the group's neighborhood, the boys have had their meetings in the clinic from the outset. They still stop by almost daily to see their advisor.

The initial 10-meeting program was focused on current relationships with school, police, and community, on vocation and the development of black pride and awareness, on sex and parenthood. Use was made of movies such as the "Lonely One" and "Nothing But a Man" and dramatizations of written material such as *Manchild in the Promised Land*.

At an early meeting of the group one of the more articulate members referred to the tape recorder and asked if this was to be like a study of ghetto youth. The intervenor said that that was not the purpose but that one project that the boys might be interested in would be to make tape recordings about life in the ghetto to educate "dumb white people." The group picked this up enthusiastically as an opportunity of showing people outside the neighborhood some of the positive things about themselves, since they thought that the papers usually talked about the bad things. The passive process of having discussions that were tape recorded turned into the active process of making tape recordings. From his position as a learner from a white middle-class background, the intervenor could ask questions and promote reflections. It became possible to highlight and underline examples of positive coping. The group became for the boys a place in which they could express the most positive aspects of themselves.

After the initial period, the group decided to become a club and the intervenor's role was then defined as that of advisor. (One of the club president's functions is to be a "go-between" between members and advisor.) The group structured itself and took a more active task focus—throwing dances, starting a basketball team, starting an odd-job service (which has since involved contracts to move furniture), writing articles for the Rebound Newsletters. Carrying on their "thing" about educating people outside their system, the boys made presentations to the staff and agency board of directors, spoke on a "soul" radio station, and wrote articles about themselves. Maximum use of these experiences was made by the intervenor in promoting recognition and development of individual assets and skills.

As a result, new opportunities for role experimentation and contact with role models have been made available to the boys. Through successful completion of tasks the group has won a "rep" in the neighborhood and gets positive reinforcement from adults. One development is that the Nobleteens have "quit the corner." As they became involved in the Nobleteens and began to see themselves as valuable people with futures, the boys spent less time hanging out with the gang and reduced their delinquent activities. This affected the fighting strength of the gang in the balance of power with other gangs, and so it challenged the Nobleteens' existence, beating up several members. The next day, a member of the gang happened to be stabbed, but when a runner came to enlist the Nobleteens for revenge, they refused to fight.

A black male community worker is now co-advisor to the Nobleteens. His focus with the group will be to further promote positive black identity through involvement in activities such as a Black Holiday marking the date of the assassination of Malcolm X. He will also be helping the boys take on a business venture of benefit to the community. The present intervenor hopes to develop a program in which a subgroup of the club will be hired as big brothers to younger boys who have been clinically identified as needing a relationship with an older black male.

The role of the intervenor

Because the intervenor or advisor is in frequent contact with group members, often on a social basis, he enters into and can influence the social context on their behalf. He also stands in a unique position in the group in that he is conversant with external systems. He can therefore provide a linking function by bringing the systems together, promoting what is hopefully a growth-producing transaction for the group member and an educational one for the representative of the external systems. In terms of communication he can act as a translator for both sides. Because accommodation has taken place between him and the group members, he is better able to use their language, and they, his.

Several examples here may illuminate the therapeutic possibilities of the intervenor's role in the interface between the natural group and the external system.

Example 1. In the first several months of the Nobleteens, Rick, a 14-year-old boy, visited as a guest, a cousin of a member. He was known by the nickname "Crazy" because of his impulsivity and lack of judgment. He impressed the worker as a depressed, nonverbal youngster. He then stopped coming.

During the summer the advisor was approached by Rick's mother to act as a character witness. Rick had been arrested for breaking into a parking meter and she was panicky because he had already been sent away once. The advisor talked with Rick while they cleaned paint brushes. Rick convinced the advisor that he really didn't want to be sent away again, and the advisor convinced Rick that it wasn't going to be as easy to stay out of trouble as Rick pretended it would be. They finally agreed that the advisor would recommend Rick's inclusion in the club and would report his impressions to the court.

Rick was known to the boys in the Nobleteens but usually hung out with a more delinquent subgroup. When the advisor recommended his inclusion in the club, one of the members (who happened to be retarded) questioned why Rick should have preference over the boys who were waiting to get in. He then recalled seeing the advisor coming down in the elevator with Rick's mother, realized that it was about the trouble Rick was in, and quickly withdrew his objection.

Beyond this there was no discussion of Rick's problem, but the message was clear. The club members included him in their leisure activities and protected him when trouble was brewing. Eventually the charge was dropped, and he has not been picked up for delinquent behavior since that time. He has responded positively to the feeling of group inclusion, appears noticeably less depressed, and is more verbal. The payoff came for Rick when he was unanimously elected captain of the basketball team.

Example 2. A well-known child psychiatrist was brought to a Nobleteen meeting to consult with the boys in writing a speech for influential people in the health and welfare field. His goal was to argue for more flexibility on the part of youth-serving agencies. The intervenor's only role was to bring the two together. The psychiatrist was familiar with the boys' language, and they were experienced in discussing topics which focused on their relationships with external systems. Tape-recorded material from the meeting was included in the speech, and the boys gained a great sense of competence in verbalizing their concerns and points of view.

Example 3. At one meeting of the "C" Street network club, two members informed the advisor that Mrs. White, the club president, was having an extremely severe asthma attack. The group discussed this informally and came to the conclusion that it was really her "nerves" and that she should go into the hospital. Mrs. White had been hospitalized several times previously and was diagnosed as a borderline schizophrenic. Mrs. White's main supports, her sister and her closest friend, were extremely anxious, their own fears of death and separation coming to the surface. This placed them in a real approach-avoidance bind. The advisor agreed to visit Mrs. White after the meeting.

Mrs. White was lying on the couch coughing in uncontrollable bursts. The advisor soon labeled the coughing (which was panicking her and the other two women) as a "good thing" and encouraged it. He sympathetically listened to Mrs. White recount her dramatic collapse on the hospital's emergency room floor and her subsequent hallucinations. While she talked, the two network members busied themselves cleaning up the house and attending to the children. Once the advisor had listened, he began exploring areas of stress with her. The most recent crisis was that she was being threatened with eviction for nonpayment of rent. She had contacted her relief worker, who had promised to contact the landlord. The advisor promised to talk to the relief worker. He also learned that in desperation she had gone to a different hospital. She had confidence in the treatment she received there, but did not see how she could go back for an early morning clinic. The advisor agreed that Rebound could provide her with a cab voucher.

Then the three women and the advisor sat and discussed the events of the club meeting. Mrs. White's coughing subsided, and she became calmer as she related to outside reality. The friend's and the sister's anxiety was also reduced. They could then respond in ways which reduced rather than heightened Mrs. White's anxiety.

The significance of this intervention lies not so much in the availability of the professional to meet the immediate dependency needs and to manipulate external systems on the woman's behalf as in his being in a position to repair her system of significant supports. A member of her own system would thenceforth be able to remind her that her rent was due when she got her check and remind her about the attendance officer if she became lax in getting her children off to school. The program continued to meet her dependency needs and support her medical care through the cab vouchers. Initially the vouchers were obtained for her by the professional; later she took responsibility for reminding him about getting them; eventually she went to the clinic's business office to get them herself. She has not suffered a severe attack or psychotic episode since the intervention.

Our commitment was to develop models for the delivery of services which multiply our therapeutic impact by bringing about change in existing systems. By focusing on competence and mutual support rather than on pathology, we have experimented with a model for the delivery of services to people who do not wish to perceive themselves as patients.

REFERENCES

1. ATTNEAVE, C. 1969. Therapy in tribal settings and urban network intervention. Fam. Proc. 8:192–211.

2. AUERSWALD, E. 1968. Interdisciplinary vs. ecological approach. Fam. Proc. 7:202–215.

3. CLARK, K. 1965. The Dark Ghetto: Dilemmas of Social Power. Harper and Row, New York.

4. LEOPOLD, E. 1969. Hidden strengths in the disorganized family: discovery through extended home observations. Paper presented at meeting of Amer. Orthopsychiat. Assn.

5. LEOPOLD, E. 1968. Rebound children and their families: a community survey conducted by the rebound children and youth project. Mimeo.

6. MALONE, C. 1966. Safety first: Comments on the influence of external danger in the lives of children of disorganized families. Amer. J. Orthopsychiat. 36:3–12.

7. MINUCHIN, S., et al. 1967. Families of the slums: An Exploration of Their Structure and Treatment. Basic Books, New York.

8. MINUCHIN, S. 1969. Family therapy: Technique or theory. In Science and Psychoanalysis, J. Masserman, ed. 14:179–187. Grune & Stratton, New York.

9. MINUCHIN, S., AND MONTALVO, B. 1967. Techniques for working with disorganized low socioeconomic families. Amer. J. Orthopsychiat. 37:380–887.

10. RABKIN, J., et al. 1969. Delinquency and the lateral boundary of the family. In Children against the Schools, P. Graubard, ed. Follett Educational Corp., Chicago.

11. SPECK, R. 1967. Psychotherapy of the social network of a schizophrenic family. Fam. Proc. 6:208–214.

12. U.S. DEPARTMENT OF HEALTH, EDUCATION AND WELFARE. 1968. Report of the President's Advisory Commission on Civil Disorders.

Selected annotated references

ATHERTON, CHARLES, "The Social Assignment of Social Work," *Social Service Review* 43:4 (December 1969), pp. 421–29.

The author argues that the assignment of social work is to provide resources to individuals which will assist them in the performance of social roles.

BARTLETT, HARRIETT, M. *The Common Base of Social Work Practice* (New York: National Association of Social Workers, 1970).

Bartlett develops a common knowledge and value base for the profession and stresses the centrality of the concept of social functioning. She takes the position that assessment is a cognitive function preceding intervention and that a wide range of interventive approaches are required by the profession.

BISNO, HERBERT, "A Theoretical Framework for Teaching Social Work Methods and Skills with Particular Reference to Undergraduate Social Welfare

Education," *Journal of Education for Social Work* 5:1 (Fall 1969), pp. 5–17.

Bisno classifies social work change strategies in nine methods and suggests two levels of skill—skill in determining the method to use and skill in the use of specific methods.

BOEHM, WERNER W., "The Nature of Social Work," *Social Work* 3:2 (April 1958), pp. 10–18.

Boehm develops a definition of social work emphasizing the functions of restoration, provision, and prevention.

BOEHM, WERNER W., "Toward New Models of Social Work Practice," *Social Work Practice, 1967* (New York: Columbia University Press, 1967), pp. 3–18.

Boehm agrees that social work activities can be organized into two broad groups to accomplish two types of change. One group of practitioners will be skillful at intervention in the social situation of individuals and small groups. A second group of practitioners will possess skills at intervening in the social resource structure.

CHAMBERS, CLARKE A., "An Historical Perspective on Political Action vs. Individualized Treatment," in *Perspectives on Social Welfare,* ed. Paul E. Weinberger (New York: Macmillan, 1969), pp. 89–106.

Chambers offers a historical analysis of the individual treatment versus social reform dispute in social work.

HEARN, GORDON, ed., *The General Systems Approach: Contribution toward an Holistic Conception of Social Work* (New York: Council on Social Work Education, 1969).

Hearn's work is a collection of original papers developing the holistic or generalistic approach in social work.

MEYER, CAROL, *Social Work Practice: A Response to the Urban Crisis* (New York: Free Press, 1970).

This author develops a model of practice calling for social workers to link clients to resources within urban settings and to assist institutions to deliver services in a humanizing manner.

PERLMAN, HELEN HARRIS, "Casework Is Dead," *Social Casework* 48:1 (January 1967).

Perlman maintains that there is a continuing need for individualized services and suggests that the profession maintain a dual focus on individual service and social action.

REIN, MARTIN, "Social Work in Search of a Radical Profession," *Social Work* 15:2 (April 1970), pp. 13–28.

Social work change theories can focus on either individuals or social conditions. Rein believes that approaches in either area can support or challenge existing standards of behavior. He identifies four social work ideologies—traditional casework, community sociotherapy, radical casework, and radical social policy. He contends that radical casework may be the modality for accomplishing the central mission of social work.

SCHNEIDERMAN, LEONARD, "A Social Action Model for the Social Work Practitioner," *Social Casework* 46:8 (October 1965), pp. 490–93.

The author proposes a documentation model whereby the practitioner documents the need for action (generalizes beyond specific clients). He acknowledges that this is not a new proposal but notes that it is not being effectuated. He suggests that the professional association has the responsibility of responding to the documented needs in terms of action programs.

SCHWARTZ, WILLIAM, "Private Troubles and Public Issues: One Social Work Job or Two?" *Social Welfare Forum, 1969* (New York: Columbia University Press, 1969), pp. 22–43.

Schwartz traces the dichotomous thinking that results in divisions of social work practice and suggests an alternative mediating approach which combines both foci of the dichotomy.

TABER, MERLIN A., and ANTHONY J. VATTANO, "Clinical and Social Orientations in Social Work: An Empirical Study," *Social Service Review* 44:1 (March 1970), pp. 34–43.

This survey of a national sample of 821 practicing social workers found that a clinical-social division does not characterize the attitudes of social workers. The study suggests that most social workers integrate the two orientations in their practice.

Chapter 2

SOURCES AND FUNCTIONS
OF KNOWLEDGE

In this chapter the sources and functions of knowledge in social work practice are discussed. Our first task is to define the various terms that are found in reading about social work knowledge. We will also discuss the confusion between confirmed knowledge, assumptive knowledge, and values in social work literature. Next, some of the very real and extremely complex problems involved in the selection and organization of knowledge for use will be presented. As part of the consideration of this matter it is suggested that one problem is the way social workers are accustomed to breaking down and testing knowledge, and it is proposed that systems theory may offer a useful framework for approaching knowledge selection and development. In conclusion we will examine questions concerning the importance of knowledge, criteria for the selection of knowledge, and how to deal with our ignorance when we are expected to be experts.

DEFINITION OF TERMS

Perhaps we should begin by asking what we mean by the term *knowledge* and by the phrase often met in social work literature, "the knowledge base of social work." Alfred Kadushin states that the "knowledge base of social work is a comprehensive topic which encompasses the facts and theories, skills and attitudes, necessary for effective, efficient practice."[1] In discussing the term *knowledge* as used in the working

---

[1] Alfred Kadushin, "The Knowledge Base of Social Work," in *Issues in American*

definition of social work practice (formulated by the National Association of Social Workers and cited in the first chapter of this text), William Gordon, a social work educator who has long been interested in the problem of defining the scope of social work knowledge, states:

> Knowledge, in the working definition, designates generalized perceptions of man in his world which can be symbolized explicitly enough to be reliably communicated and are susceptible to testing and extension by the procedures of empirical science. Knowledge differs from value assumptions not only in the degree to which its propositions have already been verified . . . but especially by the intent to verify them by scientific procedures. . . . A revised working definition should include under "knowledge" a wide range of propositions with respect to their degree of verification, but also exclude all assumptive preference rather than scientific necessity.[2]

In the above quotation Gordon attempts not only to define knowledge but also to differentiate it from another important base of social work practice which is discussed in the next chapter—social work values. In a later article Gordon elaborates more completely on this distinction:

> Thus knowledge refers to what, in fact, seems to be, established by the highest standards of objectivity and rationality of which man is capable. Value refers to what man prefers or would want to be. . . . it becomes clear that the heart of continuity and professional utility lies in what social work wants for people (values) and what it knows about them (knowledge).[3]

Bartlett, whose work has also been referred to in the first chapter, points out that "knowledge and value take priority over method and technique." She goes on to say:

> Values . . . refer to what is regarded as good and desirable. These are qualitative judgments; they are not empirically demonstrable. They are invested with emotion and represent a purpose or goal toward which the social worker's action will be directed. Knowledge propositions, on the other hand, refer to verifiable experience and appear in the form of rigorous statements that are made as objective as possible. Value statements refer to what is preferred; knowledge statements to what is confirmable.[4]

Social Work, ed. Alfred J. Kahn (New York: Columbia University Press, 1959), p. 39.

[2] William E. Gordon, "A Critique of the Working Definition," *Social Work* 7:4 (October 1962), p. 7.

[3] William E. Gordon, "Knowledge and Value: Their Distinction and Relationship in Clarifying Social Work Practice," *Social Work* 10:3 (July 1965), p. 34.

[4] Harriett M. Bartlett, *The Common Base of Social Work Practice* (New York: National Association of Social Workers, 1970), p. 63.

Bartlett points out that the statement that "there is interdependence between individuals in this society" has often been included under values in social work literature although it is a demonstrable fact, and thus should be classified as knowledge. She continues:

> At any stage in the development of scientific knowledge there are some propositions that do not appear confirmable and thus must be regarded as value assumptions. In some instances, however, statements that are identical in form can be taken as either part of knowledge or as values. The idea that home is the best place for a child is an example; it can be taken as preferred or as a hypothesis for investigation. Here it is the intention regarding the proposition, rather than the actual substance, that makes the difference. There is also a long-range shift that will take place between a profession's body of knowledge and values. As scientific knowledge increases, some propositions that were at first preferred assumptions will become established as confirmed knowledge.
>
> . . . Knowledge and value play distinctly different roles, both of which are needed. . . . Proper use of knowledge and value rests not only on distinguishing those propositions that belong in different categories but also in recognizing that the user's intent—whether as a preferred or confirmable statement—also makes a difference as to how they should be classified. According to this approach, propositions regarded as verifiable by science and research—and that are intended to be verified—are considered knowledge.[5]

As an example of the confusion possible between knowledge and values we might look for a moment at the value of "self-determination." In working with children, we may find it difficult to set appropriate limits to their behavior because we operate on "self-determination" as a primary value instead of utilizing the knowledge available as to the needs of children for both freedom to grow and the setting of limits to unacceptable behavior. Here a value is being used when knowledge is needed.[6] Another example is the way in which we often confuse the *knowledge* that "the client will change with greater ease and less pain if he is actively involved in the process of deciding about change" with the *value* that "the client as a human being has the *right to make his own decisions about what he will do*." In this instance knowledge and value support each other, but we need to be clear in discussing our work with the client whether we are acting primarily on the basis of knowledge, of value, or of both in some combination.

Theory is another word that is often encountered in social work litera-

---

[5] Ibid. pp. 63–64.
[6] Ibid.

ture. What is the difference between theory and knowledge? Two kinds of knowledge have been discussed: (1) knowledge that has been confirmed by empirical testing and observation and (2) knowledge that is accepted and acted upon as though it were true, but has not yet been confirmed, although the intent is to confirm it ultimately. The latter might be called assumptive knowledge. A theory is a coherent group of general propositions or concepts used as principles of explanation for a class of phenomena—a more or less verified or established explanation accounting for known facts or phenomena and their interrelationship. If one thinks of knowledge as discrete bits of truth or discrete facts and observations, like a pile of bricks, theory can be likened to a wall of bricks. In a theory the observations of the real world are ordered and put together in a certain way and held together by certain assumptions or hypotheses as bricks in a wall are held together by a material that cements them in place. Thus theory is a coherent group of general propositions, containing both confirmed and assumptive knowledge, held together by connective notions that seek to explain in a rational way the observed facts of phenomena and the relationship of these phenomena to each other.

Thus when we speak of the knowledge base of social work we may be speaking of tested knowledge, but we are more likely to have various theories in mind: theories about man, how he develops, and the genesis of his dysfunctioning; theories about man and his institutions and how these grow and change, as well as how they are functional and dysfunctional for man and his society. We do not often have in mind a list of unrelated facts, because a list of unrelated facts, no matter how well verified by empirical observations the facts may be, seldom tells us what they mean. It is theory (something assumed to be true—taken for granted), constructed of known facts and phenomena held together by certain conceptual notions, that speaks to the meaning of facts.

Before leaving our definitions, we should deal with one other word. The term *principle* is often found in social work literature. This term is used in two ways, and one should be aware of the context of the material to know which is meant. A principle may be an accepted or professed rule of conduct (often built on a value), or it may be a fundamental, primary, or general truth on which other truths depend. Used as an expression of a primary or general truth, a principle may have been empirically tested or it may be an assumption—a proposition taken as given.

To summarize: When we speak of the knowledge base of social work we are usually speaking of social work theory which is constructed partially of empirically tested knowledge and partially of assumptive knowledge which has not yet been empirically investigated but which can be subjected to such investigation. All this is in contrast to "values," which are statements of what is preferred. Principles of action in social work rest upon both its values and its theories.

DEVELOPMENT OF KNOWLEDGE AND THEORY IN SOCIAL WORK

Within a human services profession three levels of theory generally develop: (1) a general theory of man, his growth and development, his functioning and interrelationships; (2) the profession's practice theory, which is a statement of the nature of the principles and processes (general guides to action) of the particular profession and of the responsibilities assumed by the practitioner in the lives of the people with whom he works; and (3) specific operational procedures and skills. In social work, as in all other professions, the social worker uses knowledge that comes both from his own profession and from other disciplines. In particular, much of social work theory about man and his organizations, about how man grows, changes. and functions, is borrowed. This is true partly because as practicing professionals social workers have been more interested in the application of present knowledge than in the creation of new knowledge, and partly because in discussing their practice knowledge in the journals of the profession, social workers often write only of unique individual situations without making appropriate attempts to generalize their experiences and to connect them with what is already known and set forth in the literature.

In discussing the problem of the generation of new knowledge vis-à-vis the application of borrowed knowledge, Sidney Berkowitz, a practicing social worker and agency executive, points out that the present-day heroes in the field of medicine are the surgeons who are engaged in organ transplants. Yet these men are, strictly speaking, technicians who are dependent on borrowed knowledge supplied by research biologists, biochemists, geneticists, physiologists, and other scientists.[7] Berkowitz reminds the reader that the majority of professional social worker practitioners are largely concerned with practical and emotional motives rather than with intellectual drives; that, although they may have contributed little to theory building in the basic social, behavioral, or biological sciences, they have contributed much to the knowledge of the development and refinement of various social work methods and techniques. In addition they have developed, and passed on to others, a kind of wisdom about human behavior that can come only from skilled clinical practice over time.

---

[7] Sidney J. Berkowitz, "Curriculum Models for Social Work Education," *Modes of Professional Education*, Tulane Studies in Social Welfare (New Orleans: School of Social Work, Tulane University, 1969), vol. xi, p. 232.

It would appear that if social work is to expand its tested knowledge it needs to develop a group of social work researchers interested in the generation and testing of new knowledge; and the practitioner needs to internalize the discipline necessary to keep abreast of the literature so that there may be an orderly accretion of knowledge, a wall built gradually by the appropriate placing of bricks, rather than bricks scattered over the landscape without even a blueprint as to how they might fit together. In his inquiry into behavioral science, Abraham Kaplan, a philosopher of science, points out that "knowledge grows not only by accretion and replacement of dubious elements by more sound ones, but also by digestion, by remaking of the old cognitive materials into the substance of a new theory."[8] Although the growth of scientific knowledge is marked by the replacement of poor theories by better ones, if knowledge is to advance, each new theory must take account of the theory it seeks to replace. Each new theory must reshape and integrate the old so that there is a continuity of knowledge development, even in the most revolutionary of times. Kaplan says that the problem in the behavioral sciences is that we do not do this, that we do not steep ourselves in the theories available to us before we take off on a charge of our own. He is concerned that the lag in the behavioral sciences comes because each researcher or theoretician is busily drawing his own "new" blueprints. The social and behavioral sciences are replete with low-level empirical findings, but these remain empirical bricks, unusable until someone can find the connection to hold them together.

Actually, as pointed out by Kadushin in "The Knowledge Base of Social Work," we have an embarrassingly rich literature that details what the social worker needs to know, to do, and to feel. But that knowledge is not organized in a manner that allows us to readily specify in this chapter what you will need to know about what. Thus, nowhere will you find a book on *Knowledge Necessary for Social Work Practice.*

There have been any number of attempts to organize social work knowledge in a manner that would allow it to serve as a base for social work practice. Mary Richmond is considered by many to have made the first major attempt to pull together social work knowledge, in a pioneering work called *Social Diagnosis.*[9] In 1923, the Milford Conference brought together a panel of experts to examine and extract the common elements of social casework practice.[10] In his review of the

---

[8] Abraham Kaplan, *The Conduct of Inquiry: Methodology for Behavioral Science* (San Francisco: Chandler, 1964), pp. 304–5.

[9] Mary E. Richmond, *Social Diagnosis* (New York: Russell Sage Foundation, 1917).

[10] American Association of Social Workers, *Social Casework—Generic and Specific: A Report of the Milford Conference,* Studies in the Practice of Social Work, No. 2 (New York: AASW, 1929).

history of social work knowledge, mentioned earlier, Kadushin points out that between 1929 and 1959 there were two major reviews of social work education throughout the world and five major studies of social work education in the United States. Since Kadushin wrote, there have been other attempts to specify the knowledge base of social work. Perhaps the most comprehensive and exhaustive attempt yet made is the Curriculum Study of the Council on Social Work Education.[11] This study ran to twelve volumes and can hardly be summarized in the space available to us in this text, or utilized by students in a discrete course. A quotation from Kahn, who has studied the knowledge base of social work, gives us some notion of the possible range of data that social work may be concerned with:

> Social work knowledge is, at the present time, in fact, an amalgam of several different things: (1) propositions borrowed from or markedly like those of psychiatry and some branches of psychology; (2) propositions fewer than in (1), borrowed from, or markedly like those of, sociology, social anthropology, and a scattering from other fields; (3) apparently original propositions about how to do certain things in casework, group work, and community organizations; (4) methods, techniques, and attitudes, clearly derived from the fields of administration, statistics, and social research; (5) propositions about how to do things apparently derived from, or markedly like, those of progressive education.[12]

Bartlett says:

> These needed concepts and criteria to guide the social worker's use of knowledge come first from the core of the profession. A comprehensive concept concerned with people interacting and coping with their environment gives promise of offering a central focus and a group of related subconcepts adequate to provide the necessary guidance. Here are to be found the ideas relating to life tasks, coping patterns, environmental demands and supports, exchanges, between people and their environment, and new concepts not yet perceived, all of which require disciplined examination and testing by the profession.[13]

The Council on Social Work Education, a body which speaks with some authority for schools of social work, from time to time issues a statement of the official curriculum policy of the council as an accrediting body of social work education. Since the membership of the council consists largely of social work educators, it could be assumed that this

---

[11] Council on Social Work Education, *Social Work Curriculum Study*, vols. i–xii (New York: H. Wolff, 1959).

[12] Alfred J. Kahn, "The Nature of Social Work Knowledge," in *New Directions in Social Work*, ed. Cora Kasius (New York: Harper, 1954), p. 197.

[13] Bartlett, *The Common Base*, p. 152.

statement outlines the knowledge being taught, or seen as essential, by faculties of schools of social work. A copy of the council's latest curriculum statement is reprinted in this chapter. At least three broad areas of knowledge are referred to in this statement: (1) knowledge pertaining to human behavior and the social environment of man, (2) knowledge pertaining to social welfare policy and services, and (3) knowledge pertaining to social work practice.

This list may not seem very helpful because it is so general. The fact is that these same areas are mentioned in most lists of social work knowledge. The problem is that these large chunks of knowledge need to be assembled and formed into some kind of meaningful whole for use. However, these large areas of knowledge have been very differently conceptualized, particularly as to principles that guide action, and there are no conceptual linkages. It is as though the profession had purchased an unfinished foundation in which different types of construction blocks were put together in different ways. We cannot proceed to build on this foundation until we have found some way to complete it so that the blocks not only fit together but can bear the weight of the structure we want to put on top of it. Social workers are having great difficulty in finding what kind of construction blocks and what kind of construction can bring very diverse foundation walls together in such a way that we can build on them. Or perhaps we may have to tear down the walls already built and, using the blocks of knowledge from the walls, construct them differently.

FUNCTION OF KNOWLEDGE IN SOCIAL WORK PRACTICE

Perhaps one of the reasons that we have great trouble in selecting and organizing knowledge stems from our inability to define with any precision what social workers should be expert about in their practice. "Reliance upon empirical data has not been a hallmark of professional social work practice, partly because of our tools and objectives of research, but also, perhaps, because we have not yet agreed upon the goals and boundaries of social work practice."[14] In the above quotation Meyer speaks to the issue of the function of knowledge in social work practice. In the professions, in contrast to the basic sciences, knowledge is sought for use rather than for its own sake. What the social worker is supposed to be about dictates "and defines the boundaries of relevant knowledge as well as stimulating the search for new knowledge. Part of what makes a given profession distinctive is the nature of action

---

[14] Carol Meyer, "Direct Services in Old and New Concepts," in *Shaping the New Social Work,* ed. Alfred J. Kahn (New York: Columbia University Press, 1973), p. 38.

or practice evolving from placing knowledge within a particular frame of reference."[15]

This frame of reference is dictated by the purposes and values of the profession. Thus a profession does not seek to build knowledge outside of or beyond its purposes. However, knowledge and purpose have an interactive relationship in that, as purposes change, we search for new knowledge in order to deal with the new purposes, but also, as knowledge expands within a given purpose, we may find that the purpose itself is changed by the new knowledge (often more slowly than we would wish). Moreover, if only one solution is possible, or acceptable, there is no problem for empirical or experimental research. Thus "questions whose answers are dictated by the value system of our society, and some questions that depend upon the value system of social work," are not researchable for purposes of knowledge building.[16] So values join purpose in setting a boundary to the knowledge that we will examine and incorporate.

Another problem in utilizing empirical research as a way of knowledge building in social work is the necessity we often face of making immediate choices in crisis situations. Since our society is not very good about planning ahead in relation to human services, problems often seem to arise with such rapidity that we cannot delay planning while we investigate the relative merits of various solutions or acquire empirical knowledge about the utilization of solutions. In such situations we act in the context of the knowledge we already possess, guided by how we organize and evaluate present knowledge in light of the problem.

It is well to remember that social work is a profession concerned with the impact of social problems on the lives of people, and that the solutions that it can operationalize must fall within the value system and available resources of the times in which it acts. Thus, from the beginning, each generation of social workers has had to invest most of its energy in helping individuals, families, and institutions deal with the social crisis of the times, using the tools and knowledges available and improvising when these proved inadequate. One problem for social workers of today is the tendency to define our problems and to take action based on the past instead of determining what relevant knowledge we can bring from our past and moving beyond it by searching for new knowledge in light of the new functions that confront the profession. In other words, unless we are constantly alert we will find ourselves

[15] Sheila B. Kammerman, Ralph Dulgaff, George Getzel, and Judith Nelson, "Knowledge for Practice: Social Service in Social Work," in *Shaping the New Social Work,* ed. Alfred J. Kahn (New York: Columbia University Press, 1973), p. 97.

[16] Lilian Ripple "Problem Identification and Formulation," in *Social Work Research,* ed. Norman A. Polansky (Chicago: University of Chicago Press, 1960), p. 28.

defining our present problems in light of yestrday's knowledge base. As the needs and demands of practice change, the appropriate knowledge base changes; and as the knowledge base changes, grows, and develops, the functions and the value system of the profession also change. The constantly changing functions of social work, as dictated by our constantly changing and developing society and the constantly expanding knowledge of man in interaction with his social institutions and the physical world, demand a constantly expanding and reorganized and reformulated knowledge base so that each social worker will need to be an active learner for his entire professional life. The demand for a more adequate knowledge base always seems to move ahead of us as an unachievable goal.

We might well consider that man has, over the years, developed the wheel, the lever, and the pulley, and learned to know and use them as independent things before he has put them together in complex configurations. In the same way scientists have sought to understand the components before trying to deal with larger wholes. However, in human societies, by contrast, we have had functioning wholes (individuals, families, groups, organizations, societies, and even nations) long before we became aware of the need to analyze these phenomena in any systematic way. And even in the physical sciences, the precision of prediction declines rapidly as complexity increases, so that it is not the social sciences alone that suffer from the difficulty of making predictions in relation to complex phenomena.[17]

However that may be, as we struggle to understand human behavior for the purpose of being helping persons in planned change processes, we very rapidly become aware that in order to acquire such understanding we will need to have some grasp of the goals and purposes of the behavior. Take, for example, a friend of ours who called us one day to say that he had quit his job. We were aware that he had been having a great many disputes with his supervisor and that the supervisor had told him that he would not be recommended for the next raise for which he was eligible. In addition, we knew that his wife wanted the family to return to the state where they had lived previously and that our friend had been offered a better job with a huge increase in salary in that state. Thus we were not surprised when we heard that he had resigned. We could have predicted this behavior and, by any commonsense criterion of understanding, we could understand why he did what he did. However, we need to recognize that such prediction and understanding came from our perception of this man, his circumstances, his preferences, and their interrelationships within him, which are "wholes," rather than from any analysis of specific impulses imping-

---

[17] Alfred Kuhn, *The Logic of Social Systems* (San Francisco: Jossey-Bass, 1974) p. xvii.

ing on his nervous system and of the transformation of such impulses into others leading to the activation of effectors.

To carry this example further and make it more applicable to social work, let us suppose that Mr. X came to you as a client requesting that you help him make a decision in a situation similar to our friend's. However, Mr. X's situation is complicated by the additional fact that his youngest child is both retarded and physically handicapped and that the state in which the new job is located has no resources to continue the treatment and education his child has been receiving. Also, the new job does not provide health insurance, under which much of the cost of treatment has been covered in his present employment. Feeling overwhelmed by his problem, Mr. X really wants you to make the decision. What kinds of knowledges will you need in order to help this man resolve his problem and come to a decision? And how do you select from and organize these knowledges to bear on this particular problem of this particular man? Or consider the social worker in a large city high school located in a neighborhood in which there have recently been large population movements involving diverse racial groups. The social worker has been asked for help in handling the conflict between the school's black, Puerto Rican and white students. What knowledge does the social worker need? Knowledge of the culture and social systems of the groups, knowledge of the problems in the larger community and its organizations, knowledge of the school system and its resources, and knowledge of community leaders as individuals and leaders are all necessary. How are these to be pulled together and utilized? Or consider the social worker employed by a federation of senior citizens' clubs who is asked to help the members obtain free public transportation during certain hours of the day, a privilege enjoyed by the aged in another city. What knowledge does this worker need?

GENERAL SYSTEMS THEORY AS A CONCEPTUAL FRAMEWORK

It is the proposal of the authors of this text that general systems theory may give us a conceptual framework which will allow us to organize our knowledge in ways useful to our professional function. Others have made the same proposal before us. Therefore, in our discussion we intend to rely heavily on the writings of other authors.[18]

[18] See, among others, Gordon W. Allport, *Personality and Social Encounter* (Boston: Beacon, 1964), pp. 39–59; Robert Chin, "The Utility of Systems Models and Developmental Models for Practitioners," in *Planning of Change*, ed. Warren G. Bennis, Kenneth D. Benne, and Robert Chin (Holt, Rinehart and Winston, 1961), p. 201; Howard Goldstein, *Social Work Practice: A Unitary Approach* (Columbia: University of South Carolina Press, 1973), pp. 105–36; A. Pincus and A. Minahan, *Social Work Practice: Model and Method* (Itasca, Ill.: F. E. Peacock, 1973), pp. 530–64; Herbert Stream, *Social Casework* (Metuchen, N.J.: Scarecrow Press, 1971),

Systems theory is not in itself a body of knowledge, nor does it contain any prescriptions as to actions that a social worker might take. Rather, systems theory presents us with tools of analysis that may accommodate knowledge from many sciences. It is a way of thinking—a way of viewing and organizing data.[19] Because it is a way of thinking that requires us to abandon a linear approach to causation and to substitute an understanding of the reciprocal relationships among all parts of the field (transactional approach) and an interactive focus, in which we deal with the effects of one system on another, systems theory requires considerable study for any real understanding. It may seem difficult to grasp because it uses a vocabulary different from that found in much of social science literature. Those of its terms which come from communications theory or cybernetics often seem very mechanical to social workers. We intend to deal here with only a few central concepts of the theory. As a further help to understanding this way of organizing knowledge, an article by Ann Hartman is reproduced at the end of this chapter. We have also included additional suggestions for reading in the selected references.

We are proposing the use of systems theory as a conceptual framework for the organization of data about people and groups, as a way of originating more helpful questions and approaches to problem solving. This is very different from proposing it as a model of empirical reality with a predictive capacity (see Hartman's article for a further discussion of this point). Used in this way, systems theory helps us avoid the tendency, discussed in the first chapter, to focus on either the individual or on society as the primary locus of pathology or as the primary target of change. It reminds us that things are not so simple.

Systems theory, on the other hand, offers a conceptual framework that shifts attention from discrete units (be those units either individuals or social groups) and their characteristics to the interaction and interrelatedness of units. (See Hartman's article for the example of the ten-year-old boy.) Noting the success of the physical sciences in building knowledge by splitting "wholes" into pairs of smaller units (variables), establishing causal relationships between those variables, and attempting

---

pp. 123–95; Walter Buckley, ed., *Modern Systems Research for the Behavioral Scientist* (Chicago: Aldine, 1968), especially the following articles: Anatol Rapoport, "Foreword"; Norbert Wiener, "Cybernetics in History," p .31, Magoroh Maruyama, "The Second Cybernetics: Deviation-Amplifying Mutual Causal Processes," p. 304, Tamotsu Shibutani, 'A Cybernetic Approach to Motivation," p. 330, Geoffrey Vickers, "The Concept of Stress in Relation to the Disorganization of Human Behavior," p. 354; Walter Buckley, *Sociology and Modern Systems Theory* (Englewood Cliffs, N.J.: Prentice-Hall, 1967); Ludwig von Bertalanffy, *General Systems Theory* (New York: Braziller, 1968); Arthur Koestler, *The Ghost in the Machine* (New York: Macmillan, 1968).

[19] Sister Mary Paul Janchill, "Systems Concepts in Casework Theory and Practice," *Social Casework* 50:2 (February 1969), p. 77.

to understand a total phenomenon by the process of adding such understandings, the social sciences, too have tried to seek direct cause and effect relationships between paired variables. However, this appears to be an inappropriate method for explaining the complex behavior of living things. To demonstrate the inadequacy of this method, we might see how it would be used to explain the flight of birds. It would have no difficulty explaining the physical and chemical principles of the bird's ability to fly, but it cannot explain why the bird takes off in the first place.[20]

The "wholes" we are concerned with in social work are more than the sum of their paired variables. That "more" is found in their purpose (or goal-directed behavior) and in their interactive complexity. The analytic method that breaks a phenomenon into its separate parts only gives us a vast number of items of information and leaves us without the ability either to make sense out of the information or to reassemble the system. The systems approach allows us to replace the older analytic orientation, in which we observed the individual on the one hand and his environment on the other, with a more holistic orientation to the problem of complex organization, in which we see the individual and his social and physical environment as an interacting whole. We are, thus, concerned with the laws of interactions and transaction rather than with the intrinsic qualities of the parts. The assumption is that the behavior of the parts is different when studied in isolation than when seen within the whole because of the dynamic interactions and organizing patterns that are only observable as a part of the whole.

A system may be described as a set of interrelated elements with a capacity for certain kinds of performance. Each component of the set is related to at least some others in a more or less stable way within a particular period of time and space.[21] The assumption is that a system is a complex adaptive organization of parts which, by its very nature, continually generates, elaborates, and restructures patterns of meanings, actions, and interactions. Within a system something is continually going on, including a constant interchange with the environment across its boundary. Although a system is viewed as a constantly changing whole that is always in the process of movement toward a selected purpose, its parts are assumed to interact within a more or less stable structure at any particular point in time.

The open system

Perhaps the central concept in the theory of social systems is the view of the system as open, which means that an essential factor of

---

[20] Rapoport, "Foreword," p. xiv.
[21] Buckley, *Sociology,* p. 41.

a system's continuity and change is its engagement in interchanges with the environment. The open system receives input from and produces output to its environment. The environment and the transactions with it are basic to the existence of the system. It is because of this quality of openness that human systems grow and evolve toward increased order and complexity (negative entropy).

Closed systems are systems that do not interact with other systems, neither accepting input from them nor producing output to them. Such systems have a quality called entropy, which means that, over time, they tend toward less differentation of their elements and toward a loss of organization and function. This notion brings us to the concept of boundaries.

Boundaries

A boundary may be defined as a closed circle around selected variables, where there is less interchange of energy or communication across the circle than there is within the circle. Open systems have, by definition, semipermeable boundaries. However, the relative "openness" or "closedness" of those boundaries will vary with the system. All of us are probably familiar with certain communities that are very conscious of themselves, of their entity, and are extremely unwilling to admit strangers or new behavior. Such communities have relatively closed boundaries, and in time may well suffer some of the effects of entropy. We all have met families with such boundaries, boundaries well guarded by careful parents, and we may also know other families in which boundaries seem too open and unguarded to preserve the unit, in which social workers are allowed to intrude at will, with no challenge to their business there. To understand the boundary of a family is simple, but the concept of boundary itself is complex.

A social worker confronted with a problem involving the functioning of an individual, a family, or a social group will find that the definition of the problem and the definition of the boundaries of the social systems with which he will work are inextricably related. For example, when an individual brings a problem to a social worker, does the worker define the problem and the boundaries of the social system in such a way that he sees the problem as lying within the boundaries of the individual as a complete social system? Or does he define the problem in such a way that the system becomes the focus of concern and the individual is seen as a component of the system? Or does he believe that the problem falls within the sphere of another institution? The boundaries of a social system are established by the practitioner, and it becomes his task to determine what transactions are central to the solution of the problem.[22] Usually social science definitions of social entities are used to set boundaries, e.g., family, group, institution, organization, etc.

A concept that may help us in establishing the boundaries of the systems we are attempting to understand is that of "levels" of systems. Simon has called this notion "layering," pointing out that we can best consider the individual, primary groups, organizations, etc., as "nests of Chinese blocks" in which any activity taking place in one system at one of these layers will obviously be operating simultaneously in at least one other system (the larger block) at another level.[23]

Tension

We often view tension in human beings or in their organizations as a pathological or disturbing factor that occurs only occasionally or residually. In contrast to this notion, systems theory conceives of tension as characteristic of, and necessary to, complex adaptive systems, though there is recognition that tension may manifest itself in either destructive or constructive ways. Thus systems theory does not attribute a positive or a negative value to tension per se, or even to conflict. Rather, it sees such elements as attributes of all systems simply because they are alive and open to transactions across their boundaries. It is the identification and analysis of how and to what purpose tensions operate within a system and between systems that are of major importance for social work practitioners. Rather than consider "inertia" as a given, or sought for, quality of complex, adaptive systems, with tension occurring as a "disturbing factor, we must see some level of tension as characteristic of and vital to such systems although it may manifest itself as now destructive, now constructive."[24]

Feedback and purposive systems

A basic characteristic underlying purposive, goal-seeking mechanisms is that of "feedback." By feedback is meant "a communications network which produces action in response to an input of information and includes the results of its own action in the new information by which it modifies its subsequent behavior."[25] Feedback-controlled systems (and

---

[22] Robert W. Klenk and Robert M. Ryan, *The Practice of Social Work,* 2d ed. (Belmont, Calif.: Wadsworth), p. 21.

[23] Herbert Simon, "Comments on the Theory of Organization," *American Political Science Review* 46:3 (1952), pp. 1130–39.

[24] Buckley, *Sociology,* p. 53.

[25] Karl W. Deutsch, "Toward a Cybernetic Model of Man and Society," in *Modern Systems Research for the Behavioral Scientist,* p. 390.

all human systems are thus controlled) are goal directed "since it is the deviations from the goal-state itself that direct the behavior of the system."[26] The goal-directed feedback loop underlying the self-directing human and social systems involves a receptor that accepts information from the outside, an element that imputes meaning to the information, a selector that establishes priorities of information processed, and a mechanism which measures or compares the feedback input against a goal and passes the mismatch information on to a control center which has the capacity of activating appropriate behavior to bring the system in line with its goal.[27] The meaning of the feedback is not something in it, or something in the system, but something in the interaction between the two. In the complex adaptive system there are "multi-staged mediating processes"[28] between the reception of feedback and the "output."

The question for the social worker is, Under what conditions does the information carried on the feedback loop promote change and under what conditions does it inhibit change? Two kinds of feedback have been identified. It is generally held that negative feedback carries information that the system is behaving in such a way as to make it difficult to achieve its goal and that such feedback results in behavioral correction in line with goals. Positive feedback is generally held to mean that the system is behaving correctly in relation to its goal and that more behavior of the same quality is called for. Negative feedback is seen as deviation correcting since it results in change in behavior back to the goal, while positive feedback, since it calls for more of the same, is seen as moving toward ever greater deviation from the previous state.

Change and stability

Because of the openness of human systems and the interaction of elements within their boundaries, it is impossible to conceive of such systems as static. They are constantly in the process of change and movement. And such movements in a human system represent the system's attempt to take purposive, goal-directed action. Human systems strive for the enhancement and elaboration of internal order and for the ordering and selection of outside stimuli accepted across the system boundary in such a way that purposive movement toward a selected goal is maintained. At the same time that a system is constantly in a state of change it must also maintain a dynamic equilibrium. This notion is expressed by the concept of "steady state" or "homeostasis."

---

[26] Buckley, *Sociology*, p. 53.

[27] Ibid., p. 69.

[28] Ibid., p. 55.

This concept deals with the order and structure necessary for any effective movement—without these all is chaos and purposive movement becomes impossible. Thus, although the movement of systems toward some goal is essential to their continued existence, systems also have a need for a certain amount of order and a certain stability.

"Equifinality" and "multifinality" are two concepts relative to the change and stability of systems that are important to social workers. Equifinality means the capacity to achieve identical results from different initial conditions. If a system is open, it can be shown that the final state will not depend on those conditions. Such a system will have a goal of its own, and the end state will depend upon the interactions of the elements of the system and the transactions of the system with other systems in relation to that purpose. The concept of "multifinality" suggests an opposite principle: similar conditions may lead to dissimilar end states. Thus, similar initial conditions in any living system may or may not be relevant to or causally important in the establishment of the end state.

POTENTIAL VALUES OF SYSTEMS THEORY

Some potential values of systems theory as an organizing framework for social work knowledge are as follows:

1. Systems theory allows us to deal with far more data than does the analytical model, enabling us to bring order into a massive amount of information from all the different disciplines on which social work needs to draw. And it is the collection and ordering of the data that give structure to all else in the social work process, as all else is operational.

2. The concepts relating to systems and their development, function, and structure are equally applicable to the range of clients served by social workers, from the individual to society.

3. Systems theory provides a framework for gaining an appreciation of the entire range of elements that bear on social problems, including the social units involved, their interrelationships, and the implications of change in one as it affects all.

4. Systems theory shifts attention from the characteristics possessed by the individual or his environment to the transactions between systems, changing the vantage point of the data collector and focusing on interfaces and the communication process that takes place there. Social work has long been struggling to see man and his environment as a unit.

5. Systems theory sees man as an active personality system capable of self-initiated behavior, and thus able to contribute and alter his behavior or even to create new environments. Adaptation of the environment is as much a property of human systems as is the tendency to be affected by or adapt to the environment. These concepts negate the

tendency to see disturbances as pathology and move the worker into the present life of the system.

6. The concept of systems as purposive, combined with the concepts of equifinality and multifinality, radically changes the view of both causation and the possibilities for change, and supports the worker's concern with self-determination and with the client's participation in the change process.

7. The use of systems theory brings the purpose of the system into the center of the worker's consideration, engendering further concern with self-determination and the necessity of relating professional feedback to client purpose.

8. If a living, open system requires constant transaction with other systems and its environment for its progressive development, it becomes evident that a major function of social workers becomes the provision and maintenance of such interchange opportunities for all populations.

9. Social workers need to be increasingly concerned with populations and systems heading toward isolation, with the strains in our society that result in isolation, and with our now isolated populations.

10. If change and tension are inherent in open systems, social workers need to direct their attention to why changes they suggest may be resisted, why such changes become unbearable for a system. This further emphasizes the principle of meeting the client where he is and with self-determination. It removes the notion that tension or conflict is pathology.

11. The concept of system boundary speaks to the social worker's concern with the client's rights and recognizes that the social worker should be concerned with the ways he and the services he brings move across the boundary of a social system.

12. The recognition that change in one part of a system can often greatly affect the whole means that we must be increasingly aware of the impact of our intervention in the broader transactions of our clients. In addition it speaks to the fact that we do not have to change a whole system to bring meaningful change but that we must choose our point of intervention with care. It broadens the concept of the points at which we can enter a system, provides us with more ways of entering effectively, and may make our interventions more simple.

13. The systems perspective also places the agency as a social system and the worker and client in the same transactional field. We are a social system, and we are involved as components of our own social system network.

IS KNOWLEDGE NECESSARY?

Given all the effort to identify the knowledge base of social work, and given the fact that it keeps eluding our grasp with such persistence, we might ask, Is knowledge necessary? We hold that it is. In the first place, as pointed out earlier in this chapter, although it has proven impossible to come up with a definitive statement of the knowledge base of the profession, all statements issued over the years are in remarkable substantive agreement at a generalized level. Thus there must be more grasp of a common knowledge base by social work practitioners than one might think. In the second place, the idea that one can operate without theory and knowledge is naive. Briar and Miller discuss this point:

> The choice for the practitioner is not whether to have a theory but what theoretical assumptions to hold. All persons acquire assumptions or views on the basis of which they construe and interpret events and behavior, including their own. These assumptions frequently are not explicit but are more what has been called "implicit theories of personality." Thus, the appeal for practitioners to be atheoretical amounts simply to an argument that theory ought to be implicit and hidden, not explicit and self-conscious.
>
> It is difficult, however, to defend an argument favoring implicit theory that, by definition, is not susceptible to scrutiny and objective validation and therefore cannot be distinguished from idiosyncratic bias. The weaknesses of implicit theory are particularly serious for a profession in which a significant portion of the practitioner's activity consists in forming judgments and impressions about persons on the basis of which decisions are made affecting their lives in critical ways. . . .
>
> Whether implicit or explicit, the social worker's particular assumption about human behavior can be expected to influence his professional actions, and therefore, to have important consequences for his clients.[29]

As an example of their point, Briar and Miller indicate that the assumptions a social worker holds about the possibilities of change in human nature will probably affect the degree of optimism with which he approaches his clients and their problems; and that his premises about what can be changed will largely determine what he attempts to change.[30] Perhaps the important things to keep in mind is that the interventive repertoire (what one does) of social workers grows out of and is dependent on knowledge (what one believes is the nature of the phenomenon and what one believes will be of help) and values (what social workers see as desired ends) in interaction with the problem the client brings and the solution he seeks. The social worker's input into his work with any client system depends on social work purposes and values; on how the worker understands the situation through

---

[29] Scott Briar and Henry Miller, *Problems and Issues in Social Casework* (New York: Columbia University Press, 1971), pp. 53–54.

[30] Ibid., p. 30.

the use of social work knowledge and theory; and on where he thinks "the client is" with the problem he brings.

It is the social worker's responsibility to analyze and understand the situation with which he must deal before taking action. An essential of all professional practice is that it requires the rapid, continuous, expert selection and use of generalizations from the profession's body of knowledge, while remaining open to feedback from the client system that may force the abandonment of the first premise and the selection of another. The social worker puts his professional knowledge to its first important use through his ability to "know where the client is," so that client and worker may be actively and appropriately involved in assessing the situation in which they are involved.

To summarize the above, social workers, particularly social work educators, are continually trying to identify the knowledge base on which the profession rests. However, the problems in such identification are almost overwhelming in that (1) the primary knowledge of the profession, empirically acquired, is drawn from the immense range of human problems as they are revealed by the individual in his situation and as they emerge in their cumulative aspects; (2) knowledge needed for many of the problem-solving activities of the profession has to be drawn from allied disciplines, with all the problems that this poses for selection, translation, and use; and (3) the relevant knowledge is changing constantly and advancing rapidly; (4) the profession is engaged in multiple functions and is uncertain as to what it should be expert about. For example, as the focus shifts from concern with the internal state of the individual and his adaptive functioning to a broader, and certainly more complex, view of the individual as a participant in an interactional field of psychological and social forces, the knowledge base of social work will have to be organized differently than it is now, and an expanded range of approaches and techniques will have to be used. Helen Perlman recognizes this point when she says, "Knowledge, no sooner grasped, leaps forward again to excite new pursuit, and this is both the gratification and the frustration of trying to work on problems-in-change."[31]

It is reassuring to realize, however, that all the statements of the Council on Social Work Education, all the minutes of conferences, and all the books and articles on social work knowledge, which laid end to end might well circle the world several times, are in general agreement on the four broad areas of knowledge important to the social worker. However, as we have stated, the problem lies not in the task of finding a consensus on the broad areas of knowledge but in the task of selecting the critical concepts for use by the practitioner in social work from

---

[31] Helen Harris Perlman, *Social Casework: A Problem-Solving Process* (Chicago: University of Chicago Press, 1957), p. 27.

this immense range of knowledge and in the task of relating these concepts to one another.

CRITERIA FOR THE SELECTION OF KNOWLEDGE

In *Problems and Issues in Social Casework*, Briar and Miller discuss the requirements that any adequate theory of intervention should satisfy. They say that an adequate theory of intervention "must be explicit about the question of goals."[32] They point out that theories holding an optimistic view of human change have the practical virtue of "orienting the practitioner to potentials for change and to searching for more effective and powerful ways of bringing it about."[33] The theory should be clear about what its effective application would require of the client.[34] If statements about what is required of the client are absent, there is danger that theories will be applied to systems for which they are inappropriate. And if this knowledge is not shared with the client, he is deprived of important decisions about his involvement.

Another point that Briar and Miller make is that the theory should specify in behavioral terms what the practitioner needs to do to bring about changes. Some theories describe the practitioner's role in terms of the effect that his activities should produce rather than in terms of what he should do. Such theories leave to the practitioner the difficult task of translating theory into action, and make actions difficult to evaluate. The theory should also specify what the practitioner needs to do in order to make sure that the changes that occur are carried over into the client's ongoing life situation. Finally, the theory should set forth some guides for the assessment of outcome.[35]

In addition to Briar and Miller's formulation of the questions that theory should answer, we are including our own statement of the criteria for selection of the concepts that form the knowledge base of social work. To begin with, we should recognize that since social work is a profession, our primary task is not to generate knowledge about man and his system per se, but to select and organize knowledge in light of the nature of our tasks and the ways people change. Our knowledge base, therefore, must encompass concepts (largely borrowed from other fields) of how human systems develop, change, and dysfunction, and how the interrelationships between systems are formed, continue to operate, or dysfunction. Given the goals and purposes of social work in our society, we should select from borrowed knowledge that which helps

---

[32] Briar and Miller, *Problems and Issues* p. 180.
[33] Ibid., p. 183.
[34] Ibid.
[35] Ibid., pp. 184–85.

us determine (1) what in any given situation should be our unit of observation, (2) what events in this unit we should observe, (3) how we should observe them, (4) how we should relate them to each other in a way meaningful for the selection of methods of intervention, and (5) how we should determine whether our intervention produced the kind of change that was sought by us and the system with which we were involved (in other words, were we and our client able to achieve what we had jointly agreed was a desirable goal?). We should test out whether borrowed knowledge is really helpful in answering these questions. It is also our task as social workers to be producing our own knowledge about effective answers to the last questions.

DEALING WITH INCOMPLETE KNOWLEDGE

The practitioner-to-be is in the here and now faced with a great deal of knowledge to master—knowledge that is not very well related or integrated. Some of this knowledge is supported by empirical evidence; some of it is assumptive and supported, if at all, by only the roughest of evidence. Sometimes knowledge and value are all mixed up. And there never seem to be the appropriate interrelationships between bits of knowledge. The fact is, the amount of knowledge needed is so great and some of it is so uncertain that we are faced with the uncomfortable fact that we are constantly intervening in people's lives on the basis of incomplete knowledge (as are all other practitioners in the human services). This, however, raises some hard questions. How can we help people to feel some confidence in us as helpers while we remain tentative and often uncertain about what we know? How can we doubt our effectiveness and still be effective? How can we act as experts and be so constantly aware of our own ignorance?

The stress of acting on the basis of incomplete knowledge confronts all professionals in the human services, but it may bear heaviest on social workers because of their commitment to the individual and his worth. Some social workers handle it by trying to forget what they do not know, and they become very dogmatic people, certain of their own knowledge but unable to grow because one cannot learn if one already knows. Some social workers try to handle it by emphasizing what they don't know, how helpless they are; and they run around looking for authorities while their client suffers from the lack of a secure helper. Some practitioners try to handle it by blaming the profession for their discomfort. They then find themselves in the bind of representing a profession in which they have no confidence and with which they have no identification. That must be one of the most uncomfortable binds of all. Such workers have neither read and considered enough literature of other professions to understand that all professions are woefully lacking in knowledge of human beings and their interaction nor come to grips with their need to know.

The demand that we act on uncertain knowledge goes along with being a helping person in complex and ever-changing situations. Our best way of living with this is to commit ourselves to being active learners *all the time* and to the scientific method as a part of our equipment. We need to pledge to ourselves each and every day: "I will try everything I know to help the client system with which I am involved. In some aspects I may be too ignorant to truly know what way is best, but I will think carefully about my procedures, and I will be willing to assume the responsibility for my actions. I will not be blinded by preconceptions, nor will I be guilty of impulsively following a fleeting impulse or an easy answer. I will draw thoughtfully and responsibly upon every bit of knowledge that is available, and I will constantly and actively seek for more. I will be an insistent questioner rather than a passive taker, remaining identified with the profession while I vigorously question it. This is my solemn vow to my client. Thus, if my knowledge proves inadequate to the situation and the client's problem, my client and I will know that everything possible, given the present state of knowledge, has been done."[36]

Within the covers of this book will be offered some of the practice knowledge which we believe, from our own study, our own questioning, and our own experience as both practitioners and teachers, will be helpful to people who are interested in beginning the challenging journey of becoming a truly competent social worker—a journey that no one ever completes. We believe that any one author, or even two, can offer only partial knowledge. For example, little knowledge about either the social services network or the human condition per se will be offered here. We have chosen to offer knowledge about professional social work practice itself. We believe that the other necesary knowledge (at least for now) can be acquired from other sources within the curriculum of the university and the social work major. We also believe that the knowledge given here will be the most valuable and the most immediately needed in fieldwork or on a first job. In some ways we are building the structure and trusting that you will be able to construct the basement from other sources. This may mean that for the time being your building is setting somewhat uncertainly on jacks without the underpinnings that will gradually have to be put in place.

RECAPITULATION

In this chapter we have looked at social work knowledge and the problems involved in the selection and organization of knowledge for

[36] Based on Briar and Miller, *Problems and Issues,* pp. 184–85.

professional practice. We have pointed out that the functions of a profession determine the parameters of the knowledge that helps in the delivery of services, the maintenance of organizations, and the effecting of change. We need to know more about the processes of human and social change, the design of services responsive to the human systems that seek to utilize our help, and the evaluation of what we do.

We have suggested that systems theory, with its emphasis on transactions and interfaces between systems, on the constant activity of the open system, on the purposiveness of human systems, and on communication and information flow, may not only be of help to us as a way of organizing knowledge, but also introduces concepts that are in basic agreement with our value system and our functions. We have attempted to set forth some guidelines for the selection of theory and have offered some ways of dealing with our feelings when we are aware of the need to act on incomplete knowledge. We would further remind our readers that all knowledge of human systems and their change is incomplete.

A LOOK FORWARD

The readings that follow deal with three major divisions of this chapter. Gordon's article is a discussion of the difference between knowledge and values and of the purposes each serves. The areas of knowledge that the Council on Social Work Education thinks important in the education of social workers have been reproduced as an example of where the field is now in its thinking and as a statement of the areas of knowledge that are presently covered in the literature of the profession. Hartman's article on systems theory has been included to supplement our statement about this way of viewing man and his environment and their development. This article and the material in the chapter are both very brief accounts of a new approach that requires a new way of thinking, not simply the addition of new knowledge.

In the selected references at the end of the chapter there are more readings on the problem of establishing a knowledge base of social work and on systems theory. As the reader moves through the remaining chapters of the book, he will find various examples of the operationalizing of systems concepts.

Knowledge and value: Their distinction and relationship in clarifying social work practice*

William E. Gordon

Two of the five elements defining social work practice, as stated in the "Working Definition of Social Work Practice," are "value" and "knowledge."[1] The relevant sections read as follows:

Value

Certain philosophical concepts are basic to the practice of social work, namely:
1. The individual is the primary concern of this society.
2. There is interdependence between individuals in this society.
3. They have social responsibility for one another.
4. There are human needs common to each person, yet each person is essentially unique and different from others.
5. An essential attribute of a democratic society is the realization of the full potential of each individual and the assumption of his social responsibility through active participation in society.
6. Society has a responsibility to provide ways in which obstacles to this self-realization (i.e., disequilibrium between the individual and his environment) can be overcome or prevented.

These concepts provide the philosophical foundation for social work practice.

Knowledge

Social work, like all other professions, derives knowledge from a variety of sources and in application brings forth further knowledge from its own processes. Since knowledge of man is never final or absolute, the social worker in his application of this knowledge takes into account those phenomena that are exceptions to existing generalizations and

* Reprinted with permission of the author and the National Association of Social Workers from *Social Work*, 10:3 (July 1965), pp. 32–39.

[1] The working definition is included in Harriett M. Bartlett, "Toward Clarification and Improvement of Social Work Practice," *Social Work*, Vol. 3, No. 2 (April 1958), pp. 3–9. The other three elements of social work practice are "purpose," "sanction," and "method."

is aware and ready to deal with the spontaneous and unpredictable in human behavior. The practice of the social worker is typically guided by knowledge of:

1. Human development and behavior characterized by emphasis on the wholeness of the individual and the reciprocal influences of man and his total environment—human, social, economic, and cultural.

2. The psychology of giving and taking help from another person or source outside the individual.

3. Ways in which people communicate with one another and give outer expression to inner feelings, such as words, gestures, and activities.

4. Group process and the effects of groups upon individuals and the reciprocal influence of the individual upon the group.

5. The meaning and effect on the individual, groups, and community of cultural heritage including its religious beliefs, spiritual values, law, and other social institutions.

6. Relationships, i.e., the interactional processes between individuals, between individual and groups, and between group and group.

7. The community, its internal processes, modes of development and change, its social services and resources.

8. The social services, their structure, organization, and methods.

9. Himself, which enables the individual practitioner to be aware of and to take responsibility for his own emotions and attitudes as they affect his professional functions.

It can be seen that the working definition does not attempt to define "value" and "knowledge' 'except to refer under "value" to "philosophical concepts . . . basic to the practice of social work." The designers of the original definition apparently assumed that the meanings of "value" and "knowledge" were clear enough not to be confused.

Early in the work of the Subcommittee to Revise the Working Definition of Social Work Practice, however, it became clear that a distinction is not uniformly made between value and knowledge in social work. In the working definition itelf, which purported to make such a distinction, assertions are listed under "value" that range from "The individual is the primary concern of this society" to "There is interdependence between individuals in this society." Even without benefit of formal definition, one immediately senses a fundamental difference between these two statements. The first is obviously an assertion of an ideal, the second of an empirically demonstrable fact. Similarly, there are in the literature consensual statements classified as "philosophy and principle" that range from "Every human being is an end in himself and must not be used as a means to any other purpose" to "Man as a social being grows, develops, and matures through relationships with others, and needs these relationships to survive."[2] Again, a difference between

---

[2] Anne Winslow Oren and John C. Kidneigh, "A Note on Social Work Values," *Minnesota Welfare*, Vol. 13 (Fall 1961), pp. 26–31.

the two statements is obvious. The former asserts an ideal with its indicated action, the latter an empirically testable generalization.

The designers of the original working definition, as well as the subcommittee to revise it, saw fit to present two categories of propositions, one labeled "value" and the other "knowledge," and to subsume under each some of what was thought to be definitive of social work practice. To complete this task obviously requires more clarification of what is intended to go under each heading and some examination of the rationale for separating them.

Distinction between value and knowledge

In their basic meaning, value and knowledge are quite distinct and run on quite independent meaning tracks. In its traditional meaning, to "value" something is to "prefer" it. A measure of the extent of a preference is what price, effort, or sacrifice one will make to obtain what is preferred, whether article, behavior, or state of affairs. To identify a value held by an individual or a society, therefore, requires a description of "what" is preferred and some measure of the extent of that preference, that is, the price in effort, money, or sacrifice the individual will pay to achieve his preference, or the provision a society will make or the positive or negative sanctions it will impose to enforce the preference. As pointed out by Muriel Pumphrey, values:

> imply a usual preference for certain means, ends, and conditions of life, often being accompanied by strong feeling. While behavior may not always be consistent with values held, possession of values results in strain toward consistent choice of certain types of behavior whenever alternatives are offered. The meaning attached to values is of such impelling emotional quality that individuals who hold them often make personal sacrifices and work hard to maintain them, while groups will mobilize around the values they hold to exert approval and disapproval in the form of rewards and penalties (sanctions).[3]

The idea of strongly preferring to the point of investment of self and goods to obtain or maintain what is preferred is clearly central in value.

Knowledge, on the other hand, denotes the picture man has built up of the world and himself as it *is*, not as he might wish or fantasy or prefer it to be. *It is a picture derived from the most rigorous interpretation he is capable of giving to the most objective sense data he is able to obtain.*[4] An assertion of how things *are* that is found to hold

---

[3] Muriel W. Pumphrey, *The Teaching of Values and Ethics in Social Work Education*, Vol. XIII of the Curriculum Study (New York: Council on Social Work Education, 1959), p. 23.

[4] "Objective" is used here in the sense of data least influenced by the observer and most influenced by what is observed. "Rigorous" is used in the sense of following the rules of reasoning designed to reduce the incidence of erroneous conclusions.

when confronted with objective data rigorously interpreted is central to the idea of knowledge. Thus knowledge refers to what, in fact, *seems to be,* established by the highest standards of objectivity and rationality of which man is capable. Value refers to what man *prefers* or would *want to be* with a degree of attachment that may involve all the loyalty or devotion or sacrifice of which he is capable.

Some sources of confusion

While "valuing" and "knowing" in the sense given above are quite distinct when applied to real objects, behaviors, conditions and so forth, they are easily confused when applied to *statements about* such objects, behaviors, and the like. A statement of value and a statement of knowledge may be identical in form, and confusion arises, therefore, as to whether a given assertion should be taken as a part of knowledge (generalization) or as a statement of preference (value). For example, the statement that "the inherent dignity and worth of the individual establish his right to survive in terms which are satisfying to himself and to the world" is not from its structure identifiable as a value or as a generalization.[5]

A profession with pride in its orientation to the "real" world and to doing something about this world may be less concerned with its "statements" (generalizations, pronouncements, assertions, and the like) than it should be. Its statements, however, are the purveyors of its culture, except as it relies on example and demonstration for communicating and teaching. As social work is practiced in an increasing diversity of settings, with increasing fusion of methods, it becomes clear that the heart of continuity and professional utility lies in what social work wants for people (values) and what it knows about them (knowledge). To apply value and knowledge consciously and rationally, to communicate them in education, and to develop and extend them through research, all require their statement in some form. Social work's stance, therefore, toward these statements that constitute a large part of the profession's culture becomes critical to its practice, teaching, and research, and thus to its future. Social workers need to be aware of the extent to which they practice, teach, and research with these statements because of their preference for them or because of the statements' confirmation or confirmability.

With respect to statements purporting to describe values (what is preferred) and knowledge (what is thought to be), the distinction between value and knowledge lies largely in our sense of preference or

---

[5] Oren and Kidneigh, op. cit., p. 27.

sense of confirmation or confirmability concerning the statements. If this distinction is recognized, it is obvious that a statement may be:

1. Preferred and confirmed: "A democratic form of government leaves ultimate power in the hands of the people."
2. Preferred and not confirmed: "A democratic form of government permits man to reach the highest level of development of which he is capable."
3. Not preferred but confirmed: "Through the institution of war man has developed a socially sanctioned way of destroying millions of his fellow men."
4. Not preferred and not confirmed: "Man is the only species to have evolved to his level in the universe."

Thus the problem of separating value and knowledge becomes in one sense a more precise location of our attitude and stance toward the statements describing our perception of the world, both as we would wish it and as we think it is. How we locate a statement with regard to preference and confirmation will determine what we will do about its implications. If, for example, we believe a statement is confirmed (corresponds to reality) and we prefer it (like it that way), we will be adherents to the status quo and will feel no impulse to modify our statements to bring them into conformity with reality (no urge to inquiry) and no impulse to change reality to conform with our preference (no urge to change the world). When we believe that a statement is not confirmed and we also have no preference for it, we have the ultimate flexibility with respect to new ideas and the greatest freedom, although not necessarily the greatest drive to inquiry.

Dysfunctional outcomes

The greater difficulty in social work, however, falls when confirmation and preference do not coincide (Items 2 and 3 above). Failure to distinguish between preference and confirmation or confusion of the two when they do not coincide is highly dysfunctional at two levels of professional activity.

At the practice level, where we try to use knowledge and value as guides to action, the dysfunctional result of confusion is readily obvious. The ineffectiveness of knowingly or unknowingly substituting a preferred for an objective view of a situation is well known. Equally ineffective is substitution of the preferred proposition for the confirmed generalization as a guide to action, whether it is professional social work practice or any other activity. Knowledge and value play distinctly different roles, which, if not recognized or if mixed can greatly reduce the effectiveness of a profession and hence its ultimate development.

If a value is used as a guide in professional action when knowledge is called for, the resulting action is apt to be ineffective. If knowledge is called on when a value is needed as a guide to action, the resulting action may be unpurposeful. Both outcomes greatly reduce the potential for human welfare residing in the profession's heritage of both knowledge and values. Man's ability over time to bring some aspect of the world into conformity with his preferences (realize his values) seems to be directly proportional to his ability to bring his statements and perceptions into conformity with the world as it now is (develop the relevant science). As man develops and exercises his preference for the confirmed, he increases his ability over time to bring himself and the world into conformity with his preferences. As he masters the rules by which nature plays, he can increasingly influence the outcome of the game.

Dysfunctional results from failure to distinguish clearly between value and knowledge also express themselves in how the culture of social work itself is developed—that is, what is done about the statements that describe and delineate so much of that culture. Not separating clearly what is simply preferred from what is confirmed or confirmable restricts the active pursuit of knowledge and interferes with the constant adjustment required between preference and confirmation in any area where knowledge is expanding.

When confirmation is not clearly established for statements about *what is,* but preferences are strong for those statements, the difference between value and knowledge is expressed largely in one's intentions with respect to the preferred but not yet confirmed statement. Assertions that objective data rigorously interpreted offer the possibility of confirming can obviously be treated either as preferred states of affairs (values) or as putative knowledge (the assumptions and hypotheses of science), or both.[6] When assertions are preferred and unconfirmed but potentially confirmable, one's intentions toward them determine largely whether they are value or knowledge. For example, the proposition that the nuclear family is the best social medium for rearing mentally healthy children may be strongly preferred or valued or it may be treated as a hypothesis to be tested. Thus the difference between value and putative knowledge in this situation resides more in the stance taken toward the proposition—that is, in the intentions toward it—than in the proposition itself. These intentions involve considerable psychic interplay between preference (how we would like things to be) and reality insofar

---

[6] The distinction is quite clear in scientific work. For the same person to treat a proposition both as preferred and as a hypothesis requires that the tester be doubly alert to bias in his testing procedures, and signs of such preferences are usually cause to raise questions about the investigator's objectivity or scientific neutrality.

as it can be validly confirmed (the way things are). The fact that confirmation is especially tenuous in the social-psychological realm leaves far more room for interplay between the preferred view and that which purports to some confirmation than is the case in the physical or biological realms. The tension between preferred and thought-to-be-confirmed or confirmable propositions in the social and psychological sciences is therefore greater than in the physical and biological sciences.[7]

Convergence of value and knowledge

Unconfirmed statements vary, of course, in their degree of confirmability, ranging finally into assertions that there is no reasonable expectation of confirming, and preference becomes the final arbiter of selection. It is here that all philosophies, scientific included, meet on equal grounds. The assumption that knowledge is good for man competes on equal terms with the assumption that man has worth and dignity. Neither is confirmable, but either or both can be strongly preferred. Once, however, there is a possibility of confirmation through objective observation rigorously interpreted, preference for the confirmed or confirmable statement over the unconfirmed or unconfirmable characterizes the scientific approach—that is, the confirmed or confirmable statement is valued more than others.

The ascendancy in a society of the scientific value (preference for propositions confirmed or confirmable) constantly narrows the realm of propositions held solely or largely by perference. Expanding scientifically derived knowledge, therefore, crowds propositions held largely by preference constantly in the direction of the presently unconfirmable. When expansion of knowledge confronts preferred explanations and assumptions with confirmatory or disconfirmatory evidence, the preference or value either becomes firm knowledge or loses its preference and ceases to be a value. For example, many pre-Copernican people actively preferred the proposition that the earth was the center of the universe and applied sanctions to those who did not hold with this proposition. The confirmed proposition that the earth is a minor planet in a minor galaxy is, however, the preferred one today. On the other hand, the value attached to a highly sacrificial life in which the individual "gives" far more than he "gets" is being thrown into considerable question by the nonvalued outcome to mental health and personality development.

Knowledge and value can thus converge by two routes. One is the shifting of preference toward the confirmed, which is characteristic of a scientifically oriented society. The other is the modification of the

---

[7] This tension is sometimes erroneously referred to as a clash between science and values rather than more precisely as a conflict between preference and confirmation.

reality on which confirmation is based so that the world, as it were, comes to be in accord with preference, which is characteristic of a change-oriented society.

Two approaches

For social work the minimum first step is the separation of what social work prefers or wants for people from what social work knows about people. A recasting of its propositions into those preferred or valued assertions about man, his behavior, and his society and those confirmed or confirmable by objective data rigorously interpreted would then follow. Two approaches are open for progress in this direction. One would begin with empirical data, and the other would move directly to formulations of choices openly and frankly made by the profession.

Empirical approach. As Oren and Kidneigh demonstrated, it is entirely feasible to establish a list of assertions preferred by a defined group of social workers.[8] An extended list of value assertions tested by consensus in the profession as a whole would yield an approximate value-set or profile for social work at the time it was established. Such a list of valued behaviors, conditions, relationships, and so forth might further be crudely distributed according to their degree of confirmation or confirmability, and thus throw some light on the extent to which preference and confirmation are congruent and the extent to which preference is for as yet unconfirmed or even unconfirmable propositions. One would look for those unconfirmed assertions that have a reasonable probability of being confirmed in the future by bringing reality into conformity with them as goals rather than as scientific propositions. One would also look for those unconfirmable propositions that attempt to rationalize conflict between preference and emerging confirmed or confirmable or predictable states of human affairs. When personal values come into conflict with the yield of scientific endeavor, the offense to personal values may result in escape maneuvers that are more rationalizations than rational. It may result, for example, in casting what is really a preference as a putative knowledge assertion, but consciously or unconsciously designed to be unconfirmable by virtue of vagueness, structure, or reference to temporally and physically remote entities. The intentions one has toward a proposition—that is, to hold it notwithstanding or to modify it in accordance with objective data rigorously interpreted—are often revealed in the architecture of the proposition and its amenability to application of scientific precedures. In identifying and sorting out the propositions of social work into the value and knowledge categories, the profession needs to be aware of where it is rationally exercising its preference for things as they are or might be and where

---

[8] Op. cit., pp. 27–30.

it is rationalizing its reluctance to submit its preferences to objective data rigorously interpreted.

Direct formulation of values. A consensual approach to the identification of social work values and putative knowledge would be an illuminating exercise. Direct formulation, however, probably holds more promise for the reliable separation of values and knowledge, and especially for the selection of a value configuration of pervasive and enduring potential and the articulation of a science applicable to the attainment of the values.

Such a set of value assertions that the profession can accept and proclaim must meet several criteria. First, it must embrace, without fundamental contradiction, what the majority of the profession "feels is right" for social work and thus command practitioners' preference without reservation. Such a set must also be sufficiently basic and fundamental to remain useful over a substantial period of time in much the same way that the value implicit in the Hippocratic oath has served the physician over the ages. The focal value-set asserted by the profession should give the profession the highest possible sense of mission and suggest more immediate goals and objectives consistent with this purpose. Finally, the value-set ultimately selected should be so cast as to accommodate and encourage substantial growth of knowledge in the service of those values and encourage the treatment of preferred but unconfirmed assertions as hypotheses whenever they contain any elements of confirmability.

Value focus

Maximum realization of each individual's potential for development throughout his lifetime is a basic value that seems to meet the criteria above. As a value it may be treated as an unconfirmable assumption that it is "right" and "good" for each individual to continue to develop, grow, unfold, and attain the greatest possible elaboration of his "humanness" in his lifetime. While one might seek to rest authority for accepting the assumption in some higher ethic or value, it should need to appeal to a metaphysic to be accepted as fundamental in itself for anyone who fully appreciates man even as simply the most remarkable outcome of evolutionary history on this planet.

The core idea of human realization—unfolding of potential, continued growth in the human dimension, and so on—leaves ample room for adherence to the idea of self-determination. The faith that man when freed can be trusted to grow and develop in desirable directions is probably the highest expression of a belief in human dignity, and thus an encompassing value for social work to proclaim and use as an ultimate criterion to judge that which is good and desirable for people.

Knowledge focus

In conformity with the distinctions made above between value and knowledge (preference and confirmation), the knowledge base of social work must be formulated toward confirmed and confirmable propositions—that is, knowledge formulation must deal in generalizations that, even if preferred, are intended to give way to objective data rigorously interpreted. While the basic knowledge formulation must relate to present social work perspective sufficiently to utilize and build on social work wisdom, there are other important criteria to be met:

1. High relevance or applicability to the achievement of the values is essential if the knowledge formulation is to yield a science of social work to serve the values of social work.

2. Theoretical interest and potential for development are essential in the knowledge formulation if it is to provide the intellectual stimulation for research and the conceptual structure to formulate such research.

3. Commitment to knowledge-building further requires the selection of an area of phenomena and the selection of a few prime variables on which to focus and concentrate the scientific knowledge-building effort.

To meet these criteria it is proposed, therefore, that the central phenomenon of social work science is "social transactions," or the action interface between people, activity in the boundary between the human organism and one of the currently most important parts of his environment—other people. Theoretical interest would attach to *the relationship between the quality and the amount of this transaction and its effect on human realization* on the one hand, *and on the nature of the social environment* on the other.

Social functioning, for some time considered the ultimate concern of social work, becomes the beginning, not the end of social work interest, an interest fed by the impact of functioning patterns on both human growth and the social environment. Knowledge pursued and formulated along the feedback lines of social functioning to the individual and to his environment is a neglected area of inquiry largely untouched by psychologies and sociologies that are intent on explaining the causes of social functioning rather than its consequences.

Value-knowledge alignment

The location of the ultimate social work value in human realization and the focus of its contributing science on social functioning separate social work value and knowledge into distinct and separate dimensions—value in the growth or outcome dimension and knowledge in the pattern-of-functioning dimension. By shifting the major emphasis in valuing to outcome in the human realization realm, the behavior realm is open for scientific evaluation against that outcome. Behaviors evaluated scientifically against outcomes rather than valued according to current preferences would clearly separate the social worker's role of scientific professional from his role as social norm enforcer, a separation not always clearly made in the present mixing of values and knowledge. With the development of a science describing the relationship between social transaction patterns and outcomes both for human realization and social environment, social work would for the first time be in a position to evaluate scientifically rather than simply on the basis of preference the proposed social arrangements and behaviors thought to be good for people. Consequently, social work would place the foundation for its knowledge base clearly in the realm of a science and in the service of an emerging value of growing appeal.

Social work curriculum*

Council on Social Work Education

The professional curriculum for social work draws broadly and selectively from the humanities, from other professions and scientific disciplines, as well as from the knowledge and experience developed by social work. Application of this content to social work involves ethical as well as scientific commitment. The study and analysis of ethical considerations is an important component of social work education.

The curriculum is developed as a unified whole and achieves its coherence by viewing all courses as presenting knowledge to throw light on several broad components related to human problems and needs: social welfare policy and services, human behavior and the social environment and social work practice. These terms merely denote areas of substantive knowledge but are not intended to delineate the structure of the curriculum or the categorization of courses. It is expected that schools will provide systematic instruction relevant to the content of these spheres and that each school will develop an appropriate schema for the ordering of its particular courses. The general kinds of substantive

* Reprinted by permission of the Council on Social Work Education from the *Manual of Accrediting Standards for Graduate Professional Schools of Social Work,* revised April 1971, pp. 56–60.

knowledge and the major instructional obejctives to be pursued within the total curriculum are described below.

Content pertaining to social welfare policy and services

Opportunity should be provided all students to acquire knowledge of the general policies, conditions, legislative bases, institutions, programs, and broad range of services relevant to social welfare in contemporary society. Similarly, all students should be informed about the characteristics, functions, and contributions of social workers and of the profession in connection with social welfare problems and programs. Further, each student should have an opportunity, consistent with the school's objectives and resources, to concentrate study on a sector of social welfare having particular pertinence to his professional career interests.

The major aims of study pertinent to social welfare policy and services are to prepare professionals to act as informed and competent practitioners in providing services, and as participants or leaders in efforts to achieve desirable change. Instruction should be directed toward developing both analytic skills and substantive knowledge, with a focus on the acquisition of competence required for the development, implementation, and change of social work policies and programs.

Attention should be given to the historical as well as current forces which generate social policies and contribute to social problems. Of particular importance is knowledge and ability to make choices about the social policies that condition authorization, financing, and programming of social welfare services, and development of a broad appreciation of the human values and social norms which shape both policies and services. Students should be provided with a basis for identifying and appraising the programs and agencies characteristically involved in dealing with problems of the individual and society, as well as those which contribute to the enhancement of personal experience and of social opportunity. Study should also be addressed to the changing nature of problem conceptions, to deficiencies in contemporary programs, and to emerging forms of service or expressions of need. Specific foci for study should include agencies' structural and administrative patterns, their service-delivery systems, the populations served by agencies, their linkages with related programs and other organizations, and their social and political environments.

Provision should be made for helping students to acquire an ability for critical analysis of the problems and conditions in society and its major institutions which have warranted or now require the intervention of social work. Study should be given to the characteristics and structures of social work as a profession, with particular attention to the roles its members have served, historically and currently, in the development and implementation of social welfare policies and programs. With respect to the fields of service within which they are practitioners, students should be helped to develop the capacity to raise relevant questions and to read and evaluate research reports bearing upon these questions.

Education in this area should aim at development among students of commitment to the profession's responsibilities to promote social welfare goals and services, to work toward prevention of social problems, and to contribute to positive social change. To be fostered are motivation and competence to participate effectively in the formulation and implementation of policies, in the improvement of programs, and in the progressive change of service agencies.

Content pertaining to human behavior and the social environment

The body of content relating to human behavior is designed to contribute to the student's understanding of the individual, group, organizational, institutional, and cultural contexts within which human behavior is expressed and by which it is significantly influenced. This objective is achieved through the retrieval, specification, and extension of those theories and bodies of knowledge derived from the biological, psychological, and social sciences as well as from the humanities which are needed for an understanding of social work values and practice.

Ultimately, all sciences are concerned with and contribute, directly or indirectly, to an understanding of human behavior. There is no generally accepted unified theory of human behavior, nor is there any single theory or formulation of relevant content which is sufficient for all social workers. Rather, there are many theories and systems of knowledge which have been developed for a variety of purposes and within a wide range of perspectives. These theories and perspectives, as well as their interrelationships, should be recognized and reflected as specifically as possible in the curriculum design and modes of instruction.

While it is expected that all social work students achieve a basic understanding of individual and collective dynamics, the particular specification of the content of this component of the curriculum and the design within which it is executed should derive from and be consistent with the educational objectives and program of the individual school, the range and quality of its educational resources, the needs and composition of the student body, and the functions of social work. Opportunities should be provided for the social work student to develop the capacity to identify and master those aspects of this body of content which are relevant to the social work roles for which he seeks competence and to the tasks which he expects to perform.

Equal in importance to the mastery of relevant content for the social work student is the development of the capacity to assess critically the state of this theory and knowledge as it relates to social work practice, the assumptions which have influenced its development, and, finally, to begin to develop the skills and capacities which will ultimately permit him to fulfill his obligation to contribute to its development.

Content pertaining to social work practice

This area of the curriculum is designed to help the student learn and apply the knowledge and principles of social work practice in accordance with the values and ethics of the profession. The components of knowledge and competence to be fostered in this area of the curriculum may be combined differently in several areas of intervention for a variety of purposes and to meet diverse needs.

The development of competence in the practice of social work is a primary curriculum objective and requires provision of opportunities designed to help each student:

- Understand the relation of knowledge, value, and skill to each other and their utilization in the appraisal of problems or situations for social work intervention and in the provision of professional service.
- Develop the self-awareness and self-discipline requisite for responsible performance as a social worker.
- Recognize and appreciate the similarities and differences in the helping roles of various professionals and other personnel and in the problem-solving processes associated with service to individuals, groups, organizations, and communities.
- Understand the responsibilty and functions of the social worker in contributing from professional knowledge to the prevention of social problems and to the improvement of social welfare programs, policies, and services.
- Develop a spirit of inquiry and a commitment throughout his professional career to seek, critically appraise, contribute to, and utilize new knowledge.

Social work practice is conducted through particular professional roles, generally in organizations providing social services. These roles require the practitioner to exercise his knowledge and skill. Preparation for these roles necessitates acquisition of specialized learning and competence. To assure the provision of both basic instruction and specialized study, the graduate curriculum must include one or more concentrations. A concentration presents a distinctive pattern of instruction that organizes experiences appropriate to a specific range of professional roles and functions. Each concentration should be developed so that the student can attain a level of competence necssary for responsible professional practice and sufficient to serve as a basis for continuing professional development.

Schools may identify a variety of modes or dimensions of competence and service as their basis for development of concentrations within the curriculum. Programs of graduate education, in addition to their conservation function, must react to and encourage consideration of new or expanded roles, the changing nature of professional roles, and the conditions bearing upon practice. The pattern of concentrations within the curriculum is intended to organize instruction in preparation for competence practice, not to define or govern the nature of professional roles.

Responsibility rests with each school for definition and development of its concentration(s) for instruction in social work practice. In view of the profession's scope, no single concentration, and probably no school's composite of concentrations, should be conceived as providing instruction sufficient for the full range of social work roles. But no concentration should be so narrowly conceived that it focuses primarily on specific competencies, specific positions, or on career lines within particular service organizations.

For each concentration it offers the school is expected to formulate explicitly the following:

1. Aims and rationale of the concentration including its relevance to social work.
2. Identification of existing or emerging professional roles suitable for and available to those who complete the concentration.
3. Specific educational objectives including the professional knowledge and competence to be fostered.
4. The specific arrangement of educational experience, including courses and practice skill components.
5. Relation of each concentration to the total curriculum and to its several components including other concentrations.

It is anticipated that there will be diversity among schools in the kinds and number of concentrations offered, as well as in their designations, and in the instructional activities and learning experiences provided. Each school is expected to formulate, develop, and justify its concentration(s) oriented to the responsibilities of the profession and commensurate with the school's resources and capabilities.

To think about the unthinkable*

Ann Hartman

Time and time again the field of social work has been engulfed by waves of new knowledge and theory originating in the many fields of knowledge on which social work practice is based. Repeatedly, social workers have been challenged to learn new vocabularies and master new concepts and eventually to translate them into practice. "The psychiatric thread" of the twenties, the psychoanalytic revolution of the thirties, modern ego psychology, and the new knowledge from the social sciences have all stretched our intellectual and integrative capacities to their limits.

Once again, if my barometer is correct in assessing the intellectual climate, practitioners are shortly to be challenged by a strange vocabulary, new conceptual models, and new knowledge. General systems theory began trickling into the field with the publication of Werner Lutz's "sleeper," *Concepts and Principles Underlying Casework Practice.*[1] That trickle has now become a stream, and, as we see the yearly multiplication of references to and articles about systems theory, we might well prepare ourselves for a flood.[2]

Early reactions to this body of theory have ranged from enthusiasm, to caution, to resistance, to downright suspicion. These are reactions, to be sure, that have accompanied the introduction of every new body of knowledge or conceptual framework. In addition to natural resistances to newness and strangeness, however, there are specific aspects of systems theory that have been particularly responsible for the negative responses that have developed.

First, systems theory is highly abstract, and the task of translating it through middle-range theory into practice is immense. Social workers,

---

* Reprinted by permission of the author and the Family Service Association of America from *Social Casework,* 58:8, (October 1970), pp. 467–74.

[1] Werner A. Lutz, *Concepts and Principles Underlying Social Casework Practice,* Social Work Practice in Medical Care and Rehabilitation Settings, Monograph III (Washington, D.C.: National Association of Social Workers, Medical Social Work Section, 1956).

[2] See Gordon Hearn, ed., *The General Systems Approach: Contribution Toward An Holistic Conception of Social Work* (New York: Council on Social Work Education, 1969); Sister Mary Paul Janchill, "Systems Concepts in Casework Theory and Practice," *Social Casework,* 50:74–82 (February 1969); and Carel B. Germain, Social Study: Past and Future, *Social Casework,* 49:403–9 (July 1968).

faced with the overwhelming demands of practice in this increasingly complex world, cannot help but respond with the question, "It's all very interesting, but what does it have to do with my tasks or me?"

Second, the current nature of systems theory leads to major confusion. There is not just one definitively conceptualized and neatly packaged systems theory, but many different theories or views. Should ten people immersed in systems thinking meet to discuss their views, there would probably be ten versions and even ten vocabularies.

Third, those interested in translating systems concepts frequently do so in the systems language, which not only fails to edify but can alienate or irritate the uninitiated. Finally, of lesser importance—but perhaps somewhat relevant—is the nature of the systems language itself. Terms such as *input, throughput, coding,* and *entropy* produce such mechanistic associations that they may serve to alienate many caseworkers. We did survive and finally adopted *id, superego,* and *Oedipus,* so one hopes that if the terms are truly meaningful, they will overcome their unappealing resonances. This article will attempt to clarify some of these problems in the hope of bringing systems thinking a little closer to the casework practitioner.

The major question—the question for which there is not one but many answers—is, what is systems theory? It is my conviction that a major source of confusion has been the tendency of both social workers and writers on systems to fail to distinguish sufficiently between the use of the system as a conceptual model and the use of the system as a model of empirical reality with predictive value, a description of "what things are really like out there." The use of the system as a conceptual tool requires no verification in resarch; the only requirement is for the system to be consistent with its set of definitions. To take this conceptual model and announce that the world is so constructed is, however, another very giant step. To move from organizing data about people and groups within a systems conceptual framework is very different from going on to make statements about the way living systems "behave" as systems.

The system as a conceptual model

The conceptual model of the system is a means of ordering what Alfred North Whitehead called this "radically untidy world" in terms of relatedness rather than in terms of shared characteristics.[3] It is a relativistic and extensive rather than an absolute and essential mode of thought. In other words, it examines the nature of an entity in relation

---

[3] Alfred North Whitehead, *The Aims of Education and Other Essays* (New York: Macmillan Co., 1929).

to the things it affects and is affected by rather than in relation to essential characteristics.

For the most part, Western thought has tended to be linear, atomistic, and analytical rather than transactional and synthetic. These modes of thought may well reflect the limitations of mentation, the fact that we think in a linear stream in time, that we can think of only one thing at a time, and that we are limited in the amount of data with which we can deal. These limitations lead us to attempt to master knowledge by partializing it, and, of course, analysis and partializing distort the nature of the very reality we are attempting to understand. The inadequacy of these modes of thought has lead to a systems model of conceptualization in one after another field of science. The conceptual model of the system enables us to expand our minds and deal with infinitely more data. It helps us to think about the unthinkable.[4]

The common sense definition of a system would be a whole that is composed of interrelated and interdependent parts. To elucidate this original definition, other characteristics may be specified. The system has boundaries. Data are either a part of the system or are not. A system has structure made up of those parts of the system included in the boundaries and the more or less permanent pattern of their relationship. Function, in systems terms, is defined as the result, or the outcome, of the structure. Systems have emergent qualities. This is the familiar concept that the whole is greater than the sum of the parts and that the interrelatedness of units in a system gives rise to new qualities that are a function of that interrelatedness. A poem is more than a list of all the words that compose it. In many frames of reference, it is possible to say that we never perceive the unit parts, but only the emergent qualities. A system has a frame of reference; in using the system's conceptual model it is essential to specify that frame of reference. For example, a human being can be considered as a psychological, biological, chemical, or physical system, or as a part of many social systems. Each frame of reference generates a very different system and yet each is describing the same empirical object.

Finally, a change in one part of the system affects the system as a whole and all of its parts. This statement may appear to be substantive or predictive, but in truth, it simply follows from the original definition.

Relevance to social work practice

What has this to do with the practice of social work? Does this mode of thought offer anything of real help to the practitioner? Does it indeed stretch the mind or merely clutter it? It is my conviction that this mode

---

[4] I am indebted to Carel Germain who suggested to me that the systems model enabled us "to think about the unthinkable."

of thought is highly appropriate to the tasks and aims of social work practice. Social workers have always struggled to capture and express interactional concepts. Although there have been shifts in emphasis over the years and periods of excessive concentration on purely psychological data, our profession's concern has been primarily with the *person in relation to his environment.*

Ma.y Richmond's basic views were highly transactional, but she, of course, was a captive of the cognitive modes of her day. Most scientists were concerned with encyclopedic empirical surveys and the classification of data. Thus, in her attempt to capture the infinite complexity of the person-in-situation, Mary Richmond produced the ponderous *Social Diagnosis.*[5] Her limitations were perhaps not in her basic conceptions but in the analytic and synthetic tools available to her.

The systems model, therefore, can be helpful to social workers because if offers a conceptual framework that shifts attention from characteristics possessed by individual entities to interaction and relatedness. The following example illustrates this shift. John, age ten, may be thought of as one of the class "ten-year-old boy" with characteristics that, being a ten-year-old boy, he is likely to have. Or, he may be thought of in all of his relationships—with his father, mother, total family, school, peer group, neighborhood, social class, cultural value system, and access to the opportunity structure.

Diagnostic terms that describe interactional relationships are beginning to be developed; for example, there is the "family scapegoat," which describes a certain kind of transaction between a child and his family. Complementarity and pseudomutuality also aim at transactional diagnoses. Efforts are being made to describe dynamically more and more complex interactions with or between more and more complex systems. The conceptual model opens the door to and encourages transactional thinking and observations.

In addition, the system as a conceptual model enables us to bring order into the massive amount of data from all of the different frames of reference or fields of knowledge that provide the base for social work practice. According to one estimate, human knowledge doubled from 1950 to 1960, from 1960 to 1966, and again, from 1966 to 1970.[6] As social work students and practitioners are faced with the problem of having to master more and more knowledge, this higher order of conceptualization permits the handling of vast amounts of material and increases our ability to consider the intricate patterns of contemporaneous interactions. This conceptual model can give us a framework that

---

[5] Mary E. Richmond, *Social Diagnosis* (New York: Russell Sage Foundation, 1917).

[6] Michael J. Kami, "Planning for Change with New Approaches," *Social Casework,* 51:209–10 (April 1970).

is substantively neutral and "portable" from one frame of reference to another. The tools are equally applicable to the personality system, the social agency as a social system, the family, and a hospital. The concepts can aid in the mastery of the theories of personality, ego, crisis, family, small groups, and communication.

Helpfulness of spatial representation

Akin to Kurt Lewin's field theory, the systems model further enhances conceptualization because it lends itself to spatial representation.[7] People immersed in systems thinking are constantly drawing pictures that resemble DNA (deoxyribonucleic acid) or an urban transit system. The helpfulness of spatial representation must not be underestimated. Not only can such pictures help us to organize what we know as we see it in one moment in all of its complexity, but they can also aid in the discovery of new knowledge, or new relationships. In *The Double Helix*, James Watson describes how the structure of DNA was solved through the actual manipulation of three-dimensional models.[8] The drawing of pictures of relatedness is also an aid to communication. In the classroom, the staff meeting, and in supervision, the ability to represent spatially and visually the client, the family, and the organization in all the complexities of the "life space" is a stimulating teaching aid.

Because the systems model enables us to consider concurrently a number of interacting variables, it serves as an aid in avoiding reductionism. We have gone through periods of emphasizing causation in society's malfunction. We have also been guilty of laying all effects at the door of psychological causation. Further, we have attempted to understand social groups by applying principles of individual psychological functioning to them—principles that do not apply. With clarity of frames of reference, and with the study of the interaction among personality, social, cultural, and biological systems, we can move to a more sophisticated diagnostic view of multiple causation.

Conceptualizing reality as systems of related entities can move us to a broader conception of practice, to see practice in relation to multiple possibilities for intervention. When the mind is stretched, so too are the possibilities for action. Because an effect on one component of the system affects all the other components, the possibilities for intervention become multiple. Further, according to the systems principle of equifinality, various interventions may conclude with the same final effect. For example, let us consider John, the ten-year-old boy. Perhaps he

---

[7] Kurt Lewin, "Formalization and Progress in Psychology," in *Theory in Social Science: Selected Theoretical Papers*, ed. Darwin Cartwright (New York: Harper & Brothers, 1951).

[8] James D. Watson, *The Double Helix* (New York: Atheneum, 1968).

was referred to an agency because of poor performance in school. Direct therapeutic intervention with the boy is not necessarily the only, the most economical, or even the best choice. Intervention with the mother, the father, the family as a whole, or the school may be more helpful. Or the boy's poor school performance may be best approached through such interventions as improved housing or economic supports for the family, a vocational training opportunity for the father, or a recreation program.

Such a view does not mean that intervention should always be more and more extensive and multiple. Frequently, it can be more simple. For example, family therapists have certainly been systems oriented and have attempted, in conjoint family therapy, to alter the system as a whole by treating the system as a whole. They have sometimes neglected to consider, however, that family therapy can consist of intervention with one central family member who becomes the emissary of change for the total system.

These analytical tools for thought grow out of the original definitions of the system. Like all classification schemes, they become the means of ordering reality; they make no claim as to the nature of that reality. Social workers may use these tools to think about the unthinkable—to gain a broader and more sophisticated view of their field of operation and their professional tasks.

Systems theories in operation

Systems theorists, however, have gone far beyond the use of the system as a conceptual framework and have developed various bodies of theory and principles about the way systems operate—bodies of theory that claim empirical predictive value. These principles are concerned with the functioning of open, or living, or energy systems, as they are variously called. These systems import and export energy and are the systems of primary concern to social workers. It must be emphasized that these principles and their implications are not universally accepted, that they are in varying stages of empirical validation, and that, at this point, they can be utilized only as possible hypotheses. When bodies of scientific knowledge or theoretical structures are in conflict or inadequately established in research, social workers must move with caution. However, if we shut ourselves off from rich sources of stimulation and knowledge and await pure certainty, we seriously limit our own innovative possibilities. Further, social work practice and research can contribute, and currently are contributing, to the validation, refinement, or repudiation of empirical propositions related to these propositions.

The discussion here will be limited to the examination and possible applications of a few of these major concepts. First, most systems theorists generally agree that the open system strives toward the maintenance of some sort of inner integrity or balance between subsystems and units within subsystems. This tendency has been given various names. Walter B. Cannon, in his *Wisdom of the Body*, called it "homeostasis"; he was one of the first thinkers to describe the various control and communication subsystems that maintain the body's inner integrity in the face of inner and outer stress.[9] Psychoanalytic thinkers have used the term for a similar psychological process. Ludwig von Bertalanffy seems to have been the originator of the term "moving steady state"; this term implies a process, or a moving balance, and avoids the somewhat static implications of homeostasis as a particular state.[10]

What are the practice implications of the hypothesis that the open system strives to maintain a moving steady state? The examples are numerous. A major area of practice theory intimately related to homeostasis is "crisis theory." A state of crisis is defined as a situation in which a person's adaptive capacities (or homeostatic mechanisms) are overwhelmed by relatively sudden or intense alteration of internal or external demands. These demands may come in the form of a traumatic event, a new external situation, or new demands made upon the individual occasioned by a developmental stage in the life cycle. The concept that a crisis may be an opportunity as well as a threat follows logically from the systems hypotheses. The individual may adapt to and master the new demands through the development of new and more differentiated adaptive modes. It is this possibility that indicates that crisis intervention may not only prevent breakdown of adaptation but may offer invaluable opportunities for growth. "New occasions teach new duties; . . ."[11]

Implications for institutional change

Applications of crisis theory can move beyond the individual, the family, and the small group to an increased understanding of the impact of events and change on organizational systems, such as service organizations and social agencies. The hypotheses concerning the system's maintenance of a steady state implies a tendency that is essentially "conservative"—a tendency for the dynamics of a system to be geared to the maintenance of the system and for some resistance to change to be inevitable. Social workers have joined sociologists in examining service organizations to see how much energy is utilized in the performance

---

[9] Walter B. Cannon, *Wisdom of the Body* (New York: W. W. Norton & Co., 1932).

[10] Ludwig von Bertalanffy, "The Theory of Open Systems in Physics and Biology," *Science*. III:23–29 (January 1950).

[11] James Russell Lowell, *The Present Crisis*, Stanza 18.

of tasks and the achievement of goals and how much in self-maintenance.

Concern about practice implications on an individual or an organizational level has led to discussion of the concept of inducing crisis as a method for change, particularly for changing institutions.[12] When this strategy for change is operationalized, however, it must be remembered that, according to crisis theory, the resolution of the crisis can go either way—toward the development of new adaptive modes or toward regression and defense through the closure of the system, the isolation of the stimulus, and the rigidifying of the structure.

The hypothesis of homeostasis is not new to social workers. Cannon's work was of interest to writers and practitioners in the thirties. The homeostatic functions of the ego have been of major concern to caseworkers because the profession has increasingly moved toward a practice geared to the reestablishment and maintenance of adaptive capacities. What is perhaps added by a systems approach is the ability to move to other systems and to see some of the same phenomena in operation, and thus to broaden the base of knowledge and practice.

Von Bertalanffy has been the main proponent of a second and much more controversial principle governing the operation of open systems. This principle is a generalization of the second law of thermodynamics in physics. This law states that any closed system has the tendency to return to entropy. Entropy is the opposite of system. Without interchange with the environment, a system tends to lose inner energy differentiation (or the ability to do work in physical terms), which is bound up in systemization and released in the move toward entropy. A corollary of this principle is that an open system tends toward further elaboration, increasing complexity, and differentiation.

Initially, this principle seems remote from casework thought and practice; however, its implications for much of the thought underlying our professional practice are immense. Such systems theorists as von Bertalanffy and Gordon Allport have felt that Sigmund Freud's emphasis on the first law of thermodynamics (the conservation of energy), rather than the second, led to the traditional model of the personality system as a "semiclosed" system.[13] Allport believes that this mechanistic, Newtonian view has been corrected by modern ego psychology, which emphasizes the personality system's differentiation and development in relation to the environment, rather than its being almost solely an elaboration of the inner instinctual drives.

Some ego psychologists have opened the personality system to the

---

[12] Kami, "Planning for Change with New Approaches."

[13] Ludwig von Bertalanffy, "General Systems Theory and Psychiatry," in *American Handbook of Psychiatry*, ed. Silvano Arieti (New York: Basic Books, 1966), 3:705–21; and Gordon Allport, "The Open System in Personality Theory," *Journal of Abnormal and Social Psychiatry*, 61:301–10 (November 1960).

extent that they give instinctual status to man's drive·to interact with, to master, and to develop novel solutions in relation to his environment. Basically, they are arguing for the autonomous ego. The more conservative ego psychologists believe that the ego's autonomy is an emergent quality growing from the ego's organization and that the energy at the disposal of the ego is id energy. Ego autonomy, whether as an emergent quality or basic characteristic of the ego, serves to open the personality system and to bring metapsychology in line with twentieth century thought.

Implications for personality change

This view of the personality system radically changes both the concept of causation and the possibilities for change. The personality is no longer seen primarily as an elaboration of the drives and their early vicissitudes, the nature of which are laid down in early childhood. The comment, "give me a child till he's seven and I'll have him the rest of his life!" is expressive of this view of the tyranny of the early years.

If the personality system were thus closed, it is obvious that *real* change could only take place through psychoanalysis or a related form of intensive psychotherapy, getting back to and "redoing" these early years. All other levels and efforts at change would be "superficial." Certainly caseworkers have struggled with this designation for years. There has existed a hierarchy of interventions performed by caseworkers, ranging from "environmental manipulation," through various levels of direct intervention, to "intensive psychotherapy," accompanied by differentials in status and even in salaries. Because *real* change could only occur through an approach to the deepest levels of the personality, many caseworkers labored with their feelings that what they were doing made no *real* difference. Currently we are seeing an opposite view expressed, a view that may be equally reductionist; that is, that an approach to the individual on any level is irrelevant and that any *real* change is major social change.

Erik Erikson, in his epigenetic view of growth and change, opens the personality system to meaningful interaction with inner and outer influences without abandoning the significance of early experience.[14] His view is that throughout life, particularly in the crisis periods occasioned by new biopsychosocial demands and tasks, human beings have new opportunities for growth and change, but that the manner in which these opportunities can be utilized is reflective of the individual's success or failure in dealing with the earlier maturational tasks.

---

[14] Erik H. Erikson, *Childhood and Society*, 2d ed., rev. and enl. (New York: W. W. Norton & Co., 1950).

No matter how the change opportunities are further described, if the personality system is open throughout life, if meaningful change is possible—not only through therapeutic intervention, but through life experience, through new opportunities for mastery, for social interchange, for involvement, and for participation—the caseworker's role and assessment of possible effectiveness alters radically. The primary arena for change shifts from past to present, and new emphases in casework practice emerge. Old-fashioned "environmental manipulation" becomes a major and highly sophisticated intervention. Treatment emphasis shifts to the offering or making available of a variety of opportunities in the here and now, to the development of "inputs," or enriching experiences with accompanying supports so that these inputs can be utilized.

The medical clinical model, which focused on the correction of pathology—pathology rooted in early trauma and deprivations—is joined by the life model, the developmental model, the enrichment model, the life space model, milieu therapy, and the social competence model.[15] Although differing in detail, all of these models see change as a result of the availability of new opportunity, supplies, and experiences in the individual's social, emotional, and physical environment. These changes bring the worker into the everyday life of the client, where the action is. Interestingly enough, such models of casework intervention come close to the original Richmond definition, that casework consists of *"those processes which develop personality through adjustments consciously effected, individual by individual, between men and their social environment."*[16]

The entropy principle leads to other quite specific applications in casework practice. These applications concern the effects of stimulus starvation, isolation, or social deprivation. If the living system requires constant transaction with its environment for the maintenance of differentiation, a major area of activity of caseworkers is, evidently, the provision and maintenance of very specific opportunities for interchange and services for isolated populations.

It is possible to point out "populations at risk," populations heading toward isolation. One such population is obviously the aged. Retirement, growing lack of mobility, loss of relationships through death, and

---

[15] Bernard Bandler, The Concept of Ego-Supportive Psychotherapy, in *Ego-Oriented Casework: Problems and Perspectives,* ed. Howard J. Parad and Roger R. Miller (New York: Family Service Association of America, 1963), pp. 27–44; Eleanor Pavenstedt, *The Drifters: Children of Disorganized Lower-Class Families* (Boston: Little Brown & Co., 1967); Thomas Gladwin, Social Competence and Clinical Practice, *Psychiatry,* 30:33–37 (February 1967); and John and Elain Cumming, *Ego and Milieu: Theory and Practice of Environmental Therapy* (New York: Atherton Press, 1962).

[16] Mary E. Richmond, *What Is Social Casework?: An Introductory Description* (New York: Russell Sage Foundation, 1922), pp. 98–99.

through the loss in our culture of the meaning of the extended family, all tend to isolate the aged person. Institutionalized or hospitalized populations are also in danger of such isolation. Certain populations in the social structure—particularly the poor or immigrant, non-English-speaking groups—face pressures that tend to isolate them from the larger social structure and cut them off from educational, economic, or recreational inputs.[17] Head Start and programs geared to even younger children, such as the verbal interaction program of Family Service Association of Nassau County, in Mineola, New York, seek to overcome the isolation of children and parents who have suffered certain kinds of deprivation.

Again, illustrating the helpfulness of systems thinking, the principle of entropy can also be applied to larger and larger systems. The family, a social group, a social agency—each can be examined with respect to the nature of its boundaries and the amount of interchange that occurs with its environment. Further, an analysis can be made of the strains and characteristics of the system that tend to isolate it, and conscious plans can be made for opening the system and developing meaningful inputs. Again, it is important to remember that an excess of input can overwhelm the homeostatic mechanisms and lead to a crisis, which may offer opportunity for the development of more refined adaptive mechanisms, but which can, if too extreme, lead to the destruction of the integrity of the system.

Conclusions

The first task in evaluating systems theory and its usefulness to casework practice is to make some important definitions and distinctions. Primarily, it is important to differentiate the system as a conceptual model from the various bodies of systems theory that make extensive empirical claims about the nature of reality. If the systems model is found to be useful, it can be adopted as a conceptual tool without subscribing to all or to any of the empirical claims made by the various systems theorists currently struggling to understand and predict the behavior of different open systems.

The second task is, perhaps, to define some of the major empirical propositions concerning the nature of the open system—propositions examined in this discussion, for example. These principles can generate a number of hypotheses, and these hypotheses can be operationalized and tested out in practice. In this way, the innovation of new practice approaches and the development of new knowledge can go hand in hand. Much of this creative kind of work is already in progress.

---

[17] Ann Hartman, "Anomie and Social Casework," *Social Casework*, 50:131–37 (March 1969).

The field of social work can never be accused of maintaining a closed theoretical system. On the contrary, our theoretical system has been so open to new ideas and influences that its inner integrity has frequently been shaken. Once again, the outer intellectual environment is putting tremendous stress on social work thought through the explosion of new knowledge in every substantive field of concern to the profession. Let us hope that even in our current state of disequilibrium, we can consider this new knowledge not as a threat but as an opportunity. With the conceptual aid of the systems model, we can, perhaps, move to test and to integrate this new knowledge and emerge from the current crisis with more sophisticated and differentiated means of performing our tasks and achieving our goals.

Selected annotated references

ALLPORT, GORDON W., "The Open System in Personality Theory," *Journal of Abnormal and Social Psychology* (1960), pp. 301–11.
This article is a classic for students of the meaning of systems theory for human systems. As the title indicates, Allport puts great emphasis on the difference between closed and open systems.

AUERSWOLD, EDGAR H., "Interdisciplinary versus Ecological Approach," *Family Process* 7:2 (September 1968), pp. 202–15.
This case study illustrates the way systems theory as a base for a new way of thinking leads to a different style of operation.

BUCKLEY, WALTER, *Sociology and Modern Systems Theory* (Englewood Cliffs, N.J.: Prentice-Hall, 1967).
Buckley presents a model in which the sociocultural system is seen as a complex, adaptive system.

CHIN, ROBERT, "The Utility of Systems Models and Developmental Models for Practitioners," in *The Planning of Change,* ed. Waren G. Bennis, Kenneth D. Benne, and Robert Chin (New York: Holt, Rinehart and Winston, 1961), pp. 201–15.
This article on the meaning of systems theory for human service practitioners is an excellent one for beginning students of systems theory. The author discusses the difference for the practitioner in the use of developmental theory and systems theory as a base for practice.

JANCHILL, SISTER MARY PAUL, "Systems Concepts in Casework Theory and Practice," *Social Casework* 50:2 (February 1969), pp. 72–84.
Sister Janchill's excellent article is an attempt, paralleling Hartman's article to select and organize systems concepts for use by the caseworker.

KADUSHIN, ALFRED, "The Knowledge Base of Social Work Practice," in *Issues in American Social Work,* ed. Alfred J. Kahn (New York: Columbia University Press, 1959).

Written fifteen years ago, this statement might well be compared with the statement "Knowledge for Practice" in the latest book edited by Kahn, also listed in these references. In this earlier statement Kadushin makes a plea for a sounder knowledge base for the profession and sees it as coming from social work research.

KAHN, ALFRED, J., ed., *Shaping the New Social Work* (New York: Columbia University Press, 1973).

This collection of original papers by leading social work scholars speaks to the challenges facing social work today. The papers by Kamerman, Dolgoff, Getzel, and Nelsen ("Knowledge for Practice: Social Science in Social Work") and by Gurin ("Education for Changing Practice") and the "Epilogue" by Kahn bear on the issues discussed in this chapter of the text.

KIDNEIGH, JOHN C., "A Note on Organizing Knowledge," in *Modes of Professional Education,* Tulane Studies in Social Welfare (New Orleans: School of Social Work, Tulane University, vol. 11, Chap 9).

This is a technical discussion of ways of organizing social work knowledge for teaching and learning in the profession.

MARUYAMA, MAGOROH, "The Second Cybernetics: Deviation-Amplifying Mutual Causal Processes," in *Modern Systems Research for the Behavioral Scientist,* ed. Walter Buckley (Chicago: Aldine, pp. 304–13).

Maruyama examines the effect on human and social systems of deviation-amplifying positive feedback loops. The author holds that the secret of growth in social systems may well lie in the process of deviation-amplifying mutual positive feedback networks rather than in the initial condition or the initial push.

VICKERS, GEOFFREY, "Is Adaptability Enough?" *Behavioral Science* 4 (1959), pp. 219–34.

Vickus discusses the concept of adaptation from a system theory perspective in which adaptation is seen as an endless process of give and take between the individual, society, and the physical environment.

Chapter 3

VALUES IN SOCIAL
WORK PRACTICE

No issue can be more troublesome for social work than that of values. Efforts to make definitive statements about social work values stir heated controversy. Is there a value base which all social work practitioners must accept? Does social work possess a set of values that are in some way unique in our culture? Are there interventive methodologies that social workers should not use because they may be inconsistent with what the profession believes about the nature of man? These questions are commanding the attention of many contemporary social work thinkers. Charles Levy takes a clear stand: "The social work profession is well advised to tolerate differences in diversity about some things but not about its ideology."[1] Levy goes on to suggest a framework for conceptualization of the profession's ideology along the dimensions of preferred conceptions of people, preferred outcomes for people, and preferred instrumentalities for dealing with people. Henry Miller, in the article reproduced in this chapter, notes some of the value dilemmas encountered by contemporary social work practitioners and suggests, as one alternative, the withdrawal of social work from settings in which treatment is imposed or coerced.[2] Elizabeth Salomon, whose article is also included in this chapter, suggests the possibility of inherent conflict between the humanistic stance of social work and scientific methodol-

[1] Charles Levy, "The Value Base of Social Work," *Journal of Education for Social Work* 9:1 (Winter 1973), pp. 34–42.
[2] Henry Miller, "Value Dilemmas in Social Casework," *Social Work* 13:1 (January 1968), pp. 27–33.

ogy.[3] In a recent book Scott Briar and Henry Miller advance the intriguing suggestion that one of the profession's traditional values—client self-determination—might be conceptualized as a treatment technique rather than a basic value. They suggest that clients in one-to-one relational systems make faster progress when extended maximum opportunities for self-determination; thus self-determination might be viewed as a treatment technique geared toward facilitating client progress rather than as a basic human value which the profession promotes.[4]

Rather than offer definitive answers to these questions, in this chapter and its readings we will attempt to raise some of the issues for thought and consideration as well as to outline our own thinking. The chapter will accomplish three purposes:

1. It will arrive at a definition of the concept of social work value.
2. It will examine two value premises which we consider to be essential to social work practice.
3. It will note relationships between these value premises and practice.

WHAT IS MEANT BY SOCIAL WORK VALUE?

One of the dictionary definitions of value is "something intrinsically valuable or desirable."[5] As noted in Chapter 2, for William Gordon value refers to things which are preferred, whereas knowledge refers to things which are known or knowable.[6] Values might be thought of as things a profession prefers; to use Levy's suggestions, values might be further classified as to preferred conceptions of people, preferred outcomes for people, and preferred instrumentalities for dealing with people. Values can be thought of as beliefs which a profession holds about people and about appropriate ways of dealing with people. Paul Halmos, an English sociologist who has devoted considerable attention to the study of helping professions, suggests from an extensive review of their literature that they operate from tenets of faith concerning the nature of man. This faith, Halmos argues, is accepted without proof and provides guidance and direction for the helping professions.[7] Thus values can be considered as unproved (probably unprovable) beliefs which a profession holds about the nature of man. These beliefs are

[3] Elizabeth L. Salomon, "Humanistic Values and Social Casework," *Social Casework* 48:1 (January 1967), pp. 26–33.

[4] Scott Briar and Henry Miller, *Problems and Issues in Social Casework* (New York: Columbia University Press, 1971), p. 42.

[5] *Webster's Seventh New Collegiate Dictionary* (Springfield, Mass.: G. & C. Merriam Company, 1971).

[6] William E. Gordon, "Knowledge and Value: Their Distinction and Relationship in Clarifying Social Work Practice," *Social Work* 10:3 (July 1965), pp. 32–39.

[7] Paul Halmos, *Faith of the Counsellors* (New York: Schocken, 1966).

reflected in the day-to-day work of the practitioner and provide direction and guidance to professional practice.

But are a profession's values uniquely its own? Does a profession find its uniqueness and its distinctiveness in the value premises underlying its work? We think not. The social work profession exists within a larger cultural context; it identifies and operationalizes value premises already existing in society and not held exclusively by the profession. Schwartz's concept of the sources of limitations on professional social work practice relates to this point. Schwartz identifies three sources of limitations—the norms of the overall society, the function of the agency, and the service contract with the particular client system.[8] The social work profession exists within a culture whose value premises provide a source of limitation to the profession. A complex culture, however, is characterized by diverse value premises some of which may be in conflict with each other; like other professions, social work selects from this diversity the premises it will support and builds its practice on these. The profession may achieve a degree of uniqueness in the particular way in which it operationalizes value premises, but the premises themselves are shared with other components of the culture.

We have tried to establish that values can be construed as unproven beliefs which guide and direct the work of a professional. These beliefs however, are not uniquely the possession of the profession. They are elements of the overall culture and are shared with others in the culture. However, they may achieve a degree of uniqueness in the way they are operationalized by particular groups. What are the value premises with which the social work profession identifies, and how are these premises operationalized? Two essential value premises underlie the practice of social work: (1) belief in the uniqueness and inherent dignity of the individual and (2) belief in client self-determination. Before we examine these premises, a few comments are necessary concerning the levels of abstractness with which values are discussed.

One way of thinking of values is to picture an inverted triangle (see Diagram 1). The top or wide part of the triangle can represent values in a remote, general, or abstract sense. As we move toward the bottom and point of the triangle, the values become more proximate, specific, and concrete. The challenge to practitioners is to take abstract value concepts, such as client determination or the innate dignity of the individual, and to use these concepts in specific applied situations. When asking ourselves a "how-to-do-it" question, we are implying movement in this direction, from the general to the specific; conversely, in asking ourselves a "why" question to seek justification or explanation of our actions, we are moving from the specific to the remote level. In thinking

[8] William Schwartz, "The Social Worker in the Group," *Social Welfare Forum, 1961* (New York: Columbia University Press, 1961), pp. 153–54.

DIAGRAM 1
Values can be conceptualized at abstract or concrete levels

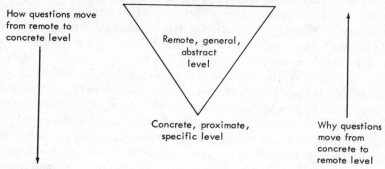

How questions move
from remote to
concrete level

Remote, general,
abstract
level

Concrete, proximate,
specific level

Why questions
move from
concrete to
remote level

PRINCIPLES:
1. Agreement about values increases with remoteness.
2. It is important to know the level of abstraction when values are discussed.
3. The challenge to social work is to apply remote value concepts in concrete situations.
   Source: This diagram was suggested by Dr. Philip Heslin, Catholic Charities Bureau, Superior, Wisconsin.

of values at these two levels—remote and concrete—one must recognize that agreement generally increases with abstractness. Agreement, for example, to the abstract principle of client self-determination is readily secured; but at the specific level, say, in working with a 15-year-old who is bent on stealing cars, there may be considerable controversy over how to make this principle concrete. In talking about value premises, it is important that we specify whether the discussion is about an abstract principle or is an attempt to apply an abstract principle in a concrete situation. Our next task is to discuss two abstract principles—client self-determination and the innate dignity of the individual—and to identify ways in which they can be operationalized by the social work practitioner.

RESPECT FOR THE DIGNITY AND UNIQUENESS OF THE INDIVIDUAL

One of the central value premises consistently accepted and supported by the social work profession is that each person is a unique individual with an inherent dignity which is to be respected. People are sufficient ends in themselves and are not to be treated as objects or as means to other ends. Diversity and variety among individuals are to be welcomed and encouraged. Paul Tillich, a theologian who has directed his attention to the philosophy of social work, refers to the uniqueness of every individual and situation as man's existential nature when he perceives social work as promoting.[9] William Gordon derived his match-

---

[9] Paul Tillich, "The Philosophy of Social Work," *Social Service Review* 36:1 (March 1962), pp. 13–16.

ing concept of the social work function (referred to in Chapter 1) from the same basic notion; Gordon has suggested that the social work profession does not attempt to move either the environment or the person toward some ideal model, but rather strives to establish linkages between individuals and their environment allowing for the widest possible diversity of both people and environments.[10]

What are some of the implications of this principle for social work practice? This is the "how" question. How can the premise that every individual is unique and has the right to be treated with respect and dignity be applied in concrete social work situations? The potential for operationalizing the value premise will be considered in two areas—first, sensitivity on the part of the social worker to messages he is giving others; and second, the relation of classification procedures to individualization.

Social psychologists have rather soundly established the theoretical position that people's image of themselves develops largely out of their communication with others.[11] Specifically, people build and incorporate their self-image from the messages they receive from other people about themselves. Further, people who feel good about themselves, see themselves as persons of worth, and have a sense of their own strength and capability, tend to be happier and have the ability to deal constructively and appropriately with their environment.

Given these positions, social workers and other professionals intervening in the lives of people are well advised to be constantly sensitive to the messages they are extending to others about their worth. Do we, in the little things we do, communicate to the other person that he is a unique individual to be highly prized? What, for example, is the message communicated when we safeguard time and provide a client with a specific time to be seen as opposed to a catch-me-on-a-catch-as-catch-can basis for visits? Do appointments in advance communicate to the client a higher sense of respect than unannounced visits or hurriedly arranged telephone appointments? And, speaking of telephoning, how about the all too frequently overlooked return call? What message does the client get from the worker in terms of the client's worth when the worker does not have the courtesy or good sense to return telephone calls promptly? How about the ability to listen to the clients, to secure from them their own account of their situation, and to avoid prejudgments. And does not privacy, both in terms of how the social worker

---

[10] William E. Gordon, "Basic Constructs for an Integrative and Generative Conception of Social Work," in *The General Systems Approach: Contributions toward an Holistic Conception of Social Work,* ed. Gordon Hearn (New York: Council on Social Work Education, 1969), p. 6.

[11] See, for example, Arnold M. Rose, ed., *Human Behavior and Social Processes* (Boston: Houghton Mifflin, 1962).

conducts the interviews and how he treats the material gained from interviews, communicate something to clients about the esteem in which they are held? A worker attempting to operationalize the premise of individual uniqueness and dignity may find it useful to repeatedly inquire of himself, "What does this action on my part communicate to the client about my perception of his personhood?"

Another thorny problem confronting the social worker attempting to operationalize the value premise of individual uniqueness and dignity is that of striking a balance between classification and the responsibility to respond to persons as individuals. Classification refers to the need to generalize beyond individuals and to organize phenomena on the basis of common characteristics. This process is essential in order to make sense out of a mass of raw data and, as discussed in Chapter 2, is an essential part of the process of knowledge building. When the phenomena we are dealing with are people, however, classification may cause us to respond to people as objects placed in a particular category rather than as individuals. The pitfalls of this process are being documented in a growing body of literature from sociologists studying deviance from a labeling perspective.[12] Not only does labeling or classification lead to distortion of individual differences, but, as labeling theorists and their supporting research are noting, a person labeled deviant, those doing the labeling, and the surrounding audience frequently respond to the deviant on the basis of the label rather than on the basis of individual characteristics. This creates conditions for the development of a self-fulfilling prophecy in which the person becomes what he has been labeled.[13] Current efforts to divert youth out of the juvenile justice system are recognition of the position that the very process of labeling a youngster a delinquent may contribute pressure toward additional delinquencies. Hans Toch states the problem succinctly:

> Playing the classification game in the abstract, as is done in Universities, is a joyful, exhilarating experience, harmless and inconsequential. Classifying people in life is a grim business which channelizes destinies and determines fate. A man becomes a category, he is processed as a category, plays his assigned role, lives up to the implications. Labeled irrational, he acts crazy; catalogued dangerous, he becomes dangerous or he stays behind bars.[14]

---

[12] For an introduction to this perspective see Earl Rubington and Martin S. Weinberg, *Deviance: The Interactionist Perspective* (New York: Macmillan, 1968); J. L. Simmons, *Deviants* (Berkeley, Calif.: Glendessary Press, 1969).

[13] Robert K. Merton, *Social Theory and Social Structure* (Glencoe, Ill.: Free Press, 1957), pp. 421–36.

[14] Hans Toch, "The Care and Feeding of Typologies and Labels," *Federal Probation* 34:3 (September 1970), p. 15.

Karl Menninger, a noted psychiatrist, has reacted with strong words to the 1968 publication of a revised set of diagnostic (i.e., labeling) categories for psychiatry:

> A committee of our worldly national body has just [1968] published a manual containing a full description of all the bewitchments to which all human flesh is err, with the proper names for each one, the minute suborder and subspecies listed and a code number for the computer. The colleagues who prepared this witch's hammer manual are worthy fellows—earnest, honest, hard-working, simplistic; they were taught to believe that these horrible things exist, these things with Greek names and Arabic numerals. And if a patient shows the stigmata, should he not be given the label and the number? To me this is not only the revival of medieval nonsense and superstition; it is a piece of social immorality.[15]

Social workers who are sometimes prone to adopt psychiatric terms and classifications might pay special heed to Menninger's concern.

But isn't classification necessary? Or, are we to agree with Salomon's position that there is an inherent conflict between the needs of science to order and classify and the humanism of social work?[16] Toch suggests that "the point of concern rests in any labels that lead to sorting or disposition."[17] Toch takes the position that the labeling is necessary for thinking or theory building but is not particularly helpful in making dispositional decisions about people; concern should occur when decisions about what is going to happen to people are based on the individual's having previously been placed in a particular category. And yet it is precisely at this point that classification appears to be most useful. Generally classifications come into play when professionals are attempting to assess or diagnose a situation as a guide in selecting appropriate procedures for dealing with the problem. Our point of view on this will be more completely developed in Chapter 8, in which assessment procedures will be discussed in terms of the participation of both the worker and the client. In general, however, we think it possible to develop assessment procedures which maximize individuality and minimize the need for categorization, yet maintain scientific rigor in dealing with valid and reliable data, vigorously pursuing facts, and conscientiously seeking alternative explanations.

We have attempted to identify one major value premise in social work—the individual is unique and should be treated with respect and dignity—and have suggested that this principle can be operationalized

---

[15] Karl Menninger, *The Crime of Punishment* (New York: Viking, 1968), pp. 117–18.

[16] Salomon, "Humanistic Values." *Social Casework* 48:1 (January 1967), pp. 26–32.

[17] Toch, "Care and Feeding."

through careful analysis of our own behavior to be sure we are communicating messages to clients that indicate their worth and through minimizing the use of classifications which may both distort the individuality of the client and provide an impetus for the client and others to react to the classifications rather than the individual. We will now turn our attention to a second major value premise—client self-determination.

CLIENT SELF-DETERMINATION

The principle of client self-determination derives logically from belief in the innate dignity of the person. If people possess an inherent dignity, then it follows that they should be permitted to become what they wish—to determine their own life-styles insofar as possible. The belief in client self-determination clearly implies that people should be permitted to make decisions for themselves and carries with it the rather clear assumption that most of the time those decisions will be responsible—responsible in the sense that people in their decision making will, for the most part, make decisions which are consistent with the welfare of the community. The social work stance has generally been to couple the concept of client self-determination with that of responsibility for the total community and to attempt to work out a balance between the two. Barring some clear-cut indication of danger to others, however, the social worker in day-to-day contacts with clients will generally attempt to maximize opportunities for client self-determination.

Inherent in the concept of client self-determination is the idea of alternatives. Self-determination implies decisions, or the making of choices between one course of action as contrasted with other courses of action. It is fraudulent to think of self-determination without alternatives. If there is only one course of action, how can there be self-determination? The client has no choice and thus no opportunity for self-determining. Much of social work activity with clients consists of a quest for alternatives in order to expand the client's opportunities for self-determination. The quest for alternatives may take various forms—helping the client develop new alternatives and resources within the environment or helping the client find and develop new ways to respond to environmental demands. Thus, interventive activity may focus on removing blockages within the environment which are limiting the client's opportunities or helping the client remove blockages within himself which are limiting his ability to see alternative courses of action. The person whose range of responses to his environment is limited by his own stereotyped and patterned behavior is as much lacking in opportunity for self-determination as the ghetto client confronted with a lack of environmental opportunities. Thus, the principle of client self-determination will lead the social worker in the direction of developing alternatives so that the client can exercise the decision making implied in the concept of self-determination.

The client exercising decision making is a key phrase in this formulation. The concept of client self-determination as operationalized in social work calls for maximizing opportunities for clients to make decisions for and about themselves. This is an area in which the social work profession may differ markedly from other professions. Clients generally go to other professionals for expert advice, that is, expecting to be told what in the view of the professional is best for the client. Patients expect the doctor to diagnose an ailment and to recommend a specific course of treatment, and clients expect the lawyer to advise them as to what action should be taken in dealing with a legal problem. In both of these situations there is, of course, an element of self-determination, inasmuch as the patient or client must ultimately decide whether or not to follow the expert's advice.

In most dealings with professionals in our culture the decision-making authority of the client is largely overshadowed by the expertise of the professional and, to a large extent, limited to the decision of whether or not to accept the professional's advice. But not so with the social work profession. The expertise of the social worker lies less in the substantive areas of knowing what is best for the client and more in the process area of assisting clients in developing alternatives for themselves, making a decision among the alternatives, and implementing the decision. To assume that one knows what is best for clients is to run the very grave risk of developing what Matthew Dumont refers to as a rescue fantasy:

> The most destructive thing in psychotherapy is a "rescue fantasy" in the therapist—a feeling that the therapist is the divinely sent agent to pull a tormented soul from the pit of suffering and adversity and put him back on the road to happiness and glory. A major reason this fantasy is so destructive is that it carries the conviction that the patient will be saved only through and by the therapist. When such a conviction is communicated to the patient, verbally or otherwise, he has no choice other than to rebel and leave or become even more helpless, dependent, and sick.[18]

Sometimes the new or even the experienced worker feels frustration in coming to grips with the reality that the social worker cannot be the fountainhead of all wisdom who can masterfully assume and resolve the client's problems. A certain humility, perhaps, is necessary to recognize that the client is the chief problem-solver. This is not to deny that the worker plays a major part in assisting the client through the process, and may at times serve rather forcefully as the client's agent.

---

[18] Matthew Dumont, *The Absurd Healer* (New York: Viking, 1968), p. 60.

Does the foregoing suggest that the social worker does not offer an opinion or make a suggestion? Emphatically not. Just as the extreme of taking over and making decisions for the client is to be avoided so is the extreme of never sharing a viewpoint with the client. Such action denies clients the benefit of the worker's judgment and may effectively deny clients alternatives that they may wish to consider in their own decision making. As Charlotte Towle has said, "The social worker's devotion to the idea that every individual has a right to be self-determining does not rule out our valid concern with directing people's attention to the most desirable alternative."[19] Workers have the obligations of sharing with clients their own thinking, perhaps their own experiences, not as a way of directing the clients' lives but rather as an additional source of information and input for the clients to consider in their own decision making. It is imperative, however, that the social worker's input be recognized as information to be considered and not as edict to be followed. Schwartz, in the article reprinted in Chapter 1, offers some very helpful suggestions in this regard. He suggests that the worker has a responsibility to contribute data to the client and that the data might include facts, ideas, and value concepts. He goes on to argue that in contributing data the worker should inform the client that he is offering only part of the total available social experience and is not the fountainhead of all knowledge. Moreover, the data contributed should be clearly related to the purpose of work with the client, and opinions, while important data, should be clearly labeled as opinions and not represented as facts.[20] Client self-determination does not imply worker nonparticipation; the skill, indeed, the mark, of a successful practitioner lies in his ability to share knowledge and thinking without imposing a judgment, but leaving the client free to accept or reject his views.

Fields of practice in which the worker possesses legal authority that may be used to coerce the client are sometimes cited as raising questions with the concept of self-determination. Does the presence of legal authority, such as that found in correctional and child protection settings, negate the concept of self-determination? No, it does not, although the presence of legal authority does place some limits on the client's self-determination and on the worker's functions which it is important for both the worker and the client to recognize. In these settings, in respect to some of their decisions, workers will be acting as agents of the society rather than as agents of the client. In this regard William Reid and Laura Epstein make a distinction between the protective and helping

---

[19] Charlotte Towle, *Common Human Needs* (New York: National Association of Social Workers, 1965), p. 26.

[20] Schwartz, "The Social Worker," pp. 153–54.

functions of the worker,[21] suggesting that the practitioner must not only recognize these differences but must also make sure the client understands them. The worker must be clear as to both the source and extent of this authority, and these matters must be clearly communicated to the client. This is an example of agency function, Schwartz's second source of limitation on worker activity,[22] limiting the kind of agreement workers can enter with clients.

While the presence of legal authority may limit areas for client self-determination, it also leaves extensive areas for the exercise of client self-determination. These include determining how the authority will be exercised as well as noting areas in addition to the legal requirements in which self-determination may be emphasized. A probation agency, for example, may enforce the legal requirement that the probationer must report to the probation officer; this is not a matter for client self-determination. But the sensitive probation officer can allow for considerable client self-determination in the frequency of reporting, the length of the interviews, the time of reporting, and the content to be discussed during the interviews. Even in correctional settings clients can be extended considerable self-determination in how they utilize the worker, including, if they choose, only using him for the minimum mandated by the probation orders. Gerald O'Connor offers a very insightful position on the question of self-determination in corrections:

> The principle of self-determination, the freedom to choose one's own destiny is based on an assumption of individual dignity. . . . The recognition of man's right to free choice guarantees that he may choose to run his life as he sees fit. This choice may run counter to society's welfare and even his own, yet essentially it is his choice and his prerogative. Society may censure, but it cannot take from him his right; nor should society strip him of his dignity by a censure. The criminal then has a right to say "crime is my choice and I am willing to pay the price. If you send me to prison, I am paying my debt to society and refuse to submit to your attempts to reform me." The principle of self-determination makes it incumbent upon society to honor such a plea.
>
> There are large numbers of inmates in correctional institutions who recognize a need for rehabilitation and are willing to become involved in programs for that end. An inmate's voluntary recognition of a need for assistance does not, in turn, give officials a free reign in outlining his rehabilitation program. It is reasonable that the offender have input into the definition of his own "problem" and have this included in the official assessment. He should have the opportunity to say what type of program would assist him and who should provide the services. Fur-

---

[21] William J. Reid and Laura Epstein, *Task Centered Casework* (New York: Columbia University Press, 1972), pp. 213–15.

[22] Schwartz, "The Social Worker," pp. 153–54.

ther, it seems appropriate that the inmates have a right, in part, to determine the conditions under which the services are delivered.[23]

Even in situations involving legal authority considerable latitude exists for clients to exercise self-determination. Skillful workers can maximize these opportunities with the client. At the very least, of course, the client has the option of determining whether he is going to do anything more than the legal minimum as well as the option of ignoring the requirements of the authority and accepting the consequences.

One other aspect of self-determination requires emphasis. Some workers confuse client self-determination with worker self-determination. We are not arguing for the latter. In taking on a professional responsibility, workers agree, tacitly at least, to limit their own self-determination in the clients' behalf. The National Association of Social Workers Code of Ethics clearly limits worker self-determination, especially in its seventh clause: "I practice social work within the recognized knowledge and competence of the profession."[24] When a worker's communication styles or dress styles arouse the antagonism of clients or others who may influence clients, the worker's professional responsibility may call for the forfeiting of his self-determination in the clients' behalf. This excerpt from an interview with a social worker functioning in a community organization capacity illustrates the frustrations which may be experienced by a worker unwilling to set aside his own self-determination in behalf of the clients.

> I remarked that it certainly must be satisfying to organize and be part of such an event. I was surprised when Alice shook her head slowly and said in a much more somber tone of voice, "No, 99 percent of the time there is very little glamour to organizing." I asked her to explain further, and she went on to say that it is hard, hard work and that one of the most discouraging things for her to realize is that oftentimes the people you are organizing aren't necessarily looking for a change in the system, but rather to become a part of that system. Usually that means playing the same games that those in power play. She talked further about the frustration she deals with constantly. I, too, began to feel that organizing was not the glamorous, romantic job I had pictured it to be.[25]

Does this worker have an obligation to set aside her own goals of "changing the system" and work with clients who want to be successful within

---

[23] Gerald O'Connor, "Toward a New Policy in Adult Corrections," *Social Service Review* 46:4 (December 1972), pp. 485–86.

[24] National Association of Social Workers, "Code of Ethics," *Encyclopedia of Social Work* (New York: NASW, 1971), vol. ii, pp. 958–59. For further discussion see also Alan Keith-Lucas "Ethics in Social Work," *Encyclopedia of Social Work* (New York: NASW, 1971), vol. i, pp. 324–28.

[25] From a student interview, University of Minnesota, School of Social Work, 1971.

the system rather than produce more revolutionary change? We think she does.

In this section on client self-determination we have attempted to establish this concept as one of the value premises underlying social work. Five points have been made. First, self-determination commits the social worker and the client to a quest for alternatives. Without alternatives there is no opportunity to make decisions and no opportunity to engage in self-determination. Second, a major responsibility of the social worker is to maximize clients' opportunities for decision making. Social workers are not experts in what is substantively best for clients and thus should avoid making decisions for clients; but social workers are expert in assisting clients in a process of joint decision making. Third, the social worker has an obligation to offer his own viewpoint and suggestions to clients. These are offered as alternatives and input which a client may consider, and not as an edict or a "right" answer for the client. Fourth, even in situations where the worker is vested with legal authority, considerable opportunity exists for client self-determination which the worker should attempt to maximize. Fifth, a differentiation must be made between client self-determination and worker self-determination. In assuming professional responsibility, workers sharply limit their own self-determination and become responsible for conducting themselves in ways which best meet the interests of clients and maximize clients' opportunities.

RECAPITULATION

This section has presented our thinking concerning social work values. Values were defined as things which a profession prefers but which cannot be proven to be true. Values are not unique to a profession but are adapted from the overall culture. The uniqueness and innate dignity of the individual and the principle of client self-determination were analyzed as two value premises underlying social work practice. The process of operationalizing these values—especially client self-determination—provides an opportunity for social work to find its distinctiveness among the professions.

Several implicit principles in the preceding discussion should be more explicitly stated. (1) Values are guides to action; they are principles which, whenever possible, are to be maximized. Values, however, are not straitjackets. Deviations from them may be necessary at times, although the primary focus will be on maximizing them. (2) In situations where the value premise and knowledge are in conflict, opt for knowledge. In Chapter 2 a potential conflict was noted between self-determination and a child's need for protection and stability in order to meet developmental needs; a lower priority was attached to the value of self-determination because of knowledge of the child's needs. (3) When knowledge is lacking, the value premises should become the prevailing standards. (4) Values limit the uses to which the profession's methodology can be placed. Group processes, for example, might well be used to subvert individualism or to stir up fear and hysteria which threaten diversity and self-determination. This use of group strategies is inappropriate because it is inconsistent with the value premises of the profession. Change strategies and methodology can be used for a variety of ends. Social work practitioners must be sure that their strategies are used to support the uniqueness of the individual and the client's right to self-determination.

A LOOK FORWARD

Two thought-provoking articles as well as the Code of Ethics of the National Association of Social Workers are reproduced in this chapter. Henry Miller identifies "value dilemmas in social casework" and reaches the conclusion that social work should "get out of the business of dealing with involuntary clients." Miller modifies this view somewhat in relation to clients who do not have the ability to make choices—children, the mentally deficient, etc.—but presents a stronger statement than that of the authors; we suggested the possibility of finding a common ground for work with the involuntary client. Elizabeth Salomon also presents a controversial position—that inherent conflicts exist between the humanism of social work and the demands of science. The points of conflict suggested by Salomon—classification, objectivity of observations, and the tendency to oversimplify complex phenomena—do not imply, of course, that social work or other humanistic undertakings can proceed in an unsystematic and undisciplined manner. The National Association of Social Workers Code of Ethics provides a statement, at an abstract level, of the present values of the profession. But there is not universal agreement that this statement reflects social work values appropriately. We do not necessarily expect agreement with these readings or with the foregoing material. This material is presented to stimulate thought and discussion about some of the difficult value questions confronting the profession.

The pages ahead will present an approach to social work practice which we believe is both humanistic and scientific. Classification is minimized; clients are involved in a partnership undertaking with workers; and individuality is maximized. The problem-solving process which is outlined requires a high degree of rationality and discipline on the part of workers. In the next chapter the concept of relationship—the medium through which much of the problem-solving work may occur—is introduced. A discussion of communication and interviewing as basic skills follows the chapter on the social work relationship. Subsequent chapters outline the phases of the problem-solving model.

Code of Ethics[*][1]

National Association of Social Workers

Social work is based on humanitarian, democratic ideals. Professional social workers are dedicated to service for the welfare of mankind; to the disciplined use of a recognized body of knowledge about human beings and their interactions; and to the marshaling of community resources to promote the well-being of all without discrimination.

Social work practice is a public trust that requires of its practitioners integrity, compassion, belief in the dignity and worth of human beings, respect for individual differences, a commitment to service, and a dedication to truth. It requires mastery of a body of knowledge and skill gained through professional education and experience. It requires also recognition of the limitations of present knowledge and skill and of the services we are now equipped to give. The end sought is the performance of a service with integrity and competence.

Each member of the profession carries responsibility to maintain and improve social work service; constantly to examine, use, and increase the knowledge upon which practice and social policy are based; and to develop further the philosophy and skills of the profession.

This Code of Ethics embodies certain standards of behavior for the social worker in his professional relationships with those he serves, with his colleagues, with his employing agency, with other professions, and with the community. In abiding by the code, the social worker views his obligations in as wide a context as the situation requires, takes all of the principles into consideration, and chooses a course of action consistent with the code's spirit and intent.

As a member of the National Association of Social Workers I commit myself to conduct my professional relationships in accord with the code and subscribe to the following statements:

- I regard as my primary obligation the welfare of the individual or group served, which includes action for improving social conditions.

---

[*] Reprinted by permission of the National Association of Social Workers.

[1] Adopted by the Delegate Assembly of the NASW, October 13, 1960, and amended April 11, 1967.

- I will not discriminate because of race, color, religion, age, sex, or national ancestry, and in my job capacity will work to prevent and eliminate social discrimination in rendering services, work assignments, and in employment practices.
- I give precedence to my professional responsibility over my personal interests.
- I hold myself responsible for the quality and extent of the service I perform.
- I respect the privacy of the people I serve.
- I use in a responsible manner information gained in professional relationships.
- I treat with respect the findings, views, and actions of colleagues, and use appropriate channels to express judgment on these matters.
- I practice social work within the recognized knowledge and competence of the profession.
- I recognize my professional responsibility to add my ideas and findings to the body of social work knowledge and practice.
- I accept responsibility to help protect the community against unethical practice by any individuals or organizations engaged in social welfare activities.
- I stand ready to give appropriate professional service in public emergencies.
- I distinguish clearly, in public, between my statements and actions as an individual and as a representative of an organization.
- I support the principal that professional practice requires professional education.
- I accept responsibility for working toward the creation and maintenance of conditions within agencies which enable social workers to conduct themselves in keeping with this code.
- I contribute my knowledge, skills, and support to programs of human welfare.

Value dilemmas in social casework*

Henry Miller

This paper is concerned with certain moral dimensions of the social casework enterprise. To the extent that it deals with what one should or should not do, it can hardly be buttressed with an empirical line of argument. Rather, the paper takes the form of an exhortation. The

* Reprinted with permission of the author and the National Association of Social Workers from *Social Work*, 13:1 (January 1968), pp. 27–33.

plea is for social caseworkers to maintain a constant focus on what has traditionally been the crucial value of their endeavor: the inherent dignity of man. This is a difficult focus to sustain, for it must inevitably clash with other professional moralities. This is especially so at the present time when the elaboration of technique has such high priority and when the cry for more knowledge, more predictability, and more control increases in modulation.

The central thesis of this paper is that social casework, as a therapeutic activity, is faced with a fundamental and perhaps insoluble value paradox. It poses for itself the ultimate end of a dignified and worthy human being; however, the methods it uses to accomplish that end are likely to be demeaning to the individual. The moral question for the caseworker, then, becomes one of deciding what he can legitimately *do* to his clients without giving offense to this intrinsic state of worth.

The dignity of man

There are at least three elements to the paradox. The first bears on the end of the casework endeavor and embodies the aforementioned assumption about the value of an individual human being. It is the fundamental tenet not only of social casework but of all social welfare. It is a rather beautiful conception and an article of faith that brings credit to any social worker. It holds that man is a creature of dignity and that he is entitled to infinite respect—simply by virtue of the fact that he is a man. He may be, at times, a bad man or a mixed-up man or a stupid man—indeed, he may be so bad or mixed-up or stupid that society is forced to constrain or punish him—but, nonetheless, he remains proud in the face of his confusion and dignified in the isolation of his confinement. Society may incarcerate, commit, punish, or otherwise reap vengeance for his malice—but it cannot strip him of his nobility.

This conception of man runs persistently throughout the thought of Western civilization. It is rooted in Homer, it reached a brilliant flowering during the Renaissance, and it is the foundation of the democratic ideal that was originally projected for the United States. It subsumes liberty and justice but, above all, equity, an equity that allows a person to say to any fellow human being: "You may be wiser, healthier, or richer than I; you may be more expert; you may be handsomer, classier, and luckier; but, where it really matters—in the innermost recesses of selfhood or soulhood, whatever and wherever that is—*you are no better than I.*"

At this point an empirically minded person may take exception and wonder about the availability of data to support the premise of a soul or a self. But this is not an argument for the existence of a soul—dignified or undignified. It is the postulation of a point of view toward mankind and it is a stance in which the writer and—it is hoped—the profession believe. It is a good belief. It may appear silly to the cynical, it may run in the face of man's long chronicle of abominable behavior, it may be contradicted by his irrefutable incumbency in the animal kingdom, but it is still a good and noble belief. And it is prerequisite for social welfare; without it the whole welfare edifice makes no sense at all.

Life is suffering

So man is dignified. But, alas, he lives in a sewer—a sewer of suffering. And this is the second element in the paradox: the human condition is one of suffering. Under the best of conditions life is cruel. It is not merely neutral—it is antagonistic. It may be unnecessary to pursue this line of argument in detail especially because it is so painfully self-evident in daily work with clients. Those who require additional documentation, however, may consult the written genius of the species: the Old and New Testaments, the scripture of Eastern theology, the incomparable poets, and, of course, the existentialists, who sometimes act as though they were the first to stumble on the fact of man's miraculous isolation.

Life is suffering because, in the first instance, we are ultimately betrayed by the mortality of our own bodies. We die and those we love die. We are ravaged by disease, we live with imminent and inevitable loss, we are harassed by the elements, we are oppressed by our institutions—in short, we suffer. Freud, the super-realist, summed up the human condition quite well when he wrote:

> Thus our possibilities of happiness are already restricted by our constitution. Unhappiness is much less difficult to experience. We are threatened with suffering from three directions: from our own body, which is doomed to decay and dissolution and which cannot even do without pain and anxiety as warning signals; from the external world, which may rage against us with overwhelming and merciless forces of destruction; and finally from our relations to other men. The suffering which comes from this last source is perhaps more painful to us than any other. We tend to regard it as a kind of gratuitous addition, although it cannot be any less fatefully inevitable than the suffering which comes from elsewhere.[1]

The terrible dilemma

In any event, this premise of human suffering provides the second prerequisite for the institution of social welfare. Suffering argues that

---

[1] Sigmund Freud, *Civilization and Its Discontents* (New York: W. W. Norton & Co., 1961), pp. 23–24.

man needs attention, human dignity argues that he merits attention, and social welfare, the third element in the paradox, is there to do the job—along, it must be noted, with several other institutions in this civilization. But it is at this point that the terrible dilemma occurs: how is one to minister to man's suffering without robbing him of his dignity?

Let us take as a starting point the traditional device that society has used to alleviate suffering—charity. It is obvious that the giving of alms is demeaning when it is accompanied by the implicit gratuity of "I, the donor, am better than you, the recipient." Such an implication can be communicated in various ways: in subtle vocalizations, in the physical bearing of the alms-giver as he drops his coin into the bowl, in the publicity given the act. Behind such a stance is always the notion: "I have given you something—be *grateful* to me!" And when the gratitude must be expressed by an obligation to listen to good counsel, the humiliation of the recipient is complete.

The current public assistance programs contain these implicit demeaning qualities. Indeed, most are all too explicit. That is why public welfare can never be a dignified source of assistance: the recipient is burdened with an expectation that he will be grateful to a more fortunate community and willing to take advice from it on how to manage his life. It is the means test, of course, that provides the sufficient condition for the degradation.

It is difficult to find an instance of a charitable institution that does not have this demeaning quality. Care must be taken here: to change the name of the device does not change its nature. Public assistance could be called "monthly reward" and the means test labeled "scholarship application," but the stigma would remain. As long as the recipient is subject to the conditional largess of another he is in a demeaning position.

But enough of charity. What about casework per se? Here the degradation may occur in a more insidious manner, but in a way that is no less real. Before proceeding further with this line of argument, however, it must be made clear what kind of casework is in question. This is casework that has been summarized under such rubrics as "aggressive casework," "reaching the unreached," "case-finding," "working with the involuntary client," and so forth. It is a casework that permits an unsolicited encounter with an initially unwilling client in the name of expertise. And it is a casework that occupies the preponderance of energies expended in the larger field of social welfare. If we consider, for example, the areas of public welfare, corrections, the services offered by the newer poverty programs, education, inpatient services, among others, we realize the enormous investment the profession has in offering a casework service to clients who make no request of it, who have little choice about their involvement and even less comprehension as to what the involvement entails.

In spite of some risk of overstatement, let us, for the sake of argument, put the case quite starkly: The social work profession presumes to confront a large number of people with the judgment that they are unhappy, confused, deviant, ill, maladapted—this list could be extended indefinitely—and, as such, require the benefits of our attentions. This judgment is based on either the conclusions of society in the form of legal adjudications or commitment procedures or the diagnostic acumen of our own expert knowledge. In the latter instance we look upon an individual and say that he suffers from an ailment, and we can say this because we are expert; he may not realize that he is afflicted—he may not even care that he is afflicted—but we know he is and it is our responsibility to minister to him. In the former instance we concur in the judgment of society that he is ailing and we accept the charge of that society to effect a remedy.

What is wrong with this stance and how does it impinge on the client's dignity? The wrong inheres in the assumption that we have a right to impose unsolicited advice upon another human being—*and he is not free either to withdraw himself from the situation or even to discount the advice.* If he is on welfare, his benefit is contingent on being counseled in the use of his money or more; if he is on probation or parole, his physical freedom becomes a condition of his receptivity to counsel; if he hangs around on street corners he is assaulted by the insinuations of the street worker; if he is insane and hospitalized, the duration of his confinement becomes a function of a willingness to be counseled. He may not choose to be so advised—but if he is to eat or wander without constraint in the world he must submit himself to the good intentions of the expert.

By this position we deprive an individual of the one freedom that is primary to all others and that endows him with the core of his dignity: the freedom to make a shambles of his life. This may sound like a strange doctrine—that people should be free to err, to make mistakes, to fail, to be "ill." But, in a very basic sense, it is the mainspring of all other freedoms, especially in a culture premised on scientific determinism and reaching ever closer to an end wherein mankind *can* exercise control over his world and his brethern. The profession *does* have the expertise to diagnose maladaptive behavior. Our judgment is far from perfect in this regard, but it is improving and it will continue to improve. We are working in our research toward an end when we can control society and behavior, and, if we are not careful, we may succeed in that end. Then the awesome and terrible dilemma is immediately upon us: what happens to the humanity of man, to the rewards of failure, to the dignity of real choice when that day arrives?[2]

Voluntary use of casework services

What is argued, then, is that man be offered the possibility of choice—and that includes the choice of being maladaptive or deviant or even "ill." Society may—indeed, it must—demand a price for deviance; it cannot operate without a minimum degree of conformity and compliance. But the individual in question should be given the option of paying the price; the old convict notion of "serving one's time and paying a debt to society" has always been a most dignified formulation. The dignity inheres in a conception of responsibility. How humiliating to be told that one behaves in a particular manner because one cannot help it, that one is not responsible for one's actions, that X is a result of poor socialization and Y is a result of good socialization, that good deeds are as predetermined as are bad deeds, that narcissism and altruism are consequences rather than choices, and that man is nothing more than a wisp of straw caught in the winds of instinct and environment.

This moral stance should not be misunderstood: It is not an argument for bigger and better jails. It is not a testimony to a belief that poverty is ennobling. It does not advocate a doctrine of laissez-faire in terms of our social institutions. If people are poor, let us either produce well-paying jobs or give them money; if people are ill, let us offer them hospitals and medicine and physicians; let us have schools and universities and houses and parks. We can be magnanimous in our construction of these resources and ingenious in making them available to all. But let us not wrap these goodies with strings that dangle so that if a man needs food he must suffer the insolence of well-intentioned advice or if he needs training he must submit to counsel about the legitimacy of his offspring. Alas, there will always be crime and criminals, and we will need prisons. By all means, let the prisons be infused with the spirit of humanism. But humanism does not mean group therapy as a precondition to parole.

If the poor want advice, let us advise them—but at *their* initiative and not ours. If criminals wish their criminality treated, let us treat it—but after *they* request it. Let us have our clinics and our adjunctive services; indeed, let us advertise these remedies so that they are known—but let us not dare to act the parent with adult human beings

---

[2] It is in the creative imaginations of novelists that the terror of a controlled society becomes most evident. The writer does not have in mind here the political authoritarianism of *1984*, but rather the benign "scientific" worlds of *Walden II* [B. F. Skinner (New York: Macmillan Co., 1948)] or the society pictured in *A Clockwork Orange* [Anthony Burgess (New York: Ballantine Books, 1963)].

and exclaim: "We know what's best for you, poor afflicted one, and—like it or not—take our medicine."

The plea, then, is for the voluntary use of casework services. But there are certain problematical situations that make such a dictum an oversimplification. The voluntary use of service presumes a clientele that is capable of making choices, and such a presumption does not hold in the case of children, the mentally deficient, and, probably, certain types of the mentally ill. With such classes of clients we have very little choice and society must impose its good intentions, but let us do this reluctantly and with parsimony and with the certainty that there is, in fact, no other viable alternative assumption.

Some would argue that there is another type of client who merits our attention but he has been so oppressed by a hostile society and so impoverished by deprivation that he has neither the knowledge nor the will to ask for our help. We must be careful, in this line of argument, that we are not merely substituting new pejoratives, in the guise of technical jargon, for old pejoratives. Of course Negroes are not racially inferior or lazy. But is it any less patronizing—or humiliating—to see them as culturally deprived, aspirationally stultified, lacking in a sense of basic integrity and identity because of a brittle family structure, or otherwise "not with it"? Let us beware the possibility of the more hideous colonialism that can stem from the white man's casework—a colonialism disguised by the language of science and an immaculate empiricism. It is not at all clear that if opportunities were available to the "deprived" they would use them. And, if they choose not to, it is nobody's business but their own.

So we deal, then, with the voluntary client. But even in this instance there are many value problems. Three of these stand out as being of primary importance.

Inevitable moral concern of casework

The first problem is perhaps the most difficult. It is premised on the notion that man's ailments are essentially disorders of moral style rather than disease entities per se. That is to say, clients come to us, not with mental illnesses of a classic medical order, but with problems of ethics— with confusions about values, with concerns of rightness and wrongness.[3] If this premise is true, the traditional therapeutic injunction of

---

[3] Evidence for this assertion can be found in Thomas Szasz, *The Myth of Mental Illness* (New York: Harper & Row, 1961); O. Hobart Mowrer, *The Crisis in Psychiatry and Religion* (Princeton, N.J.: D. Van Nostrand Co., 1961); Mowrer, *The New Group Therapy* (Princeton, N.J.: D. Van Nostrand Co., 1964); and Perry London, *The Modes and Morals of Psychotherapy* (New York: Holt, Rinehart & Winston, 1964).

moral neutrality—which, by the way, is in itself a morality—becomes an absurdity. The caseworker cannot disengage himself from the moral concerns of his client when such happen to be the core of his difficulty and the very reason he asked for help in the first place. But if the caseworker must then enter into this once forbidden realm, he assumes the functions of a priest—but a priest without an explicit theology, a secular priest with an idiosyncratic dogma.

Again, we must be careful not to be seduced by our own language. As marriage counselors, for example, we cannot claim to be indifferent to divorce; if we try to salvage a marriage we are rather explicit in the positive value we put on the institution. If we claim to let the parties decide for themselves—a claim that, in most instances, is a self-deception—we still hold an implicit value toward marriage, namely, that marriages can legitimately be dissolved. Either way we take a position and subscribe to a morality.

We take such positions all the time: we hold to dogmas about the worth of human relationships, about love, about fidelity, about honesty, about autonomy, about child rearing, about work and creativity—and these are the very concerns that torture the minds of our clients. They come to us for help with these agonizing issues and, if we are honest, we cannot help but admit our influence on them. In a very real sense we become proselytizers of our own morality. And that, it must be acknowledged, is a horrendous burden. God may be dead, but fifty thousand social workers have risen up to take his place!

Do clients share social work's goals?

This is not our only problem with the voluntary client, however. Let us accept the premise that we are experts; surely, if we are not experts now, we will become so in the not-too-distant future. To the extent that we are experts we truly *do* know what is best for our clients—and for our voluntary clients at that. They come to us for help and we are then privileged to posit goals or outcomes to our endeavors. But would our clients share these goals or posit the same ones for themselves? Our client may want sexual restraint—we may offer a guiltless sexual license. He may want to forget—we may help him remember. He may want simplicity—we may offer complexity. He may want adaptation—we may offer autonomy. He may want a soft dream—we may confront him with a sharp reality. As experts we *do* posit goals: we study, we diagnose, we set a goal based on a diagnosis, and we work to that end in our treatment. We do, of course, consider what our client wants for himself, but that consideration is incorporated into the diagnosis; it is one more bit of data for us to take into account when we construct our own—usually private—objectives.

Physicians do the same thing. They know what is best and they know what a reasonable outcome may be. It would be a foolish physician who allowed his patient to make the prognosis and set the therapeutic regimen. It does not take many visits to the doctor to know that dignity is not a characteristic of the examining table; one's body is treated as an object. How much more undignified is it to have one's mind or thoughts or fantasies or dreams or hopes or needs treated as manipulable things? We may know what is best, but perhaps it is more in keeping with a tradition of decency to keep our knowledge and our prognoses to ourselves.

Capitalizing on clients' hope

There is one final problem for social work, and this has to do with the nature of the therapeutic process itself. A great deal of evidence has accumulated by this time which suggests that the therapies stemming from a myriad different theoretical orientations have approximately the same efficacy.[4] These diverse orientations include the more traditional or primitive procedures of witchcraft, faith healing, magic, and other folk therapies. In many ways this accretion of evidence is quite remarkable; it concludes that in spite of some quite different technical procedures and rationales most patients get better and their improvement probably lies in what is common to all such procedures—the authority of the healer and the faith or expectation of the patient. What we do, then, is to capitalize on the gullibility of our clients: we are magicians who exploit their ignorance, their misery, their dependence, and their need. We do this, again, for their own good. Our intentions are honorable; we are not dabblers in black magic, but we are magicians nonetheless. Attention is called once more to the pitfall of self-deceptive language: a diagnosis in terms of libidinal energies, interaction patterns, and alienation may sound quite learned, but is no more relevant to the outcome of treatment than is a diagnosis in terms of mana, possession, and juju. The shaman treats troubled souls much as we do—and quite as effectively. And he treats in the same way: he capitalizes on the desperate hope of his client.

If this assumption is correct we are again faced with an ethical dilemma: How far can we go in an exploitation of gullibility and desperate need? Shall we summon up our charismatic voice and lay hands on an ailing client if we have reason to believe it will help him? Do

---

[4] See, for example, Jerome Frank, *Persuasion and Healing* (New York: Schocken Books, 1961); and Ari Kiev, *Magic, Faith and Healing* (New York: Free Press of Glencoe, 1964). The classic paper on the disparate effects of therapy is by Hans J. Eysenck, "The Effects of Psychotherapy," *International Journal of Psychiatry*, Vol. 1, No. 1 (January 1965).

we deal in talismans and amulets? Some would say, "No, never—that is hypocrisy and fraud," but we are clever, so we support instead of charm; we modify defensive structures instead of burning candles; we offer interpretations instead of sacrificial goats.

All these considerations raise a basic question for the caseworker who must decide what things are permissible in the name of therapy. What means can be utilized to accomplish our ends—indeed, what ends are permissible for us to conjure? At this point professional integrity leads us to conclude: "I don't know"—but, surely, it is time to worry ourselves about these matters.

Our business is with dignity

But perhaps it is possible to offer a solution to our trouble or, at least, a direction in which we can move. It has been argued that any unsolicited treatment of clients is an affront. The consequence of this argument is clear: Social workers must get out of the business of dealing with involuntary clients, with people who do not want us. This is not out of sulk, but out of respect. It has also been argued that the treatment of even the voluntary client is shot through with ethical difficulties, but in these instances the client, in a sense, asks for it; he risks an intrusion into his ethical system. Social work's obligation with the voluntary client is to explicate these risks for him and to be careful and extremely critical of what we do.

But this was to be a paper on the dignity of man, and herein lies a wide and virgin domain for social work. There are in the world people who need us and want us. Confronting them is an array of frightful institutions and the inevitable tribulation that stems from human encounters. Let us join with these clients in a search for and reaffirmation of their dignity. Let us become their allies and champion their cause. Let us become mercenaries in their service—let us, in a word, become their advocates. There is no degradation in engaging the service of a mercenary; a mercenary is there to be used. Let our clients use us, then, use us to argue their cause, to maneuver, to obtain their rights and their justice, to move the immovable bureaucrats.[5] Social casework once had a marvelous tradition of advocacy. This writer would like to see us return to the best of that tradition, to see social caseworkers available to people who need an ally—an expert ally--who would advocate for them in this mad struggle of living. Our business is with

---

[5] There is no need here to discuss the role of advocate. This theme is covered by Scott Briar, "Dodo or Phoenix? A View of the Current Crisis in Casework," *Social Work Practice 1967* (New York: Columbia University Press, 1967); and Irving Piliavin, "Restructuring the Provision of Social Services," *Social Work* 13:1 (January 1968), pp. 34–41.

people—not with organizations. And, above all, our business is with dignity.

Humanistic values and social casework*

Elizabeth L. Salomon

[His heart] had ceased to partake of the universal throb. He had lost his hold of the magnetic chain of humanity. He was no longer a brother-man, opening the chambers of the dungeons of our common nature by the key of holy sympathy, which gave him a right to share in all its secrets; he was now a cold observer, looking on mankind as the subject of his experiment, and, at length converting man and woman to be his puppets . . . .

Nathaniel Hawthorne, *Ethan Brand*

The professional casework process has two fundamental parts, or elements: one is personal, intuitive, sympathetic, and empathic; the other is scientific, abstractive, and generalizing. As the social work profession builds an ever more sophisticated body of scientific knowledge, however, it runs the risk that its members will achieve technical proficiency at the cost of increasing separation or estrangement from truly deep feelings of concern for those it is dedicated to help. Although the extent of this estrangement varies enormously from one practitioner to another, no one can escape it entirely, if only because we are all part of the American culture, which is a highly technological one. The only remedy is an increased consciousness on the part of the casework practitioner that the two elements intersect in the professional relationship, and that both are based on philosophical assumptions that should be examined.

In the early years of modern social work, Mary Richmond found the element she called "the charitable impulse" to be too often a "blind force," even though she described it as "perhaps the very best thing we have." As a result she began the attempt to evolve a scientific method to harness this force effectively in the service of the client. This method, which has come to rely on objectivity, detachment, neutrality, and the ability to conceptualize, was intended to serve as a balance to moral intuition, which is most strikingly characterized by its immediacy. The

---

* Reprinted by permission of the author and the Family Service Association of America from *Social Casework*, 48:1 (January 1967), pp. 26–32.

tension between these two forces today was seen by Gordon Hamilton in her identification of the curious paradox of distance and intimacy in the casework relationship.[1]

Some believe that "analysis and immediacy fear each other's rights, and there is good reason to keep them separated."[2] Although, in fact, they cannot be kept separate, we must be more sensitive to both and more deeply aware of some of the dangers of scientific objectivity in particular. For while it can lead us to become more proficient and precise in diagnosis and treatment method, we may dull our hearing of the deeper calls of human suffering if we always listen with a narrow diagnostic formulation in mind. Scientific precision, though its validity is undeniable, may, if it becomes the central preoccupation, produce social work technicians who increase the distance between themselves and their clients on the assumption that they will, thereby, obtain a clearer and more objective understanding of them. This overemphasis on technique has been called "one of the chief (if not *the* chief) blocks to the understanding of human beings in Western culture . . . an overemphasis which goes along with the tendency to see the human being as an object to be calculated, managed, 'analyzed.' "[3]

Obviously we could not transmit the valuable experience and observations of practitioners and theorists if we did not have a body of scientific knowledge. Without organization and classification there are only chaos and good impulses. If we sometimes envy Lady Bountiful her spontaneity, we need only remind ourselves that her innocence was corruptible, prejudiced, ignorant, and ultimately both harmful and useless; we can remind ourselves, more immediately, of the untrained worker whose preference is for the "good" or "deserving" client. Even here, however, the coin has another side, as recognized in another context by Harold Nitzberg and Marvin Kahn. With the sophisticated and well-intentioned caseworker whose ardor is dampened by a diagnostic classification suggesting "untreatability," they contrast the welfare worker, who, unaware of the connotation of "untreatability" suggested by some diagnostic labels, empathizes with the clients' elemental needs for food, shelter, and medicine.[4] In brief, my position is not antiscientific. But I *am* suggesting that scientific objectivity is a double-edged sword when applied to human relationships.

---

[1] Gordon Hamilton, *Psychotherapy in Child Guidance,* Columbia University Press, New York, 1947, pp. 126–27.

[2] *Philosophy of the Social Sciences: A Reader,* Maurice Natanson (ed.), Random House, New York, 1963, p. 4.

[3] Rollo May, "Contributions of Existential Psychotherapy," in *Existence: a New Dimension in Psychiatry and Psychology,* Rollo May, Ernest Angel, and Henry F. Ellenberger (eds.), Basic Books, New York, 1958, p. 76.

[4] Harold Nitzberg and Marvin W. Kahn, "Consultation with Welfare Workers in a Mental Health Clinic," *Social Work,* Vol. VII, July 1962, p. 91.

The dominance of positivism

Modern social work rests on certain unspoken philosophical assumptions, on a framework of positivism with its credo of a new enlightenment, its cult of objectivity, and its empirical scientific methodology—the currency of the world of Freud and Mary Richmond. According to the positivist point of view, the world is discoverable and knowable. Its scientific method, induction, consists of breaking down natural objects into their characteristic elements and then elaborating these elements into types—or concepts, judgments, conclusions, and theories. Most significant, the inductive method of positivism holds that a real world can be observed and that the observer can be divorced from the objects he observes. Even when we observe ourselves (as social workers are enjoined to do to become self-aware), we turn ourselves into objects that can be observed: we make ourselves foreign to ourselves.

Positivism is the dominant philosophy in the world today. Perhaps that is why we so rarely acknowledge its influence. It leads us to seek a statistical kind of knowledge of individuals; certain recurring similarities become the basis for generalization and are then thought of as characteristics. This method of acquiring knowledge explicitly denies value, because it is objective. We see its reflection in social work's philosophy and in its methodology of being "nonjudgmental" or "ethically neutral," though questions of value are more and more being raised. Dale Harris has said that "[caseworkers] have often described the aim of their activities as helping others to help themselves. This statement implies respect for the integrity of the client. In practice it has sometimes implied either a naïve belief in innate goodness, or the validity of the social relativity viewpoint, or both."[5] Actually it is impossible to act outside the context of a value system: even the tone of voice one uses with a client reflects it. In truth one must be aware of one's own value orientation. What should be avoided is a narrow ideological point of view, which is then imposed on the client in a judgmental fashion.

The problem of values is not the only one raised when a positivistic view is applied to human behavior. Because the scientist, to be useful, must order and classify, he may try to fit all life experience into the vise of his own set of constructs (for example, ego, id, superego) and believe that his set explains all human life. In social work and psychiatry, for example, people are sometimes reduced to no more than the sum of their psychic conflicts; their current experiences are devalued. In this context, "What does this *really* mean?" suggests that the reality sought is the reality of psychic origins only. And a narrowly reductionist attitude is not restricted to a few second-rate practitioners but seems

---

[5] Dale B. Harris, "Values and Standards in Educational Activities," *Social Casework*, Vol. XXXIX, February–March 1958, p. 161.

to be prevalent even among the faculty of schools of social work. Muriel Pumphrey has written: ". . . the most consistent student complaint about class teaching was that they felt faculty members did not accept students' questions in a value area as being philosophic and speculative, but usually interpreted them narrowly as manifestations of personal conflict."[6]

Scientific knowledge as an abstraction

Though all human activity has a psychological aspect, a psychological explanation does not exhaust its meaning. We need to understand that a patient's diagnosis does not define him as a person, as Gerald Rubin has pointed out: "In addition to a person's striving to reduce anxiety and achieve pleasure (Freud), or to attain a state of social well-being (Adler), there is also present a striving for actualizing one's 'uniqueness' and attaching to one's unique being a sense of 'value' in a context that is 'meaningful' to others."[7] Rubin's corollary is that not all psychological suffering is necessarily neurotic and that suffering *can* be spiritually enriching. Those who tend to reduce all reality to the level of psychological reality tend, in fact, to elevate psychobiological adaptation to the status of the ultimate value.

What we must realize is that scientific knowledge is always an abstraction from the *Lebenswelt,*† or complex life-world—what Stanley Hyman has referred to more poetically as "the tangled bank of life," with its perplexities, ambiguities, and, ultimately, its unpredictability and mystery. I believe that Erik Erikson has the *Lebenswelt* in mind when he contrasts Freud's idea of objective reality, the "outer world" with its criteria of science, with actuality, "the world of that intuitive and active participation which constitutes most of our waking life." He goes on to say: "This term [reality, or objective reality] more than any other, represents the Cartesian strait jacket we have imposed on our model of man. . . ."[8] The neatly arid world of explicit cause and effect is caught by William Golding in his novel *Free Fall.* "All day long the trains run on rails. Eclipses are predictable. Penicillin cures pneumonia and the atom splits to order. All day long, year in, year out, the daylight

[6] Muriel W. Pumphrey, *The Teaching of Values and Ethics in Social Work Education,* Social Work Curriculum Study, Vol. XIII, Council on Social Work Education, New York, 1959, p. 31.

[7] Gerald K. Rubin, "Helping a Clinic Patient Modify Self-destructive Thinking," *Social Work,* Vol. VII, January 1962, p. 79.

† I should like here to acknowledge my obligation to Professor John Wild of the Yale University Philosophy Department for this helpful concept.

[8] Erik H. Erikson, *Insight and Responsibility: Lectures on the Ethical Implications of Psychoanalytic Insight,* W. W. Norton & Co., New York, 1964, p. 163.

explanation drives back the mystery and reveals a reality usable, understandable, and detached."[9]

The world described by Golding exists, of course, but I believe that it is not the whole of reality. We should not, for example, mistake the case history, with its dehydrated abstractions of symptom, syndrome, diagnosis, and prognosis for the vital human being about whom it is written. When we say "oral dependent personality," we are telling a truth—often a "usable" truth—about an individual. But we cannot believe it is the whole or the most fundamental truth even when we flesh in the history with other relevant facts. There are many, many oral dependent personalities, but how different, as individuals, people with the same diagnosis can be! Diagnosis and classification are true, as maps are true; they are abstractions, not reality. The scientific method used narrowly can lead from abstraction to dehumanization and fragmentation by the very professions dedicated to restoring the individual to wholeness.

The dangers of positivism

Another unfortunate result of a positivistic belief that the world is ultimately "knowable"—and the corollary conviction that human behavior and human motives are ultimately "knowable" in terms of cause and effect—is the corruption of the positivistic stance by those who are influenced by its ethos but do not have the scientist's appreciation of the complex interrelationships among multitudinous causal factors. This naïve attitude lends itself to grossly oversimplified explanations of human motives. It binds bits of information together into a one-to-one relationship and creates a sort of vise in which, for example, a mother's sickness during pregnancy necessarily means she *really* rejects her child. Even among positivistic practitioners, there are many sophisticated and often humane persons who are impatient with this sort of oversimplification and who demand a much more complex and a much richer network of cause-and-effect relationships, including all manner of subtle historical, cultural, and personally idiosyncratic patterns. Certainly such a base makes possible a closer, more informed look at the client's world. Nevertheless it is still a look from the outside; it still assumes that reality is objective and that the only real world is the world of biological determinism.

The problem is that these practitioners demand too much of objective knowledge, push it too far. Life refuses to be so rigidly ordered and classified. That such an attempt at ordering and classifying life fails to correspond with reality stems from what Camus calls *démesur,* a limiting measure of things and of man, according to Erich Kahler's trans-

---

[9] William Golding, *Free Fall,* Harcourt, Brace and Co., New York, 1960, p. 252.

lation. Arguments to the effect that knowledge can be only approximate
are opposed by the assumption that man's behavior would be predictable
and measurable if only we had a gigantic computer into which we
could feed the most complex sort of data, which might range from
projections of weather conditions to the most minute cultural discrimina-
tions—and if only the life span were long enough to wait for the machine
to come out with an answer. So even these more truly scientific practitioners make an object out of man, an object to be studied and observed
"objectively."

In our efforts to be objective, in our attempts to be self-understanding
and self-aware, we even go so far as to view ourselves as objects or
as "cases." As an illustration of the wider implications of this attitude
in modern culture Kahler notes:

> . . . a human life becomes a case that can be filed under certain cate-
> gories . . . . These non-personal criteria take hold of our private, per-
> sonal attitudes toward ourselves, so that a person will view and experi-
> ence his self through that completely non-personal criterion. So a person
> instead of immediately succumbing to his pain, instead of being unhappy,
> will at once scrutinize the cause of his frustrations objectively and in
> a detached manner. Instead of using his personal judgment as derived
> from his own experiences, wisdom and values, instead of trying to resolve
> his situation independently in his unique fashion, including his pain,
> and in some way acknowledging the legitimacy of his suffering and
> unhappiness, he will analyze himself by means of pre-established psycho-
> logical and sociological categories—he will manipulate himself as a
> psycho- or socio-clinical case. Thus he makes himself into an object
> visualized by an alien transpersonal eye.

Kahler concludes that this attitude results in both *"a new sensibility"*
that perceives nuances and penetrates into new levels of reality, and
"a new insensibility" that we are not aware of—a kind of callousness.[10]

The ideals of the Enlightenment

The picture that has been given of the social worker as scientific
practitioner and as neutral observer is not, of course, the whole picture.
It does not take into account the dedication and social evangelism so
characteristic of social work from the very beginning. The long humanitarian tradition of social work, distinguished by a passion for social
justice and a fervent belief in the possibility of human betterment, fills
in the value-vacuum of positivism with the ideals of the Enlightenment.
Democracy, human perfectibility, self-determination, and the dignity

[10] Erich Kahler, *The Tower and the Abyss: An Inquiry into the Transformation of the Individual*, George Braziller, New York, 1957, pp. 91–93.

of man are not only acknowledged but proclaimed. Both positivism and the Enlightenment are rooted in the Lockean *tabula rasa* doctrine, which, in denying original sin—that unyielding, irrational stumbling block— promised that man could be changed and shaped by his environment. It is the ethos of the Enlightenment that is so congenial to this nation's activism, pragmatism, and optimism, and to the social and human sciences in particular. At the same time, however, a fundamentally materialistic philosophy inheres in it, suggesting that man is passive and wholly subject to external stimuli in his environment. The ultimate development of this concept was behaviorism.

The contemporary social worker, schooled in depth psychology, is too sophisticated to put much stock in "environmental manipulation" except as "first aid." It should be pointed out, however, that while Freudian psychology acknowledges genetic differences and emphasizes the dynamics of interpersonal relationships, it also postulates universal stages of human development. In so doing, it lends itself to distortion by those who confuse general formulations and abstractive prescriptions for psychic health with a response to man that acknowledges the full complexity of human experience. For persons such as these, psychic formulas become as reductive as the environmental formulas of the behaviorists.

I believe that social work has been hampered by the shallowness of assumptions of the Enlightenment about the nature of man. Though the values of the Enlightenment, which represent a secularization of Judeo-Christian ethics, are by no means to be despised, neither do they take into account the ambiguity, complexity, and mystery of human nature. May has made a useful distinction between what he calls "ecstatic reason," in the seventeenth and eighteenth centuries, and "technical reason," in the nineteenth century. As he defines it, ecstatic reason included "the capacity to transcend the immediate situation, to grasp the whole, and such functions as intuition, insight, poetic perception were not rigidly excluded. The concept also embraced ethics: reason in the enlightenment meant justice."[11] Technical reason, however, became equated with science and married to technique. It is, therefore, faith in technical reason based on such assumptions as human perfectibility that gives social work the hope that it can solve such problems as delinquency, and then leaves it little to fall back on if all material and therapeutic resources are provided and the problem remains or takes new forms.

Humanistic values

While social work follows the *ethics* of the Judeo-Christian tradition, particularly as they have been interpreted through the democratic tradi-

---

[11] May, op. cit., p. 34.

tion of the Enlightenment, it has neglected an exploration of man's spiritual dimensions, partly because of the essentially pragmatic method out of which social work principles are evolved. As a result, then, of a detachment from value, on the one hand, and of the inadequacy and vagueness of its ideals, on the other, the profession of social work has a kind of *de facto* ideology—one that is insidious, because unacknowledged; one that permits moralistic judgments by the very caseworker who eschews "judgmentalism." I call it the "ideology of mental health." The caseworker may, without awareness, judge a compulsively tidy housewife as severely as his nineteenth-century predecessor judged a slovenly one. Because he is more concerned with human *behavior,* than with human *nature,* he tends to accept Freudian principles in doctrinaire fashion. Despite the fact that many social workers are creative enough to break through stereotypes, there is a tendency for insights to harden into doctrine and psychiatric clichés, and it is very difficult not to become mechanistic in the use of techniques and deterministic in attitude.

In trying to free themselves from the fetters of moralistic attitudes, social workers have been hampered by confusing a moralistic with a moral view of life. What is really needed, it seems to me, is a concept of man and the human condition that will deepen the social worker's understanding of man's moral and spiritual nature. This means that social work should affirm the priority of humanistic values above scientific method, which is essentially based on abstractions from life. Erikson points out that in medicine the Hippocratic Oath "subordinates all medical method to a humanistic ethic."[12] The humanistic disciplines give us a synthetic view of man to balance the analytic view. Tragedy, for example, shows us the ambiguity of man's experience as "fated but free, free but fated." It suggests that we can acknowledge the possibility of choice even as we observe one chain of human misery linked from generation to generation. Jung stresses that there are *two* modes of existence—the organic, or biological, pointing to the "inexorable cycle of biological events," and the mode of the human spirit, which offers us the only way of breaking "the spell that binds us to the cycle of biological events."[13]

Today, ego psychology is allowing some autonomy to the ego. But the thoroughgoing positivist can only see freedom as an illusion—or at best a "subjective feeling," by implication, of an inferior order of reality—and can only see improvement in treatment as a result of a causal network mechanically set in motion by therapy. I believe that the "subjective feeling" is the primary stuff of reality and that the "causal network" is an abstraction of a deductive nature. Psychological determi-

---

[12] Erikson, op. cit., p. 237.

[13] Floyd W. Matson, *The Broken Image: Man, Science and Society,* George Braziller, New York, 1964, p. 213.

nism offers no real opportunity for dealing creatively and meaningfully with pain or the hope of self-knowledge. If human destiny is determined solely by a combination of objectifiable inner and outer forces that shape the individual, then meaning is destroyed along with choice: the individual is left a helpless victim of fate without responsibility for himself.

Rubin seems also to have tired of endlessly sharpening technique to the neglect of the broader understanding of the human condition. He describes a particular case in which he looked beyond the patient's diagnosis of "schizophrenia," and helped the patient look beyond it, because it was not the important thing about the man. What mattered—and he was able to transmit this conviction to the patient—was what he *did* with his unhappiness, his situation. In this instance he was able to help the patient affirm his power to make choices rather than see himself as a "schizophrenic," with the connotations of hopelessness. He was also able to discuss the patient's suicidal thoughts as something every human being has to weigh and consider. I suspect that Rubin is able to transcend the patient's diagnosis and enter his life-world in the way that was described by Jung: "If I want to understand an individual human being, I must lay aside all scientific knowledge of the average man and discard all theories in order to adopt a completely new and unprejudiced attitude."[14] I am sure Jung does not mean that he is abandoning scientific knowledge, but rather that he does not allow scientific detachment to hamper the relationship. According to such a view the individual and his world come first, and deductions and inferences are secondary; the therapist dares to forego preconceptions.

Many writers have dealt with the logical extension of an attitude that gives primacy to empathy over detachment. *Encounter* is the term most frequently used to describe the somewhat mystical (in the sense of ultimately spiritual) transaction between the patient and therapist, the existential psychiatrists having dealt most fully with this phenomenon. But they pretend to no monopoly. Harry Stack Sullivan speaks of participant-observation, Martin Buber of "healing through meeting," with the ground of meeting ". . . on this side of the objective, on the narrow ridge, where *I* and *Thou* meet, there is the realm of 'between.'" Gabriel Marcel writes of "inter-subjectivity"—implying an intimate communication on the order of communion. Each communicant recognizes the other in himself (to recall Rank's phrase) and recognizes himself in the other. Tillich also says "you must participate in a self in order to know and understand what it *is*. By participation you change it."[15] Detachment is felt to be "useful" but subordinate to participation. This point of view implies that the therapist must be willing to risk himself

[14] C. G. Jung, *The Undiscovered Self*, Mentor Books, New York, 1959, p. 18.
[15] See Matson, op. cit., pp. 238–41.

136   *Social work processes*

in the encounter, and most of these writers put a great deal of emphasis on the reality of the encounter's taking place between two real people, both of whom must be touched and changed by the experience.

May emphasizes that a person is taken seriously in the encounter: his guilt, for example, is treated as guilt, that is, a profound quality in man's total humanity, and not automatically changed to "guilt feelings." He speaks through Binswanger of the need to "wake or rekindle that divine 'spark' in the patient which only true communication from existence to existence can bring forth and which alone possesses, with its light and warmth, also the fundamental power that makes any therapy work—the power to liberate a person from the blind isolation, the *idios kosmos* of Heraclitus, from a mere vegetating in his body, his dreams, his private wishes, his conceit and his presumptions, and to ready him for a life of *koinonia*, of genuine community."[16]

The stakes are high when social workers enter into a helping relationship with other human beings. When we emphasize skill and technique at the expense of human feeling, we are only reflecting a larger cultural problem: a complex technological world in which individuals are regarded "functionally." Because of our commitment to restore "wholeness," we must first restore wholeness to our own vision of life. Unless we are able to do so, the price could be the same as that paid by Ethan Brand, the price of our humanity—our heart. Perhaps if we seek a deeper understanding of our human condition and undertake a more thoughtful examination of our professional and personal values, we shall be reminded of Erikson's interpretation of the Golden Rule: "The doer of the Golden Rule, and he who is done by, is the same man, *is* man."[17]

Selected annotated references

APTEKAR, HERBERT H., *An Intercultural Exploration: Universals and Differences in Social Work Values, Functions and Practice.* (New York: Council on Social Work Education, 1966).

This volume is a summary of the highlights of a ten-day seminar undertaken by 22 social work educators from ten different countries. The primary focus of the conference was on values and their relationship to other social work issues. The volume allows students to explore values in international perspectives.

BIESTEK, FELIX, *The Casework Relationship* (Chicago: Loyola University Press, 1957).

---

[16] May, op. cit., p. 81.
[17] Erikson, op. cit., p. 243.

Biestek defines and discusses the principles of individualization, purposeful expression of feelings, controlled emotional involvement, acceptance, nonjudgmental attitude, client self-determination, and confidentiality as they relate to work with individuals.

HALMOS, PAUL, *Faith of the Counsellors* (New York: Schocken, 1966).

From an examination of the published literature from psychiatry, clinical psychology, psychiatric social work, and educational counseling, the conclusion is reached that these counseling professions operate from an unproven set of tenets of faith. The tenets are identified and discussed.

KENDALL, KATHERINE A., ed., *Social Work Values in an Age of Discontent* (New York: Council on Social Work Education, 1970).

This is a collection of lectures on social work values given over a period of three years in honor of Ann Elizabeth Neely.

LEVY, CHARLES, "The Value Base of Social Work," *Journal of Education for Social Work* 9:1 (Winter 1973), pp. 34–42.

Social work has an ideology which can be conceived along three basic dimensions—preferred conceptions of people, preferred outcomes for people, and preferred instrumentalities for dealing with people.

McLOED, DONNA L., and HENRY, J. MEYER, "A Study of Values of Social Workers," in *Behavioral Science for Social Workers*, ed. Edwin Thomas (New York: Free Press, 1967), pp. 401–16.

Major value premises of social work were conceptualized from the literature. A scale was developed to measure these values, then used to compare students with experienced social workers and social workers with teachers.

NATIONAL ASSOCIATION OF SOCIAL WORKERS, *Values in Social Work: A Re-examination*, monograph ix in the series sponsored by the Regional Institute Program, NASW (New York: NASW, 1967).

This is an excellent monograph for social work students. It is a collection of papers on values presented at the Regional Institute Program that focused on values. Among others, there are papers by Biestek, Perlman, Keith-Lucas, and Bernstein.

O'CONNOR, GERALD, "Toward a New Policy in Adult Corrections," *Social Service Review* 46:4 (December 1972), pp. 581–96.

Changes in adult corrections policy are suggested to increase self-determination and respect for client dignity while also protecting society. Specific suggested changes include the discontinuance of enforced therapy, the greater use of a determinate sentence, and the development of correctional communities, initiated by inmates, to achieve their own rehabilitation.

TILLICH, PAUL, The Philosophy of Social Work," *Social Service Review* 36:1 (March 1962), pp. 13–16.

Social workers individualize, listen with empathy, and are directed to the aim of helping every person find a place where he can consider himself necessary.

TOCH, HANS, "The Care and Feeding of Typologies and Labels," *Federal Probation* 34:3 (September 1970), pp. 15–19.

Toch offers four principles to avoid the harmful effects of classifying people-participant classification; no label should transcend its criteria; work with clients should facilitate declassification; and classification is of behavior and not people.

Chapter 4

THE SOCIAL WORK
RELATIONSHIP

In this chapter we will discuss the social work relationship and its use. During our lifetime each of us has experienced the connections of emotion and intimacy with others that we call "human relationships." Everyone needs these connections with other human beings, although not everyone finds it easy to accept the thought that he does. When we cannot find these connections with other people, we often name and personalize trees and animals, or perhaps our car, and derive comfort from acting as if another human being were present. In fact, though we may rarely be conscious of what these relationships mean to us and what powers they contain (except at certain points in life when we are suddenly bereft of a meaningful relationship or are in the process of becoming involved in a new one), the most critical characteristic of our humanity is that we live our lives within relationships to other people. Thus "relationships" do not originate for any of us within the social work process, or the professional helping effort (and therein may lie the rub, as we shall discuss later). Nor can social work claim to have been the lone discoverer of this attribute of mankind or the only group interested in pursuing its investigation. Psychology and psychiatry, among other professions, have also been very active in attempting to research the helping relationship.

However, social work can take pride in the fact that from its earliest beginnings it recognized the importance of human interaction and attempted to employ the concept of relationship in a conscious and deliberate way for the benefit of the people it served. In the early formulations

138

describing social work activity the relationship between worker and client was given a special importance—and no concept appears more frequently in the literature of the profession. Although the goals toward which this early activity was directed were those which the worker thought desirable for society and personally redemptive for the client, there was a beginning of the principle of self-help and a very clear conviction of the power of personal influence in the stimulation of this process.[1]

Perhaps the outstanding author and teacher in the field of social casework at the beginning of the 20th century was Mary Richmond. In her writings we find considerable material about the social work relationship. She asserted that social casework stands for the "intensive study and use of social relationships." She defined the focus of casework activity in terms of "skill in discovering the social relationships by which a given personality has been shaped; an ability to get at the central core of the difficulty in these relationships; power to utilize the direct action of mind upon mind in their adjustment."[2] The importance of the effect of "mind upon mind" was recognized in the development of "friendly visitors" in early social work.

In spite of the early recognition of relationship as a basic concept in social work theory, and in spite of the years of concern with the development and use of relationship in practice, a clearly defined concept of the social work relationship has yet to be articulated. There is great unanimity about the importance of human relationships in the promotion of growth and change, but there is little common understanding about just how these relationships promote such development. In the professional literature authors often merely describe qualities of the relationship that they consider important, or they record very specific instances of their use of relationship in the helping process.

Being convinced that the concept of relationship is central to all of social work practice, we intend in this chapter to consider some attempts of selected social work authors to express the nature of social work relationships, and to examine some of the notions, implicit or explicit, in such statements. We shall consider the roles that social workers carry and how these affect and shape social work relationships and the qualities of social workers who would work effectively with others.

---

[1] See Ralph and Muriel Pumphrey, *The Heritage of American Social Work* (New York: Columbia University Press, 1961); Bertha C. Reynolds, *Unchartered Journey* (New York: Citadel Press, 1963); Mary E. Richmond, *Friendly Visiting among the Poor: A Handbook for Charity Workers* (New York: Macmillan, 1899).

[2] Mary E. Richmond, "The Social Case Worker's Task," *Proceedings of the National Conference of Social Work* (Pittsburgh, 1917), pp. 211–15.

A REVIEW OF THE LITERATURE

In 1957 Felix Biestek collected a number of excerpts illustrating the attempts of social workers to express the nature of the relationship. He points out that relationship has been compared to an atmosphere, to flesh and blood, to a bridge, and to an open table.

> The essence of the relationship has been called an interplay, a mutual emotional exchange, an attitude, a dynamic interaction, a medium, a connection between two persons, a professional meeting, a mutual process. The concept "interaction" seems to be the most generic and it was most commonly described as "dynamic."
>
> The purpose of the relationship was described as creating an atmosphere, the development of personality, a better solution of the client's problem, the means for carrying out function, stating and focusing reality and emotional problems, and helping the client make a more acceptable adjustment to a personal problem.[3]

Biestek sees the relationship between caseworker and client as the medium through which the knowledge of human nature and the individual is used. "The relationship is also the channel of the entire casework process; through it flow the skills in intervention, study, diagnosis and treatment."[4] He defines the casework relationship as

> the dynamic interaction of attitudes and emotions between the caseworker and the client, with the purpose of helping the client achieve a better adjustment between himself and his environment.[5]

In a book on social casework Helen Harris Perlman says of "relationship" that

> it is a condition in which two persons with some common interest between them, long term or temporary, interact with feeling. . . . Relationship leaps from one person to the other at the moment when some kind of emotion moves between them. They may both express or invest the same kind of emotion; they may express or invest different or even opposing emotions or . . . one may express or invest emotion and the other will receive it and be responsive to it. In any case, a charge or current of feeling must be experienced between two persons. Whether this interaction creates a sense of union or of antagonism, the two persons are for the time "connected" or "related" to each other.[6]

---

[3] Felix Biestek, *The Casework Relationship* (Chicago: Loyola University Press, 1957), p. 11.

[4] Ibid., p. 4.

[5] Ibid., p. 12.

[6] Helen Harris Perlman, *Social Casework: A Problem-Solving Process* (Chicago: University of Chicago Press, 1957), pp. 65–66.

Perlman goes on to say that the identifying mark of a professional relationship "is in its conscious purposiveness growing out of the knowledge of what must go into achieving its goal"; that "all growth-producing relationships, of which the casework relationship is one, contain elements of acceptance and expectation, support and stimulation."[7] She also identifies authority as an element of the professional relationship. Perlman clearly differentiates between the relationship and other aspects of the helping process. She sees the caseworker as helping people to deal with their problems through (1) the provision of resources, (2) the problem-solving work, and(3) the therapeutic relationship, which she defines in another work as the "climate and the bond" between worker and client that "acts to sustain and free the client to work on his problem."[8]

Social workers who attempted to help people through the use of groups were also concerned with the development and use of relationships. Grace Coyle, who was very influential in the early development of group work, defined relationship as "a discernible process by which people are connected to each other, and around which the group takes its shape and form."[9] Gisela Konopka, an international authority in group work theory, does not define the relationship in her writings. She does discuss it as one of the major helping media available to the social group worker, and sets forth its elements as purpose, warmth, and understanding.[10]

In her book *Social Work with Groups* Helen Northen says:

> Relationship has been described as consisting "primarily of emotional responses which ebb and flow from person to person as human behavior evokes different affective reactions." The social worker in a group situation develops a unique relationship with each member, based on an understanding of the individual.[11]

Writing about the giving and taking of help, Alan Keith-Lucas defines the helping relationship as "the medium which is offered to a person in trouble through which he is given the opportunity to make choices, both about taking help and the use he will make of it."[12] He identifies the qualities of the relationship as (1) mutuality, (2) reality, (3) feeling,

[7] Ibid., pp. 64–84.

[8] Helen Harris Perlman, *Perspectives on Social Casework* (Philadelphia: Temple University Press, 1971), p. 58.

[9] Grace L. Coyle, *Group Work with American Youth* (New York: Harper and Row, 1948), p. 91.

[10] Gisela Konopka, *Social Group Work: A Helping Process* (Englewood Cliffs, N.J.: Prentice-Hall, 1963), pp. 107–18.

[11] Helen Northen, *Social Work with Groups* (New York: Columbia University Press, 1969), pp. 53–58.

[12] Alan Keith-Lucas, *The Giving and Taking of Help* (Chapel Hill: University of North Carolina Press, 1972), p. 47.

(4) knowledge, (5) concern for the other person, (6) purpose, (7) takes place in the here and now, (8) offers something new, and (9) is nonjudgmental.[13]

In a recent book Pincus and Minahan write that a relationship "can be thought of as an affective bond between the worker" and other systems with which he may be involved and that relationships may involve an "atmosphere of collaboration, bargaining or conflict." They classify all social work into three types: collaborative, cooperative, and conflicted.[14] These authors go on to identify the common elements of all social work relationships as (1) purpose, (2) commitment to the needs of the client system, and (3) objectivity and self-awareness on the part of the worker.[15]

SOCIAL WORK ROLES AND RELATIONSHIP

In studying this brief review of relationship, one will readily note that with the exception of Pincus and Minahan the concept of the professional relationship has been most thought about, and most written about, by persons concerned with the one-to-one or one-to-group *helping* relationship. However, as Pincus and Minahan point out, in addition to the direct helping relationship social workers carry many other types of relationships. They may be involved with landlords, teachers, employers, and even boards of directors and executives of other agencies on behalf of their clients. Or a worker, noting that a number of the parents with whom he works are concerned about drug problems, may help his agency develop a special seminar for workers on the subject of drug use. Another worker may be helping agency representatives develop plans for increased agency coordination on the assumption that this will be helpful to clients. A third may be lobbying for a law requiring that all group insurance carried by employers for employees must cover the pregnancies of unmarried as well as married employees and the pregnancies of minor daughters of employees. In all of the above situations the workers would be involved in relationships with others. However, these relationships are not with clients, nor are they helping relationships per se, in that the worker offers no services to the other persons in the relationship and carries no professional responsibility to help them with their personal problems or their personal development.

Social workers engaged in administration, policy, planning, and organization activities often carry a client relationship with the system in

[13] Ibid., pp. 47–65.

[14] A. Pincus and A. Minahan, *Social Work Practice* (Itasca, Ill.: F. E. Peacock, 1973), pp. 69–73.

[15] Ibid.

which they are involved, but the responsibilities they assume within this relationship are quite different from those of the direct services helping relationship. In these relationships, too, they carry no responsibility to help the other system with personal problems or to provide personal growth experiences for any individual member or the group as a unit. Rather, they are involved in helping the client system to change another (target) system in regard to certain professional policies and programs.

It is our position that all social work relationships carry certain common elements but that the mix and importance of the elements are different in different types of relationships. When one is working as an administrator, policymaker, and/or researcher, the use of self is always involved, but one selects and emphasizes different aspects of the skills in relationships. All social work relationships have purposes, and these purposes will always embody the normative purposes of the profession, though not necessarily the operational and the unique aspects. All social work relationships involve elements of power and authority, but these elements may be lodged in persons other than the social worker especially in situations involving policymaking or organizational change.

All professional relationships involve self-discipline and self-knowledge paired with the capacity for free, genuine, and congruent use of self. However, different types of relationships may involve different qualities of awareness and the use of different elements in the self. Some relationships may call for self-awareness in the areas of power and status problems, competitive feelings, and impatience with colleagues; others may call for awareness of one's fear of dependency or the need to do for others. One can deal with other persons and systems better if one has some sensitivity to their situation and goals and some empathy for them. However, the content of the empathetic understandings will vary greatly. All social work relationships are emergent and are affected by time and place. In all professional relationships the social worker is representing something beyond himself, either his agency or his profession, and all practitioners share a commitment to client welfare as a base for their professional activities. There are seven essential elements that are a part of social work relationships: (1) concern for others, (2) commitment and obligation, (3) acceptance and expectation, (4) empathy, (5) genuineness, (6) authority and power, and, overriding and shaping all the rest, (7) purpose. In order to carry his professional relationships with professional skill the worker will need to make the following qualities a part of his professional self: maturing, creativity, the capacity to observe self, the desire to help, courage, and sensitivity.

Although it is our belief that all social workers need to have a grasp of the elements discussed in this chapter, we also believe that these elements of the professional social work relationship are used differentially and that the variables affecting their use may be expressed in the following model:[16]

1. The purpose of the relationship;
2. The role of the worker and the role of the other in interaction;
3. The position of the worker in terms of agency and job;
4. The position of the other with whom the social worker is in interaction;
5. The goal toward which the social worker is directing his activity (note that in the helping relationship worker and client share a goal but that this may not be true in social work relationships involving advocacy or conflict);
6. The goal toward which the other person is directing his activity;
7. The form of communication (in the helping relationships the form of communication between worker and client is usually verbal, but in other relationships letters, reports, etc. may be principal forms utilized);
8. The forms of intervention to be utilized by the worker;
9. The type of system with which the worker interacts.

PURPOSE AS AN ELEMENT OF RELATIONSHIP

As was pointed out at the beginning of this chapter, all human beings have experienced connections with other human beings that we call relationships. Most of us are capable of, and most of the time are involved in, many sets of simultaneous relationships. In social intercourse many of us drift into "relationships" with others without being aware of just how or why they developed. However, few of us continue relationships with others without some reason; there is something that brings us into contact with them and some reason why we continue the interaction. When we become involved with another person, the nature of our purpose, goals, or intent, together with our perception of the other person's purpose, goals, or intent will determine how we behave toward him and how the relationship will develop.

If purpose is a part of all relationships, why does it need to be discussed as a special part of professional relationships? And how does purpose differ in professional relationships as compared with personal relationships? That the relationship is purposive and goal directed does not give the social work relationship its special mark. What makes the social work relationship special is that its purpose and goal are conscious and deliberate and come within the overall purpose and value system of the profession.

---

[16] Taken in part from Yvonne L. Fraley, "A Role Model for Practice," *Social Service Review* 43:2 (June 1969), pp. 145–54.

In Chapter 1 we discussed the purpose of social work practice—the changing or altering of something in the interaction of people and their environment so as to improve the capacity of individuals to cope with their life tasks in a way reasonably satisfying to themselves and to others, thus enhancing their ability to realize their aspirations and values. In Chapter 3 we saw how our professional values limit and shape what we do as social workers. These two factors, the overall purpose of the profession and its value system, limit and focus the purpose of the social work relationship so that influence is not used capriciously. We will call this the normative limits of purpose in the social work relationship— the normative purpose of all social work relationships is some kind of change in, or development of, a human or social system to the end that the capacity of individuals to cope with their life tasks and to realize their aspirations and values is improved.

In addition to being shaped by the normative purpose, each social work relationship will be deliberately and consciously shaped, in part, by the purpose of the given "type" of encounter. For example, the "helping relationship" is distinguished by a particular type of purpose—an increase in the coping capacity of the client system. However, a social worker may attempt to convince a legislative committee of the necessity for increasing state aid to school systems so that special education classes or open schools for dropouts may be established. The different purpose of this interaction will be critical to the way the relationship develops and is utilized. We can call this aspect of purpose the operational purpose of the relationship. One of the critical differences among types of social work relationships is that they are governed by different operational purposes even though they share a normative purpose. Within the overall limits set by the normative purpose, the operational purpose determines the outer parameters of a relationship.

Besides the normative and operational purpose, each social work relationship will have a unique, individual purpose. And these unique purposes will be affected by time: the immediate, unique purpose of this particular interaction will differ from the long-range purpose of a series of interactions. Thus, Mrs. Jones may have become involved in a helping relationship because she wants to have an enduring and happy marriage (a longtime purpose), but when she comes in today she may want help about the way she responded this morning to her husband's criticism of her housekeeping (an immediate goal which is a step to the long-term goal). The outreach worker at a community center may be involved with a street group in discussions about using the center for its meetings. The worker's immediate purpose is to provide the group with a better meeting place, while his longtime purpose may be to help the group develop less destructive activities.

It is the position of the authors that, while the normative and operational purposes of any social work relationship may be implicit, the social worker needs to be able to clearly formulate the unique, immediate purposes of professional contacts with others and that such purposes should be verbally shared with them. (With some clients who have little acquaintance with the "talking therapies," it might be helpful to discuss the normative and operational purposes as well.) A study by Mayer and Timms[17] shows that one difficulty in establishing a helping relationship with certain clients is their lack of understanding of the purposes and values of the professional person. Ideally, in the helping relationship, the unique purpose should come out of mutual consideration of what the client wants; but be that as it may, it is the worker's obligation to see that purpose is established. A professional relationship is formed for a purpose consciously recognized by all participants, and it ends when that purpose has been achieved or is judged to be unachievable. This understanding or perception of purpose sets certain norms for how persons will behave toward one another in the relationship and how the relationship will develop. (Purpose will be considered again in Chapter 6.)

DEVELOPMENT OF RELATIONSHIP

This brings us to a critical point. Relationship in a social work helping process does not emerge out of some mysterious chemistry of individuals in interaction, but develops out of purposive interaction, out of the business with which the worker and the client (or other system) concern themselves. We do not presume that the client is looking "for a helping relationship" when he enters the social work situation, but rather that he comes out of concern about a problem in which the professional relationship is instrumental in working toward a solution. This means that we do not speak of the worker's "establishing a relationship" or "offering a relationship"; neither do we speak of needing a good relationship before we can talk about difficulties. The relationship comes out of the communication about difficulties. It grows and develops out of purposive work. The professional relationship as an affective, experimental interaction should develop as necessary to the task. It is not necessarily pleasant or friendly; sometimes the problem is worked out in reaction and anger, in conflict as well as in collaboration or bargaining. A wise social worker writes that "the attempt to keep the relationship on a pleasant level is the greatest source of ineffectual helping known to men."[18] Seek relationship as a goal, "and it will generally elude one."

---

[17] John E. Mayer and Noel Timms, *The Client Speaks: Working Class Impressions of Casework* (New York: Atherton Press, 1972).

[18] Keith-Lucas, *Giving and Taking Help*, p. 48.

But in a helping situation a relationship will grow wherever one person demonstrates to another by his actions and his words that he respects the other, that he has concern for him and cares what happens to him, that he is willing both to listen and to act helpfully.[19]

The fact that the relationship develops out of purposive work means that it has motion and direction and emergent characteristics. It grows, develops, and changes; and when the purpose has been achieved, it comes to an end. The time structure is another variable which directly affects the nature and rate of the development of the relationship. Whether time limits are imposed on the process arbitrarily by outside forces or are imposed as necessary for task accomplishment, they have a deep effect on the emergent quality of the relationship. It is generally known that the frequency of meetings and the amount of time the participants spend together affects the climate of the relationship and the speed with which it develops. The authors believe that the imposition of individualized time limits consonant with a shared unique purpose will increase the effectiveness of the joint purposive work. The setting in which the worker and the other system find themselves will also affect relationship, since the setting interacts with time and purpose. In every instance, the operational purpose will be affected by the setting and the worker's position within it; and in most instances the limits of the purpose will also be imposed by the setting and the worker's position within it. This is to be expected, since the unique purpose of the relationship must fall within the parameters of the operational purpose.

Relationship is subject to differentiation and differential use. The kind of relationship that develops between the social worker and the system with which he is interacting will depend on the particular combination of a number of variables. The overriding variable is purpose, but other variables combine with purpose to form the relationship: the setting in which the worker and the system come together; the time limits of the process; the individuals or groups involved and the interests they represent; the capacities, motivations, expectations, and purposes of those involved; the problem which brings practitioner and system together and the goals each has for its resolution; the qualities of the worker and what he brings of himself, his knowledge, and his skill; and the actual behaviors of the members of the relational system in transactions over time.

We are now ready to turn to the worker and what he, as a professional helping person, is expected to bring to the helping relationship. Both the worker and the client (or the other system, if this is not a helping relationship) bring to the relationship irrational elements, nonrational

---

[19] Ibid., pp. 48–49.

elements (emotion, feeling, affect), and rational elements (intellectual and cognitive qualities). In the case of both the worker and the other system these elements come from (1) past experiences that have affected and developed the ability of the individuals to relate to others; (2) the here and now physical and emotional state of those involved; (3) the here and now thoughts or mental images of each individual about himself, the process, and the problem; (4) each person's anxiety about the present situation and about himself in it; (5) each person's expectations of how he should behave and what should come out of the interaction; (6) each person's perception of the other, or others, involved; (7) the values and ideals shared in common by the participants in the process; and (8) the influence of other social and environmental factors.[20] However, since the worker presents himself as the professional person in the relationship, and because of this is often allowed to share in the most private and sensitive aspects of vulnerable people, he carries special responsibilities for what he brings to the helping process.

If the reader will now reexamine the attempts of earlier authors to explain or describe what the worker should bring to the helping relationship he will find that most of these attempts deal with the communication of certain affective attitudes. While through the years social workers have used different words to express what they saw as the nature of the helping relationship, the notions of what kind of worker behavior is necessary to that particular relationship have changed relatively little. They have simply been better elaborated and differentiated over the years. The literature of other human service professions also discloses that their professional helping persons have developed very similar concepts. Some of these concepts have been broken down into smaller units and have been the object of experimental study, some are very well established because they are based on the clinical observations of many professional helping people over many years with many clients.[21] Thus most human service professionals use similar words to describe the emotional quality of the helping relationship. It is generally agreed among professional people in the human service professions that certain qualities are necessary within a human relationship for growth and change to take place.

We believe that all these various qualities can be classified into six groups of essential elements of all professional relationships: (1) concern

[20] Howard Goldstein, *Social Work Practice: A Unitary Concept* (Columbia: University of South Carolina Press, 1973), pp. 139–50.

[21] See, for example, Charles B. Truax and Kevin M. Mitchell, "Research on Certain Therapist Interpersonal Skills in Relation to Process and Outcome," in *Handbook for Psychotherapy and Behavior Change,* ed. Allen E. Bergin and Sol L. Garfield (New York: Wiley, 1971), pp. 299–342.

for the other, (2) commitment and obligation, (3) acceptance and expectation, (4) empathy, (5) authority and power, and (6) genuiness and congruence. These elements will be used according to the purpose and type of relationship.

ELEMENTS OF THE RELATIONSHIP

Concern for the other

To put this as simply as possible, concern for the other means that the worker sincerely cares about what happens to the client system and is able to communicate this feeling. In the helping relationship concern for the other involves "the sense of responsibility, care, respect, knowledge of another human being and the wish to further his life."[22] It is an *unconditional* affirmation of the client's life and needs—a wanting him to be all he can be, and to do all he wants to do, *for his own sake*. Those last four words are critical.

It is obvious that if we want to help others we must become deeply involved with them, and we need to want for them what they would want for themselves as we would want for ourselves what we want for ourselves. However, there is a danger in this, as the closer our emotional relationship with an individual the more likely we are to become overinvolved out of desire to see the trouble removed from him or the problem solved for him. When we feel that someone else's problem is our own problem, when we are unable to tolerate the thought of our own pain and need to have the client succeed because that is what we want, rather than to offer what the client wants or needs, then we too are involved.

True concern for another in the helping relationship means that we offer our skills, our knowledge, ourselves, and our caring to the client to be used by him (or not used, as the case may be) in his movement toward his goals. It means that (within certain limits of purpose, time, and place) we respond as the client needs us rather than as our need to help demands, that we care enough for the other to leave him free to fail. For most of us it is so much easier and more satisfying "to do" than to stand and wait (but "he also serves who only stands and waits") that we convince ourselves that concern is expressed through "doing" rather than through "an active waiting." To be truly concerned means that we are willing to be the "agent of a process rather than the creator of it."[23]

---

[22] Erich Fromm, *The Art of Loving*, p. 47.
[23] Keith-Lucas, *Giving and Taking Help*, p. 104.

Keith-Lucas gives us an excellent summary of this notion when he writes that concern

> means the willingness to let the helped person decide to what extent, and under what conditions he is willing to be helped. It does not mean necessarily agreeing to help under these circumstances, or even refraining from pointing out that help is not possible under them. Nor does it mean refraining from offering what help is available, or even, if the need is desperate, intervening in an attempt to get help started. But it does mean, ever and always, treating the helped person as the subject of the sentence, serving his interest, allowing him all possible freedom to be what he wants to be.[24]

Sometimes we equate this business of concern for others with "liking." It is the position of the authors that notions of "liking" or "disliking" are misleading, and that to ask workers to "like" everyone often results in the denial or repression of feeling rather than a change in it. What we are speaking of in our use of the concept of concern is a sense of so caring for the other (as the subject of our interactions together) that personal feelings of liking or disliking (which are, after all, related to the person as the object of our response) no longer have any meaning. Again we quote Keith-Lucas:

> What the helping person develops is a feeling to which liking and disliking are wholly irrelevant. This is what is meant by concern. It means to care what happens to another person quite apart from whether one finds him attractive or unattractive.[25]

Under the rubric of the concept of concern we would place many descriptive words used by other authors in discussing the helping relationship, words such as *warmth, liking, support, nonjudgmental respect, expectation,* and *understanding.* Some of these words are descriptive of emotions and attitudes that also fall partially under other concepts; for example, "nonjudgmental respect" is also a part of acceptance and will be discussed in some detail when we take up that concept.

"Understanding" may also be a part of other attitudes, but we would like to point out here that it is an important part of this concept that we seek understanding out of our concern for the other and out of our desire to help him in a way that he can use, not out of our own need to know, or understand, for our purposes. It is always disturbing to hear a social worker use the amount and extent of the material that the client "felt free to share with me" as the test of a helping relationship or the "success of an interview." Sharing oneself with a helping person is never an easy or an unmitigatedly positive experience. Knowing this, and being concerned for the privacy and rights of the client, we seek

---

[24] Ibid., p. 103.
[25] Ibid., p. 106.

knowledge about a person, or understanding of him, only because we are concerned to help. And we seek only so much understanding as is necessary for the process of helping. To seek knowledge for the sake of knowing, or in order to demonstrate our skill at interviewing to others, is, again, to make the client the object rather than the subject of our efforts.

We communicate our attitude of concern and respect in any type of relationship to the person with whom we are working by, among other things, being on time for our interviews or conferences; by making appointments before we go to his home or office (which says that we respect him and his privacy and we want him to have the opportunity to present himself to us as he wishes to); by seeing that our interviewing or conference space is as attractive as we can make it; by dressing in the way that his culture says is "appropriate to a helping person offering service to a *valued* person"; and by concerned listening.

For the worker, concerned listening is not a passive "hearing." It is an active search for the meaning in, and an active understanding of, the client's communication. One may well disagree with what is being said, but one must value the sharing that is going on. In a helping relationship particularly, the worker values the client's offering of his feelings, thoughts, and ideas. The high feeling in a situation heavy with conflict should not obscure the worker's need to hear accurately. In the helping relationship the worker must, in one way or another, convey his recognition of the value of the client's communication and his desire to understand it. Responding to the content of the client's communication with relevant questions or comments in the search for understanding is one indication of responsive caring; an expressed desire to understand often conveys concern better than a statement of already achieved understanding.

Concern for the other means that we view the client as a uniquely valuable human being, and in a helping relationship it means that, in addition, we transcend our own needs and our own view of the problem and lend ourselves to the serving of the client's interests and purposes in his coming to us or in our going to him.

Commitment and obligation

Persons cannot enter into interrelationships with other persons in a meaningful way without assuming the responsibilities that are linked to such interactions. These responsibilities may best be expressed in the concept of commitment and in its corollary, obligation. In the helping relationship, both client and worker must be bound by commitments and obligations if the purposes of the relationship are to be achieved. A commitment to the conditions and purposes of the relationship and to an interdependent interaction, built upon involvement and investment, allows the client to feel safe and thus to reduce the testing behavior and trial-and-error searching that usually mark the beginning of a relationship. This allows him to turn his attention and his energy to the task at hand rather than to employ it in self-protection. Once a commitment to the relationship has been established, and the limits of time, place, and purpose have been accepted, each participant is able to depend on the predictability of the other's behavior, attitudes, and involvement.

The earlier writings on the helping relationship seldom mention commitment and obligation, but recently we have had more and more social work literature that speaks of the helping contract. Usually, we mean by this phrase that the expectations and terms of the commitments and obligations of both client and worker are explicitly shared. We consider this defining of commitment and obligation, along with the clarification of purpose, time, and setting, to be an important process and will discuss it in greater detail in Chapters 6 and 7. However, whether or not commitments and obligations are explicitly defined, they are an important, and inescapable, part of every professional relationship involving the giving and taking of help.

Any person asking for help from another is acutely, if unconsciously, aware of the necessity for commitments and the taking on of obligations; and it is often the fear of what may be involved for him in the expectations and obligations of the commitments that keeps him from seeking help. The general obligations that clients are usually expected to assume are: an open and honest presentation of the problem, of his situation, and of his ways of coping that relate to the problem; an accommodation to the minimum procedural conditions of the helping relationship, such as coming to a certain place at a certain time for an interview and working as he can on the selected problem. The client is expected to assume these obligations as he can, and his commitments can be renegotiated without penalty.

The worker assumes more binding commitments and obligations. He cannot renegotiate the contract without the consent and participation of his client. His obligations include the responsibility to meet the essential procedural conditions of the relationship in the fullest way—being present at prearranged times and places and in certain emergency situations as well; keeping the focus of the work together on the client's problem; offering a relationship that is conducive to sharing, growth, and change. If we violate our commitments to our explicit or our implicit contract without adequate reason and adequate explanation to our client, we can be very sure that the client will question our desire to help—our investment in our involvement with him. Perhaps worse, the client may interpret such a violation as a message that we do not consider him important. Being present when we are needed carries a connotation that we think the client important, and being absent or late when we are obligated to be present carries a connotation of rejection.

Thus far we have focused on the helping relationship. However, in summary, we would broaden our comments to define commitment as an involvement with a client, a client system, or other systems that is unqualified by our idiosyncratic personal needs. It is a freely determined wish to further the purpose of the relationship without the expectation of returns that support our sense of worth, add to our self-esteem, or preserve our status. This commitment is communicated through a resolute consistency, constancy, responsible follow-through, and the preservation of the other's dignity and individuality. This preservation demands more than an awareness of the other's dignity and individuality; it involves actions based on sensitive and thoughtful understanding of the other and his position. Commitment requires that the worker assume a simultaneous responsibility and accountability for what he says and does to the client, the client system, or other systems; to the professional system which sanctions his right to offer help; and to himself.[26]

Acceptance and expectation

In most discussions of acceptance in helping relationships one finds notions to the effect that this means the communication of a nonjudgmental attitude as well as efforts to help workers differentiate between accepting the person and accepting his actions. We would prefer that the worker regard acceptance as more than a refusal to judge and that he try not to distinguish between a person and his actions. We would like him to consider acceptance as an active verb—*to accept*—meaning to receive as adequate or satisfactory, to regard as true, to believe in, to receive what the other offers. To accept another means to receive what he offers of himself, with respect for his capacity and worth, with belief in his capacity to grow and mature, and with awareness that his behaviors can be understood as attempts at survival and coping. Acceptance means acting in the recognition that the essence of being human is having problems, making choices (good and bad, wise and foolish), and participating in the shaping of one's destiny with the resources at one's command. Rather than meaning "to refuse to judge," acceptance means "to actively seek to understand."

The basic elements in acceptance are perhaps knowing, individualization, and trust or expectation. Knowing relates to our efforts to take in and understand another's reality and experience, his values, needs, and purposes; to acquire some idea of where the other person comes

---

[26] Goldstein, *Social Work Practice*, p. 74.

from, of his life and frame of reference. Individualization means the capacity to see the person as a unique human being with distinctive feelings, thoughts, and experiences. The individual must be differentiated from all others, including ourselves. We must not make assumptions about others based on generalized notions about a group, a class, or a race, although there is a need to appreciate and understand the manner in which race, class, and sex influence client-worker transactions. Trust or expectation means that we have a belief and faith in the capacity of individuals for self-determination and self-direction—that we consider it the right and responsibility of each individual to exercise maximum self-determination in his own life with due regard for the welfare of others.

Acceptance of the client does not just occur. It grows from the roots of a fundamental belief and faith that the inherent processes of individual development will lead a person toward greater maturity when such processes are fostered and matured, and it develops as we seek to understand the feelings, thoughts and experiences, resources and lack of resources, opportunities and deprivations that have led the individual to the choices he has made. In fact, it is our conviction that one finds it almost impossible to be judgmental when one is fully engaged in a cooperative journey to the understanding of another. One cannot understand if one is observing another through the lenses of what is right or wrong, good or bad. Most human behavior is purposive, and if we can understand the purpose of behavior, then it becomes understandable rather than right or wrong.

Acceptance does not mean that we always agree with another person. It does not mean that we forgo our own values to agree with or support the client's values. It does not mean that we "excuse him from the world in which he must live." It means rather that we may present the importance of, and our belief in the importance of, behaving in socially appropriate ways in keeping with established laws and regulations at the same time that we seek to understand the intense anger that drives him to act impulsively against certain limits and regulations and that we can empathize with his need to strike out. True acceptance carries with it an assumption that people act as they must in the complexity of their particular human situation and that they are what their nature and their environment, coupled with their vision, permits them to be.

Thus we see that self-determination, nonjudgmental respect, sensitivity, individualization, expectation of growth, and understanding are all part of the general notion of acceptance. One of the most effective ways to communicate acceptance is to try to understand the client's position and his communication of his feeling. This can be done by commenting on his communication in ways that indicate a desire to understand or to further understanding of what he is saying, or by asking questions that are related to the content he is trying to communicate and thus to reveal that you heard him and are interested in understanding him.

Empathy

All the authors cited in the first section of this chapter agree that empathy is a necessary quality of the helping relationship. Empathy is the capacity to enter into the feelings and experiences of another— knowing what he feels and experiences—without losing oneself in the process. The helping person makes an active effort to put himself in the perceptual frame of the other person without losing his own perspective, but, rather, using that understanding in order to help the other person. The story of the cowboy and his lost horse at the end of this chapter is an example of empathy. The cowboy found the horse because he was able to feel as if he were the horse—to feel and think as the horse might feel and think. However, since he was not a horse, having found the horse he brought it back.

Carl Rogers defines empathy as "the perceiving of the internal frame of reference of another with accuracy, and with the emotional components which pertain thereto, as if one were the other person but without ever losing the 'as if' condition."[27] Keith-Lucas points out that empathy is the worker's understanding of the feelings the other has about the situation, knowing inside oneself how uncomfortable and desperate these feelings may be for the client, but never claiming these feelings for oneself as the helping person. He goes on to differentiate between pity, sympathy, and empathy with a very cogent illustration:

> Consider three reactions to someone who has told us that he strongly dislikes his wife. The *sympathetic person* would say, "Oh, I know exactly how you feel. I can't bear mine, either." The two of them would comfort each other but nothing would come of it. The *pitying person* would commiserate but add that he himself was most happily married. Why didn't the other come to dinner sometime and see what married life could be like? This, in most cases, would only increase the frustration of the unhappy husband and help him to put his problem further outside himself, on to his wife or his lack of good fortune. The *empathetic person* might say something like, "That must be terribly difficult for you. What do you think might possibly help?" And only the empathetic person, of the three, would have said anything that would lead to some change in the situation.[28]

[27] Carl Rogers, "Client-Centered Therapy," in *Theories of Counseling and Psychotherapy,* ed. C. H. Patterson (New York: Harper and Row, 1966), p. 409.

[28] Keith-Lucas, *Giving and Taking Help,* pp. 80–81. Italics are authors'.

Empathy requires what may seem to many beginning workers to be antithetical qualities—the capacity to feel an emotion deeply and yet to remain separate enough from it to be able to utilize knowledge. Methods of reasoning are necessary if one is to make an objective analysis of the problem and the possibilities of solution. Even as the worker lets the full awareness of the client's emotion wash over him, he is aware that he is feeling, not as the client feels, but *as if* he were the client. He must remember that the client came to him, not to have someone share his feeling (although this is relieving) but to enlist aid in coping with a situation that feeling alone cannot resolve. If it could, the client would not need help, for he has feeling enough invested, and undoubtedly he has hard thinking and trying invested too. He needs a worker who, in standing apart, can bring some difference in feeling and thinking, and who is able, with a clear head, to manipulate or secure resources that were unavailable to the client's influence, were unknown to the client, or were not thought of by him.

In learning to be empathetic we have to develop the capacity for imaginative consideration of others and to give up any fixed mental image that may lead us to change reality to fit any preconceived expectation. In this we are handicapped by two factors: the set of stereotypes we all carry with us, which are useful in enabling us to quickly grasp the meaning of encounters in daily life but which block greater discernment; and the limited symbols—words, gestures, and reports—available to us to convey another's reality. Thus the accuracy of our interpretation is dependent on our sensitivity and intuition; our ability to put this together in a dynamic way with all that we know about the other (his experiences, behavior, problems, and associations), our conception of his potentials and what we know about what he wants and hopes for; all our theoretical knowledge and helping experiences; and all our other experiences with similar kinds of people and situations—real or fantasied. Then, when we have this mental representation of the other, we must hold it lightly, recognizing that there is always something unknown and unfelt about the other that makes any mental representation of him tentative, no matter how hard we have struggled to attain it, and no matter how much understanding we bring to it. Full knowledge of another being is something forever beyond attainment by anyone; it can only be approached, never achieved. It is questionable whether any client wants to be fully and totally known. There is something very frightening about someone's knowing everything about us, for in knowledge lies control; so in the ordinary course of living we reveal our intimate selves only to those we trust. Without the pain of the problem and the hope that the worker can offer some help toward coping with it, few clients would be willing to share themselves with an unknown other.

The fact that we can never fully know another, that the client does not come to have us join him in his intimate feeling, except in a limited way, and that if we felt like him we would be unable to introduce the differences in thinking and feeling that bring change, all require that we be able to maintain a certain detachment. This demand is often more difficult for the beginning worker than the demand to feel. Each worker maintains this balance differently. This is an area in which supervision can be of great help. By comments and questions the effective supervisor helps the practitioner to observe himself and to be aware of his contribution to the relationships he forms with others. Thus self-awareness—an essential quality of all social work relationships—grows.

While some degree of empathy is needed at the very beginning of a relationship (and without this quality a relationship cannot be formed), it is a quality of the relationship and thus is not something which the helping person constructs by himself. It comes, grows, and develops from the process of interaction of client and worker in which the client can be encouraged to express his feelings more and more specifically, fully, and precisely, and the worker grows in his capacity to feel with the client and in his understanding of what is expressed. What the client seeks, especially at the beginning of the relationship, is not (as we said earlier) full understanding, but rather to enter a relationship with a helping person in which he senses that his feeling and thinking are acceptable and that what he expresses is understandable as a possible human response to his situation.

Acceptance and empathy are seldom discussed in social work literature dealing with the social worker's relationship with other than client systems. However, it would seem that such elements could be of help in either cooperative or conflicted relationships that involve purposive change in nonclient target systems. Resistance to change, and conflict, will be prevented to the degree that the practitioner is able to help the target system develop its own understanding of the need for change as well as an awareness of how members of the target system feel about change and what change will mean to the target system. If conflict is the chosen method of bringing change, the practitioner's ability to empathize with the feelings of the other will enable him to choose the most effective way to engage himself in the conflict. The practitioner who is able to accept the members of a client, or a target, system as individuals with both rational and nonrational positions and who can empathize with those positions will, other things being equal, be more productive than the practitioner who does not possess these skills. The way the worker uses these skills will differ in different situations. In the helping relationship the worker may communicate empathy directly. In other types of relationship he may use it to shape other communications.

Authority and power

The two remaining elements of a helping relationship that we will discuss are (1) authority and power, and (2) genuineness and congruency. Not only are these perhaps the most difficult concepts to understand, but it is the misunderstanding of the element of authority and power in helping relationships that often affects our genuineness with clients. Among other things, authority may be defined as a power delegated to the practitioner by client and agency in which the practitioner is seen as having the power to influence or persuade resulting from his possession of certain knowledge and experience and from his occupying a certain position. Thus there are two aspects of authority in the helping relationship. The first might be called the institutional aspect, in that it comes from the social worker's position and function within the agency's purpose and program. The second aspect is psychological, in that the client gives the worker the power to influence or persuade because he accepts him as a source of information and advice—as an expert in his field. A person in need of help seeks someone who has the authority of knowledge and skill to help him. The worker's acceptance of the client's assumption that he carries this authority may infuse the relationship with a sense of safety and security when the client's own powers of self-dependence fail him.

The primary characteristic of the concepts of power and authority in the helping relationship is that they are neither good nor bad in themselves. Some aspects of these elements are always present, and the attempt of the social worker to abdicate his role and pretend that he carries no authority only leaves the client troubled by suspicions and doubts about why the worker is unwilling to admit what he, the client, is so aware of. This incongruence between what the client feels and what the worker says makes an authentic relationship impossible. The crucial significance of power and authority lies in how they are utilized for help.

Social workers have had a hard time with the concepts of authority and power. There has been too little examination of authority and power as factors that enter into all human relationships—all human relationships develop laws about acceptable behavior of the people involved within those relationships.[29] This is one of the problems that workers often face in using professional relationships for other purposes than the direct helping process. The clients of the community organization worker, the research worker, and the consultant are in a different power relationship to the worker than are the clients in the helping relationship.

---

[29] See Jay Haley, *Strategies of Psychotherapy* (New York: Grune and Stratton, 1972), pp. 1–68.

If what this factor means for the workers and those with whom they work is unexamined (or, worse, even denied), they lack knowledge they need to guide them. Social workers need to be able to deal with power and authority both when they exercise it and when others exercise it in relation to them.

In his discussion of authority in social work relationships Goldstein points out that when persons require what another has to offer "that cannot be obtained elsewhere—whether one is seeking the adoption of a child, financial assistance, help with a personal problem, or professional services to assist in a social action enterprise—the relationship cannot be equalized." As the social worker's needs have no relevance to the task, "the seeker cannot reciprocate or supply the provider with any reward that can restore the balance. The fact that the seeker has limited alternatives to meet his needs, is further heightened by the fact that the worker is seen as having competence and knowledge."[30] When the social worker says, "We will meet once a week on a Monday, if that is convenient to you," or when he decides to include another family member in treatment, he is setting the conditions of the relationship. Or he may refer the client elsewhere. These are all examples of power and authority.

Genuineness and congruence

In the research that has been done on helping relationships by Truax, Carkhuff, and Rogers, among others, it has been found that in an effective helping relationship the helping person needs to communicate four things: empathy, acceptance, unconditional positive regard (we have called this quality "concern for the other," as we find this phrase more expressive of the essential notion), and congruence.[31] Congruence means that we bring to the relationship a consistent and honest openness and realness and that our behavior and the content of our communications with, and in regard to, the client must at all times match each other (be congruent) and must match our underlying value system and our essential selves as professional people. (We will discuss the qualities we need to have as helping people later in this chapter.)

In order to be congruent and genuine, we must seek three things: (1) an honest knowledge of ourselves, of who and what we really are; (2) a clear knowledge of agency procedures and policies and of our professional role, both in their meaning to us and in their meaning

---

[30] Goldstein, *Social Work Practice*, pp. 84–86.

[31] For references to this work see Truax and Mitchell, "Research on Therapist Skills," pp. 299–342: and Charles B. Truax and Robert R. Carkhuff, *Toward Effective Counseling and Psychotherapy: Training and Practice* (Chicago: Aldine, 1967), pp. 1–2.

to our clients; and (3) an internalization of the first two and of our concern for the other, our acceptance of him, our commitment to his welfare and to the authority aspects of our role and position, so that these qualities are so much a part of us that we no longer need to be consciously aware of them and can turn our full attention to the client and his situation.

A person who is real, genuine, and congruent in a helping relationship is one who knows himself and is unafraid of what he sees in himself or of what he is. He can enter a helping relationship without anything of himself to prove or protect, so he is unafraid of the emotions of others. For example, our unwillingness to be honest with our clients about our authority in a relationship, or about what we are going to do with the information they share (see Seymour Halleck's article on professional dishonesty) may be a consequence of negative experiences with authority in our own lives. Therefore, we try to deny (to lie about) what the client sees so clearly is really there. To be congruent we need to have faced and examined our own feelings about many central life experiences that clients share with us, so that we know which feelings are ours and which are the client's. What are our feelings about the lies we encounter? We are angry about them and so we must be different? We want the client to see we are different and that we understand better than anyone else? Do we really? Can we free ourselves of certain behaviors and feelings we dislike? Will our being free of them help our client? Or is it better to admit that they are there so that the two of us can examine what they mean for the client? What are we afraid of, or what do we want, in denying to the client the facts about certain agency restrictions on service and about our capacity to skew these so that they do not bear so heavily on him?

This brings us to the second half of the worker's awareness—the meaning of his agency role and position to him and to his client. Not how he wants the client to see him, but how the client does see him—as a representative of a particular agency or service. Workers and clients come together, as a rule, within some kind of bureaucratic structure. The client usually does not pay for the costs of service, or at least does not pay the full costs. So the worker is paid by someone other than his client. What do the structure of the agency, its position in the community, and the source of the funds to support its services mean to the client? The worker who has not honestly examined these questions and who has not faced what they mean both to himself and his client will often appear to the client to be somewhat divorced from the reality of the client's life. So being honest and real means that he has examined his role and task in relation to agency, client, and target systems and that he can assume them fully and honestly with an openness about all their parts and of their impact on the client.

Our popular culture tends to place emphasis on irrationality in caring relationships with others, to hold that true caring ought to be something impulsive and instinctive, from the heart as it may be as of this moment, uninhibited and "natural." There is a belief that to think about a feeling distorts it and makes it less an expression of what we are—as though our head were not a genuine part of us; or as though only the heart were good, and the head must perforce be evil. This stance neglects the common theme of much of the literature of human emotion, in which the heart is held to be fickle and inconsistent, unwilling to be committed to another. Actually, to be congruent people we need a warm and nurturing heart, and an objective, open, aware, and disciplined mind, and an open channel of communication between head and heart so that we appear all of one piece to others.

There is a tendency to view "professionalism" and "objectivity" as though these qualities meant "coldness," "cautiousness," and an impersonal, restricted reaction to the expressed feeling of others. Actually, these ways of presenting oneself in a relationship are totally unprofessional and are related to one's own need to be self-protective, to be afraid of oneself and thus of others. Both this impersonal way of operating with others and the undisciplined, personal expression of one's impulses of the moment are self-serving modes of behavior that are destructive of the capacity to communicate congruence and genuineness in the helping relationship, which requires that we keep the client squarely in the center of our concern.

Perhaps an example will illustrate this point. When we watch a really competent figure skater in a "free skating" program, we do not feel that she is incongruent, or unreal, or dishonest. Instead we feel the spontaneity and creative force with which she puts her whole self into the performance. But the performance required years of slow and painful learning—it required more than a little of self-discipline and persistence, of hard, slow growth and change in the use of self. The creative, free movements of this skater are quite unnatural to the untrained beginner on ice skates. They are not in any way the "natural" movements of the skater the first time she put on skates and tried the ice. Yet the skater does not think of each movement or gesture. In fact, if she does she will not give a free performance. Her performance has the effect it does because she has so internalized the demands of the task that she can give herself to it entirely and can respond freely and spontaneously to what is in herself and in the here and now situation. And as we watch her we are aware that she gets great satisfaction from the use of her competence in a disciplined yet free way. She knows herself and her capacity, and there is a joy in what she does. So we, too, should enter all professional relationships with a clear knowledge of what we can and cannot do, a sense of our competence and a belief in what we are doing. We, too, should get satisfaction from the use of ourselves in helping. How can we believe that the creative use of self in helping others demands less time, and work, and discipline, and knowledge of self and of the limits of action than does the performance of a figure skater?

Rational and irrational elements in the helping relationship

Obviously there are cognitive elements in the professional relationship. Both the worker and those with whom he interacts think as well as feel in a helping transaction. Both bring knowledge and values to their association. In all professional relationships the social worker needs to be actively cognitive—relating what is said and done to his knowledge—and making sense out of the interchange of feelings. Much of the rest of the text will be devoted, as have the first three chapters, to setting forth the values and knowledge that the worker needs to master. It is enough to mention here that cognition is an important element of the relationship.

The irrational elements of the relationship are those elements—feelings and attitudes, inherent patterns of behavior—which are not called forth by the present situation but are brought to it, relatively unchanged by the here and now and by reality, from earlier relational experiences. They are irrational in that they are usually unconscious (and thus not available to our present awareness) and in that they are, in the form in which they appear, inappropriate to the present situation.

As an example of the power of the irrational: One of the authors was once involved in a helping relationship with a family which had been referred by the school social worker because a son was emotionally disturbed. Bob was one of two sets of twins. Besides the twins there was one other child in the family. None of the other children showed any unusual difficulty in school. After some observation of the mother's relationship to her children it became obvious that she treated Bob differently from the others. She indulged him more than his brothers and sisters and was totally unable to limit him. When confronted with examples of the different way in which she reacted to Bob, she burst into tears and said she could not deny him because he was just like her. It seems that she had always felt "picked on" as a child, and she was sure Bob felt the same way. She had been the younger and smaller of a set of twins, as Bob was, and she was sure he felt just as she did, so she was trying to help him feel better. In reality, she had no evidence that Bob felt the way she assumed he did. Nor had she ever faced the fact that she and Bob were two very different persons with two very different childhood situations. Her response to Bob was an irrational one with roots in her own painful childhood.

A further, and important, example of the effects of the irrational in all our lives is found in the attempt to create a congruent, honest working relationship across racial, cultural, or social class barriers. We may master all the knowledge about the history and culture of another race; we may plan rationally how to use ourselves in the relationship; but, too often, when we actually come together with a member of another race we find feelings and thoughts rising inside us that may be quite contrary to what we want to feel and think. We condemn ourselves for these forbidden feelings and deny them both to ourselves and to others, yet they persist. They persist because they are irrational responses that are learned as a part of our culture. Each of us lives and grows up in a racist society, so we all absorb, to a greater or a lesser extent, the irrational attitudes of that society in regard to race. These attitudes become a part of us, and are all the more difficult to understand and eradicate because of the very fact that they are irrational.

It is important that the worker recognize that such irrational elements are a part of the helping relationship (indeed, of all relationships) because such realization enhances his capacity to understand and accept the expressions of his clients, and because it helps him to accept the importance of his own self-awareness. The presence of irrational elements in the most knowledgeable and thoughtful of us makes the demand for self-awareness a constant one. We need to exercise all the care of which we are capable in order to keep such elements in ourselves from intruding inappropriately into the helping relationship.

THE HELPING PERSON

It is difficult to discuss "the helping person" because there are almost as many kinds of helpers as there are people who need help. There is probably no one person who is equally effective in creating helping relationships with all people. And there is probably no one person who is an ideal helping person, so that each of us will probably lack some of the qualities a helping person should have. There are, however, certain qualities, attitudes, and approaches toward life that are found to an uncommon degree among helping people—and, thus, among social workers. We are going to discuss six of those qualities here—six qualities that we see as central to effective social work functioning. Someone once wrote that "helping relationships are created by helping people, not by helping techniques." From our point of view, this means that the social work practitioner brings about system change through his use of self—of what he is—of what he has made a part of himself, including his being, his thinking, his feeling, his belief system, his knowledge. In other words, what we do must be congruent with what we are seeking to become as persons.

Let us acknowledge that there are many people who do not have the capacity to help others—just as there are many people who do not have the capacity to design computers or perform surgery. And neither of these jobs is simply a matter of knowledge. Both require certain kinds of people with certain kinds of talents. Among the kinds of people who are not good helpers are: those who are interested in knowing about people rather than in serving them (coldly objective students of humanity); those who are impelled by strong personal needs to control, to feel superior, or to be liked; those who have solved problems similar to the problems of the people in need of help but have forgotten what it cost them to do so; and those who are primarily interested in retributive justice and moralizing.[32]

Maturing people

The most effective helping people usually experience themselves as living, growing, developing people who are deeply involved in the process of becoming. They do not exclude themselves from the "human condition," but view all people, including themselves, as engaged in problem solving. Not only are they unafraid of life, but they frankly enjoy the process of being alive with all the struggle that this may involve. They find change and growth exciting rather than threatening. Their anxiety and tension are at an optimum level, so they are free to take on new experiences. Thus they do not need to be "right" to defend where they are. Perhaps most of the other qualities that we will discuss stem from this quality.

Creativity

The helping person needs to be a nonconformist in that he needs to hold most solutions to the problems of life as tentative. Conformity involves accepting prevailing opinion as fact and thus stymies openness to other solutions. However, we need to distinguish nonconformity from "counterconformity," a term which has been used to characterize a person who is always "against" authority or accepted ways of doing. Such a person is not truly independent, but is motivated by a need to defend his identity and by hostile and/or aggressive needs. Intellectual openness and receptivity suggest a state of freedom to detach oneself from certain theoretical positions or systems of thought. The creative person can allow himself to be dominated by the problem with which he is grappling rather than search for a known solution. It is not that the creative person is not knowledgeable, that he has not given a great deal of himself to learning what is known, but that he is able, in spite of the

---

[32] Keith-Lucas, *Giving and Taking Help,* pp. 89–108.

heavy investment he has made, to hold this knowledge tentatively. This seems paradoxical to many people, and it is indeed a heavy demand, for when we invest heavily in things we tend to hold them dearly.

This brings us to another paradoxical quality of the creative person. Although he is often deeply committed to a problem, he is at the same time detached from it. The creative person likes complexity. He does not seek premature closure, but can maintain an openness and joy in the contradictory or obscure, and a tolerance for conflict.

Capacity to observe self

Capacity to observe self is usually discussed in social work literature under the rubric of self-awareness, and we have discussed it as an element of genuineness and congruence. It is an important capacity for the social worker and is discussed in most material that deals with the helping relationship. Perhaps the two previously discussed qualities are an important part of this capacity, which really means to be sensitive to one's own internal workings, to be involved with oneself and one's needs, thoughts, commitments, and values, yet to stand back enough from oneself to question the meaning of what is going on. This means that the helping person must take a helping attitude toward himself as well as toward others.

We chose not to use the term *self-awareness* for this quality because we think that it is more than self-knowledge. There have to be other qualities. Self-love and love of others, self-respect and respect for others, self-confidence and confidence in others, acceptance of self and acceptance of others, faith in self and faith in others develop together or not at all. So the capacity to observe self probably requires the ability to care deeply about oneself and one's goals, to respect and to believe in oneself and yet to be able to stand back and observe oneself as an important piece of the complex activity of helping.

This way of regarding self leads to flexibility, a sense of humor, a readiness to learn, an acceptance of one's limitations, and an openness— all of which are important qualities of the helping person. And most of all, the capacity to observe self demands courage—we need to be unafraid of what we will find. All of us, to some extent, distort in one way or another feelings that we do not want to acknowledge, but the more this is true of us the less we can help others. It is the need for self-protection, the fear for self, that gets in the way of sincerity, openness, genuineness, and honesty.

Like all other human beings, social workers cannot make themselves over simply because they wish to do so. Like all other human beings, we are the product of our intellectual and physical attributes, we are shaped by the range, expansiveness, and richness of our life experiences, including our educational experiences, and by how we have used those experiences in developing our basic beliefs, values, and attitudes. However, even if we cannot remake ourselves at will, it is important in observing ourselves that we have the capacity to see ourselves as growing and developing people.

Desire to help

A deep desire to increase the ability of people to choose for themselves and to control their own lives is an absolutely essential quality of a helping person. Effective helping relationships or other social work relationships simply cannot be created and sustained without this desire. Basically, the desire is a commitment to ourselves rather than to others because it must be our desire, be related to us and our commitment to ourselves. It is this commitment that gives us the courage to know ourselves and the willingness to risk ourselves in the service of others.

Courage

It takes great courage—not the courage of the unaware and insensitive but the courage of the man who is thoroughly aware yet does what he knows needs to be done—to take the risks with oneself and others that social work relationships inevitably demand. Workers must be willing to assume the risks of failing to help, of becoming involved in difficult, emotionally charged situations that they do not know how to handle, of having their comfortable world and ways of operating upset, of being blamed and abused, of being constantly involved in the unpredictable, and perhaps of being physically threatened. "It is only the person who can be afraid and not be afraid of his fear who is in a position to help."[33]

It takes great courage to be able to think about ourselves and others as we are. And, even more, it takes great courage and great strength to directly face clients with the reality of their problems when this reality threatens us. And it takes courage to engage in honest thinking about others and yet to be basically for people—to be skeptical and inquiring in our thinking, yet trusting in our attitude toward others.

Sensitivity

Our methods of sharing ourselves completely with others are awkward and imperfect even when we are committed to that sharing. For troubled people the ability to share themselves and their situation is incredibly more difficult because of all their feelings about their problems and

---

[33] Keith-Lucas, *Giving and Taking Help,* p. 100.

about themselves as people with problems, and because of the threat of the unknown in the helping process. Therefore, the worker who would help needs a capacity for feeling and sensing—for knowing in internal ways—the inner state of others without specific clues. This quality probably depends on our ability to observe even small movements and changes in others and to make almost instantaneous inferences from them, to put ourselves into the feeling and thinking of others, and to avoid stereotypes. It is probably closely related to our capacity to be open to the new and to our readiness for change.

RACE AND THE SOCIAL WORK RELATIONSHIP

We cannot leave a discussion of the professional relationship without some mention of the impact of racial or cultural difference on the develoment and use of the professional transaction. It is particularly fitting that this discussion should follow the sections on rational and irrational elements in the change process and on the helping person himself. Racist attitudes and actions are so deeply embedded in American society that it is impossible for any of us to have escaped their impact on our conscious and unconscious selves and on the ways we relate across racial lines. It is easy to underestimate the extent of the impact of racist attitudes on individuals of all races because of the multivarious sources which subject all of us to both explicit and implicit negative stereotypes. Implicit negative messages are more insidious, hence more devastating and difficult to deal with, yet they affect every part of us and all our relationships.

Shirley Cooper expresses it well when she says: "Clearly racism bites deeply into the psyche. It marks all its victims—blacks and whites—with deep hurt, anger, fear, confusion, and guilt."[34]

Cooper urges that we examine our own thinking with special care as our "efforts to acknowledge and deal with racial factors are affected by highly emotional attitudes." She points out that white people "influenced by a culture rampant with racism and unfamiliar with the intricacies and nuances of the lives of ethnic people may, even with the best of intentions, fail to recognize when social and cultural factors predominate" in their professional attitudes. Cooper notes that "ethnic therapists are vulnerable to the opposite form of clinical error. Because they are so centrally involved, they may exaggerate the importance or impact of ethnic factors."[35] She goes on to say that in color blindness individuals

[34] Shirley Cooper, "A Look at the Effect of Racism on Clinical Work," in *Dynamics of Racism in Social Work Practice*, ed. James Goodman (New York: National Association of Social Workers, 1974), p. 128.

[35] Ibid.

tend to lose their particular richness and complexity; and that there is a danger of no longer relating to individuals as they are but rather of relating to individuals as though they were "only culture carriers."[36]

Cooper discusses the unavoidable guilt experienced by white practitioners who live in a privileged and segregated society and says that in their struggle with this guilt they may deal with it through "unrealistic rescue fantasies and activities—a form of paternalism."

> When white guilt remains unconscious it can lead to overcompensation, denial, reaction formation, an intense drive to identify with the oppressed, and a need to offer the victim special privileges and relaxed standards of behavior no more acceptable to minorities than to the general population.[37]

In the black practitioner, oppression produces its own personality and distortion. It may lead to costly overachievement at the expense of more normal development. Whether one achieves or does not achieve, there is the anxiety that hard-won gains, or battles lost, are not, in fact, the consequence of one's performance but rather the result of considerations based on race. With the actuality of one's own productivity in doubt, there are anxieties about self-worth and competence and there is no real way to measure one's own behavior.[38]

In speaking of the white-black encounter within the professional relationship, Gitterman and Schaeffer say:

> One direct consequence of the institutionalized racial positions of blacks and whites is social distance. . . . As a result of these conditions, there emerge two separate and distinct experiences, each somewhat unknown and alien to the other. It is this very quality of mutual strangeness which characterizes the initial black-white encounter. It may be camouflaged, denied, or rationalized. The void may be filled by stereotyped "knowledge" and preconceptions, but the essential unknownness remains. Not only are the two different, but, not having lived or known each other's differences, they can only speculate about them. They see each other and the world, and are in turn viewed . . . by the world, in different ways. . . .
>
> Thus separated . . . white . . . and . . . black . . . come together . . . face each other and are confronted with the necessity of doing something together. . . . First, there is suspiciousness and fear between them. . . .
>
> There is also anger between them. Once again, much has been written, especially in recent years, of the rage that is felt by black people. The white worker also feels anger of which he may or may not be aware. He may be angry at the black client for being so troubled,

[36] Ibid.
[37] Ibid.
[38] Ibid.

or helpless, or dependent, or hard to reach. He may be angry at himself for his inability to do very much to really help his client; or he may be angry at the client for being angry at him. The anger is there on some level. It is most likely that the client perceives it even if the worker does not.

There is also pain between them. This pain is one of the most complex dynamics because it stems from so many different sources . . . pain and suffering connected with whatever presenting problems caused the client to seek service . . . pain at being black in white America . . . pain felt by the worker in response to his client's pains . . . pain from the guilt felt by each party. . . . Most profoundly, there is guilt caused by repressed anger and other negative feelings experienced by both.[39]

Gitterman and Schaeffer recommend some ways of dealing with the racial gap between worker and client. Essentially, their recommendations reflect the factors in the relationship that we discussed earlier in this chapter. They point out that the helping process is a mutual endeavor between active participants, that it takes both participants to do the job, and that they must listen to each other. They emphasize that the white worker cannot ignore or minimize the social factors that contribute to the plight of the racially different client.[40]

Perhaps the best way to end this too brief discussion of race is to quote from the preface of the volume in which Gitterman and Schaeffer's contribution appears. Here the editor says:

The profession of social work cannot afford to sustain practices that would diminish the humanity of any group. It must deny that only blacks can treat blacks, or only whites can treat blacks, or only people of the same culture can understand each other well enough to provide help.

Social work must teach that different is not "better," nor is it "worse," it is *different*. And its technology must be developed, in every sense, to propagate a multiracial set of identities that will continue and extend the search for a common basis in humanity.[41]

RECAPITULATION

In this chapter we have discussed the professional relationship. The chapter has been long and complex, but even so it does not fully express the richness and complexity of the professional relationship as it is known by the worker and the other systems with which he interacts in the daily struggle with human problems. We have attempted to summarize the development in social work literature of the concept of relationship,

[39] Alex Gitterman and Alice Schaeffer, "The White Professional and the Black Client," in Goodman, *Dynamics of Racism*, pp. 154–56.

[40] Ibid., p. 157.

[41] James A. Goodman, "Preface," in Goodman, *Dynamics of Racism*, p. xiii.

to identify the various components of relationship, to deal briefly with some of the differences in the use of these components in various types of relationships, to discuss the worker himself and his capacities, and to deal with the issue of racism in professional relationships.

A LOOK FORWARD

In this chapter are two articles that deal with special problems in professional relationships. These articles deal with empathy and the problem of dishonesty. We present them to you as increasing the richness of the chapter, but with no pretense that they are an adequate sampling of the rich and diverse literature on relationship. We would strongly recommend that you sample the selected references for further reading in this important area. In the following chapters we will be discussing what the worker does within the relationship.

---

*The impact of professional dishonesty on
behavior of disturbed adolescents**

Seymour L. Halleck

The role of dishonesty on the part of those who treat the emotionally disturbed has been inadequately examined. Thomas Szasz, a provocative psychiatric theoretician, has made a beginning effort in this direction by examining the issue of lying, both conscious and unconscious, as it relates to communication of the patient to the worker.[1] There has been no attention paid, however, to the problem of dishonesty in the other direction, namely, for the professional worker to the client or patient. Szasz touched on this issue when he discussed the need of persons in our society to maintain traditional cultural patterns by lying to their children. He postulates that much of adolescent rebellion may be related to the fact that it is during this time of life that the adolescent first becomes intellectually mature enough to perceive that significant adults in his life have lied to him repeatedly.

---

* Reprinted with permission of the author and the National Association of Social Workers from Social Work, 8:2 (April 1963), pp. 48–55.
[1] Thomas S. Szasz, *The Myth of Mental Illness, Foundations of a Theory of Personal Conduct* (New York: Harper, 1961).

These concepts raise intriguing issues for those who are entrusted with the professional management of disturbed adolescents. Is it possible that they communicate information, values, and morals to adolescent clients that they themselves do not believe fully? Do professional workers contribute to the perpetuation of rebellious behavior or do they perhaps even precipitate it by a failure to present themselves and their world in an honest, straightforward manner? The answer to these questions may unfortunately be a qualified "yes."

Most adults, including child care workers, do fail at times to communicate an honest picture of the adult and adolescent world to their patients. They are often less than straightforward in presenting themselves as helping persons. In subtle ways they communicate a wish for the adolescent to develop values and moral codes that many adults would themselves have difficulty in accepting. The dishonesty described in this paper is frequently perpetuated by parents and other adults who come into contact with adolescents. While such behavior is obviously deleterious when nonprofessionals are involved, it is especially harmful when employed by a professional youth worker.

In approaching an issue as emotion-laden as lying, the author is tempted to be provocative, cynical, or pessimistic. It is not his intention to communicate these attitudes. He contends, however, that adult workers in all the clinical behavioral sciences tend to lie to their adolescent patients. The lying may at times be on a fully conscious basis; at other times it may be more or less beyond awareness. The net effect of this behavior is to confuse and at times infuriate the adolescent, which in itself may produce greater rebellion, more symptoms, and more pain—or exactly the opposite of the original goals. As is true for most dynamic situations, whether one is dealing with individuals or with groups, positive growth must often follow a painful appraisal of less acceptable behavior and motivations. A realistic examination of dishonest behavior on the part of professional workers can then be considered a painful but necessary procedure that may encourage freedom to develop new and more effective techniques.

This discussion is focused primarily on the interaction of professionals with adolescents who are either institutionalized or who are involved with community agencies. This group certainly constitutes a great majority of adolescents who come into contact with psychiatrists, psychologists, sociologists, and social workers. In some instances, particularly in private practice, when the worker may function only as the patient's—or at most the family's—agent, some of the aspects of dishonest behavior may not apply, and these exceptions will be noted. There are at least seven areas in which adolescent clients are deceived either through conscious fabrication or through subtle and unconscious communication of attitudes to which professional workers do not adhere.

The lie of adult morality

In confronting the chaotic sexuality and poorly controlled aggressiveness of the adolescent, most professional workers tend to communicate the possibility of a world in which such impulses are resolved easily. They imply that adults control their impulses and that success in the world is dependent upon such restraint. To a limited extent this is certainly true. Too often, however, they present a picture of the world that is far removed from reality and does not take cognizance of the social usefulness of certain kinds of aggressive and sexual behavior. The adolescent boy knows that aggressiveness, and sometime unscrupulous aggressiveness, may be a prerequisite for success. He knows that the interviewer sitting behind the desk has probably struggled aggressively to gain the status of a professional position. The sexually promiscuous adolescent girl knows (even if she has not read the Kinsey report) that on a statistical basis the professional person with whom she interacts has probably at some time in his life been guilty of the same behavior for which she is being punished.

It may be unrealistic to communicate readily the worker's own deficiencies and therefore provide the adolescent rationalizations for disturbed behavior. There is a frequent tendency, however, to err in the other direction. Professionals communicate a picture of themselves and their world as one in which only the highest type of values and moral standards prevail. The adolescent cannot understand this. His personal experiences, his observational powers, and his intuitiveness tell him that something is wrong. He wants to like and to identify with adults, but he is painfully aware of an inconsistency or basic dishonesty in their approach. He may then come to believe that adults are incapable of being anything but "phony" and react by rebellious behavior or isolation from the adult world.

This type of dishonesty is seen with considerably less frequency in private psychotherapeutic interactions, especially with adults. Here the worker tries to produce a climate in which the universality of antisocial impulses is accepted and usually discussed freely. An unwillingness to extend this same honesty to a large portion of adolescent patients is a serious error. The adolescent is struggling to understand the adult world. He will learn the truth about it whether he is told or not.

The lie of professional helpfulness

The professional worker who confronts adolescents in the courtroom, the community clinic, or the state institution serves a dual role, as an agent of the community and as a helping person. The community wants him to control, attenuate, or in some way modify the behavior of an individual who is causing it some distress. The worker is also interested in his client; he feels some wish to make the disturbed adolescent a more comfortable and effective person. It is important to understand, however, that in the majority of these situations (there are exceptions in private practice) the worker does not function as an agent of the adolescent patient. His salary is paid by the community. When the community's needs conflict with the adolescent's needs, it is the community that must be obeyed and decisions are not always made entirely in the patient's interest. It is still possible within the limitations of this role for the worker to maintain an honest identification as someone who wants to help the adolescent. If he does not communicate, however, that one of his most basic roles is other than help oriented, he is being dishonest.

Most adolescents do not seek help; they are sent. For example, take the case of an adolescent boy who has been a behavior problem in school and has been referred to the school psychologist. The boy is told that he must see a professional person and that the psychologist will try to help him. He knows, however, that the school is somewhat provoked with him and that its officials are going to act to prevent him from being an annoyance. He does not know what will be done. He does know that the school psychologist, functioning as the agent of the community, may exert a tremendous amount of power over him. As a result of his interaction with this professional worker he may be removed from school, forced to attend special classes, or even removed from his home and sent to an institution. No matter how benign a person the school psychologist then turns out to be, it is very difficult for the adolescent to perceive him as a helping person.

As long as the worker and the adolescent are aware of the fact that the professional may be participating in mutually antagonistic roles, effective communication is possible. The situation is complicated, however, when the worker pretends that his only motivation in seeing the adolescent is to help him. The adolescent realizes that this is obviously untrue. He then perceives the adult worker as dishonest, which only makes him want to be dishonest in return. Experienced workers have learned that the word "help" rarely evinces a positive response from the adolescent. He experiences it as a kind of "Kafka"-like double talk. In many settings, then, the word "help" is perceived by the adolescent as an unreliable and perhaps dangerous word.

The lie of confidentiality

The issue of confidentiality is closely related to the problem of helpfulness. Most caseworkers, psychologists, and psychiatrists have been taught that the model for a professional helping relationship is derived from the psychotherapeutic situation. In traditional forms of psychotherapy the communications of the patient or client to the worker are considered private material to be shared with no one outside the treatment situation. Many of the techniques professional workers use in interviewing, evaluating, diagnosing, or counseling the adolescent are derived from what they were taught about psychotherapy. Often the worker behaves as though the adolescent is entitled to expect confidentiality and as though it were going to be provided. It is extremely rare for the adolescent to be told directly who is going to see the report the worker writes, who is going to read it, and with whom the case is going to be discussed.

The issue here, as with helpfulness, is that the worker cannot guarantee confidentiality to the patient since he is not the agent of the patient. The worker has obligations to the child's family, his clinic, his agency, or his institution. Even if after submitting an initial diagnostic report he begins to see the adolescent in a more traditional psychotherapeutic relationship, complete confidentiality can rarely be promised. While it is true that useful communication can take place between the worker and the adolescent without the guarantee of confidentiality, it is also true that to imply that this guarantee is extended, or to extend it with the full knowledge that it is not meant to be kept, can result in development of situations that inhibit communication. It does not take a very clever adolescent to understand that the worker has primary responsibilities to his agency and to the community. He may fully understand that whatever information he gives will be shared with others and can be used in making important decisions about him. If professionals do not let him know this, he will perceive their behavior as dishonest, and his communications to the adult world will be effectively diminished.

The lie of rewards for conformity

The necessity of conforming to adult standards is most often communicated to adolescents whose behavior deviates from the norms of the community. To this sizable proportion of disturbed adolescents, professional workers seem to be saying, "Your behavior is unacceptable, it produces more difficulty and leads you to experience more pain. It is to your own infinite advantage to be passive, to conform, to obey." There is ample evidence, however, that in attacking the behavioral defenses of the adolescent, workers remove character armor, leaving him more susceptible to anxiety. There is really little in the way of pleasure that can be promised to the adolescent if he risks giving up characterological defenses. This has been discussed previously in terms of the problems imposed on the criminal when he is viewed as a "patient."

Society and the psychiatrist in particular may be imposing an almost intolerable burden on the delinquent in asking him to exchange the "bad" role for the sick role. It is not surprising that the criminal looks upon the usual rehabilitation program with cynicism and distrust. Only when those in charge of treatment searchingly ask themselves what they are trying to do to the delinquent when they try to make him into a conforming citizen and are able to appreciate what he is giving up in accepting the sick role, can therapy be successful.[2]

It is always a moving, sometimes an overwhelming, experience to see an adolescent abandon behavioral expressions of conflict for a more introspective way of life. This is never accomplished without considerable pain and sometimes despair. If the adolescent is told that the simple expedient of conforming to adult standards produces pleasure, he is told a lie. Conformity on the part of the adolescent certainly meets the immediate needs of the community; whether it meets the needs of the individual adolescent is questionable. When workers pretend to him that it does, they encounter only confusion and anger, especially when he experiences the inevitable anxieties that come when he attempts to control his behavior.

Denial of limitations

The majority of adolescents who come to the attention of community agencies are from troubled homes and lower socio-economic groups. Many of them have been subjected to severe psychological and economic deprivations. Their educational experiences have been limited. Psychiatric studies have produced data which indicate that the effects of early emotional deprivation are to a certain extent unmodifiable.[3] Deficiencies in early educational experiences may also seriously limit potentialities for achievement in the world.

The average professional worker comes from a middle-class background, which in our culture implies a far greater potentiality than that seen in most adolescent clients. (Here we must, of course, exclude selected disturbed adolescents of superior intelligence, of middle-class background, or from reasonably well-integrated homes.) Many workers fail to see that with a few exceptions they are dealing with people of limited potential who will never be like them. Failing to realize this fact, the worker may then encourage identifications, ambitions, and

---

[2] Seymour L. Halleck, "The Criminal's Problem with Psychiatry," *Psychiatry*, 23:4 (November 1960).

[3] J. Bowlby, "A Note on Mother-Child Separation as a Mental Health Hazard," *British Journal of Medical Psychology*, 31:3–4 (1958), pp. 247–48; G. Engel, F. Reichsman, and H. Segal, "A Study of an Infant with Gastric Fistula in Behavior and the Rate of Total Hydrochloric Acid Secretion," *Psychosomatic Medicine*, 18:5 (October 1956), pp. 374–98; H. Harlow, "The Nature of Love," *The American Psychologist*, 13 (1958), pp. 673–85.

achievements that are not possible for his client and which leave the adolescent with a feeling of frustration.

Few workers are guilty of consciously pushing their clients to achieve beyond their limits. Many of them, however, repeatedly deny the impressive limitations of some of their patients and assure them that the development of certain identifications and goals is entirely possible. This is a type of unconscious dishonesty that may produce considerable harm. The adolescent may righteously say to himself, "Who is this guy kidding? Is he trying to reassure me or reassure himself? Maybe he's trying to humiliate me by throwing my inadequacies in my face. He'll never understand me."

"Open up; trust me; all will go well"

A close relationship is a foundation of any successful therapeutic interaction. Experiencing closeness to another person leads to the possibility of examining one's behavior in such a way that unfavorable personality defenses can be modified or exchanged for more useful ones. Most professional workers leave school with the feeling that they will be successful with clients if they can persuade them to be open and close. The adolescent, however, especially the disturbed adolescent, frequently is struggling with some of the negative aspects of closeness that he experiences as stultifying or smothering. He has begun to find certain types of relationships among his peers that provide him with a feeling of considerably more safety. To abandon movement in this direction and again attempt to develop a close relationship with an adult involves grave risk-taking for him. He is well aware that the little freedom he has gained may have to be surrendered if too much closeness develops.

If the worker realizes this, he can gently, tactfully, and with some humility gradually allow a meaningful, nonsymbiotic relationship to develop between him and the child. In a healthy close relationship between adolescent and adult, the adolescent is allowed certain kinds of independence, dignity, and, of course, distance when he wants it. The social structure in which most professional workers function makes it extremely difficult to provide this kind of relationship. They usually begin in settings in which they have tremendous power over the adolescent, who is thrown into a forced dependency. The adolescent is often forced into a relationship that he, at least on a conscious level, has not sought. The possibility of prolonged relationships is often limited by the fact that both professionals and their clients are extremely mobile, frequently changing responsibilities, jobs, and geographical locations. A sustained, intensive relationship is not a common occurrence in most situations developed in community agencies.

Professional workers are guilty, nevertheless, of continuously exhorting the adolescent to "open up; trust me; if you rely on me and share things with me, all will go well." But the disturbed adolescent knows that this is not true! He knows that the person who is pleading with him to expose himself may be a person with whom he will have only limited future contacts and whom he can see few reasons for trusting. He is further aware of the possibility that he can lose much in such a relationship and that the worker may not really be offering a true intimacy between equals. To the adolescent it seems like a poor bargain. He feels that the worker is dishonest in offering this type of bargain and he reacts with fear, distrust, and cynicism.

"We like you but not your behavior"

Anyone who has spent much time with adolescents knows that their behavior can be provocative, frustrating, and at times infuriating. It is distressing to see how few professional workers are willing to admit honestly how angry they get with their adolescent clients. This anger frequently is rationalized with statements to the effect that "I like you but not your behavior." Sometimes the worker's anger is totally denied but comes out only through his behavior toward the adolescent. In these types of situations workers sometimes tell the adolescent that they are not really angry with him but they feel that he must be disciplined for his own good, and that by depriving him of privileges or changing his situation, they are really trying to help him. Frequently this anger is displaced onto the parents or onto other professional workers. Anyone who works with adolescents in a community or institutional setting is painfully aware of the extreme rivalry and sometimes open animosity between individual professionals and their groups. The fact is that it is almost impossible to work with adolescents for any period of time without becoming periodically angered.

It is dishonest and unfair both to the worker and to the adolescent to deny, rationalize, or displace this anger. It belongs in the therapeutic situation and should be communicated with as much restraint, tact, and honesty as the worker is capable of providing. To do less than this establishes a basically dishonest pattern of interaction and precludes the possibility of the adolescent experiencing positive emotional growth. He knows that adults at times find him intolerable and cannot be expected to cooperate or communicate with people who are unwilling to admit this fact.

Prerequisites to an honest approach

By the time the professional worker comes to his first meeting with the adolescent, he is encountering a child who has probably been lied to repeatedly by his parents and relatives. If the adolescent has also had experiences with welfare agencies this situation may have been compounded through dishonest behavior on the part of professional workers. The child may by this time have learned a variety of techniques of resistance to cope with what he perceives to be the "phoniness" of adults. This situation is one of the most important contributing factors to the sullen inertia and negativism so often found with adolescent clients. A good portion of the malignant effects of this factor can be ameliorated through a change in techniques and attitudes on the part of the worker directed toward a more honest interaction. When efforts are made toward more scrupulous honesty with adolescent patients it is almost invariably gratifying to discover a child who is more open, talkative, and willing to discuss areas of life that are not ordinarily communicated. The child seems almost delightfully surprised to discover that he can talk to an adult in a free and easy manner.

The methods of developing an honest approach to an adolescent patient or client are uncomplicated and straightforward. They are based on a conviction on the part of the worker that he is going to be scrupulously honest with himself and the child when he discusses or implies attitudes toward the seven areas considered earlier. It is only necessary for the worker to be aware of any tendency to convey untrue attitudes and ideas and to make a constant effort to avoid doing so. A useful illustration can be obtained through outlining the behavior and attitudes of a professional who is trying to avoid the pitfalls previously discussed. The techniques and attitudes employed by this hypothetical worker in his interactions with adolescent patients will be described. These techniques, whether utilized by youth workers, teachers, or parents, can effectively increase communication between adults and adolescents.

With respect to the "lie of adult morality" no effort is ever made by the worker to criticize, disparage, or in any way condemn the adolescent's antisocial behavior. Rather, it is considered as something the community (rightly or wrongly) will not tolerate if done openly and, most important, as something that *has not served the social or personal needs* of the adolescent. A routine and essential part of an initial interaction with any adolescent consists of a careful assessment of the net gains and losses caused by this behavior. The social usefulness of certain kinds of aggressive behavior is never disparaged. No attempt is made to discuss behavior in terms of right or wrong, neurotic or normal, or good or bad. The worker will attempt at times to communicate his own moral standards, which may or may not be more stringent than those of the patient. These are always clearly labeled as the worker's personal beliefs and it is made clear that they may not be relevant for the patient.

The lies of professional helpfulness and confidentiality are handled directly by explaining the evaluator's own position as precisely as possible during the initial interview. The child is told who is employing the examiner, what the examiner's responsibilities to his employer are, what kind of report will be written, and exactly who will see and discuss it. Contrary to what might immediately be expected most adolescents respond favorably to such an approach. When the rules of the "game" of interviewing are wholly apparent to them, there is little need for defensiveness or negativism. The sheer surprising impact of having an adult be so direct with them often in itself produces a favorable effect that encourages them to be more open.

To avoid taking the stand that conformity or adjustment to adult standards breeds comfort and contentment, the worker must have a deep and thorough understanding of the role of antisocial behavior in maintaining the adolescent's equilibrium. He must be thoroughly able to empathize with the "fun" and at times pleasure associated with behavior that flaunts rules. He must also realize that such behavior may be all that stands between feelings of hopelessness and despair. Adjustment to the adult world is not presented as something that necessarily brings pleasure but rather as a necessary and sometimes unpleasant requisite to survival. At times the worker might even openly discuss conformity as a burden and warn the patient as to some of the dangers of such behavior. Such an approach provides leverage when the issue of the adolescent's rigid conformity to his own peer group inevitably arises during a prolonged relationship.

Avoiding the communication that most adolescent clients have the same potential as the professional worker involves a careful attention to not confusing the worker's own needs with those of the child. Our hypothetical worker freely discusses with adolescents the problems of moving from one social class to another and makes no effort to pretend that class distinctions do not exist. The barriers to advancement which minority group adolescents profess are more often accepted as realities than interpreted as projections. The adolescent boy who has a long police record and who has missed out on many educational opportunities is not deluded into believing he can "be anything he wants." The girl who may have had one or more illegitimate children is not assured of her potential for making a favorable marriage. The worker's general attitude is that this can be a "tough world" in which only a determined few manage to overcome the deprivations of their early background.

While the worker may firmly believe that a relationship with an understanding and skilled adult promulgates favorable personality change, all efforts are made to let the adolescent develop the relationship at his own pace and without extravagent, implied promise of its value. The patient is told exactly when and for how long the worker will be available. Full attention is paid to the risks the client takes in developing a relationship; sometimes these risks are actually spelled out.

Strenuous efforts are made to deal with the adolescent's fear of being swallowed up in his dependency needs. "Openness" is encouraged as a necessary prerequisite to gaining understanding but it is not held out as a "cure-all" or as a goal in itself. Exhortations to trust the worker are avoided rigorously. Rather, the adolescent is told that he will have to decide himself about the worker's trustworthiness on the basis of his own experience.

Perhaps the most outrageous dishonesty perpetrated against adolescents by professionals involves their tendency to cover up their own angry feelings, which invariably develop toward the patient. It is surprisingly easy to tell an adolescent when he is annoying and such communications, when presented in a restrained but straightforward manner, rarely have a negative effect upon the relationship. A communication such as "I find your behavior during this interview extremely difficult and I'm having trouble keeping from getting annoyed myself" may in many instances be preferable to "What's bothering you?" or "How can I help?" or even to passive acceptance of provocative behavior. The adolescent appreciates this kind of straightforwardness. It tells him where he stands and enables him to look at his behavior without having to deceive either himself or the adult.

Conclusions

Anyone who has reared children knows that occasional dishonesty is essential if the child is to grow up with a reasonable degree of security. The truth to children, if understood, may be unbearable. If an orderly, sane, and relatively nonchaotic way of life is to be maintained, it is essential that children at times be deceived or at the very least kept in the dark as to issues they are not yet ready to master. In the treatment of adults there are clear landmarks for the worker to follow. Adults who enter psychotherapy are greeted with an atmosphere that not only condones but puts a premium on truthfulness on the part of all participants. Exceptions are made only when it is felt that the patient is too seriously ill to comprehend or tolerate the impact of truth. In these cases various deceptive practices may be used for the patient's benefit.

If one could argue convincingly that the great majority of disturbed adolescents were similar to children or to the severely disturbed adult, there would be considerable justification for withholding truth and practicing deception for the adolescent's own gain. Anyone who works with adolescents, even seriously disturbed ones, however, is quickly aware that such a comparison is invalid. Adolescents are extremely open to learning. They are in the process of discovering new aspects of the world around them, and are also increasingly preoccupied with their own inner world. Even the most disturbed adolescent has rarely developed a fixed pattern of rigid personality defenses that preclude being able to look at the truth in a reasonably open way.

The professional worker knows that the adolescent is capable of serious volatile impulsive behavior and does not have available to himself the controls that most adults have learned. Perhaps much of the explanation for an unwillingness to be honest with adolescents is related to a fear that they will not be able to tolerate the truth and that it will be used in a destructive, unhelpful way. One can also speculate that dishonest behavior might be related to the frightening impact of aggressive and sexually provocative adolescent behavior that touches upon areas of our own problems which have not been completely understood or worked through. When we present a dishonest picture of the world to our clients, we may really be trying to avoid the despair of facing the frightening world in which we live and thereby to reassure ourselves.

To interact honestly with an adolescent, all interested adults must believe that the growth of useful personality traits is more likely to take place in an atmosphere of truth than of dishonesty. This involves a willingness to take the risk of presenting communications that temporarily disturb the adolescent and a tolerance of the possibility that many of these disturbances will be directed against the adult. Any adult who wishes to communicate effectively in this manner must of course come to terms with self-deceptions in his own life so that they do not interfere with his ability to face reality with others.

Being understanding and understood: Or how to find a wandered horse*

Wendell Johnson

I want to talk with you from the point of view of the person on the other side of the desk. I want to try to tell you, if I can, what the handicapped child or adult would tell you if he could, if he knew enough about you, about your work, and if he knew enough about his own difficulties.

To begin with, I think that the representative handicapped child would tell you, if he could, that he is very grateful for the work you

* Reprinted from *ETC*, 8:3 (Spring 1951), by permission of the International Society for General Semantics.

are trying to do. I think he would be impressed by your tests, your standardized interviews, if you have any (there are psychologists who do not believe in them), remedial procedures, your play therapies, etc. He would try to tell you that he thinks you are doing great work and he would mean it. I say this with considerable conviction, because I have been on the other side of the desk. As a stutterer, I am very grateful to everyone who has attempted to help me.

But the handicapped child would also want to tell you something else. He might find it very difficult to find the words, but somehow he would want to say to you that there is something missing, that he wishes that we, as professional workers, were able to understand him a little better. He realizes that we understand him to a certain extent, but he feels that our understanding of him is often rather highly specialized. We understand him only as a particular type of individual. The understanding is somehow partial. It may even be the kind which precludes our paying any attention to certain phases of his problem, or of him as an individual, or of the situation in which the problem has meaning for him. There are, for example, psychologists and other kinds of clinical workers, who tend to become very dogmatic about their methods and points of view, and who refuse to consider certain aspects of a given case. The child on the other side of the desk feels that such a worker is not paying attention to certain things that to the child are very important. There are times, I think, when he would feel that he was just being out-and-out misunderstood.

I want to try now to get on the other side of the desk—your side—for a moment. As a clinical worker, I want to talk today more or less from the point of view of one who works with general semantics, and those of you who know general semantics will catch the overtones of it in my remarks. I trust that all of you will realize, however, that I cannot, in the time available, make clear explicitly what I mean in detail by general semantics. Some of you will sense the semantic basis of the view that an important reason why we do not understand handicapped children and adults better than we do is that we tend to see them through our own individual evaluational filters. We never really see a unique individual child. We see only what we are prepared, psychologically and evaluationally, to see. We are able to feel only what we are prepared by training and experience to feel. We understand, of course, that the child on the other side of the desk is now behaving the way he behaves, partly because of his background, certain childhood experiences, the way he has been trained, and the things that he has learned and not learned. Well, the individual behind the desk has had a childhood, too. He has had a background too. He has had parents. After all, maladjustments begin in the home, and the man behind the desk has had a home, too. He does the things he does and he has the attitudes he has for just about the same general kinds of reasons that the child operates with, and such reasons are individualized in the way they work out their effects. So you never see the child as a whole. You see only what you are prepared to see. You can understand only what you are prepared to understand. It does not matter what books you have read, either—at least, it does not matter as much as we sometimes think it does. You had a childhood in which conditions determined and limited what you are now going to do with the books you have read. The child will look different to you from the way he will look to any other worker. The net result is that the child somehow feels that he is being understood or evaluated only by one individual, and that he is not being evaluated in anything like a complete sense.

There is another reason why we do not understand these children better than we do, a very obvious reason. It is that we do not have their handicaps. In fact, we feel very often that it is a rather important part of the qualifications of a worker in this area that he not have handicaps. I wonder, however, whether it is possible for an individual who has never had a problem—if there are any individuals like that—to have any significant insight into the difficulties of individuals who do have serious problems. The point is that if you have not had a handicap, then all you can ever have in the way of knowledge of the individual that you are attempting to help is the kind of knowledge that is verbal. I do not believe that we shall ever develop a really adequate understanding of the feeble-minded, for example, as long as only intelligent individuals work with the problem. Somehow, we are going to have to get some feeble-minded persons to specialize in this field! I do not think that we should pretend that we understand the deaf, for example, as long as we are able to hear. Oh, yes, we can understand in a kind of verbal way; we are able to make measurements and we are able to work out relationships statistically, and study the individuals in terms of what these relationships tell us about them. We are able to "dope out" what a person would miss in the way of auditory stimulation with a given hearing loss. We are able to understand what that might mean to a person when it comes to learning how to talk or to maintain clear speech, but when all is said and done, we have never been deaf. I do not know what it is like, and I think that the best thing I can do in working with the deaf is to take that into account.

And how can we do that? Well, I think we do it mainly in two ways. One is by never being dogmatic when it comes to how the other individual feels. We do not know for sure how he feels, and I think we ought frankly to face that. The other thing we tend to do, I think, if we have this point of view, is to be more ready to ask the child what he thinks about the problem and about our approaches to it.

Those who have attempted to help me have always wanted to ask me a good deal about how I felt about my speech problem, and about my mother and father, etc., but seldom, if ever, has a clinical worker asked me how I felt about him, how I felt about what he was doing, how I felt about his ideas. There was always a feeling that the expert was attempting somehow to force on me a point of view, an interpretation, a kind of understanding. And almost always when I would ask questions, or say perhaps, "No, no you don't quite understand. . . ," there was a tendency on the part of the clinical worker to take that to be evidence of what the psychoanalysts call "resistance." It is a rare clinician who listens really effectively to what "the case" tries to tell him. It could be that as clinicians we are wrong and that "the case" has something to tell us, that he is not resisting at all. He may be trying to teach us something. Some of our methods, for example, sound very good to us and they are backed up by great authorities, but when applied to a particular individual, they do not work. Some of the children and adults on the other side of the desk might be trying to tell us why they do not work.

I had a very strong feeling, most of the time, when I was on the other side of the desk, that the clinician working with me was *interested in the work.* I hardly ever had the feeling that the interest was directed exclusively to me, and I think I have noticed that sort of thing in other cases. In my own clinical work I feel quite sure that I, too, have a tendency to get interested in the theory and the techniques and somehow to lose sight of the child. It is actually hard to stay interested *in him.*

Consider, for example, what goes on in a training course in mental testing. You have to give possibly fifty Stanford-Binet tests to pass the course. Every child who gets one of those fifty is going to sense that you are testing him—not to *test him,* not because you are interested *in him,* but *because you want to pass the course.* You have to give fifty Stanford-Binets; and he will do as someone to test; but he also feels that anybody else would do, too. Now, there is a great deal of clinical work like that—work done by somebody trying to learn a method, somebody very much interested in the method, who spends his leisure hours talking to his friends about it, who spends his nights reading about it and trying to write about it; and then when he finds a case, he rubs his hands to say to himself, "Ah, that's fine, now I've got a case to work on." A handicapped child finds it hard to trust a clinical worker like that. He understands that *he* is not being examined; *the method* is being examined. The child is being used as the file, or the hammer—the tool—to refine the method. The method is not being used as a tool to solve his problem.

This all adds up to the feeling that almost all individuals have, I think, when they go to clinics, that somehow they are not being understood. They are being helped, of course, and a lot of people are putting in a great deal of time doing things which are very impressive and which they, the handicapped, are very happy to have done; but they are just a little lonely in the midst of all these activities. Somehow, someone seems to be working *on* them for some reason other than to help them. The clinical workers are doing things to them and for them in order to satisfy certain requirements that have been set up by the State Board of Education perhaps. They are doing all these things in order to write an article for some professional journal possibly. The "case" is perfectly willing to cooperate and he may even see the value of the activities in which he is asked to participate. It is just that he feels the clinicians never quite get to know him.

Moreover, most clinical workers tend to fall rather easily into a particular kind of language habit. For the most part, we use a language that tends to have a certain kind of structure. By that, I mean that it tends to involve certain types of sentences and it tends to enforce only certain types of distinctions. For example, the ordinary language we use tends to make us talk as though there were *two* kinds of people in the world, two kinds of political possibilities, two kinds of everything. It is largely an "either-or" language. The world, however, is not "either-or" and the nervous system of the individual using the language is not "either-or." Nevertheless, when we use our common language, we tend to talk as though there were only two possibilities in any given situation. The language we use tends to relate these two possibilities in a particular way. Almost always we talk as though we were dealing with relationships that work only one way. For example, we commonly talk about handicaps as though they were to be broken down in any one case into "symptoms" and "causes," and then our language does our thinking for us in terms of these two categories. There are no "symptoms" and there are no "causes" in nature. The categories, of course, are man-made, they are abstractions, they are verbalisms. Together, the categories of cause and symptom are a kind of system for organizing facts in a particular way. It is not the only way to organize them. There is nothing "natural" about it—it is just the way our particular kind of language works. If it works in such a way that we are led automatically to assume that the cause is somehow more "basic" than the symptom, nevertheless, it is to be fully realized that anybody who tells you that you should always work on the causes and never on the symptoms, is seldom, if ever, reporting the hard-earned conclusions of long and laborious investigation. *Such a person is usually echoing a kind of statement that has somehow become traditional.* It is part and parcel of the language forms of our culture. You do not have to think at all in order to talk about "causes" and "symptoms" as though they were distinct and as though "causes" were more "basic." That is just the way the language does your thinking for you.

What are the facts in the meantime? I think almost all of the serious mistakes that are made by the workers I have tried to train, and almost all the serious mistakes I have made and still make as a clinician, tend to be of two kinds. We tend either to ignore the "symptoms" or we over-emphasize them. There are some speech pathologists, for example, who are so hypnotized by the stutterer's "surface noises" that they devote all their time to these "noises." There are others who take the attitude that they are merely "symptoms," so they start to hunt for the "causes," so that they will have something on which to work. If you have ever stuttered, however, you know very well that what we call the "symptoms" are very important; and the attitude that they should be ignored is strange, indeed.

Stuttering can be very painful. I have had stutterers in my clinic who would go through contortions so severe that they would fall over. Now what kind of a psychologist is it who would stand there and watch them fall over and say, "Oh, that's not important—that's just a symptom." That sort of behavior is much more than a "symptom." It is the cause of a complex pattern of social relationships; and if you do not think it is, I suggest that you go into a department store today and stutter severely to one of the clerks. Get all blocked up, all tied up, and do not tell anyone what you are doing. When the clerk gets through telling you that she does not have whatever you have asked for, pretend to try to say, "Thank you," as you move away about eight or ten feet—and then suddenly blurt it out. That sort of thing happens to stutterers. You carry out this assignment and then decide whether that sort of behavior is "just a symptom." Note carefully whether it has any effects. Any stutterer can tell you that it has effects—tremendous effects.

The facts are that anything can be called a "symptom" and anything can be called a "cause." It depends on where you are standing; and if you are standing inside the quandary, so to speak, then the things which from the outside look like symptoms look like causes. Often the individual on the other side of the desk feels that we do not understand that, that somehow we are ignoring what is very important to him. Recently, for example, a clinical psychologist told me that she was working with a cerebral-palsied boy, about 17 years old. She said she was giving him psychotherapy, which in my judgment is highly desirable for a large proportion of cerebral palsy cases. When I asked her, however, "Aren't you doing anything else?" she said, "No," as if to say, "Well, what else is there to do?" Now, it should not take too much imagination to emphasize with a cerebral-palsied individual and to realize that if anything could be done to help him directly to achieve a little more relaxation and a little more coordination in the performance of everyday activities, it would be very important to him. If he could attain these kinds of improvement, the chances are that he would react much more effectively to psychotherapy.

Let us make this very absurd. What I am trying to say is that one of the things we do which tends to keep us from understanding handicapped children and adults better is that we do not spend enough time trying to appreciate the symptoms, as we call them. To them, they are not symptoms so much as they are causes of frustration and misery. They want to have everything possible done to alleviate or remove the symptoms. They want to work on the so-called causes, too, of course. But in the meantime, they are in pain or distress.

Now, as I suggested, let us make the situation very absurd. Suppose that we were out in the woods and we came upon a man who had accidentally got his foot caught in a bear trap. There he is, howling and carrying on frightfully, weeping and straining in a most profane fashion. Then two psychologists come by and one of them wants to give the man the Rorschach test and an intelligence test and take a case history. The other psychologist, however, has undergone a different kind of training; and he says, "No, let's start intensive psychoanalysis right now." So, they talk it over. They have their differences, of course, but they agree eventually that what this man in the bear trap needs is obviously psychotherapy. If he would just be trained to be a more mature individual; if he could have the release therapy he needs; if he would undergo the needed catharsis, achieve the necessary insight, and work through the essential abreaction, he would develop more maturity, he would understand the difficulty he is having, and he would then be able to solve his problem himself. Obviously, the psychologists agree, that is the only sound way to deal with the poor fellow. Suddenly, however, a farmer comes by and lets the man out of the bear trap. To the utter amazement of the psychologists, the man's behavior changes greatly and quickly. Besides, he seems to take a great liking to the farmer, and goes off with him, evidently to have a cup of coffee.

The basic principle illustrated by this absurd example is that psychotherapy is more beneficial when it is carried on under optimal conditions. And one way to prepare optimal conditions for psychotherapy, or for classroom teaching, for that matter, or for any kind of special instruction, is to do everything possible first—or as you go along—to relieve any distressing symptoms that may be distracting the individual you are trying to help. If the symptoms make a difference to the individual, if they are producing impaired social relationships, impaired self-evaluations, impaired parent-child relationships, or tantrums, or anxiety—then clearly anything that can be done directly, by means of literal or figurative aspirin, to relieve the symptoms will be all to the good in helping to bring about favorable conditions for therapy.

I started out by saying that we tend to find it hard sometimes to understand handicapped youngsters because we see them through our own individual evaluational filters. The general point I want to make in this connection can be well illustrated by reference to a kind of experience I am sure we have all had at one time or another in going to a large hospital. There are many clinics, divisions, or departments in such a hospital, and you hardly know where to begin. You go to one of them, and either a doctor there examines you and makes a diagnosis, or else he refers you to another clinic. In this other clinic you will either be diagnosed and treated, or referred back, or referred on to a third clinic. By the time you reach the other side of the hospital at the end of the week, you have begun to wonder, "Who is going to tie all this together for me? Who is going to tell me what all these examinations mean in functional relationship to each other? Who has the whole story here?" In one clinic someone examined your heart; in another someone examined your liver; but no one has examined you in any comprehensive fashion, and you begin to feel that you are not quite sure that anyone knows the whole story. By some sort of process that is not too easy to figure out, you end up having a last talk with somebody, and what you get then is *his* evaluation. He may take into account all of the individual reports from the various clinics, and he may not. If he does, it is not always easy to see just how he takes them into account. At any rate, he tells you something and that is what you have to tell the folks when you get home and they ask you, "What did they say at the hospital?"

What is the matter here? I think one of the things that is the matter is that in our tendency to specialize—and we have to specialize in this complicated world—we tend to develop a pride in our own specialties, and we tend to develop the illusion that we study only facts when we specialize. Now, there is a great deal to be said for the proposition that when you study pediatrics, or neurology, or psychology, or speech pathology, you study a special language. It is hard to determine how much you study facts, as such—whatever that means. It is perfectly obvious that you study languages or special terminologies; and each one of them, considered separately, tends to leave out much more than it includes about the individual. You can not possibly get the whole picture, you can not possibly tell the whole story about the individual, in any one language. I take that to be perfectly obvious. Also, these languages do not always serve as handy gadgets for reporting. After you learn the language of neurology, for example, it tends to have a determining effect on your observational reactions, it tends to affect your perceptions, to direct your investigations. You look only for certain things you have words for. *You do not look for things you do not have words for.* So the neurologist looks only for certain things. That is not all that his language does for him, however. The facts he does get from his language—from his directed observation—are organized by his language in a particular way. There is nothing 'fundamentally natural about this organization—it simply represents the way the language works. The language is a thinking machine. Our language does our thinking for us.

Consequently, one way to improve our ability to understand the person on the other side of the desk is to learn all the special languages we can. We need the language of neurology, of physiology, of anatomy, of psychology, the language of Freud, Pavlov, Thorndike, Hull, Carl Rogers, the language of general semantics. We need them all, because we are not able to make adequate observations or to organize our observations in the most adequate way, or to report our findings and evaluations fully effectively with any one language. With all of them, we stand a chance of doing at least a little better job, which the individual on the other side of the desk will interpret in his way by saying that we understand him better.

Finally, I have a practical suggestion to leave with you, and then I shall be ready to conclude my remarks. I think we can understand the person on the other side of the desk somewhat better if we will develop an ability which the old western cowboys carried to a high point of perfection. The experienced western cowboy was able to find a lost horse with uncanny ability. I understand that he did this by working at the job of trying to feel like a horse. He asked himself, "Now what kind of reason would I have for wandering away if I were a horse? With such a reason where would I go?" Apparently, it is possible to empathize with a horse a good deal—to feel like a horse to a surprising degree.

At any rate, the cowboy would imagine that he was a horse, that he had the horse's reason for going, and then he would go to the place he would go if he were a horse—and usually he would find the horse.

I think this is something one is able to work at effectively in trying to help handicapped children. You simply ask yourself, "Now what are the possible reasons for behaving as this child does? If I were the child, what would be my reason for doing what he does? Just what would I be trying to achieve? What would I be trying to avoid?"

You can go from there to ask a lot of questions, such as, "How could I achieve my purposes differently? What other motives could I have? What other effects could I try to achieve, and by what other means? What changes would I have to achieve before I would be able to use other procedures, or work toward other goals?" And so forth.

The next time you see a stutterer holding his breath with all his might when he is supposedly trying to say, "Hello!" see whether you can do what the old cowboys did, and ask yourself, "Why would I hold my breath if I were he?" It is a very simple thing to practice—this thing of trying to get inside the other fellow's skin—and I think that one can develop a great deal of skill in doing it. It is the kind of skill that the child on the other side of the desk will interpret by saying that he feels as though he were being understood. With the risk that a pun always involves, perhaps we might say that it is a skill that the child on the other side of the desk will recognize as horse sense.

Selected annotated references

BENNIS, WARREN G., KENNETH D. BENNE, and ROBERT CHIN, *The Planning of Change* (New York: Holt, Rinehart and Winston, 1961).
This is an excellent collection of readings on the dynamics of change. See especially Strauss's article "Transformations of Identity" and the editors' analysis of "Dynamics of Influence."

BIESTEK, FELIX, *The Casework Relationship* (Chicago: Loyola University Press, 1957).
Biestek attempts to explain, define, and analyze the casework relationship. The attempt, however, gathers a great many things under the umbrella of the relationship.

CARKHUFF, ROBERT B., *The Art of Helping: An Introduction to Life Skills* (Amherst, Mass: Human Resource Development Press, 1973).
An interesting, brief presentation of the effective ingredients of all helping relationships from the experience and research of the author.

CHAIKLIN, HARRIS, "Honesty in Casework Treatment," *Social Welfare Forum, 1973* (New York: Columbia University Press, 1973), pp. 266–74.
Honesty in treatment means that worker and client share themselves and a mutual understanding of treatment and the details of this practice. Examples include the sharing of self, professional information, test information, and notes, and sharing in the creation of the record. Honesty in practice relates to competence.

GITTERMAN, ALEX, and ALICE SCHAEFFER, "The White Professional and the Black Client," *Social Casework* 53:5 (May 1972), pp. 280–91.
The authors attempt to define some of the specific obstacles within the white professional–black client relationship and to make some suggestions for dealing with them. A specific case illustration demonstrates how one worker and one client struggled against the obstacles keeping them apart as separate, distrusting individuals.

HARDMAN, DALE, "The Constructive Use of Authority," *Crime and Delinquency* 6:3 (July 1960), pp. 245–54.
Hardman notes the constructive potential for authority relationships and identifies specific steps the worker in an authority position may take to maximize that potential.

HARDMAN, DALE, "The Matter of Trust," *Crime and Delinquency* 15:2 (April 1969), pp. 203–18.
This article analyzes the counseling use of trust in relation to a variety of theoretical positions. Published literature in the basic source of data.

KEITH-LUCAS, ALAN, *The Giving and Taking of Help* (Chapel Hill: University of North Carolina Press, 1971).
This very helpful little book sets forth in simple, warm language the complex elements of the giving and taking of help. It contains chapters on the helping relationship, the helping factors, and the helping person.

MAHONEY, STANLEY C., *The Art of Helping People Effectively* (New York: Association Press, 1967).
This slim book will be useful to anyone who is in a helping relationship to another. Mahony sees helping as involving acceptance, presence, listening, and information giving.

OVERTON, ALICE, "Establishing the Relationship," *Crime and Delinquency* 11:3 (July 1965), pp. 229–38.
Overton discusses the ingredients necessary to establishing a relationship in settings where the client is not voluntarily seeking help. These ingredients include clarity of purpose, clearly conveying that one has respect for the client, and dealing with resistances on the part of both worker and client.

ROGERS, CARL, "Characteristics of a Helping Relationship," *Canada's Mental Health,* Supplement #27 (March 1962).
Rogers reviews research on the nature of relationship and suggests ten approaches which will facilitate the worker's establishing a relationship.

ROGERS, CARL, "The Therapeutic Relationship: Recent Theory and Research," in *The Human Dialogue* ed. Floyd Matson and Ashley Montagu (New York: Free Press, 1967), pp. 246–59.
The three essential conditions in the therapist's relationship to client growth are: congruence of feelings, thoughts, and communications; unconditional positive regard for the client; and an accurate empathetic understanding of the client.

SINSHEIMER, ROBERT, "The Existential Casework Relationship," *Social Casework* 50:2 (February 1969), pp. 67–73.
Writing from a philosophic base in existential philosophy, Sinsheimer discusses the casework relationship as an attitudinal framework within which the practitioner functions and characterized by love, active caring, acceptance and concern for the other.

VONTRESS, CLEMMONT E., "Racial Differences: Impediments to Rapport," *Journal of Consulting Psychology* 18 (1971), pp. 7–13.
This article discusses the difficulties of establishing and maintaining productive helping relationships across racial lines in our society. Vontress makes suggestions for the training of helpers that may be productive in creating interracial understanding.

OXLE, GENEVIEVE B., "The Caseworker's Expectations in Client Motivation," *Social Casework* 47:7 (July 1966), pp. 432–37.
The importance of expectation and stimulation in client progress is discussed, with particular emphasis on the responsibility of the worker to maintain the expectations of the client somewhat beyond where the client is.

Chapter 5

COMMUNICATION AND INTERVIEWING

Interviewing is a basic social work skill. The interview is the major tool utilized by the social worker to collect data from which to make intervention decisions. While other data collection tools are available to the worker (these will be discussed further in Chapter 8), the interview remains the primary tool and the client the primary source of data. Many social work interventive strategies are also dependent on interviewing, with the interview used as the modality through which strategies directed toward change are applied. Because of the ubiquitousness of interviewing in social work practice, some brief consideration of interviewing and communication is essential in any book purporting to develop a practice model. A number of excellent recent books have appeared on the social work interview,[1] and social work educational programs usually devote considerable time to the development of interviewing skills. We do not intend either to provide a comprehensive treatment of interviewing or to give the student a bag of tricks. Rather, this chapter will introduce the use of social work interviewing as a central tool of social work practice, identify some of the barriers to

---

[1] Alfred Kadushin, *The Social Work Interview* (New York: Columbia University Press, 1972); Margaret Schubert, *Interviewing in Social Work Practice* (New York: Council on Social Work Education, 1971); Annette Garrett, *Interviewing: Its Principles and Methods,* 2d ed., revised by Elinor P. Zaki and Margaret M. Mangold (New York: Family Service Association of America, 1972); Karl and Elizabeth de Schweinitz, *Interviewing in the Social Services* (London: National Institute for Social Work Training, 1962); John Rich, *Interviewing Children and Adolescents* (New York: St. Martin's Press, 1968).

communication, offer ideas concerning the role of the social work interviewer, and, present briefly some techniques we have found useful in the data collection interview. Interviewing skills will continue to be refined and developed throughout a social work career.

COMMUNICATION AND INTERVIEWING

Communication can be defined as an interactional process which gives, receives, and checks out meaning,[2] and occurs when people interact with each other in an effort to transmit messages, receive transmitted messages, and check out meanings. The checkout phase of the communication process is essential and is discussed as an interviewing technique by Robert Brown in the article reproduced in this chapter.[3] A, for example, sends a message to B, which B receives. But how does B know that he has recived the message A intended to send? Perhaps his receptors were faulty, perhaps A's transmitter was faulty, or perhaps there was noise or interference between A and B which distorted the message. B checks out the message with A by indicating what has been received in order to confirm that the message B received was the message A

DIAGRAM 2
The communication process

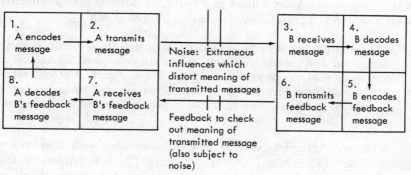

intended to send. (See Diagram 2.) Communication difficulties result when this checkout process is omitted.

The communication theory concepts of encoding, transmitting, receiving, decoding, and noise provide a useful framework for understanding

[2] For a succinct presentation of communication theory as applied to social work practice see Virginia Satir, *Conjoint Family Therapy* (Palo Alto, Calif: Science & Behavior Books, 1964), chaps. 8 and 9.

[3] Robert A. Brown, "Feedback in Family Interviewing," *Social Work* 18:5 (September 1973), pp. 52–59.

problems which may arise in the social work interview. Encoding refers to the process of putting the message to be sent into symbol form in preparation for transmission. Transmitting refers to the process of sending the encoded message; receiving to the process of interpreting the stimuli received; noise to extraneous influences that may have distorted the message when it was on its way from the transmitter to the receiver. Checkout or feedback provides a way of overcoming problems created by noise as well as by inadequate encoding or decoding or faulty transmission or reception.

Communications occur simultaneously on many levels. We can speak of verbal and nonverbal communications or overt and covert communications. Virginia Satir speaks of denotative and metacommunication levels of messages. By the denotative level, she means the literal content of the symbols (usually words). She defines metacommunications as messages about the message; a metacommunication refers to such things as a voice inflection, gestures, manner of speaking, etc., all of which provide additional clues about the meaning of the denotative level of communication.[4] The ability to communicate several messages simultaneously provides opportunity for the famous double bind—the simultaneous transmission of contradictory messages leaving the receiver in a "be damned if I do, be damned if I don't" position.[5]

But what is the meaning of all of this to interviewing in social work? Interviewing can be looked upon as a particular kind of communication. Robert Kahn and Charles Connell define an interview as a

> specialized pattern of verbal interaction—initiated for a specific purpose, focused on some specific content area, with consequent elimination of extraneous material. Moreover, the interview is a pattern of interaction in which the role relationship of interviewer and respondent is highly specialized, its specific characteristics depending somewhat on the purpose and character of the interview.[6]

The social work interview is a set of communications with four special characteristics: (1) it has a context or setting; (2) it is purposeful and directed; (3) it is limited and contractual; and (4) it involves specialized role relationships. The context or setting for the interview will usually be that of a particular agency offering defined services to clients bringing specified problems to the agency. The context, of course, provides a limit to the communications and becomes a basis for the "elimination of extraneous material"—i.e., material not related to the particular con-

---

[4] Satir, *Conjoint Family Therapy*, p. 76.

[5] Gregory Bateson, Don D. Jackson, Jay Haley, and John H. Weakland, "A Note on the Double Bind—1972," *Family Process* 2 (1963), pp. 154–61.

[6] Robert Kahn and Charles Connell, *The Dynamics of Interviewing* (New York: Wiley, 1957), p. 16.

text. Social work interviews are purposeful and directed in the sense that they are conducted to accomplish specific goals (a legitimate purpose may certainly be the definition of the goals of furthering worker-client communications). Conversely, interviews are not casual exchanges of information or informal conversations. The purposes of interviews provide a basis for limiting communications and eliminating extraneous material. Interviews are limited and contractual in the sense that the interviewer and the interviewee come together in a specific context for defined purposes and that their communications are limited to meeting those purposes. And, finally, interviewer and interviewee occupy specialized roles and interact with each other on the basis of those roles. This, again, is a limiting factor inasmuch as client-worker interactions will usually be confined to the expected behaviors of the specialized roles.

To summarize, communication can be viewed as an interactional process involving the giving, receiving, and checking out of meaning; communication occurs on many levels and may not always be congruent. Interviewing is a specialized form of communication which is contextual, purposeful, and limited and which involves specialized role relationships. This chapter focuses on interviewing to secure information which client and worker will use jointly in decision making about the nature of the problem and of intervention. The primary source of data is the client; interviewing techniques are used to encourage the client to share data for joint client-worker use.

Since the data is to be used in decision making about intervention, the social worker must be concerned about the reliability and validity of data collection procedures. The concepts of reliability and validity are defined for an interviewer in social work as they are defined in other scientific and research activity. Reliability refers to the extent to which data collection tools (in this case, the interview) produce consistent information. If different messages are received from the client at different times, the social worker wants to be reasonably certain that the differences reflect actual changes in the client and are not a consequence of the worker's interviewing style; otherwise a reliability problem exists. Validity refers to the extent to which the information being obtained reflects the actual perceptions, thoughts, feelings, and behaviors of the client. If the client is not sharing his actual perceptions, thoughts, feelings, and behaviors, a validity problem exists, the worker will have to adjust the interviewing techniques in order to secure more accurate information. One responsibility of the social worker is to create a climate in which the client is comfortable in sharing valid and reliable information.

The next section considers some potential barriers to communication—barriers which will affect the validity and reliability of our data. In subsequent sections the role of the interviewer will be analyzed and suggestions will be offered which will assist the social work interviewer to increase the probability of securing valid and reliable data.

BARRIERS TO COMMUNICATION

Barriers to communication may occur at any phase in the communication process—encoding, transmitting, receiving, decoding, and checkout. Many of these barriers are obvious—inability to conceptualize and use symbols (encoding problems), speech impediments, hearing or receptor impediments, failure to understand the concepts received (decoding problems), and environmental influences (noise which interferes with the messages or prevents them from traveling clearly from the transmitter to the receiver). While these barriers are real and are of continual concern to the worker desirous of reliable and valid data on which to base decisions, they are also reasonably obvious sources of error in communications. In this section we will consider a series of subtler, less obvious, but equally serious barriers to communication which will affect the validity and reliability of the data on which intervention decisions are based. Six worker barriers and the barrier of client resistance will be considered. Approaches on the part of the worker which may serve as barriers to the collection of valid and reliable data include anticipation of the other, the assumption of meaning, stereotyping, confusion of purpose, the urge to change, and inattentiveness.

The first worker barrier to communication—anticipation of the other—is alluded to by Carl Rogers as follows:

> But what I really dislike in myself is when I can't hear the other person because I'm so sure in advance what he is going to say that I don't listen because it is afterwards that I realize I have only heard what I have already decided he is saying. I have failed really to listen at those times when I can't hear because what he is saying is too threatening, because it might make me change my ideas and my behavior.[7]

The assumption of meaning, a second worker barrier to communication, occurs when a worker receives an ambiguous message, fails to check out its meaning with the client, and proceeds on the basis of a meaning which the worker has read into the client's message. The words themselves may be ambiguous, the way in which they are uttered may convey unclear feelings or thoughts, or the client's behavior may be communicating messages inconsistent with the words. In all of these situations the checkout of meaning with the client may prevent erroneous assumptions

---

[7] Carl Rogers, "Some Personal Learnings about Interpersonal Relationships," filmed lecture produced by Academic Communications Facility, University of California at Los Angeles.

and proceeding on the basis of invalid and unreliable data. An example of assumption of meaning occurs in this brief excerpt from an interview with a 16-year-old boy on parole:

> I asked how things had gone this past week. He looked at me with a grin and said, "Fine." He added that he had not done anything. During this time he kept leafing through the magazine and pointed out someone's picture to me. At this point I told him that we were here to talk and that he should put the magazine away. It is very obvious that this boy knows very little or at least practices few of the common courtesies of everyday living.[8]

This worker assumed from the boy's grin and his leafing through the magazine that he was trying to avoid entering into conversation. The worker, however, erroneously acted on the basis of this assumption without first checking it out with the youngster. A few minutes taken to ask the boy what it was about the magazine that interested him or to make a more direct checkout—"I get the message that you are not too interested in talking with me now"—might have clarified the situation and produced a more reliable and valid basis on which to act.

Worker stereotypes of clients are a third barrier to communication. This barrier relates directly to the problems of classification and categorization discussed in Chapter 3. It exists when clients are seen as members of groups—low income, delinquent, schizophrenic, black, etc.—and action is taken without permitting the client's individuality to transcend to stereotype of his group. Stereotyping leads to the two previous problems—anticipating the other and assumptions of meaning occur because of stereotypes held by workers. Stereotyping can be very subtle; after experience with several similar clients, workers may note similarities on the basis of which they begin to develop a stereotype of that particular kind of client. The stereotype then interferes with the worker's perceptions of new clients and may well serve to block out communications inconsistent with it.

Failure on the part of the worker to make explicit the purpose of an interview may lead to a condition in which the worker and client hold differing, perhaps contradictory, purposes. Given such confusion of purpose, both client and worker will then interpret their own and each other's communications in light of their particular understanding of the objective of the interview. As these subtle distortions continue, the client and the worker will be going in two entirely different directions.

One of the more serious barriers to communication, arises from prematurely urging clients to change. This is a very easy pitfall for the social worker. *Change* is a common word in the profession; by and large,

---

[8] Student interview, University of Iowa, School of Social Work, 1966.

social workers are committed to being change agents, both to improve the conditions of the community and to assist individuals to utilize the resources of the community more effectively. Difficulties occur, however, when change efforts are attempted without sufficient data on which to base an assessment of the problem. Although change may occur through any human interaction, effecting change is not the primary purpose of the data collection interview—change efforts should be based on valid and reliable data and on a considered decision of the client and worker to engage in such efforts. The purpose of the data collection interview is to gather the information on which decisions about intervention can be based. To urge change at this early stage may create a barrier to communication—a barrier which limits the availability of important information that could influence decision making. A secondary problem is that change efforts in these early contacts frequently take the form of directive approaches—such as persuasion and advising—which are seldom effective until a high degree of trust has been developed and which, used prematurely, create barriers to continuing communication. And it is the process of continuing communication which provides opportunities for the development of increased trust.

A very potent worker barrier to communication is inattentiveness. A worker whose mind wanders during an interview, who is thinking about other clients or planning future activities, creates barriers for continued client-worker communication. Clients can reasonably expect the worker to give undivided attention to their present communications, and the worker has a responsibility for establishing a time frame that will enable him to attend to other matters that require attention without diverting attention from the interview of the moment.

As workers learn to avoid anticipating what the client will say, to check out the meanings of the communications received, to avoid stereotyping, to clarify purposes, to avoid attempts at change until the necessary data is available and change decisions can be made jointly, and to give all clients opportunities for undivided attention, the likelihood of securing reasonably valid and reliable information should be enhanced considerably. But clients may also create barriers to communication. These barriers may be thought of as resistances on their part against entering into a problem-solving process. Resistance may be considered as a specialized kind of defense utilized by the client to ward off the worker and to protect himself from any discomfort involved in participating in a problem-solving process.

Three sources of resistance can be distinguished. Resistance may stem from the usual discomfort of dealing with a strange person and situation. Essentially this is a "normal" anxiety and discomfort with which many of us approach new situations. Second, resistance may stem from cultural and subcultural norms regarding involvement with service agencies and asking for help. Norman Johnston, for example, identifies a number of variables in the prison milieu which contribute to distortion and deception in the communications between inmates and prison counselors.[9] Because of cultural norms, some persons may find it particularly difficult, to admit the existence of a problem and to seek a solution. Agencies may exacerbate such cultural differences by establishing procedures which intensify the discomfort of persons of certain cultural backgrounds. An agency emphasis on scheduled appointments and office visits, for example, may aggravate the resistance of clients from lower socioeconomic groups and hamper their ability to utilize more traditional social service agencies. Finally, some clients may be securing a degree of gratification from their problems. This type of pathological involvement with a problem is a serious source of resistance, which interferes with the client's ability to communicate and makes seeking a solution more difficult.

What is the worker's responsibility in relation to client resistance? To facilitate communication, the worker may need to help the client identify and deal with any of these obstacles to communication. Dealing with obstacles to communication will become a necessary preliminary goal before the client and worker can move into any other problem-solving work. Dealing with resistances is one manifestation of the worker's second task as conceptualized by Schwartz in the article appearing in Chapter 1—"the task of detecting and challenging the obstacles which obscure common ground."

RESPONSIBILITIES OF THE WORKER

What are the social worker's responsibilities in the data collection interview? They can be conceptualized in three interrelated areas. First, social workers are responsible for creating a productive climate in which the client can comfortably participate and in which the client—the primary source of data—will share the thoughts, feelings, and perceptions necessary for intervention decisions. The climate should help secure valid and reliable data. To a large extent, the creation of such a climate involves the worker's skill in avoiding the worker barriers to communication noted earlier and in helping clients to deal with the obstacles to communication presented by their own resistances. The creation of a productive climate for participation might be construed as synonymous with the development of a helping relationship. In Chapter 4 we referred to relationship as a climate or an atmosphere and suggested strongly that relationship is not the end of service but a stepping-stone

---

[9] Norman Johnston, "Sources of Distortion and Deception in Prison Interviewing," *Federal Probation* 20:1 (January 1956), pp. 43–48.

toward the provision of problem-solving service for the client. One way to operationalize the concept of relationship is to define it as a climate or milieu which is characterized by open and verbal communications. Thus the presence of relationship might be inferred from the extent to which communications are open and verbal. Creating this kind of climate is a basic responsibility of the worker, a responsibility which is met primarily by the nature of his communications and interactions with clients.

A second major responsibility of the worker is to provide a focus for the interview. This occurs by establishing a purpose for the interview very early and focusing the interactions in relation to the purpose. Tangents should be avoided; questions that lead into extraneous areas are not helpful; and the worker, when pursuing what the client has said, should pick up on areas related to the interview's central focus. Focusing the interview does not mean dictating the purpose, nor does it mean cutting off the client; it does mean, however, jointly establishing with the client a particular purpose for an interview and fulfilling the responsibility of maintaining that focus. Material brought out in a particular interview may suggest a purpose and focus for subsequent interviews; the worker may deliberately not respond to this material initially but may bring it up later. Aaron Rosen and Dina Lieberman report on an experimental study of the extent to which workers' responses are content relevant—"the extent to which the content of an interactive response is perceived by a participant to be relevant to, and in agreement with, his own definition and expectations of the content to be dealt with in the treatment relationship."[10] With compliant clients, workers with more training did significantly better at maintaining content relevance. Workers with less training had more content-relevant response with aggressive clients; however, many of the responses were harsh and retaliatory and thus perhaps ineffective in helping. Rosen and Lieberman suggest that their findings point to the need for clear worker and client orientation as to the purpose of the interview.[11] A clear purpose may assist the worker in keeping the interview focused, although this is apparently difficult with an aggressive client.

A third major responsibility of the worker is to separate and identify the client's levels of response. Responses are typically on one of four levels—perceptual, cognitive, feeling, and behavioral. The perceptual level of response refers to interactions and communications around what the client perceives or has perceived—what was seen and heard. The cognitive level refers to interactions and communications around what

---

[10] Aaron Rosen and Dina Lieberman, "The Experimental Evaluation of Interview Performance of Social Workers," *Social Service Review* 46:3 (September 1972), p. 398.

[11] Ibid., pp. 410–11.

the client thinks—what meaning he ascribes to what was seen and heard. The feeling, or affective, level refers to interactions and communications around the feelings that were generated in the client by either his perceptions or his cognitions—how the client feels about what was thought or about what was seen and heard. And the behavioral level refers to interactions and communications around either the client's past behavior or his anticipated behavior—how the client behaved and how he might behave in relation to what was and will be seen and heard. It is possible to interact with clients at all these levels. For data collection, however, a thorough exploration of the perceptual and cognitive levels is necessary before moving into the feeling and behavioral levels.

Perhaps an example will clarify this responsibility. Put yourself in the position of the worker whose client is a 16-year-old boy who has frequent arguments with his father and angrily left the house and drove off in a neighbor's car after a recent argument. In discussing this situation, the youth will probably initiate the conversation on the cognitive level—with some comment to the effect that he and his dad do not get along, that his dad does not understand him, or that his dad is unfair. These are all cognitive statements: they reflect a meaning or interpretation which the youngster has placed on perceived events. A frequent interviewing error is to simply accept the meaning which the client has reported and to move immediately into the areas of feelings and behavior. However, a careful prior exploration with the client of his perceptions of the events which led to this interpretation that his father and he do not get along will be very useful. What took place? What did the boy see and hear? What did his father say? What did the boy say? What happened then? After exploring the incidents in detail, the client-worker are prepared to consider alternative interpretations of the events. After moving back to the perceptual level (What did you see and hear?) and reconsidering the cognitive level (What meanings do you ascribe to what you saw and heard?), the client-worker may then move legitimately to the question of feelings. (What did you feel when this was occurring? Do I still detect a note of anger in your voice? As you look back on it now, what kinds of reactions are you having?) And from the feeling level the next logical step is to behavior. (What did you do when this happened? As you look back, what might have been other ways of handling yourself? In view of such experiences, if you and your father have future arguments, what are ways in which you think you might behave?) Before moving into a consideration of the client's feelings and behavior, considerable effort is expended to collect from him an account of the incidents that occurred and his interpretation of those incidents. Failure to explore the perceptual and cognitive levels in detail may lead to very incomplete data with which to engage the client in problem-solving plans.

To sum up, the worker has three primary responsibilities in the interview—creating a productive climate, focusing the interview, and separating and clarifying levels of response.

While the purpose of this chapter is not to offer a bag of tricks or to deal at any length with interviewing techniques, a few suggestions may help the reader to make a start in building a repertoire of interviewing methods for creating a productive climate, focusing the interview, and separating levels of response.

SOME IDEAS ABOUT TECHNIQUE

Open-ended questions are useful, especially in early phases of an interview or a subpart of an interview.[12] An open-ended question is one that cannot be answered yes or no—one that requires an essay-type answer. Questions such as "Tell me a little about yourself" or "What would you like us to do?" are extremely open-ended. Open-ended questions are good questions to start with because they allow the client considerable leeway in beginning where he wishes. If the client fumbles, the worker can come back with a much more focused question. Diagram 3 illustrates several open-ended responses that permit the interviewer to focus the interview and invite additional participation from clients. An interview can be thought of as a funnel—starting with very broad, open-ended questions that become much more specific and focused as worker and client narrow in on specific areas of concern.

The interviewer attempting to secure data on which to base interventive decisions must become adept at probing for additional information. *Probing* may be an unfortunate word—the intent is not to indicate an abrasiveness or harshness but rather an invitation to pursue a particular area. Questions such as "Can you tell me more about that?" or "I'd like to hear a little more in this area" are both open-ended and probing inasmuch as they are related to something the client has said and are asking for more information. Diagram 3 illustrates a wide number of probing questions which are nonabrasive and which both invite the client to continue to express himself and enable the worker to provide direction to the interview.

The data collection interview requires that the worker maintain neutrality and carefully avoid biasing questions. While we may joke about the "You do love your wife, don't you?" kind of question, biases creep in in subtler ways. The requirement of neutrality does not negate our earlier remarks about worker input. The purpose of the data collection interview is to secure reliable and valid information about the client's perceptions and interpretations of his experiences; worker input at this

---

[12] For a very good discussion of open-ended questions see Stanley Payne, *The Art of Asking Questions* (Princeton, N.J.: Princeton University Press, 1951), chap. 3.

DIAGRAM 3
Interviewing responses[13]

The hypothetical situation I will use is one you will meet many times as a counselor. A client will say, "I don't get along with my parents." Here are numerous responses which can be used to fulfill the two important requirements of interviewing: (1) allowing the client to express feelings, and (2) helping you to direct the interview.

—You don't get along with your parents.
—Your parents?
—What do you mean when you say. . . .
—I don't understand what you mean when you say. . . .
—Help me understand what you mean. . . .
—Give me an example of how you. . . .
—Tell me more about this.
—Uh-huh.   —and   —For instance?   —Go on.
—Oh?   —but   —I see.
—When did you first notice that. . . .
—How do you feel about this? (Perhaps the most important question one could ask.)
—What are some of the things you and your parents disagree about?
—What are some problems kids like you have—not just you but all kids in general?
—What are your parents like? What is your dad like? What is your mom like? (General questions.)
—You seem to be very upset about this.
—You look worried (or you look unhappy).
—(Avoid asking a question which calls for a yes or no answer.)
—(Just be silent. A word about silence. In patients and particularly in adolescents, silence tends to provoke anxiety. Silence generally loses its effect if too prolonged.)
—You say you have trouble getting along with your parents. What are some of your troubles?
—Perhaps you could share some of your ideas about what has caused these problems.
—(It probably never helps to ask the question why. If they knew why they were having trouble with their parents, they wouldn't be seeing you.)
—Maybe it would help to talk about this.
—Compared to you, what type of people are your parents?
—If your parents were here, what would they say about this problem?

stage would have a biasing effect and should be avoided. First the worker learns the client's position and thinking, and then he may consider offering his own experience to the client. The sharing of worker input comes when various intervention strategies are under consideration.

Throughout this chapter frequent references have been made to checkout. Checkout requires the use of feedback in which the worker consciously and deliberately reflects back to the client what the worker is perceiving in order to determine whether the communication is correct. This is what I hear you saying. Or, I seem to be hearing this. Or, I see you're doing this. Or, am I understanding what you are saying in this? These are all feedback probes and are an effort to refer back to the client what the worker is hearing in order to allow the client to correct any errors in meaning. Feedback is a very useful and necessary technique for clarifying communications. While it may sometimes seem

[13] This material was developed by Dr. Richard J. Bealka, psychiatrist, Mental Health Institute, Independence, Iowa.

awkward, because we seldom employ this technique in everyday activity, reflecting back to the client what we are seeing and hearing can avoid both pitfalls and misunderstandings and also serves the function of encouraging the client to pursue conversation in a particular area. Rosen and Lieberman examined the use of feedback among workers of different levels of training. They used the concept of stimulus-response-congruence—"the extent to which a response by one participant in the relationship provides feedback to the other participant that the message he sent was actually received"[14]—and found that trained workers maintained a lower rate of incongruent responses than untrained workers.[15] This finding suggests that the use of feedback is a skill acquired by training and helps explain an initial awkwardness with its use.

One final suggestion for enhancing communication is to avoid asking why. *Why* is a frequently used word in our language. But the "why" question is basically defense producing—it is a question that asks a person to explain his behavior. Social workers, by and large, are not interested in asking clients to explain their behavior but are interested in asking them to describe the situation in which they are behaving and to explore alternative ways of interpreting and reacting to that situation. Such questions as, What was happening then? What seemed to be going on? Can you tell me what you were doing? and What seemed to be the nature of the situation? are much more likely to elicit material which can be used constructively with the client in problem solving.

RECAPITULATION

In this chapter we have tried to establish a number of points. Interviewing for data collection purposes can be regarded as a set of communications which the social worker uses to secure valid and reliable data from the client concerning the client's perceptions, and, perhaps, the feelings the client attaches to both perceptions and meanings. The process involves giving, receiving, and checking out meanings. The client is the primary source of the data on which decisions concerning problem solving are based; thus social work interviewing techniques must be considered in terms of whether or not they contribute to the climate in which the client can share reliable and valid data. The reliability and validity of data may be impaired by six worker barriers to communication—anticipation of what the other is going to say, assumptions of meaning about communications from the other, stereotyping, inexplicit purposes for the interview, premature efforts to produce change, and inattentiveness. The quality of the data may also be affected by resis-

---

[14] Rosen and Lieberman, "Evaluation of Interview Performance," p. 398.
[15] Ibid., p. 409.

tances stemming from the client's hesitancy to enter into strange situations, cultural norms affecting his ability to enter into problem solving, and his pathological involvement with the problem. The social worker collecting data has the primary responsibility for creating a climate in which the client can participate productively, for providing a focus, and for securing data on the perceptual and cognitive levels as well as on the affective and behavioral levels. Open-ended questions, probing, neutrality, extensive use of feedback, and avoiding "why" questions are all useful interviewing approaches to data collection.

One final note. We regard interviewing as a disciplined art. But does discipline interfere with spontaneity? Does learning interviewing techniques make the interviewer mechanical and nonhuman? We think not. Learning interviewing techniques may increase the social worker's spontaneity for two reasons. First, in the process of learning about interviewing the social worker becomes aware of and able to deal with barriers to communication in his usual responses to people. Second, interviewing techniques expand the repertoire of responses available to the worker. The increased repertoire permits increased spontaneity because the worker is not locked into an earlier, limited set of responses. Alfred Kadushin expresses this last point eloquently:

> The interviewer should, of course, be the master of the techniques rather than the obedient servant bound by rules. Technical skill is not antithetical to spontaneity. In fact, it permits a higher form of spontaneity; the skilled interviewer can deliberately violate the techniques as the occasion demands. Technical skill frees the interviewer in responding as a fellow human being to the interviewee. Errors in relation to technique lie with rigid, and therefore inappropriate, application. A good knowledge of techniques makes the interviewer aware of a greater variety of alternatives. Awareness and command of technical knowledge also has another advantage. To know is to be prepared; to be prepared is to experience reduced anxiety; to reduce anxiety is to increase the interviewer's freedom to be fully responsive to the interviewee.[16]

In Chapter 4 we noted that the graceful figure skater could not become spontaneous and "free" without many hours of disciplined practice. So it is with interviewing. Spontaneity and freedom do not come naturally but with discipline, with practice, and with learning.

A LOOK FORWARD

The two articles reproduced in this chapter further explore two themes which have already been established. Robert A. Brown reports on a research project studying the use of feedback with the client system—especially in family interviewing—and finds feedback to be a use-

---

[16] Kadushin, *Social Work Interview*, p. 2.

ful technique. We have not specifically discussed interviewing across racial or cultural barriers. Drawing on several research projects, Alfred Kadushin discusses the racial factor in the interview. He notes that the question is not, Can a white worker communicate with a black client? but, How can such contact be established? The communication principles discussed in this chapter assume increased importance as the social, racial, or ethnic gulfs between worker and client increase.

In the next chapter the problem-solving model is outlined. Later chapters will elaborate phases of the model. The material on knowledge, values, relationship, and interviewing provides a necessary prerequisite for problem solving.

*Feedback in family interviewing**

Robert A. Brown

Social work interviews are complex transactions that may provide clues to understanding change in clients. Bartlett, Briar, Greenwood, and Gordon suggest that the interview process should be investigated so that elements of professional practice may be identified.[1] Whereas counseling was once characterized by free association and nondirective techniques, it now includes such constructs as aggressive intervention, confrontation, and feedback. For many years social workers did not provide specific information to clients about themselves. However, this is not characteristic of contemporary practice.

The concept of feedback is not well defined as it applies to interviews. Feedback may be communicated both verbally and nonverbally. In its simplest form, it represents one person's attempt to communicate information to another. Although the information may be provided surreptitiously through questions or inferential statements, its most direct form is the declarative statement. When a social worker uses a declara-

* Reprinted with permission of the author and the National Association of Social Workers from *Social Work*, 18:5 (September 1973), pp. 52–59.
[1] Harriett Bartlett, "The Place and Use of Knowledge in Social Work Practice," *Social Work*, 9 (July 1964), p. 40; Scott Briar, "The Casework Predicament," *Social Work*, 13 (January 1968), p. 10; Ernest Greenwood, "Research on the Clarification of Casework Concepts: A Review of and Commentary on the Nolan Study," p. 67, unpublished manuscript, University of California at Berkeley, 1965; and William Gordon, "A Critique of the Working Definition," *Social Work*, 7 (October 1962), p. 11.

tive statement to communicate information concerning the client with whom he is interacting at the moment, he is using a specialized form of feedback. Because this occurs repeatedly in social work interviews, the process should be more clearly understood.

The author calls this type of feedback "ascription." Because it occurs repeatedly and should therefore be under the conscious control of the interviewer, it should be considered an interviewing technique. With this in mind some important questions are raised: to what extent is feedback sanctioned by current theories of social work practice? What information is provided and how is it received by clients? When does the technique appear to work? In this article the author discusses the various applications of ascription utilized by the major social work theorists and describes a research project that identified ascriptive statements made by social workers in interviews and their clients' responses.[2]

The author defines "technique" as one of the many specific acts each participant in a relationship uses to accomplish his purposes. "Client system," as he defines it, includes the interfacing of biological, psychological, and social systems within the individual client, as well as the similar interfacings of individuals who are related to the client and each other through a family system. Thus a client system may comprise one or many persons.

"Ascription" is the act of attributing or imputing a characteristic to someone.[3] For the purposes of this article, the characteristic ascribed may be any one that the social worker perceives in the client and communicates to him. It may refer to physical, psychological, or social attributes of an individual or a group, including their relationships. It may have a socially positive or negative meaning and it may refer to the past, present, or future. The only criterion is that the statement clearly impute something to the client with whom the worker is interacting in the interview. For instance, a worker may say to a client "You look depressed" or tell a family "You have been having fun together."

This definition of ascription includes interpretations given to clients but also something more. Whereas interpretations bring "an alternative frame of reference to bear on a set of observations or behaviors with an end in view of making them more amenable to manipulation," ascriptions may also reinforce an existing frame of reference in the client.[4] For example, a simple statement of agreement ("Yes, you are right!")

---

[2] Findings are reported in greater detail in Robert A. Brown, "The Technique of Ascription," Unpublished doctoral dissertation, University of Southern California, 1971.

[3] C. L. Barnhart, ed., *The American College Dictionary* (New York: Random House, 1964), p. 73.

[4] Leon H. Levy, *Psychological Interpretation* (New York: Holt, Rinehart & Winston, 1963), p. 7.

or of support ("You certainly handled that well!") may seek to reinforce the client's own interpretation.

The author defines an "ascriptive episode" as that part of the interview which begins with an ascriptive statement, spoken by a social worker, and ends with a shift away from the ascribed characteristic. In most instances the episode includes a client's responses to the ascription.

Social work theories

All the major theorists in social casework, social group work, family treatment, and combined practice include provisions for workers to offer their observations, discoveries, and conclusions to clients.

Social casework. In Hollis's framework, the purpose of such statements is to help clients reflect on themselves and their environmental situation (e.g., "I have a feeling that you may be afraid I will criticize you.").[5] Perlman uses ascriptive comments that may reflect the client's feelings and offer interpretations or support to maximize the client's participation in the problem-solving process.[6] Other casework theorists use ascription to interpret the client's behavior in the treatment relationship,[7] to point out recurrent behavioral patterns,[8] or to help clients achieve valid ego identities.

Social group work. Social group work theorists have tended to focus on the social workers' actions and goals that precipitate change in clients. Ascriptions are used by Northen principally to enhance the client's perception of reality by calling attention to an emotion so that an integration of cognitive and affective components within the client may be promoted.[10] However, ascriptions also lend themselves to other aspects of the social worker's role, such as providing support, improving communication, enhancing competence, and modifying the environment.[11]

[5] Florence Hollis, *Casework: A Psychosocial Therapy* (New York: Random House, 1964), pp. 71–75, 91–93, and 104–6; and Hollis, "Crisis-Focused Casework in a Child Guidance Clinic," *Social Casework*, 49 (January 1968), p. 41.

[6] Helen Harris Perlman, *Social Casework: A Problem-Solving Process* (Chicago: University of Chicago Press, 1957), p. 159.

[7] Herbert H. Aptekar, *The Dynamics of Casework and Counseling* (New York: Riverside Press, 1955), p. 236.

[8] Alice Ullman and Milton Davis, "Assessing the Medical Patient's Motivation and Ability to Work," *Social Casework*, 46 (April 1965), p. 201; and Ann W. Shyne, "An Experimental Study of Casework Methods," *Social Casework*, 46 (November 1965), pp. 535–41.

[9] Elizabeth Meier, "Interactions between the Person and His Operational Situation: A Basis for Classification in Casework," *Social Casework*, 46 (November 1965), p. 547; and Herbert S. Strean, "Casework with Ego-Fragmented Parents," *Social Casework*, 49 (April 1968), p. 226.

[10] Helen Northen, *Social Work with Groups* (New York: Columbia University Press, 1969), p. 73.

[11] Ibid., pp. 52–85.

Schwartz uses ascriptions to present the client's problem to him in a new form.[12] Ascriptions may be used in all the worker's tasks (e.g., to detect and challenge the obstacles that obscure and frustrate the client).[13]

Phillips limits ascription to providing information clients could not provide themselves. Her purpose is to enhance the client's sense of his relation to others through a shared experience.[14] The interview itself, which is a shared experience, offers the best perspective for ascriptive statements because it is immediately accessible to all the participants.

Vinter uses ascription to modify the behavior of group members. In his framework ascriptive statements are made by workers who act as "spokesmen of norms" and "stimulators of potentials."[15] The purpose of Konopka's use of ascription is to individualize and enhance the social functioning of group members as well as the entire group. She would probably stress the worker's dynamic, conscious use of himself while implementing an interview technique and would use only ascriptive statements that have socially positive implications.[16]

Family treatment. Theorists of family treatment, such as Overton and Tinker, utilize ascriptive statements as "shared observations." These observations focus empathically on the behavioral indicators, both positive and negative, that constitute the reason for a professional investment in the family. The purpose of these observations is to bring about a change-oriented partnership of the worker and the family. From this perspective, most ascriptive statements would be directed toward the family-as-a-whole rather than individual family members.[17]

Satir stresses two roles for the worker: a model of communication and a resource person who provides a family with impartial information

[12] William Schwartz, "Group Work and the Social Scene," *Issues in American Social Work* (New York: Columbia University Press, 1959), pp. 134–135; and Schwartz, "Toward a Strategy of Group Work Practice," *Social Service Review,* 36 (September 1962), pp. 268–79.

[13] William Schwartz, "The Social Worker in the Group," *The Social Welfare Forum, 1961* (New York: Columbia University Press, 1961), pp. 157–158.

[14] Helen U. Phillips, *Essentials of Social Group Work Skill* (New York: Association Press, 1957), pp. 93, 133–34, and 149–53.

[15] Robert D. Vinter, "Approach to Group Work Practice" and "The Essential Components of Social Group Work Practice," in Vinter, ed., *Readings in Group Work Practice* (Ann Arbor, Mich.: Campus Publishers, 1967), pp. 3 and 26, respectively.

[16] Gisela Konopka, *Social Group Work: A Helping Process* (Englewood Cliffs, N.J.: Prentice-Hall, 1963), pp. 163–171. This represents a shift in thinking from Konopka's earlier position that only the client may draw interpretations. For further details see Konopka, *Group Work in the Institution* (New York: William Morrow & Co., 1954), p. 123; and Konopka, "Social Group Work: A Social Work Method," *Social Work,* 5 (October 1960), p. 59.

[17] Alice Overton and Katherine Tinker, *Casework Notebook* (St. Paul, Minn.: Greater St. Paul Community Chest & Councils, 1957), pp. 39–40.

about itself.[18] Others in family treatment use ascriptive statements to confront clients with their inconsistencies,[19] to challenge individual family members,[20] or to draw attention to transactonal family patterns.[21]
Combined practice. Smalley's and Polansky's theories relate to combined practice with individuals and groups. Smalley uses ascription for the purpose of enhancing a client's psychological growth through the worker's frank expression of his own understanding.[22] Polansky notes that a client's willingness to communicate is partially dependent on the worker's skill in receiving a client's communication.[23] Use of ascriptions may be considered one such skill.

Thus one may see that in some form ascription is sanctioned by all major social work theorists. These theorists agree that experiences shared by workers and clients result in self-awareness and changes in behavioral patterns in clients. They differ regarding the worker's role in providing these experiences and the purposes behind his actions. That is, most theoreticians provide for ascriptive statements that vary in their degree of directness, ranging, for instance, from reflective consideration to aggressive intervention.

Although theories of social work are descriptive of practice situations, they do not suggest how ascriptions produce change in clients. Buckley has proposed a systemic model of interaction that emphasizes the client's learning of symbols and the exchange of information in client-system functioning.[24] From Buckley's model it may be concluded that ascriptive statements produce change in two ways: as instruments of communication and as feedback to client systems.

[18] Virginia M. Satir, *Conjoint Family Therapy: A Guide to Theory and Technique* (Palo Alto, Calif.: Science and Behavior Books, 1964), p. 97; and Satir, "Conjoint Family Therapy," in Bernard L. Green, ed., *The Psychotherapies of Marital Disharmony* (New York: Free Press, 1965), pp. 132–33.

[19] David Hallowitz, Ralph Bierman et al., "The Assertive Counseling Component of Therapy," *Social Casework*, 48 (November 1967), p. 546.

[20] Robert M. Nadal, "Interviewing Style and Foster Parents' Verbal Accessibility," *Child Welfare*, 46 (April 1967), p. 211.

[21] Donald R. Bardill, "A Relationship-Focused Approach to Marital Problems," *Social Work*, 11 (July 1966), p. 76; Murray H. Sherman, Nathan Ackerman, Stanford N. Sherman, and Celia Mitchell, "Non-Verbal Cue and Reenactment of Conflict in Family Therapy," *Family Process*, 4 (March 1965), pp. 133–62; Rae B. Weiner, "Adolescent Problems: Symptoms of Family Dysfunctioning," *Social Casework*, 47 (une 1966), pp. 373–77; Frances H. Scherz, "Multiple-Client Interviewing: Treatment Interpretations," *Social Casework*, 43 (March 1962), pp. 234–40; and Arthur Leader, "The Role of Intervention in Family-Group Treatment," *Social Casework*, 45 (June 1964), p. 328.

[22] Ruth E. Smalley, *Theory for Social Work Practice* (New York: Columbia University Press, 1967), pp. 130 and 139.

[23] Norman A. Polansky, "The Concept of Verbal Accessibility," *Smith College Studies in Social Work*, 36 (October 1956), pp. 4–6.

[24] Walter Buckley, *Sociology and the Modern Systems Theory* (Englewood Cliffs, N.J.: Prentice-Hall, 1967).

As instruments of communication or statements in a conversation, ascriptions represent an opportunity for social workers and clients to achieve a "common mapping of the environment" or an exchange of information that alters the cognitive organization and hence the concept of self and the environment of both the client and worker.[25] They are not labels with which clients must wrestle, but statements in conversation that generate new understanding for everyone. Consider, for example, what happens when a client rejects an ascription with: "No, in fact I feel rather good."

Research design

In research conducted by the author between September 1969 and December 1970, tape-recorded interviews with families were used to identify selected statements made by social workers and to note clients' responses. Twenty fieldwork instructors from schools of social work in the Los Angeles metropolitan area agreed to tape-record a one-hour interview with a family. This was both a random sample and a universal survey of instructors conducting family interviews who were willing to participate.

Characteristics of social workers in the sample were compared with characteristics of an NASW membership survey.[26] The sample was biased in favor of interviews conducted by social workers in private practice, in psychiatric services, or in family services other than public services. Characteristics of social workers in the sample and in the NASW survey were not otherwise significantly different.

Characteristics of the clients in the sample did not differ significantly from a Los Angeles County population survey with respect to ethnic backgrounds; however, clients in the sample had greater social position and status than had been assumed. Thus, except for the biasing factors noted, the interviews that were studied were typical of all social work family interviews.

A total of 526 ascriptions were identified in 20 one-hour interviews. Each example was analyzed by the researcher and two other judges through the use of questionnaires, completed by the workers.[27] Descriptive and evaluative data were gathered that related to the purpose for

---

[25] Ibid., p. 124.

[26] See Alfred M. Stamm, "NASW Membership: Characteristics, Deployment, and Salaries," *Personnel Information*, 12 (Mary 1969), p. 1.

[27] The .05 level of significance was required to reject the null hypothesis. Findings reported here were at or well beyond this level. In many instances, alternative probability models were used to confirm findings. The criterion level of .02 determined reliability of judgments.

which each statement was made, its content, various factors related to the communication process, and the client's reactions. A linguistic analysis of selected phrases and words used by clients and workers during ascription was done by computer.

All social workers in the sample used ascriptive statements, which indicates that the technique is used extensively. The average number of ascriptive statements used in each interview was 26. However, the frequency of use was subject to great variation among the workers.[28]

Of a total of 526 statements, 85 percent stimulated immediate verbal responses from clients. Thus one may conclude that the ascriptive episode was an experience shared by participants in the interviews and from which a mutual view of the environment could result. What type of experience was it? Apparently it focused on the individual at the time of the interview.

Instruments of communication

Although these were family interviews, workers tended to focus on individual members instead of the family-as-a-whole or some subgroup. Most ascriptive statements (83 percent) were addressed only to one person and relatively few (17 percent) to subgroups. Therefore, the "shared experiences" were primarily experiences shared by a social worker and one family member while other members observed or shared the experiences in a secondary way.

It is the author's impression that few ascriptive statements stimulated an overt dialogue among family members. This finding is in contrast to Overton's and Tinker's concept of the worker's partnership with the family-as-a-whole and suggests that workers may be overlooking one method of increasing family interaction by not addressing ascriptive statements to the entire family. The author believes that if a substantial number of ascriptions were directed to the family-as-a-whole, a sense of relationship would increase among family members. For example, consider the difference between the worker stating: "You missed her message" and "That message got lost between you."

It is also interesting to note that 52 percent of the ascriptive statements related to what had just occurred in the interview (e.g., "You seemed angry just then."). This supports Phillips's belief that the present offers the best perspective for enhancing a sense of relationship through shared experiences. However, if the purpose of an ascription is to provide feedback, clients are more likely to evaluate critically the ascribed characteristic when it is expressed in a universal time reference (e.g., "You spend a great deal of time being angry.").

---

[28] Range: 1–51; standard deviation: 12.7.

If the goal is to enhance a sense of relationship or to achieve a common mapping of the environment, the worker should project himself, as a real person, into the interview. Yet, ascriptions contained few statements that specifically included the worker (e.g., "You seem to me . . ."). In effect, clients were asked to consider ascribed characteristics as characteristics by themselves, not as the perceptions of a worker. The author believes that these statements should be clearly identified as the interviewer's perceptions.

The frequency with which social workers and clients use common symbols is a measure of the extent to which they share a common environment. The workers referred to others by name (noun or pronoun) twice as frequently as they did to themselves ("I, me"), and they referred to themselves in singular form seven times more frequently than in plural form. When a social worker refers to himself and his clients together, calling attention to "us," "our," or "we," he is focusing on their mutual relationship in treatment and, in effect, is mapping a common environment.

The extent to which ascriptive statements lend structure to an interview is another indication of how "shared" the experience really is. Using the number of ideas contained in the statements and clients' responses as a measure, ascriptive episodes were found to be rather simple instruments of communication that provided little overall structure to the interview. Most such statements (69 percent) and most responses of clients (57 percent) contained no more than two distinct ideas.

A client's opportunity to respond is another indication of structure in the interview. Workers gave clients an opportunity to respond to 85 percent of the ascriptive statements. However, when clients were blocked from responding, the worker's activity was the most apparent cause. Generally, this activity consisted of the worker oververbalizing or otherwise diverting the client's attention from the ascribed characteristic.

Feedback to client systems

The second major way in which ascriptions produce change is as feedback to systems. In feedback the worker gives clients specific pieces of information about themselves. Feedback produces change because the ascribed characteristic turns experience of the individual or the family group back on itself, producing a symbol of the individual or the family. This "organized self" represents a learned set of attitudes the individual and the family members maintain about themselves and their environment.

Self-consciousness and self-control are mechanisms of feedback that are internal to the client system. Ascriptions represent feedback that is external to the system. If they are understood and accepted by the client, ascriptions become a part of the client's self-consciousness. To be accepted by a client, an ascription must in some way relate to his goals and must meet criteria he sets.[29]

The feedback provided in ascriptive statements reflects the fundamental concern of the social work profession for relationships between people. However, an analysis of selected phrases spoken by social workers and clients during ascriptive episodes indicates that although both workers and clients focused on a discussion behavior, workers expressed relatively more interest in the clients' relationships than did the clients themselves.

A classification of the observed ascriptive statements is presented in Table 1. Relationship statements—the most frequently observed

TABLE 1
Types of ascriptive statements

Type of statement	Number	Percent
Relationship	164	31.2
Behavior	117	22.2
Feeling	105	20.0
Value	72	13.7
Other	68	12.9
Total	526	100.0

type—included statements such as "You and your mother argue about things" and "You were beginning to say you wished something different from her." Behavior-oriented statements included "You are talking about your mother and she is sitting next to you" and "You said you try not to give way to yelling quite so much." Feeling statements included "You noticed him getting scared" and "I think what you want is for him to feel more cheerful." Value statements included "I think we should keep on working on this last thing" and "I think we will have to think about the good start he has made and not get lost." Other ascriptive statements referred to cognition, environment, agreement, and disagreement.

Although the author recognizes that agreement can be communicated without using words, such as nodding, it was thought that verbal feedback expressing agreement would be used by workers (e.g., "Yes, you are right!"). However, no examples were identified in the data. It is believed that this type of feedback is an important facet of bringing about change in clients. Thus if workers did not use ascription to express

---

[29] Buckley, op. cit., p. 174.

agreement, what were their motives? As Table 2 shows, the principal reasons for use of ascription were to improve the client's perceptions of reality and to improve communication with the client.

TABLE 2
Social workers' judgments of their purpose in making ascriptive statements[a]

Purpose of statement	Number	Percent
To improve the client's perception of reality	239	46.05
To improve communication with the client	161	31.02
To help the client achieve competence in his actions	59	11.37
To support the client	54	10.40
To use environmental resources	6	1.16
Total	519[b]	100.00

[a] Assuming an equal probability of occurrence among the categories, the probability associated with the observed frequencies in each category was beyond the p = .0000 level.
[b] The remaining seven statements were not classified in this framework.

It is of interest to note that the purpose of 90 percent of the ascriptive statements was to produce change and only 10 percent to support clients. Providing supportive information, such as bringing out the client's strengths, is surely a viable facet of producing change. Intuitively, at least, it would seem to warrant proportionally greater use than was revealed in these data.

What evidence is there that clients are involved in the feedback process? Evaluation by the judges indicated that 82 percent of the ascriptive statements were perceived and 80 percent were considered by clients, but only 46 percent were critically evaluated. This suggests that workers may need to redirect their clients' attention to the ascribed characteristic and to ask them to evaluate it. This was rarely done among the sample tested.

In general, clients used profitably those statements they considered but did not evaluate. They used them, for example, as a point of departure to another subject or to be woven into another overriding thought. The judges found that 62 percent of the ascriptions that were evaluated were accepted and only 9 percent were clearly rejected by clients. They further found that children rarely evaluated ascriptions critically, whereas adults, especially men, did. Some questions are raised, therefore, concerning the effect of ascriptions on children. Together, these data indicate that about half the ascriptive statements were used by clients in a meaningful way. To the author's knowledge, there are no other research findings available that indicate whether a 50 percent level is cause for alarm, indifference, or celebration.

The judges agreed that ascriptions were most helpful when they were expressed clearly, simply, and directly and when workers explained that the statements were their perceptions, not objective facts. Ascriptions were helpful when their expression reflected a sensitive awareness of the client, when they were not judgmental, and when they permitted responses from the client. They were also helpful when their content related to the client's feelings, behaviors, or central problem area or to the communication process within the family or the interview.

Conclusion

In this article some facets of the feedback process have been examined as they apply to social work interviews with families. Feedback is sanctioned by theories of practice and is widely used by social workers. The information given to clients reflects the profession's concern with human relationships. However, because its use is undisciplined, many opportunities are missed to use the process more effectively. If the worker considers the feedback process as an interview technique, he might bring its use under conscious control. For instance, before using an ascription, he should know whether his purpose is to increase a sense of relatedness or to provide needed information, or both. Used as a technique, ascriptions can produce changes if they bring the worker and client together in a way that is dynamic and meaningful to both.

The racial factor in the interview*

Alfred Kadushin

Ethnicity, broadly speaking, means membership in a group that is differentiated on the basis of some distinctive characteristic which may be cultural, religious, linguistic or racial. The nonwhite experience in America is sufficiently differentiated so that race can be regarded as a specific kind of ethnicity. Although the term nonwhite includes Mexican-Americans, American Indians, orientals, and blacks, this article on the racial factor in the interview is almost exclusively concerned with black-white differences, not only because blacks are the largest single nonwhite minority, but because most of the descriptive, clinical, and experimental literature concerned with this problem focuses on blacks.

The black client often presents the interviewer with the problem of socioeconomic background as well as differences in racial experience.

* Reprinted with permission of the author and the National Association of Social Workers from *Social Work*, 17:3, (May 1972), pp. 88–98.

Although the largest number of poor people are white, a disproportionate percentage of the black population is poor. Hence the racial barrier between the white worker and black client is frequently complicated further by the class barrier—white middle-class worker and black lower-class client. However, the exclusive concern here is with the racial factor, i.e., the differences that stem from the experiences in living white and living black.

The problem

Racial difference between worker and client is an ethnic factor that creates problems in the relationship and the interview. Understanding and empathy are crucial ingredients for an effective interview. But how can the white worker imagine what it is like for the black client to live day after day in a society that grudgingly, half-heartedly, and belatedly accords him the self-respect, dignity, and acceptance that are his right as a person or, more often, refuses outright to grant them to him? How can the worker know what it is like to live on intimate terms with early rejection, discrimination, harassment, and exploitation?

A relaxed atmosphere and comfortable interaction are required for a good interview. But how can this be achieved when the black client feels accusatory and hostile as the oppressed and the white worker feels anxious and guilty about his complicity with the oppressor? In such a situation the black client would tend to resort to concealment and disguise and respond with discretion or "accommodation" behavior.[1] Concealment and "putting the white man on" have been institutionalized as a way of life—they are necessary weapons for survival, but antithetical to the requirements of an effective interview. Often the black client openly refuses to share, as expressed in the following poem, "Impasse," by Langston Hughes:

> I could tell you,
> If I wanted to,
> What makes me
> What I am.
>
> But I don't
> Really want to—
> And you don't
> Give a damn.[2]

---

[1] Thelma Duvinage, "Accommodation Attitudes of Negroes to White Caseworkers and Their Influence on Casework," *Smith College Studies in Social Work*, Vol. 9, No. 3 (March 1939), p. 264.

[2] Copyright © 1967 by Arna Bontemps and George Huston Bass from *The Panther and the Lash*. Reprinted by permission of Alfred A. Knopf, Inc.

The attitude toward permeability of the racial barrier for the social work interview has changed over the last twenty years. In 1950 Brown attempted to assess the importance of the racial factor in the casework relationship by distributing questionnaires to social agencies in Seattle, Washington.[3] Eighty percent of the practitioners responded that the racial factor did intrude in the relationship, but it was not much of a problem for the experienced worker with some self-awareness.

By 1970 blacks' disillusionment with the integrationist stance and a greater accentuation on their special separate identity from the white culture and the unique effects of their historical experience resulted in frequently repeated assertions that no white could understand what is meant to be black. Consequently, it is said, an effective interview with a black client requires a black interviewer. Many who have studied this problem, although not ready to go this far, generally concede that currently the racial barrier in the interview makes rapport and understanding much more difficult than was previously imagined.[4]

Obviously people who share similar backgrounds, values, experiences, and problems are more likely to feel comfortable with and understand each other. In sociology the principles of homophyly (people who are alike like each other) and homogamy (like marries like) express these feelings. Synanon, Alcoholics Anonymous, and denominational agencies are organizational expressions of this idea.

Social workers tend to follow the same principles by selecting for continuing service those clients who are most like themselves and subtly discouraging or overtly rejecting those "who cannot effectively use the service." The rich research literature about differential access to mental health services by different class groups tends to confirm that this is a euphemism for people who are different from "us."

There is similar research with regard to agency selectivity relating to race. For example, a study of patients seen for ten or more individual psychotherapy interviews at a metropolitan psychiatric outpatient clinic found that "Caucasian women were seen proportionally longest, followed

---

[3] Luna B. Brown, "Race as a Factor in Establishing a Casework Relationship," *Social Casework,* Vol. 31, No. 3 (March 1950), pp. 91–97.

[4] See, for example, George P. Banks, "The Effects of Race on One-to-One Helping Interviews," *Social Science Review,* Vol. 45, No. 2 (June 1971), pp. 137–46; Dorcas Bowles, "Making Casework Relevant to Black People: Approaches, Techniques, Theoretical Implications," *Child Welfare,* Vol. 48, No. 8 (October 1969), pp. 468–75; Marylou Kincaid, "Identity and Therapy in the Black Community," *Personnel and Guidance Journal,* Vol. 47, No. 9 (May 1969), pp. 884–90; Jean Gochros, "Recognition and Use of Anger in Negro Clients," *Social Work,* Vol. 11, No. 1 (January 1966), pp. 28–38; Clemmont Vontross, "Counseling Blacks," *Personnel and Guidance Journal,* Vol. 48, No. 9 (May 1970), pp. 713–719; Vontross, "Cultural Barriers in Counseling Relationships," *Personnel and Guidance Journal,* Vol. 48, No. 1 (September 1969), pp. 11–16; and Vontross, "Racial Differences— Impediments to Rapport," *Journal of Counseling Psychology,* Vol. 18, No. 1 (January 1971), pp. 7–13.

by Caucasian men.[5] Racial minority group patients had proportionately fewer contacts—black males had the lowest number of interviews. Non-whites not only had fewer contacts, but their attrition rate was higher. All therapists, including psychiatric social workers, were Caucasian. Therapist ethnocentricity was measured with the Bogardus Social Distance Scale. Those who scored low in ethnocentrism were more likely to see black patients for six or more interviews; those who scored high treated black patients for this length of time much less often. (Differences were statistically significant.) Worker ethnocentrism may help account for the higher attrition rate of black clients who apply for social services. It is certainly true for black clients in family service agencies and black applicants for adoption.[6]

But the following statement by a black mental health worker, retrospectively analyzing her own personal experience, indicates that a therapeutic relationship with a white person, although difficult, is possible:

> In answering the question of whether a white middle-class psychiatrist can treat a black family, I cannot help but think back over my own experiences. When I first came to New York and decided to go into psychotherapy I had two main thoughts: (1) that my problems were culturally determined, and (2) that they were related to my Catholic upbringing. I had grown up in an environment in which the Catholic Church had tremendous influence. With these factors in mind, I began to think in terms of the kind of therapist I could best relate to. In addition to being warm and sensitive, he had to be black and Catholic. Needless to say, that was like looking for a needle in a haystack. But after inquiring around, I was finally referred to a black Catholic psychiatrist.
>
>   . . . he turned out to be not so sensitive and not so warm. I terminated my treatment with him and began to see another therapist who was warm, friendly, sensitive, understanding, and very much involved with me. Interestingly enough, he was neither black nor Catholic. As a result of that personal experience, I have come to believe that it is not so much a question of whether the therapist is black or white but whether he is competent, warm, and understanding. Feelings, after all, are neither black nor white.[7]

Thus the question of whether a white worker can establish contact with a black client is more correctly stated as "How can such contact be established?"

---

[5] Joe Yamamoto et al., "Factors in Patient Selection," *American Journal of Psychiatry*, Vol. 124, No. 5 (November 1967), pp. 630–36.

[6] See "Non-White Families Are Frequent Applicants for Family Service," *Family Service Highlights*, Vol. 25, No. 5 (May 1964), pp. 140–44; and Trudy Bradley, *An Exploration of Caseworkers' Perceptions of Adoptive Applicants* (New York: Child Welfare League of America, 1966).

[7] As quoted in Clifford J. Sager, Thomas L. Brayboy, and Barbara R. Waxenberg, *Black Ghetto Family in Therapy—A Laboratory Experience* (New York: Grove Press, 1970), pp. 210–11.

White worker–black client

What can be done to ease the real difficulties inherent in white worker–black client cross-racial integration? Because the white worker is initially regarded as a potential enemy, he should carefully observe all tʰᵉ formalities that are overt indications of respect—e.g., start the interview promptly, use Mr. and Mrs. rather than the client's surname or first name, shake hands and introduce himself, listen seriously and sincerely. Rituals and forms are not empty gestures to people who have consistently been denied the elementary symbols of civility and courtesy.

Discussions about racism have left every white with the uneasy suspicion that as a child of his culture he has imbibed prejudices in a thousand different subtle ways in repeated small doses and that the symptoms of his racism, although masked to himself, are readily apparent to a black person. These suspicions may be true. Thus a worker must frankly acknowledge to himself that he may have racist attitudes and make the effort to change. To paraphrase a Chinese maxim: The prospective white interviewer who says, "Other white interviewers are fools for being prejudiced, and when I am an interviewer I will not be such a fool," is already a fool.

To conduct a good interview, the worker must be relatively confident that he knows his subject matter. But how can he feel confident if he is aware that there is much about the black experience he does not and cannot know? Certainly he can dispel some of his ignorance by reading about and becoming familiar with black history, black culture, and black thinking and feeling. This is his professional responsibility. When a worker lacks knowledge about the client's situation, he appears "innocent." Thus he is less respected, more likely to be "conned," and less likely to be a source of influence.

The white worker may find it helpful to be explicitly aware of his reactions to racial differences. In making restitution for his felt or suspected racism, he may be overindulgent. He may oversimplify the client's problems and attribute certain behavior to racial differences that should be ascribed to personal malfunctioning. When color is exploited as a defensive rationalization, race is a weapon. Burns points out that black children "have learned how to manipulate the guilt feelings of their white workers for their own ends. They have also learned to exploit the conceptions most white workers have about the anger of black people."[8]

In interracial casework interviews the participants are keenly aware of the difference between them. Yet they rarely discuss the racial factor

---

[8] Crawford E. Burns, "White Staff, Black Children: Is There a Problem?" *Child Welfare*, Vol. 50, No. 2 (February 1971), p. 93.

openly.[9] It is not clear whether this is because race is considered irrelevant to the work that needs to be done or because both participants agree to a conspiracy of silence about a potentially touchy issue. Nevertheless, race—like any other significant factor that contaminates interaction—must be at least tentatively discussed because to be "color-blind" is to deny real differences.[10]

The presumption of ignorance, necessary in all interviews, is more necessary when interviewing a black client because the worker is more likely to be ignorant of the client's situation. Therefore, he must listen more carefully, be less ready to come to conclusions, and be more open to having his presuppositions corrected by the client, i.e., he must want to know what the situation is and be receptive to being taught.

It is frequently asserted that lower-class black clients lack the fluency and facility with language that are required for a good interview. Yet studies of speech behavior in the ghetto suggest that blacks show great imaginativeness and skill with language.[11] Thus the worker has the obligation to learn the special language of the ghetto. The agency can help by hiring black clerical and professional staff. If the black client sees members of his own group working at the agency, he has a greater sense of assurance that he will be accepted and understood.

Black worker–black client

If both worker and client are black, different problems may arise. The pervasiveness of the cultural definition of blackness does affect the black client. Thus he may feel that being assigned to a black worker is less desirable than being assigned to a white worker because the latter may have more influence and thus be in a better position to help him.

The fact that the black social worker has achieved middle-class professional status suggests that he has accepted some of the principal mores of the dominant culture—e.g., motivation to achieve, denial of gratification, the work ethic, punctuality. To get where he is, he probably was educated in white schools, read the white literature, and associated with white classmates—as he now associates with white colleagues.

The black middle-class worker may feel estranged not only from

[9] See Roger Miller, "Student Research Perspectives on Race," *Smith College Studies in Social Work,* Vol. 41, No. 1 (November 1970), pp. 1–23; and Michele Seligman, "The Interracial Casework Relationship," *Smith College Studies in Social Work,* Vol. 39, No. 1 (November 1968), p. 84.

[10] Julia Bloch, "The White Worker and the Negro Client in Psychotherapy," *Social Work,* Vol. 13, No. 2 (April 1968), pp. 36–42.

[11] See, for example, Thomas Kochman, "Rapping in the Black Ghetto," *Transaction,* Vol. 6, No. 4 (February 1969), pp. 26–34.

whites but from his own blackness. The problem of establishing a clearly defined identification is more difficult for "oreos"—those who are black on the outside, but white on the inside because of their experiences while achieving middle-class status.

The black worker who returns to the ghetto after professional training may be viewed with suspicion.[12] An alien returning from the outside world, where he has been "worked over" by the educational enterprise to accept white assumptions, values, and language, he has supposedly lost contact with the fast-changing ghetto subculture in the interim.

If the black client sees the white worker as representing the enemy, he may see the black social worker as a traitor to his race, a collaborator with the establishment. Therefore, barriers to self-disclosure and openness may be as great between the black worker and black client as between the white worker and black client.

The black client is also a source of anxiety to the black worker in other ways. A black psychiatrist stated it as follows: "For the therapist who has fought his way out of the ghetto [the black patient] may awaken memories and fears he would prefer to leave undisturbed."[13] Thus Brown's findings that black workers were less sympathetic to black clients than to white clients is not surprising.[14] They were made anxious by black clients' failure to live up to the standards of the dominant culture and felt that such deviations reflected on the race as a whole— thus decreasing the acceptability of all blacks, including themselves.

Calnek aptly defines overidentification in this context as a "felt bond with another black person who is seen as an extension of oneself because of a common racial experience."[15] A black AFDC client described it as follows: "Sometimes the ones that have had hard times don't make you feel good. They're always telling you how hard *they* had to work— making you feel low and bad because you haven't done what they done."[16] The black worker also may be the target of displacement, i.e., the black client's hostility toward whites is expressed toward the black worker because he is less dangerous.

One clear advantage in the black worker–black client situation, however, is that the black professional provides the client with a positive

---

[12] Orville Townsend, "Vocational Rehabilitation and the Black Counselor: The Conventional Training Situation and the Battleground Across Town," *Journal of Rehabilitation,* Vol. 36, No. 6 (November–December 1970), pp. 26–31.

[13] As quoted in Sugar, Brayboy, and Waxenberg, op. cit., p. 228.

[14] Brown, op. cit.

[15] Maynard Calnek, "Racial Factors in the Counter-Transference: The Black Therapist and the Black Client," *American Journal of Orthopsychiatry,* Vol. 40, No. 1 (January 1970), p. 42.

[16] As quoted in Hugh McIsaac and Harold Wilkinson, "Clients Talk About Their Caseworkers," *Public Welfare,* Vol. 23, No. 2 (July 1965), p. 153.

image he can identify with. Kincaid states that "a Black counselor who has not rejected his own personal history may be most able to inspire a feeling of confidence and a sense of hope in his Black client."[17]

When the worker is black and the client is white, other problems may arise. The client may be reluctant to concede that the black worker is competent and may feel he has been assigned second best. If the client is from the South, he may be especially sensitive to the reversal in usual status positions.[18]

If the client sees himself as lacking prejudice, he may welcome being assigned to a black worker because it gives him a chance to parade his atypical feelings. He may be gratified to have a black worker since only an unusually accomplished black could, in his view, achieve professional standing. On the other hand, because the white who turns to a social agency for help often feels inadequate and inferior, he may more easily establish a positive identification with the "exploited" and "oppressed" black worker.[19]

Matching

Any discussion of the problems inherent in cross-cultural interviewing inevitably leads to the question of matching. On the whole, would it not be desirable to select a worker of the same race as the client? Would this not reduce social distance and the resistance and constraints in interactions that derive from differences in group affiliation, experiences, and life-style? If empathic understanding is a necessary prerequisite for establishing a good relationship, would this not be enhanced by matching people who are culturally at home with each other?

Obviously, empathic understanding is most easily achieved if the worker shares the client's world. However, the difficulties of empathic understanding across subcultural barriers can be exaggerated and the disadvantages of matching worker and client can be underestimated.

The world's literature is a testimonial to the fact that people can understand and empathize with those whose backgrounds and living situation are different from their own. For example, an American Christian, John Hersey, demonstrated empathic understanding of a Polish Jew in *The Wall;* an American Jew, Elliot Liebow, demonstrated his ability to understand ghetto blacks in *Tally's Corner;* and a white South

---

[17] Kincaid, op. cit., p. 888.

[18] Andrew D. Curry, "Negro Worker and White Client: A Commentary on the Treatment Relationship," *Social Casework,* Vol. 45, No. 3 (March 1964), pp. 131–36.

[19] William Grier, "When the Therapist Is Negro: Some Effects on the Treatment Process," *American Journal of Psychiatry,* Vol. 123, No. 12 (June 1967), pp. 1587–92.

African psychiatrist, Wulf Sachs, showed his sensitive understanding of a Zulu in *Black Hamlet*.[20]

If the worker's professional training enhances his ability to empathize with and understand different groups and provides the knowledge base for such understanding, the social and psychological distance between worker and client can be reduced. If the gap is sufficiently reduced, the client perceives the worker as being capable of understanding him, even though he is a product of a different life experience.

Some of the relative merits and disadvantages of close matching and distant matching are succinctly summarized in the following statement by Carson and Heine: "With very high similarity the therapist may be unable to maintain suitable distance and objectivity, whereas in the case of great dissimilarity he would not be able to empathize with, or understand, the patient's problems."[21] Thus it is not surprising that relevant research suggests effective interviewing is not linearly related to rapport, i.e., it is not true that the more rapport, the better. The relationship appears to be curvilinear, i.e., little rapport is undesirable, but so is maximum rapport. The best combination is moderate closeness or moderate distance between participants. Weiss, in a study of the validity of responses of a group of welfare mothers, found that socially desirable rather than valid responses were more likely to result under conditions of high similarity and high rapport.[22]

Clinical evidence also suggests that racial matching is not always a crucial variable in the interview. A study that tested the degree of distortion in responses to black and white psychiatrists by patients in a county psychiatric ward concluded that "the factor of race did not significantly affect the behavior of the subjects in the interview situation."[23] The patients perceived and responded to black psychiatrists as psychiatrists rather than as members of a different race. In a California study AFDC recipients were asked to assess the help they received

[20] New York: Alfred A. Knopf, 1950; and Boston: Little, Brown & Co., 1967 and 1947, respectively.

[21] R. C. Carson and R. W. Heine, "Similarity and Success in Therapeutic Dyads," *Journal of Consulting Psychology*, Vol. 26, No. 1 (February 1962), p. 38.

[22] Carol H. Weiss, *Validity of Interview Responses of Welfare Mothers—Final Report* (New York: Bureau of Applied Social Research, Columbia University, February 1968). See also Herbert H. Hyman, *Interviewing in Social Research* (Chicago: University of Chicago Press, 1954); Barbara S. Dohrenwend, J. A. Williams, and Carol H. Weiss, "Interviewer Biasing Effects, Toward a Reconciliation of Findings," *Public Opinion Quarterly*, Vol. 33, No. 1 (Spring 1969), pp. 121–29; and Dohrenwend, John Colombotos, and B. P. Dohrenwend, "Social Distance and Interviewer Effects," *Public Opinion Quarterly*, Vol. 32, No. 3 (Fall 1968), pp. 410–22.

[23] William M. Womack, "Negro Interviewers and White Patients: The Question of Confidentiality and Trust," *Archives of General Psychiatry*, Vol. 16, No. 6 (June 1967), p. 690.

from their caseworkers. The study group was large enough so that black and white caseworkers were able to contact both black and white recipients. The general conclusion was that the "race of the worker, per se, did not make a significant contribution to the amount of 'help' recipients received from the social service."[24]

Paraprofessionals

The shortcomings of matching have become more apparent as a result of experience with indigenous paraprofessionals in the human services. In efforts to find new careers for the poor during the last few years, many social agencies have hired case aides from the area they serve. These indigenous case aides live in the same neighborhood as the client group, generally have the same racial background, and often struggle with the same kinds of problems. Therefore, they are in an excellent position to empathize with and understand the problems of the poor, blacks, and poor blacks—and in fact they often do.

In a study of agency executives' and supervisors' evaluations of paraprofessional performance, it was found that these workers were rated high on their ability to establish rapport with clients. One agency administrator described this ability as follows:

> In intake interviewing, paraprofessionals are very good at picking up clues and cues from the clients. They have a good ear for false leads and "put-ons." Their maturity and accumulated life experience, combined with firsthand knowledge of the client population, assists the agency in establishing communication with clients rapidly. . . . The new client is more comfortable with a paraprofessional because he or she is someone like himself.[25]

Riessman, however, notes the following difficulties:

> Frequently professionals assume that NP's [nonprofessionals] identify with the poor and possess great warmth and feeling for the neighborhood of their origin. While many NP's exhibit some of these characteristics, they simultaneously possess a number of other characteristics. Often, they see themselves as quite different from the other members of the poor community, whom they may view with pity, annoyance, or anger. Moreover, there are many different "types" of nonprofessionals; some are earthy, some are tough, some are angry, some are surprisingly articu-

---

[24] *California Welfare: A Legislative Program for Reform* (Sacramento: Assembly Office of Research, California Legislature, February 1969), p. 10.

[25] Karolyn Gould, *Where Do We Go From Here?—A Study of the Roads and Roadblocks to Career Mobility for Paraprofessionals Working in Human Service Agencies* (New York: National Committee on Employment of Youth, 1969), pp. 5–6.

late, some are sick, clever wheeler-dealers, and nearly all are greatly concerned about their new roles and their relationship to professionals.[26]

Much of the research on nonprofessionals confirms the fact that with close matching, the problems of overidentification and activation or reactivation of problems faced by the worker are similar to those that concern the client. The client, feeling a deep rapport with the worker and anxious to maintain his friendship, may give responses that he thinks will make him more acceptable. He has an investment in the relationship and does not want to risk it by saying or doing anything that would alienate the worker.

If the effects of matching are not invariably advantageous, the effects of difference in cultural background between worker and client are not always disadvantageous. The problem that is created when a worker is identified with one subculture (e.g., sex, race, age, color, or class) and the client is affiliated with another is one specific aspect of in-group–out-group relations generally. The worker, because of his higher status, may encourage communication from the client. In addition, because he is an outsider, he does not reflect in-group judgments. If the client has violated or disagrees with in-group values, this is an advantage. Currently, for instance, a middle-class white-oriented accommodative black client might find it more difficult to talk to a black worker than a white worker.

If the client with upwardly mobile aspirations is looking for sources of identification outside his own group, contact with a nonmatched worker is desirable. Thus the lower-class client, anxious to learn middle-class ways, would seek such a worker. The fact that the worker does not initially understand him may be helpful. In trying to make his situation clear, the client may be forced to look at it more explicitly than before—i.e., in explaining it to an outsider, he may explain it better to himself. Further, the client may feel that the white worker has more influence in the community. Thus he may feel more hopeful.

In contrast, however, numerous studies indicate that in most instances some disadvantages derive from racial difference between interviewer and interviewee.[27] With white interviewers blacks are more likely to

---

[26] Frank Riessman, "Strategies and Suggestions for Training Nonprofessionals," in Bernard Guerney, ed., *Psychotherapeutic Agents—New Roles for Nonprofessionals, Parents and Teachers* (New York: Holt, Rinehart & Winston, 1969), p. 154. See also Charles Grosser, "Manpower Development Programs," and Gertrude Goldberg, "Nonprofessionals in the Human Services," in Grosser, William Henry, and James Kelly, eds., *Nonprofessionals in the Human Services* (San Francisco, Calif.: Jossey-Bass, 1969); and Francine Sobey, *The Nonprofessional Revolution in Mental Health* (New York: Columbia University Press, 1970).

[27] See, for example, Jerome A. Sattler, "Racial 'Experimenter Effects' in Experimentation, Testing, Interviewing and Psychotherapy," *Psychological Bulletin*, Vol. 73, No. 2 (February 1970), pp. 137–60.

make acceptable public responses; with black interviewers they give more private answers. For example, blacks are less ready to share their feelings about discrimination with white interviewers. Carkhuff, in a study in which black and white therapists from middle- and lower-class backgrounds interviewed white and black patients from various class backgrounds, found that both class background and race affected the readiness with which patients shared intimate material. They were most open to therapists of similar race and class.[28]

Client preference

Research on client preference does not uniformly support the contention that clients invariably select professionals from their own group. Dubey, for example, offers empirical support for the contention that blacks do not overwhelmingly prefer black workers.[29] Using black interviewers, he asked some five hundred ghetto residents questions such as "Would you rather talk with a Negro social worker or with a white social worker?" and "Would you rather go to an agency where the director is Negro or to one where the director is white?" About 78 percent of the respondents said they had no preference. Only 10–11 percent said they strongly preferred a black worker or agency director.

Backner encountered this problem over a three-year period as a counselor in the City College of New York's SEEK program, established to help high school graduates from poverty areas with problems encountered in college.[30] Eighty percent of the students in the program were black and 15 percent were Puerto Rican. Backner was constantly admonished by students that "a white counselor can never really understand the black experience" and that "no black brother or black sister is really going to talk to whitey." However, the results of a questionnaire completed by about half of the 325 students in the program tended to substantiate the staff's impression that although the students responded negatively to white counselors in general, they reacted differently to their own white counselors. One item asked, "What quality in your counselor would make you feel most comfortable?" Only 12.7 percent of the respondents said that a counselor of the same racial background

---

[28] Robert R. Carkhuff and Richard Pierce, "Differential Effects of Therapist's Race and Social Class Upon Patient Depth of Self-Exploration in the Initial Clinical Interview," *Journal of Consulting Psychology*, Vol. 31, No. 6 (December 1967), pp. 632–34. See also Eugene C. Bryant, Isaac Gardner, and Morton Goldman, "References on Racial Attitudes as Affected by Interviewers of Different Ethnic Groups," *Journal of Social Psychology*, Vol. 70, No. 1 (October 1966), pp. 95–100.

[29] Sumati Dubey, "Blacks' Preference for Black Professionals, Businessmen and Religious Leaders," *Public Opinion Quarterly*, Vol. 34, No. 1 (Spring 1970), pp. 113–16.

[30] Burton L. Backner, "Counseling Black Students: Any Place for Whitey?" *Journal of Higher Education*, Vol. 41, No. 8 (November 1970), pp. 630–37.

was the most important consideration. In response to the question, "Which SEEK teachers, counselors, and tutors are most effective and helpful to you?" 4.9 percent of the students checked "teacher, counselor, or student with the same ethnic and racial background," whereas 42 percent checked "those whose ability as teachers, counselors, tutors seems good."

In a subsequent survey of all SEEK students, using a mail questionnaire that was completed anonymously and returned by 45 percent of the students, the relevant question was, "Your own counselor's ethnic background (a) should be the same as yours, (b) doesn't matter." Although 25.3 percent of the respondents answered that their counselors should have the same background, 68.4 percent said it did not matter. Subsequent studies indicated that when a student felt ethnicity was important, he was often expressing his feelings about the counselor as a person rather than a white person. However, in another study in which respondents had the opportunity to view racially different counselors via video tapes in a standard interview based on a script, blacks selected black counselors and whites selected whites.[31]

Brieland showed that client preference was dependent on certain conditions.[32] Black and white social work students asked black ghetto residents the following question: "If both were equally good, would you prefer that the (doctor, caseworker, teacher, lawyer, parents' group leader) be Negro (Black, Colored) or White?" One interesting result demonstrated the important effects of similarity or dissimilarity between interviewer–interviewee pairs. The white interviewers had a significantly larger percentage of respondents who said they had no preference as compared with black interviewers to whom respondents confessed they preferred a black doctor, caseworker, teacher, and so forth. However, only 55 percent of the respondents interviewed by black interviewers said they preferred a black caseworker, and 45 percent had no preference or preferred a white caseworker. The basis for respondents' preference for a black caseworker, other factors being equal, was that a black interviewer was more likely to be interested in his problems, less likely to talk down to him or make him feel worthless, more likely to give him a feeling of hope, and more likely to know the meaning of poverty.

A second question, which introduced the factor of competence, asked the respondent to state his preference for a black or white worker if the white worker was better qualified. A large percentage of those who preferred "equally good" black caseworkers preferred a white caseworker

[31] Richard J. Stranges and Anthony C. Riccio, "Counselee Preferences for Counselors: Some Implications for Counselor Education," *Counselor Education and Supervision*, Vol. 10, No. 3 (Fall 1970), pp. 39–45.

[32] Donald Brieland, "Black Identity and the Helping Person," *Children*, Vol. 16, No. 5 (September–October 1969), pp. 170–76.

if his qualifications were better. Competence, then, proved to be more important than race in determining black respondents' caseworker preferences.

Barrett's and Perlmutter's study of black clients' responses to black and white counselors at the Philadelphia Opportunities Industrialization Center—which offers training, placement, and vocational guidance services—supports Brieland's findings.[33] Although black clients preferred black counselors in the abstract (the interviewers in the study were black), actual ongoing client-counselor contact indicated that competence was a more crucial and significant variable than race. However, Barrett and Perlmutter suggest that the importance of matching may be greater when the problems discussed focus on personal concerns rather than on concrete services and when the client initially contacts the agency.

Conclusion

After making the usual cautious provisos about the contradictory nature of the findings, the tentativeness of conclusions, the deficiencies in methodology, the dangers of extrapolation, and so forth, what do all these findings seem to say? They seem to say that although nonwhite workers may be necessary for nonwhite clients in some instances and therapeutically desirable in others, white workers can work and have worked effectively with nonwhite clients. They seem to say that although race is important, the nature of the interpersonal relationship established between two people is more important than skin color and that although there are disadvantages to racially mixed worker-client contacts, there are special advantages. Conversely, there are special advantages to racial similarity and there are countervailing disadvantages. In other words, the problem is not as clear cut as might be supposed.

Not only is the situation equivocal, it is complex. To talk in terms of white and nonwhite is to simplify dichotomously a variegated situation that includes many kinds of whites and nonwhites. For example, interview interaction with a lower-class black male militant is quite different from interview interaction with a middle-class female black integrationist.

Findings like the ones reviewed here are understandably resisted, resented, and likely to be rejected because of the political implications that can be drawn from them. Nonwhite community leaders, in fighting for control of social service institutions in their communities, point to the special advantages to community residents of nonwhite staff and administration. Some studies tend to suggest that the need for nonwhite

---

[33] Franklin T. Barrett and Felice Perlmutter, "Black Clients and White Workers: A Report from the Field," *Child Welfare*, Vol. 50, No. 1 (January 1972), pp. 19–24.

staff and administration is not that urgent. However, this ignores the current underrepresentation in social agencies of nonwhite workers and administrators, the clear preference of some nonwhite clients for a worker of similar racial background, the fact that many clients need workers of similar racial background as sources of identification for change, and the fact that although white workers may be able to understand and empathize with the nonwhite experience, nonwhite workers achieve this sooner, more thoroughly, and at less cost to the relationship.

Selected annotated references

ARCAYA, JOSE, "The Multiple Realities Inherent in Probation Counseling," *Federal Probation* 37:4 (December 1973), pp. 58–63.
Arcaya analyzes the multiple realities of the probation officer–probationer relationship in four areas—relevant features in the situation, conflicts, ways the conflicts are handled, and suggested approaches to mitigate the conflicts. The mitigating approaches include active listening, responsive talking, and contextualization of language.

BENJAMIN, ALFRED, *The Helping Interview* (New York: Houghton Mifflin, 1969).
This small paperback is a profoundly simple treatment of the helping interview that social workers use every day. It treats the interview as a serious and purposeful conversation between two people. Our students tell us that they find this one of the most helpful books they read as they begin fieldwork.

DUNCAN, STARKEY, JR., "Nonverbal Communication," *Psychological Bulletin* 72:2 (1969), pp. 118–37.
Duncan reviews research concerning the role of nonlanguage behaviors in communication.

GARRETT, ANNETTE, *Interviewing: Its Principles and Methods* (2 ed., revised by Elinor P. Zaki and Margaret M. Mangold) (New York: Family Service Association of America, 1972).
This is a revision of a classic in social work literature. Much of the revision lies in the updating of the case examples. The book has two sections, the first dealing with the art of interviewing and the second consisting of case examples.

HARTMAN, HENRY L., "Interviewing Techniques in Probation and Parole," *Federal Probation* 27:1–4 (March, June, September, and December 1968).
This series of four articles analyzes steps a probation worker might take to establish a relationship and maximize communication with clients in an authority setting.

ITTELSON, WILLIAM, and HADLEY CANTRIL, "Perception: A Transactional Approach," in *The Human Dialogue*, ed. Floyd Matson and Ashley Montagu (New York: Free Press, 1967), pp. 207–13.
The three major characteristics of perception are that it occurs as part of a total transaction, that it is unique, and that it is as much an externalization as an internalization.

JOHNSTON, NORMAN, "Sources of Distortion and Deception in Prison Interviewing," *Federal Probation* 20:1 (January 1956), pp. 43–48.

The general attitudes of the prison community, the dehumanizing process of reporting for an interview, the frequent officiousness of the interviewers, the emotionally unrewarding nature of the prison environment, and the cultural gap between the professionals and the inmates are identified as variables which may create distortion and deception in information secured by professionals from inmates in a prison setting.

KADUSHIN, ALFRED, *The Social Work Interview* (New York: Columbia University Press, 1972).

This book describes the general art of interviewing as it is practiced by social workers in social agencies. It deals with the general definition and purpose of the social work interview, analyzes the interview in terms of its elements, and introduces the special factors of class, race, sex, and age for consideration.

MULLEN, EDWARD, "Casework Communication," *Social Casework* 49:9 (December 1968), pp. 546–51.

Mullen reports the results of a research study using a typology of casework responses developed by Hollis and summarizes other research.

PAYNE, STANLEY, *The Art of Asking Questions* (Princeton, N.J.: Princeton University Press, 1951).

Payne describes the formulation of various kinds of questions in reference to the development of questionnaires. Chapter 3, which deals with the open-ended question, offers useful suggesions for the interviewer.

PFOUTS, JANE H., and GORDON H. RADER, "Influence of Interviewer Characteristics on the Interview," *Social Casework* 43:10 (December 1962), pp. 548–52.

This is a study of diagnostic interviews conducted with 71 patients by 31 fourth-year medical students as part of their rotating clerkship in the Department of Psychiatry at the University of North Carolina Medical School. The most significant finding was that regardless of the social class or the age of the patients, they tended to equate warmth of the doctor with self-assurance, sensitivity, and competence. Patients tended to rate highest the students whose judgment and understanding they felt they could trust and whose actions suggested that they could help them do something about their problems.

RICH, JOHN, *Interviewing Children and Adolescents* (New York: St. Martin's Press, 1968).

This is a practical guide to interviewing skills which are helpful in working with children and youth.

ROSEN, AARON, and DINA LIEBERMAN, "The Experimental Evaluation of Interview Performance of Social Workers," *Social Service Review* 46:3 (September 1972), pp. 395–412.

This is an experimental study of trained (MSW) and untrained (non-MSW) social workers in two public welfare agencies. The interviewer was simulated by an actress. Interview performance was evaluated in relation to stimulus-response congruence and content relevance. Both aggressive and compliant clients were represented.

SCHUBERT, MARGARET, *Interviewing in Social Work Practice* (New York: Council on Social Work Education, 1971).

Schubert's brief monograph, written for beginning students, covers various aspects of interviewing pertinent to the social work interview and gives insights into the techniques used in applying the interview method.

STEWART, JOHN, ed., *Bridges Not Walls: A Book about Interpersonal Communication* (Reading, Mass.: Addison-Wesley, 1973).

This collection of articles on communication is based primarily on dialogical philosophy and humanistic psychology. It contains articles by Rogers, Kelly, Reusch, and Scheflen, among others. It deals, among other things, with empathetic listening, self-perception, perception of others, and verbal codes.

TRUAX, CHARLES B., and ROBERT CARKHALL, "Concreteness: A Neglected Variable in Research in Psychotherapy," *Journal of Clinical Psychology* 20:2 (April 1964), pp. 264–67.

Truax and Carkhall's research report suggests that concreteness defined as specificity of expression correlates highly with three measures of the therapeutic process. The concreteness of the therapist's expressions seems to ensure emotional proximity between client and therapist, increases the accuracy of the therapist's responses, and encourages specificity on the part of the client.

Chapter 6

PROBLEM SOLVING: A MODEL FOR SOCIAL WORK PRACTICE

The last two chapters discussed the need for social workers to have well-developed capacities in relating to and communicating with others. Such capacities are ways of bridging distances between ourselves and others. They are ways of achieving understanding between the client system and the practitioner, and of communicating that understanding. However, as was stated in the earlier chapters, relationship and understanding do not develop just because two bodies, one called the worker and the other the client, find themselves in a common enclosed space. Relationship, understanding, and a freedom of communication develop as practitioner and client system work together toward some purpose. Thus the social work process can be considered in terms of cooperation—resting on the ability of each to relate to and communicate with the other—between the client, who has available information about what (1) brings him in contact with the social work practitioner and (2) what he expects of this contact, and the social work practitioner, who has at hand (1) a fund of information about a variety of problems and (2) an orderly way of proceeding (a pattern of thinking, if you will). This orderly way of proceeding increases the probability of appropriate selection and utilization of (1) what the client brings to the situation and (2) the practitioner's knowledge and information toward the end of improving the client's ability to realize his aspirations and values.

In Chapter 1 we spoke of the skills necessary to social work practice as skill in deciding, skill in doing, and skill in resolving the questions that come out of the doing. These skills are the essential elements that are utilized to move the social work process toward the ends set forth above. They are the central elements of a framework we have called the "problem-solving model."[1] The model rests on the belief that effective movement toward purposive change, or altering something that one wishes to alter, rests on the ability of the worker to engage in rational, goal-directed thinking and to divide his activities into sequential steps, each characterized by some broad goal of its own which must be accomplished before the succeeding phase can be successfully completed. The achievement of such interim goals depend on the active participation of worker and client, and there must be agreement between these partners that the interim goals have been achieved before they can move on to the following stages. This position on the interaction of the participants in the process will be further developed in the following chapters. For now let us move on to consider the worker's input into the "problem-solving model."

DEWEY AND PROBLEM SOLVING

The ancestor to problem solving is typically identified to be *How We Think*,[2] a volume written by John Dewey in 1933, in which he attempted to describe the thought processes of a human being when confronted with a problem. In doing so, Dewey was interested in clarifying reflective or rational thinking, goal-directed thinking, or problem solving. According to Dewey, problem-solving behavior is based on reflective thought that begins with a feeling of perplexity, doubt, or confusion. The person wants to eliminate the difficulty or solve the puzzle, but in order to do this effectively he must follow a rational procedure. If he fails to do so he can act uncritically or impulsively, leaping to inappropriate conclusions, mistaking the nature of the problem, becoming involved in searching for the answer to the wrong problem, or making a number of other errors. Any one of these behaviors may very

---

[1] We are neither the first nor the only persons to have used this term for this approximate way of conceptualizing practice. In social work, Helen Harris Perlman must be considered the originator of the "problem-solving framework." Her work is well known. She has written extensively and her principle work is cited in the annotated bibliography at the end of this chapter. Our development of the concept differs somewhat from Perlman's, but both Perlman and the authors have based their formulations on John Dewey's work on problem solving.

The scientific method itself may also be considered a model of problem solving, and problem-solving frameworks have been developed by other authors in the behavioral sciences. Notable among these efforts is the wrok of Benne, Bennis, and Chin in their development of strategies of effecting change in human systems. These authors, however, see the problem-solving process as a normative reeducative approach to change. It is our position that the formulation is broader than that.

[2] John Dewey, *How We Think*, rev. ed. (New York: D. C 'Ieath, 1933).

well compromise his capacity to cope with the situation and undoubtedly makes it likely that the problem will remain unsolved.

Dewey held that effective problem solving demands the active pursuit of a set of procedural steps in a well-defined and orderly sequence. These steps Dewey referred to as the "five phases of reflective thinking," and they include: recognizing the difficulty; defining or specifying the difficulty; raising suggestions for possible solutions and rationally exploring the suggestions, which includes data collection; selecting an optimal solution from among many proposals; and carrying out the solution. Since Dewey, many persons, working in various areas of endeavor, have come to recognize that when one engages in investigation and problem solving there is a preferred model for orderly thought and action that can be laid out in progressive steps and pointed toward the reaching of a solution, and that the conscientious implementation of such a model materially increases the likelihood that one's objectives can be achieved.

It has been recognized that Dewey's list of five successive phases can be broken down into finer incremental steps and that orderly precision follows when this is done. Further, it has been recognized that Dewey's list failed to include the terminal aspects of problem solving— the evaluation of the effectiveness of the attempted solution, and the use of feedback loops (see Chapter 2) into the process, by which modifications can be made in the procedures employed even as one is engaged in employing them. In social work literature one will find a number of models which divide the activities of a social worker into sequential phases, each phase characterized by some broad goal of its own which must be accomplished before he moves on to complete the next phase. In general such models demand that the worker be successively involved with: (1) recognition or definition of the problem and engagement with the client system, (2) data collection, (3) assessment of the situation and the planning of action, (4) intervention, or the carrying out of action, (5) evaluation, and (6) termination.

PROBLEM SOLVING AND THE PRACTITIONER'S RESPONSIBILITY

We have our own outline of such a model, which we will present at the end of this discussion and which we will discuss in the following chapters. But first, we wish to speak to another important matter in this business of problem solving in social work. While we believe that such a process is orderly, that it is sequential, and that any one phase depends on the successful completion of the preceding phase, we also feel that any linear sequencing of tasks is an oversimplification of the process. In any given situation the worker may be operating in more than one phase at a time. In spite of the fact that the phases follow each other in some rough order, one phase does not wait upon the completion of another before it begins. Problem solving in social work probably proceeds, not linearly, but by a kind of spiral process in which action does not always wait upon the completion of assessment, and assessment often begins before data collection is complete. In fact, one often becomes aware that he has not collected enough facts, or the proper facts, only after he begins the process of trying to put all he knows together in some sort of summing-up process. Also, when the worker and the client system begin to take action toward some solution of the problem, the worker might well discover that he is proceeding on the wrong problem and must start all over again. However, in this case, he begins again with the distinct advantage of having some knowledge and some observations and some working relationships that he did not have before.

The fact that the problem solving process is a squirming, wriggling, alive business which may be grasped as an intellectual concept that concerns what goes on in the worker's head but also vitally concerns the social reality between the worker, the client, and all the interrelated systems of which the worker and the client are a part, makes it a difficult model to carry out in practice. All parts of the model may be present at any one time in a way that may obscure for the ordinary viewer, and often for the worker as well, the fact that there is "rhyme and reason" in what is being done. But it is the worker's business to know, in general, what phase is the primary focus of his and the client's coming together, and it is his business to check out constantly to see that all phases are dealt with. Failures in helping stem as often from the worker's impulsive leap to some action from what he sees at the moment as the problem, with no pause for thought and consultation in between, as from the worker's inability to engage in a helping relationship. In fact, these two parts of the helping process (the capacity to relate to and communicate with others and problem-solving efforts) are so firmly interwoven that we often do not pause to see them as separate things.

The problem-solving process itself, in and of itself, is the process by which worker and client decide (1) what the problem or question is that they wish to work on; (2) what the desired outcome of this work is; (3) how to conceptualize what it is that results in the persistence of the problem in spite of the fact that the client wants something changed or altered; (4) what procedures should be undertaken to change the situation; (5) what specific actions are to be undertaken to implement the procedures; and (6) how the actions have worked out.

For the worker, the use of the process involves considerable skill and the cultivated capacity to keep a clear head as well as an understanding heart. However, the problem-solving framework gives the worker no specific guides to specific procedures. It does not promise that if one does this type of thinking and exploring he will come out with *the* (or with *this*) answer. It promises rather that one must do this type of thinking and exploring, consciously and knowingly, in about this order if he wants to increase the probability of coming out with *an effective answer* that is in the direction of the client's goals. What the answer is, specifically, will depend on (1) what the question is, specifically, (2) what the client wants, specifically, and (3) what the worker and the client can bring to the process in terms of knowledge, understanding, resources, and capacity for joint action.

Although there are other frameworks for social work practice, the authors like the problem-solving framework for a number of reasons:

1.   No assumptions as to the nature or location of the problem are built into the framework itself. Thus the framework allows the problem to be defined as lying within the client system, as lying within the other systems with which the client system has transactions, as lying in some lack in social resources that should be supplied by the environment, or as lying in transactions among these factors.

2.   The way the problem is defined and the goal is established determines "which data are relevant and where the emphasis and direction of inquiry will lie."[3] This allows for data collection that is relevant, salient, and individualized. There are no set demands as to the data collected.

3.   The framework allows for the use of systems theory both as a guide (once problem and goal are established) to data collection that is relevant, salient, and individualized, and as a framework within which the data collected may be organized and viewed.

4.   The framework is not based on any one theoretical orientation and thus allows for the selection of such theoretical orientations as may be appropriate to the specific problem and client system involved.

5.   The framework is congruent with the function and purpose of the social work profession in that it supports the client's right to his definition of the problem and, in case the worker has a different view, demands that some negotiation be undertaken in defining the problem-to-be-worked (which simply means that worker and client must agree on what they are going to undertake together). The framework also recognizes the importance of the purposes of the client system.

6.   In addition to supplying a method applicable to a wide variety of situations and settings in which social work is practiced, and to different sizes and types of systems, the problem-solving framework demands that the tasks and activities of the social worker be stated at a very specific level and related to client goals. This seems to the authors to

---

[3] See Carel Germain article at the end of this chapter.

be a distinct advantage over frameworks that allow for a more abstract treatment plan.

THE CLIENT SYSTEM AND PROBLEM SOLVING

We have been speaking of what is required of the worker in the use of the problem-solving model. What is required of the client? There may be a tendency to think that since the model requires a large dose of rationality on the part of the worker it is appropriate only for clients who come with a well-developed ability to weigh and measure alternative courses of action. Nothing could be farther from the truth. One of the authors originally used such a model with families who were seen as totally unable to cope in a meaningful way with life tasks. However, these families whose capacity for understanding was held to be totally deteriorated, could participate as partners in the problem-solving process once they understood that we really wanted to know them as people and were willing to help them pursue their own goals (and once the practitioner learned to listen). They could tell us something about goals they had for themselves that were impossible of achievement because changes were needed that they alone couldn't effect. And it was here that we began the problem-solving process. In other words, this process demands of the client (1) that he be able to share with the worker information about something that he would like to have changed (2) in order to achieve something that is of value to him, and that (3) as the worker is able to demonstrate his concern and his competence to help through the exploration of this problem, the client is able to trust this concern enough (4) to allow the worker to continue to meet with him around this purpose. That is all that is demanded of the client system.

BASIC ASSUMPTIONS OF THE MODEL

This model does not in any way deny the irrational and instinctive characteristics of man, but it also accepts the findings of social scientists who have studied the social milieu of the mental hospital that even the most regressed psychotic patients are at least as responsive to changes in external reality as to their internal fantasies, that altering their external reality alters their ways of coping, and that "given a chance to participate in making decisions that affected their lives, inmates generally did so in a responsible manner and with constructive results for all concerned—professionals as well as themselves."[4] This model further accepts the view that social work processes are not a set of techniques

---

[4] Barbara Lerner, *Therapy in the Ghetto: Political Impotence and Personal Disintegration* (Baltimore: Johns Hopkins Press, 1972), p. 161.

by which an expert who understands what "is really wrong," seeks in his wisdom to improve, enlighten, plan for, or manipulate a client system. Rather, it sees social work processes as an attempt "by one human being with specialized knowledge, training and a way of working to establish a genuinely meaningful, democratic, and collaborative relationship with another person or persons in order to put his special knowledge and skills at the second person's (or group's) disposal for such use as he/they choose to make of it."[5] It recognizes that decisions about what individuals and groups of individuals should be, have, want, and do are cognitive decisions that involve rational and nonrational processes, perceptions of the describer and the possible, and values, an area in which "every man is a legitimate expert for himself and no man is a legitimate expert for others."[6] The model rests on the assumption that the given in each human being is his desire to be active in his life—to exercise meaningful control of himself for his own purposes. Systems theory tells us that living systems are purposive, and we believe that practitioners are more effective when they start with the client's purposes and the obstacles to their achievement. This does not mean that one is naive about unconscious and irrational factors. It simply means that one starts with the rational with consciously expressed problems and goals.

PRESENTATION OF THE PROBLEM-SOLVING OUTLINE

At the end of this chapter you will find two outlines of the problem-solving model. The first outline is a short outline—just the bare bones of the model. It is included here so that the reader can grasp the essentials of the model before he is confronted with all the details. The second is a long outline, but in use it is a good deal simpler and a good deal more complex than it appears to be on these pages. It appears more complex than it is because one section, IVC, contains a suggested outline for data collection on five separate systems: the individual, family, group, organization, and community. No practitioner is likely to collect information about all five systems in any one situation. In fact, the practitioner is not expected to become fully and completely knowledgeable about all the factors listed under IVC for any one system. The factors are listed for consideration and selection, and not for unthinking adoption. However, because of the complexity of the long outline a shorter one, which may be more usable, is also presented.

This notion of selectivity is what makes for the complexity in the effective use of the model. Every part of it is designed to be used differentially by the worker, given the problem, the goal, and the client

---

[5] Ibid., p. 11.
[6] Ibid., p. 161.

system. Effective use depends on the worker's capacity for deciding and selecting. The type of client system (individual, family, group, organization, or community) that is involved, the type of need, the lack or felt difficulty that has been identified, and the goals and expectations of the client system in interaction with the worker's knowledge of what is usually involved in such instances and his sensitivity to the individual differences in this instance, will determine the range of the data to be secured and how and when it is collected.

RECAPITULATION

In this chapter we have introduced the concept of problem solving as a model for social work practice. This model demands that the worker recognize that when people engage in investigation and problem solving there is a preferred model for orderly thought and action that can be laid out in defined, progressive steps. We take the position that while this demands a rational approach on the part of the worker, the demand on the client is that he be able to share with the worker something that he would like to change to some purpose. Our model is based on the assumption that people want to control their own lives and that, given a chance to participate in such decisions, they are able to do so.

The problem-solving framework presented in this chapter should be used selectively by the worker.

A LOOK FORWARD

"A Problem Focused Model of Practice" is reprinted in this chapter. It is another development of the problem-solving model. It departs from that of the authors in the unilateral authority it gives the worker. Also reprinted is an article on the use of systems theory as a base for the social study. The article should serve as a bridge between this chapter and the next, which will deal with data collection. In the next three chapters we will be continuing our discussion of the phases of the problem-solving model.

OUTLINE OF PROBLEM SOLVING MODEL—SHORT FORM

Contact phase

 I. Problem identification and definition
   A. The problem as the client system sees it
   B. The problem as defined by significant systems with which the client system is in interaction (family, school, community, others)

    C. The problem as the worker sees it

    D. The problem-for-work (place of beginning together)

II. Goal identification

    A. How does the client see (or want) the problem to be worked out?

        1. Short-term goals

        2. Long-term goals

    B. What does the client system think is needed for a solution of the problem?

    C. What does the client system seek and/or expect from the agency as a means to a solution?

    D. What are the worker's goals as to problem outcome?

    E. What does the worker believe the service system can or should offer the client to reach these goals?

III. Preliminary contract

    A. Clarification of the realities and boundaries of service

    B. Disclosure of the nature of further work together

    C. Emergence of commitment or contract to proceed further in exploration and assessment in a manner that confirms the rights, expectations, and autonomy of the client system and grants the practitioner the right to intervene

IV. Exploration and investigation

    A. Motivation

        1. Discomfort

        2. Hope

    B. Opportunity

    C. Capacity of the client system

Contract phase

V. Assessment and Evaluation

    A. If and how identified problems are related to needs of client system

    B. Analysis of the situation to identify the major factors operating in it

    C. Consideration of significant factors that contribute to the continuity of the need, lack, or difficulty

    D. Identification of the factors that appear most critical, definition of their interrelationships, and selection of those that can be worked with

    E. Identification of available resources, strengths, and motivations

    F. Selection and use of appropriate generalizations, principles, and concepts from the social work profession's body of knowledge

      G. Facts organized by ideas—ideas springing from knowledge and experience and subject to the governing aim of resolving the problem—professional judgment

VI. Formulation of a plan of action—a mutual guide to intervention
    A. Consideration and setting of a feasible goal
    B. Determination of appropriate modality of service
    C. Focus of change efforts
    D. Role of the worker
    E. Consideration of forces in the client system or outside forces that may impede the plan
    F. Consideration of the worker's knowledge and skill and of the time needed to implement the plan

VII. Prognosis—what confidence does the worker have in the success of the plan?

Action phase

VIII. Carrying out of the plan—specific as to point of intervention and assignment of tasks; resources and services to be utilized; methods by which they are to be used; who is to do what and when

IX. Termination
    A. Evaluation with client system of task accomplishment and meaning of process
    B. Coping with ending and disengagement
    C. Maintenance of gains

X. Evaluation
    A. Continuous process
    B. Was purpose accomplished?
    C. Were methods used appropriate?

OUTLINE OF PROBLEM-SOLVING MODEL—LONG FORM

Contact phase

I. Problem identification and definition
    A. The problem as the client system sees it
        1. Nature and location of need, lack, or difficulty
        2. Significance and meaning assigned by the client system to the need, lack, or difficulty
        3. Length of existence, previous occurrences, precipitating factors identified
        4. Conditions that bring client system and worker into interaction at this time
        5. Significance and meaning assigned by the client system to this interaction

B. The problem as defined by significant systems with which the client system is in interaction (family, school, community, others)
   1. Nature and location of need, lack, or difficulty as seen by these systems
   2. Significance and meaning assigned by these systems to this need, lack, or difficulty
   3. Significance and meaning assigned by these systems to client's interaction with interventive agent
C. The problem as the worker sees it
   1. Nature and location of need, lack, or difficulty
   2. Precipitating factors that the client system knows about and believes to be related and that the worker knows about and believes to be related
   3. Significance of conditions that bring client system and worker into interaction
   4. Nature and degree of effort that client system has put into coping with problem and client system's feeling about such efforts
D. The problem-for-work (place of beginning together)
   1. Problem or part of problem that the client system feels is most important or a good beginning place
   2. Problem or part of problem that in the worker's judgment is most critical
   3. Problem or part of problem that in the worker's judgment can most readily yield to help
   4. Problem or part of problem that falls within the action parameters of the helping system
II. Goal identification
   A. How does the client system see (or want) the problem to be worked out?
      1. Short-term goals
      2. Long-term goals
   B. What does the client system think is needed for a solution of the problem?
      1. Concrete resources
      2. Specific assistance
      3. Advice, guidance, or counseling
   C. What does the client system seek and/or expect from the agency as a means to a solution?
      1. Specific assistance (concrete service to enable the client system to do something)
      2. Specific resources (concrete things)
      3. Change in the environment or other social systems

        4. Change in specific individuals
        5. Advice or instruction
        6. Support or reassurance
        7. Change in self
        8. Change in interaction between client system and others

    D. What are the worker's goals as to problem outcome?
        1. Long-term goals—are they different from client system's goals?
        2. Short-term goals—are they different from client system's goals?
        3. Does worker believe client system's goals to be realistic and acceptable?
        4. What facilitating and intermediate goals can be identified?
        5. Level of agreement between workers and client system on goals

    E. What does the worker believe the service system can or should offer the client to reach these goals?
        1. Specific assistance
        2. Specific resources
        3. Change in the environment or other social systems
        4. Advice or instruction
        5. Support or reassurance
        6. Change in self
        7. Change in interaction between client system and others

III. Preliminary contract
    A. Clarification of the realities and boundaries of service
    B. Disclosure of the nature of further work together
    C. Emergence of commitment or contract to proceed further in exploration and assessment in a manner that confirms the rights, expectations, and autonomy of the client system and grants the practitioner the right to intervene

IV. Exploration and investigation
    A. Motivation
        1. Discomfort
            a. Quantity and quality of discomfort
            b. Is discomfort generalized to total life situation?
            c. Is it attached to present situation?
            d. Is it focused on presenting problem?
            e. How much discomfort is attached to help-seeking or help-taking role?
        2. Hope
            a. Quality and quantity hope
            b. Is there a generalized quality of optimism based on evaluation of past successes in coping?

    c. Are past experiences separated from present situation with realistic perception of the differences involved?

    d. Does client system perceive means of dealing with problem that he can accept and does client system perceive ways of access to such means?

    e. Gratifications from efforts toward solution including relationship to worker, other critical systems, and resources

B. Opportunity

    1. What opportunities have there been for client system to experience success in coping?

    2. What feedback has been available to client system as to value of these successes?

    3. What opportunities have there been for client system to acquire knowledges and skills needed for coping with present problem?

    4. What part of present problem is a result of departure from average level of opportunity made available to individuals, families, and groups in our society?

    5. What opportunities for solution of problem does the worker see in the present situation?

        a. Socioeconomic

        b. Within individual, family, or group as primary system

        c. Within family, group, or community as secondary sources

        d. In worker's skill, service system, and community or outside resources

        e. Other

C. Capacity of the client system

    1. Factors in the study and evaluation of the individual in any system—dyad, family, small group, organization, or community

        a. Physical and intellectual

            (1) Presence of physical illness and/or disability

            (2) Appearance and energy level

            (3) Current and potential levels of intellectual functioning

            (4) How the individual sees his world—translates events around him—perceptual abilities

            (5) Cause and effect reasoning—ability to focus

        b. Socioeconomic factors

            (1) Economic factors—level of income, adequacy of subsistence, and way this effects life-style, sense of adequacy, self-worth

        (2)   Employment and attitudes about it

        (3)   Racial, cultural, and ethnic identification—sense of identity and belonging

        (4)   Religious identification and linkages to significant value systems, norms, and practices

c. Personal values and goals

        (1)   Presence or absence of congruence between values and their expression in action—meaning to individual

        (2)   Congruence between individual's values and goals and the immediate systems with which he interacts

        (3)   Congruence between individual's values and practitioner's—meaning of this for interventive process

d. Adaptive functioning and response to present involvement

        (1)   Manner in which individual presents self to others—grooming—appearance—posture

        (2)   Emotional tone and changing levels

        (3)   Style of communication—verbal and non-verbal —level of ability to express appropriate emotion —to follow train of thought—factors of dissonance, confusion, uncertainty

        (4)   Symptoms or symptomatic behavior

        (5)   Quality of relationship individual seeks to establish—direction—purposes and uses of such relationships for individual

        (6)   Perception of self

        (7)   Social roles that are assumed for ascribed— competence with which these roles are fulfilled

        (8)   Relational behavior

            (*a*) Capacity for intimacy

            (*b*) Dependency-independency balance

            (*c*) Power and control conflicts

            (*d*) Exploitative

            (*e*) Openness

e. Developmental factors

        (1)   Role performance equated with life stage

        (2)   How developmental experiences have been interpreted and used

        (3)   How individual has dealt with past conflicts, tasks, and problems

        (4)   Uniqueness of present problem in life experience

2. Factors in the study and evaluation of the family
   a. The family as a social system
      (1) The family as a responsive and contributing unit within a network of other social units
         (*a*) Family boundaries—permeability of rigidity
         (*b*) Nature of input from other social units
         (*c*) Extent to which family fits into the cultural mold and expectations of larger system
         (*d*) Degree to which family is considered deviant
      (2) Roles of family members
         (*a*) Formal roles and role performance (father, child, etc.)
         (*b*) Informal roles and role performance (scapegoat, controller, follower, decision maker)
         (*c*) Degree of family agreement on assignment of roles and their performance
         (*d*) Interrelationship of various roles—degree of "fit" within total family
      (3) Family rules
         (*a*) Family rules that foster stability and maintenance
         (*b*) Family rules that foster maladaptation
         (*c*) Conformation of rules to family's life-style
         (*d*) How rules are modified—respect for difference
      (4) Communication network
         (*a*) Way family communicates and provides information to members
         (*b*) Channels of communication—who speaks to whom
         (*c*) Quality of messages—clarity or ambiguity
   b. Developmental stage of the family
      (1) Chronological stage of family
      (2) Problems and adaptations of transition
      (3) Shifts in role responsibility over time
      (4) Ways and means of problem solving at earlier stages
   c. Subsystems operating within the family
      (1) Function of family alliances in family stability
      (2) Conflict or support of other family subsystems and family as a whole

      d. Physical and emotional needs
          (1) At what level does family meet essential physical needs?
          (2) At what level does family meet social and emotional needs?
          (3) Resources within family to meet physical and emotional needs
          (4) Disparities between individual needs and family's willingness or ability to meet them
      e. Goals, values, and aspirations
          (1) Extent to which family values are articulated and understood by all members
          (2) Do family values reflect resignation or compromise?
          (3) Extent to which family will permit pursuit of individual goals and values
      f. Socioeconomic factors (see list under IVC1b)
   3. Factors in the study and evaluation of small groups
      a. Functional characteristics
          (1) How group came to be
             (*a*) Natural group
             (*b*) Group formed by outside intervention
          (2) Group's objectives
             (*a*) Affiliative, friendship, and social groups—mutuality and satisfaction derived from positive social interaction—tendency to avoid conflict and to stress identification
            (*b*) Task-oriented groups—created to achieve specific ends or resolve specific problems—emphasis on substantive rather than affective content
            (*c*) Personal change groups—emphasis on psychological and social content—dynamics of interpersonal behavior
            (*d*) Role enhancement and developmental groups—recreational, educational, and interest clusters—emphasis on rewards and on gratifications of participation, observation, learning, and improved performance
          (3) How group relates to contiguous groups—how it perceives itself and is perceived as conforming to or departing from outside values

    b. Structural factors

        (1) How the members were selected and how new members gain entry

        (2) Personality of individual members

            (*a*) Needs, motivations, personality patterns

            (*b*) Homogeneity-heterogeneity

            (*c*) Age of members

            (*d*) Factors of sex, social status, culture (see appropriate entries under IVC1 and IVC2) in relation to functions and purposes

            (*e*) Subgroups, their reasons for being, and the purposes they serve

            (*f*) Nature and locus of authority and control

                (1) How leadership roles develop

                (2) How decisions are made

    c. Interactional factors

        (1) Norms, values, beliefs, guiding values

        (2) Quality, depth, and nature of relationships

            (*a*) Formal or informal

            (*b*) Cooperative or competitive

            (*c*) Freedom or constraint

        (3) Degree to which members experience a sense of interdependence as expressed in individual commitments to the group's purposes, norms, and goals

4. Factors in the study and evaluation of organizations

    a. The organization as a system with a mandate

        (1) Organization's task—its mission within the social structure

            (*a*) Clarity with which task is stated

            (*b*) How task is perceived by organization's members

        (2) Individual and group roles relevant to the task

            (*a*) Which persons have the responsibility for carrying out the mandate of the organization?

            (*b*) Elements and parameters of their roles

            (*c*) Congruence between expected role behaviors and how these roles is seen by role bearers and others

            (*d*) Are roles assumed, delegated, earned, or appointed?

        (3) Location of organization within system of organizations
           (*a*) Population group organization is designed to serve
           (*b*) Kind of problem for which it is accountable
           (*c*) Organization's isolation from or cohesion with other organizations
           (*d*) Quality of interorganizational communication
           (*e*) Way organization manages input from other systems

b. Culture of the organization
        (1) Style with which organization operates
           (*a*) Governing beliefs of members
           (*b*) Expectations and attitudes of members
           (*c*) Theories that govern and guide organizational action
        (2) Modes of interaction with external groups or within organization itself
           (*a*) Formal or informal
           (*b*) Deference to authority—hierarchical
           (*c*) Ritual
           (*d*) Channels of communication
        (3) Organization's technologies—resources, methods, and procedures in implementation of organization's task
           (*a*) Jargon
           (*b*) Routine and protocol
           (*c*) Accepted and approved modes of communication

c. Competence of the organization
        (1) Availability and adequacy of funds, physical plant, equipment
        (2) Scope of authority vis-à-vis the community
        (3) Special status, force, and control in relation to larger community
        (4) Merit of guiding policies, flexibility, and responsiveness
        (5) Efficiency of internal decision-making process
        (6) Level of morale, spirit of commitment of members
        (7) Degree to which above factors combine to make the organization more than the sum of its parts

5. Factors in the study and evaluation of a community
    a. The community as a social system
        (1) Organizations, institutions, and groups of the community which effect existing condition and how they are linked with one another
        (2) Location of the problem and community units related to it
        (3) Units that can be engaged to deal with the problem—their stake in change—their accessibility
        (4) How will change in anyone unit affect other units?
    b. The community as an organic entity
        (1) Attitudes toward social control and conformity
        (2) Opportunities for social mobility
        (3) How the community defines success or failure
        (4) Beginning appraisal of the community power structure and how it exercises controls
        (5) How power is achieved in the community
        (6) How prevailing problems are identified and by whom
        (7) Beliefs held about causes of social problems
        (8) How the community labels the victims of social problems
        (9) Problem-solving capacity and resources
    c. Intercommunity structures and processes
        (1) Relationships and negotiations within governmental and nongovernmental sectors

Contract phase

V. Assessment and evaluation
    A. If and how identified problems are related to needs of client system
    B. Analysis of the situation to identify the major factors operating in it
    C. Consideration of significant factors that contribute to the continuity of the need, lack, or difficulty
    D. Identification of the factors that appear most critical, definition of their interrelationships, and selection of those that can be worked with
    E. Identification of available resources, strengths, and motivations
    F. Selection and use of appropriate generalizations, principles, and concepts from the social work profession's body of knowledge

      G.   Facts organized by ideas—ideas springing from knowledge and experience and subject to the governing aim of resolving the problem—professional judgment

VI.   Formulation of a plan of action—a mutual guide to intervention

      A.   Consideration and setting of a feasible goal

          1.   Goal is set as the direct result of, and during the process of, problem definition and analysis

          2.   Goal should be mutually agreed upon and time-limited

          3.   Goal should be within the commitment and the capacity of client system and worker to achieve, given the opportunities the environment can offer, the worker's resources and skills, and what the client system can bring to bear.

      B.   Determination of appropriate modality of service

      C.   Focus of change efforts

          1.   Client system (what particular aspect of functioning?)

          2.   Family system (what aspect?)

          3.   Significant others in the client system network

          4.   Agencies and other institutions in the community

          5.   Worker's own service system

      D.   Role of the worker

          1.   Advocate: when legitimate resources are resistive or resources must be created

          2.   Broker or mediator: locates resources for client system, interprets client system's needs to others, attempts to modify others' behavior toward client system, mediates between client system and others

          3.   Teacher: provides information, explanations, and expressions of opinions and attitudes

          4.   Enabler: attempts to help the client system to find within the system itself and the system's situation the necessary answers and resources by communication of interest, sympathy, understanding, and the desire to help; encourages exploration or ventilation of content concerning the nature and interactions of the client system and the client system's situation; encourages the reflective consideration, awareness, and understanding of the present person-situation-problem gestalt; plans with the client system and encourages the client system to act independently

          5.   Therapist: makes communications that contribute to or encourage reflective consideration, awareness, and understanding of the psychological patterns and dynamics of the client system's behaivor; or aspects of the client

system's earlier experiences that are thought to be relevant to such present behavior; or aspects of the person-
situation gestalt that lie in the past
   E. Consideration of forces in or outside of the client system
that may impede the plan
   F. Consideration of the worker's knowledge and skill and of
the time needed to implement the plan
VII. Prognosis—what confidence does the worker have in the success
of the plan?

Action phase

VIII. Carrying out of the plan—specific as to point of intervention and
assignment of tasks; resources and services to be utilized; methods
by which they are to be used; who is to do what and when
  IX. Termination
    A. Evaluation with client system of task accomplishment and
meaning of process
    B. Coping with ending and disengagement
    C. Maintenance of gains
  X. Evaluation
    A. Continuous process
    B. Was purpose accomplished?
    C. Were methods used appropriate?

A problem focused model of practice*

Kurt Spitzer and Betty Welsh

Social work is in serious danger of losing its sense of direction, its
purpose, and its relevance to today's fast moving and ever changing
world. Much of the literature reflects the frustrations experienced when
one attempts to bring traditional approaches to bear on a society that
operates within a value system and political frame of reference totally
different from the one that existed even ten years ago.[1]

* Reprinted by permission of the authors and the Family Service Association of
America from Social Casework, 50:6 (June 1969), pp. 323–29.
[1] The authors wish to dedicate this article to Ella Zwerdling, professor, School
of Social Work, Wayne State University, whose memory will serve as a constant
inspiration to all who are committed to the cause of human betterment, just as
her presence served to inspire those whom she taught and those who were fortunate
enough to work closely with her.

Concern is frequently expressed in regard to the need for the social work profession and the individual social worker to become meaningfully involved in political and social action and the need for social work to develop a position of greater influence in order to bring about more constructive social change.[2] By contrast, many other groups that are far less knowledgeable about social problems are perched in positions of influence in relation to social legislation and the provision of resources and programs.

Scott Briar identifies other frequently mentioned areas of concern.[3] He points to the need to develop more effective ways of reaching "clients from the more deprived segments of our population . . . who are not disposed to see a prolonged and often indefinite series of interviews as a solution to their problems" and expresses concern about caseworkers' putting "commitment to a method before human need." Doubtless the implied criticism is equally applicable to workers trained in other methods.

Other factors frequently identified as limiting social workers' functioning are "the infusion of the disease model of psychiatry into the central stream of casework" and the "bureaucratization of practice."[4]

Another area of concern is the matter of staying in touch with the realities of today's rapidly changing society and modifying social work functions in line with the changes. In an address to social work educators Mitchell I. Ginsberg made reference to the changing nature of clients, many of whom do not currently present themselves as helpless, passive requesters or recipients of service.[5] Rather, they are frequently verbal and outspoken and demonstrate considerable capacity to form themselves into viable action groups. Social workers should be aware of the fundamental change in the client stance and should welcome and support it as a sign of the increased participation and social consciousness of the deprived segments of society.

The rapid, dynamic changes in social problems occurring in our complex society require that the social worker also adopt a new stance. It should be a problem focused stance that will provide the worker with (1) the means for evaluating a given problem and its impact at various levels of society, all the way from the individual to the community level; (2) guidelines to determine the level at which it is feasible to intervene; (3) a wide range of intervention procedures that will be needed for problem prevention, resolution, or amelioration; and (4)

---

[2] Mitchell I. Ginsberg, "Changing Values in Social Work," 16th Annual Program Meeting of the Council on Social Work Education, Minneapolis, Minnesota, January 23–26, 1968.

[3] Scott Briar, "The Casework Predicament," *Social Work*, 13:6 (anuary 1968).

[4] Briar, "The Casework Predicament," . . . 7 and 8.

[5] Ginsberg, "Changing Values." . . .

the ability to evaluate objectively the effectiveness of his interventions in order to determine the direction of the next steps in the process and the new tasks he may need to undertake.

This article represents a beginning attempt to conceptualize a problem focused practice model that embraces these basic elements. It identifies the prerequisites needed for the problem focused approach, describes the essential nature of the problem solving process involved in the application of such an approach, presents an illustration of the practice model in action, and highlights some of the implications for the development of social work theory and for social work education.

Prerequisites for practice

The attempt to address a social problem comprehensively obviously cannot be the task of one social worker alone. It is the task of work groups within an entire program, an agency, or a network of services, which are identified in this article as the social welfare response system.[6]

A work group may be made up of a variety of professional services. It may include members of several human service professions, social workers of various degrees of competence, and ancillary personnel.[7] Its structure has to be flexible, so that it may be constantly responsive to the ever changing nature of the problem. All staff efforts must be geared toward problem prevention, resolution, or amelioration. False loyalties to parts of the social welfare response system or perpetuation of subsystems that are no longer helpful must be considered dysfunctional. The entire system should thus develop a group sense of self-awareness that keeps it in tune with the needs of the client system or systems—a concept that general systems theoreticians refer to as *feedback*. Feedback is an important process operating to keep a system viable, effective, and moving toward the achievement of the objectives for which it was originally established or to change the original objectives in line with newly emerging needs or changed conditions. The social workers involved in such an effort have to take leadership to provide the conditions that are conducive to such a stance. They must guide the building of meaningful working relationships and constructive group processes, the development of staff, and the provision of support

[6] We are indebted to Howard Buchbinder and Virginia Ebbinghaus for the concept of the social welfare response system, which they include in their conceptual model related to the development of the integrated curriculum at the St. Louis University School of Social Work.

[7] A meaningful description of such work groups (seen as "people working together on client tasks") was presented by Elliot Studt in a paper at the 16th Annual Program Meeting of the Council on Social Work Education, Minneapolis, Minnesota, January 23–6, 1968. See Elliot Studt, "Social Work Theory and Implications for the Practice of Methods," *Social Work Education Reporter*, 16:22 ff. (June 1968).

to staff in times of difficulty in order to ensure consistent effort on everyone's part. Clarity of the specific role that each member of the work group carries in relation to specific tasks also should enhance constructive and effective working relationships.

The problem focused stance requires of the social worker the ability to be creative, innovative, purposeful, and fully identified with the basic value system of the social work profession and its emphasis on the inherent worth of every individual. The worker has to have knowledge of the various client systems with which he will be interacting. He needs the skills that will allow him to become effectively involved in relationships with individual persons and families, with small groups and neighborhood groups, and within large and small systems and institutions.

The problem solving process

The first step to be taken by the social worker addressing himself to a problem area is the identification and definition of the problem. He makes an attempt to gain some understanding of the implications of a given problem and its impact on the individual, the family, the neighborhood, and the systems and institutions in the community. Fuller understanding is gained through detailed exploration and identification of relevant casal factors. Using the concept of "priorities and feasibility" suggested by Franklin Zweig and Robert Morris,[8] the social worker next decides on short range and long range objectives and the strategy of intervention; he identifies specific tasks to be carried out and decides when and where to take action and what resources should be used.

Problem focused practice requires an ongoing and continuing process, since problems are rarely totally resolved. As a result of intrapsychic or environmental events, the impact of the social welfare response system, or the responses to the problem by other segments of society, new elements are introduced and the nature of the problem constantly changes. The changes require ever changing forms of response by the social welfare response system and ever changing emphases—from the individual to the family to the neighborhood level, back and forth, depending on what seems feasible or possible or seems to require priority consideration. Thus, continuous feedback based on evaluation of the impact of interventions by the worker or the social welfare response system is an indispensable part of the process. The essential steps of the problem solving process may be outlined as follows:

1. Statement of the problem
2. Identification of causal factors

---

[8] Franklin M. Zweig and Robert Morris, "The Social Planning Design Guide: Process and Proposal," *Social Work*, 11:13–21 (April 1966).

3. Development of a plan of action (service design)
   a. Identification of needs
   b. Determination of objectives
   c. Selection of intervention procedures and tasks
4. Evaluation and feedback.[9]

In carrying out the tasks identified as necessary and appropriate, the social worker applies his knowledge of human behavior and the social environment, as well as his relationship skills, within the framework of professional ethics and values, in the context of one-to-one, group, and organizational interaction. In the process he may be carrying out a wide variety of tasks, including prevention, treatment, innovation, advocacy, consultation, supervision, research, and administration.[10] The essential point, however, is the way in which the worker utilizes himself, and that depends primarily on the kinds of tasks he sets for himself. Direction, form, and focus, therefore, are determined by the nature of the worker's tasks. Effective implementation of the tasks requires of the social worker a clear understanding of his objectives and of the nature of the relationships in which he is involving himself in working toward his objectives; a considerable amount of flexibility; and an ability to modify focus, objectives, and response as dicated by the ever changing picture of the problems on which he is working.

It is necessary for the social worker to have no special commitment to a particular method. He is thereby in a position to see the possible use of a variety of interventive methods, procedures, or tasks as they seem most applicable in the light of his assessment of the problem.

Clearly, the problem focused stance leads the social worker in many directions in practice, including social action activity and social policy development whenever feasible and appropriate. At the same time the worker does not ignore the needs of the individuals and the groups struggling with the immediate impact of social problems on their current lives. Again, help is not perceived as being available only on a one-to-one basis or through group process alone. Rather, help may be viewed as being available through various combinations of processes.

Illustration. The following illustration is drawn from the practice experience of a field work unit of four graduate students of the Wayne State University School of Social Work, located in one of the largest inner city junior high schools with a student population of 2100.

---

[9] This conceptualization is based, to a large extent, on the five classes of design tools that make up the Social Planning Design Guide developed by Zweig and Morris.

[10] It is our belief that most social workers now engage in many such tasks almost daily, though frequently without recognition on their part of the nature of the task(s) they are engaged in or the tools (in terms of knowledge and skills) that they should possess for most effective carrying out of these tasks. Schools of social work will need to build into their curriculum designs adequate procedures for the preparation of their students of the effective performance of these tasks.

Statement of the problem. At a meeting with the student unit the female counselors of the school, with whom the social work unit had close working relationships, presented their concerns about the large number of girls requesting return to school following pregnancy. Almost all the girls had not given up their infants. They lived in their own homes or parents' homes and had child caring responsibilities. The study patterns of the girls had been disrupted by their long absence from school, since school policy required the immediate suspension of any student upon evidence of her pregnancy.

The counselors reported that the girls had difficulty maintaining regular attendance, were chronically late for classes, or had to be home early in the afternoon. Although class schedules had been adjusted, the counselors thought the girls needed many more additional services and much more concerted help.

Identification of causal factors. In order to gain a fuller and more dynamic picture of the problem, it was necessary to identify some of the pertinent factors and implications in relation to the problem as it pertained to the school's tasks and to the girls' tasks and their situations. They were identified as follows:

1. The girls' current life situation—being needed at home—resulted in disrupted attendance patterns and tardiness. In addition, the role of mother, with its attendant implication of maturity and independence, frequently was in conflict with the implications of the student role. The girls' poor attendance prevented the school personnel from having the opportunity to teach and, by policy, being able to maintain the girls on the rolls.
2. The demands and the structure of the educational system were in conflict with the girls' child caring responsibilities.
3. The curriculum had nothing to offer that the girls could directly put to use in their roles of mother and homemaker.
4. Carrying out those roles tended to isolate the girls from their peers.

All the information about the girls was in the realm of inference and speculation, based on the material presented by the counselors. What was needed, however, was firsthand information about the impact of the problem on the girls and their families. The task of gathering it was assigned to one of the social work students. Five girls were referred to the student by the counselors, with the twofold purpose of providing social work services to them based on their needs and, at the same time, gaining some understanding about the nature of the problem, which would enable the unit to decide on future intervention objectives and strategy formulations.

It was apparent from the initial interviews that each girl wished to attend school and ultimately to be graduated from high school. Also apparent were several stumbling blocks, such as the following:

1. A lack of money for books and supplies
2. A need for arrangements for child care
3. Established patterns of nonattendance at school prior to pregnancy
4. The difficulty of returning to a rigorous school schedule
5. Little time for study at home
6. The complication of being new in a school and class and being a year older than classmates.

Each of the girls' situations was further complicated by individual factors similar to those of Joanne and Sally:

> Joanne was sixteen years old and married. She had had difficulties with her husband and had returned to her parents' home. Although she wanted to attend school, her immediate need was to work out her marriage situation and find a source of financial support, since she was no longer an AFDC dependent. Because her husband was not the father of the child, he was not required to support him. She was struggling with being rejected by her husband.
>
> Sally, fifteen years old, lived with her mother, who was a deaf mute. The mother had recently lost her job because of illness, and Sally's sister and her child had moved into the home to help financially. The sister worked, and Sally's mother was frequently out of the home seeking employment or public welfare support while Sally took care of the home. An eviction notice had been served, and electricity had been cut off.

Development of a plan of action (service design). The next step consisted of an examination of what had been learned. This involved an identification of the needs of the pregnant schoolage girl, an examination of the social welfare response system, and determination of feasible objectives and appropriate intervention procedures.

The problem was identified as relating each year to about two thousand schoolage girls in the city of Detroit.[11]

As a more complete view of the problem was obtained, needed interventive tasks became clearer, including tasks related to prevention of

---

[11] According to data compiled by the Program Development and Research Department of United Community Services of Detroit, obtained from the Michigan Department of Public Health, there were 1,847 recorded illegitimate births to mothers 18 years of age and younger in 1965, 2,102 such births in 1966, and 2,387 in 1967. We do not have data on "non-illegitimate births" by age groups. The total number of births annually by schoolage girls is obviously larger than these figures indicate.

the situations the girls found themselves facing. The following needs were identified:

1. Comprehensive sex education programs in the schools during the latency and adolescent years
2. Services during pregnancy: health care; continuing education; individual and group counseling for the schoolage pregnant girl and her family, such as counseling in child care, adoption procedures, and future planning, and guidance for the mother of the girl; classes in child care and motherhood; and social work services for the father
3. Increased research activity in relation to the problems of the pregnant schoolage girl to establish a broad and accurate basis for more comprehensive community services for unmarried mothers
4. Development of constructive policies by the school system relative to the schoolage pregnant girl.

The selection of specific intervention procedures is often greatly influenced by such considerations as feasibility—in terms of community readiness and support. And at the time at which this development occurred there was a heightened sense of awareness of the problem of the pregnant schoolage girl in many sectors of the community. As a result, the students took the initiative to call together a number of people from the human service professions who were particularly interested in doing something about the problem. In view of an assessment that it was not possible to change existing policies and procedures, a proposal was drafted for the creation of a Continuing Education for Girls program, consisting of neighborhood education centers for pregnant schoolage girls. The proposal called for qualified teachers and official credit for the course work completed in the program. The program was to be essentially interdisciplinary in nature. Public health nurses were to conduct courses on physical health, sex education, and child care and child development. Social work agencies were to provide counseling for the girls, their families, and the fathers.[12]

It should be noted that the active moral support of community resources and agencies made it possible for the proposal to be developed and ultimately to receive favorable consideration. Much support also came from the Detroit public school system. The final draft of the proposal as formulated by a staff member of the Detroit Board of Education represented a synthesis of several ideas developed by concerned organizations and individuals. Few school systems in the country have taken such an enlightened step.

Evaluation and feedback. The implementation of the program also brought the magnitude of the problem into full view. Although the

---

[12] The writers of the original draft of the proposal were Ella Zwerdling and Betty Welsh.

proposal was adopted, necessary funding was obtained, and the program is currently in operation, the problem solving process has not ended. Indeed, it goes on *ad infinitum*, since the needs are continuous and the problem, extremely complex. No one single intervention procedure can ever provide total resolution. Continuous evaluation is necessary to determine future needs and tasks. Further steps in the selection of objectives, tasks, and implementation procedures will depend on the nature of the findings of continuing evaluation of the effectiveness of the program, as well as identification of unmet needs. For example, consideration now must be given to the role and responsibilities of schools in providing sex education and meaningful social services as an integral part of the public school program and in revising policies in relation to pregnancy. The community, however, will have to support such efforts by means of programs providing effective maternal and infant health care, community mental health services, family life education, family planning, and above all more adequate provision of resources for basic survival needs.

Review of essential aspects.   First, it was recognized that the provision of traditional social work services, such as casework or group work, was inadequate, since one of the major factors in relation to the problem was the interruption of the educational process. Whatever casework or group work services could be offered could only be labeled "picking up the pieces after the damage was done." In view of the negative over-all environmental situations of the majority of the girls, this was clearly a totally impossible task. Even granting that casework or group work services might have been helpful, they could have reached only a small number of the girls. In addition, social work services were less significantly related to pregnancy and more related to the effects of policies adopted by the educational system (which is part of the social welfare response system) in regard to pregnancy. In other words, the situation was illustrative of a not uncommon situation in our society: namely, a large number of our social problems are frequently more significantly the results of the nature of the response—the stance—of the social welfare response system than of the causative factors outside the social welfare response system.

An assessment led to the conclusion that the policies and procedures regarding the pregnant schoolage girl could not be readily changed within the existing public school structure. At that time, however, there was considerable broad community concern about the needs of unmarried mothers and the fate of their babies, as evidenced by the many conferences held in relation to the problem, newspaper publicity, and concern expressed by large segments of the public school community. All were attempting to find new and more effective approaches to the problem and demonstrated a general readiness for *innovation*. The readiness of the community is a very important factor in the selection of intervention procedures.

Moreover, when large segments of the community can be meaningfully engaged in the development of a program, continued significant community involvement can be relied upon after the inception of the program, in the ongoing problem solving process, as new needs are identified and require action by the social welfare response system.

Another important aspect of the Continuing Education for Girls program is its *preventive* feature, not only in terms of the problems that plague students attempting to return to school after pregnancy, which is a form of secondary prevention, but also a much more fundamental one. When a girl is able to complete her high school education and thereby acquire the basic tools for meaningful employment or higher education, is provided with basic knowledge about child care and child rearing, and is benefiting from social services, she is able to rear her infant under much more advantageous circumstances than those under which she herself was reared. She can be expected to provide better care for her child, thus breaking the multigenerational cycle of poverty, dependency, and family pathology.

Many other important programs that can further enhance preventive efforts must be developed and made available on a wider scale in order for social work services to be effective in the area of prevention.

Summary

This article has presented a formulation of a new social work practice model. The model was devised on the basis of the contention that such a new model is needed if social workers are to begin making a more viable impact on the social problems of our era. The approach suggested by the model is problem focused, in that the identification and definition of the problem leads to a determination of objectives, tasks, and priorities; the levels at which intervention should take place; and the methods of intervention to be used. To be most effective, the entire social welfare response system should be related to the prevention, resolution, and amelioration of a specific problem entity and the impacts it makes on the client systems at the individual, family, small group, or neighborhood level or in societal and institutional systems.

The social work profession will have to exert considerably more effort in developing useful guidelines for the application of appropriate theories of human behavior and the social environment. A basic need is the development of a unifying theoretical system,[13] providing for the

---

[13] We believe that General Systems Theory, which addresses itself to a study of living systems at various levels of organization, holds excellent promise for providing such a unified theory base.

integration of many theoretical systems into a meaningful whole, that is useful to social work and, possibly, other helping professions.

A group of faculty members at the Wayne State University School of Social Work developed an experimental curriculum for the preparation of students for problem focused social work practice as outlined in this article. After a year of planning, the program was begun in September 1968 with an initial enrollment of sixteen first-year students. Although the period of time that has elapsed since its inception is too short to provide any definitive findings, the impressions of the learning outcomes are encouraging in terms of the students' ability to relate to the needs of a variety of client systems at various levels of organization and to address themselves to social problems intelligently.

Education for *social work practice* is unquestionably one of the soundest ways of educating students. As Herbert Aptekar points out:

> Learning the role of social worker and learning social work practice are comparable to learning to draw the human body. One can break either into parts, if one wants to. The question that must now be faced, and the scientific obligation that the profession must carry out, is to see if there is a better way of introducing students to the integrated role of *social worker* (not caseworker, groupworker, or community organization worker) and if there is a better way of introducing students to *social work practice* (not casework, groupwork, or community organization practice). If a better way can be found, it will certainly be in keeping with the present developments in agencies and programs, and social work education will take a giant step forward.[14]

It is hoped that this article will give impetus to further innovation in social work practice and education geared to meeting the ever changing demands of society.

Social study: past and future[*]

Carel B. Germain

New approaches to the practice of social casework are now being considered, implemented, and evaluated in all sectors of the profession. The impetus for innovation derives from a number of sources, including

[14] Herbert H. Aptekar, a review of *Theory for Social Work Practice* by Ruth Elizabeth Smalley, *Journal of Education for Social Work*, 3:105 (Fall 1967).

[*] Reprinted by permission of the author and the Family Service Association of America from *Social Casework*, 49:7 (July 1968), pp. 403–9.

the application of crisis concepts in various areas of practice, the growing use of family treatment, the efforts to develop more effective modes of intervention in work with the poor, the concern about treatment dropout and treatment failure, and the need to use the limited supply of trained personnel more productively. Innovation is an appropriate professional response to new knowledge, to the emergence of new problems and needs, and to the impact of social change on old problems and needs. Nevertheless, the implications of innovation must be recognized. And certain implications in current new approaches seem to cast doubt on long-accepted notions of the psychosocial study as a formalized process essential to the diagnostic understanding on which treatment intervention is based.

The crisis approach assumes a time-limited period of upset, when the usual coping capacity is weakened, anxiety is high, and the individual or family is most accessible to help. Immediacy of preventive or restorative intervention is seen as paramount; a period of study and exploration as a basis for action appears inconsistent with the concept of crisis.

Similarly, family treatment appears to emphasize the here-and-now interaction of family members as the arena for the caseworker's intervention, and longitudinal study-diagnosis of the individual family members is eliminated or at least subordinated to a horizontal focus on current transactions, communication patterns, and role relationships. The successes and economies of this approach give weight to prevalent doubts about the usefulness of social study as it has been conceptualized.

Experiences in the use of reaching-out techniques over the past decade and in contemporary efforts to understand and apply social and cultural differentials in casework practice have led to the realization that social study pursued in traditional terms is often experienced by the poor or lower-class client as a frustration and rejection.

Recent research findings have suggested that the dropout problem in the early phase of contact may be referred, in part, to difference in the objectives of caseworker and client, in that the caseworker's goals in the early interviews have been traditionally related to the gathering of information, albeit in a therapeutically oriented way, whereas the client's goal has been to secure immediate help with the presenting problem. Too often the caseworker is left with facts, we are told, but no client. Moreover, concerns about the manpower shortage carry the implication that the days of long-term treatment are over and with them the interview hours spent on study and exploration in order to uncover the "real" problem underlying the request for help.

Perhaps these emphases on speeding up the helping process mean that study, as it has been conceived and taught, is no longer appropriate or even possible. They may represent a growing polarity between theory and practice, and it seems urgent that social casework re-examine its tenets and assumptions concerning social study. Are we so in the grip of yesterday that we are clinging in theory to a time-honored principle no longer valid for the requirements of current and future practice? Or, at the other extreme, are we in danger of discarding, through expedience and disuse, what is actually a necessary component in all casework?

It is my conviction that study continues to be an essential element in a scientifically based practice. Indeed, the spirit of scientific inquiry on which study rests is more than ever necessary in the face of the constant change in social needs and conditions that now confronts the caseworker. Yet it must be study that serves today's demands, not yesterday's ideologies.

In order to reshape the study process, the first task is to identify the fundamental concepts in the traditional model of study. They will be identified in this article as relevance, salience, and individualization. It will be suggested that the resolution of practice dilemmas that emerge as these concepts are modified may depend on broadening conceptions of casework practice.[1] The study process will be recast within the framework of systems theory. Attention will be drawn to ways in which such a recast study process can match up with new treatment modalities to deliver services that make more productive use of time and resources for the client, the agency, and the worker.

Relevance, salience, and individualization

Mary Richmond set forth the principles of social investigation that gave to social study its initial shape and direction.[2] According to her model, the caseworker's first responsibility in planning treatment was to secure any and all facts that, taken together, would reveal the client's personality and his situation. Thus, the beginning thread of a scientific orientation appeared in the insistence on a factual base that, through logical and inferential reasoning, would lead to a plan of action. It was as if knowledge of all the evidence would reveal the cause of the problem and hence its remedy; consequently, every source of information was to be utilized.

In the light of increased experience and accretions of knowledge, particularly from psychoanalysis, the routine gathering of massive amounts of data gradually gave way to a more discriminating approach. Social history was obtained with more understanding of its relation to

---

[1] See Morris S. Schwartz and Charlotte G. Schwartz, *Social Approaches to Mental Patient Care,* Columbia University Press, New York, 1964.

[2] Mary E. Richmond, *Social Diagnosis,* Russell Sage Foundation, New York, 1971, and Mary E. Richmond, *What Is Social Case Work?,* Russell Sage Foundation, New York, 1922.

personality dynamics. Concepts clarifying the ego's functions in relation to social reality and to inner forces led away from the earlier preoccupation with repressed content to what is still the unit of attention, the person-in-situation. The impact of these developments on study culminated in Gordon Hamilton's conceptual model.[3]

Whereas Richmond had urged the exhaustive collection of facts followed by separation of the significant from the insignificant, Hamilton introduced the concept of relevance. Sources of data were respecified as the client's own account, the reports of collaterals, documentary evidence, findings of experts, and the worker's observations. Viewed in terms of newly defined psychological and environmental dimensions, they were to be tapped selectively according to the nature of the problem, the wish of the client, the purpose of the agency, and the availability and preventive value of the information itself. Study, guided by professional knowledge, was to be related quantitatively to the degree of intervention indicated and the difficulty of establishing the diagnosis. An important distinction was made between history-taking for diagnosis in the early contacts and the use of history for abreaction in the treatment phase.

Hamilton described two types of social study, the *patterned* type and the *clue* type. The most clearly conceptualized examples of the patterned type are the eligibility study made in public assistance work and the psychogenetic study made in cases focused on behavior disorders or emotional disturbances. In such studies priorities are assigned to certain areas considered relevant, and these areas are held in the foreground of attention. In making the clue type of social study, the worker feels his way on the basis of the request and clues, consciously and unconsciously furnished, in order to collect facts relevant to the problem. It has been recently pointed out, however, that, "as Miss Hamilton suggests, clue and pattern are really interrelated and are perhaps more indicative of ways of envisaging the process of securing data than they are clear-cut types of study. The patterned study may involve a matter of priorities, but it is best developed on a basis of explaining the relevance of the inquiry to the request, and with the client's participation, than on a questionnaire basis. Similarly, the clue approach involves a concept of pattern since criteria for relevance give significance to the clue. Further, the worker controls this approach by injecting attention to priority of subjects for exploration at appropriate points."[4]

The scientific orientation that began in Richmond's approach to social

---

[3] Gordon Hamilton, *Theory and Practice of Social Case Work* (2nd ed., rev.), Columbia University Press, New York, 1951. See especially Chapter VII, pp. 181–212.

[4] Lucille N. Austin, on "clue and pattern," as discussed in a doctoral seminar in social casework, Columbia University School of Social Work, New York, Spring 1966.

study is firm and clear in the Hamilton model. Since the model requires systematic inquiry into relevant facts, it is useful in considering the model to note *Webster's* definition of *relevant* as "bearing upon, or properly applying to, the case in hand; of a nature to afford evidence tending to prove or to disprove the matters in issue. . . ."[5] It follows that the way in which the problem is cast determines which data are relevant and where the emphasis and direction of inquiry will lie. How the problem is defined, and to some extent the mode of intervention available or selected, determines what data will be perceived as relevant and consequently observed, collected, and interpreted for professional judgment. An inquiry into a set of circumstances viewed as indicative of a personality disturbance, for example, will result in the collection and interpretation of certain data. These data will be quite different from those collected and interpreted when the same set of circumstances is viewed as indicative of a disjunction between the individual and his familial, organizational, or cultural system or between the individual and his physical environment.

An observation underscored in Hamilton's work but sometimes lost sight of in practice had been made as long ago as 1936 by Fern Lowry, namely, that "the decision what to treat frequently demands greater skill than the decision how to treat."[6] As Lowry suggests, early dropout and treatment failure is frequently attributed to the client or to external factors when it should be attributed, rather, to the caseworker's tendency to assume responsibility for every discoverable need. Such a tendency may even conflict with the client's wish for immediate help in a specific area. Accordingly, Lowry urges that the impulse to treat every need and the urge to cure be restrained.[7] From such a standpoint, study is not an inquiry into all areas and needs.

The work of Schwartz and Schwartz introduces the concept of salience[8]—and *Webster's* defines *salient* as "prominent; conspicuous; noticeable. . . ."[9] A salient feature, then, is one that has an emphatic quality that thrusts itself into attention.

According to the foregoing concepts of relevance and salience, treatment is not properly focused on the total person. It becomes, in fact, more individualized and differential when it is particularized for particu-

---

[5] *Webster's New International Dictionary of the English Language* (2nd ed.), G. & C. Merriam Co., Springfield, Massachusetts, 1950, p. 2104.

[6] Fern Lowry, "The Client's Needs As the Basis for Differential Approach in Treatment," in *Differential Approach in Case Work Treatment,* Family Welfare Association of America, New York, 1936, p. 8.

[7] Ibid., p. 9.

[8] Schwartz and Schwartz, op. cit., pp. 111–35.

[9] *Webster's New International Dictionary of the English Language* (2nd ed.), op. cit., p. 2204.

lar clients having particular needs or problems in particular situations.[10] Individualization is based on choice among needs, modes of treatment, and possible goals. From this perspective, social study must become more individualized in order to specify the salient need or needs for which social casework has professional accountability. Specifying the salient need, however, is not the same as partializing the problem. What is described here is still an organismic approach in which the caseworker remains constantly aware of the whole, and the changing relationships of the parts to the whole, while singling out salient need for individualized treatment.

Although caseworkers have long known of the importance of the role of norms in the assessment of functioning within specific social and cultural contexts, the concept of salience requires a shift in the concept of normalcy and a shift from setting treatment goals in terms of cure. Some shift has already occurred insofar as goals are conceptualized as restoration of a prior level of social functioning or return to a previous equilibrium. A further shift away from notions of cure is required so that some resolution of the presenting problem, easing of precipitating stress, and even remission of symptoms, for example, can be embraced as goals. These become appropriate additions to the array of possible goals as new models of casework intervention develop in response to new knowledge and new conditions. The individual and social value of such goals, in relation to conservation of the client's resources and to manpower issues, seems clear. Moreover, the resemblance of these goals to the processes of natural life situations is striking.

Broadening the conceptions of help

In social casework theory and education, if not always in practice, study-diagnosis-treatment has been conceptualized on a psychotherapeutic model in which the worker—and, it is hoped, the client—"will peer down the long avenue of the client's past life," as John Dollard puts it, "to see how the present event matured."[11] This conceptualization has often led to searching for, and giving primacy to, the problems underlying the presenting request, or even unrelated to it.

The dilemma that presents itself when such an approach is viewed in the light of the foregoing discussion and may be resolved through broadening the conceptions of casework help within the framework proposed by Schwartz and Schwartz. They distinguish between *treatment* as conventionally accepted clinical procedures and *help* as a large variety

---

[10] Schwartz and Schwartz, op. cit., p. 124.

[11] John Dollard, *Criteria for the Life History*, Yale University Press, New Haven, Connecticut, 1935, p. 27.

of attempts to influence clients in a therapeutic direction. They suggest that the conceptions of help should

> include considerations such as a wider arena within which help might proceed, a different conception of who and what is to be helped, and a different view of the conditions and processes that affect therapeutic progress. . . . Thus, broadening the conceptions of help involves some reorientation. From looking upon the process exclusively as a clinical activity, directed at a disease entity, and undertaken within the boundaries of the conventionally defined therapist-patient relationship, the change is to seeing it, in addition, as a sociopsychological process that attempts to deal with problems in living that are not necessarily serious or well-defined emotional disorders.[12]

The authors advance four objectives to be achieved in broadening the conceptions of help. They are interrelated, and although each may be discussed separately for heuristic purposes, each can only be understood in relation to the other three. These objectives are "reconceptualizing the unit of help, changing the . . . object of help, expanding the role of helper, and re-orienting . . . [the] approach to help processes."[13]

The unit of help. The unit of attention in social casework has been the person-situation, although history reveals a shifting in emphasis at times from one to the other side of the hyphen. The newer ego concepts have made possible the appropriate study of psychosocial factors in social functioning. Newly conceptualized elements of the dynamic environment—such as role, class, ethnic and other reference groups, value orientations, family structure, and the agency as a social system—have permitted more accurate definitions of the situation.[14] In spite of much effort, however, there has until recently been no way to integrate psychological and social phenomena without invoking the fallacy of reductionism. In this regard, general systems theory offers a fruitful approach to reconceptualizing the unit of attention in a way that will permit a valid redefinition of social study.

The object of help. Caseworkers have tended to modify their traditional stance in relation to the client whenever the family, rather than the individual, has been viewed as client—and have frequently misconstrued family-focused treatment of individuals as family treatment. Much work lies ahead in developing, from the knowledge and experience of casework itself, useful study-diagnostic concepts and derivative treatment principles and techniques for the family as a social system.

Also required is an enlarged definition of the object of help to encompass not merely the personality, but the whole human being within

---

[12] Schwartz and Schwartz, op. cit., p. 85.

[13] Ibid.

[14] Herman Stein, "The Concept of the Social Environment in Social Work Practice," *Smith College Studies in Social Work*, Vol. XXX, June 1960, pp. 187–210.

a fluid, real-life situation, in order to utilize the therapeutic potential of life processes, adaptive and coping capacities, and social supports.

Still another possibility lies in viewing the agency itself as the object of change or as an instrument for change rather than as a given in the situation. Such a view has some similarity to conceptions of milieu therapy as applied in hospitals and other institutions; it implies the use of organizational structure and the organizational roles of clients and workers within the agency to effect organizational or individual change. Given such a view, social study would embrace a consideration of the impact on clients of organizational variables, of the potential of those variables for fostering or inhibiting growth, and of sources of organizational resistance to change.

The helper. The discipline of social casework has moved in several ways toward redefining the role of the worker from that of clinician-therapist to that of helper. Whereas the formal, instrumental, functionally specific role was traditionally the only one available to the caseworker, a more informal, expressive, functionally diffuse role has been evolving. Its inception was in the development of reaching-out techniques in several fields of practice. And the dimensions of the role have become clearer in the course of current attempts to reduce social distance, which are based on increasingly sophisticated knowledge of socialization experiences and life styles in deprived groups.

In addition, there has been expansion in the leadership role of the caseworker on service teams, which may include homemakers, volunteers, case aides, and indigenous helpers. Such a team approach appears to offer varied experiences and interpersonal relationships for clients with salient needs in those areas. Continued experimentation and research in programs in which one practitioner makes combined use of casework, group work, and community organization methods are also expected to expand the caseworker's repertory of roles.

The help processes. Conventional treatment procedures require verbal skills, introspection, and motivation, which are not infrequently lacking among clients of casework services. Now, however, the idea of help is being broadened to include informal processes and activities. New uses of the home visit are being developed; searches are being made for ways to provide experiences in a social context that will promote growth and maturation in the client; and new techniques of concretization and demonstration are being utilized.[15] In such efforts the relationship offered the client is viewed as a training ground for living and for assuming social roles in more rewarding ways. The caseworker supports adaptive responses and progressive forces, rather than uncover-

---

[15] See, for example, Louise S. Bandler, "Casework with Multiproblem Families," in *Social Work Practice, 1964,* Columbia University Press, New York, 1964, pp. 158–71.

ing coping failures, since the latter tactic tends to foster transference and the attendant regressive needs.

The concept of casework help has been broadened to include the provision of consultation services, and, increasingly, caseworkers are being enlisted to provide consultation to community caretakers with respect to the needs and responses of their clientele, either as specific individuals or total groups. Those being helped are not cast in the role of client and are not subject to its prescriptions and proscriptions. They may be merely present, perhaps in a helping arena, such as a day care center, a school, or a sheltered workshop.

These broadened conceptions of help call for new models of intervention and new ways to provide help more appropriately and effectively to supplement the psychotherapeutic model and increase the caseworker's flexibility and adaptiveness. Some, such as the crisis model[16] and the life model,[17] are now being developed. They furnish new ways of conceptualizing needs and problems and new methods and techniques of intervention. The relevance and salience of data vary with a shift from one model to another. For example, it may be necessary to reconceptualize certain disturbances as life crises, maturational or situational, or as role transitions imposing new statuses and ego tasks or as psychosocial disabilities requiring help in developing social competence. Defining problems in these terms demands that study produce new kinds of environmental data for the understanding and utilization of life processes as treatment media. Implicit is an emphasis on rapidity in the collection of data so that decisions can be reached to take action that is timely in terms of the model.

A systems approach

Because systems theory, as a way of viewing biological, psychological, and social phenomena, cuts across disciplines and bodies of knowledge, its constructs may be useful for the identification of the relevant and salient data in individualized study. The unit of attention is reformulated as a field of action in which the client—his biological and personality subsystems—is in transaction with a variety of biological, psychological, cultural, and social systems within a specific physical, cultural, and historical environment. Though there are important differences among these types of systems, all, as open systems, have important properties in

---

[16] Developments in the crisis model are found in Howard J. Parad (ed.), *Crisis Intervention: Selected Readings,* Family Service Association of America, New York, 1965.

[17] Bernard Bandler, "The Concept of Ego-Supportive Psychotherapy," in *Ego-Oriented Casework: Problems and Perspectives,* Howard J. Parad and Roger R. Miller (eds.), Family Service Association of America, New York, 1963, pp. 27–44.

common.[18] Some of these characteristics have to do with the input, trans-formation, and output of energy from and to the environment, which highlight the interdependence of systems, exchanges across boundaries, and degrees of openness to the environment. Other features pertain to the maintenance of a steady state or dynamic homeostasis—that is, the preservation of the general character of the system—and these highlight feedback processes, subsystem dynamics, and the relation between growth and survival. These and other characteristics draw attention to the functional and dysfunctional consequences, the reciprocal effects and reverberations that occur in the field of systems as the result of the operations of each. Similar observations can be made concerning the relation of its parts to any single system.

In contrast to the two-dimensional person-situation approach, this conception offers a wide range of system variables and encourages a holistic view. It leads to a focus on the disruptive factors in the usual steady state and on the mechanisms for restitution, coping, adaptation, and innovation in all systems. The systems perspective also places the agency as a social system and the worker and the client in the same transactional field. The helping relationship has a larger purview, which adds the reciprocal influences of the roles, norms, and values of several transacting social systems to the clinical aspects of the relationship. The worker's entrance into the client's field changes it *de facto,* not only through his effect as an observer on the observed but also through the reverberations of his entrance through the various other systems in the client's field, particularly secondary role networks. Similarly, the client's organizational roles have an impact on agency role-sets, whether they are designed by client groups as in some current public welfare agencies or by other agencies that have provided for planned participation for citizen-clients. In either instance, Heinz Hartmann's view of adaptation, which takes into account the individual's potential for contributing to the modification of existing environments and the creation of new ones, is more likely to be implemented through the systems approach.

Conclusions

We tend to observe and recognize as relevant what is closest to our conceptual model, and the systems perspective allows more indicators of salient and relevant variables to filter through the worker's perceptual

---

[18] For further discussion of the characteristics and operations of open systems, see, for example, Daniel Katz and Robert L. Kahn, *The Social Psychology of Organizations,* John Wiley & Sons, New York, 1966, pp. 14–70, and Roy R. Grinker (ed.), *Toward a Unified Theory of Human Behavior,* Basic Books, New York, 1967. All the material in this work is valuable. See also Gordon Hearn, *Theory Building in Social Work,* University of Toronto Press, Toronto, 1958, pp. 38–51.

screen. This does not mean that in any one case the entire field is covered.[19] On the contrary, the systems perspective enables the worker to comprehend the salient features of the problem as it is systematically conceived, to recognize relevant data within the relevant system or systems, and to reach professional judgments more rapidly. Paradoxically, it enlarges the unit of attention while it sharpens the focus by suggesting additional possible points of entry to effect change, as well as by illuminating the feasibility of change in specific systems. In a systems approach, a rapid gathering of relevant facts related to the salient features of the presenting need requires, however, greater breadth of knowledge, more skill in diagnosis, and greater capacity for communication, relationship, and self-awareness than are required in a traditional person-situation approach. Rapidity requires confidence in a knowledge base amplified to include all systems, their characteristics and linkages. Even in the first interview, the caseworker's broad knowledge is available to lead him to an understanding of the psychological and social commonalities revealed empirically through verbal and nonverbal clues. Increased knowledge and skill permit him to rely on these clues and signs as indicators that it is not then necessary to explore many phenomena and large areas of the client's experience. As Joseph Eaton has pointed out, this kind of professional confidence and security calls for tolerance of some degree of uncertainty and error.[20]

No matter what types of casework intervention may arise from broadened conceptions of help, the worker with a scientific orientation will always think diagnostically, using logical procedures with respect to evidence, inferential reasoning, and the relating of empirical data to theory and knowledge. He will make disciplined use of prognosis and evaluation, as formulated by Hamilton, against which predicted probable outcomes are measured. Careful analysis will be made of cases that do not have the expected outcome in order to uncover previously unknown variables, which may themselves add to the refinement of study. The worker will be guided in study, as in the total helping process, by social work values. His effectiveness will be enhanced by diversified patterns of communication, differential roles, and helping relationships that give attention to the emotional, cultural, and cognitive forces in growth and change.

For the new demands of practice, social study remains the scientific

---

[19] This view departs from that suggested in a pioneer paper, Werner A. Lutz, *Concepts and Principles Underlying Social Casework Practice*, "Social Work Practice in Medical Care and Rehabilitation Settings, Monograph III," Medical Social Work Section, National Association of Social Workers, Washington, D.C., 1956, pp. 72–75. In contrast, the present article is an attempt to apply systems theory to more models than the clinical.

[20] Joseph W. Eaton, "Science, 'Art,' and Uncertainty in Social Work," *Social Work*, Vol. III, July 1958, p. 10.

inquiry Hamilton conceptualized, but it is becoming accelerated and more sharply relevant in its focus on salient system variables. Its newer form and content must go hand in hand with newer treatment modes, newer levels of intervention, and broader conceptions of the flexible helping process that is social casework.

Selected annotated references

BALES, ROBERT F., and FRED L. STRODTBICK, "Phases in Group Problem-Solving," *Journal of Abnormal and Social Psychology* 46 October (1951) pp. 485–95.

The authors discuss the various phases of problem solving by a group.

BENNE, KENNETH D., WARREN G. BENIS, and ROBERT CHIN, "General Strategies for Effecting Changes in Human Systems," in *The Planning of Change*, ed. Warren G. Bennis, Kenneth D. Benne, and Robert Chin (New York: Holt, Rinehart and Winston, 1969).

This excellent basic article discusses three models for planned change: rational-empirical, normative-reeducative, and power-coercive. The problem-solving model is discussed under the normative reeducative approach to change.

BETZ, BARBARA J., "The Problem-Solving Approach and Therapeutic Effectiveness," *American Journal of Psychotherapy* 20:1 January (1966), pp. 45–56.

Betz presents psychotherapy as essentially a problem-solving process. She maintains that good results are based on accurately defining the problem right from the start. The article deals primarily with work with psychotics.

DAVIS, SHELDON A., "An Organic Problem-Solving Method of Organizational Change," in *The Planning of Change*, ed. Warren G. Bennis, Kenneth D. Benne, and Robert Chin (New York: Holt, Rinehart and Winston, 1969).

This paper features laboratory training and problem solving as the strategy of change. The author places emphasis on man as an active growth-seeking person and on a value influence process that is transactional, rather than one-way. There is an interesting discussion of problem solving.

HALLOWITZ, DAVID, "The Problem-Solving Component in Family Therapy," *Social Casework* 51:2 (February 1970), pp. 67–75.

This article deals with the problem-solving component in family therapy.

PERLMAN, HELEN H., *Social Casework: A Problem-Solving Process* (Chicago: University of Chicago Press, 1957).

Perlman conceives casework as a problem-solving process. She discusses the knowledge that the worker needs to possess about the nature of the person, the place, and the process, and makes a clear distinction between relationship and the work the client and worker may engage in.

Chapter 7

THE CONTACT PHASE: PROBLEM IDENTIFICATION, INITIAL GOAL SETTING, AND DATA COLLECTION

The problem-solving process may be divided into three large phases, each with its own tasks: (1) the contact phase, which involves problem identification, initial consideration of goals, and data collection; (2) the middle or contract phase, which involves putting together the collected data, reconsidering and restating goals, making plans for action, and carrying out the plans made; and (3) the ending or termination phase, which includes evaluation and termination. This chapter will deal with the contact phase, in which client and worker come together and begin the initial exploration that will in the next phase result in a decision as to whether they will go on together and, if so, how.

The social worker and the client system may come together in several different ways; the individual, family, or group may reach out for help with a problem that they have identified as being beyond their means of solution, or an individual or group may identify another individual or group as having a problem and request that the social work agency or the social worker become involved. An example of such a request is found in the Spitzer and Welsh article "A Problem Focused Model of Practice" at the end of the last chapter. In that example the teachers in a school identified a group of girls who the teachers thought needed help, since the girls were struggling with responsibilities beyond those assumed by the average schoolgirl, and the school social worker was asked to offer her services to the girls.

In our culture, asking for or taking help (at least from others beyond one's intimate circle of associates) is often a severe blow to one's sense of adequacy. The person who accepts help has to face the fact that: (1) there is something in his situation that he wants changed but that he cannot change by himself; (2) he must be willing to discuss the problem with another person; (3) he must accord that other person at least a limited right to tell him what to do or to do things for him; and (4) he must be willing to change himself or his situation or, at the very least, to go along with changes that others make in his situation.[1] How difficult these steps are depends on several things. The difficulty in asking for help is greatly increased if the problem is one that is generally seen in our culture as being a fault in the person who has it. If a person has usually been taken advantage of or if his confidence has been abused when, in the past, he revealed his situation to another, or if his previous attempts to live in a supposedly better way have always resulted in defeat, the business of asking for help may be excruciatingly difficult. On the other hand, for parents who support a group work agency financially so that their children can have positive developmental group associations, the enrollment of their children in various helping programs, while it is a recognition that they as parents need help in offering their children growth experiences, is usually seen as a positive and normal thing to do. Or the neighborhood group which seeks the worker's help as an advocate to change another system, such as the school or the housing project, may also see this quest for help as a positive step to control its own situation. However, since the social problems of poverty and unemployment are often viewed as the result of individual pathology, the family faced with them may feel inadequate.

Anyone who has driven through miles of confused streets before stopping to ask someone for directions might well ask himself why he had to waste time, gas, and energy before admitting that he did not know where he was going. And how many persons have said to themselves that there was little point in asking because very few "natives" are ever able to give adequate directions? This attitude is a way of preserving our sense of adequacy, if not superiority, while asking for help.

In the beginning phase of their work together worker and client have to clarify what the difficulty is that they are going to work on. (Such clarification is the end product of the considerations outlined in Section I of the problem-solving model in Chapter 6). They have to determine the expectations and goals that the client holds for the outcome of the work together. They have to jointly understand the realities and boundaries of the practitioner's abilities and the service system's resources (Section IIIA of the model). The client has to have some realistic understanding of what the work together is going to require of him. As a result of the execution of these tasks, a preliminary contract to proceed

---

[1] Alan Keith-Lu as, *The Giving and Taking of Help* (Chapel Hill: University of North Carolina Press, 1972) p. 20.

with the necessary exploration and data collection is formulated. The mutual decision as to problem, goals, and expectations will determine the focus of the data collection. We do not seek to know all there is to know about a client, but rather to understand what knowledge is necessary in order to solve the problem and achieve the outcomes sought. (See Carel Germain article at the end of Chapter 6.)

GETTING STARTED

Regardless of the size or type of client system, in the accomplishment of these tasks the practitioner will be involved in two major forms of human association that are typical of social work practice: the interview and the group meeting. The following discussion relates to principles that are important in either instance. (In that discussion we will sometimes refer to the client rather than to the client system simply because this allows us to use the pronoun *he*—a human term—rather than the mechanistic *it* which seems to be called for in references to the client system.) The first task the practitioner faces is that of preparation for the initial contact. Because one cannot divide individuals, or groups, or human interactions, into discrete and entirely orderly parts, this first meeting will undoubtedly involve some elements that bear on all the tasks outlined in the preceding paragraph. However, the primary focus of the beginning will concern Section IA through Section IC in the model—the problem as it is seen by the client system, by systems with which the client system is in interaction, and by the worker. Certainly these aspects will need to be clarified before the problem-for-work (Section ID) can be settled, and focused work on data collection (as apart from incidental data collection) cannot begin until this point has been established.

In preparation for the initial contact, the worker will want to collect and review any pertinent data he has about the client system and the purposes of the coming encounter. In addition, he may want to discuss with others in the setting the kinds of help that the service system can offer. Because beginnings are important in establishing the pattern of ongoing relationships, and because he wishes to demonstrate respect and concern for the client system, the worker will want to do everything possible to reduce unnecessary obstacles to complete and free communication. An understanding about the time and place is essential, as are arrangements to ensure that the meeting will be comfortable, private, and as free from interruptions as possible. The worker may also want to give some thought to contact with other elements of the client system or other systems whose interest and/or participation may impinge on the change endeavor, such as the family of a referred adolescent or the school which suggested that a certain neighborhood group might find a home in a nearby community center. Thought should be given to contact with referral sources—very serious thought, because this action will have many implications for both the practitioner and the client system as they begin work together.

We cannot set forth any universally applicable rules for information collection before the worker meets with the client system, but we can discuss some principles of data collection for the practitioner's consideration. The key principles of data collection in social work are: (1) the client system should be the primary source of information; (2) data is collected for use so that the data collected should be related to the problem at issue; and (3) the practitioner should not acquire information that he would be unwilling to share with the client system. In addition he should be willing to share with the client system the process by which he secured the information and to explain why it was secured in the way it was. Further, it is our conviction that if a worker has information about a particular aspect of the problem he should share this information with the client before asking the client how he feels and thinks about that particular point. In this way, the worker scrupulously avoids trapping the client and gives him the opportunity, before taking a position, to reconcile what the worker knows with what the client thinks and feels. If the worker must seek information in advance of the initial contact with the client system, he should limit that data to the situation that brings client and worker together, nothing more. It is possible that amassing large amounts of information unrelated to the problem at hand may well get in the way of the worker's really hearing what the client is saying about the here and now. In general, it is our position that, if information should be sought from other sources than the client system and the files of the worker's agency, this can be done *after* the first meeting when the practitioner and the client have established the need for such information and the purposes it serves. Thus, most data collection will take place after worker and client have agreed to work together and have defined the problem on which they will work and the ends that will be sought.

Perhaps we should pause here to clarify the above discussion in its relationship to two types of clients: (1) the voluntary client who comes to the worker of his own free will with a problem he has identified, and (2) the involuntary client who comes to the worker either because someone in a power position has demanded that he do this or because the worker has been asked to see him and has initiated the transaction. At the first meeting the involuntary client may or may not be willing to share with the practitioner what the client sees as the problem, but usually advance information about the client has been supplied by the individual or agency that took the initiative in forcing client and worker to come together. It is our position that the principles of data collection outlined earlier apply to the worker's contacts with both the voluntary and the involuntary client.

The involuntary client may not (and usually will not) have given permission for information to be shared with the worker or have knowledge of what information was shared. This makes it very important that the worker, at the very beginning, share the advance information and, if possible, the source of that information with the client. Sometimes the worker cannot share the source of information, for example, in cases involving the neglect and abuse of children in which the informant asks not to be identified. In the interest of protecting the children, such requests are granted. With the involuntary client it may also be necessary, in order to protect the rights of others or in the client's own interest, for the worker to collect certain information without the client's permission. This does not relieve the worker of the responsibility to inform the client that he intends to take such action, and to report to the client the content of the information he collects. In fact, in order to give the client as much control of the involuntary relationship as possible, the sharing of the worker's intent is essential. If one cannot decide the action taken, having knowledge of the action and the reasons for it gives one some sense of being in at least partial control.

As previously mentioned, there are two types of beginnings: in the first the client has decided that he needs to explore what can be done about some felt need, lack, or difficulty, and has asked for help; in the second someone other than the client has been concerned about this matter, and the worker has initiated the contact with the client at that other person's request. When someone has asked to see the social worker, the most sensible thing to do is to let him state in his own terms why he has come. But the first contact starts on a different note when the worker has initiated it. Then the worker must be prepared to explain why he has taken this action, being careful to allow the client time to respond to his statement of purpose and concern.

When the practitioner initiates contact with the client around a problem identified by someone other than the client, he often feels like an intruder. In such instances it is easy to become more worried about oneself than about the client's problem. Following the natural human course of wanting to be liked and accepted by people, we often hope to somehow slip into a pleasant relationship and then to get down to business. This seldom results in a helpful beginning. When a social worker reaches into other people's lives uninvited he must be able to define his reasons so directly, so simply, and so clearly (not with "weaselly" double-talk or words that do not quite portray the situation) that they do not need to worry about what the worker knows or what he is going to find out—clients do not need to ask themselves why he is *really* here. The worker needs to be so concerned about the client system that he is concerned about the stress that his presence may add to it.

DEFINING THE PROBLEM

So the worker begins with a consideration of the problem that he and the client see as a beginning place. For many individuals and groups, needs and wants come in bulk size. But one cannot do everything at once, so the first job the practitioner has is to engage with the client in the business of deciding where to start. The client's selection of a starting point is where one would ordinarily hope to begin. But if the client's choice is dangerous to him or others, or if it promises more trouble and failure, the worker has the responsibility of pointing out the risks. A social worker cannot be a part to planning that is destructive, but he needs to be very sure of his ground before he rejects out of hand the client's starting place.

All of the above indicates that the practitioner must utilize the skills of interviewing, communication, and use of relationship discussed in the preceding chapters to help him in arriving at some understanding of the client's perception of the problem. This does not mean that any worker needs to be, or can be, an instant expert on problems. The primary job at this point is to seek to understand, to take the time and ask the questions necessary to help one gain understanding. Not understanding immediately is not necessarily an indication of inadequacy. The worker can simply ask the client to help him see what is in the situation. In working with a problem beyond his understanding or a system very different from his own it is important that the practitioner not burden either himself or the client with the unrealistic expectations of immediate mutual understanding. This is particularly true when the practitioner is talking with someone whose life experiences are very different from his own. On the basis of his perception of what the client is telling him, on the basis of some understanding of his reaction to the client's problem, and on the basis of information that he may already have about the problem, the worker will need to formulate a notion of the problem and its meaning. He then shares this view with the client. Arriving at a notion of the problem is no more an instant process than is arriving at understanding. It may well take several meetings. The client's perception of the problem and the worker's perception of the problem may not be the same. Frequently, they are not. Then it becomes necessary for the worker and the client to enter into a series of negotiations and discussions directed toward arriving at a definition of the problem on which they are to begin work.

An example of this is found in "The House on Sixth Street," one of the readings reprinted in this chapter. When Mrs. Smith comes to the agency for help about her housing, the worker sees the problem as broader than Mrs. Smith's troubles. The worker defined the problem as one belonging to all the tenants of the house and became an advocate for that particular client system. The critical principle in problem definition is that worker and client must find a common ground which both understand and on which they agree that the beginning interventive efforts will be focused.

Sometimes the development of a common ground for work can be established quickly, sometimes a series of interviews may be necessary, and sometimes a common ground cannot be found. However, without a common place to begin the worker and the client cannot proceed further. When a common ground cannot be reached, the worker and the client may find it necessary to simply acknowledge this fact and, for the present at least, discontinue their efforts. In an authority-related setting, where the worker has a legal mandate to provide supervision and the client has a legal mandate to report his activities, there are two possibilities. The worker may return to the court and acknowledge that there is nothing he and the client can meaningfully accomplish together and ask that the court decide the next steps. This might be a wise course of action if the situation involves, for example, the court's charge that the practitioner work with a mother who has been abusing her child and the worker is concerned about the danger of such behavior to the physical well-being of the child. Or the worker might agree with the client that the worker will only attempt to meet the responsibilities mandated by law. In either of these situations, however, the possibility of reaching a common ground at a future date should be kept alive by leaving the door open for future negotiations.

Partialization is an important aspect of problem definition. Partialization refers to the process of separating out from the universe of problems brought by the client and/or identified by the worker the specific problem or problems which are to become the focus of worker-client attention. No one can deal with a whole range of problems at one time, even when they are closely related, and an attempt to do so may lead to floundering, lack of focus, and an overwhelming sense of despair as worker and client recognize the multiplicity of the client's stress experience. These difficulties can be avoided by partializing out from the universe of problems a specifically defined problem (the problem-to-be-worked[2]) as the beginning point. Later other problems may be

---

[2] One of the authors first heard this phrase used by Helen Harris Perlman in a lecture. It seemed so expressive of the concept we have in mind here that we adopted it. It carries, for us at least, the connotation of worker activity with the client toward problem solution.

tackled. Partialization also provides greater opportunities for finding a common ground—client and worker do not have to agree on all problems in order to find a beginning place.

Another word of caution: at this stage in the exploration of the problem one must be careful not to assume that it lies with the person who first approaches the agency. Although the problem may be very troublesome for this person, it may lie in another system. The target of change may not be the client. This point is very well illustrated in Francis Purcell and Harry Specht's case example, "The House on Sixth Street."

If the client does not have any suggestions as to where to start (as was true for the mother who said to the worker that she didn't know which problem was the largest one: "All I know is that we are in a mess for sure"), the worker may introduce suggestions as to a starting place. Sometimes the worker and the client system may find that where to begin can very well turn into the immediate problem-to-be-worked. In other words, it is perfectly possible that the problem-for-work is the definition of the problem. And if that sounds like double-talk, it isn't. In order to work on something one has to decide where one should begin and where one is going. The inability of various interests involved in a situation to perceive the problem in the same way—to define it in a congruent way that allows work to be done on it—may well be a central problem. Consider the following example:

> Miss B, a 29-year-old schoolteacher, was admitted to a rehabilitation service following a massive stroke. She had been diabetic since she was five years old and, despite constant medical attention and rigid personal self-discipline in diet and medication, the disease was becoming progressively worse. During the last five years she had been losing her sight, and now she is considered legally blind. The stroke, which was also related to the diabetic condition, had resulted in a paralysis of her right side. Miss B had always been a very goal-directed person and, in spite of an ever more handicapping illness, has an advanced degree in the education of handicapped children. She sees her problem as one of getting well quickly so she can return to her classroom; and she has a somewhat unrealistic notion of what is involved in such an accomplishment, denying the hard and difficult work of learning to walk with a cane and of learning to read by the use of braille. She is angry with the nurses and often refuses to cooperate with them because she feels that they are trying to keep her dependent. The diagnosis of her doctors (which has been shared over and over again with her) is that she is in the last stages of an irreversible terminal condition and that she can never return to teaching. From their view, the problem is that Miss B is unwilling to accept the diagnosis and behave properly. The staff feel that the problem is that the patient won't accept the massive damage that she has and will not participate

with them in the small, painful, and difficult tasks necessary to achieving minimal self-care. A social worker sees the problem as getting Miss B to apply for welfare because her own funds are almost exhausted and to engage Miss B in planning for a move to a nursing home, as the rehabilitation facility cannot keep her much longer.

In this situation, the problem-for-work probably has to be that of attempting to resolve the incongruence among the various views of the problem and of finding a beginning that can permit the client and the various other necessary systems to interact to some productive purpose for the client.

GOAL SETTING

This case situation leads us to another consideration that interacts closely and constantly with the definition of the problem-to-be-worked. That is the question of how the client system or other systems see the problem as working out. Not only did each of the significant participants in this situation have his view of the problem, but each view of the problem encompassed an objective or an answer to it. Professional people involved with Miss B wanted her to accept both the inevitability of her physical deterioration and a "realistic" plan for future care—although they differed on the plan. Miss B wanted to return to teaching.

We often find that persons involved in a problem situation present us with the solution rather than with the problem. The client comes to request our help in implementing an already-decided solution rather than in examining alternatives to action. This makes eminently good sense, in that the search for some desired end is a constant thrust of all of us. Goal seeking is what gives the problem-solving process its thrust and purpose, and the consideration of client goals is an important part of each phase of the problem-solving model. The way workers recognize goals and the way they work with goals will differ in each phase, but client goals must never be ignored. In the beginning contact it is important that the practitioner separate problem from goal so that each may be considered separately. Thus when a mother comes to a child-welfare agency saying that she needs to place her child, she may well be presenting the worker with her goal in the shape of a problem. This may be her answer to any one of a whole range of problems; but while it is the only answer she can see, it may be an answer that will cause her great pain and despair. The worker will need to become involved in the question to which placing the child is the client's answer. Worker and client may or may not find a better answer, but in any case the worker should not confuse question and answer. However, in the process of defining and exploring the client's problem, the worker must never lose sight of the fact that the client's original goal was placement, and it is essential for the worker to understand the meaning that this goal had for her. We do not dismiss client goals lightly—we simply seek to separate goal and problem for more effective work.

Let us return to Miss B, a real person whom one of the authors knew. How does one reconcile the disparate views of the goals in this situation? Miss B, desperately needing to deny the diagnosis, is determined that she will get well and return to teaching. All she wants is recognition of this goal and help in achieving it. The medical staff are certain that she can never return to teaching, that the illness is progressing rapidly, that her only hope is to stay its progress somewhat by certain attempts at self-care, and they want her to accept these conclusions. A social worker, concerned over the limits of hospital care and Miss B's finances, wants Miss B to plan soon for other care.

There are different types and dimensions of goals that need to be recognized and discussed at this point. One may be concerned with an optimal goal—or an ultimate goal—which is the final desired outcome to which the effort is directed. Or one may be concerned with interim goals—objectives that are significant steps on the journey toward the optimal goal. Before the ultimate objective can be realized, a series of intermediate objectives usually need to be met. Often these intermediate objectives can be a way of testing whether the ultimate goal is sound. There are usually several layers, or levels, of interim goals. The first goal achieved becomes an aid to the achieving of more complex or more advanced interim goals. Just as one needs to determine a problem-for-work with which to begin, one often finds that the initial steps have to do with facilitative or interim goals as a way of collecting data and making decisions on the feasibility of the ultimate goal.

If one examines the different levels of goals stated at the time the social worker entered Miss B's case, one finds that the interim goals are not different for the various systems involved. The struggle is over ultimate goals. All the professional people involved in the situation want Miss B to participate in rehabilitative efforts that will keep her functioning as well as possible for as long as possible. These same efforts are necessary if Miss B is to be able to carry through her ultimate goal of returning to teaching.

The worker's efforts may very appropriately be directed to sharing with Miss B (1) that the medical staff and Miss B see the problem differently, (2) that they are in strong disagreement over the ultimate goals, (3) that the worker questions whether Miss B can return to full-time teaching, but (4) that perhaps the place to start is with the problem of her ability to work on certain interim goals that are necessary to *either* ultimate goal. So they can begin with what is involved for her in trying to walk again, to read braille, to care for herself in certain physical matters, while collecting data about her progress and planning for the future. Eventually there will come a time (and there did) when the worker and Miss B will have to put the results of their efforts together and make an ultimate plan—either she returns to the community as an independently functioning person or she accepts some alternate plan for at least partially sheltered care. The time of assessment and renegotiation of goals and of planning for the longer future will have to come. But for now they can explore the problem and the feasibility of certain long-term goals by starting with interim goals that become the facilitative goals in that all can agree on them and that they allow further data collection before assessment and decision making.

We believe that both ultimate goals and the means of change are obtained from objective study, evaluation, and planning. These procedures are essential to the effective use of the problem-solving model. But all too often we see cause, truth, and knowledge as absolutes. Sure of ourselves and our understanding, we manipulate our data into firm conclusions, or we use the information to arrive at a psychosocial explanation that seems reasonable to us and set off on a course of action toward our immediate goals—goals that may not be shared with the client or take account of his expectations. Instead, the contact phase of the problem-solving process demands that the practitioner begin with an exploration of the common definition of a problem-to-be-worked and a common understanding of and acceptance of goals which at this stage may only be (and probably should only be) facilitative goals that serve to engage the client systems and the worker in jointly unearthing the ongoing knowledge that will eventually establish (in the contract phase) firmer means and ends around the central issues such assessment will identify. The problem-solving model, as we use it, demands that the client's purposes and expectations in joining the worker in interaction be explored and understood and kept in the center of concern. It is our firm conviction that lack of initial exploration of expectations and goals and lack of careful selection of the starting place in the contact phase of the worker-client interaction account for a large percentage of the failures of the helping process.[3]

PRELIMINARY CONTRACT

In arriving at the preliminary contract, which is in essence an agreement between the worker and the client on the problem-to-be worked and the facilitative goals, there are some other absolutes that must be clarified with the client. The worker must clarify the realities and boundaries of what he can offer, and must behave in such a way as to help the client understand the nature of further work together. To make

---

[3] For empirical evidence of this see John E. Mayer and Noel Timms, *The Client Speaks: Working Class Impressions of Casework* (New York: Atherton Press, 1970).

a brief comment on the first point: this requires that the worker be able to convey to the client the limits of the service he can offer while at the same time conveying to him the worker's belief in his ability to help within those limits, and his interest in helping the client find another resource should the service he can offer be too limited. In other words, the worker does not want to promise more than he can deliver and so trap the client by false hopes, but neither does he want to operate in such a way as to imply hopelessness to the client. The client may come to the worker out of pain, or despair, or anger, but he will only become involved in action with the worker when this feeling of discomfort is joined to a hope that something can be done.

One usually finds clients confused about how the helping process will work. As was pointed out in the first chapter of this text, people find it difficult to grasp the nature of the social work job. There are seldom visible technologies or artifacts that will give others some notion of what the process is all about. The practitioner's actions in the beginning phase can give the client a sample of the social work method. That is one reason the beginning is so important. Another reason is the pattern-setting nature of communication between elements of a system or among systems.

At the end of the beginning phase of problem identification and goal determination, client and worker decide whether they wish to continue together. If they do, the worker is then free to begin to collect the information that will be the data on which assessment and planning will be based. The problem-solving model at the end of the last chapter includes a long list of the kinds of information that may need to be collected, given certain problems and certain client systems. We would caution again that nothing is more sterile than information collecting for the purpose of information collecting. Information is collected for the purpose of taking effective action, and all efforts must be directed to that end. The kind and amount of information collected will be dictated by the defined problem-for-work and the preliminary goal that is established.

AREAS OF DATA COLLECTION

We set forth in our model some general kinds of data that the practitioner might want to consider, but he will have to do the deciding that is involved in specific selection. There are two areas of information that we suggest be considered very seriously in every situation. These areas are motivation and opportunity and their relationship to each other. We want to speak briefly about motivation and opportunity as specific areas of data collection because we believe they are generally misunderstood by practitioners.

What causes any of us to act? As was stated earlier, for action to take place, discomfort with things as they are must be felt, but this is not enough. If any of us is to act, to our discomfort, mild or severe, must be added the hope of being able to reach a goal that we see as the answer to our wants, and in addition there must be some ability to consider what has gone wrong and some opportunity for change in the situation. An important research study[4] on the factors that contribute to effective casework service concludes with the observation that productive engagement in the casework process is dependent on the client's "hope-discomfort balance" and on the extent to which the practitioner is able to engage that pressure by the hope and clearly defined opportunity he offers. The study states that before work can begin on a problem the client must be uncomfortable about the present state of affairs and hope that something can be done about it, and the worker must be able to communicate understanding (empathy, if you will) of the client's discomfort and, even more important, he must engage himself with the client's hope. As was once said, when hope is weak the practitioner must find a way of "hitching his motor to the client's wagon." For this reason, we would urge that the worker always be concerned, with all client systems and in all problem situations, with the level of the client's hope-discomfort balance and with his early activity with the client in this area and the way he engages himself and the client with the opportunities for reaching objectives.

SOURCES AND METHODS OF DATA COLLECTION

Before closing this chapter, we would like to make some general observations about the sources from which worker and client will collect the information that is needed to make an assessment. The first, and most important principle, is that the client system must be aware of the resources the worker is using and why he is using them. If at all possible (as was noted earlier in the chapter), the client's permission should be secured before any particular source of information is used. However, whether or not his permission is secured, the client *must know* about the sources used, the information sought, and why the information is believed to be appropriate to the task at hand. If our commitment is to the clients' participation in decision making that will lead to action toward their goals, then we must share with them all information on which decisions may be based. Otherwise, we deprive them of an opportunity for representative participation in the discussion about themselves.

---

[4] Lilian Ripple with Ernestina Alexander and Bernice W. Polemis, *Motivation, Capacity, and Opportunity: Studies in Casework Theory and Practice* (Chicago: School of Social Service Administration, 1964).

In general, modes of data collection can be divided into three groups: (1) questions, verbal or written; (2) observation; and (3) other professional or institutional systems. Perhaps the most widely used tool for data collection is the interview or group meeting with the client system in which questioning and observation are used to gain information. The interview or the meeting requires a knowledge of the principles of relationship and communication that have been discussed in previous chapters of this text. In addition to the material in these chapters there are selected references that give guidance for further reading in this area. In his use of the face-to-face meeting the practitioner will need to decide its purpose, the information he needs to obtain from it, and how he wants to structure it. At one extreme is the nondirective interview or meeting in which the worker follows the feeling and thinking of the interviewee or allows the group to reveal itself as it will. At the other extreme is the completely structured interview or meeting, in which the worker has a scheduled set of questions from which he will not depart. However, the worker is also giving some structure to the interview and determining what data may be collected when he decides where and when it will be held, when he establishes ground rules and norms for content and participation, and even when he arranges the chairs of the persons involved. Careful thought should be given to the place of the first meeting: Is it to be on "his turf or yours"?

Obviously, the interview may be used to collect information from sources other than the client system. In using these other systems, the worker will want to consider carefully the kinds of information he thinks they can provide and the need he has for this information. He will need to give thought to the fact that certain sources of information may expect the interview to involve a sharing of information. If the worker is to share information he will need to discuss this with the client system. If he is unwilling to share information he must make this known to his source when he requests the interview.

Many kinds of written questioning techniques are in use. Clients are often asked to fill out application or information forms when they first approach an agency. There are various questionnaires that may be used with various client systems for various purposes. If a group is trying to decide a focus for future meetings, and members seem reluctant to share their views openly with other members, an anonymous written questionnaire may be helpful. It allows members to express an opinion without penalty. Written exercises are sometimes used in work with families to allow members to express themselves without feeling that they have directly attacked other members of the family. In certain community organization projects, the use of a survey based on a written questionnaire is a very valuable technique. Obviously, one would not want to use a written questionnaire with a client who does not express himself well in writing, or a client who might see it as a dehumanizing device, or a client to whom it might imply that he was being classified into just one of a similar group of persons.

In speaking of both verbal and written questioning as data collection tools, we should mention the use of other persons to collect information for the worker. In certain situations, someone close to the client system and knowledgeable about the situation may conduct an interview for the worker. An indigenous Spanish-speaking community worker might be asked to talk to a Chicano woman who has just suffered the loss of her husband and who should not be asked to take on the additional burden of speaking in English to a stranger at such a time. Also the worker may have other professionals, such as psychologists, administer tests to gain certain knowledge. These tests may be oral or written. Psychologists often use projective techniques, which allow the respondent to impose his own frame of reference upon some stimulus, such as a picture. Or, in order to have two sources of information, the worker may ask a psychiatrist, or perhaps his supervisor, to interview the same client system that he is dealing with.

Along with questioning, the worker usually utilizes observation as a way of gathering data. Though we all use observation of others in all our daily interactions, much will be lost unless we learn to make deliberate, planned use of the technique. As with verbal questions, observation can be structured or unstructured, and the worker can be a totally uninvolved observer, or a participant observer, or a leader-and-initiator observer. For example, the worker might give a group of children a game to play and then observe and record their actions without being in any way involved in the game. Or he might be a member of a committee, both involved and observing. Or he might serve as a committee chairman while trying to observe the interactions of the members. This last possibility will probably cause many to ask how effectively a chairman can observe the interactions of his committee members. This is an example of questions that are often raised about the use of observations. What about the bias and the selectivity of the observer? None of us can possibly observe all the interactions of a group, or even all the facial expressions and changes in posture of one person, in an interview. Observation requires a sensitivity to others, the capacity to see small changes. In addition it requires that we know ourselves and our biases. It requires us to have given thought to what we want to learn through this process and to how we do it. Since we cannot collect all the data on any one transaction we must recognize that we collect only certain information and are, therefore, selective. We must know what framework guides this selectivity. The article "Of Plums and Thistles" in this chapter speaks to the problem of observation. It asks that practitioners not only observe the client system, but also that they be self-observant, and that these two kinds of observations be related.

The last general way one collects information is from the use of existing written material—material not gathered specifically for the present situation. Often the worker may find that his agency, or some other place has records of previous contacts with the client system. Usually, it is wise for the worker to know the contents of such records and to discuss them with the client. Otherwise the client may waste valuable time and trouble in worrying over what you may know about him. If previous written materials are available, they can be a very efficient means of data collection. Their use places little demand on the client system and is within the worker's control. But therein lies a seductive danger—such records can be used so easily without the client's knowledge. There is another danger—when we read something we have a tendency to feel that we really know it. For these reasons we would like to especially caution the practitioner against the indiscriminate use of such material. He must question written material as he does a human informant. Does it give the facts? Are the facts documented? Or does the material merely reflect another person's judgments? The practitioner must also recognize that such material deals with the past; that it may not bear on the present problem and may even confuse the issue in that it was written or gathered for a purpose unconnected with it; and (to repeat) that it may reflect the biases and selective perceptions and evaluations of the persons who collected it. Often there is a tendency to see written material as holding more of the truth than the practitioner's present experiences. This tendency should be strongly resisted. On the other hand, appropriate written material can be an effective source of data.

RECAPITULATION

In this chapter we have discussed the contact phase of the problem-solving process. We have pointed out that this phase involves eight essential tasks that can be summarized as: (1) the initial contact, (2) the determination of the problem-for-work, (3) the clarification of goals, (4) the clarification of the limits of service, (5) the clarification of what will be asked of the client system, (6) the development of appropriate relationships, (7) the emergence of a commitment to work together, and (8) data collection. It will be noted that these tasks demand the activity of the worker as well as the client.

This beginning part of the problem-solving process is extremely important because, it sets the pattern for the phases of work that follow. We have suggested that, given the limits of any specific situation, we collect information about at least three elements of the client system:

the hope-discomfort balance that the client brings to the first encounter; the opportunities that the client sees and that the worker can bring to bear; and factors within the client system and in its relationships to the world around it.

One further caution: It is perhaps a misunderstanding of the level and magnitude of problem-definition and goal-setting that leads some professionals to view the problem-solving model as only of value to the client capable of highly rational functioning. It is our view that every human being has wants (if only to get rid of the worker) and that these wants can be translated into wishes and wishes into goals. The meaning and value of the goals has nothing to do with the worker's evaluation of their value, rather it relates to the client's wishes. Practitioners often see the only goals worth setting as those that seem to the practitioner to involve a generally better life. However, for many clients the securing of essential survival needs and life supports are the only goals worth setting, at least when he has no reason to trust either the practitioner or life itself. If the problem that the client sees is the lack of certain concrete essentials of life this can become the problem-to-be-worked, client and worker can agree that the securing of these essentials is the first and most important goal at the moment, and the plan can well be that the worker will find a way to supply this resource. In this situation, the worker may have done a good deal of the initial work in defining the problem and the achievement of the goal may have come from the worker's concrete giving. The essential factor here is not the level of goal or who works toward the goal but that the client was involved in the thinking and planning that was done and that what was given was related to the client's wishes and not something that the worker unilaterally thought was needed. Our inability to see small concrete goals as important objectives for work and our assumption that the worker's supplying of concrete needs to apathetic, withdrawn, depressed, or angry people need not involve mutual problem-definition and goal-setting (no matter how primitive the level) are built upon certain unconscious, or not so unconscious, practitioner assumptions about what is meaningful professional interaction that need to be seriously examined.

A LOOK FORWARD

In the last part of the chapter we discussed some of the modes of information gathering that are available to the practitioner. Thus ends our discussion of the contact phase of the problem-solving process. Articles of two other authors are reprinted in this chapter to extend the development of the points made in it. In the next chapter we will consider the contract phase of the transaction. The contract phase is the core of the work together.

Of plums and thistles: The search for diagnosis*

Doris Campbell Phillips

> Simple Simon went to look
> If plums grew on a thistle;
> He pricked his finger very much,
> Which made poor Simon whistle!

Apply Mother Goose's moral to the search for diagnosis, and you may avoid suffering the stings of reaching for diagnostic plums on thistle "trees"! For the secret of diagnosis is in knowing where to look for it. And you don't have to be so simple to make poor Simon's mistake of looking in the wrong place.

But where should you look? There are four places where the odds are in favor of your finding plums instead of thistles. The first place to look for clues to a diagnosis is in your spontaneous reactions to your client; another is in his reactions to you; the third is in your client's problems; and the fourth is in his proposed solution to those problems.

The obvious reason for this search—or, in other words, the purpose of diagnosis—is to enable the worker and client to begin and carry through a relationship and mutual activity which help the client solve his problems. The sooner the diagnostic search begins, the better it serves this purpose. And the search might well begin at home.

Worker's reactions to client

To get off to a prompt start and "begin at home," the school social worker should, as she meets her clients for the first time, search out her own spontaneous reaction to the youngsters and their parents. It's a good time to do this, simply because the worker's spontaneity is not yet influenced by her professional *self*-consciousness. She has not yet studied her client's behavior and thereby modified and objectified her own response. Her understanding, after the diagnostic search bears all its fruit, may turn out to be quite objective and nearly completely correct—a tribute to her professional ability. But before that comes about,

---

* This is a revision of an article originally published in *Social Work*, 5:1 (January 1960), pp. 84–90. It has been revised and brought up to date esp·cially for this volume.

she may well find the first of her diagnostic plums in her initial subjective, spontaneous reaction.

That's because the worker's reaction is not something that wells up in her without provocation. Instead, it is elicited by the behavior of the client. Everything a person does, everything he is, depends on what he learns in his interaction with the world. He behaves in certain ways that bring forth certain responses from those around him. Even though the responses he learns to bring about may cause problems for himself and others, they *are* what he has learned in his own individual life experience. In some cases, a person repeats again and again some sequences of behavior that aren't appropriate or that are hurtful to himself or to others.

Let me illustrate this point. Larry, a nine-year-old, is referred to a school social worker by his teacher, Miss Morris, about two months after school started. About one-and-one-half days out of every week Larry is "absolutely impossible"—he turns the classroom upside down, is wildly disobedient, and leads other children into temptation, adroitly extricating himself from the situation just as the others fall into sin. The rest of the time he is thoughtful, helpful, and lovable, and Miss Morris knows of no reasons for his blowups.

When Larry comes to the worker's office for the first time, he enters with a swagger, smiles winningly, sits down, and says, "Well, it's like this. . . ." He waves his arms expansively and pushes a pile of papers off the worker's desk onto the floor. It was an "accident," of course, but his eyes never leave the worker's face, and the smile on his lips broadens. "Oops," he says, and very slowly gets down and begins picking up each paper. There's something maddening about it, and the social worker, Mrs. Verry, who is, after all, a real person with the usual complement of vulnerable feelings, *burns*. But when he gets the papers picked up, he stacks them neatly, and steps close to Mrs. Verry. "Is that okay?" he asks, looking at her like a little kindergarten boy. He remains standing close beside her, and picks up her clock, holding it carefully and asking her if he can move the hands, how the alarm works, and so on. His shoulders, thrown back so arrogantly when he came in, now look a bit frail, his head is bent over the clock, and his long lashes hide his eyes. His slender young figure is half-turned to her, and his sleeve touches hers. Mrs. Verry is only human. She feels drawn to this defenseless little guy, and it is with a bit of effort that she begins talking to him about why he is here. He replies to her beginning gambit with "Yes, I'm too noisy," and his innocent, respectful, wide-eyed face turned to her is so gravely concerned that she feels like saying, "Fellow, you can be as noisy as you like with me." But she doesn't say that, of course. Instead she encourages him to tell her more about that. He moves to the other side of the desk—and the spell is broken.

There he puts on an exhibit that makes Mrs. Verry feel like Miss Morris's long-estranged and now-reconciled blood kin. He's smart-alecky, cleverly belittling of her—maddening. Then, just as she is beginning to think that corporal punishment might not be such a bad method for social workers, Larry comes close to her, smiles his heart-tugging smile, and says, "I have to go now, but I'd like to come again. Could I come next Monday?" Mrs. Verry weakly says yes. She's had it.

Then, in the week that follows, the social worker goes over her interviews with Larry's divorced mother, and tries to understand Larry in the light of his life experience. She becomes involved in this other kind of diagnostic thinking, and if she is not careful she overlooks the diagnostic revelation in his behavior with her.

Mrs. Verry can be fairly sure that she is not the first who has felt the stir of anger, together with the sense of closeness and identity and tenderness, when in the presence of this youngster. When Larry was in the third grade, his teacher nipped his classroom cutting-up in the bud. She simply drew herself up in a commanding posture, and with the authority of a dominating personality said, "We'll have none of this." And when Larry drew close to her, she stared through him and ordered, "Go back to work." But even this teacher had an Achilles' heel. She was proud of certain science projects which had brought her recognition. Larry became a science devotee, and after a while Miss Murray felt very close to the boy, whose interest and accomplishments in her project elicited her identity with him, and awakened her latent motherliness. Or so it did until, on three successive demonstrations to parents and other teachers, Larry broke a test tube, spilling its contents; dropped a live frog; and knocked over a bottle of blueing. His fourth-grade teacher, Miss Morris, was not a forceful disciplinarian, and so it was not hard for Larry to act out his learned behavioral pattern in this area with her.

What did Larry's behavior with Mrs. Verry, as expressed in his words and actions and bearing, reveal? What is it in his past experience and in his ongoing interactions at school and at home that brings about this behavior? We learn that he behaved in a similar sequential fashion with Miss Murray—is this behavior repeated in numerous situations and with many people? These are questions to consider, not in isolation, of course, but in relation to other diagnostic intimations.

Now, of course, if a social worker is to find a diagnostic plum and not a thistle in her own reactions, she must not only be aware of her spontaneous reaction, but must also be able to measure and evaluate it. That means that she must be self-knowledgeable without feeling the necessity to deny or transform what she knows about herself. With Larry, for instance, Mrs. Verry must first be aware of her anger and her feeling of identity with him. Then she must ask herself, "Is there something in my own experience that causes me to feel this way at this particular time, something that hasn't much to do with Larry's actual presence and behavior?" Probably then she'll need to learn from others who know Larry, particularly his teacher, what their reactions are—their honest to goodness, down-to-earth reactions, which sometimes are not discovered because the teacher, too, may feel a professional obligation to present her more sophisticated insights. In summary, a Mrs. Verry should trust her own reactions, but not trust them blindly, or she may sting herself with a prickly thistle.

Before leaving this point, give some thought to one of its related aspects having to do with the school social worker's obligation to help teachers help children. If the social worker forgets the personal impact of her client's appearance and behavior, then the worker's helpfulness to teachers may be limited. For example, the first time Miss Shannon, a school social worker, sees 12-year-old Sharon's thick makeup hiding a dirty face, her shifty eyes, her hip-swinging suggestiveness, and her lying evasiveness, Miss Shannon reacts with some repulsion and uneasiness. But almost immediately the worker brings to bear her professional self-discipline and her professional consideration of what this means, and of why Sharon is this kind of girl. Maybe, even by the end of the first interview, Miss Shannon has lost sight of her own immediate response, and has translated the descriptive words used here into language that is less personal and less judgmental.

But the teacher, even though she too may have achieved some understanding of Sharon, cannot remove the girl from the group, and must cope with her in the midst of the other youngsters—not at all an easy task. For in that context the teacher experiences the impact of Sharon's appearance and behavior day in and day out. How hard it is for her to hold on to a professional attitude under the pressure of that impact! And along the way Miss Shannon, now almost completely innocent of even the memory of her own repulsion, loses sympathy with the teacher, so that she cannot really understand how hard it is to have Sharon in the classroom day by day. A wedge is driven between worker and teacher, which limits the worker's helpfulness.

Now let us go on to discuss the other "places" a worker may find diagnostic plums.

Client's reaction to worker

Let us say that the social worker has taken note of her initial reaction to her client, and has begun her diagnostic inquiry. Next, then, let us look for a diagnostic plum in the reverse: the client's reaction to the worker. And remember, the client's reaction to the worker is influenced by feelings and attitudes toward the *school* which developed before the request for help from the client or referral by someone else brings client and worker together. Moreover, his feelings and attitudes toward the problems he is bringing will influence his response to the worker.

Most school social workers, even those who have been in school social work for many years, think of themselves as a part of the school, and not as *the school.* That's only natural. When the worker introduces herself to parents or children she has to explain her *difference* from the classroom teacher, principal, nurse, and janitor, all well-known school personnel. This encourages her to see herself as a part, a *different* part, of the school, and naturally to expect parents and children to see her this way. And they do, up to a point. Some need to see her as different; others, perhaps, sense her desire to have them see her differently, and oblige. And yet, without being fully aware of it themselves, they may also look upon the worker as the *school,* (1) seeing the *school* as a kind of entity and (2) having feelings and attitudes directed toward their conception of it as a whole. To the child that means the worker represents all of what school has appeared to be in his experience. To each of the parents, the worker represents an idea of *school* that has been formed through the years, beginning with early experience as a pupil and nurtured by ongoing relatedness to the school as parent and as citizen-taxpayer. Remember that the position of a parent of a pupil now in school is conducive to some strain, for the parent demands from the school but also must answer to the school; he has a measure of control, but, on the other hand, the school also has its control, which could be exercised to the detriment of his child.

Clients' expectations of what the social worker will be like and how she will relate to them are also influenced by their attitudes toward the problems they need help in resolving. How they feel about their own problems and related ones of other family members—overwhelmed, baffled, ashamed, troubled, etc.—will help shape their expectations of what the worker's attitudes and actions will be. This means that the client may be prepared to react to the worker as a potential helper, or perhaps as a judge and critic who will threaten and maybe mete out punishment, or as a derider, or a supporter, or an interloper. The worker's diagnostic inquiry will reach further if she knows what the reaction is. If there is a "problem behind the problem" in the client's expectations of what the worker will be like and will do, worker and client will have to clear away misconceptions before they can understand each other.

Now we've discussed the diagnostic clues in a client's reaction to the worker which began before he saw her. The reaction will continue, either in full flow or ebb tide, throughout the contact. The important point is that the reaction always bears watching in the interest of development of insight into his problems.

And while we're talking about the client's reaction to the worker, let's remember that he also reacts to her as the person she appears to be to him, especially in his first contacts with her. He reacts to the worker's ethnic and racial origin, to the worker as an older or younger person, man or woman, married or unmarried, better or less well educated, richer or poorer, likable or unlikable, more passive or more active than he, more or less "successful" in the areas he values. Not all, but some, of these reactions will show through, and they should help the worker know what it means to this person to reveal himself to her and to use her help, especially if she carefully relates them to her other diagnostic findings.

The client's problems

Let us say that the worker has noted her own reaction to her client, and his to her. Where else will she look for diagnosis? In her client's problems, of course: the problems described by the child's teacher and his parents; those the client, whether youngster or parent, tells about; those observed by the worker.

So much has been written about problems as symptoms and signs, so much has been discovered and revealed about the sources of problems and their ultimate meaning, that it would be impossible to treat the subject fully here. Instead, let us adopt a simpler diagnostic approach, which may be helpful in everyday practice. This suggests that the worker view her client's problems as *reactions*, and that she then make it her diagnostic job to figure out what these problems are reactions to; what it is in his surroundings which encourages these reactions; how well established they are in the client's personality and behavior; and finally what it would mean to him to relinquish these reactions.

Now, then, what may be the objects of the client's reactions which have turned into the problems that bring him to the worker? *First, the client may be reacting to the fact that his behavior—the kind of person he is—is not supported by the culture in which he lives, or is supported by one part of our complex culture but not by another.* Quite often, sadly enough, it is that part of our culture with which school personnel is identified which rejects the client and his behavior. Take, for instance, 13-year-old Pete, who is referred for truanting, and closemouthed, sinister-appearing defiance when he is in school. To the school he represents the feared and hated "juvenile delinquent," an epitome of a cast-off segment of our society. And don't think he doesn't know it. He reads the papers, watches TV, sees the expressions on people's faces, senses the attitudes of teachers and principal. He is supported and encouraged in his behavior by the neighborhood in which he lives. But he is not living in an era when he expects to live and die in that neighborhood. Even it is changing, and Pete knows that there is no future for him there. After all, he is subject to the conforming drives in our society, and he recognizes many of the same success symbols that boys in more favored neighborhoods covet. And so he has aspirations to find acceptance with the dominant cultural group. But these secret aspirations meet with frustration in rejection for reasons he does not fully understand, and he reacts with his problem behavior. The social worker's job is not only to recognize this, but to try to see whether this boy has the capacity and the potential motivation to take the really portentous course of moving away from behavior which accords him recognition and approval in his cultural corner, and to behavior that may—but he does not know it will—bring him recognition and approval in what now seems to him a hostile and rejecting corner, the enemy's corner.

Second, the client's problems may be a reaction to restrictions imposed on him by inadequacies of his person—real or imaginary, genuine or self-imposed. In that case, it is not enough to know that he has a handicap. To find her diagnosis the worker will need to know specifically how the client views the handicap, what overtones it has for him, and how others who are important to him view it. And above all, the worker should be sure she understands what handicap he is reacting to. Nine-year-old Richard cannot read, and spends his time in school and in special tutoring sessions engaged in anxious kinds of behavior, twiddling with his pencil, balancing the eraser on his head, laughing nervously when there's nothing to laugh about. The children call him "Dummy." His teacher winces, his parents are frantic. When the worker talks with the boy about his reading problems, Richards says frankly, "I'm just dumb." But wait a minute: is that why he's anxious? If the worker is perceptive, she will notice that Richard is the only one who is *not* worried about his reading problem. And so, when the worker broadens her inquiry, she finds that what the boy is really worried about is the fact that he cannot catch a ball, although her father has sweated and cursed and shamed him in many a practice session. And the other boys won't let him play. He is convinced that he will never be a real man anyway, so why worry about a little thing like reading?

Third, the client's problems may be a reaction to his inability to relate successfully to others—parents and siblings and all the others who represent them, once or more removed. It is not possible to discuss here the intricacies of relationship and the various kinds of disturbances that may occur. Besides, thinking of the client's problems as *reactions* to disturbances in his relations with others may be helpful in the beginning because it keeps the worker focused on the problem as it is known and felt keenly by the client.

To illustrate, Mary, a high school senior, comes to the worker at the suggestion of a teacher. Mary says that she has an argument with her mother every morning before her mother goes to work. Afterward, Mary feels upset and goes back to bed. When she finally gets up she is late to school or doesn't attend. She says she's worried about this because she wants to graduate. Mary's immediate problem, the one she's bringing to the worker, is her reaction to disturbing events in the mother-daughter relationship. At this time the worker and Mary need to focus on Mary's reactive behavior, how it came about, how well established it is, how it satisfies and frustrates her, whether she wants to and can change it without first changing the relationship with her mother. It may not be necessary—or possible, for that matter—to alter profoundly the relationship to which Mary is reacting. If it should prove necessary to go beyond Mary's reaction to the disturbances themselves, nothing has been lost through early focus on the presenting problem.

Fourth, problems which bring the client to the worker may be a pattern of behavior he engages in whenever he enters certain kinds of situations or interacts with people who have some particular significance for him. The reason such reactive behavior becomes a problem for him is that it gets him into trouble with other people, or with himself, yet it persists. It may be a problem that a person can "live with" rather comfortably, such as that of Roy's father, Mr. Peterson, who "falls over his feet while he's kowtowing" whenever he meets a man with superior athletic ability. It becomes a more serious problem if Mr. Peterson defers without question to a high school coach's version of an occurrence involving Roy without listening to the boy's story.

A still more serious example of repetitive behavior reaction is Larry's behavior, described earlier. Mrs. Verry observes in her first interview with Larry a cycle of behavior reported to her earlier by the referring teacher, a cycle of behavior in which Larry first does things that he has learned make people feel kindly or affectionate toward him, then does things that he has learned are offensive to them. This behavior apparently has some momentary satisfaction for Larry; it may, in some way we don't understand, discharge tension that neither we nor Larry can identify, but it has caused problems for him with teachers and with classmates. What is it about the situation and the people in it that brings forth the behavior? Do the teachers and the social worker have some particular significance for him? A pivotal question has to do with his relationships with his divorced parents: Was it in his relationships with either or both that this behavior pattern developed? What keeps it going?

In summary, then, the social worker will be helped to find her diagnosis if she approaches her client's problems as reactions, and searches for the objects of these reactions. Having done this, and having also examined her client's reactions to her and hers to him, she will be further rewarded if she looks for diagnosis in the solutions proposed by the client, directly or indirectly, to his own problems or those of his child, and his ability or inability to use his own solutions successfully.

Solutions proposed by the client

Rarely does a client come to a social worker without first having tried out solutions of his own. The school social worker is apt to have a double-barreled solution presented to her—the child's and the parents'—which may or may not be the same. The fact that a referral has been made is, in itself, evidence that someone is dissatisfied with the solution. It does not work for the child, or for his parents, or for other children in the classroom or on the playground, or for the teacher—one or more of these are sufficiently dissatisfied for the child to be considered "in trouble." By looking closely at both barrels of the solution, the worker can learn much about the child and his parents. The worker should ask such questions of herself as, "Why was this solution chosen?" "Why doesn't it work?" or even, "Does anyone really want it to work?" "What does it tell about the problems it purports to solve?"

For example, six-year-old Bobby, in the second half of the first grade, refuses to go to school in the morning and on several occasions goes home without permission before school is over. He is direct about it: he likes school and his teacher, and he will come if his mother will bring him. His mother proposes to the school social worker that she will bring him every day for a while. That is their solution to his reluctance. But it does not solve anything, because Bobby won't go without his mother when the time comes for him to go. And his mother seems unable either to persuade or "make" him go alone—as she "makes" him do other things. Now is the time for the worker to ask questions such as those above. Then, perhaps, she will note that Bobby is not willing to give up his "solution," which he has found in forcing his mother to assure him that she really wants him to go to school. He does this through placing her in the position of parting from him instead of vice versa. And the worker will note that Bobby's mother needs to go to the extreme of taking him every day—to protect herself from admitting that she really wants to keep him at home with her. The worker, in recognizing how the "solution" fits in with the needs of both mother and child, now has the beginning of more "why" questions, which will pave the way toward diagnosis.

What has been given is a description of a diagnostic approach rather than a discussion of diagnostic formulations. It is meant to be helpful to the worker, who, because of the nature of things, will encounter many a thistle "tree," and may be able to make use of a few simple directions to find the real plum trees.

The house on Sixth Street[*]

Francis P. Purcell and Harry Specht

The extent to which social work can affect the course of social problems has not received the full consideration it deserves.[1] For some time the social work profession has taken account of social problems only as they have become manifest in behavioral pathology. Yet it is becoming increasingly apparent that, even allowing for this limitation, it is often necessary for the same agency or worker to intervene by various methods at various points.

In this paper, the case history of a tenement house in New York City is used to illustrate some of the factors that should be considered in selecting intervention methods. Like all first attempts, the approach described can be found wanting in conceptual clarity and systematization. Yet the vital quality of the effort and its implications for social work practice seem clear.

The case of "The House on Sixth Street" is taken from the files of Mobilization For Youth (MFY), an action-research project that has been in operation since 1962 on New York's Lower East Side. MFY's programs are financed by grants from several public and private sources. The central theoretical contention of MFY is that a major proportion of juvenile delinquency occurs when adolescents from low-income families do not have access to legitimate opportunities by which they can fulfill the aspirations for success they share with all American youth. The action programs of MFY are designed to offer these youths concrete

---

[*] Reprinted with permission of the authors and the National Association of Social Workers from *Social Work*, 10:4 (October 1965), pp. 69–76.

[1] Social work practitioners sometimes use the term "social problem" to mean "environmental problem." The sense in which it is used here corresponds to the definition developed by the social sciences. That is, a social problem is a disturbance, deviation, or breakdown in social behavior that (1) involves a considerable number of people and (2) is of serious concern to many in the society. It is social in origin and effect, and is a social responsibility. It represents a discrepancy between social standards and social reality. Also, such socially perceived variation must be viewed as corrigible. See Robert K. Merton and Robert A. Nisbet, eds, *Contemporary Social Problems* (New York: Harcourt, Brace, and World, 1961), pp. 6, 701.

opportunities to offset the debilitating effects of poverty. For example, the employment program helps youngsters obtain jobs; other programs attempt to increase opportunities in public schools. In addition, there are group work and recreation programs. A wide variety of services to individuals and families is offered through Neighborhood Service Centers: a homemaking program, a program for released offenders, and a narcotics information center. Legal services, a housing services unit, a special referral unit, and a community development program are among other services that have been developed or made available. Thus, MFY has an unusually wide range of resources for dealing with social problems.

The problem

"The House on Sixth Street" became a case when Mrs. Smith came to an MFY Neighborhood Service Center to complain that there had been no gas, electricity, heat, or hot water in her apartment house for more than four weeks. She asked the agency for help. Mrs. Smith was 23 years old, Negro, and the mother of four children, three of whom had been born out of wedlock. At the time she was unmarried and receiving Aid to Families with Dependent Children. She came to the center in desperation because she was unable to run her household without utilities. Her financial resources were exhausted—but not her courage. The Neighborhood Service Center worker decided that in this case the building—the tenants, the landlord, and circumstances affecting their relationships—was of central concern.

A social worker then visited the Sixth Street building with Mrs. Smith and a community worker. Community workers are members of the community organization staff in a program that attempts to encourage residents to take independent social action. Like many members in other MFY programs, community workers are residents of the particular neighborhood. Most of them have little formal education, their special contribution being their ability to relate to and communicate with other residents. Because some of the tenants were Puerto Rican, a Spanish-speaking community worker was chosen to accompany the social worker. His easy manner and knowledge of the neighborhood enabled him and the worker to become involved quickly with the tenants.

Their first visits confirmed Mrs. Smith's charge that the house had been without utilities for more than four weeks. Several months before, the city Rent and Rehabilitation Administration had reduced the rent for each apartment to one dollar a month because the landlord was not providing services. However, this agency was slow to take further action. Eleven families were still living in the building, which had twenty-eight apartments. The landlord owned the electric company several thousand dollars. Therefore, the meters had been removed from the house. Because most of the tenants were welfare clients, the Department of Welfare had "reimbursed" the landlord directly for much of the unpaid electric bill and refused to pay any more money to the electric company. The Department of Welfare was slow in meeting the emergency needs of the tenants. Most of the children (forty-eight from the eleven families in the building) had not been to school for a month because they were ill or lacked proper clothing.

The mothers were tired and demoralized. Dirt and disorganization were increasing daily. The tenants were afraid to sleep at night because the building was infested with rats. There was danger of fire because the tenants had to use candles for light. The seventeen abandoned apartments had been invaded by homeless men and drug addicts. Petty thievery is common in such situations. However, the mothers did not want to seek protection from the police for fear that they would chase away all men who were not part of the families in the building (some of the unmarried mothers had men living with them—one of the few means of protection from physical danger available to these women—even though mothers on public assistance are threatened with loss of income if they are not legally married). The anxiety created by these conditions was intense and disabling.

The workers noted that the mothers were not only anxious but "fighting mad"; not only did they seek immediate relief from their physical dangers and discomforts but they were eager to express their fury at the landlord and the public agencies, which they felt had let them down.

The circumstances described are by no means uncommon, at least not in New York City. Twenty percent of all housing in the city is still unfit, despite all the public and private residential building completed since World War II. At least 277,500 dwellings in New York City need major repairs if they are to become safe and adequate shelters. This means that approximately 500,000 people in the city live in inferior dwelling units and as many as 825,000 people in buildings that are considered unsafe.[2] In 1962 the New York City Bureau of Sanitary Inspections reported that 530 children were bitten by rats in their homes and 198 children were poisoned (nine of them fatally) by nibbling at peeling lead paint, even though the use of lead paint has been illegal in the city for more than ten years. Given the difficulties involved in lodging formal complaints with city agencies, it is safe to assume that unreported incidents of rat bites and lead poisoning far exceed these figures.

The effect of such hardships on children is obvious. Of even greater significance is the sense of powerlessness generated when families go

---

[2] *Facts About Low Income Housing* (New York: Emergency Committee For More Low Income Housing, 1963).

into these struggles barehanded. It is this sense of helplessness in the face of adversity that induces pathological anxiety, intergenerational alienation, and social retreatism. Actual physical impoverishment alone is not nearly so debilitating as poverty attended by a sense of unrelieved impotence that becomes generalized and internalized. The poor then regard much social learning as irrelevant, since they do not believe it can effect any environmental change.[3]

Intervention and the social systems

Selecting a point of intervention in dealing with this problem would have been simpler if the target of change were Mrs. Smith alone, or Mrs. Smith and her co-tenants, the clients in whose behalf intervention was planned. Too often, the client system presenting the problem becomes the major target for intervention, and the intervention method is limited to the one most suitable for that client system. However, Mrs. Smith and the other tenants had a multitude of problems emanating from many sources, any one of which would have warranted the attention of a social agency. The circumstantial fact that in individual contacts an agency offers services to individuals and families should not be a major factor in determining the method of intervention. Identification of the client merely helps the agency to define goals; other variables are involved in the selection of method. As Burns and Glasser have suggested: "It may be helpful to consider the primary target of change as distinct from the persons who may be the primary clients. . . . The primary target of change then becomes the human or physical environment toward which professional efforts via direct intervention are aimed in order to facilitate change."[4]

The three major factors that determined MFY's approach to the problem were (1) knowledge of the various social systems within which the social problem was located (i.e., social systems assessment), (2) knowledge of the various methods (including non–social work methods) appropriate for intervention in these different social systems, and (3) the resources available to the agency.[5]

The difficulties of the families in the building were intricately connected with other elements of the social system related to the housing

[3] Francis P. Purcell, "The Helping Professions and Problems of the Brief Contact," in Frank Reissman, Jerome Cohen, and Arthur Pearl, eds., *Mental Health of the Poor* (New York: Free Press of Glencoe, 1964), p. 432.

[4] Mary E. Burns and Paul H. Glasser, "Similarities and Differences in Casework and Group Work Practice," *Social Service Review,* Vol. 37, No. 4 (December 1963), p. 423.

[5] Harry Specht and Frank Riessman, "Some Notes on a Model for an Integrated Social Work Approach to Social Problems" (New York: Mobilization For Youth, June 1963). (Mimeographed.)

problem. For example, seven different public agencies were involved in maintenance of building services. Later other agencies were involved in relocating the tenants. There is no one agency in New York City that handles all housing problems. Therefore, tenants have little hope of getting help on their own. In order to redress a grievance relating to water supply (which was only one of the building's many problems) it is necessary to know precisely which city department to contact. The following is only a partial listing:

No water—Health Department
Not enough water—Department of Water Supply
No hot water—Buildings Department
Water leaks—Buildings Department
Large water leaks—Department of Water Supply
Water overflowing from apartment above—Police Department
Water sewage in the cellar—Sanitation Department

The task of determining which agencies are responsible for code enforcement in various areas is not simple, and in addition one must know that the benefits and services available for tenants and for the community vary with the course of action chosen. For example, if the building were taken over by the Rent and Rehabilitation Administration under the receivership law, it would be several weeks before services would be re-established, and the tenants would have to remain in the building during its rehabilitation. There would be, however, some compensations: tenants could remain in the neighborhood—indeed, in the same building—and their children would not have to change schools. If, on the other hand, the house were condemned by the Buildings Department, the tenants would have to move, but they would be moved quickly and would receive top relocation priorities and maximum relocation benefits. But once the tenants had been relocated—at city expense—the building could be renovated by the landlord as middle-income housing. In the Sixth Street house, it was suspected that this was the motivation behind the landlord's actions. If the building were condemned and renovated, there would be twenty-eight fewer low-income housing units in the neighborhood.

This is the fate of scores of tenements on the Lower East Side because much new middle-income housing is being built there. Basic services are withheld and tenants are forced to move so that buildings may be renovated for middle-income tenants. Still other buildings are allowed to deteriorate with the expectation that they will be bought by urban renewal agencies.

It is obvious, even limiting analysis to the social systems of one tenement, that the problem is enormous. Although the tenants were the clients in this case, Mrs. Smith, the tenant group, and other community groups were all served at one point or another. It is even conceivable that the landlord might have been selected as the most appropriate recipient of service. Rehabilitation of many slum tenements is at present nearly impossible. Many landlords regard such property purely as an investment. With profit the prime motive, needs of low-income tenants are often overlooked. Under present conditions it is financially impossible for many landlords to correct all the violations in their buildings even if they want to. If the social worker chose to intervene at this level of the problem, he might apply to the Municipal Loan Fund, make arrangements with unions for the use of non-union labor in limited rehabilitation projects, or provide expert consultants on reconstruction. These tasks would require social workers to have knowledge similar to that of city planners. If the problems of landlords were not selected as a major point of intervention, they would still have to be considered at some time since they are an integral part of the social context within which this problem exists.

A correct definition of interacting social systems or of the social worker's choice of methods and points of intervention is not the prime concern here. What is to be emphasized is what this case so clearly demonstrates: that although the needs of the client system enable the agency to define its goals, the points and methods of intervention cannot be selected properly without an awareness and substantial knowledge of the social systems within which the problem is rooted.

Dealing with the problem

The social worker remained with the building throughout a four-month period. In order to deal effectively with the problem, he had to make use of all the social work methods as well as the special talents of a community worker, lawyer, city planner, and various civil rights organizations. The social worker and the community worker functioned as generalists with both individuals and families calling on caseworkers as needed for specialized services or at especially trying times, such as during the first week and when the families were relocated. Because of the division of labor in the agency, much of the social work with individuals was done with the help of a caseworker. Group work, administration, and community organization were handled by the social worker, who had been trained in community organization. In many instances he also dealt with the mothers as individuals, as they encountered one stressful situation after another. Agency caseworkers also provided immediate and concrete assistance to individual families, such as small financial grants, medical care, homemaking services, baby-sitting services, and transportation. This reduced the intensity of pressures on these families. Caseworkers were especially helpful in dealing with some of the knotty and highly technical problems connected with public agencies.

With a caseworker and a lawyer experienced in handling tenement cases, the social worker began to help the families organize their demands for the services and utilities to which they were legally entitled but which the public agencies had consistently failed to provide for them.

The ability of the mothers to take concerted group action was evident from the beginning, and Mrs. Smith proved to be a natural and competent leader. With support, encouragement, and assistance from the staff, the mothers became articulate and effective in negotiating with the various agencies involved. In turn, the interest and concern of the agencies increased markedly when the mothers began to visit them, make frequent telephone calls, and send letters and telegrams to them and to politicians demanding action.

With the lawyer and a city planner (an agency consultant), the mothers and staff members explored various possible solutions to the housing problem. For example, the Department of Welfare had offered to move the families to shelters or hotels. Neither alternative was acceptable to the mothers. Shelters were ruled out because they would not consider splitting up their families, and they rejected hotels because they had discovered from previous experience that many of the "hotels" selected were flop-houses or were inhabited by prostitutes.

The following is taken from the social worker's record during the first week:

> Met with remaining tenants, several Negro men from the block, and [the city planner]. . . . Three of the mothers said that they would sooner sleep out on the street than go to the Welfare shelter. If nothing else, they felt that this would be a way of protesting their plight. . . . One of the mothers said that they couldn't very well do this with most of the children having colds. Mrs. Brown thought that they might do better to ask Reverend Jones if they could move into the cellar of his church temporarily. . . . The other mothers got quite excited about this idea because they thought that the church basement would make excellent living quarters.

After a discussion as to whether the mothers would benefit from embarrassing the public agencies by dramatically exposing their inadequacies, the mothers decided to move into the nearby church. They asked the worker to attempt to have their building condemned. At another meeting, attended by tenants from neighboring buildings and representatives of other local groups, it was concluded that what had happened to the Sixth Street building was a result of discrimination against the tenants as Puerto Ricans and Negroes. The group—which had now become an organization—sent the following telegram to city, state, and federal officials:

> We are voters and Puerto Rican and Negro mothers asking for equal rights, for decent housing and enough room. Building has broken windows, no gas or electricity for four weeks, no heat or hot water, holes in floors, loose wiring. Twelve of forty-eight children in building sick. Welfare doctors refuse to walk up dark stairs. Are we human or what? Should innocent children suffer for landlords' brutality and city and the state neglect? We are tired of being told to wait with children ill and unable to attend school. Negro and Puerto Rican tenants are forced out while buildings next door are renovated at high rents. We are not being treated as human beings.

For the most part, the lawyer and city planner stayed in the background, acting only as consultants. But as the tenants and worker became more involved with the courts and as other organizations entered the fight, the lawyer and city planner played a more active and direct role.

Resultant side-effects

During this process, tenants in other buildings on the block became more alert to similar problems in their buildings. With the help of the community development staff and the housing consultant, local groups and organizations such as tenants' councils and the local chapter of the Congress of Racial Equality were enlisted to support and work with the mothers.

Some of the city agencies behaved as though MFY had engineered the entire scheme to embarrass them—steadfastly disregarding the fact that the building had been unlivable for many months. Needless to say, the public agencies are overloaded and have inadequate resources. As has been documented, many such bureaucracies develop an amazing insensitivity to the needs of their clients.[6] In this case, the MFY social worker believed that the tenants—and other people in their plight—should make their needs known to the agencies and to the public at large. He knew that when these expressions of need are backed by power—either in numbers or in political knowledge—they are far more likely to have some effect.

Other movements in the city at this time gave encouragement and direction to the people in the community. The March on Washington and the Harlem rent strike are two such actions.

---

[6] See, for example, Reinhard Bendix, "Bureaucracy and the Problem of Power," in Robert K. Merton, Alisa Gray, Barbara Hockey, and Horan C. Sebrin, eds., *Reader in Bureaucracy* (Glencoe, Ill.: Free Pess, 1952), pp. 114–134.

By the time the families had been relocated, several things had been accomplished. Some of the public agencies had been sufficiently moved by the actions of the families and the local organizations to provide better services for them. When the families refused to relocate in a shelter and moved into a neighborhood church instead, one of the television networks picked up their story. Officials in the housing agencies came to investigate and several local politicians lent the tenants their support. Most important, several weeks after the tenants moved into the church, a bill was passed by the city council designed to prevent some of the abuses that the landlord had practiced with impunity. The councilman who sponsored the new law referred to the house on Sixth Street to support his argument.

Nevertheless, the problems that remain far outweigh the accomplishments. A disappointing epilogue to the story is that in court, two months later, the tenants' case against the landlord was dismissed by the judge on a legal technicality. The judge ruled that because the electric company had removed the meters from the building it was impossible for the landlord to provide services.

Some of the tenants were relocated out of the neighborhood and some in housing almost as poor as that they had left. The organization that began to develop in the neighborhood has continued to grow, but it is a painstaking job. The fact that the poor have the strength to continue to struggle for better living conditions is something to wonder at and admire.

Implications for practice

Social work helping methods as currently classified are so inextricably interwoven in practice that it no longer seems valid to think of a generic practice as consisting of the application of casework, group work, or community organization skills as the nature of the problem demands. Nor does it seem feasible to adapt group methods for traditional casework problems or to use group work skills in community organization or community organization method in casework. Such suggestions—when they appear in the literature—either reflect confusion or, what is worse, suggest that no clearcut method exists apart from the auspices that support it.

In this case it was a manifestation of a social problem—housing—that was the major point around which social services were organized. The social worker's major intellectual task was to select the points at which the agency could intervene in the problem and the appropriate methods to use. It seems abundantly clear that in order to select appropriate points of intervention the social worker need not only understand individual patterns of response, but the nature of the social conditions that are the context in which behavior occurs. As this case makes evident, the social system that might be called the "poverty system" is enduring and persistent. Its parts intermesh with precision and disturbing complementarity. Intentionally or not, a function is thereby maintained that produces severe social and economic deprivation. Certain groups profit enormously from the maintenance of this system, but larger groups suffer. Social welfare—and, in particular, its central profession, social work—must examine the part it plays in either maintaining or undermining this socially pernicious poverty system. It is important that the social work profession no longer regard social conditions as immutable and a social reality to be accommodated as service is provided to deprived persons with an ever increasing refinement of technique. Means should be developed whereby agencies can affect social problems more directly, especially through institutional (organizational) change.

The idea advanced by MFY is that the social worker should fulfill his professional function and agency responsibility by seeking a solution to social problems through institutional change rather than by focusing on individual problems in social functioning. This is not to say that individual expressions of a given social problem should be left unattended. On the contrary, this approach is predicated on the belief that individual problems in social functioning are to varying degrees both cause and effect. It rejects the notion that individuals are afflicted with social pathologies, holding, rather, that the same social environment that generates conformity makes payment by the deviance that emerges. As Nisbet points out, ". . . socially prized arrangements and values in society can produce socially condemned results."[7] This should direct social work's attention to institutional arrangements and their consequences. This approach does not lose sight of the individual or group, since the social system is composed of various statuses, roles, and classes. It takes cognizance of the systemic relationship of the various parts of the social system, including the client. It recognizes that efforts to deal with one social problem frequently generate others, with debilitating results.

Thus it is that such institutional arrangements as public assistance, state prisons, and state mental hospitals or slum schools are regarded by many as social problems in their own right. The social problems of poverty, criminality, mental illness, and failure to learn that were to be solved or relieved remain, and the proposed solutions pose almost equally egregious problems.

This paper has presented a new approach to social work practice. The knowledge, values, attitudes, and skills were derived from a generalist approach to social work. Agencies that direct their energies to social

---

[7] Merton and Nisbet, op. cit., p. 7.

problems by effecting institutional change will need professional workers whose skills cut across the broad spectrum of social work knowledge.

Selected annotated references

LEWIS, HAROLD, "Morality and the Politics of Practice," *Social Casework* 53:7 (July 1972), pp. 404–17.

This excellent article presents two primary problems for the social worker in his efforts to engage the client in beginning work on his problem: the problem of establishing trust between worker and client, and the problem of the distribution of justice in our society. Lewis develops some guides for the worker's consideration. We would recommend his article to all readers of this text.

PERLMAN, HELEN HARRIS, "Intake and Some Role Considerations," *Social Casework* 41:4 (April 1960), pp. 171–76.

This article considers the bearing of role expectations and role performance on the ability of worker and client to engage in problem definition. Perlman sees the concept of role as important in determining the quality of client engagement.

PERLMAN, HELEN HARRIS, *Social Casework: A Problem-Solving Process* (Chicago: University of Chicago Press, 1957).

See Chapters 8, 9 and 10 for an excellent discussion of process, content, and method in the beginning phase of work with clients.

Chapter 8

THE CONTRACT PHASE: JOINT ASSESSMENT, GOAL SETTING, AND PLANNING

This chapter is about decisions—decisions concerning the nature of the client's problem, desired outcomes (goals), and how the outcomes will be achieved. The chapter will define the contract phase of the problem-solving model in Chapter 6, present an outline of the process by which worker and client jointly arrive at the contract, and enumerate a set of principles to guide the worker's participation in this process.

DEFINITION OF THE SERVICE CONTRACT

In discussing the problem-solving process, identification of the problem, and data collection, we have maintained a consistent emphasis on the partnership nature of the interaction between client and worker. The partnership is working together to define and explore a common task. Mutuality between client and worker needs to be established at the very outset and to continue through all their associations. In the service contract, however, the partnership concept is fully developed and made explicit. Anthony Maluccio and Wilma Marlow, in an article reprinted in this chapter, say:

> Webster's *Third New International Dictionary* defines contract as a "covenant," a "compact," or "an agreement between two or more persons to do or forbear something." These words suggest mutuality, participation, and action.
> For the purposes of social work, the contract may be defined as *the explicit agreement between the worker and the client concerning*

312

the target problems, the goals, and the strategies of social work interven-
tion, and the roles and tasks of the participants. Its major features
are mutual agreement, differential participation in the intervention process, reciprocal accountability, and explicitness. In practice these features
are closely interrelated.[1]

Increasingly research into "outcome" in social work practice is accu-
mulating evidence that social work is often not helpful because the
worker and the client are not working toward the same purposes.[2] When
a client approaches an agency expecting a certain kind of help toward
a certain kind of goal he will be confused, and perhaps he will feel
even more inadequate if the worker offers something that the client does
not understand and was not aware he wanted. In such situations the
client often leaves the agency in frustration and disappointment.

When considering the importance of mutuality in the partnership
and in the joint understandings and operating principles that are involved in the concept of contract, one should not lose sight of an equally
important notion—that of difference. The concept of partnership does
not mean that client and worker bring the same knowledge, understanding, feeling, and doing to the business of working together. Partnership
and contract also highlight the differences that worker and client can
contribute to the process. "The contract is a tool for such delineation,
and for both client and worker it is an ongoing reminder of their collaborative relationship and different responsibilities."[3]

The service contract involves input, decision making, planning, and
commitment from both the client and the social worker. The process
of arriving at a service contract protects the client's individuality and
maximizes his opportunities for the exercise of self-determination. In
discussions, negotiations, and choosing among available alternatives, or
in making commitments to engage in developing new alternatives, the
client's opportunities for meaningful decisions about self and situation
are greatly increased.

The next section describes what goes into the process of arriving
at a service contract, and a final section will make explicit a number
of principles which are implicit in the process. In many respects the
process may appear similar to that described in the last chapter on
the beginning phase of working together. The similarity exists partly
because of the "spiral" nature of work with clients (a process which

---

[1] Anthony N. Maluccio and Wilma D. Marlow, "The Case for the Contract,"
Social Work 19:1 (January 1974), p. 30. Italics in original.

[2] See, for example, John E. Mayer and Noel Timms, *The Client Speaks: Working
Class Impressions of Casework* (New York: Atherton Press, 1970); Barbara Lerner
Therapy in the Ghetto: Political Impotence and Personal Disintegration (Baltimore:
Johns Hopkins Press, 1972); Norman A. Polansky, Robert D. Borgman, and Christine
de Saix, *Roots of Futility* (San Francisco: Jossey-Bass, 1972).

[3] Maluccio and Marlow, "The Case for Contract," p. 31.

will be made more explicit in Chapter 10, "Evaluation") and partly because the concept of contract also appears in the initial contact phase. A preliminary contract is developed to facilitate the process of collecting data—a prerequisite for joint worker and client decision making concerning the problem-to-be-worked, the desired outcomes, and the means or interventive efforts to be utilized in achieving those outcomes.

Arriving at a service contract involves a series of client-worker negotiations directed to answering these questions: Is the problem we want to work on the one that was identified when we began work together? Why has the problem persisted despite earlier client attempts to solve it? What is the desired solution (i.e., what outcomes or objectives should the interventive effort be directed toward achieving in relation to the problem)? How will this solution be achieved? (Remember that the client may be an individual, a family, a group, or representatives of a community and that the worker may be interacting with the client in a variety of settings.)

JOINT ASSESSMENT AND DECISION MAKING

Joint assessment and decision making is at the very heart of the development of the service contract. In the contact phase worker and client have arrived at an initial definition of the problem-to-be-worked. They have set initial goals, collected some data, and done some exploration together related to the identified problem and goals. Now they must put this data together to determine what the problem is, what the client wants done about it (a reworking of the goal), and how they are going to do it. This process involves the ordering and organizing of the information, intuitions, and knowledge that client and worker bring so that the pieces come together into some pattern that makes sense, at least in the here and now, in explaining the problem and in relating this explanation to alternative solutions. There is movement from what is observed, inferred, or deduced, based on knowledge and experience, to some conclusive explanation of what we make of it, and thence to a determination of goals and how they can be implemented. Such assessments evolve not from one person's head, or from the simple addition of one item to another, but rather from a combination of data in relevant ways. They evolve from viewing the relationships of all elements to one another as client and worker appraise the client-in-situation, and from the assessment of their total significance to the client in light of what he wants to accomplish. Harriett Bartlett, in material reprinted in this chapter, refers to these processes as "analysis of a situation to identify the major factors operating within it" and "identification of those factors which appear most critical, definition of their interrelationships, and selection of those to be dealt with."[4] At its best the processes involve both client and worker in assembling and ordering all information and in making judgments as to their meaning for their work together.

Social workers often mistakenly assume that only the worker engages in these tasks. We do not deny that both the worker and the client must do hard and independent thinking (for the worker this is a professional obligation), but the test of the soundness of such thinking is how well their thinking fits together. Sometimes the culmination of this process is erroneously seen as putting the client in a category or affixing a label. That is emphatically not the purpose of the process! The process is not focused on the client alone; it is focused on the client, the problem, and the situation in a systematic interaction. In work with human beings, thinking and action cannot move in a straight line from cause to effect. Systems theory teaches us that problems are the result of complicated interactions among all system variables, and that to seek a single ultimate cause or reason is to doom oneself and, more important, one's client to frustration and failure. So our aim is not to come up with an answer in terms of labels or categories, but to order our understanding of the client-situation-problem for purposes of decision making concerning goals and actions.

Sometimes this process is called "diagnosis." We dislike this term for several reasons. First, the preferred definition of the term in Webster's is, "The art or act of identifying a disease from its signs and symptoms."[5] Thus the term carries the implication that there is something wrong with the client. Second, the term implies that the decision about what is wrong is made by the professional person through an examination. There is no inkling of dynamic interaction and joint responsibility in the term. Finally, diagnosis is often seen as a process by which a professional arrives at a label for something. After all, that is what happens when a doctor diagnoses. He assigns a label signifying what is wrong. This is his assessment as the knowing authority, and, at even greater variance with our notions of the contract, the doctor usually tells us what he has determined to be the most satisfactory form of treatment. We hope that the process of assessment and decision making in social work is understood to be quite different from diagnosis. The phrase *process of assessment* is used because we think that this is the way assessment must be regarded—as an ongoing, joint process, a shared endeavor.

Consistent with the approach outlined in Chapter 1 the problem may

---

[4] Harriett M. Bartlett, *The Common Base of Social Work Practice* (New York: National Association of Social Workers, 1970), p. 144.

[5] *Webster's Seventh New Collegiate Dictionary* (Springfield, Mass.: G. & C. Merriam Co., 1971), p. 229.

be defined as residing with the client, as outside the client but experienced by him, or as the result of the client-situation interaction. The target of change may or may not be the client. This point is very well illustrated in "The House on Sixth Street," the case example in Chapter 7. After client and worker have jointly defined the problem-for-work (this may or may not be the same as the presenting problem), the next decision is to define goals—what is to be done?

SETTING GOALS

What are the desired outcomes of the client and worker's joint work? What is perceived as the appropriate solution for the problem? What are the goals of our actions? Essentially the same process is utilized in arriving at an answer to these questions as in developing a definition of the problem-for-work. The worker's first responsibility is to use interviewing skills to elicit from the client his view of the desired outcome. The worker may also have developed a view of the desired outcome which he shares with the client. If the two views are not congruent, then this difference must be negotiated, just as incongruent perceptions of the problem were negotiated. Unless the worker and client can arrive at mutually agreeable goals, there is no sense in proceeding further because they will be working in opposed directions.

Specifying goals is a crucial element of the service contract. Particular attention must be paid to two characteristics of the goals. First, goals should be sufficiently specific and concrete to be measurable. Only in this way can the client and worker know whether the goals have been accomplished, and only in this way can the profession of social work establish its accountability. Broadly stated goals, such as helping the client feel better, or increasing the client's opportunities for socializing experiences, or improving the parent-child relationship, are meaningless. We will have more to say on this topic in the chapter on evaluation and will be introducing a set of procedures—Goal Attainment Scaling— which require the setting of specific, measurable goals that will enable the client and worker to determine the extent of goal attainment.

Second, there should be a reasonable chance of attaining the goals set. In establishing goals, worker and client will, of course, consider such variables as the client's degree of interest in attaining them, the client's abilities, and the resources available to the client. Lilian Ripple and others have referred to these variables as motivation, capacity, and opportunity, and, of course, goals may be established in any of these areas— that is, legitimate objectives of client-worker activity might be to increase the client's motivation, abilities, or opportunities in defined areas.[6] Re-

---

[6] Lilian Ripple and Ernestina Alexander, "Motivation, Capacity and Opportunity as Related to Casework Service: Nature of the Client's Problem," *Social Service Review* 30:1 (March 1956) pp. 38–54.

gardless of the areas in which goals are established, consideration is given to the variables of motivation, capacity, and opportunity with a view toward establishing goals with a reasonable chance of attainment.

In recapitulation, goal setting in social work is a joint client-worker process in which mutually agreeable solutions to the problems are developed. These solutions, or goals, should be specific enough to be measurable and proximate enough to be attainable.

PLANNING FOR INTERVENTION

Given a mutually determined definition of the problem and its solution, the task of planning a way to move from problem to solution remains. The development of an intervention plan consists of decisions, again jointly made by the client and the worker, as to the steps which will be taken to solve the problem, i.e., reach the goals. The steps taken in making these decisions parallel those taken in defining the problem and arriving at goals. The worker will first discover from the client what steps the client would like to take to reach the solution and what steps the client expects the worker to take. The worker must establish what is expected of the client as well as what the worker expects to do to accomplish the goals, and, again, any differences in these expectations must be negotiated and resolved.

Social workers, while negotiating interventive means, are responsible for considering four important limitations on worker activity. These limitations are time, skill, ethics, and agency function. No worker can make unlimited time available to a specific client. Time constraints on the worker must always be considered in entering into a service contract. A worker cannot responsibly commit himself to activities which extend beyond the time he has available; conversely, a client can reasonably expect a worker to do what the worker says he will do. Consider, this incident, for example. A skilled, generally capable worker recently placed a 14-year-old boy in a foster home. The worker was cognizant of the fact that the youth might have some initial adjustment problems and indicated that they would be visiting together on a weekly basis to talk about any problems that arose from the placement. This worker, however, was employed in a large agency with a heavy case load and, because of the pressure of time, was unable to visit with the boy until four weeks after the placement was made. By this time, the boy had justifiably become disillusioned and angry with the worker and rejected efforts by the worker to become jointly involved in problems that were occurring in the placement. The youth ran away and eventually became institutionalized. Had this worker made a realistic contract—to see the boy once a month instead of once a week—the client and worker might have been able to maintain their communication and to engage in more effective problem solving. A common misconception held by many new workers is to confuse the intensity of service with the quality of service. Poor-quality service is provided when workers make commitments that they cannot meet, and, conversely, frequent contacts between worker and client do not necessarily imply high-quality service. What is required is the ability of the worker to plan his time so he will not make commitments beyond the time available.

Second, the worker will not enter into a service contract that calls for activity on his part which exceeds his skills. It is a professional's responsibility to be aware of his strengths and weaknesses and not to enter into agreements that exceed his ability. When a client requires a specialized skill which a particular worker does not possess, such as marriage counseling or bargaining with a large bureaucracy, then the negotiated intervention plan will include involvement of another resource to assist with this aspect of the intervention.

Third, the worker will avoid involvement in intervention plans that commit him to unethical behavior. An obvious example would be the securing of economic resources through illegal means. An economic crisis might be alleviated by a burglary, but it would not be appropriate for a worker to participate in planning or executing such an action.

Fourth, as Schwartz noted in Chapter 1, worker-client contracts are always limited by the functions of the agency in which the worker participates. This unfortunate limitation derives from the tendency to organize social services in this country around functional specializations rather than to provide generic services.[7] Workers can seek to define agency functions broadly and, when necessary, will consider the possibility of requesting exceptions to agency limitations or attempting to work within their agency to secure a broader definition of its functions. Some ways to accomplish such changes are discussed further in Chapter 13. So long as agencies do have specialized functions, however, workers must be cognizant of this source of limitation on the commitments they make to clients.

In the next chapter worker activity in moving from problem to solution will be discussed as interventive roles. Before these roles are utilized, however, a service contract must be developed to specify the nature of both worker and client activity. As in the definition of the problem and of goals, any differences between worker and client in these areas is to be resolved prior to implementing any intervention plan.

RECAPITULATION

The service contract is a plan jointly negotiated by the worker and the client which defines the problem-for-work, specifies the objectives,

---

[7] For additional discussion of this point see Harold L. Wilensky and Charles N. Lebeaux, *Industrial Society and Social Welfare* (New York: Free Press, 1965) pp. 233–82.

and provides an intervention plan designed to move from the problem to the objectives. The process of negotiating the service contract culminates in a commitment on the part of both worker and client to implement the plan. Once negotiated, the service contract is binding on both the worker and the client and is not subject to unilateral changes—changes can, of course, be jointly negotiated.

Four principles have been implied in this chapter which can be stated explicitly.

1. Joint negotiation of the service contract connotes precisely what the words imply. The contract involves input from both worker and client. We indicated disagreement with the concept of diagnosis because of a lack of client input in the decision making that leads to a diagnosis. But frequently workers also err in the other direction—in failing to provide their own input for fear that it might hamper the client's right to self-determination. A worker's professional judgment, experience, and background are all sources of knowledge and information that should be available to the client in joint decision making. The key is to arrive at a service contract which is truly joint—one representing the best merged collective judgment of both worker and client.

2. The worker is expected to bring a broad knowledge base to the process of arriving at a service contract. This base will include knowledge of human functioning, of the social environment, and of the interaction of the two. The worker will be expected to draw on the sources of knowledge identified in Chapter 3 and to apply those sources to the specific client situation under consideration.

3. The focus of the service contract and the intervention plan will be consistent with the concept of social functioning. This means that the worker and the client must be alert to the widest possible range of goals and interventive approaches. The target of change may be the client, forces in the environment, or the interaction of the two. Although no worker can be expected to master all change strategies, the worker can be expected to be aware of the broad repertoire of change strategies available to the profession and to be able to select jointly with the client the strategy most appropriate for the client and, if the worker cannot provide that service, to be able to locate it elsewhere in the community. Methodological specialties may be necessary, but they cannot be justified as blinders.

4. The development of a service contract is a cognitive process involving thinking, reasoning, and decision making. Feelings are important, but planning should be done on a rational basis. The planning may, of course, involve plans to deal with feelings. Further, rational planning precedes interventive activities. This does not deny the spiral concept of practice which has been identified in earlier chapters and which

will be made more explicit in the chapter on evaluation. But whenever the worker is consciously engaged in interventive efforts, those efforts should be based on a deliberate, rational service contract negotiated with the client.

A LOOK FORWARD

This chapter has treated a crucial component of social work processes. The joint client-worker development of a rational plan that defines the problem-to-be-worked, establishes objectives, and specifies an interventive plan is a prerequisite to intervention. In Chapter 9 we will discuss worker intervention activities which are conceptualized as interventive roles. Evaluation is discussed in Chapter 10. This essential part of work with clients shows social work processes to be more dynamic and continuous than has been implied in our linear description of the problem-solving process.

The two articles reprinted in this chapter offer additional ideas concerning assessment and contracting. Harriett Bartlett stresses the cognitive aspects of assessment and offers her view of the assessment process. Bartlett is less explicit about client involvement than we have been. The article by Anthony Maluccio and Wilma Marlow offers a very useful discussion of contracting which provides for explicit client involvement and is applicable with client systems of various sizes.

---

*Professional judgment in assessment**

Harriett M. Bartlett

Professional judgment

All professions rest on bodies of values and knowledge in the form of principles and generalizations. It is generally agreed that it is through the professional judgment and skill of the practitioner that they are applied. However, concepts of skill vary widely in social work. Some people would include the ability to use knowledge effectively in performance, but this aspect has received little emphasis. In the writer's opin-

* Reprinted with the permission of the author and the National Association of Social Workers from Harriett M. Bartlett, *The Common Base of Social Work Practice* (New York: NASW, 1970), pp. 139–46.

ion, *professional judgment* is of such importance that it should receive greater recognition in its own right.[1]

Professional judgment is one of the most important features distinguishing occupations from professions. In occupations many activities can be routinely outlined so that workers can be given regular instructions about how to carry them out. Varying degrees of judgment and discretion are of course always necessary but not to the degree required in professional practice. In a profession the complexity and variability of the situations to be dealt with require the exercise of individual judgment by the practitioner in each new situations. Such judgment is a key operation in any profession. The praciticner must be able to select the relevant principles from his profession's body of knowledge and values and apply them appropriately in assessing the situation before him. While some writers who discuss criteria for professions, like Carr-Saunders and Wilson and Flexner, emphasize the importance of professional judgment, others do not.[2] In the author's view it must be stressed in any consideration of social work because social workers deal with complex, rapidly changing social situations and make decisions influencing the lives of many people in important ways. A high degree of responsibility is implied for which an equivalent degree of expertise and accountability are required.

Features of assessment in social work practice

In this chapter we will consider the use of professional judgment by social workers in assessing social situations, which is the point at which judgment first comes into operation in practice. It is important to visualize and understand how such professional judgment is exercised in social work. We need to understand social workers' ways of assessing the full range of situations they face, whether in relation to individuals and families, groups of people, neighborhood services, community devel-

[1] The expert judgments of social workers have been used in social work research. See Ann W. Shyne, ed., *Use of Judgments as Data in Social Work Research* (New York: National Association of Social Workers, 1959). Jack Stumpf refers to professional judgments as interventive acts in "Community Planning and Development," *Encyclopedia of Social Work* (New York: National Association of Social Workers, 1965), p. 194. In a working paper, the NASW Committee on the Study of Competence mentions one component of responsible, self-regulated practice as being the ability to "dependably exercise critical judgment in making wise decisions," a concept to be developed further as the committee's work proceeds. See "An Outline of Qualitative Components Relevant for Assessment of Professional Practice in Social Work" (New York: National Association of Social Workers, 1965), p. 1. (Mimeographed.)

[2] A. M. Carr-Saunders and P. A. Wilson, *The Professions* (Oxford, England: Clarendon Press, 1933); and Abraham Flexner, "Is Social Work a Profession?" *Proceedings of the National Conference of Charities and Correction* (Chicago: National Conference of Charities and Correction, 1915), pp. 576–90.

opment, large governmental programs, or issues of national social policy. In today's expanding and changing practice, all social workers must be able to assess, at least in a preliminary way, a wide range of situations. This is one of the new challenges being presented to the profession.

Certain conditions are necessary for such a broadened use of professional judgment in assessment. (1) There must be some common concept of the profession's central focus, so that practitioners can think together in comprehensive terms. (2) Assessment must be consistently directed to an examination of the phenomena, conditions, and situations to be dealt with, since decisions regarding action and intervention must be based on understanding the problem. (3) A body of relevant propositions and generalizations, related through a growing system of theory, must be available to practitioners to guide them in their assessments.

These conditions, however, have not been present in social work practice. The method-and-skill model emphasized feeling and doing. Assessment as a distinct intellectual process, common to all social workers, has not been recognized and defined. "Diagnosis," as conceived in social work, has been customarily associated with and confined to a particular method and thus has been narrowly perceived. Developed first in casework and then in the other methods, it has followed the medical model, which is based on a classification of diseases and pathologies. Lacking a typology of problems in social work, however, social workers have defined many kinds of diagnosis, oriented toward causal factors, current dynamics, clinical categories, problem types and problem-solving, assessing and establishing objectives, and similar approaches.[3] The fact that social workers were using clusters of knowledge from separate sources, mainly about individuals, groups, and communities or agencies, programs, and settings, meant that this diagnostic thinking was still further fragmented.

Another important characteristic of social work practice has been that the diagnostic process was customarily shared with the people served and other associates, with conscious use of the professional relationship. This way of working with others developed from the social worker's respect for people and the recognition that the results of assessment are less effective when decisions are imposed upon others. Early in social work history, through psychiatric theory social workers became aware of the importance of using the professional relationship with the individual skillfully and responsibly because of the risk of developing

---

[3] See Helen Harris Perlman, *Social Casework: A Problem-solving Process* (Chicago: University of Chicago Press, 1957), pp. 164–82; Florence Hollis, *Casework: A Psychosocial Therapy* (New York: Random House, 1964), pp. 179–203; Gisela Konopka, *Social Group Work: A Helping Process* (Englewood Cliffs, N.J.: Prentice-Hall, 1963), pp. 79–106; and Meyer Schwartz, "The Problem of Defining Community Organization Practice," *Defining Community Organization Practice* (New York: National Association of Social Workers, 1962), pp. 15–17 (mimeographed).

emotional dependence rather than stimulating growth. Theory regarding group process extended these insights to small groups. More recently, there has been recognition of the forces operating to further or block the efforts of the professional worker to help larger groups assess their situations or to carry through joint thinking with professional planners and experts.[4]

Of further significance is the concept of "study, diagnosis, and treatment" as developed in social work. Although these can logically be considered as separate and sequential steps, in social work practice they were found to involve considerable overlapping. Here the use of the client-worker relationship in casework treatment was of particular importance. There was general agreement, as stated by Hamilton, that "treatment begins at the first contact."[5] Thus the three parts of the casework method traditionally have been viewed in practice and taught in schools as intertwined, simultaneous occurrences.[6]

Several results followed from these features of assessment as it developed in social work practice. The concept of treatment as beginning with the first contact moved practitioners into immediate action, not only in casework but also in other areas of practice. The social worker's responsibility to analyze and understand the situation with which he must deal *before* taking action—an essential of all professional practice—was not fully recognized. Emphasis on skill as feeling and doing and on sharing assessment with others in the situation prevented assessment from standing out in its own right as an intellectual process based on knowledge and value. Furthermore, because of the incorporation of diagnostic thinking within the three methods, assessment was necessarily limited in scope. Thus the unintended consequences of these perceptions of social work practice were to retard movement toward recognition of the use of professional judgment in assessment as a distinct and basic process in social work practice.

Assessment as a cognitive process

In its general outlines, professional assessment is a form of logical analysis that would be carried through by any person with a trained

---

[4] In a current examination of community organization, Arnold Gurin divides the professional tasks into two kinds, "analytical, or the rational treatment of the substantive problems involved; and interactional, or the interpersonal relationships that are involved in dealing with the problem." "The Community Organization Curriculum Development Project: A Preliminary Report," *Social Service Review*, Vol. 42, No. 4 (December 1968), p. 426.

[5] Gordon Hamilton, *Theory and Practice of Social Case Work* (New York: Columbia University Press, 1940), p. 166.

[6] Helen Harris Perlman, "Social Casework," *Encyclopedia of Social Work* (New York: National Association of Social Workers, 1965), p. 706.

mind. It requires the kind of objective and rigorous thinking characteristic of the scientific method. However, this is not all. It is also a *social work* assessment and therefore must demonstrate the characteristics of the profession's approach to situations and problems. Since the common base of practice is only partially defined, we are breaking new ground here in trying to describe assessment in this way. But the attempt seems worthwhile because there is currently a gap in the practice model at this point—between knowledge and value, on the one hand, and their application in practice on the other hand—which needs to be filled. we shall consider first the general outlines of assessment as a cognitive process and then examine some of its social work characteristics.

The process of assessment can be viewed as covering the following steps: (1) analysis of the situation to identify the major factors that are operating in it; (2) identification of those factors that appear most critical, definition of their interrelationships, and selection of those to be dealt with; (3) consideration of possible alternatives for social work action, based on prediction of possible outcomes; and (4) decision as to the specific approach and action to be taken.[7]

Analysis. In facing any one of a wide variety of situations with which he may be concerned, the social worker must first analyze the situation to identify the major factors operating in it. The initial examination, known as the process of study, involves the use of observation, interviews, documents, and similar means. Various criteria to guide the collection of relevant data have been developed in the past in connection with the three methods. However, the situations can now be expected to be of wider scope and variety than previously dealt with because diagnosis can no longer be confined within a single method.

Interaction between people and environment, the area of social work's central concern, involves multiple factors—biological, psychological, social, economic, and others—all of which must be identified and related in assessing a single social situation. Concepts adequate in either clarity or breadth for enabling social workers to deal with so many variables in a systematic manner distinctive of their profession have not been available.

Another aspect, which has not received the recognition it deserves, is that such analysis requires rapid, continuous, expert selection and use of appropriate generalizations from the profession's body of knowledge. It is because the selection must be so rapid that the knowledge must be visible and readily available to the practitioner. The wider

---

[7] Descriptions of assessment as a basic process in social work practice do not seem available in the literature. Boehm has described some of the steps under "Activities of Social Work." See Werner W. Boehm, *Objectives of the Social Work Curriculum of the Future* (New York: Council on Social Work Education, 1969), p. 53. See also, Gary A. Lloyd, "Integrated Methods and the Field Practice Course," *Social Work Education Reporter*, Vol. 16, No. 2 (June 1968), pp. 39–42.

the range of situations faced, the broader must be the knowledge. Social change in our society now requires that all social workers be able to operate flexibly and respond intelligently to the full range of social work's concern.

Identification of critical factors. The next step in assessment involves identifying the particular factors (from among those regarded as major in the situation) that appear most critical and defining their interrelationship. This is, of course, a key step in assessment and often must be repeated several times as understanding grows or situations change. The factors to be dealt with are then selected in terms of their significance in creating the problem or their probable response to social work interventive efforts. Just as a physician makes a prognosis in relation to the probable course of the disease in an individual case, so the social worker considers—as far as his knowledge permits—the ongoing course and possible trends in the social situation. Such analysis might, for instance, point most strongly to deficiency in coping capacity or deficiency in environmental supports or some combination of the two. According to the concept of social functioning, coping capacity and environmental demand can no longer be considered separately but always in interaction with each other.

Alternatives for action. In the third step, alternatives for social work action are considered and a prediction of their possible outcomes is made. This involves defining objectives and weighing the relevance and feasibility of various alternative lines of action. The social worker may decide that all or part of the situation does not belong to social work. If it is within social work's scope, then he must decide which aspects are likely to be most responsive to social work's interventive approaches and why. Note that what is involved is not a "group worker" assessing a "group work problem" but a *social worker* scanning the profession's full interventive repertoire.

Deciding what action to take. The final step in assessment is that of deciding on the specific approach and action to be taken. The social worker may decide that some combination of interventive approaches is needed, such as direct help to families combined with neighborhood services. As a social worker, he will have competence in at least one type of intervention and if he is an experienced worker, probably at least initial competence in several others. If the situation he faces is in an early stage of development, he may decide to offer consultation at first, with the aim of drawing in other social workers possessing the necessary competence at a later date.

Having made the necessary decisions, the social worker moves into the action to which this whole process of assessment has been directed. The assessment may be telescoped into a brief period or greatly extended. As has been pointed out, it is shared with others in the situation and interwoven with interventive action as situations evolve. In social work, as in other professions, assessment can only be effective if it is recognized by the practitioner as a conscious intellectual process, to be carried on deliberately, responsibly, and expertly.

The case for the contract*

Anthony N. Maluccio and Wilma D. Marlow

The contract is among the basic concepts utilized in social work that are inadequately formulated and incompletely incorporated into practice. There has been little effort to clarify its theoretical foundations, delineate its uses, and test its validity. It has been mentioned frequently in the literature as a pact, working agreement, or therapeutic alliance. Referring to clients' and workers' hidden or double agendas, writers have spoken of covert, implicit, and "corrupt" contracts. However, a review of the literature reveals no comprehensive discussion or formulation of a conceptual framework.

Lack of clarity about the contract, its limited development, and its restricted application to social work practice may be factors that contribute to the clash of worker-client perspectives, client discontinuance, and the frustrations that clients and practitioners encounter when they try to work together meaningfully and productively.

This article attempts to stimulate interest in examining, conceptualizing, and using the contract. To do so seems timely in light of the current critical reassessment of roles and methods of social work, changing attitudes toward consumers of services, and new ideas about the helping process.

A pertinent aspect of changing theory and practice is the growing conviction that the client or consumer has an important role in formulating policy and planning program. One model of service delivery proposes that the consumer have a choice in what services are provided, some control over how and by whom services are delivered, and a real opportunity to participate.[1] It is logical to extend the concept of "maximum feasible participation" in policy-making and planning to direct and per-

* Reprinted with permission of the authors and the National Association of Social Workers from *Social Work*, 19:1 (January 1974), pp. 28–36.

[1] Thomas M. Meenaghan and Michael Mascari, "Consumer Choice, Consumer Control in Service Delivery," *Social Work*, 16 (October 1971), pp. 50–57.

sonal interaction between social workers and clients, whether the latter are individuals, families, groups, or communities. Clearly conceived and properly used, the contract can serve as an important tool in helping consumers achieve such participation. It might also become an integral feature of the emerging "life model" of practice, which stresses optimum utilization of the client's own life processes and resources.

The contract in theory

The origins of the term "contract" as applied to social work are not clear. Writings on group work in the 1940s and 1950s include implicit references to the contract, as seen in Coyle's discussion of the "grouping process" in group formation and Trecker's formulation of the group worker's role as "agent of the agency."[2] In 1951, Hamilton alluded to the contract, without naming it, in discussing the application process. She saw as fundamental the worker's responsibility to make explicit the conditions and the terms of help available from the agency.[3] In 1957, Perlman made one of the earliest references to the contract as a pact.[4]

Major social work scholars gave the contract some attention at a 1969 symposium on comparative theoretical approaches to casework. In formulating the problem-solving model, Perlman indicated that the person establishes a contract when he decides to use the agency and the worker for help in coping with his problem, thus moving from the role of applicant to that of client.[5] Rapoport identified the contract as a significant step in crisis intervention, noting that by the end of the initial interview goals should be agreed upon and mutual expectations spelled out between client and worker.[6] Scherz defined the contract in family therapy as a "conscious agreement between family and worker to work in certain ways toward certain goals."[7] In the behavior modification approach to casework, Thomas saw validity in an explicit contract

---

[2] Grace L. Coyle, *Group Work with American Youth* (New York: Harper & Bros., 1948), pp. 88–90; and Harleigh B. Trecker, *Social Group Work—Principles and Practices* (rev. ed.: New York: Whiteside, 1955), pp. 23–35.

[3] Gordon Hamilton, *Theory and Practice of Social Casework* (2d ed., rev.; New York: Columbia University Press, 1951), pp. 148–80.

[4] Helen H. Perlman, *Social Casework: A Problem-Solving Process* (Chicago: University of Chicago Press, 1957), p. 149.

[5] Helen H. Perlman, "The Problem-Solving Model in Social Casework," in Robert W. Roberts and Robert H. Nee, eds., *Theories of Social Casework* (Chicago: University of Chicago Press, 1970), p. 155.

[6] Lydia Rapoport, "Crisis Intervention as a Mode of Brief Treatment," in Roberts and Nee, op. cit., p. 291.

[7] Frances H. Scherz, "Theory and Practice of Family Therapy," in Roberts and Nee, op. cit., p. 237.

and spoke of written as well as verbal agreements.[8] In Smalley's discussion of the functional orientation, the concept of the contract is implicit in her use of time phases related to beginnings and endings of treatment; according to her, a time-limited contract may be fulfilled, renewed, or renegotiated.[9] In the psychosocial approach, Hollis acknowledged that the term was widely used and that practitioners increasingly preferred to state explicitly the end results of the initial phase of casework before engaging in treatment.[10]

Although these scholars represent differing philosophical and theoretical orientations to casework, the concept of the contract appears compatible to practice within the separate frameworks. In particular, they convey a sense that the client is emerging from his traditional role as a passive recipient of service to an active, self-determining person who cooperates with the worker more and more consciously and deliberately in the helping process.

The literature on community organization has given limited consideration to using the contract for reaching a working agreement between the worker and the client. On the contrary, goals and roles have usually been analyzed from the perspective of the worker.[11]

In group work, Schwartz has stressed that the establishment of a "working agreement" is a fundamental task of the worker. According to his formulation, the rules and boundaries within which worker and group members operate determine their working contract and influence their functions.[12] The contract essentially corroborates the convergence of the worker's and the client's tasks and "provides the framework for the work that follows, and for understanding when the work is in process, when it is being evaded, and when it is finished."[13] Other writers on group work concur with Klein that the contract is "an agreement about expectations of the reciprocal roles of the worker, the members, and the sanctioning agency."[14]

Thus the contract has received some attention in social work, but

---

[8] Edwin J. Thomas, "Behavioral Modification and Casework," in Roberts and Nee, op. cit., p. 196.

[9] Ruth E. Smalley, "The Functional Approach to Casework Practice," in Roberts and Nee, op. cit., pp. 98–121.

[10] Florence Hollis, "The Psychosocial Approach to the Practice of Casework," in Roberts and Nee, op. cit., p. 45.

[11] See Jack Rothman, "An Analysis of Goals and Roles in Community Organization Practice," *Social Work,* 9 (April 1964), pp. 24–31.

[12] William Schwartz, "The Social Worker in the Group," *The Social Welfare Forum, 1961* (New York: Columbia University Press, 1961), p. 158.

[13] William Schwartz, "On the Use of Groups in Social Work Practice," in Schwartz and Serapio R. Zalba, eds., *The Practice of Group Work* (New York: Columbia University Press, 1971), p. 8.

[14] Alan F. Klein, *Social Work Through Group Process* (Albany: State University of New York at Albany, 1970), p. 51.

its elaboration has remained at a limited and simplistic level. In general, theorists have tended to equate it with the working agreement that concludes the initial, exploratory phase of social work intervention. Similarly, writing from a psychoanalytic perspective, Menninger has argued that the contract can be used to clarify the mutual expectations of patient and therapist, reach agreement about appropriate expectations, and spell out the conditions of their cooperation.[15]

The underlying thesis of this article is that the contract has potential value as an ongoing, integral part of the total process of intervention. Further elaborated in theory and deliberately applied to practice, the contract can crystallize and exploit to the maximum degree the process and substance of the work in which practitioner and client engage. The use of a contract can help facilitate worker-client interaction, establish mutual concerns, clarify the purposes and conditions of giving and receiving service, delineate roles and tasks, order priorities, allocate time and constructively for attaining goals, and assess progress on an ongoing basis.

The contract defined

Although it is a much-talked-about term among practitioners, the contract has not been clearly defined in social work. The legal profession has attempted to define it since the contract constitutes the basic framework for a substantial portion of legal practice. Although the diversity of elements and perspectives inherent in the concept has prevented the devising of an entirely satisfactory or universally accepted legal definition, one that is widely quoted in the following: "A contract is a promise, or set of promises, for breach of which the law gives a remedy, or the performance of which the law in some way recognizes as a duty."[16] Except for the idea that the contract is a legally enforceable agreement, the elements in this definition are pertinent to social work, especially the notions of mutual promise and duty between the contracting parties.

Webster's *Third New International Dictionary* defines contract as a "covenant," a "compact," or "an agreement between two or more persons to do or forbear something." These words suggest mutuality, participation, and action.

For the purposes of social work, the contract may be defined as *the explicit agreement between the worker and the client concerning the target problems, the goals, and the strategies of social work intervention, and the roles and tasks of the participants.* Its major features are mutual agreement, differential participation in the intervention process, recipro-

---

[15] See Karl Menninger, *Theory of Psychoanalytic Treatment* (New York: Harper & Row, 1964), pp. 15–42.

[16] Samuel Williston, *A Treatise on the Law of Contract*, edited by Walter H. E. Yeager (3d ed.; Mt. Kisco, N.Y.: Baker, Voorhis, 1957), Sect. 1.

330   *Social work processes*

cal accountability, and explicitness. In practice these features are closely interrelated.

Mutual agreement

Mutual agreement between worker and client concerning the nature and course of interaction is an essential component of practice. Many writers agree that mutuality must be established at the outset and maintained throughout contact.[17] Agreed-upon goals, roles, and tasks are fundamental in determining the direction, quality, and content of intervention.

Research studies and clinical reports substantiate the fact that difficulties and frustrations result from a lack of agreement between client and worker or from a clash in their perspectives.[18] Worker and client may be operating under different assumptions—especially if varying expectations were not adequately discussed—and thus may not always have the same perception of what constitutes help or treatment.

Practitioners often find it difficult to establish mutuality in the crucial areas of goals and methods. Some resort to a double agenda, in which the worker formulates for himself a set of goals that is different from the one he shares with the client. Greenhill reports that he used to set up therapeutic contracts with families that included agreement to work together in relation to a child's problems. Covertly, however, he would intend to work with the entire family's problems, a plan he divulged to family members only after they became involved in treatment.[19] Greenhill was referring to experiences of his early years in family therapy, but seasoned practitioners sometimes superimpose their own goals on those of clients. Beall warns of the dangers of a "corrupt contract," when the client's stated goals conceal implicit and opposing ones. Operating with such a contract in a clinical setting can reinforce neurotic aims rather than promote therapeutic change.[20]

Deliberately considering the contract in each situation can help reduce clashes in perspectives, clarify vague or confusing expectations, and enhance the possibility of meaningful cooperation in working toward realis-

[17] See Werner Gottlieb and Joe H. Stanley, "Mutual Goals and Goal-Setting in Social Casework," *Social Casework*, 38 (October 1967), pp. 471–81.

[18] See John E. Mayer and Noel Timms, "Clash in Perspective Between Worker and Client," *Social Casework*, 50 (January 1969), pp. 32–40; and Phyllis R. Silverman, "A Reexamination of the Intake Procedure," *Social Casework*, 51 (December 1970), pp. 625–34.

[19] Laurence Greenhill, "Making It," in Andrew Ferber, Marilyn Mendelsohn, and Augustus Napier, eds., *The Book of Family Therapy* (New York: Science House, 1972), p. 509.

[20] Lynette Beall, "The Corrupt Contract: Problems in Conjoint Therapy with Parents and Children," *American Journal of Orthopsychiatry*, 42 (January 1972), pp. 77–81.

tic, mutually agreed-upon goals. Client and worker must share their understanding of assistance sought and to be given. Without this, the concept of mutuality is hollow. Furthermore, exploring and spelling out mutual expectations can help client and worker stay attuned to the reality of the current situation and can reduce the tendency toward regressive transference and countertransference.[21]

As Schubert notes, the contract is useful at an early stage for formulating certain basic understandings in order to determine whether the client has come to the appropriate agency, whether the service needed can be offered, who is going to give it, what if any are the conditions for providing the service, whether any eligibility requirements are to be met, what fees if any will be charged, and what other persons may be involved.[22] Client-worker agreement about these important aspects can be a powerful force in mobilizing energies for a common cause.

In group work, Garvin describes research showing that agreement between the worker and the group member on their expectations of each other is positively correlated with the worker's performance and with progress in group problem-solving.[23] Similarly, Brown's intensive investigation of early group sessions reveals that developing mutual expectations as early as possible is significantly related to later group functioning and member satisfaction.[24] The findings of studies of small groups support these results. They indicate that members' agreement about a group's goals and means of achieving goals leads to improved motivation and functioning.[25]

In community organization, the contract might be applied, for example, when worker and clients are preparing to negotiate and bargain with their change target. It is essential that group and worker agree on proposed demands, lines of attack and defense, potential concessions, allocation of roles, and choice of strategies.[26] Discussing and adopting an explicit contract that establishes consensus on these points could clarify planning and give the participants a sense of solidarity.

---

[21] Rapoport, op. cit., p. 291.

[22] Margaret Schubert, *Interviewing in Social Work Practice: An Introduction* (New York: Council on Social Work Education, 1971), p. 7.

[23] Charles Garvin, "Complementarity of Role Expectations in Groups: the Member-Worker Contract," *Social Work Practice, 1969* (New York: Columbia University Press, 1969), pp. 127–45.

[24] Leonard N. Brown, "Social Workers' Verbal Acts and the Development of Mutual Expectations with Beginning Client Groups," pp. 99–115. Unpublished doctoral dissertation, Columbia University School of Social Work, New York, 1971.

[25] See Bertram H. Raven and Jan Rietsema, "The Effects of Varied Clarity of Group Goal and Group Path Upon the Individual and His Relation to His Group," in Dorwin Cartwright and Alvin Zander, eds., *Group Dynamics: Research and Theoy* (Evanston, Ill.: Row, Peterson & Co., 1960), pp. 395–413.

[26] See George A. Brager and Valerie Jorrin, "Bargaining: A Method in Community Change," *Social Work*, 14 (October 1969), p. 82.

Differential participation

Practice theory has focused primarily on the worker's functions and responsibilities, devoting limited attention to the client's role and tasks. The respective contributions of client and worker to social work intervention have not been clear, especially with regard to the client's perception of the worker's role.

The concept of the contract not only emphasizes the importance of *joint* participation in the common enterprise of intervention, but also highlights the *differential* participation of client and worker. As Grosser points out: "A view of worker and client as having different but equal roles is not simply a theoretical concept; it is a practical prerequisite to operationalizing such innovations as worker partisanship and client participation."[27]

The worker has a major responsibility to delineate with the clients the unique aspects of their participation at each phase of the process. The contract is a tool for such delineation, and for both client and worker it is an ongoing reminder of their collaborative relationship and different responsibilities.

Efforts have been made recently to differentiate between tasks and roles of clients and workers. Reid formulates the worker's primary roles as follows: to define with the client the most effective course of action in resolving the problem and to direct his intervention toward helping the client achieve his necessary tasks.[28]

Vattano speaks of the "power-to-the-people movement" as a challenge to traditional practice through its emphasis on self-help groups. Members of the groups provide direct services to each other, while social workers function as peers, catalysts, researchers, or theory builders.[29]

Zweig depicts the role of the legislative ombudsman, in which the worker is a bridge between the client and his elected representative. The worker may motivate the applicant who initially in seeking help with his own needs to deal with policies affecting him. The client then becomes an activist rather than a target for intervention. As an administrative ombudsman, the worker expedites the bureaucratic processes involved in service delivery and guides the client or consumer through them.[30]

---

[27] Charles F. Grosser, "Changing Theory and Changing Practice," *Social Casework*, 50 (January 1969), p. 19.

[28] William J. Reid, "Target Problems, Time Limits, Task Structure," *Journal of Education for Social Work*, 8 (Spring 1972), p. 67.

[29] Anthony Vattano, "Power to the People: Self-Help Groups," *Social Work*, 17 (July 1972), pp. 7–15.

[30] Franklin M. Zweig, "The Social Worker as Legislative Ombudsman," *Social Work*, 14 (January 1969), pp. 26–27.

Studt proposes a basic framework for social work practice that incorporates the following features: (1) The client is the "primary worker in task accomplishment" and carries the major responsibility. (2) The social worker has a secondary responsibility "to provide the conditions necessary for the client's work on his task." (3) No one but the client can perform the tasks that his own life-stage and specific situation require.[31]

Implementation of the contract is founded on the belief that the client ultimately must exercise his right to self-determination. When the client assumes the responsibility for choosing among alternatives and using his own skills and resources to deal with his agreed-upon tasks, this enhances his motivation, investment, and self-esteem. The client's meaningful participation in making decisions and formulating the contract is based on the recognition that people are spontaneously active, seeking, and striving beings. The insights of ego psychology highlight the fact that the active, seeking person who carries out his commitments and who takes responsibility for his actions experiences a sense of achievement and competence in performing his role. In the process of developing the contract, the worker can discover ways to enhance the client's sense of identity and independence by offering opportunities for choice, self-determination, and self-mastery.

The possibilities inherent in this approach are increasingly evident as social workers move away from the traditional view of service planned for and provided to the client by a worker who is more knowledgeable, objective, or expert. For example, involuntary clients in a correctional setting were able to engage in meaningful decision-making once the opportunity was offered and stimulated.[32] In a child care agency an innovative focus on decision-making was constructive, time saving, and advantageous to adoptive applicants and children awaiting placement. Applicants were given the responsibility for deciding, on the basis of photographs shown them early in the adoption process, which child they wished to adopt—a decision traditionally made by the worker at the end of the evaluation process.[33]

Reciprocal accountability

The client and the worker are accountable to each other in various ways, each having an ongoing responsibility to fulfill agreed-upon tasks

---

[31] Elliott Studt, "Social Work Theory and Implications for the Practice of Methods," *Social Work Education Reporter,* 16 (June 1968), pp. 22–24 and 42–46.

[32] Ibid.

[33] Joan Shireman and Kenneth W. Watson, "Adoption of Real Children," *Social Work,* 17 (July 1972), pp. 29–39.

and work toward agreed-upon goals. The contract can help make both parties as aware as possible of their reciprocal obligations.

The client's responsibility must be emphasized. Insufficient attention to it may partially account for the limited involvement of some clients in the helping process or their withdrawal from it. In child welfare settings, this lack may help explain parents' psychological abandonment of placed children. A contractual alliance with parents of emotionally disturbed children in residential treatment would clarify their accountability, bring into sharp focus their role in treatment, and make the concept of a family-centered program more dynamic.

Beck points out that "professionals tend to be accountable to other professionals rather than to the consumers of their services."[34] In social work, accountability has typically been related to the worker's role as agency representative and to the agency's mandate from the community. It has been stressed that being within an agency complicates the worker's efforts to be accountable to the client. But this view is changing. Patti and Resnick argue that, although organizational expectations realistically constrain workers, "the professional can work within an agency and retain his primary commitment to client welfare."[35]

The increased responsiveness to clients that is inherent in the use of a contract helps shift the worker's sanction away from the community toward the client. This is especially evident in situations of advocacy, in which a worker's engagement by the client system is established through a contractual alliance featuring mutual accountability.

Explicitness

Explicitness is the quality of being specific, clear, and open. Although its importance is obvious, the degree to which it is implemented in practice is debatable. Frequent double agendas, implicit or covert contracts, and discrepant client-worker expectations have been mentioned. Often in casework practice the client sees one problem or target of intervention, while the worker sees another—usually related to a subtle or underling difficulty. The client is interested in obtaining tangible help with an immediate need but "the caseworker doggedly pursues a different agenda, namely one of trying to get the client to see the 'real' problem underneath it all."[36]

The contract offers an opportunity to spell out as openly as possible the conditions, expectations, and responsibilities inherent in the planned

---

[34] Bertram M. Beck, "Community Control: A Distraction Not an Answer," *Social Work*, 14 (October 1969), pp. 14–20.

[35] Rino J. Patti and Herman Resnick, "Changing the Agency from Within," *Social Work*, 17 (July 1972), p. 57.

[36] Reid, op. cit., p. 61.

interaction. Therefore a fundamental task of the worker is to clarify contractual expectations and obligations. Research on brief treatment has corroborated the value of formulating explicit and specific goals.[37] To the traditional exhortation to "start where the client is" might be added: "and let him know where you are, and where you are going." An explicit contract can help give the client more ethical protection than is possible through unspoken or covert contracts.

The client must be explicit as well as the worker. Emphasis on explicitness in contract formulation would actively engage the client's cognitive functions and resources—and such engagement has proved valuable in crisis intervention. In addition, the worker would be more likely to be continually "tuned in" to the needs that the client feels. In his formulation of task-centered casework, Reid suggests requiring "that the client himself explicitly acknowledge the problem and express a willingness to work on it."[38] The rationale is derived from evidence that in social work practice the client's perception of his situation is more important than the worker's view of the problem.

Application to practice

Little experimentation with the contract has been reported in social work practice. At present, its formal use appears to be atypical or innovative rather than regularly incorporated in practice.

Child welfare workers have used a written contract to delineate mutual responsibilities between agency and foster or adoptive parents. However, no published account of their experiences is available.

In a mental health setting oriented toward transactional analysis, the concept has been used with patients briefly hospitalized following a crisis. The initial interview was focused on establishing "a clear verbal contract" that outlined specific problem areas, appropriate goals, and methods of treatment. The contract alleviated "many of the fears of the patient concerning "strange" things that might happen to him on a mental health unit. The patient knows exactly the nature of the therapeutic contract and realizes that he will have an important role to play in determining the course of his treatment."[39]

A family agency serving an upper-middle-class community reports successful experiences with the written contract as an integral tool in treatment. Goals and tasks of participants, schedules for contacts, fees and methods of payment, options for renegotiation, and other pertinent

[37] See William J. Reid and Ann W. Shyne, *Brief and Extended Casework* (New York: Columbia University Press, 1969).

[38] Reid, op. cit., p. 61.

[39] See Donn M. Brechenser, "Brief Psychotherapy Using Transactional Analysis," *Social Casework*, 53 (March 1972), pp. 173–76.

factors are spelled out. The agency has noted a clearer understanding
of treatment goals by client and worker, wiser use of time, and greater
awareness of time limits. There was also a growing realization that the
contract could be used in setting boundaries for the treatment
relationship.[40]

The written contract has considerable merit with clients requesting
help with interpersonal problems. Whether it can be validly adapted
to others needs further testing.

Flexibility

To be a truly dynamic tool, the contract should be used flexibly.
If either the worker or the client rigidly adheres to its conditions—which
they may tend to do with a written contract—this limits its usefulness,
especially when the client's or the worker's perception of the situation
changes. The binding restrictions and penalties of legal contracts would
be inapplicable to social work and would constrain the creativity and
spontaneity of both client and worker.

To guard against rigidity, there should be provisions for reformulation
or renegotiation by mutual consent as circumstances change, problems
are resolved, or the focus of intervention alters. Changes in the contract
should be based on open discussion by all parties and should not be
subverted by client, worker, or agency. Emphasis should remain on
the client's perceived need rather than on the worker's interpretation.
When a short-term contract expires, a client wishing further help over
a protracted period could ask to negotiate a new one.

Questions may be raised in connection with flexibility. How meaningful is a contract if its breach does not incur some form of punishment,
loss, or suffering? Will contract modifications be discussed so frequently
that the real issue of working on the problem is delayed or avoided?
Will the contract become the goal of client-worker interaction rather
than the means of attaining the client's goals? These are potential problems to explore.

As social workers formulate contracts more actively and deliberately,
they should also consider the legal ramifications. In our society a contractual agreement may be legally binding even when it is not written.
Will partial or total failure to fulfill its terms therefore render the practitioner or agency subject to law suits or malpractice claims?

It is evident that much more must be done in exploring the use
of the contract, putting it into operation, and developing principles of
action applicable to different client populations in diverse settings. Im-

---

[40] See Richard Lessor and Anita Lutkus, "Two Techniques for the Social Work
Practitioner," *Social Work*, 16 (January 1971), pp. 5–6.

plementation must take into account the client's characteristics, capacities, and motivation. For example, using the contract with children or with involuntary clients may require special modifications of techniques and procedures.

In effect, the contract can be more or less complex, depending on how ready and able the client is to engage in formulating and utilizing it. In many situations, the client's social, physical, or psychological characteristics limit his ability to formulate an explicit contractual agreement. It is important to experiment with use of the contract to test its validity, identify its limitations, and derive specific operational guidelines.

Potential of the contract

The contract can contribute significantly to the positive outcome of social work services. In particular, it can bring focus and meaning to inherent values and principles implicit in social work practice and make the contracting parties more aware of them. If the worker has conviction about the contract and implements it fully, he can help the client participate more actively in dealing with his own situation. In so doing, he can affirm the client's preeminent role in social work intervention.

The contract has the potential to serve as an active instrument for engaging worker and client in meaningful and productive interaction for the following reasons:

- It is derived from their shared experience in exploring a situation and reaching agreement on goals and tasks.
- It gives both practitioner and client a sense of immediate involvement and meaningful participation and signifies their mutual commitment and readiness to assume responsibility.
- It provides a base line for periodically reviewing accomplishments, assessing progress, and examining the conditions of agreement.

At its present stage, the contract does not offer specific propositions and principles of action for use with different types of consumers of social services. But there is sufficient evidence from clinical practice and from research on crisis intervention, brief treatment, and client discontinuance to suggest that the use of some form of contract in social work merits systematic experiment and research in various settings, with varying periods of service, and with clients having different characteristics and problems.

This article aims to contribute to developing cumulative theory for practice in this important area. Analysis of practice experiences and research findings could refine the concept further, formulate its specific components and operational guidelines, validate its incorporation into the helping process, and explore its efficacy in enhancing the client's perception and use of social services.

Selected annotated references

CROXTON, TOM A., "The Therapeutic Contract in Social Treatment," in *Individual Change through Small Groups* ed. Paul Glasser, Rosemary Sarri, and Robert Vinter (New York: Free Press, 1974), pp. 169–83.
Croxton summarizes legal/historical perspectives on contracts as well as the use of contracts in social work and social practice. He conceptualizes the contracting process into six phases—exploration, negotation, the preliminary contract, the working agreement, secondary contracts, and termination and evaluation.

GOTTLIEB, WERNER, and JOE H. STANLEY, "Mutual Goals and Goal-Setting in Casework," *Social Casework* 48:8 (October 1967), pp. 471–77.
The development of mutually acceptable goals is essential if casework with families is to be effective. Casework consists of worker and client goal-directed activities to bring about constructive change.

LEIFER, RONALD, "The Medical Model as Ideology," *International Journal of Psychiatry,* vol. 9 (New York: Science House, 1970–71), pp. 13–21.
The acceptance of the medical model in psychiatry obscures important differences between psychiatry and medicine which in turn obscures the social functions of psychiatry.

LESSOR, RICHARD, and ANITA LUTKUS, "Two Techniques for the Social Work Practitioner," *Social Work* 16:1 (January 1971), pp. 5–6, 96.
Lessor and Lutkus report the use of chart pads and contracts in a private family service agency.

SCHAPLER, JAMES H., and MAIDA J. GALINSKY, "Goals in Social Group Work Practice: Formulation, Implementation and Evaluation," in *Individual Change through Small Groups,* ed. Paul Glasser, Rosemary Sarri, and Robert Vinter (New York: Free Press, 1974), pp. 126–48.
This article discusses who sets goals and how they are set, implemented, and evaluated in group work. It is an interesting article to compare and contrast with our statement on goal setting.

SUNDEL, MARTIN, NORMA RADIN, and SALLIE R. CHURCHILL, "Diagnosis in Group Work," in *Individual Change through Small Groups,* ed. Paul Glasser, Rosemary Sarri, and Robert Vinter (New York: Free Press, 1974), pp. 105–26.
This article discusses the content of diagnosis, the information required in a diagnostic assessment, and the diagnostic procedures in a particular model of group work.

SHEVRIN, HOWARD, and FREDERIK SHECTMAN, "The Diagnostic Process in Psychiatric Evaluations," *Bulletin of the Menninger Clinic* 37:5 (September 1973), pp. 451–95.
This article on the process of clinical diagnosis was written to help the psychiatric practitioner to develop a concept of the diagnostic method. It is not an easy article to read but would be of value to students who want to pursue the concept further.

Chapter 9

INTERVENTIVE ROLES: IMPLEMENTATION OF THE PLAN

The service contract has been negotiated and agreement achieved, and client and worker are now prepared for the hard business of intervention. The worker is confronted with the challenge of actually using his abilities, skills, knowledge, and contacts to assist the client in reaching their mutually defined goals. The worker's activity in this area will be discussed in terms of interventive roles. The concept of interventive roles will be defined, and three such roles—broker, enabler, and advocate—will be discussed. Some general considerations about conceptualizing intervention in terms of roles will be noted, and finally we will set forth a configuration of interventive roles which is very appropriate for the generalist worker.

THE CONCEPT OF INTERVENTIVE ROLES

A more explicit statement of the concept of interventive roles can be developed by examining meanings for the terms *intervention* and *roles*. Throughout this book we have been using the term *intervention* in a more restricted and narrower sense than do many of our social work colleagues. Our usage of the term refers to activities undertaken subsequent to the development of a service contract and directed toward the achievement of goals specified in the service contract. Some social work scholars and practitioners use the term in a more global way to refer to all social work activities, including data collection and contracting (or assessment) functions as well as actual change efforts. This concept is often expressed by the statement that "treatment begins at the opening of the first contract between worker and client."

We do agree with the notion that patterns of relationship and communication begin to develop when the client and the practitioner first meet, but we wish to differentiate the exploration of problem and goals and data collection on the part of both worker and client from goal-directed, jointly planned change efforts. We prefer a more limited use of the concept of intervention, first, to maintain the focus on activities directed toward goal attainment and, second, to minimize the danger of making the concept of contracting secondary, or perhaps losing it, in efforts to produce change. We see danger in the desire of workers, and sometimes clients, to produce change quickly and move ahead with change activities without first developing a contract which clearly specifies the problem, objectives, and interventive activities to be utilized in accomplishing the objectives. Maintaining a narrower definition of intervention and also stressing the functions of data collection and contracting will tend to keep these three aspects of social work processes in a more balanced perspective. Intervention in our usage therefore refers to social work processes which occur after a service contract has been arrived and are directed specifically to the achievement of goals specified in that contract.

Role is a global concept with wide usage in the sociological, social-psychological, and psychological literature. The term is not always used consistently.[1] For our purposes, role refers to the behaviors expected of a person. Role enactment will refer to the actual translation of these expectations into behavior. In a global sense a person's role, or roles, can be conceived as comprising the total universe of expectations which he holds for his own behavior as well as the expectations of his behavior which are held by others. But our focus is much narrower; interventive roles will refer to the behavior by means of which both the client—an individual, a family, a group, or a community—and the worker expect the worker to accomplish goals specified in the service contract. One of the central points stressed in Chapter 8 was that intervention, along with all other social work processes, is undertaken jointly by the worker and the client. This chapter, however, focuses specifically on the worker's interventive activity.

In this chapter discussion will center on three interventive roles—those of social broker, enabler, and advocate. This is not an exhaustive

---

[1] See Bruce J. Biddle and Edwin J. Thomas, *Role Theory: Concepts and Research* (New York: Wiley, 1966), chaps. 1–3. Brief discussions of role theory concepts are found in Neal Gross, Ward Masson, and McEachern, *Explorations in Role Analysis* (New York: Wiley, 1958), chap. 3; and Lionel J. Neiman and James W. Hughes, "The Problem of the Concept of Role—A Re-Survey of the Literature," in *Social Perspectives on Behavior* ed. Herman D. Stein and Richard A. Cloward (Glencoe: Free Press, 1959), 177–85.

listing. Some authors conceptualize the social worker's roles differently or add other roles. Charles Grosser's article in this chapter discusses these three roles in relation to community development programs and also adds a fourth role—that of activist. The literature also includes references to such additional roles as therapist,[2] encourager,[3] ombudsman,[4] bargainer,[5] and lobbyist.[6] The readings in this chapter include an excerpt from a report of the Southern Regional Education Board which conceptualizes social work activity into twelve functions and roles. In Chapter 1 we noted Bisno's conceptualization of nine social work methods ("methods," as the term is used by Bisno, appear very similar to our concept of role).[7] The interventive roles of broker, enabler, and advocate, however, provide a useful framework for the beginning social work practitioner to utilize in conceptualizing interventive activity. The value of the framework is further enhanced because, as is true of the concept of contract, it is not limited by the size of the relational system; workers can use it to conceptualize their interventive roles whether they are working with individuals, small groups, or larger systems.

Our limiting of the definition of intervention and our organization of this chapter around the concept of interventive roles is not meant to deny or ignore the importance of specific change modalities.[8] Rather than attempt to catalog change modalities (many of which wax and wane as the culture and the profession emphasize different approaches), we chose to conceptualize intervention in a way which transcends spe-

[2] Scott Briar, "The Current Crisis in Social Casework," *Social Work Practice, 1967* (New York: Columbia University Press, 1967), pp. 19–33.

[3] William W. and Loureide J. Biddle, *The Community Development Process: The Rediscovery of Local Initiative* (New York: Holt, Rinehart and Winston, 1965), p. 82.

[4] James E. Payne, "Ombudsman Roles for Social Workers," *Social Work* 17:1 (January 1972), pp. 94–100.

[5] George A. Brager and Valerie Jorcin, "Bargaining: A Method in Community Change," *Social Work* 14:4 (October 1969), pp. 73–83.

[6] Mary Ann Maheffey, "Lobbying and Social Work," *Social Work* 17:1 (January 1972), pp. 3–11.

[7] Herbert Bisno, "A Theoretical Framework for Teaching Social Work Methods and Skills with Particular Reference to Undergraduate Social Welfare Education," *Journal of Education for Social Work* 5:2 (Fall 1969), pp. 5–17.

[8] For one such list of modalities with additional references see James K. Whittaker, *Social Treatment: An Approach to Interpersonal Helping* (Chicago: Aldine, 1974), 200–248. Other works which may be of use include Robert W. Roberts and Robert H. Nee, eds., *Theories of Social Casework* (Chicago: University of Chicago Press 1970); Jack Rothman, "Three Models of Community Organization Practice," *Social Work Practice, 1968* (New York: Columbia University Press, 1968), 16–47; Emanuel Tropp, "The Group: in Life and in Social Work," *Social Casework* 49:5 (May 1968), 267–74; and James K. Whittaker, "Models of Group Development: Implications for Group Work Practice," *Social Service Review* 44:3 (September 1970), pp. 308–22. See also articles under "Social Casework," "Social Group Work," and "Social Planning and Community Organization" in the *Encyclopedia of Social Work* (New York: National Association of Social Workers, 1971).

cific modalities. The concept of interventive roles (broker, enabler, and advocate) provides a framework for the analysis of interventive activity that is independent of the change modalities currently in vogue.

THE SOCIAL BROKER ROLE

How does a worker enact the role of social broker? Analogies from other fields may be useful. How is the role of stockbroker enacted? Presumably a stockbroker assists clients in defining their resources and developing investment objectives; once this has been accomplished, the broker utilizes his contacts and knowledge of the market to select stocks that will assist clients in reaching the defined investment objectives. How about the real estate broker? Again, the realtor will assist a client in analyzing his resources and needs to define objectives in terms of the type of home the client wishes to buy. Then, using his knowledge of the available resources, the realtor will assist in matching the client's needs to the available housing. And so it is in the enactment of the social broker role. The worker serves as a linkage between the client and other community resources. Harold McPheeters and Robert Ryan, writing for the Southern Regional Education Board, note that the primary function of the broker is linkage, which they describe as follows:

> The primary objective is to steer people toward the existing services that can be of benefit to them. Its focus is on enabling or helping people to use the system and to negotiate its pathways. A further objective is to link elements of the service system with one another. The essential benefit of this objective is the physical hook-up of the person with the source of help and the physical connection of elements of the service system with one another.[9]

In linkage the activities of the worker are directed toward making connections between the client and the community in order to accomplish the objectives specified in the service contract. Serving as a social broker requires a broad knowledge of community resources as well as a knowledge of the operating procedures of agencies so that effective connections can be made.

What are some examples of social brokering? The worker who arranges for a client to receive marital counseling, for job placement of an unemployed person, or for improved housing functions as a social broker if these activities involve connecting the client to other resources. The worker who brings specialized resources to groups—outside experts who may provide valuable information to the groups—is functioning

---

[9] Harold L. McPheeters and Robert M. Ryan, *A Core of Competence for Baccalaureate Social Welfare and Curricular Implications* (Atlanta: Southern Regional Education Board, 1971), p. 18.

as a social broker in that he provides linkages between the client and additional community resources. Or, when working with a community group, the worker can assist the group by identifying sources of funding for programs or additional outside expertise that can assist the organization in moving toward defined goals. A common element in all these examples is making a referral in order to connect the client to another resource. Referral is a basic part of the enactment of the social broker role, and frequently assisting a client to find and use a needed resource is the most important service a worker can provide. The process of making a referral will be reintroduced in the concluding portions of this section as we discuss the integration of the roles of brokers, enabler, and advocate, and will be further developed in Chapter 10.

THE ENABLER ROLE

The worker enacts the enabler role when his intervention activities are directed toward assisting the client to find the coping strengths and resources within himself to produce the changes necessary for accomplishing objectives of the service contract. The major distinguishing element of the enabler role is that change occurs because of client efforts; the responsibility of the worker is to facilitate or enable the client's accomplishment of a defined change. A common misconception in discussion of the enabler role is to see it only as a change that occurs within the client or in the client's pattern of relating to others or the environment. However, the enabler role can also be used to help the client find ways of altering his environment. The distinguishing feature of the enabler role is that the client effects the change with the worker performing a supporting or enabling function for him.

The worker who assists a group of neighborhood residents in thinking through the need for a new day-care center, in identifying factors that must be considered in establishing the center, and in planning the steps that might be taken to provide day care will be serving as an enabler to a community group. The worker who helps a group to identify sources of internal conflict as well as influences that are blocking the group from moving towards its defined goals and then to discover ways of dealing with these difficulties is serving as an enabler in relation to the group. Likewise, the worker who assists a mother in identifying problems in her relationship with her child and in identifying and selecting alternative courses of action to improve that relationship is also serving as an enabler.

Teaching is an important aspect of the enabler role. Frequently workers will provide clients with information necessary to decision making; in some situations information may be all that a client needs to accomplish his defined goals. Giving information must be clearly distinguished, however, from giving advise. "Giving information" implies supplying the client with data, input, or knowledge which the client is free to use or not to use on his own behalf; "giving advice" implies that the worker knows what is best for the client. Workers rarely give advice, but providing information is an important service they render to clients.

One of the five tasks of the social work function as identified by Schwartz is the contribution of data which may help the client cope with social reality and the problem which is being worked. Schwartz also, however, offers three important warnings: (1) the worker must recognize that the information he offers is only a small part of the available social experience; (2) the information should be related to the problem that brings the client and worker together; and (3) opinions should be clearly labeled as opinions and not represented as facts.[10] Virginia Satir, a noted family counselor, clearly identifies the worker's responsibility to contribute from his own experience in working with troubled families. She also notes a second major function of the educational component of counseling—modeling communication.[11] In their approach to clients and to problem solving, workers provide a model of behavior which the client, if he wishes, may emulate. Albert Bandura, a behavioral psychotherapist, further describes the use of modeling as a device for teaching clients new behavior patterns.[12] In the sense both of providing information and of providing modeling behavior, teaching is an important aspect of the enabler role.

Encouraging verbalization, providing for ventilation of feelings, examining the pattern of relationships, offering encouragement and reassurance, and engaging in logical discussion and rational decision making are also avenues by which the enabler role might be enacted. In an article included in this chapter Nicholas Hobbs discusses enabler approaches which assist clients to make progress in one-to-one relational systems. Utilizing enabling as the interventive role will, of course, involve the worker primarily in contacts with the client system rather than with external systems. But, as noted, the client system can be an individual, a group, or a community.

THE ADVOCATE ROLE

Advocacy is a concept which social work has borrowed from the legal profession. As advocate, the social worker becomes a spokesman

---

[10] William Schwartz, "The Social Worker in the Group," *Social Welfare Forum, 1961* (New York: Columbia University Press, 1961), pp. 164–66.

[11] Virginia Satir, *Conjoint Family Therapy* (Palo Alto, Calif.: Science and Behavior Books, 1964), pp. 97–100.

[12] Albert Bandura, "Behavioral Psychology," *Scientific American* 216:3 (March 1967), pp. 78–86.

for the client by presenting an arguing the client's cause when this is necessary to accomplish the objectives of the contract. As Charles Grosser notes, the advocate in social work is not neutral but, like the advocate in law, is a partisan spokesman for his client. The advocate will argue, debate, bargain, negotiate, and manipulate the environment on behalf of the client. A report of the Ad Hoc Committee on Advocacy of the National Association of Social Workers, reproduced in this chapter, notes the techniques and issues involved in the use of advocacy. Like the broker and enabler roles, the advocate role can be utilized with client systems of various sizes.

Advocacy is becoming an increasingly popular role of social workers. In the article on value dilemmas reproduced in Chapter 3, Henry Miller, like others, argues for a reemphasis on advocacy. Unlike the broker and enabler roles, however, advocacy can be used without the direct involvement of the client. This creates a danger of falling to the temptation of serving as a client's spokesman without having a clear contract with the client to do so. A lawyer does not become a spokesman for a client until the client has retained him and authorized him to extend this service; likewise, the social worker should be sure he has an explicit contract with the client prior to engaging in advocacy activities.

ROLES ARE NOT FUNCTIONAL SPECIALIZATIONS

Our discussion of social work intervention roles as discrete entities can lead to misconceptions. We are not recommending this conceptualization of interventive roles as a basis for functional specializations; we think it would be inappropriate for workers to consider themselves as specializing as brokers, enablers, or advocates. Any such specialization would limit a worker's ability to be of service to a client. Rather than specializations, all workers will require abilities in all three roles so that they can select the most appropriate interventive role for each client situation. Each of the roles may be used in some client situations; this provides the worker and the client with alternative approaches to use in achieving goals. Consider, for example, the following excerpt from a report made by a social worker in a Head Start program. At the request of Mrs. B, the worker had come to her home to take an application to enroll the child in the program; the discussion described here occurred right after the application was completed.

> The last question was, "Why do you want your child in Head Start?" Mrs. B answered by saying that he had to learn to behave better and he needed to be around other children more than he was. Putting the form aside, I asked her what sort of problems she was having with Jimmy. He had been sitting at her side, suprisingly quiet for a three-year-old. In response to my question Mrs. B told me about

taking Jimmy to the child guidance center and what the doctor had told her. Apparently the doctor had tested Jimmy and then talked to Mrs. B. She had complained of his bad behavior and that she didn't know how to discipline him. Apparently the doctor told her that the problem might be hers and not Jimmy's. He said that she was lonely and insecure and maybe needed some guidance in handling her children. She discussed this freely and admitted that this might be true. I asked her whether she would like to have me come over to talk to her about ways to handle Jimmy. She said definitely yes, that she couldn't do a thing with him.

In this excerpt we note the development of a preliminary service contract. There appears to be agreement that Mrs. B is having difficulty in the way she is handling Jimmy, and the goal is for her to learn new ways of handling him. The interventive step by means of which the worker proposes to accomplish this is to talk with Mrs. B about her parenting of Jimmy. The worker is proposing the enabler role, but this is a situation where the role of broker and perhaps even the role of advocate might have been used. Had this worker explored the situation more completely with Mrs. B, the intervention plan might have been different. For example, further exploration with Mrs. B about what happened at the child guidance center, about her perceptions of what the doctor said, about her thinking and feelings concerning the experience, and about her willingness to return to the clinic might have led to an intervention plan involving the worker's serving as the linkage between Mrs. B and the clinic. Or, possibly, if there appeared to be a problem with the manner in which the clinic related to Mrs. B, the worker might have used an advocate role and served as Mrs. B's spokesman at the clinic. Note that the objective remains the same—to help alter Mrs. B's way of relating to her son—but that the intervention plan to accomplish it may involve counseling with Mrs. B, serving as the linkage between Mrs. B and the clinic, or acting as Mrs. B's spokesman at the clinic. Consideration of all three alternatives is not likely to occur, however, unless the worker is both willing and able to use all three roles and is prepared to explore the client situation adequately before arriving at an intervention plan.

A second misconception that can grow out of our discussion of roles is that a worker will use only one role with each client. To the contrary, an intervention plan may combine elements of various roles. This can be illustrated by discussing the referral process—a major part of the social broker role. If a contract has been negotiated which calls for referral in order to achieve its objectives, three distinct subsequent steps are involved. These are preparation of the client, preparation of the referral organization, and follow-up. Preparation of the client includes discussion of what the referral will involve, what the referral agency expects, etc., and requires enabling skills. At this stage the worker is attempting to enable the client to make effective use of the referral agency. Ethel Panter offers a useful discussion of client preparation in terms of its ego-building impact on clients.[13] Referral also generates feelings and reactions to loss on the part of both client and worker; this aspect of referral will be discussed further in Chapter 11, "Referral, Transfer, and Termination." Enabling skills are used to help clients deal with their reactions to new agencies or workers and are necessary to successful completion of a referral.

Preparation of the referral agency involves the sharing of information about the client (with the client's full knowledge and usually with his consent). In some situations an agency may be reluctant to accept a referral and to provide a service which it is mandated to provide. When this happens, the worker may need to become the clients' spokesman and to utilize advocacy approaches. After the actual referral has been made (i.e., after the client makes initial contact with the referral organization), the worker will follow up with both the client and the organization. Ideally, follow-up should be a part of the initial planning. As a result of follow-up, the worker may learn about client resistances to continuing the service or the referral organization's resistance to continuing with the client. In the former situation additional enabling approaches may be utilized with the client, and in the latter additional advocacy approaches may be utilized on behalf of the client.

This model of social brokerage supplemented by advocacy and enabling skills to help a client secure services he requires is one which will frequently be used by the generalist social worker. A worker skilled at involving the client in developing a service contract and skilled at helping the client to find and utilize the resources necessary to meet the objectives of the contract will provide an extremely useful, largely unavailable, service to clients. Such an approach, however, requires the ability to use enabling skills both to humanize the ways in which services are delivered and to assist agencies in meeting their responsibilities to clients.

RECAPITULATION

Intervention has been defined as the social worker's activity directed toward achieving the objectives of a service contract. Three major interventive roles have been discussed—social broker, enabler, and advocate. Any of these roles may be used to reach the same contract objectives: this provides client and worker with alternative approaches to intervention. In addition, the roles may be used in conjunction with

---

[13] Ethel Panter, "Ego Building Procedures That Foster Social Functioning," *Social Casework* 47:3 (March 1966), 142–43.

one another to reach the same objectives. A focus on social brokerage in which enabling is used to assist the client in utilizing community resources and advocacy is used to influence the way the resources are delivered to the client may be a major part of the services provided by the generalist social worker.

A LOOK FORWARD

The readings in this chapter elaborate further on interventive roles. The article by Charles Grosser discusses the application of roles in a community development program. The paper by Nicholas Hobbs offers a statement on enabling approaches which can be used effectively in supporting clients, and the statement of the National Association of Social Workers Ad Hoc Committee on Advocacy notes approaches and issues that can be used in implementing advocacy roles. Harold Mc-Pheeters and Robert Ryan provide an alternative conceptualization of social work roles.

In the next chapter we discuss evaluation, an essential part of the problem-solving model which will lend a more systemic dynamic quality to social work processes. Evaluation provides feedback loops through which worker and client negotiate changes in their plans; through the continuous use of evaluation and feedback social work becomes less linear and more systemic.

Social welfare objectives and roles*

Harold L. McPheeters and Robert M. Ryan

To describe social welfare work adequately, one must know not only what is being done, but also to what objective is it directed. The task has meaning only when one knows to what end it is being done. This was described as the difference between *what the worker does* and *what gets done.* In human service work there are often several alternative approaches that may be taken to reach the same objective. From these concepts the participants [a task force of social work educators and practitioners who met with members of Southern Regional Education Board

* Reprinted with permission of the authors and the Southern Regional Education Board from *A Core of Competence for Baccalaureate Social Welfare and Curricular Implications* (Atlanta: Southern Regional Education Board, 1971), pp. 17–20.

to attempt to define the core of competence needed for the baccalaureate worker] began to think about *roles* that would represent a set of alternative activities that might be carried out to a common major objective. The list of major objectives to which social welfare work might be directed and the corresponding roles that workers might play in meeting the objectives varied from time to time in the discussion, but the participants finally settled on 12 broad *centers of gravity* for the field of social welfare. These centers were found to be almost never mutually exclusive. They might be collapsed or extended or given other names. The 12 objectives and their corresponding roles were:

1. DETECTION—*Outreach Worker.* The primary objective is to identify the individuals or groups who are experiencing difficulty (at crisis) or who are in danger of becoming vulnerable (at risk). A further objective is to detect and identify conditions in the environment that are contributing to the problems or are raising the level of risk.

2. LINKAGE—*Broker.* The primary objective is to steer people toward the existing services that can be of benefit to them. Its focus is on enabling or helping people to use the system and to negotiate its pathways. A further objective is to link elements of the service system with one another. The essential benefit of this objective is the physical hook-up of the person with the source of help and the physical connection of elements of the service system with one another.

3. ADVOCACY—*Advocate.* The primary objective is to fight for the rights and dignity of people in need of help. The key assumption is that there will be instances where practices, regulations, and general conditions will prevent individuals from receiving services, from using resources, or from obtaining help. This includes the notion of fighting for services on behalf of a single person, and fighting for changes in laws, regulations, etc., on behalf of a whole class of persons or a segment of society. Advocacy aims at removing the obstacles or barriers that prevent people from exercising their rights or receiving the benefits and using the resources they need.

4. EVALUATION—*Evaluator.* This involves gathering information, assessing personal or community problems, weighing alternatives and priorities, and making decisions for action.

5. MOBILIZATION—*Mobilizer.* The foremost objective is to assemble and energize existing groups, resources, organizations, and structures, or to create new groups, organizations, or resources and bring them to bear on problems that exist, or to prevent problems from developing. Its principal focus is on available or existing institutions, organizations, and resources within the community.

6. INSTRUCTION—*Teacher.* Instruction is used in the sense of an objective rather than a method. The primary objectives are to convey and impart information and knowledge and to develop various kinds

of skills. A great deal of what has been called casework or therapy is, in careful analysis, simple instruction. This is also needed for prevention and enhancement of social functioning.

7. BEHAVIOR CHANGE—*Behavior Changer.* This is a broad one. Its primary objective is to bring about change in the behavior patterns, habits, and perceptions of individuals or groups. The key assumption is that problems may be alleviated or crises may be prevented by modifying, adding, or extinguishing discrete bits of behavior, by increasing insights, or by changing the values and perceptions of individuals, groups, and organizations.

8. CONSULTATION—*Consultant.* This involves working with other workers or agencies to help them increase their skills and to help them solve their clients' social welfare problems.

9. COMMUNITY PLANNING—*Community Planner.* This involves participating and assisting neighborhood planning groups, agencies, community agents, or governments in the development of community programs to assure that the human service needs of the community are represented and met to the greatest extent feasible.

10. INFORMATION PROCESSING—*Data Manager.* This objective is often ignored within social welfare. Its primary focus is the collection, classification, and analysis of data generated within the social welfare environment. Its contents would include data about the individual case, the community, and the institution.

11. ADMINISTRATION—*Administrator.* Again, the term is used as an objective rather than a method. The principal focus here is the management of a facility, an organization, a program, or a service unit.

12. CONTINUING CARE—*Care Giver.* The primary objective is to provide for persons who need ongoing support or care on an extended and continuing basis. The key assumption is that there will be individuals who will require constant surveillance or monitoring or who will need continuing support and services (i.e., financial assistance, 24-hour care), perhaps in an institutional setting or on a community basis.

These objectives and their corresponding roles are "goal oriented" and not "process oriented." However, there have been continuing problems with definitions since some of these same words are commonly used with process meaning—especially "evaluation," "data processing," "administration," and "consultation."

These *roles* are not roles in the usual sociological definition of the word. However, the word *role* seemed to be the most useful and appropriate label for participants to use to describe this concept of a set of alternative functions, all directed to a common objective.

Community development programs serving the urban poor*

Charles F. Grosser

A discontinuity exists between the theory and the methodology of community organization. Recognition of this is evidenced in the recent literature. Kahn notes:

> One cannot plan for the education, job training, placement, or counseling of deprived inner-city youth without new concentration on the public sector generally. What was often tokenism in welfare council participation would not do for these endeavors. . . . One must learn to deal with, involve, plan with, bring pressure upon, or even to cause changes in, local and state governmental bodies. . . .
> . . . until recently, the community organization method was conceptualized entirely in relation to the enabling role. . . . The enabling took the form of facilitating leadership development of consensus about direction to be taken or winning local assent to leadership-sanctioned direction and plans—not of shaping planning out of true community-wide involvement in goal setting.[1]

Morris and Rein similarly indicate that

> the requirements of the new community demand skill in invoking special points of view and in living with other professionals who advocate competing points of view.[2]

One major factor impelling new developments in community organization practice is the increased attention by the field to the client group with which it is engaged: specifically, beginning to work directly with the recipients—rather than exclusively with the providers—of social welfare service. As the term is used in this paper, *neighborhood community development* means community organization efforts being made with lower-class, minority group, urban slum residents. The goals of these efforts are to engage the poor in the decision-making process of the

---

* Reprinted with permission of the author and the National Association of Social Workers from *Social Work*, 10:3 (July 1965), pp. 15–21.

[1] Alfred J. Kahn, "Trends and Problems in Community Organization," *Social Work Practice, 1964* (New York: Columbia University Press, 1964), pp. 9, 19.

[2] Robert Morris and Martin Rein, "Emerging Patterns in Community Planning," *Social Work Practice, 1963* (New York: Columbia University Press, 1963), pp. 174–75.

community, both to overcome apathy and estrangement and to realign the power resources of the community by creating channels through which the consumers of social welfare services can define their problems and goals and negotiate on their own behalf. Much of the experience gained from these efforts can be generalized for application to most groups of deprived persons.

The purpose of this paper is to explore some of the consequences emerging from community organization's growing engagement with the poor man. Briefly discussed are (1) the substantive areas and issues with which community organization practice will have to deal, (2) a consideration of the role of the community worker, and (3) a brief review of the issue of the organizational forms that practice will take.

Substantive areas and issues

Community organization in neighborhood development programs signifies direct engagement with the problems of the poor man. More than any other group in our society, the poor expend a major portion of their efforts to achieve the "good life" through interaction with agencies of city government. It is with the local branches of the department of welfare, the police, the housing authority, the board of education, and similar agencies that the poor man negotiates for his share of the community's resources. Striving toward the equitable distribution of these resources is the programmatic strategy that must accompany any bona fide effort to encourage the residents of the inner-city slum to help themselves. If neighborhood development denies or ignores this fact, in the eyes of the local residents it is at best sham and window-dressing, at worst, deceit. Lower-class, minority group individuals cannot be expected to feel that they have a part in the determination of their own destinies in the face of such grievances as denial of welfare to nonresidents, forcing parents to take legal action against their child under the relatives' responsibility laws, categorization as an "undesirable tenant" with no right to face one's accusers and no recourse to appeal, arrest and interrogation characterized by prejudice and brutality, and an inferior, segregated school system. To attempt to facilitate a client's adjustment to such a social system is to betray his interests. Therefore, if local community development programs are to be successful, it must be recognized that local efforts at self-expression will be directed at the agents of government in an attempt to bring about solutions to such injustices as these.

Further, in order to arouse people who have been systematically socialized into apathy and inaction—in some cases, over several generations—it may be necessary to teach them that the solutions to their problems lie in the hands of certain governmental agencies, and that these agencies are sensitive to well-publicized mass efforts, particularly in election years. Lower-class, alienated, nonparticipating people will not be induced to organize by appeals to their sense of civic duty, patriotism, or morality, or other exhortations to exercise their obligations of citizenship. Such individuals will organize only if they perceive organization as a means to an immediate end. It should be pointed out—without becoming involved in a means-ends, process-content discussion—that these programs require a great deal more attention to material objectives than has been true in the past. Community development in slum neighborhoods is, after all, essentially a process for the redress of grievances that are the cumulative result of the differential distribution of community resources. To avoid partisanship in the name of objectivity and service to the "total community" is, in effect, to take a position justifying the pittance that has been allotted from the health, educational, and social welfare coffers to the residents of the inner-city slum.

An applied example of the foregoing was a voter-registration campaign conducted in New York City by Mobilization For Youth last summer and fall.[3] Geared to the registration of eligible minority group nonvoters, the campaign was not run on the model of the League of Women Voters, which presses voters to fulfill their civic duty. Instead, it was focused on the ballot's Proposition 1, which provided for additional low-income housing, and on the recently enacted "stop-and-frisk" and "no-knock" laws. Because these issues have great pertinence for the Lower East Side slum community, they were used to encourage voter registration. MFY was careful to avoid creating unrealistic expectations of immediate success regarding these issues; rather, it argued that Proposition 1 was sure to be defeated unless the people of New York City carried it by a large enough plurality to overcome the upstate opposition, and that the "stop-and-frisk" and "no-knock" laws violate the rights and dignity of the suspect and are a reflection of a general lack of political accountability and of abstinence from voting by the poor man, who is more often arrested and interrogated than any other citizen.

The enabler role

The traditional stance of the community organizer as enabler is based on two assumptions, one valid, the other invalid. The valid assumption is that self-imposed actions growing out of a community's assessment of its own needs have a value and permanence that do not inhere in actions imposed from the outside. The invalid assumption is that the enabling role is the only one by which this desirable end may be brought

---

[3] Betty Jo Bailey and Sidney Pinsky, "1964 Voter Registration Drive," Unpublished report, Mobilization For Youth, New York, 1965.

about. In this section several alternatives are suggested that are believed to be viable.

It should be noted, first, that the role of enabler, geared to process, may itself be limited as a strategy for facilitating community self-help. For example, one text on community organization method draws on the experience of a special governor's committee set up in Colorado to deal with pervasive problems in the state's mental institutions as illustrative of proper work by a community organizer. Conditions within the institutions were unsatisfactory, and individuals were being improperly and illegally committed:

> . . . the legislation [directed at the problems] recommended by the governor's committe did not get very far in the ensuing session of the state assembly, although a more substantial program might have resulted if the committee, or even a considerable bloc within the committee, had been willing to manipulate or use undemocratic methods. It was rightly felt, however, that this might jeopardize future working relationships—in short, that process or means was as important as the immediate goal.[4]

Although such judgments may be possible in statewide interdisciplinary committees, direct contact with those immediately affected by such decisions in a neighborhood community development program precludes any such cavalier determination of the client's fate.

The "broker" role

Familiar in such non–social work contexts as real estate and the stock market, the role of "broker" was instituted in the Mobilization For Youth program in 1962. It appears to have been first suggested for social work practice by Wilensky and Lebeaux in 1958. These writers postulated a need for "guides, so to speak, through a new kind of civilized jungle," and spoke of social work as "an example par excellence of the liaison function, a large part of its total activity being devoted to putting people in touch with community resources they need but can hardly name, let alone locate."[5]

The community organization worker brings the component of collective action to the broker role, adding a potent factor to the process. Through collective "brokerage activity," the notion of collective solutions is introduced; that is, administrative and policy changes are undertaken to affect whole classes of persons rather than a single individual. The

---

[4] Campbell Murphy, *Community Organization Practice* (Boston: Houghton Mifflin Co., 1954), p. 22.

[5] Harold L. Wilensky and Charles N. Lebeaux, *Industrial Society and Social Welfare* (New York: Russell Sage Foundation, 1958), p. 286.

following comment, taken from a report of a Mobilization For Youth community organizer, illustrates the point:

> Residents of the Lower East Side have brought their welfare problems . . . such as late checks, insufficient funds to pay large utility bills, no winter clothing, dispossess notices, and a host of others . . . to Casa de la Communidad, since it first opened in February 1963. These problems were handled by the caseworkers . . . who shared the facilities with the C.O. worker. . . All too often, no real change seemed to result either in the lives of the clients or in the procedures of welfare. The same clients tended to come over and over again from emergency to emergency.[6]

It was as a result of this experience that two community organization efforts in the welfare area were launched: a welfare information center and an organization of welfare clients holding court support orders. The latter group sought a collective resolution to the problems created by the determination of budgets on the basis of income ordered by a court but rarely received by the family.

The advocate role

It has been the experience of workers in neighborhood community development programs that the broker role is frequently insufficiently directive. Therefore the role of advocate has been co-opted from the field of law. Often the institutions with which local residents must deal are not even neutral, much less positively motivated, toward handling the issues brought to them by community groups. In fact, they are frequently overtly negative and hostile, often concealing or distorting information about rules, procedures, and office hours. By their own partisanship on behalf of instrumental organizational goals, they create an atmosphere that demands advocacy on behalf of the poor man. If the community worker is to facilitate productive interaction between residents and institutions, it is necessary for him to provide leadership and resources directed toward eliciting information, arguing the correctness of a position, and challenging the stance of the institution.

In short, the worker's posture, both to the community residents and to the institutional representatives with whom he is engaged, is that of advocate for the client group's point of view. While employing these techniques, the worker is not enabler, broker, expert, consultant, guide, or social therapist.[7] He is, in fact, a partisan in a social conflict, and

---

[6] Daniel Kronenfeld, "Community Organization and Welfare." Unpublished report, Mobilization For Youth, New York, 1965.

[7] Murray G. Ross, *Community Organization* (New York: Harper & Brothers, 1955), pp. 220–28.

his expertise is available exclusively to serve client interests. The impartiality of the enabler and the functionalism of the broker are absent here. Other actors in this social conflict may be using their expertise and resources against the client. Thus the community organizer may find himself arguing the appropriateness of issuing a permit while the police argue its inappropriateness, or the worker and tenant may take the position that building-code violations warrant the withholding of rent while the landlord argues their nonexistence. There may even be differences among social workers. For example, a community organization worker may claim certain welfare benefits for a group of clients over the opposition of a social investigator, or a community worker and a city housing authority worker may take opposite sides over the criteria the housing authority uses to evict tenants in city projects as undesirable.

In jursidictional disputes or if organizational prerogatives are at issue, it is not uncommon to find social workers at odds with each other. When issues of professional ideology or politics are involved, vigorous advocacy is the rule rather than the exception, as a casual glance through the professional journals shows. Why is it not possible for such advocates to be recruited for the poor from the ranks of social workers? This is one of the orders of today's business.

Outside the courtroom, attorneys for defendants and plaintiffs often mingle in an atmosphere of congeniality and good fellowship. Social workers do not enjoy this kind of professional relationship. It is likely that the partisan advocacy postulated will evoke virulence from the public agency that is directed against the worker. The following charges were made by school principals of a local district as a result of the actions of a group of parents who were part of the MFY community organization program:

> We find that a group of its staff is fomenting suspicion and enmity toward the schools . . . this group is largely in the CO program. . . .
>
> Mobilization workers have been engaged in a war on the schools. . . .
>
> Parents and children are encouraged to make such complaints. This means the MFY is accumulating a secret dossier on the teachers in the area. . . .
>
> The social worker from MFY began to assume the mantle of "guardian." . . .
>
> It should be noted . . . how a controversy between MFY and the principals is transformed into a conflict between the community and the schools.[8]

Such a response is not surprising since advocacy, if effective, will cause public agencies to spend more money, create more work for their already

---

[8] Report of twenty-six principals of Districts 1–4 (New York: City of New York, 1964). (Mimeographed.)

harassed staff, and focus the community's attention on the agencies' shortcomings.

The activist role

Once the fact is recognized that community development efforts on behalf of the poor will produce partisan situations, it must be conceded further that the community organizer—or, for that matter, any other service worker in the urban slum—must choose which side he is on. The same logic that legitimates the roles of broker and advocate leads inevitably to another role, that of activist. Morris and Rein have pointed out:

> Political knowledge and skill to achieve one's ends have often been considered by social workers to be unprofessional. We have somehow believed that strong advocacy of a particular point of view and the development of techniques to achieve those ends violate our professional commitment to the democratic process. The question for us is whether our commitment to professional neutrality and noninvolvement is to continue to sustain our professional practice.[9]

The traditional neutrality of the social work profession has much to recommend it, but it has been exercised to the detriment of certain client groups. Morris and Rein suggest that if this policy of noninvolvement persists, the function of community organization practice will be limited to coordination. If community organization is to find a role in community development, it cannot be exclusively neutral, hence the role of activist must also be embraced

Except for the heroes of the American Revolution, this nation has had a culturally estranged view of the political and social activist. Despite their ultimate vindication, the abolitionist, suffragette, and labor organizer are still viewed as historical mutants by the community at large. Activists are characterized as "outsiders" and "agitators" to this very day, whether they play their roles in Selma, Alabama, or between Houston and Delancey Streets in New York City.

However, the activist role is and has been a legitimate stance for the social worker, especially the community organizer, and it must be available to be chosen from among other strategies when community needs require such activity. The passivity and objectivity of the service professions is after all something of a myth: people are urged to action of all sorts—to visit a dentist, sit up straight, curb their dogs, contribute to the Red Cross, and, in some communities, to register and vote and to support the PTA. In neighborhood community development, students are urged to stay in school, tenants to keep off project lawns, dropouts

---

[9] Morris and Rein, op. cit., p. 174.

to join the Job Corps, and mothers to use well-baby clinics. Why should not tenants who are without heat also be urged to withhold rents, parents with grievances to boycott the schools, or citizens without franchise to take to the streets in legal public demonstration as a means to redress their grievances?

The answer to this point has been a matter of contingency, not reason. Some members of the profession have expressed concern that recourse to roles other than that of enabler—particularly that of activist—entails manipulation of the client group or community. The writer is convinced that the choice of role bears no relevance whatsoever to the issue of manipulation. As an attempt to achieve goals determined by the worker rather than the clients, manipulation can be accomplished by many techniques. Activists and advocates, no less than enablers and brokers, must make judgments on the basis of their professional appraisal of the client's needs, without regard to political expedience, personal ideology, or the vested interests of the agency.

Who is doing significant neighborhood community development with the impoverished today, and where? It is being done in the Negro ghettos of the North and South by nonprofessional activists in such organizations as the Congress of Racial Equality, Council of Federated Organizations, Student Nonviolent Coordinating Committee, and Southern Christian Leadership Conference. With few exceptions, neighborhood community development is taking place outside the field of social work, reflecting a narrowness of concept, not a paucity of resources in social work. Law students already have participated systematically in organizing drives for such organizations as SNCC and CORE. For a number of years, community organization practice and training of community organization students has taken place within such groups as the NAACP and the National Urban League. Therefore, it would seem appropriate for social work to place students in more activist areas within the civil rights movement.

Although techniques of activism are being sought, they are, in the main, unformulated. A body of literature is beginning to evolve, however, based on the philosophy and tactics of nonviolent direct action. For example, Oppenheimer and Lakey describe such techniques as haunting, renouncing honors, hartal,[10] boycott, demonstrations, leafleting, picketing, vigils, and role-playing.[11] They also suggest forms for record-keeping any typical budgets for voter-registration projects, provide notes on security in the Deep South, and offer advice on how to conduct

---

[10] "Hartal" is defined by *Webster's Third New International Dictionary* (Springfield, Mass.: G. & C. Merriam Co., 1961), p. 1036, as "concerted cessation of work and business esp. as a protest against a political situation. . . ."

[11] Martin Oppenheimer and George Lakey, *A Manual for Direct Action* (Chicago: Quadrangle Books, 1965).

oneself if arrested (including such specific suggestions as wearing two sets of underwear to absorb the shock of being dragged and using a bucket of water to remove traces of tear gas). Social workers should not be intimidated by the notion of incorporating some of these suggestions into their method: their strangeness stems largely from unfamiliarity. It might be noted that the many civil rights workers who have sought counsel and technique from social workers have frequently found social work methods somewhat strange also and have wondered how they might be incorporated into the methodology of nonviolence.

Organizational forms of neighborhood development

Those in community organization practice who have wrestled with the problems of neighborhood development in urban slums have found the issue of the organizational forms that their efforts should take a troublesome one. In what form should slum residents organize to mount efforts toward self-help? When the forms that voluntary associations take in the middle-class community are examined, a proliferation of styles, purposes, and patterns of participation, as varied as the personalities and social circumstances of those who participate in them, is discovered. Social workers do not have the temerity to suggest that there is a single optimal form that middle-class voluntarism should take. The assumption that such a form exists for collective action in the slum community is equally untenable.

Rather than debate on the relative merits of various alternatives, what is needed is to determine the strategies that will be most effective.

> Forms of organization, their structure, and their affiliations if any will depend on the job decided on and the personnel available. The worker may want to join an existing group in order to influence it; he may want to set up an ad hoc or temporary group composed either of individuals or of representatives of other groups; or he may want to create a new group.[12]

Neighborhood work has been conducted with groups on the basis of common cultural patterns (hometown clubs), common social problems (welfare or housing organizations), physical proximity (building or block organizations), social movements (civil rights groups), specific task orientation (voter-registration campaigns), and the operation of a resource center (storefronts). If it has not yet created the technology or method of neighborhood community development work, social work efforts at community organization in urban slums have at least established the legitimacy of such efforts.

---

[12] Ibid., p. 43.

Commenting editorially on this issue as reflected in the MFY experience, the *New York Times* stated:

> If Mobilization For Youth is to do more than merely ameliorate the lot of the poorest elements of the community, it must teach them to help themselves by concerted efforts. . . . Any form of social protest is bound to generate controversy, and some forms clearly raise serious questions of propriety for an agency that draws so much of its support from government funds. . . . But the poor must be encouraged to believe that there are ways to express their views on the need for social betterment. . . . The right to fight City Hall is as much a prerogative of the poor as of any other group of citizens; it is only when those who dwell in the slums and have to little to keep themselves and their families in dignity surrender to a supine sense of total futility and helplessness that the community has real cause to worry.[13]

Sources of gain in psychotherapy[*][1]

Nicholas Hobbs

This paper needs a subtitle. Let it be: "Five Hypotheses in Search of a Theory." One of the firmly rooted assumptions in psychotherapeutic practice is that the development of insight on the part of the client is both a major goal of the therapeutic endeavor, intrinsically worth promoting, and a primary means of achieving, step by step in the therapeutic process, the overall objective of more effective functioning. If a client can be helped to understand why he behaves as he does or to recognize and understand the origin of the neurotic tactics that continually defeat him, he will gradually abandon the inappropriate behavior and substitute therefor more rational tactics in the management of his life. Increased self-understanding is regarded as inherently good and as a means to the end of good psychological health.

The promotion of insight is thus the tactic most heavily relied upon by most therapists who write about their work. Other strategies—the encouragement of catharsis, of abreaction, of transference—are valued

---

[13] Editorial, *New York Times,* November 11, 1964.

[*] Reprinted from Nicholas Hobbs, "Sources of Gain in Psychotherapy," *American Psychologist,* 17:11 (November 1962), pp. 741–47. Copyright 1962 by the American Psychological Association. Reprinted by permission.

[1] This paper was presented as the Presidential Address to the Division of Clinical Psychology at the 1961 meeting of the American Psychologial Association.

to the extent that they lay the groundwork for the achievement of insight. The interpretation of behavior, perhaps the most widely used tactic of all, is aimed directly at the promotion of self-understanding. Furthermore, the achievement of insight by a client is a welcomed signal to the therapist that his efforts are paying off, and that his client, armed with new understanding, will gain a new measure of control over his life. All of this is a part of the folklore, both amateur and professional, of helping people by talking with them. But I have come seriously to doubt the presumed relationship between the achievement of insight and the achievement of more effective functioning.

My doubts about the efficacy of insight as a change agent were first aroused a number of years ago while working in a clinic with a staff with diverse theoretical persuasions. In staff discussions of therapy cases, the occurrence of a significant insight on the part of a client was greeted with approval and satisfaction and with the expectation that there should follow some change for the better in the client's behavior. When anticipated changes did not occur there was general discomfort. If the client persisted in behaving contrary to theory, as some obstinate clients did, we countered with a very useful, theory-preserving gambit. We said, "Well, it is obvious that the client did not have real insight. He may have had 'intelligent insight'," we said, "but he did not have 'emotional insight'." This was always an after-the-fact adjustment. We were not attracted to the obvious alternate interpretation, namely, that insight need not lead to changes in behavior. We were too much a part of our culture, both general and professional, to question the time-honored relationship between self-understanding and effective functioning.

I began to wonder why we never examined the alternate explanation of the failure of insight to produce changes in behavior. Once jarred from the point of usual perspective on this issue, I began to see a number of arguments for an alternate explanation, namely, that insight may have nothing to do with behavior change at all, or is, at best, an event that may or may not occur as a result of more fundamental personality reorganizations. Here are some of the arguments:

Item 1. In interpretive therapies, great stress is placed on the exquisite timing of interpretations. The thought occurs that an interpretation may be acceptable to a client only after he has achieved sufficient self-reorganization for the interpretation no longer to be relevant. He can accept, but he no longer "needs," the interpretation.

Item 2. In play therapy with young children most therapists do not bother to try to develop insight. Rational formulations are adult fare, a consequence of the adult's addiction to words. Instead, therapists provide children concrete experiences in relationship with a particular kind of adult and get good results.

Item 3. The equipotentiality of diverse interpretations is a bothersome thing. It is quite apparent that therapists of different theoretical persuasions seem to promote different but equally effective insights. An Adlerian interpretation based on assumed relationships between organ inferiority and life style seems just as effective as a Freudian interpretation based on disjunctions among id, ego, and superego requirements. A Jungian interpretation based on the relationship between the individual and the cosmos seems as effective as an existential interpretation of the estrangement of man resulting from the subject-object dichotomy, currently described as an invention of Descartes. Or the therapist can get equally good results by making no interpretations at all, as Rogers has shown. All this suggests that the occurrence of an insight merely means that the client is catching on to the therapist's personal system for interpreting the world of behavior. The therapist does not have to be right; he mainly has to be convincing.

There are other arguments but these will suffice. They do not, of course, disprove the accepted relationship between insight and change in behavior but they do suggest that one should give serious consideration to an alternate hypothesis. It seems to me that the traditional formulation of the relationship between self-understanding and effective behavior may be backwards. I suggest that insight is not a cause of change but a possible result of change. It is not a source of therapeutic gain but one among a number of possible consequences of gain. It may or may not occur in therapy; whether it does or not is inconsequential, since it reflects only the preferred modes of expression of the therapist or the client. It is not a change agent, it is a by-product of change. In a word, insight is an epiphenomenon.

The role of insight in therapeutic progress has probably escaped detailed analysis because we have no good definitions of what is meant by the term. Particularly are we lacking in criteria for differentiating between intellectual insight and emotional insight, if there are, indeed, two such entities, which I doubt.

The best definition that I have been able to come up with is this: Insight is manifested when a client makes a statement about himself that agrees with the therapist's notions of what is the matter with him. This is not a particularly useful formulation.

The acceptance of insight as the sovereign remedy for all neuroses represents both an unwarranted extrapolation from Freud's position and a failure to take into account the kinds of neuroses generated by Viennese life at the turn of the century and by American or European life today. Freud could not have been more explicit in insisting that his method worked best, if not solely, in cases of massive repression with accomanying conversion symptomatology. Contemporary culture often produces a kind of neurosis different from that described by Freud. Contemporary neuroses are frequently characterized not so much by repression and conversion as by an awful awareness and a merciless raw anxiety. The problem of the contemporary neurotic is not lack of insight but lack of a sense of identity, of purpose, of meaning in life. Because of a dehumanization of existence, as Kierkegaard pointed out, he has a sickness unto death. Indeed, in many of the people I work with there seems to be a substantial component of realism in their neurotic condition. Nothing can make a person more anxious, or more guilty, than an unrelentingly clear appreciation of the absurd and desperate condition of man today.

Let us suppose for the moment that insight plays no significant role in the therapeutic process. How then does change come about? What are the sources of gain in psychotherapy? My effort will be to identify sources of change that are common to all approaches to therapy, with the hope that the analysis will provide a theoretical matrix for more adequate quantitative and comparative studies of the therapeutic process. At present it seems to me that there are five major sources of gain, five kinds of experiences that are the well-springs of personality reorganization. I might add that these experiences often occur in daily life quite apart from psychotherapy and are the sources of healthy integrations and reintegrations that develop throughout the life span. Psychotherapy is a unique life situation deliberately designed to make these five sources of gain available in an intense and usable form in a compressed time span, especially for those people who are unable, because of their neurotic tendencies, to avail themselves of the normal healing and nurturing experiences of life. Psychotherapy may thus be practiced, as indeed it is, by anyone who comes into intimate contact with a client on a professional basis.

The first source of gain is in the therapeutic relationship itself. This is a widely accepted notion, and I only wish to specify, which is seldom done, what it is about the relationship that has therapeutic impact. It is this: The client has a sustained experience of intimacy with another human being without getting hurt. He has an experience of contact, of engagement, of commitment. He learns directly and immediately, by concrete experience, that it is possible to risk being close to another, to be open and honest, to let things happen to his feelings in the presence of another, and indeed, even to go so far as to dare to include the therapist himself as an object of these feelings. The neurotic, on the basis of earlier attempts at intimate relationships with important life persons, primarily his mother and father, has come to the deep-seated conviction that other people cannot be trusted, that it is terribly dangerous to open oneself up to them. This conviction may well have a very realistic basis: When he reached out to his parents he was rebuffed. When he made tentative, affective overtures to other important life persons, he got clobbered. On the basis of these hurtful experiences, he has adopted the tactic of alienation that is so characteristic of the neurotic. He may simply withdraw from significant human contacts. He may live and work in proximity with others, but let it be known that the relationship stops where his self begins. Or he may get engaged with others in intense relationships that should lead to intimacy but always with reservations, always on terms that guarantee that he is not really exposed. These are the counterfeit friendships and marriages of the neurotic. And in all this, of course, he will not even be intimate with himself; he cannot let himself feel how he actually feels about himself and others. Now I argue that human intimacy is necessary for human survival. Intimacy may be an instinctual, a biological requirement. But even if it is not a built-in requirement, the prolonged period of dependency of the human infant with its all but inevitable experience of some sustaining intimacy provides ample time to require, to learn a need to be close to others. The risking and handling of intimacy are learned by immediate experiencing; talking about intimacy, acquiring insight about intimacy, do not help much.

Now psychotherapy is a situation carefully designed to make it possible for a client to learn to be close to another person without getting hurt. For example, the therapist does not, or should not, punish the client's tentative and fearful efforts at being open and honest about his feelings. On the contrary, he is alert to and reinforces any reaching-out behavior. The therapist permits the client to use him to learn how to be intimate, but he does not make reciprocal demands of a personal character, such as those inevitably involved in friendship or marriage, for these would be too threatening to the client. The therapist may make formal demands but not personal ones. In this special accepting situation, where the ground rules are clear, the client dares to establish a fully honest relationship with another person, and finds it a tremendously reinforcing experience. He is encouraged on the basis of this concrete learning experience to risk more open relationships outside of therapy. Of course, he takes the chance of getting hurt again, as in childhood, but more likely than not he finds that others are responsive and that he is after all capable of richer, of more giving and more sustaining relationships with other people. This first source of gain lends itself readily to analysis in learning theory terms.

Now, source number two. Much of the time in psychotherapy is spent, or should be spent, in helping the client divest verbal and other symbols of their anxiety-producing potential. Shaffer is the author of the rich declarative sentence: "Man is forever signalling to himself." It is man's ability to acquire, store, and manipulate symbols, and signal to himself in symbolic form, that makes him so distinctive, and so interesting. It also makes him uniquely susceptible to neurosis. Each of us has a tremendous store of symbols that are the residuals of experiences with which they were originally associated. In the domain of interpersonal relationships, some people have a collection of symbols that, for the most part, set off in them at the deepest and most pervasive somatic level feelings of well being, of comfort, of safety, of assurance. Other people, the ones we call neurotic, have a collection of symbols that set off in them, for the most part, feelings of anxiety and guilt or of somatic distress of specific or pervasive character. Actually, most of us have a mixed collection of distressing and sustaining symbols, and we call ourselves psychologically healthy if we have a clearly favorable algebraic balance of the positive and the negative. The negative symbols, associated with earlier life experiences of a hurtful nature, tend to stick tenaciously with us. In ordinary life circumstances we do not have an opportunity to learn new and more appropriate responses to them. Here is what seems to happen. A child suffers more than he can tolerate at the hands of his father. The concrete experiences get associated with specific symbols that are a product of this unique relationship and its attending circumstances. As an adult, even after his father has long been dead, experiences with authority figures evoke the symbols which evoke anxiety, guilt, hostility, or perhaps headaches, nausea, or other somatic reactions. Because of the distress that has been aroused, he retreats either literally or psychologically from the situation. His distress diminishes, thus reinforcing the avoidance of the authority relationship, and leaving the symbols as strong as ever. But authority cannot be avoided, and the cycle gets repeated over and over again. The crucial thing to note is that he never has an opportunity to learn new and more appropriate responses to the symbols that are evoking in him what we call neurotic behavior. The conditioned response cannot get extinguished.

The task of the therapist is not to help the client gain insight into the fact that he has trouble with authority figures because of his unfortunate experiences with his own father. This is far too abstract a formulation to be of help. He has got to be helped to identify and use comfortably the specific symbols that are elicited in him by authority figures. The symbols must be divested of their anxiety-producing potential.

At this point my communication problem becomes exceedingly difficult because there is no general way to identify or categorize these symbols. They are all highly personal, highly concrete, highly specific to the particular individual. And they have got to be talked about by the client in highly specific, hot, personal, intimate terms. The terms used must get as close as possible to the client's own idiosyncratic symbol system. A bright girl who had frequent attacks of nausea explained early in therapy that she feared she was homosexual and that she recognized the unsatisfactory character of her relationship with her mother, a fine insightful statement. Much later, after she was sure that it was safe to talk to the therapist using the same symbols that she used when talking to her most private self, she described in specific detail the experiences she felt had warped her relationship with her mother. At the end of the very difficult hour, she said, "This is the blackness that I have been trying to vomit."

The transference relationship is a third source of gain in psychotherapy. It also provides the clearest illustration of the differences between therapies which stress, respectively, the rational, abstract, and verbal, or the nonrational, concrete, and experiential components of the therapeutic process. Freud's discovery of the transference situation was a brilliant achievement. It made available to the therapist a most valuable instrument, comparable to the microscope or telescope in its clarifying powers. The essence of the situation is this: The client does not talk about his neurosis, he acts it out. His neurotic strategems are no longer filtered through semantic screens; they are tried out in concrete, specific acts of hostility, overdependency, seduction, dissimulation, and so on. The therapist and the client are both immediately involved in the client's desperate and always self-defeating and yet so very human ploys and gambits.

In the Freudian prescription for the handling of transference one finds the great psychoanalytic paradox: The cure for unreason is reason. Freud gave us a twentieth-century discovery that unreasonable (i.e., neurotic) behavior is determined by specific life experiences, thousands of them probably, and that neurotic behavior is unconscious and preeminently nonrational in origin. He could have said that neurosis is a summary term describing an extensive matrix of conditioned responses built up in a lifetime of hurtful relationships with important life persons, hardened around an armature of assumed guilt. He might further have observed that no man by taking thought becomes neurotic. But for his twentieth-century diagnosis, Freud had a nineteenth-century prescription. Be rational. Transference represents the neurosis in microcosm; when transference appears it should be interpreted. As Fenichel so clearly instructs us, the client should be shown that he is behaving in an irrational manner.

Now I think it likely that this tactic will result in the client's learning that certain neurotic stratagems are not approved of, and they may well be abandoned in favor of other protective mechanisms. In the face of repeated interpretations, he may learn to repress particular transference symptoms. But nothing has been done about his need for these symptoms; his underlying distrust of himself and of other people remains untouched by the therapist's efforts to promote insight by interpreting the transference.

Transference develops when the client feels that the relationship with the therapist is becoming too dangerous, that he is losing control of the situation. He does not know how to handle the growing intimacy of the relationship without resorting to well established neurotic defenses. He does not need to be told that his tactics are inappropriate, that they are characteristic of his way of life, but he needs to learn through an immediate experience with another human being that the tactics are not necessary. Transference is best handled by providing the client with the kind of understanding and unqualified acceptance that have been so notably absent in his life. Transference stratagems disappear when the client has an opportunity to learn through concrete experience that it is possible to establish a simple, honest, open relationship with another person.

A fourth source of gain is available in those therapies which place the locus of control of the situation in the client rather than in the therapist. The client has hundreds of opportunities to practice decision making, to learn to be responsible for himself, to develop a concept of himself as a person capable of managing his own life. Here again, you will note the emphasis not on insight but on specific opportunities for the acquisition of new ways of behaving.

Before proceeding to examine a fifth source of gain which seems to be different in character from the four already mentioned, I should like to discuss briefly two possible explanations for our confident advocacy of insight as a primary change agent in psychotherapy.

Insight and understanding appeal to us as central mechanisms in therapy because of our strong general commitment to rationality in problem solving. As F. S. C. Northrup has pointed out, western culture (in spite of its immense irrationalities) has a deeply ingrained rational component. For us, reason is a faith. From earliest childhood we are taught to apply rational principles to the solution of many kinds of problems. If our automobile breaks down we do not ordinarily kick it, pray over it, or assume that its spirit has departed, as a person from a primitive culture might do. We first try to discover what is wrong and then make appropriate interventions to correct the difficulty. It is perhaps the very strength of our faith that has led to a curious short circuiting in the domain of psychotherapy. Faced with a breakdown of personal functioning, we seem to assume that the development of understanding itself is a sufficient intervention to correct the difficulty. If a person can be helped to understand the origins and current manifestations of his neurotic behavior, particularly if he feels deeply while he is gaining this insight, the neurotic behavior should disappear. A good rational question is: Why should it disappear unless appropriate learning experiences follow?

Even if we do have a cultural bias regarding the importance of insight and understanding, our convictions would gradually be extinguished in the therapy situation if they were not occasionally reinforced. And they are. Insight sometimes does lead to changes in behavior—but not for the reasons commonly assumed. Insight is usually thought of as a freeing or releasing mechanism. I think it may actually operate through the facilitation of repression and the elimination of a particular symptom. A good example is provided by Dollard and Miller. A girl had a habit of thumbing rides with truck drivers at night and then being surprised when men "took advantage of her." The therapist pointed out to her what she was doing and she stopped doing it, thus seeming to validate the assumption of insight as a releasing influence. But Miller's conflict theory provides a better explanation of her behavior, I think. She could either give up hitch hiking or run the risk, as she would see it, of incurring the disappointment of her valued therapist. She might be expected to repress her hitch hiking symptom. But nothing would have been done about her neurotic need for affection.

The same insight-related mechanism may operate outside of therapy to change behavior through repression. A person who expresses his hostility through malicious gossiping reads in a newspaper column that if he gossips he will inevitably alienate all his friends. If this prospect arouses enough anxiety, he will feel much in conflict and may repress his tendency to gossip. But since he is as hostile as ever, he may now become sarcastic or learn to excel at bridge. Again nothing would have been done about his neurotic need to be hostile. It should be pointed out that the repression of some symptoms may have subsequent therapeutic benefits if the person is thereby brought into more intimate human relationships that are intrinsically healing in accordance with the four sources of gain already described. Some symptoms are better than others. The worst symptoms are those that engender most alienation from significant others, for this cuts the person off from the normal sources of therapeutic gain in daily living.

There is a fifth source of gain common to all psychotherapies that is qualitatively quite different from the four sources that have already been described. You may have noted in the preceding arguments not only a disavowal of the efficacy of insight as a change agent but also the strong emphasis on specific and concrete opportunities for learning new ways of responding, new ways of relating to other people, and new ways of perceiving oneself. The stress is on immediate experience and specific behaviors. Throughout the discussion there is an implicit invitation to recast the analysis in terms of learning theory of a general reinforcement type. Now the fifth source of gain involves a different level of abstraction and can best be talked about in terms of cognitive processes. I, of course, imply no disjunction between learning and cognition, but simply accept the fact that, at its current stage of development, psychology tends to use different constructs to describe these two aspects of human behavior.

All approaches to psychotherapy seem to have a more or less elaborated conception of the nature of man, which they, in essence, teach to the client. In doing so, they tie in with an ongoing process which is a unique and most exciting and engaging characteristic of man. Man constantly engages in building and repairing and extending and modifying cognitive structures that help him make personal sense of the world. The individual has got to have a cognitive house to live in to protect himself from the incomprehensibilities of existence as well as to provide some architecture for daily experiencing. He has to build defenses against the absurd in the human condition and at the same time find a scheme that will make possible reasonably accurate predictions of his own behavior and of the behavior of his wife, his boss, his professor, his physician, his neighbor, and of the policeman on the corner. He must adopt or invent a personal cosmology. When he invests this cosmology with passion, we may call it his personal mystique.

There are many available cosmologies for ordering the universe and increasing predictive efficiency in daily life. One of the first of these was provided by Pythagoras, some 3,000 years ago. Contemporary religious systems seem useful in reducing uncertainty in at least some realms of experience, and for some people. Religions with established dogmas, elaborated rituals, and extensive use of personification appear to have widest appeal, as one would expect. Those with almost no formal doctrine probably appeal most to people who have at hand alternate systems for construing the world. Psychoanalysis provides a cognitive structure of remarkable cogency. Its range of applicability is not cosmic but mundane, which is one source of its appeal among pragmatic people. Its metaphor is engaging; its extensive use of reification simplifies matters, but not too much; its formulation of behavior dynamics is occasionally useful in predicting one's own behavior and the behavior of others. On the other hand, existential therapies would seem to be most acceptable to people who have come to suspect all institutionalized solutions (such as psychoanalysis) to the problem of meaning. Albert Ellis' rational therapy seems eminently suited to his clientele. I would guess that he works largely with bright, articulate, nonreligious, and reasonably well educated but not too disenchanted people who find the process and the model of rational analysis appealing and convincing. Client-centered therapy probably works best with clients who already have well developed but conflicting cognitive structures; they do not need to be taught a system for bringing order into their lives, but rather need to be helped to discover which system makes sense and feels right to them. George Kelly's fixed role therapy is, of course, the most forthright and charming method for providing a client with a cognitive structure for construing his world.

I think it possible to identify some criteria for assessing the adequacy of a personal cosmology and thus provide a therapist with some guidelines for dealing with the cognitive structures of the individual. Above all a person's cosmology must be convincing to him; when doubt occurs, anxiety mounts. Second, it should overlap reasonably well with the cosmologies of the people with whom he associates. If a person adopts a too divergent cosmology, he runs the risk of being declared psychotic and incarcerated. Then it should be perceived by the individual as internally consistent—or relativey so. When there is too great a discrepancy between self and self-ideal, for example, discontent ensues. It should contain, on the other hand, some dissonances of either internal or external origin. With a bit of dissonance, the individual will work to strengthen his major propositions about himself and his world. In addition, it should bring him into more intimate relationships with other people, for without such sustenance the spirit withers. Finally, it should have built-in requirements for revision, for to live is to change, and to remain static is to die.

The individual seeks psychotherapy (or some other source of cognitive control) when his cosmology, his personal system for imposing order on the world, breaks down to an alarming degree. With increasing anxiety, order must be restored.

There are two summary points that I would make about this fifth source of gain in psychotherapy: (a) Man by his nature is going to erect cognitive structures to increase his feeling of control over his destiny, and (b) there is no way of establishing the validity of a particular order-giving structure independently of the individual who is going to use it. The concept of insight can have meaning only as a part of the process of elaborating on some particular system for interpreting events. There are no true insights, only more or less useful ones.

All systems of psychotherapy involve in varying measures the five kinds of experiences that I have described. Their effectiveness will depend on the extent to which they provide an opportunity for the client to experience closeness to another human being without getting hurt, to divest symbols associated with traumatic experiences of their anxiety-producing potential, to use the transference situation to learn not to need neurotic distortions, to practice being responsible for himself, and to clarify an old or learn a new cognitive system for ordering his world. I am not prepared at the moment to assign beta weights to these several functions.

The social worker as advocate: Champion of social victims*

The Ad Hoc Committee on Advocacy, National Association of Social Workers

The new interest in advocacy among social workers can be traced directly to the growing social and political ferment in our cities in the past decade. Social workers connected with Mobilization For Youth[1] (which took its form in the context of this ferment) first brought the advocacy role to the attention of the profession.[2] But the notion that the social worker needs to become the champion of social victims who cannot defend themselves was voiced long ago by others, and has recently been revived.[3]

Present events are forcing the issue with new urgency. Externally, the urban crisis and the social revolution of which it is the most jarring aspect are placing new demands on social work; internally, the profession is re-examining itself with an intensity that has few precedents. The profession's faith in its own essential viability is being severely tested. It is especially timely that social work turn its attention to the role of advocate at this time, both because of its clear relevance to the urban crisis and because it has been an integral part of the philosophy and practice of the profession since its earliest days.

What is advocacy?

The dictionary defines advocate in two ways. On one hand, he is "one that pleads the cause of another."[4] This is the meaning given to the legal advocate—the lawyer—who zealously guards the interests of

---

* Reprinted with permission of the National Association of Social Workers from *Social Work*, 14:2 (April 1969), pp. 16–22.

[1] Mobilization For Youth, Inc., started as an action-research program in juvenile delinquency control on New York City's Lower East Side.

[2] See George A. Brager, "Advocacy and Political Behavior," *Social Work*, Vol. 13, No. 2 (April 1968), pp. 5–15; and Charles F. Grosser, "Community Development Programs Serving the Urban Poor," *Social Work*, Vol. 10, No. 3 (July 1965), pp. 18–19.

[3] See, for example, Nathan E. Cohen, ed., *Social Work and Social Problems* (New York: National Association of Social Workers, 1964), p. 374.

[4] *Webster's Third New International Dictionary* (Springfield, Mass.: G. & C. Merriam Co., 1961), p. 32.

his client over all others. Another definition describes the advocate as "one who argues for, defends, maintains, or recommends a cause or a proposal."[5] This definition incorporates the political meaning ascribed to the word in which the interests of a class of people are represented; implicitly, the issues are universalistic rather than particularistic.

Both meanings of advocacy have been espoused in the social work literature. Briar describes the historical concept of the caseworker-advocate who is "his client's supporter, his adviser, his champion, and, if need be, his representative in his dealings with the court, the police, the social agency, and other organizations that [affect] his well-being."[6] For Briar, the social worker's commitment to the civil rights of *his own client* "takes precedence over all other commitments."[7] This is, in essence, the orientation of the lawyer-advocate.

Brager takes another view. He posits the "advocate-reformer" who "identifies with the plight of the disadvantaged. He sees as his primary responsibility the tough-minded and partisan representation of their interests, and this supersedes his fealty to others. This role inevitably requires that the practitioner function as a political tactician."[8]

Brager does not rule out of his definition the direct-service practitioner who takes on the individual grievances of his client, but his emphasis is on the advocacy of the interests of an aggrieved *class* of people through policy change. The two conceptions do overlap at many points, as for instance when the worker must engage in action to change basic policies and institutions in order to deal effectively with his client's grievances.

Social work's commitment to advocacy

Advocacy has been an important thread running throughout social work's history. Some individuals have been elevated to heroic status because they have fulfilled this role—Dorothea Dix and Jane Addams come most readily to mind. However, it would be safe to say that most social workers have honored advocacy more in rhetoric than in practice, and for this there are at least two reasons.

To begin with, professional education and practice have tended to legitimate a consensus orientation and oppose an adversary one, and this has been perpetuated in the literature. A combative stance, often

---

[5] Ibid.

[6] Scott Briar, "The Current Crisis in Social Casework," *Social Work Practice, 1967* (New York: Columbia University Press, 1967), p. 28. See also Briar, "The Casework Predicament," *Social Work*, Vol. 13, No. 1 (January 1968), pp. 5–11.

[7] Scott Briar, "The Social Worker's Responsibility for the Civil Rights of Clients," *New Perspectives*, Vol. 1, No. 1 (Spring 1967), p. 90.

[8] Op. cit., p. 6.

an essential ingredient in the kind of partisan alignment implied by the concept of advocacy, is not a natural one for many social workers. As a result, most social workers lack both the orientation and the technical skills necessary to engage in effective advocacy. Finally, the employee status of social workers has often restricted their ability to act as advocates.[9]

At the same time that the current upheaval in society adds a note of urgency to the issue of social work's commitment to advocacy, it also adds complications to the task of fulfilling that commitment because of the emotion surrounding many of the issues. For example, some members of the profession feel strongly that fighting racism and deepening the social conscience are the only means to combat these social evils; others—equally adamant—feel that social workers are not equipped to solve these ills, which are a problem of the whole society. There is still another group of social workers who tend to avoid involvement with controversial issues at any cost. What is needed is a consistent approach on the basis of which each social worker can feel confident in fulfilling his professional commitment, an approach that can be responsive to the current crisis but must also outlive it.

Obligations of the individual social worker

The obligation of social workers to become advocates flows directly from the social worker's Code of Ethics.[10] Therefore, why should it be difficult for a profession that is "based on humanitarian, democratic ideals" and "dedicated to service for the welfare of mankind" to act on behalf of those whose human rights are in jeopardy? According to Wickenden: "In the relationship of individuals to the society in which they live, dignity, freedom and security rest upon a maximum range of objectively defined rights and entitlements."[11]

As a profession that "requires of its practitioners . . . belief in the dignity and worth of human beings"[12] social work must commit itself to defending the rights of those who are treated unjustly, for, as Briar asserts: "The sense of individual dignity and of capacity to be self-determining . . . can exist only if the person sees himself and is regarded

---

[9] It is not the intent to blame the agencies entirely for lack of advocacy in the discharge of a worker's daily duties. It is recognized that progressive agencies have already inculcated advocacy in their workers, often in the face of adverse community reactions and resistance by staff.

[10] This code was adopted by the Delegate Assembly of the National Association of Social Workers, October 13, 1960, and amended April 11, 1967.

[11] Elizabeth Wickenden, "The Indigent and Welfare Administration," in *The Extension of Legal Services to the Poor* (Washington, D.C.: U.S. Department of Health, Education, and Welfare, 1964).

[12] "Code of Ethics."

as a rights bearing citizen with legitimate, enforceable claims on, as well as obligations to, society."[13]

Each member of the professional association, in subscribing to the Code of Ethics, declares, "I regard as my primary obligation the welfare of the individual or group served, which includes action to improve social conditions." It is implicit, but clear, in this prescript that the obligation to the client takes primacy over the obligation to the employer when the two interests compete with one another.

The code singles out for special attention the obligation to "the individual or group served." The meaning seems clearest with respect to the caseworker or group worker who is delivering services to identified individuals and groups. It would appear to be entirely consistent with this interpretation to extend the obligation to the line supervisor or the social agency administrator who then is bound to act as an advocate on behalf of clients under his jurisdiction. A collateral obligation would be the responsibility of the supervisor or administrator to create the climate in which direct-service workers can discharge their advocacy obligations. As one moves to consider other social work roles, such as the consultant, the community planner, and the social work educator, the principle becomes more difficult to apply. But how can an obligation be imposed on one segment of the profession and not on another?

The inherent obligation is with respect to the work role and to those persons on whose lives the practitioner impinges by dint of his work role. It is in this role that the individual social worker is most clearly accountable for behaving in accordance with professional social work norms. Through this role he is implicated in the lives of certain groups of people; thus his actions affect their lives directly, for good or ill. Similarly, his work role gives him authority and influence over the lives of his clients; thus he has special ethical obligations regarding them. Finally, there are expected behaviors inherent in the work role on the basis of which it is possible to judge professional performance.

At this point it is important to remind ourselves of the distinction between the obligation of the social worker to be an advocate within and outside of his work role, both of which constitute an obligation of equal weight. However, the obligation to be an advocate outside the work role is general, not specific, and does not have the same force as the obligation to the client. In a sense, this obligation is gratuitous, or, as some might say, "above and beyond the call of duty." An additional problem is that there are no external criteria for judging whether a person is fulfilling this broad responsibility adequately. To use an extreme example: voting might be considered a way of carrying out the role of the advocate-reformer, yet would one say that failure to vote

---

was failure to fulfill a professional obligation? To lump together the two obligations, i.e., to be an advocate in one's work role and outside of it, might appear to reinforce the latter. In reality, it only weakens the former.

Yet the profession as a whole has consistently treated the broad social responsibilities of social workers as important to fulfillment of their responsibilities. Schools of social work make an effort to provide their students with both the orientation and skills to become involved in social issues well outside their future assigned responsibilities. The difference between the two obligations is a moral, not a formal, one. In other words, enforcement of the obligation to be an advocate outside the work role would have to be self-enforcement.

Competing claims

Until now, most discussions of the advocacy role in social work have limited their consideration of competing claims to those of the employing agency[14] or society as a whole.[15] These have overlooked the possibility that in promoting his clients' interest the social worker may be injuring other aggrieved persons with an equally just claim. Suppose, for instance, that a child welfare worker has as a client a child who is in need of care that can only be provided by a treatment institution with limited intake. Does he then become a complete partisan in order to gain admission of his client at the expense of other children in need? What of the public assistance worker seeking emergency clothing allowances for his clients when the demand is greater than the supply? Quite clearly, in either case the worker should be seeking to increase the total availability of the scarce resource. But while working toward this end, he faces the dilemma of competing individual claims. In such a situation, professional norms would appear to dictate that the relative urgency of the respective claims be weighed.

A second dilemma involves conflict between the two types of advocacy—on behalf of client or class. Such conflicts are quite possible in an era of confrontation politics. To what extent does one risk injury to his client's interests in the short run on behalf of institutional changes in the long run? It seems clear that there can be no hard and fast rules governing such situations. One cannot arbitrarily write off any action that may temporarily cause his clients hardship if he believes the ultimate benefits of his action will outweigh any initial harm. Both ethical commitment and judgment appear to be involved here. (Is it, perhaps, unnecessary to add that institutional change does not always involve confrontation?)

---

[14] See George A. Brager, op. cit.

[15] See Scott Briar, "The Current Crisis in Social Casework," p. 91.

A third dilemma is the choice between direct intercession by the worker and mobilization of clients in their own behalf. This is less an ethical than a technical matter. One can err in two directions: it is possible to emasculate clients by being overly protective or to abdicate one's responsibility and leave them to fend for themselves against powerful adversaries.

Technical competence

Questions of competence can compound these dilemmas, for good intentions are not enough for the fulfillment of the advocacy role. Workers must not only be competent, they must also be sophisticated in understanding the appropriate machinery for redressing grievances and skilled in using it. If social workers are required by the profession to carry the obligation to be advocates, they must be equipped to fulfill the role.

While any responsible profession constantly strives to improve its technology, the dissatisfaction of social workers with their skills at advocacy seems to go beyond this. For a variety of reasons, most social workers seem wholly deficient in this area. On the direct practice level, the traditional techniques of environmental manipulation have tended to become peripheral to the practice of social workers, as they have become more sophisticated in the dynamics of inter- and intrapersonal functioning. Second, knowledge of the law, which is vitally tied up with client entitlements, has had less emphasis in the social work curriculum in recent years. Even though increased attention has been given to the client in deprived circumstances—the one who is most likely to need an advocate—this emphasis in the curriculum must be further strengthened.

Regardless of the type of advocacy in which the practitioner engages, knowledge of service delivery systems, institutional dynamics, and institutional change strategies are crucial. Although great advances in this technology have taken place in certain sectors of practice and education, they must be disseminated to the field.

Among the basic content areas that need development and expansion both in school curricula and in continuing education of social workers are the following:

1. Sensitization to the need for and appropriateness of advocacy.
2. Techniques of environmental manipulation and allied practice components.
3. Knowledge of the law, particularly as it bears on individual rights and entitlements.
4. Knowledge of service delivery systems and other institutions that impinge on people's lives and from which they must obtain resources.

5. Knowledge and skill in effecting institutional change.
6. Knowledge and skill in reaching and using the influence and power systems in a community.

The relative emphasis on these different components would vary, depending on the specific work role, although all are necessary in some degree for all social workers.

Professional autonomy and the role of NASW

But lack of technical skills is not the greatest deterrent to advocacy by social workers; actually, it is their status as employees of organizations—organizations that are frequently the object of clients' grievances. Unless social workers can be protected against retaliation by their agencies or by other special interest groups in the community, few of them will venture into the advocacy role, ethical prescripts notwithstanding. It would seem to be a sine qua non of a profession that it must create the conditions in which its members can act professionally. For the profession to make demands on the individual and then not back them up with tangible support would betray a lack of serious intent.

This does not mean that all risks for the worker can or should be eliminated. A worker's job may be protected—but there is no insurance that he will advance within his organization as far or as fast as he would have if he had not been an advocate. Rather, the object is to increase the social worker's willingness to take risks to his self-interest in behalf of his professional commitment.

This brings us to the role and obligation of the professional association—NASW—and once again back to the context of social unrest, social change, and militancy in which this discussion is taking place. In view of the need for the profession to act quickly and decisively to focus on advocacy as being germane to the effective practice of social work, a program is needed—one that should be undertaken by NASW as soon as possible.[16] This program would do the following:

1. Urge social workers to exercise actively and diligently, in the conduct of their practice, their professional responsibility to give first priority to the rights and needs of their clients.
2. Assist social workers—by providing information and other resources—in their effort to exercise this responsibility.
3. Protect social workers against the reprisals, some of them inevitable,

---

[16] As the first step in implementing the program, the Commission on Ethics reviewed these findings of the Ad Hoc Committee on Advocacy and recommended that they be widely disseminated. The commission interprets the Code of Ethics as giving full support to advocacy as a professional obligation.

that they will incur in the course of acting as advocates for the rights of their clients.[17]

Certain assumptions are implicit in these three program objectives, namely:

- That the social worker has an obligation under the Code of Ethics to be an advocate.
- That this obligation requires more than mere "urging."
- That under certain circumstances, as discussed later, the obligation is enforceable under the Code of Ethics.
- That the *moral* obligation to be an advocate is not limited to one's own clients, although this cannot be enforced in the same way.
- That encouragement of advocacy and provision of certain kinds of assistance to advocates need not be limited to members of the professional association.

To return to the relationship of NASW to the social work advocate who gets into trouble with his agency because of his attempts to fulfill a professional obligation: *NASW has an obligation to the worker that takes priority over its obligation to the agency.* In effect, the worker is acting in behalf of the professional community. While the conditions of such responsibility of NASW must be spelled out precisely (to avoid misleading members or jeopardizing the interests of the profession), there can be no question about the member's prior claim on NASW support. Without this principle, the association's claim on the member is meaningless.

The Committee on Advocacy considered two extensions of NASW's obligation. One was in relation to the social work employee who is not a member of NASW. Should the same aids and protections be offered to nonmembers of NASW as to members? It was recognized that a majority of social work positions are held by nonmembers and that they are concentrated particularly in public agencies, which are often the object of client grievances. Furthermore, many indigenous workers in poverty and other neighborhood programs are especially likely to be performing an advocacy function. Obviously, the profession cannot impose a professional obligation on such persons, yet it is consistent with professional concerns that such efforts be supported even when NASW members are not involved. The committee recommends that certain types of help be provided, but states that NASW is not in a position to offer the same range of support to nonmembers as to members.

The other extension of NASW's obligation is the possible assumption

---

[17] This is the wording of the charge given to the Ad Hoc Committee on Advocacy by the NASW urban crisis task force.

by NASW of the role of advocate when a client has no alternative channel for his grievances. The committee agreed that NASW could not become, in effect, a service agency, offering an advocacy service to all who request it, although it was felt that the association should work toward the development of such alternative channels. The association should be encouraged to engage in selected advocacy actions when the outcome has potential implications for policy formulation and implementation in general. An example of this would be participation in litigation against a state welfare agency for alleged violation of clients' constitutional rights; in this instance NASW would be using the courts to help bring about social policy change instead of interceding in behalf of the specific plaintiffs in the case.

Broadly stated, then, the proposed program for NASW calls for concentrated and aggressive activities co-ordinated at local, regional, and national levels, to achieve the needed involvement by individual social workers, backstopped by members in policy-making and administrative positions and community leaders, through education, demonstration, and consultation in program planning; adaptation of NASW complaint machinery to facilitate the adjudication of complaints against agencies with stringent sanctions when indicated; and assistance to individuals who may experience retaliatory action by agencies or communities, ranging from intervention with employers to aid in obtaining legal counsel or finding suitable new employment.

Selected annotated references

BRAGER, GEORGE A., "Advocacy and Political Behavior," *Social Work* 13:2 (April 1968), pp. 5–15.
Five considerations should be evaluated before engaging in class advocacy via political action—who benefits and who is hurt by this behavior, who is the target of this behavior, what values are behind the behavior, and what action is being taken.

BRAGER, GEORGE A., and VALERIE JORCIN, "Bargaining: A Method in Community Change," in *Social Work* 14:4 (October 1969), pp. 73–83.
Brager and Jorcin analyze a bargaining role for practitioners in relation to the variabtes of the bargainers' power resources, how the issues are formulated, and the strategies used.

BRIAR, SCOTT, "The Current Crisis in Social Casework," *Social Work Practice* (New York: Columbia University Press, 1967), pp. 19–33.
Briar notes the overemphasis on the therapeutic role in social casework and suggests the need for greater use of the broker and advocacy roles.

380   *Social work processes*

DAVIDOFF, PAUL, "Advocacy and Pluralism in Planning," *Journal of the American Institute of Planners* 31:4 (November 1965), pp. 331–38; also in *Readings in Community Organization Practice,* ed. Ralph M. Kramer and Harry Specht (Englewood Cliffs, N.J.: Prentice-Hall, 1969), pp. 438–50.
Davidoff suggests moving away from unitary planning in cities and instead of having planners attached to special interests groups and serving as their advocates, decisions concerning which plan to implement would be made through a political process.

HALLOWITZ, DAVID, RALPH BIERMAN, GRACE P. HARRISON, and BURTON STULBERG, "The Assertive Counseling Component of Therapy," *Social Casework* 48:9 (November 1967), pp. 543–48.
This article develops the concept of assertive counseling within the context of a positive therapeutic relationship. Six elements are essential to this component—crisis intervention, the confrontation of disparities between perception and reality, the confrontation of discrepancies between behavior and goals, acceptance of responsibility, active direction finding, and direction implementation.

McCORMICK, MARY J., "Social Advocacy: A New Dimension in Social Work," *Social Casework* 51:1 (January 1970), pp. 3–11.
McCormick discusses the concept and history of advocacy and explores its advantages and disadvantages as an instrument of social action within the context of democratic and treatment processes.

ROTHMAN, JACK, "The Models of Community Organization Practice," *Social Work Practice, 1968* (New York: Columbia University Press, 1968), pp. 16–47.
Rothman conceptualizes and contrasts three types of community organization—locality development, social planning, and social action.

SANDER, IRWIN, "Professional Roles in Planned Change," *Centrally Planned Change: Prospects and Concepts,* ed. Robert Morris (New York: National Association of Social Workers, 1964), pp. 102–16.
Sander conceptualizes and discusses the roles of analyst-planner, organizer for change, and program administrator.

SHARTTUCK, GERALD, and JOHN M. MARRIN, "New Professional Work Roles and Their Integration into a Social Agency Structure," *Social Work* 14:3 (July 1969), pp. 13–20.
This article analyzes the integration of new roles in a project to prevent school dropouts. The new roles are conceptualized as convener, mediator, interpreter, advocate, and collective bargainer. The problems of integrating these roles into a traditional agency are noted, and suggestions for future planning are offered.

SPECHT, HARRY, "Social Policy Formulation: The Role of the Social Caseworker," *Social Work Practice, 1967* (New York: Columbia University Press, 1967), pp. 72–94.
Specht presents an eight-step model of social policy formulation—identification of the problem, analysis and fact gathering, bringing the problem to the attention of the public, the development of policy goals, building public support, formulating a legislative program, implementation and administration of the program, and evaluation. Understanding this process will enable caseworkers to make a contribution to social policy.

THURSZ, DANIEL, "The Arsenal of Social Action Strategies: Options for Social Workers," *Social Work* 16:1 (January 1971), pp. 27–34.
Thursz calls for a disciplined, planned approach to social action which is not necessarily in opposition to militancy. Violence is not acceptable as a social work strategy, although disruption to symbolize wrongs may be used. Thursz warns against faddism

and suggests that in addition to action in the political arena a watchdog role in relation to existing programs is needed.

VINTER, ROBERT D. "The Essential Components of Social Group Work Practice," *Readings in Group Work Practice*, ed. Robert D. Vinter, (Ann Arbor, Michigan: Cowpers Publishers, 1967), pp. 1–7.

In this article Vinter presents a statement of the essential elements of a problem— focused group work practice. This is an excellent article for student study in that it addresses very succinctly the core competencies needed to utilize the multi-person group session as a medium of problem solving in which worker's role is that of enabler.

WADE, ALAN, "The Social Worker in the Political Process," *Social Welfare Forum, 1966* (New York: Columbia University Press, 1966), pp. 52–67.

Involvement of the social worker in the political arena necessitate overcoming the barriers associated with the notion that politics is dirty, the preoccupation with micro intervention, and the employment of most social workers in bureaucratic agencies. Social workers are a source of data for political policy decisions and must involve themselves in the hurly-burly world of politics to use their interpersonal relationship skills effectively in the political world.

WARREN, ROLAND, "Types of Purposive Social Change at the Community Level," in *Readings in Community Organization Practice*, ed. Ralph M. Kramer and Harry Specht (Englewood Cliffs, N.J.: Prentice-Hall, 1969), pp. 205–22.

Warren conceptualizes three types of change strategies in relation to the extent of issue consensus. He labels them collaborative strategies, campaigning strategies, and contest strategies.

ZWEIG, FRANKLIN, "The Social Worker as Legislative Ombudsman," *Social Work* 14:1 (January 1969), pp. 25–33.

Zweig reports favorably on the experience of students placed in legislative offices. The experience included the use of political power to achieve professional ends; study, assessment, goal setting, implementation, and evaluation were found to be indispensable; a wide range of assessment tools and skills was necesary; and no magic formula for producing positive legislative change was found.

Chapter 10

EVALUATION

This chapter, although brief, may be one of the most crucial in the text. The 70s will be looked upon as the dawning of the age of accountability for the social work profession. Demands for evidence that interventive efforts produce results are being advanced by both funding sources and clients. Social work, along with other human service professions, is moving rapidly to develop evaluation procedures that give demonstrable indication of the impact of its interventive activities. Individual social workers have a professional responsibility to engage in evaluative efforts on at least two levels. First, evaluation efforts are an essential part of the service to specified clients. The worker helping an individual, a family, a group, or a community organization to achieve defined goals has a responsibility to engage the client in regular evaluative efforts to determine whether his interventive activities are producing the desired results. These efforts are the final phase of the problem-solving model presented in Chapter 6. Second, workers have a responsibility to cooperate and assist in more formal evaluations of agency programs and policies; line-level practitioners may not be called upon to give leadership to these formal evaluation efforts, but their assistance and cooperation are essential if such evaluation is to be conducted. Both types of evaluation—the worker's continuous evaluation with clients and formal program evaluation—should create feedback for the worker to integrate into practice.

CONTINUOUS CLIENT EVALUATION

Diagram 4 offers a schematic representation of the problem-solving process showing evaluation as providing feedback loops permitting client and worker to assess continuously the problem they have defined for

DIAGRAM 4
The problem-solving model

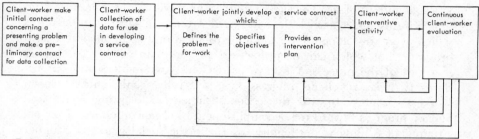

Evaluation provides feedback loops enabling client and worker to continuously reevaluate the adequacy of the data base and/or renegotiate the service contract by changing the problem definition, the objectives, or the intervention plan.

work, the objectives they have selected, and the interventive plan they have formulated. Client and worker are continuously involved in an ongoing evaluation of their experiences in trying to produce change. Their evaluation may indicate a need to redefine the problem (or define an entirely new problem), to reassess objectives (or develop new objectives), or to alter the intervention plan. The impact of evaluation and feedback loops is to reduce the linearity of the problem-solving model and to permit the model to take on a dynamic, systematic, constantly changing quality. The opportunity to change problem definition, goals, and intervention plans does not, however, remove from the worker the responsibilities of being sure that any changes are negotiated with the client and that any intervention activities are undertaken on the basis of a clearly specified service contract. Experience with interventive activities may indicate a need for a change in the contract, but changes in contracts cannot be made unilaterally.

In Chapter 8 we stressed the importance of clearly specifying goals. This is an essential prerequisite to evaluation. Without client and worker clarity as to goals, the evaluation of progress toward the accomplishment of goals is impossible. Likewise, a clear specificaton of the intervention plan is necessary to assess whether client-worker activities are appropriate for reaching the desired goals. Without a clear specification of the intervention plan, client and worker cannot evaluate whether what is happening leads or fails to lead to goal accomplishment. Intervention activities on the part of the client and the worker may be construed as inputs or independent variables, and the goals as outcomes or dependent variables. The process of evaluation is one of determining whether or not the independent variables are leading to the desired dependent variables (the latter would indicate a need to change the intervention plans).

The specification of measurable, concrete goals is one of the more difficult tasks of the social work practitioner. The article by Thomas Kiresuk and Geoffrey Garwick provides him with a useful evaluation tool. Kiresuk and Garwick describe Goal Attainment Scaling procedures which were developed to evaluate patient progress in mental health programs but which can be utilized in any program where goal setting is a part of the process. We have used Goal Attainment Scaling procedures to measure client progress toward service goals, student social workers' progress toward the accomplishment of learning goals, and agency progress toward the accomplishment of organizational goals. Goal Attainment Scaling is particularly useful to the social work practitioner because it permits the individualization of goals; there is no effort to impose predetermined, standardized goals. Rather, client and worker work toward the accomplishment of goals individually tailored to a particular situation. The procedures, however, only measure the extent of goal attainment; they do not in any way measure the importance or significance of the goals themselves, nor do they determine the intervention methods. How goals are achieved is not a part of Goal Attainment Scaling.

The grid used in Goal Attainment Scaling is reproduced in Diagram 5. It provides for the development of scales—one for each goal—with five levels of predicted attainment; the levels range from the most unfavorable to the most favorable outcome thought likely, with the expected level of outcome at the midpoint on each scale. At least one scale should be developed for each problem area, and a heading should be provided for each scale. As many scales as are necessary may be developed. Once the scale headings have been provided, a follow-up date should be set and the predicted level of outcome for each scale as of the follow-up date should be indicated.

Where do client and worker expect to be at the specified follow-up date? The entire goal may not be attained by that time; the task, therefore, is to indicate the expected level of accomplishment by the follow-up date. The next steps are to indicate the most unfavorable outcome and the most favorable outcome thought likely by the follow-up date; then the intermediate levels—less than expected success, expected level of success, and more than expected success—can be completed. The levels of predicted attainment should be specified objectively enough to be reliably scored on the follow-up date. Whenever possible, quantification

DIAGRAM 5
Goal attainment follow-up grid

Program using GAS _____

Date of scale construction _____
Follow-up date _____

LEVELS OF PREDICTED ATTAINMENTS	SCALE HEADINGS AND SCALE WEIGHTS			
	SCALE 1: ($w_1 =$)	SCALE 2: ($w_2 =$)	SCALE 3: ($w_3 =$)	SCALE 4: ($w_4 =$)
Most unfavorable outcome thought likely				
Less than expected success				
Expected level of success				
More than expected success				
Most favorable outcome thought likely				

is desirable, but it is not absolutely essential in establishing the scale levels.

A second concern is to be sure that each scale is both exhaustive and mutually exclusive. None of the five levels of success should overlap (each should be mutually exclusive), and the scale levels should account for all outcome possibilities thought likely (be exhaustive). After the scales have been developed, they can be set aside for scoring until the designated follow-up date. Scoring consists of checking what has been accomplished on each scale at the designated follow-up date. Kiresuk and Garwick present a formula for calculating an overall Goal Attainment Scale and also discuss the procedures for weighting scales if some are thought to be more important than others.

Diagram 6 illustrates a completed set of Goal Attainment Scales which might have been developed with Mrs. B in the situation described in Chapter 9. After study of this example as well as careful study of the Kiresuk and Garwick article, the student might begin experimenting with Goal Attainment Scaling. The procedures can be used in any situation where goals are set, so Goal Attainment Scaling can be learned

DIAGRAM 6
Goal attainment follow-up grid (Examples of scales which might have been developed with Mrs. B)

Program using GAS Intercity
                    Head Start

Client   Mrs. B

Date of scale construction___8-1-73___
Follow-up date_____9-1-73_____

LEVELS OF PREDICTED ATTAINMENTS	SCALE HEADINGS AND SCALE WEIGHTS			
	SCALE 1: Irritability (w_1 =) with Jimmy	SCALE 2: Mrs. B's (w_2 =) loneliness	SCALE 3: Referral to (w_3 =) Child Guidance	SCALE 4: (w_4 =)
Most unfavorable outcome thought likely	Mrs. B reports angrily yelling at Jimmy daily or oftener during last week in August.	No action on or discussion of Mrs. B's loneliness.	No discussion or action about returning to clinic.	
Less than expected success	Mrs. B reports angrily yelling at Jimmy more than 3 times but less than daily during last week in August.	Mrs. B discusses her loneliness but can not make plans to deal with it.	Mrs. B is discussing her reaction to the clinic but has not formulated plans to return.	
Expected level of success	Mrs. B reports angrily yelling at Jimmy no more than three times during last week in August.	Mrs. B is discussing her loneliness and making plans to join a group.	Mrs. B has discussed her reaction to the clinic and plans to secure a return appointment.	
More than expected success	Mrs. B has discontinued angrily yelling at Jimmy but has not discovered another way to discipline him.	Mrs. B has initiated contacts with a group.	Mrs. B has telephoned the clinic for a return appointment.	
Most favorable outcome thought likely	Above, and Mrs. B is using another form of discipline before becoming angry with Jimmy.	Mrs. B has attended one group meeting.	Mrs. B has been into the clinic for a return appointment.	

without actually working with clients. Personal learning goals can be set. How many books will be read next month? How many articles? What are the student's goals in terms of grades this term? What percent of written assignments will be completed on time? The student's learning plans will provide ample opportunity to begin work with Goal Attainment Scaling.

ASSISTING WITH PROGRAM EVALUATION

Increasingly social agencies are being called upon to establish the effectiveness of their services. Accountability extends beyond the evaluation by worker and client of the extent to which they are achieving service contract goals. It also utilizes the principles of scientific research to measure the extent to which agency programs goals are being attained and at what cost. The article by Leonard Rutman and Joe Hudson identifies phases in program evaluation and discusses issues and problems of each phase. Studies can be made of outcomes (the extent to which programs are achieving defined goals) or of efforts (the processes agencies utilize to reach goals). Process studies are particularly necessary to enable social agencies to more adequately conceptualize and identify the program inputs they utilize to reach goals. Just as interventive means must be conceptualized and related to objectives defined in the service contract, so at the level of program evaluation inputs must be conceptualized and related to program goals or outputs. The need to adequately conceptualize inputs and goals is the same whether the effort is to evaluate a client's progress or a program's accomplishment.

A recurring theme noted by Rutman and Hudson is the conflict between practitioner and researcher. They think both must make compromises if program evaluation is to be conducted, and they regard program evaluation as essential to the establishment of accountability. Practitioners may be asked to more completely conceptualize their activity and goals. However, practitioners utilizing the service contract we have described should find this a comparatively easy process. In addition the practitioner may be asked to fill out forms and maintain records which are essential for the evaluation function. Just as the evaluation of client progress provides feedback from which the worker and client can renegotiate their service contract, so formal program evaluation should provide feedback to the worker concerning the effectiveness of particular interventive means. While cooperating with researchers may involve additional effort on the part of the practitioner, ultimately the payoff in knowledge and better service should justify the effort.

RECAPITULATION

The practitioner's involvement with evaluative efforts occurs at two levels. Worker and client will be involved in a continuous process of evaluating the extent to which the goals of the service contract are being accomplished. This evaluation provides feedback loops and an opportunity for client and worker to continuously renegotiate their contract for work, objectives, and interventive means in relation to the problem. Workers may also be called upon to cooperate and assist with broader agency program evaluation. Such efforts should also provide feedback concerning the interventive approaches which appear to be most effective in given circumstances. Evaluation at both levels requires an explicit statement of goals and conceptualization of interventive means or program inputs. One model for measuring goal attainment—Goal Attainment Scaling—was discussed in relation to the measurement of client progress.

A LOOK FORWARD

The articles reproduced in this chapter relate directly to the material discussed previously. Beulah Compton offers an example of joint family-worker evaluation of progress toward the accomplishment of previously established goals. Kiresuk and Garwick provide a further discussion of Goal Attainment Scaling procedures which should be very useful to practitioners. Rutman and Hudson discuss the program evaluation process, conceptualize different phases in the process, and note issues and problems of each phase.

The next chapter will confront the student with the difficulty of bringing a working relationship to a conclusion. Earlier we discussed the process of establishing a relationship—a process which is given considerable attention in the social work literature. Frequently, however, writers fail to deal with the difficulties of constructively terminating a relationship. In Chapter 11 this process will be discussed as it occurs when a client is referred to another agency or transferred to another worker, or the service is brought to a planned termination.

Basic goal attainment scaling procedures*

Thomas J. Kiresuk and Geoffrey Garwick

Background on goal attainment scaling

Goal Attainment Scaling is a methodology for developing personalized, multi-variable, scaled descriptions which can be used for either therapy objective-setting or outcome measurement purposes. Originally developed as an assessment approach for individual clients in a community mental health milieu, Goal Attainment Scaling has since been applied to goal setting for both individuals and organizations across the whole spectrum of human services.

The Goal Attainment Scaling concept was first proposed in a 1968 article by Drs. Kiresuk and Sherman (Kiresuk and Sherman, 1968). The methodology was then implemented by the staff of the Program Evaluation Project which was directed by Dr. Kiresuk and funded by the National Institute of Mental Health. The Program Evaluation Project staff has undertaken a variety of efforts to examine the feasibility, reliability, and validity of the basic Goal Attainment Scaling approach.

* Reprinted by permission of the authors and the National Institute of Mental Health, United States Department of Health, Education and Welfare, from *Project Evaluation Report, 1969–1973*, chap. 1, of the Program Evaluation Project, Minneapolis, Minnesota. This project was supported by Grant #5 R01 1678904 from the National Institute of Mental Health.

The investigation of new possibilities and variations of Goal Attainment Scaling has continued through the efforts of both the Program Evaluation Project staff and persons in other agencies.

This chapter begins with an overview of the core of the Goal Attainment Scaling methodology. The second section discusses the characteristics of utilizing the Goal Attainment Follow-up Guide for assessment purposes. The final section briefly outlines some of the major possibilities which have been implemented or suggested for varying the basic Goal Attainment Scaling format while retaining the basic Goal Attainment Scaling approach.

I. Basic goal attainment scaling procedures

Designed for great flexibility, Goal Attainment Scaling is neither a specific set of instructions, nor a particular collection of pre-specified scales. Instead, it is a combination of an ideology, a type of record-keeping, and a series of techniques. The basic future-oriented, reality-testing approach on which Goal Attainment Scaling is based, duplicates in part the informal goal setting so often used by effective therapists and educators. In brief, Goal Attainment Scaling involves four steps:

a. collection of information about the person or organization for which goals will be scaled;
b. specification of the major areas where change would be feasible and helpful;
c. development of specific predictions for a series of outcome levels for each major area; and
d. scoring of the outcomes as they have been achieved by the time of a later follow-up interview.

(Even this fourth step is not essential to all uses of Goal Attainment Scaling. In some settings Goal Attainment Scaling has been used only to plan therapy and help the client set goals, so that the follow-up interview is not held and scoring is not carried out.) Roughly the same procedures are utilized when using Goal Attainment Scaling with organizations. (See chapter on Using Goal Attainment Scaling with Organizations in *P.E.P. Report 1969–1973* for more specialized suggestions for goal setting for groups or organizations.) These four basic points will be discussed in greater detail below.

A. The collection of information

From the client's statements, reports from the spouse, from other agencies, from relatives, from friends, and from any other available information source, a pool of information is accumulated. In the original

Program Evaluation Project staff research at the Hennepin County Mental Health Service Adult Outpatient unit one or two fifty-minute interviews plus examination of the client's information forms were the most common sources of knowledge for the clinician. In other settings, however, different schedules have been used for information collection. For an inpatient setting, information may be collected through records and contacts with the client over a period of several days.

B. Designation of problem areas

The information collected about the client will often be a relatively amorphous mass of facts. This pool of information could be analyzed in a variety of ways, but Goal Attainment Scaling is based on separating the mass of facts into a series of "problem areas." These problems indicate areas where an undesirable set of behaviors should be minimized, or where a favorable set of behaviors should be increased. The most significant, relevant problem areas should be selected for inclusion.

The Goal Attainment Scaling selection of problem areas may be carried out by a professional working alone, by the client, by both client and professional working together, by the family of the client and the professional, or through other possibilities. The procedures should be varied to meet the needs and capabilities of the agency. For example, if client participation is highly valued by the agency, then the client should be involved in the development of the problem areas.

The specified person(s) will select the problem areas most relevant to the client or organization involved. Each of these problem areas will be used to develop a continuum or scale of behaviors individually tailored to the client. In Figure 1, a completed form for the recording of the problem areas appears. This form is called the Goal Attainment Follow-up Guide, and each vertical scale represents a scale of outcomes related to a problem area for a client.

In Goal Attainment Scaling as used in the Program Evaluation Project research, there is no upper limit on the number of scales to be prepared for each client. The follow-up guide in Figure 1 has only four completed scales, but others could have been added. If necessary, a second or even a third form could also be used if more than five scales were desired. The highest number of scales known to have been constructed for one individual is ten. For organizations, from 10 to 60 scales have been utilized on the Goal Attainment Follow-up Guide. It is recommended that at least three or four problem areas be chosen, although a few clients may have only one or two scales.

Once the problem areas have been picked, each should be given a title. This title is designed to focus the attention on the problem areas of someone inspecting the follow-up guide. Each title should sum-

FIGURE 1

	GOAL ATTAINMENT FOLLOW-UP GUIDE				
SCALE ATTAINMENT LEVELS	SCALE 1: Employment (interest in work) self-report (w_1 = 10)	SCALE 2: Self-concept (physical appearance) patient interview (w_2 = 15)	SCALE 3: Interpersonal relation-ships (in training program as judged by receptionist—do not score if he does not go to train-ing program) (w_3 = 5)	SCALE 4: Interpersonal relationships (report of client's spouse) (w_4 = 8)	SCALE 5: (w_5 =)
a. Most unfavorable treatment outcome thought likely	Client states he does not want to ever work or train for work.	Client (1) has buttons missing from clothes, (2) unshaven (but says he is growing beard), (3) dirty fingernails, (4) shoes unshined (if wearing shoes needing shine), (5) socks don't match.	Never spontaneously talks to anyone. May answer if spoken to.	No friends and no close friends (i.e., "close" equals friends with whom he can talk about serious, intimate topics and who he feels like his company).	
b. Less than expected success with treatment	Client states that he may want to work "some-day" (a year or more later) but not now, and wants no training.	4 of the above 5 conditions.	Spontaneously talks to his own therapists or caseworkers, but to no other clients.	One person who is a friend or acquaintance but not a close friend.	
c. Expected level of treatment success	Client states that he might be interested in working within the next 12 months, but only if no training is required.	3 of the above 5 conditions.	Spontaneously talks to therapists, caseworkers, and one other client.	Two or more persons who are friends, but not close friends.	
d. More than expected success with treatment	Client states that he might be interested in working within the next 12 months and training for no more than 30 work days.	2 of the above 5 conditions.	Spontaneously talks to therapists, caseworkers, and 2 to 4 other clients.	One close friend, but no other friends.	
e. Most favorable treatment outcome thought likely	Client states that he might be interested in working within the next 12 months. Will train for as many days as are necessary.	One of the above 5 conditions.	Spontaneously talks to therapists, caseworkers, and 5 or more other clients.	One or more close friends, plus one or more other friends or acquain-tances.	

marize a problem area in a few words and should be placed in the blanks across the top of the follow-up guide. The title may be abstract, theoretical, or vague. This possibility is mentioned to emphasize that though the titles may be abstract or generalized, the remainder of the descriptions on the follow-up guide should be relatively specific and objective. In Figure 1, the titles selected are Employment, Self-concept, and Interpersonal relationships.

When titles have been selected for the client's follow-up guide, a numerical weight can be added to each scale, beside the title. The weighting system utilized by the Program Evaluation Project staff to indicate the relative importance of the scales does not incorporate any pre-specified weights, but allows any one- or two-digit number to be used. The higher the number used in the weight, the more significant the scale is, relative to the other scales. In Figure 1, the weights selected are 10, 15, 5, 8, so that Scale 2 for the problem area "Self-concept" with the weight of "15" is seen as the most important.

The title box can also be used to indicate any special sources of information for the scale. Special information sources might include "speak to spouse," "contact police department," "employer should help score this scale," and so on.

C. Predictions for each problem area

Goal Attainment Scaling operates within a time frame or time limit, and all outcomes should be linked to this time frame. Thus, all Goal Attainment predictions should refer to specific outcomes at a specific target date in the future. In the original research at the Hennepin County Mental Health Service, clinicians constructed the follow-up guides and were allowed to set their own time frame for the follow-up guide. The most common option was the Program Evaluation Project–suggested schedule of a follow-up interview six months after the time the Goal Attainment Follow-up Guide was constructed. In the Hennepin County Crisis Intervention Center, where clinicians and clients worked together on most scales on the follow-up guides, the follow-up interview was usually scheduled for from one to three weeks after the construction of the follow-up guide. Currently, under the new evaluation system being developed for the Hennepin County Mental Health Service Out-patient Unit, follow-ups on therapy effectiveness are held three months after the follow-up is constructed. In a special study at the Hennepin County Mental Health Service Day Treatment Center, clients are constructing follow-up guides to be followed up four months later. In short, the Goal Attainment scales should be constructed to be applicable to a future follow-up interview, and the length of time between follow-up guide construction and the follow-up interview should be adjusted to suit the needs of the individual agency. (See chapter on Follow-up Goal Attainment Scaling in *P.E.P. Report 1969–1973.*)

With the problem areas selected and the date of the follow-up interview established, a series of predictions about the client's outcomes should be made. For each problem area, a number of variables are probably applicable as sources of measurement of outcome. The person (or group) constructing the Goal Attainment follow-up Guide should select a variable for each problem area—a variable which is maximally useful for indicating treatment outcome and which can be efficiently, cheaply, and reliably measured at the time of follow-up. (See Figure 2.)

For each variable, a range of outcomes is possible at the time of follow-up. These outcomes should be presented in accord with the descriptions along the left edge of the Goal Attainment Follow-up Guide. (See Figure 1.) These five descriptions range from the "most favorable outcome thought likely" to "more than expected level of outcome" to "expected level of outcome" to "less than expected level of outcome"

FIGURE 2
Hypothetical field of information collected about the client on the follow-up guide
in Figure 1

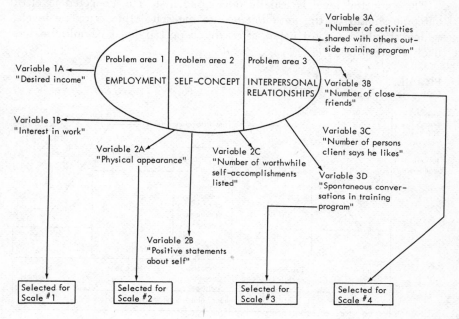

to the "most unfavorable outcome thought likely." Judgment of the persons constructing a follow-up guide is used to assign a part of the range of a variable to each of these five levels. These five levels with behaviors assigned to them comprise an individually developed continuum or scale for each variable relevant to the client.

The key level for predictive purposes is the middle or "expected" level on each variable's five-point scale. The expected level presents the best and most realistic prediction possible of the outcome which will have been reached by the client by the date of the follow-up interview. The expectations ought to be pragmatic, so that the expected level of each scale reflects what outcome actually "could" be attained by the follow-up date, not necessarily what "should" be attained.

The estimate of the "expected" outcome ought to be independent of the client's current level of functioning. As a matter of fact, for some very regressed or chronic clients, the most accurate and realistic expectation might be that they would have deteriorated by the time of follow-up, so that their level of functioning when the follow-up guide is constructed might be better than the expected level of outcome. Of course, it is hoped that such cases are rare, but Goal Attainment Scaling is based on obtaining the best prediction possible so that the clinician is not penalized by being forced to set over-optimistic goals for very difficult clients.

The expected level is usually developed first. The expected level of outcome should be the *most likely* outcome. The other outcome levels, which should be constructed after the expected level, should be less likely to occur.

FIGURE 3
Outcome probabilities

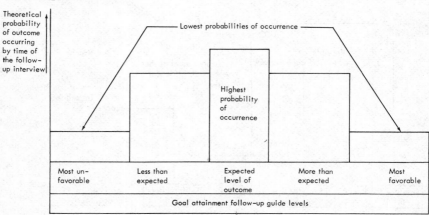

The client's level of functioning at the time the follow-up guide is developed can be noted on a separate, standard form. (See Figure 4.) This form, called the "Client's Status at Intake," is intended to show the level on each scale on the Goal Attainment Follow-up Guide which is equivalent to the client's current functioning. When the initial level of functioning is known, the *Goal Attainment Change score* can be calculated after the level of functioning at the time of the follow-up interview is scored. (See chapter on Goal Attainment Change Score in the *P.E.P. Report 1969–1973.*) Thus, at least two different kinds of effectiveness measures can be collected from the Goal Attainment Scaling system:

a. Whether or not the "expected" levels of outcome are reached.
b. Whether or not change occurred.

Experience with Goal Attainment Scaling suggests that an experienced follow-up guide constructor is able to complete the Goal Attainment Follow-up Guide in 15 to 30 minutes. If the follow-up guide is constructed jointly with the client, the process will require more time but there is greater opportunity for therapeutic interaction. At the Hennepin County General Hospital Mental Health Service, clinicians of all disciplines have constructed follow-up guides and have predicted outcomes

FIGURE 4
For the client in the Goal Attainment Follow-up Guide in Figure 1

Client Status at Intake

To facilitate the retention of the "level at intake" date, please complete this form for each Goal Attainment Follow-up Guide, using the following format.

Indicate the "level at the time of intake" with an asterisk in the appropriate cell for each scale completed. If the client's "level at intake" does not appear on a scale, put an asterisk in the cell marked "D.N.A." Any additional comments concerning the client's "level at intake" should be indicated on the reverse side of this form.

Scale 1	Scale 2	Scale 3	Scale 4	Scale 5
Much less than expected	Much less than expected	Much less than expected	Much less than expected	Much less than expected
Less than expected	Less than expected	Less than expected	Less than expected	Less than expected
Expected	Expected	Expected	Expected	Expected
More than expected	More than expected	More than expected	More than expected	More than expected
Much more than expected	Much more than expected	Much more than expected	Much more than expected	Much more than expected
D.N.A.	D.N.A.	D.N.A.	D.N.A.	D.N.A.

fairly accurately. More than one third of the scales scored at follow-up were scored at the "expected" level, with another one third of the scales scored above that level. The types of problems and clients which are particularly difficult to predict are being studied by content analysis methods of the Project staff. (See the chapter on Clinicians' Ability to Predict Outcomes in the *P.E.P. Report 1969–1973.*)

D. The follow-up interview

At the Hennepin County General Hospital Mental Health Service study, the follow-up guides are prepared by one clinician, while a different clinician undertakes therapy. The follow-up interviews are carried out by still other persons, who are not part of either the Mental Health Service staff or the regular Program Evaluation Project staff. The bulk of the interviews have been carried out by master's degree Social Workers, but bachelor degree Social Workers, Registered Nurses, and under-

graduates majoring in the social sciences have also participated as follow-up interviews.

The Program Evaluation Project follow-up interview begins with a
standardized series of questions about the client's satisfaction with the
services received. (See chapter on Consumer Satisfaction in the *P.E.P.
Report 1969–1973.*) Then the follow-up interviewer, without actually
showing the follow-up guide to the client, will ask questions designed
to lead to enough information to score the scales on the Goal Attainment
Follow-up Guides. Other agencies using Goal Attainment Scaling have
used different procedures and follow-up workers, with a variety of backgrounds, including therapy teams, psychiatric aides, and secretaries. The
interviewer should score the most appropriate level of each scale on
the follow-up guide, and the follow-up results are then collected by
the Program Evaluation Project staff. These procedures are described
in "Interviewer Procedures for Scoring the Goal Attainment Follow-up
Guide" (Audette and Garwick, 1973).

II. The Goal Attainment score

The most commonly used Goal Attainment score is based on the
Kiresuk-Sherman formula, and is calculated based on the weights assigned to each scale and the level of outcome attained for each scale

FIGURE 5

$$GAS = 50 + \frac{10 \sum_{i=1}^{n} w_i x_i}{\sqrt{(1 - \rho) \sum_{i=1}^{n} w_i^2 + \rho \left(\sum_{i=1}^{n} w_i \right)^2}}$$

where

x_i is the outcome score on the $_i$th scale of
the Goal Attainment Follow-up Guide,
w_i is the relative weight attached to the
$_i$th scale,
ρ is a weighted average intercorrelation of
the scales, and
n is the number of scales on the Goal Attainment Follow-up Guide.

as is shown in Figure 5. This formula is used to produce a single summary score for each Goal Attainment Follow-up Guide with a mean
of 50 and a standard deviation of 10 plus a correction for the possibility

of differing variances among the variables on the scales. Two manuals giving the Goal Attainment scores without calculation are available (Baxter, 1973 and Garwick and Brintnall, 1973).

The basic Goal Attainment score converts the —2 to +2 values presented in Figure 6 to a score with a theoretical range from 15 to 85. A simplified "Scale-by-Scale" score can also be calculated by directly using these —2 to +2 outcome values.

FIGURE 6
The values of the level of a single Goal Attainment Scale

Much less likely than thought	-2
Less than expected	-1
Expected	0
More than expected	+1
Much more than thought likely	+2

If a summary score with a —2 range is desired, the mean value can be determined, or a specialized formula, developed by Sherman and shown in Figure 7, can be used.

FIGURE 7

$$\text{GAS} = 50 + C \cdot \sum_{i=1}^{n} x_i$$

where C is a constant dependent only upon n:

Table of computational constants, $\rho = .3$

number of scales, $n =$	1	2	3	4	5
computational constant, $C =$	10.00	6.20	4.56	3.63	3.01

The scores based on the follow-up Goal Attainment Follow-up Guide can be used for feedback to adinistrators, supervisors, clinicians, or clients. (See the chapter on Feedback in *P.E.P. Report 1969–1973.*) The baic Goal Attainment score reflects "whether or not the treatment accomplished what it was expected to accomplish." Thus, the Goal Attainment score is probably most valuable as a comparative measure, not an absolute measure. In the next section, a few new possibilities for producing or scoring the Goal Attainment Follow-up Guide are presented. Both procedures and type of score used should fit the agency.

III. Varieties of Goal Attainment Scaling

The Goal Attainment Scaling methodology has been continually expanded ever since it was initiated. Part of this expansion is based on new and better knowledge of the way in which the Goal Attainment methodology operates. Another portion of this expansion is possible because of the development of new ideas and forms, such as the *Guide to Goals, One* format or the idea of collaborative client-therapist follow-up guide construction.

Actually, the title of this section is somewhat misleading, for there are no clear-cut "varieties" or specific variations of Goal Attainment Scaling. Instead, there are several points within the Goal Attainment Scaling process where procedures can be varied and options can be added. Thus, there is a whole spectrum of applications and "variations" of Goal Attainment Scaling and the scores produced which can be used to meet the specific needs of agency clients, administrators, and clinicians.

The four major steps within the Goal Attainment Scaling process were listed in Section I. Some recent possibilities for varying Goal Attainment Scaling within each of these steps will be discussed below. (See chapter on the Varieties of Goal Attainment Scaling in the *P.E.P. Report 1969–1973* for a more exhaustive list of possibilities.)

A. The collection of information

Many clinicians express interest in changing the Goal Attainment Follow-up Guide as new information about the client is accumulated. Some persons have suggested that the follow-up guide be altered when new problems appear or when earlier problems disappear. It is recommended that such alterations of the Goal Attainment Follow-up Guide be undertaken only on a systematic basis, if at all. For example, if an agency staff decides to permit the alteration of the follow-up guide, it should only be altered within a given time after the original construction.

Short-term goals could, however, be represented on special forms. One possibility is shown in Figure 8. With this form, the clinician may indicate short-term goals changes without destroying the predictive value of the original long-term Goal Attainment Follow-up Guide.

FIGURE 8
Linking long-term to short-term objectives

Program_____   Date_____
Scorer_____   Short–term follow–up number_____

Current status of_____
(Client's name)

A.

Long–term goals (to be scored ___ in months)

Much less than expected	Much less than expected	Much less than expected	Much less than expected	Much less than expected
Less than expected	Less than expected	Less than expected	Less than expected	Less than expected
Expected	Expected	Expected	Expected	Expected
More than expected	More than expected	More than expected	More than expected	More than expected
Much more than expected	Much more than expected	Much more than expected	Much more than expected	Much more than expected
D.N.A.	D.N.A.	D.N.A.	D.N.A.	D.N.A.

B.

Short–term objectives (to be scored ___ per week)

OBJECTIVE 1A:	OBJECTIVE 2A:	OBJECTIVE 3A:	OBJECTIVE 4A:	OBJECTIVE 5A:
Method to be Used _____	Method _____	Method _____	Method _____	Method _____
Date _____ Objective Should be Reached	Date _____ Objective Should be Reached	Date _____ Objective Should be Reached	Date _____ Objective Should be Reached	Date _____ Objective Should be Reached
Is Objective Reached ? _____ (Yes, No, Un– sure)	Is Objective Reached ? _____ (Yes, No, Un– sure)	Is Objective Reached ? _____ (Yes, No, Un– sure)	Is Objective Reached ? _____ (Yes, No, Un– sure)	Is Objective Reached ? _____ (Yes, No, Un– sure)
OBJECTIVE 1B:	OBJECTIVE 2B:	OBJECTIVE 3B:	OBJECTIVE 4B:	OBJECTIVE 5B:
Method _____	Method _____	Method _____	Method _____	Method _____
Date _____ Objective Should be Reached	Date _____ Objective Should be Reached	Date _____ Objective Should be Reached	Date _____ Objective Should be Reached	Date _____ Objective Should be Reached
Is Objective Reached ? _____ (Yes, No, Un– sure)	Is Objective Reached ? _____ (Yes, No, Un– sure)	Is Objective Reached ? _____ (Yes, No, Un– sure)	Is Objective Reached ? _____ (Yes, No, Un– sure)	Is Objective Reached ? _____ (Yes, No, Un– sure)

1. Indicate the "current status or outcome" with a mark in the appropriate level for each scale. If the client's "current status" does not appear on a long–term scale, put a mark in the cell marked "D.N.A."

2. Link at least one short–term objective to each long–term scale.

3. This form is derived from the Client Status at Intake form.

B. Designation of problem areas

Some agencies may wish to specify some types of problem areas which should be scaled for all clients. A criminal justice agency, for instance, may wish to have "Re-arrest" used as the basis for a scale for all of its parolees.

It may be useful for record-keeping purposes to outline a number of general types of problems. Each type could be given a number. When a problem area is selected, its number could be inserted at the top of the scale. These numbers are easily data-processed and enable an agency to get a rapid survey on the general types of problems being confronted by its clients.

C. Predictions for each problem area

The *Guide to Goals, One* format is a programmed version of Goal Attainment Scaling designed to lead the user through step-by-step development of a useful Goal Attainment Follow-up Guide (Garwick, 1972). This format has been applied to the Hennepin County Day Treatment Center, where clients appeared to be able to produce their own Goal Attainment Follow-up Guides with a mean of about five minutes of assistance from the clinical staff. A group of these Goal Attainment Follow-up Guides have been scored at follow-up, and the results indicate a fairly high degree of reliability. If the clients can set their own predictions, the possibilities for cost-saving in evaluation with Goal Attainment Scaling are considerable.

D. The follow-up interview

As commented earlier, one of the most striking developments in Goal Attainment Scaling utilization has been the popularity of clinical uses where the interactional aspects of the Goal Attainment Scaling process are emphasized more than evaluative uses. One survey suggested that of all the agencies considering Goal Attainment Scaling utilization, 52 percent were interested in the non-evaluative uses where the follow-up and scoring are not stressed. (See chapter on Dissemination, Consultation, and Utilization in *P.E.P. Report 1969–1973.*)

The dynamics of using Goal Attainment Scaling in this way have not been extensively studied by the Program Evaluation Project staff. However, the interactional, reality-testing features of developing the Goal Attainment Follow-up Guide as part of therapy may be eventually as important as program evaluation with Goal Attainment Scaling.

Conclusion

Further instruction on Goal Attainment Scaling may be obtained from various chapters of the *P.E.P. Report 1969–1973* and from manuals such as the Programmed Instruction Manual (Garwick, 1973). The Newsletter Compendium may also be helpful (Brintnall, 1973). For more information, please write to Ms. Joan Brintnall, Program Evaluation Resource Center, 501 Park Avenue South, Minneapolis, Minnesota 55415.

REFERENCES

AUDETTE, D., GARWICK, G. Interviewer procedures for scoring the goal attainment follow-up guide. Unpublished Project Report, July, 1973.

BAXTER, J. Goal attainment score conversion key for equally weighted scales. Unpublished Project Report, February, 1973.

BRINTNALL, J. P.E.P. newsletter compendium. Unpublished Project Report, July, 1973.

GARWICK, G. Guide to goals, one. Unpublished Project Report, October, 1972.

GARWICK, G. Programmed instruction in goal attainment scaling. Unpublished Project Report, September, 1973.

GARWICK, G., BRINTNALL, J. Tables for calculating the goal attainment score. Unpublished Project Report, August, 1973.

KIRESUK, T. J., SHERMAN, R. E., Goal attainment scaling: a general method for evaluating comprehensive community mental health programs, *Community Mental Health Journal*, 1968, 4 (6), 443–53.

Family-worker joint goal evaluation*

Beulah Roberts Compton

The word *evaluation* in social work usually conjures up visions of "researchers" who appear at our door to put our practice under their microscope of "effective outcome." And to many caseworkers the results seem costly and meaningless. The evaluation research that we as practitioners with individuals and families are most vitally interested in is not that which has a broad concern with the effects of large-scale programs on total populations groups and/or with their impact on the community. It is not that we see this as unimportant, but that we would like information from research that would provide us with an understanding of what happens when a social worker attempts to help a

---

* Original article prepared for this volume.

client resolve his problem. We want to gain an increased understanding of effective practice: why did a particular treatment bring a certain desired outcome, and would it have brought that outcome if variables relating to community reaction to the client, community structure, or institutional opportunities, that were completely out of the control of the worker, changed during the course of treatment?

Practitioners deeply involved in an effort to understand their own practice know very well that social work is not a total, undifferentiated problem-solving process, or a collection of discrete interviewing techniques that can be understood apart from a given social problem for which individual solutions must be found. Such practitioners know that it is meaningless to try to measure treatment by such variables as whether it was done by a Master of Social Work (MSW), or how often the client was seen, or whether the agency classifies it as "intensive." This essentially assumes that all MSW workers do the same thing, or that, since all wokers administer the same medicine, as it were, the only concern is whether it is taken once a week or once a month. And "intensive treatment' 'is usually based on the concept that if some is good more is better, without regard to problem or client.

Yet, even as one protests, one realizes that much of the problem is of our own making. We have oversold ourselves and our influence, have promised what boards and supporters have wanted to hear in order to continue to expand our programs. We were so sure our programs were worthwhile that we felt that such selling techniques were honorable. Thus we promised, often very vocally and explicitly, that if we just had more "trained" (MSW) workers we could move the poor and unskilled off relief, never mind the economy, and we could rehabilitate the handicapped, never mind the type of handicap. We promised that we could deal with the results of the longtime complex social problem by changing the victim. We blurred the distinction between the social problem and the individual who suffered its attack. We need to recognize clearly that if social and economic conditions are such that the basic elements for a minimally decent living are unavailable to the client's changed efforts, or the caseworker does not have it within his control to make them available, or if they do not even exist, then the social worker's service will be of little value in the client's central concerns.

But the purpose of this paper is not to belabor either ourselves or researches who are interested in program outcome. It is to examine what the individual worker can do about evaluation in his own practice. Used selectively and discriminatingly, with the understanding that it is valueless if isolated from a given social and human problem, the problem-solving process, set within the climate of a working partnership, can serve as a guide for such work. The goal of such evaluation is twofold: (1) to help the client assess gains made as a part of the process of termination, and (2) to help the worker better understand what is effective in his use of self with the client.

The first step toward the evaluation of the outcome of an individual case begins with the problem definition. One cannot evaluate effectively unless he knows what he is evaluating. In casework practice, it is usually a problem that brings worker and client together. Sometimes the client comes to the worker with the problem; sometimes the worker goes to the client with a problem the community has identified. Either way, client and worker must find a problem, preferably as identified by the client, which can be identified as the problem on which they will begin. We may define the boundaries of the case broadly, but we should be able to define with some specificity the problem on which we will work at any one time, remembering that casework is most effective when the focus is kept on the problem as the client understands it. It is further important that the problem be one that is appropriate for practice interventions. Casework practitioners cannot do everything.

Once the problem has been defined, it is necessary to establish an interim goal. The reason for establishing an interim goal at this point is that this goal in conjunction with the defined problem will determine the focus of the exploration and knowledge collection that is to follow. In casework practice the question of goals remains unsettled. Obviously, all professional people have general goals that relate to the vision of "the good life" that they hold in some way for all clients. These goals may be stated by the practitioner as: helping increase the capacity of the client to make choices about his own life, including making resources available, to help enhance the possibility of the client's self-actualization; helping people maintain and increase coping skills when confronted with crisis and threat. However, these are general goals and are not what we mean when we speak of setting individualized goals for each case. When we talk of goals in the problem-solving process we mean specific goals that give an answer or some solution to the identified problem.

These goals should be set in conjunction with the client and the way he sees the problem working out as well as what he believes that the agency and practitioner can contribute to the solution. It is our firm conviction that any goal that is to guide the course of work together must be known to and accepted as reasonable by both participants in the process. Probably one of the most common errors that practitioners make is to set goals that are too lofty. It may be that the great expectations we hold for ourselves and our clients contribute to our disappointment with our results.

Mr. and Mrs. D had been referred to the agency because of numerous problems. Mr. D had not worked for many years. He was severely alcoholic, and the children were often without food because he used the welfare food money for alcohol. The children were without adequate clothing and had had no medical attention. Mr. D often appeared before the court and spent an occasional 30 days in jail for simple assault on another man in a bar or for beating Mrs. D and the children when he had been drinking. The worker was assigned the case because of the neglect and abuse of the children.

When the worker came to visit the family for the first time, he asked the family what they saw as a place to begin. Mr. D said that the worker should not plan his getting a job as he had not been looking for quite a while. Mrs. D said that things were such a mess that she did not know which way to turn. In the face of the client's reluctance to define a question for work, the worker suggested that the children's health was a problem and that perhaps they should start with the goal of getting the children to the well-baby clinic.

There were many problems indeed in the D family. Workers for over ten years had been trying to get the D family off welfare by getting Mr. D a job. But for ten years this had not been an effective way of helping the family. The child welfare worker wanted to start with the problem as the family saw it, but faced with their inability to define any one problem, he defined one and set a goal—a goal that, given the fact that a well-baby clinic was just around the corner, seemed to be a realistic one. Given its specificity, this goal was also one that lent itself easily to evaluation.

Once the problem-to-be-worked is determined and the initial goal is set, the worker and the client need to collect information that will enable decisions about problem and goals to be finalized. Since this is not a paper on the whole problem-solving process, we will not discuss the collection of information or the processes of assessment. Once the information is collected and put together, it then becomes the responsibility of worker and client to rework the problem and the goals set earlier to be sure, that in light of the information, they are still valid and desirable.

Once the final goals are set, worker and client can begin to plan for the kinds of actions needed to reach those goals. If problem and goal must be specific and clear, certainly plans and actions to carry them out have to be at least equally clear and specific. As client and worker begin to carry out actions, the processes of evaluation come into play. Evaluation can be of two kinds: (1) interim evaluation that one engages in from time to time to be sure that worker and client are moving toward the desired goals and are carrying out the specified actions, and (2) the final evaluation in which client and worker attempt to assess whether the goal has been reached and what actions were effective for that purpose.

In one program in which the author worked, it was a general principle that we would stop for an interim evaluation at least every six months.

We called these "consolidations of gains" and used them to focus the client's attention on what he had achieved as well as on what the worker had contributed.

> I told Mrs. F that next week I came out I didn't want to talk about what we were doing about her problem, but rather I wanted us to spend the whole hour discussing how she thought things were working out.
>
> In our first evaluation session I asked Mr. J what had been most helpful to him in our work together in the last few months. He said that the best thing was that for the first time he had found that he could trust a social worker, and he thought that that was why things had gone well. Being able to trust me made it easier for him to try to do some of the things we talked about. I asked him what it was I had done or said that made him feel that he could trust me. He said that he didn't know what it was; it probably was not any one thing. Certainly people didn't wear trust on their sleeves when they came in a person's house.

Consolidations of gains, an attempt to assess progress toward goals during the process of working together, serve two important purposes: first, they enable the worker to make some assessment as to whether the plan is working well or poorly in time to make changes if it should not be working will; second, they help the client to evaluate his participation. Our experience has been that often clients want to give the social worker all the credit and need to have their own efforts pointed out to them. Thus, evaluation is not a one-way process, but involves both client and worker in an attempt to assess what each has put into the process.

When it appears to worker and client that the initial problem has been dealt with in the best way possible, it may be time to terminate a case. However, the client may identify new problems that he would like to work on so that a new problem and goal may be set for future work.

> We had originally attempted to make contact with Mrs. S around several complaints of child neglect from the school and the neighbors. Mrs. S, however, had managed to avoid becoming involved with us for the first few months, and when we finally did succeed in talking with her we found that her primary problem was to learn how to deal with the welfare board. From a beginning with this problem worker and client defined several other problems and achieved several other goals during the next three years. Eventually the time came when it was decided that Mrs. S was no longer in need of the worker, and arrangements were made to terminate the relationship. The worker asked Mrs. S for her evaluation of what they had been able to achieve together. Mrs. S identified the following achievements:
> 1. She had learned more about the requirements of the welfare board

and how to deal with the problems she might have with them. Now that she was more confident about herself she no longer let the board panic her into wild actions.

2. One of the problems identified had been the difficulty her oldest child was having in school. In her evaluation she not only pointed out how much better her son was doing as the result of the worker's initial efforts with the school and her ability to follow up on the plans, but she also felt that she was more confident in handling both her son and the school. She said that she had moved from hating the school and refusing to go there to becoming a room mother.

3. One of the other goals had been to help Mrs. S become more secure in dealing with her mother who had become very domineering and was interfering in every aspect of Mrs. S's life, including wanting Mrs. S to live with her. Mrs. S now lives alone and makes decisions.

4. Mrs. S said, "We are more secure and happy as a family. You started out to help me deal with my children without losing my temper and screaming at them, but we have ended up a better family all around."

This joint evaluation at the termination of the case helps the client to recognize the gains he has made. It gives him an opportunity to bring to the fore all his positive skills in coping independently with his own life and to examine them. He thus becomes aware of what has happened in this experience. It helps the worker to evaluate how helpful he has been in helping the client toward the goals set and what ways of using self work best in this type of situation. It also provides the worker with some opportunity to discuss the future with the client, to help him anticipate incidents in the future when he will need all his gains to cope adequately. It also allows the worker to share with the client the idea that all gains are not for all time. Thus there may well be a time when the client will want to return for further help. Such a return should be made as simple as possible for the client.

There is no one "evaluation for all seasons"; rather, there are different types of evaluations for different purposes. While program evaluation is necessary in the struggle to assess priorities in human service, it is neither the only nor the most important type of evaluation. Workers in the field need to know more about "what works" for this client with this problem. Social work is not a specific action, or a specific set of actions, applied routinely in controlled conditions to bring about a definable cure after an accurate diagnosis of the difficulty has been made. Rather, it is an individualized problem-solving process in which both client and worker find themselves dealing with many uncontrollable variables and in which client and worker are involved in jointly defined goals individualized for the particular client, situation, and problem. We know a lot about this individualized problem-solving process and how to go about it. We need to know more.

In thoughtfully using the client-worker evaluation in terms of specific goals set, both at the end of the case and during its progress, the worker can learn a great deal about his own effectiveness. If all workers in an agency did this and pooled the results of their work, some learning could take place that might help us find better ways of "doing." Workers must learn not answers, but principles of effective practice. And once such principles are learned, workers must also learn their appropriate applications. Individualized evaluation by the worker of individualized goal-achievement may contribute toward this end. One does not forget evaluation statements like the following:

> You helped me because you were willing to go right to the school and find out what was going on and what were possible things I could do about it. That helped because I could never have done that by myself. I just sat and said, "It's all their fault." And now things are just the best they could be, and I've learned how to do these things myself.
>
> I think what helped me most was her expectations that I could do what we planned. We talked about my wanting a high school diploma, and she found out about the GED test. If I passed I would get my diploma. And she thought I could do it. So I went down there and I did—I passed. Then she heard of a school where I could learn mechanics, and I went there and I got accepted. Now I have a job—and I think that this all happened because she thought I had it in me to do something.

Evaluating human services process approach*

Leonard Rutman and Joe Hudson

In the past several years there has been a growing demand for the formal evaluation of human service program.[1] This increased interest has been reflected most dramatically in the increasing amount of funds being allocated for program evaluations, particularly by the federal government. For example, Buchanan and Wholey have noted that in the

---

* Original article prepared for this volume.
[1] See Scott Briar, "The Age of Accountability," *Social Work* 18:1 (January 1973) p. 2.

three federal departments of Health, Education, and Welfare, Housing and Urban Development, and Labor there was a 30 percent increase in the amount of evaluation research funds allocated between fiscal years 1971 and 1973.[2]

In conjunction with this trend, evaluation research is becoming increasingly accepted as an integral part of program planning and policymaking in the human services. It is expected that evaluation research can meet two major goals: (1) identify the manner in which programs are carried out, particularly to determine whether they are actually implemented in the manner intended; and (2) assess the impact of these human service programs on the target group of consumers. In other words, the expectation is for evaluation research to provide a basis for both the monitoring and accountability of programs. Ultimately, soundly conducted evaluative research aims at contributing to the more effective and efficient delivery of human service programs.

The increased demand for evaluation research stems from several sources. Most obviously, funding organizations are exerting greater demands for rigorous research on the programs they support. Due in part to the relative scarcity of funds available for human service programs, funding bodies are searching for relatively objective measures on program effectiveness as a condition for the provision of ongoing financial support. No longer are funding sources satisfied with testimonials from program personnel regarding the value of their service. Assessments of program effectiveness provided by practitioners and administrators can be viewed with some skepticism inasmuch as any criticism of the worth of these programs naturally poses a threat to professional practice, status, and, ultimately, job security.

In addition to the increased skepticism of funding organizations toward potentially self-serving statements by program managers regarding the worth of the services being provided, descriptive reports which provide little more than bookkeeping information on the numbers, characteristics, and per unit cost of clients served by the agency are being viewed as insufficient to warrant the allocation of scarce funds. Instead, human service programs are being asked to provide evidence derived from outcome studies to demonstrate the extent to which stated goals are being met.

Concern about the effectiveness of human service programs has been accelerated with the appearance of research reports showing that such programs have not achieved significant positive effects for the clients served. In fact, it has become almost axiomatic that the more rigorous the research conducted, the less significant the demonstrated outcomes

---

[2] Garth N. Buchanan and Joseph S. Wholey, "Federal Level Evaluation," *Evaluation* 1:1 (Fall 1972) p. 17.

of a variety of programs.[3] A consequence of such research findings is a growing disenchantment with human service programs on the part of the public as well as of various funding organizations.

Aside from the general concern with determining the effectiveness of programs, human service professionals have become increasingly interested and involved in evaluative research for the purpose of testing theory and improving practice. This trend is particularly evident in the considerable amount of research conducted on various learning theories and the "behavior modification" approaches developed from them.

The increasing demand for rigorously conducted evaluative research has also been influenced by the growing popularity of the demonstration project as a strategy for program development and policymaking. Many federal departments have taken the initiative in stimulating the growth of demonstration projects through legislation providing for the funding of "innovative" programs. The usual pattern in funding demonstrations has been to support the development of small-scale pilot programs which include an extensive research component. Through demonstrations, it is expected that information will be provided having relevance for more general program developments and policy formulations.

Despite the optimism about the possibilities of evaluative research in monitoring and measuring the impact of human service programs, there are formidable obstacles to pursuing these aims. Several factors contaminate efforts to implement adequate research procedures: latent purposes held for conducting the evaluation study, particularly as these result in the distortion of research to justify decisions about the possible termination, continuation, or expansion of programs; ethical issues, especially in regard to denying service to a control group; administrative constraints; legal requirements; and professionals' prerogatives. Because of these factors there is a desperate need for better understanding the sociopolitical process of planning and implementing evaluative research. Such an endeavor would place particular emphasis on adjustments in the stages of planning and conducting the research, with particular attention paid to the potential consequences of such alternatives in the development of the final research design. Also required is an understanding of the factors related to the use of research findings for program changes or policymaking. In this context, a sociology of evaluative research would help to explicate the numerous issues relevant to evaluative studies of human service programs.

---

[3] See Walter C. Bailey, "Correctional Outcome: An Evaluation of 100 Reports," *Journal of Criminal Law, Criminology and Police Science* 57:2 (June 1966), pp. 153–60; H. Eysenck, "The Effects of Psychotherapy," in *Handbook of Abnormal Psychology*, ed. H. Eysenck (New York: Basic Books, 1961); Joel Fisher, "Is Casework Effective? A Review," *Social Work* 18:1 (January 1973), pp. 5–20; James Robison and Gerald Smith, "The Effectiveness of Correctional Programs," *Crime and Delinquency* 17:1 (January 1971), pp. 67–80.

Perspectives for evaluating human service programs

Judgments regarding the relative worth of human service programs are common. The general public has varying opinions regarding the success of programs such as Aid to Families with Dependent Children in meeting the problem of low income among these families, of health insurance programs in meeting the medical problems of the aged and/or indigent, and of such child welfare services as foster care in meeting the needs of children requiring substitute care. In the absence of a factual basis for making such decisions, judgments are largely based on values. Programs are viewed as being "good" or "bad" in relation to the characteristics of people availing themselves of the service, attitudes toward the social problems manifested by the target population, cultural attitudes toward work and independence, and differing views about the appropriate role of the state in attempting to ameliorate social problems and personal difficulties.

In addition to the common process in which the public formulates opinions about various programs, assessments about the relative worth of human services are also continually made by practitioners and administrators who are responsible for implementing the services as well as by the funding organizations supporting these programs. Having a deep investment in the services being provided, practitioners and administrators quite naturally extol the virtues of their programs. And it is such subjective testimonials which all too commonly are presented to funding organizations in an effort to gain continued support. Not having access to more rigorous types of information for assessing the value of particular programs, funding organizations are frequently placed in the position of relying on the subjective information provided by the program personnel.

While evaluation research also entails making judgments of worth about particular programs, it differs from the relatively simple and common process of informal evaluation based largely on opinion. In evaluation research, emphasis is placed on the application of commonly accepted research procedures to collect data which provides the basis for judgments of worth. Evaluation research is, first and foremost, a process of applying scientific procedures to accumulate reliable and valid evidence on the manner and extent to which specified activities produce particular effects or outcomes. The focus is on the end product—the effects of programs and policies—as well as on the efficiency and effort involved in achieving these outcomes. In addition to providing a basis for determining the relative success or failure of human service programs, the evidence derived from evaluation research can be used to suggest needed modifications in the current operation of the target programs.

The evaluation research process

As indicated previously, a crucial feature of the planning and conduct of evaluation research is the sociopolitical process in which the researcher and the relevant program participants (clients, practitioners, and administrators) develop the focus of the evaluative task, engage in working through the design, specify the procedures for implementing the research, cooperate in the research undertaking, and consider the implications of the research findings for future planning. There are numerous reasons for engaging in such a collaborative process. Through this involvement, the researcher can become more familiar with the organizational context within which the program operates, the explicit purposes of the research, the goals which the service presumably attempts to accomplish, and the attributes of the program being evaluated. Out of this process there is a greater likelihood that the evaluation will deal with the concerns which are considered most important by those intimately involved with the program as opposed, for example, to those which are of interest only to the researcher. Involvement in this process would also increase the probability of obtaining the cooperation of practitioners who are often anxious about having their work evaluated. Finally, the likelihood of implementing the study's recommendations are increased when program personnel have been involved in the entire planning process.

The sociopolitical context in which the evaluative task is formulated and conducted having been mentioned, it is now possible to identify the various stages of the evaluation process. First, the purposes or motives for undertaking evaluation research must be made explicit. Second, the program must be clearly defined. Third, program goals need to be stated in clear and relatively simple language, free of jargon and ambiguous terminology. Fourth, measures must be developed which can provide information on the relative progress that the program has made toward the attainment of the stated goals. Fifth, a research design must be developed which incorporates the purpose of the investigation as well as peculiarities of the program and its goals. Sixth, the implementation of the research requires continuous monitoring to facilitate reliable data collection as well as to determine whether the program is actually carried out in accordance with the originally agreed-upon procedures. Seventh, the findings are interpreted and the implications of the results for program changes and policy formulations are drawn.

It should not be assumed that the endeavor entails a linear progression from one discrete stage for the planning and conduct of an evaluation research project. Rather, these stages should be viewed as dynamically interrelated. The resolution of critical issues at any one stage will often have implications for other stages. For example, an original purpose for conducting evaluative research may have been a desire to test program effects. Such a purpose is likely to be modified if there is no clearly defined program with specific goals to be evaluated. The revised purpose may then be to conduct research aimed at "discovering" the specific nature of the program and eliciting the relevant goals. In turn, this revised purpose has direct implications for the research design, since the focus is on exploration and discovery as opposed to verification.

Unlike research conducted in laboratories, the stages of evaluation research are usually exposed to a variety of constraints in the "real world" and, as a consequence, are subject to a number of contaminating and confounding factors. These factors pose major problems to the evaluation effort. Such annoying realities dictate that the planning and conduct of evaluation research as well as the implementation of the research findings be viewed as a sociopolitical process involving the joint efforts of the researcher, the administrator, and practitioners.

Aside from their service orientation, which usually involves relatively little appreciation of the benefits and requirements of research, practitioners are generally anxious about having their practice scrutinized under the microscope of the researcher because of the possibility of having practice weaknesses revealed. In addition to fears about disclosure of the shortcomings of their programs, agency administrators are naturally concerned about the extent to which the introduction of research procedures will disrupt the provision of service to clients. For his part, the researcher is mainly concerned with applying rigorous research procedures to the agency setting despite the administrative or programmatic constraints. By becoming sensitive to these differing orientations and commitments to the human service program, he can anticipate potential conflicts which often emerge in evaluative research studies and, it is hoped, deal with them to the benefit of the evaluative task. Consequently, there is a great need in the field of evaluation research to explicate such research/program conflicts and to work toward providing alternative and mutually satisfying resolutions to them. This kind of perspective on the part of both the researcher and agency representatives can help develop potentially fruitful negotiations to the mutual benefit of the research and, ultimately, the program.

1. *Purpose.* Evaluation research efforts are generally justified on the basis that they contribute to the assessment and modification of human service programs through a rigorous investigation of the relationship of particular interventions to the outcomes produced. Viewed in this light, evaluation research is a feedback mechanism providing the necessary information for adapting programs to more effectively meet client needs. For the funding organizations, evaluation research can provide the necessary justification to terminate, continue, or expand human

service programs. In addition to these explicit or overt rationales for conducting evaluative research, there may be hidden or covert reasons for conducting such studies that may be at variance with the explicit or overt purposes (i.e., better understanding of the nature of human service programs and the assessment of their impact). Suchman[4] has termed studies guided by such covert purposes as "pseudoevaluations." Included in his list of such misuses of evaluation are: (1) "eye-wash"—a deliberate focus on the surface appearance of a program to make it look good; (2) "white-wash"—an attempt to cover up program failures during the investigation; (3) "submarine"—the political use of research to destroy a program; (4) "posture"—evaluation research as a ritual having little substance; (5) "postponement"—using evaluation to postpone needed action.

For the specification and clarification of research purposes, it is necessary to clearly identify the type of information which the research is expected to produce. This entails a process involving the researcher and the program representatives in joint clarification of the explicit purposes of the evaluation prior to the formal initiation of the project.

Three major purposes of an evaluative project can be identified—assessing program effort (inputs), program effects (outcomes), and program efficiency (economy). The evaluation of program effort is typically geared toward an assessment of the amounts and kinds of inputs used in pursuing program goals. These inputs may take the form of money, equipment, personnel, work activities, and so on. In the human services, program inputs typically constitute the experimental or treatment variable. That is, assessments of program effort involve descriptive accounts of the program "means" assumed to be causally linked to the program "ends" of goals. However, the mere assessment of program effort does not provide a test of this assumption. While a necessary condition, effort is not in itself sufficient for the achievement of program goals. Suchman,[5] for example, has compared studies of effort to assessing the number of times a bird flaps its wings without attempting to determine the distance it flies.

Evaluations of effort in human service programs are common. However, they are rarely used in the context of testing program effects. Most agencies are expected to provide yearly reports on the number of clients served by the program, the number of client contact hours, the size of staff, and the allocation of staff to various duties. These "service bookkeeping" reports or output measures are roughly analogous

---

[4] Edward A. Suchman, "Action for What? A Critique of Evaluative Research," in *Evaluating Action Programs* ed. Carol H. Weiss (Boston: Allyn and Bacon, 1972), p. 81.

[5] Edward A. Suchman, *Evaluative Reearch* (New York: Russell Sage Foundation, 1967), p. 61.

to stockholder reports, with the major difference that statements of profit and loss—the effects of the effort—are excluded.

Two assumptions about program effort are crucial. First, it is assumed that there is a logical and empirical relationship between the goals which have been specified for the program and the procedures used in achiev- ing them. Second, it is usually assumed that the program is implemented in the originally specified manner. Both assumptions point to the need for outcome studies to provide descriptive accounts of the effort ex- pended. In short, evaluations designed to measure the effects of programs should include a relatively clear specification of the amounts and types of effort expended toward the accomplishment of the desired outcomes.

The effects or program outcomes are the extent to which a program achieves its stated goals. Questions of effect deal with the ends or goals of the program and in this way provide a yardstick for assessing the central concern of an evaluation project: Does the program accomplish what it is designed to do? To use Suchman's[6] analogy again, the assess- ment of program effectiveness attempts to determine how far the bird has flown and only secondarily, as in the case of effort studies, how many times it flapped its wings.

Efficiency in achieving specified program goals is another explicit purpose for conducting evaluative studies. Essentially, this means testing the relationship between the amount and type of effort expended and the effects accomplished. In other words, efficiency is a function of the relationship of inputs to outcomes. In assessing program efficiency, one is concerned with obtaining information on the extent to which alterna- tive and less costly means could have been used to achieve comparable results.

All too often people involved in human service practice react to ques- tions of program efficiency as somehow below their professional dignity. This reaction seems to be based on the assumption that where humans are receiving services, questions relating to the efficiency of those services are callous or are irrelevant to professional practice. However, the con- cern with efficiency merely acknowledges an obligation to provide such services in the least costly form compatible with considerations of the dignity and respect which is due to their recipients.

Each of these three explicit purposes of evaluation research warrants serious consideration. Ideally, provision should be made in the research design to collect information pertinent to each purpose. The extent to which measures can be included for the achievement of these purposes, however, is related to the nature of the program being evaluated (i.e., its stage of development, the specificity of the program and its goals, etc.) and the overall reasons for undertaking the research.

⁶ Ibid., p. 62.

2. Articulation of the program's components. Prior to the implementation of an evaluative study, a program's components must be identified, conceptualized, and standardized. This should result in a clear explication of the "experimental" or independent variable. Rather than refer to programs by such a vague term as *counseling*, it then becomes possible to clearly conceptualize and operationalize this term into such varied activities as budgeting, job finding and placement, particular behavior modifications, and group therapy. Unless the program's components are clearly specified, questions regarding which program ingredients have a major effect on the accomplishment of specific as well as overall goals cannot be adequately answered.

The specification and measurement of the impact of a program's components are particularly important since experts in the field of evaluative research generally agree that evaluation of entire programs is often beyond the capabilities of existing methodology.[7] Since evaluations of total programs are so complex and such evaluations are of limited generalizability, a more common strategy is variable testing—singling out specific components of the program and testing their effectiveness in meeting limited goals. Despite the obstacles involved in conducting program evaluations, they are commonly undertaken because such information is used as a basis for decision making about continuation, expansion, or termination of programs. On the other hand, variable testing is commonly viewed as a means of improving particular interventions without posing a threat to entire programs.

3. Specification of goals. Since evaluation research attempts to determine the manner and extent to which a program achieves particular effects, a basic precondition of conducting such research is the clear articulation of program goals. In many respects, clearly stating the goals of human service programs is one of the most difficult and vexing problems of the evaluative process. A major reason for this is that such programs commonly set lofty and vague goals. Such goal statements as "the improvement of social functioning," "increasing mental health," "the prevention of criminality," and "strengthening family ties" are so vague as to make it difficult, if not impossible, to develop empirical referents or measures.

The formulation of operationalized program goals requires a joint effort between agency personnel and the researcher.[8] In this collaboration both the agency representatives and the researcher can make major contributions by bringing their respective expertise to the process. The

---

[7] Joseph S. Wholey, John W. Scanlon, Hugh G. Duffy, James S. Fukumoto, and Leona M. Vogt, *Federal Evaluation Policy: Analyzing the Effects of Public Programs* (Washington, D.C.: The Urban Institute, 1971), p. 107; and Edward Suchman, *Evaluative Research*, p. 59.

[8] For an excellent discussion of the formulation of program goals see Robert F. Mager, *Goal Analysis* (Belmont, Calif.: Fearon, 1972).

agency representatives should have a clearer understanding of what the program entails in its day-to-day work and what they consider program priorities, particularly as these relate to possible indicators of "success" or "failure." On the other hand, the researcher—especially if he is an external evaluator—presumably brings a more objective perception to the program and should therefore be able to view it in a relatively detached manner which can be of assistance to program personnel in ferreting out and articulating simply stated and relevant goals.

Besides helping to facilitate the articulation of specific and discrete program goals, the researcher must constantly emphasize the necessity of formulating goals which have direct relevance to the program being evaluated. Goals stated in specific and practical terms are useless as focal points for evaluating a program unless they clearly relate to the program services being provided. Otherwise, program failure can be attributed to the existence of irrelevant goals and not to the weakness of the program itself.

A problem to bear in mind constantly in the goal specification stage is the possible existence of conflicting goals. When viewed independently, each goal statement may appear to be appropriate, but when goals are appraised in conjunction with each other, potential conflicts may become apparent. An example of conflicting program goals would be combining the goal of increasing police manpower on walking beats in a part of a city with the goal of reducing "juvenile delinquency" as measured by police apprehensions since increasing the number of police walking beats may very well increase the number of young people who will be apprehended and brought to court.

Deciding whose goals should be used as the basis for evaluation is another thorny problem. The program may not be pursuing the goals which have been listed in organizational manuals or conveyed to the general public. On the other hand, a potential danger of having the researcher identify goals for the program is that program personnel can disclaim such goals as their priorities in the provision of services. A similar danger exists if the funding organization specifies the goals of the program to be evaluated. The funding body should, however, examine the goals which program personnel have identified and make decisions regarding the allocation of funds on that basis. This provides further justification for relying on a joint process in which researcher and program personnel articulate relevant goals.

A further task of the goal specification stage is the careful consideration of goal levels. For most human service programs a number of different goal levels can be specified—from the most ideal or ultimate level to the most immediate and practical level. An assumption is made that there is a logical connection between the most immediate and the most ideal goals. That is, the achievement of the immediate goals should have relevance for goal achievement at more remote levels.

In evaluation research, theory should be an important consideration in goal-setting and particularly in terms of the generalizability of results, the replication of the test in different situations and in suggesting further related studies. Goals can be specified on the basis of some a priori theoretical rationale underpinning the program. Conversely, it is possible to proceed in reverse order and generate theoretical propositions from the test of efforts in accomplishing program goals.[9]

4. *Specification of measures.* The human services program and its goals having been identified, a major task is the development of measures or indicators which provide a basis for determining whether or not the services were successfully implemented and whether or not they succeeded in achieving the stated goals. A number of considerations are crucial at this stage. First, in addition to developing measures on the overall goals of the program (e.g., reducing poverty), there is also the need to specify measures aimed at the outcome of discrete program goals (e.g., increased employment, improved education and health, etc.). Measures for the program's components (i.e., its methods and procedures) must also be developed. In evaluating group treatment, for example, it would be possible to develop measures which would yield data on the frequency of meetings, attendance at meetings, the focus of group sessions, the nature of the members' participation, the particular approaches used by the group leader, and the quality of the worker's intervention.

A second consideration is the criteria used to reflect the accomplishment of program goals. On this question the use of "soft" versus "hard" data is relevant and basic to the question of the reliability and validity of the measures used. Such tangible measures as age, sex, time, and grades in school, as well as relatively objective data on standardized personality and attitudinal tests, can be assumed to have a known degree of reliability and validity. There are also relatively "soft" criteria which are commonly used in less rigorous evaluation studies—personal opinions, subjective estimates, ratings obtained from participant observations, case illustrations, and so on. While these types of information can be used to reflect the flavor of a program and to document typical or extreme situations which may occur in the life of a program, their use as indicators of program success is limited. Such measures are commonly biased both by the interests of the evaluator as well as by the unrepresentative character of the events or cases to which the evaluation is applied.

---

[9] See Barney A. Glaser and Anselm L. Strauss, *The Discovery of Grounded Theory: Strategies for Qualitative Research* (Chicago: Aldine, 1967).

A third major issue centers on data collection procedures. Evaluation research studies vary in the extent to which practitioners are relied upon for the accumulation of data. Although relying on information collected by practitioners may be less expensive and threatening to these workers, the possibility of bias is great.

5. *Developing the design.* The design for evaluative studies must take into consideration the purpose of the investigation as well as the nature and goals of the program to be evaluated. Once these considerations have been taken into account in developing an "ideal" design, modifications are often called for because of ethical issues and a host of administrative and political constraints pertinent to the implementation of the design.

In those situations where it is both administratively feasible and relevant to the type of information desired, the model of a controlled experiment represents the ideal design for evaluative studies. It is depicted in the accompanying diagram.[10]

	Before	After	After − Before
Experimental group	X_1	X_2	$d = X_2 - X_1$
Control group	X'_1	X'_2	$d' = X'_2 - X'_1$

To implement this design, two equivalent groups are developed. Equivalence is best obtained through random assignment to experimental and control groups. The "before" measure provides the base line from which change is determined. The experimental group is exposed to the program being evaluated, while the control group is not. At a determined follow-up period, "after" measures are made. By comparing the "before" measures with the "after" measures, it is possible to indicate the changes logically assumed to have been produced by the experimental program.

This controlled experimental design can provide information on: (1) effectiveness—by comparing the difference in outcome between the experimental and control groups; (2) the nature of the program—by monitoring the program and showing how it is actually implemented in practice, particularly in regard to desired outcomes; and (3) efficiency—by purposefully manipulating program components to determine comparative expenditures in time, staff, money, and other resources.

Although the experimental design can yield various types of fruitful information, it is extremely demanding in regard to the preconditions which must be met for its proper implementation. The use of this design assumes that the experimental variable (i.e., the program or treatment) is clearly articulated and operationalized, accessible to manipulation,

---

[10] Samuel A. Stouffer, "Some Observations on Study Design," *American Journal of Sociology* (January 1950), pp. 356–59.

and able to be monitored. It also assumes the existence of clearly defined goals which can be used as a basis for determining the effectiveness of the program.

Even if the purpose of the investigation and the preconditions for employing the experimental design exist, there are formidable obstacles in implementing such an approach for the evaluation of human service programs. Ethical arguments concerning the denial of service have been advanced in opposition to the development of experimental and control groups. Such arguments assume that the service being evaluated is highly beneficial to potential clients and that denying it to some people would be cruel. However, considering the evidence on the outcomes of human service programs, this assumption is not terribly convincing. Rigorously conducted evaluation studies have revealed that such programs do not produce major changes. In this light, there would seem to be some merit in denying or delaying the provision to some people of a service which is of questionable value in order to improve it ultimately. This issue can also be dealt with in another manner. Rather than deny service entirely, the experimental program can be compared with an alternative approach which is administered to a control group.

In addition to difficulties posed by ethical arguments, administrative constraints may prevent the establishment of control groups, since such constraints often make it impossible to use random assignment procedures. Since cases are generally assigned on the basis of geography, the nature of the service seen as needed, or the characteristics of the client, random assignment procedures often necessitate major changes in the delegation of cases to practitioners. Such changes can create havoc in implementing the program (e.g., by having probation officers cover a very wide geographical area). Alternative methods of developing control groups are available. The most common alternative is to establish a control group through matching procedures as this involves the selection of cases which are comparable on variables which seem to have some relationship to the outcome.

6. *Monitoring the program and the research.* Once the research design has been developed and plans for implementing the research as part of the everyday routine of the agency have been arranged, the task of monitoring the project becomes a primary concern. It is not sufficient to initiate a research project and then to assume that the agreed-upon program procedures and data collection arrangements will be closely followed throughout the life of the project. Rather, carefully conducted evaluation research demands that close attention be devoted to a determination of the extent to which the program as well as the research procedures are in fact carried out in accordance with the originally stated plans.

A major reason for monitoring the evaluation project is the common conflict which often develops between the service goals of the program, which require relative freedom to operate, and the demands of research for control. The crucial question here is whether research can be done in settings where a prime concern is the care and treatment of people and where the control of all factors influencing the results may be impractical. Marris and Rein,[11] for example, found that the claims of research and action were hard to reconcile. In a controlled experimental design it is usually necessary for the researcher to act like a snarling watchdog ready to oppose any alteration in program and procedure for fear that it might contaminate the agreed-upon procedures and render the evaluation useless. On the other hand, some writers view the relationship between research and program development as dynamic and reciprocal.[12] In this view, feeding back information from the evaluation to the program in order to affect both the objectives and the procedures is held to be paramount. The extent to which there are controls on the program's operation and feedback of research findings are largely dependent on the purpose of the evaluative study. If information is needed on the ultimate worth of program ideas as a basis for continuation or termination of a particular program, then a controlled situation would be insisted on. And there would only be deliberate manipulation of program variables which have been predetermined for their contribution to the overall experiment. On the other hand, if evaluative research is viewed mainly as an ongoing means for modifying programs, then feedback of information can be provided to change the program.

7. *Utilization of findings.* The ultimate payoff of evaluation research is the incorporation of the research findings into program policies and procedures for the more effective and efficient delivery of services. The degree to which such an aim is accomplished will be largely a function of the extent to which relevant program staff are aware of, involved in, and committed to the research. This leads to our major thesis; the most accurate view of evaluation research is that it is a sociopolitical process involving the application of research methods to an organizational context. It requires a partnership between research specialists and those directly involved in the delivery of program services. Such a partnership should, ideally, be initiated and formalized during the initial planning and negotiating stages and maintained through the conduct of the research to the assessment of the information obtained and the discussion of the implications of the findings for needed modifications in the program. This is not meant to underemphasize the political and

---

[11] Peter Marris and Martin Rein, *Dilemmas of Social Reform* (New York: Atherton Press, 1969), p. 201.

[12] See Edward Suchman, *Evaluative Research,* p. 88; and Howard Freeman and Clarence Sherwood, *Social Research and Social Policy* (Englewood Cliffs, N.J.: Prentice-Hall, 1970), p. 21.

social factors extraneous to the research which will exert a major influence on the manner in which and the extent to which the findings will be used. Nevertheless, a high degree of involvement by the administrative decision makers in the evaluation process should help at least minimally to ensure the relevance and use of the information obtained for the central issues confronting the organization.

Conclusion

This paper has identified and discussed the major components of the evaluation research process. Particular emphasis has been placed on the linkages between each of the stages in the research and the sociopolitical aspects of planning and conducting evaluation research of human service programs. The ways in which relevant parties—practitioners, administrators, and representatives of funding organizations—are actively involved in the research process will, in large part, determine the quality of the information obtained as well as its relevance and utility for improving the human services.

Selected annotated references

KIRESUK THOMAS J., and R. E. SHERMAN, "Goal Attainment Scaling: A General Method for Evaluating Comprehensive Community Mental Health Programs," *Community Mental Health Journal* 4:6 (1968), pp. 443–53.
Kiresuk and Sherman describe the development, use, and scoring of Goal Attainment Scaling.

MAGER, ROBERT F., *Goal Analysis* (Belmont, Calif.: Fearon, 1972).
This is a practical step-by-step guide for reducing abstract statements of objectives to observable, measurable goals.

PROGRAM EVALUATION PROJECT, "Four Ways to Goal Attainment," *Evaluation,* Special Monograph, #1, 1973 (Minneapolis: Program Evaluation Project, 1973).
This special issue of *Evaluation* presents and compares four methods of assessing goal attainment. The methods are Concrete Goal Setting (CGS) by Theodore Bonstedt, goal-oriented Automated Progress note (GAP) by Richard H. Ellis and Nancy Wilson, Goal Attainment Scaling (GAS) by Thomas J. Kiresuk, and Patient Progress Record (PPR) by Gilbert Honigfeld and Donald F. Klein.

SUCHMAN, EDWARD A., *Evaluative Research* (New York: Russell Sage Foundation, 1967).
Suchman's book is an introduction to evaluative research. It discusses types of evaluation, the conduct of evaluation studies, evaluative design, measurements issues, and the relationship between evaluation and program administration.

Chapter 11

THE ENDING PHASE: REFERRAL, TRANSFER, AND TERMINATION

This chapter will deal with three endings of the client-worker relationship: referral, transfer and termination. So often, a worker is deeply concerned about the client only as long as he is involved in the interaction, but when he is no longer the primary professional he may leave the client to find his own way. It should be recognized that how a client-worker relationship ends may be crucial to what the client takes with him in terms of gains. In situations involving nonvoluntary adolescent clients, one cannot help but be struck at the way, in which we make ourselves indispensable at the beginning of our contacts with them; and when they feel they need us most, which is always at the time of termination or transfer, we are often so preoccupied with our own new beginnings either with other clients or with a new setting that we are unavailable to them. Referral, transfer, and termination have three factors in common: (1) some kind of problem identification has brought the worker and the client together for a greater or a lesser period of time; (2) the client is being sent on to a new phase, a new experience, another source of help, leaving the worker behind or being left behind by the worker; and (3) more is involved than simply saying good-bye and wishing everyone well. However, as each of the three tasks is different, they will be discussed separately in this chapter. We will begin with referral.

REFERRAL

Referral is a process that comes into play whenever a client or a service instigator requests our involvement in a situation that falls outside the parameters of our agency's defined services or whenever we define a problem as beyond our expertise or our agency's parameters of service. In its simplest terms, referral means that, rather than explore the situation ourselves, we suggest that someone who has come to us for help should go to another source. Since the request for help has been defined as falling outside our agency's service responsibilities, it is often tempting to see our responsibility as ending when we state this fact to the person who requested our involvement. This is perhaps the end of our responsibility as an agent of a particular bureaucracy. But it is not the end of our professional responsibility. Our professional commitment requires us to assume responsibility not only for our judgments and our actions but for the results of our judgments and our actions. If we hold ourselves out as persons concerned with the struggles of others, with problems of coping, then we must be concerned not only with offering adequate service in connection with those problems that fall within our defined "turf," but also with offering the same skilled help to enable persons to reach the proper source of help. The first step in developing skills in referral is to know what it means to an individual to ask for help either for himself or for others. (The subject of asking for help was discussed in Chapter 7.) That knowledge is crucial in considering referral.

As a way of considering referrals, let us examine again the case example discussed in "The House on Sixth Street." Mrs. Smith came to the neighborhood center to request help with her housing situation. Fortunately, she came to an agency which could offer help not only to her but to all the tenants who shared her problem. Thus, Mrs. Smith's original request came within the agency's parameters of service, and in the process of exploring her request the practitioner was able to redefine the problem so that it became a community organization problem. This resulted in more effective action than would have been taken if the worker had defined the problem as only Mrs. Smith's. But suppose that Mrs. Smith had turned to her Aid to Families with Dependent Children (AFDC) worker (as the only worker she knew) to talk about her problem, and suppose that the worker had pointed out to her that the welfare board already had knowledge of the situation and had reduced the rent it was paying the landlord and that that was all it could do. What would have happened? Or suppose that Mrs. Smith had felt that her AFDC worker really cared very little about her troubles and that she had then gone to a family agency she had heard about, and that the worker there had pointed out that the agency could not offer help in a situation that was primarily between her, the welfare board and the landlord. Is it not conceivable that Mrs. Smith would decide that there was no help for a person in her situation and that all the tenants would have gone on living in the same situation?

Now suppose instead that the worker at the private agency had told Mrs. Smith that she couldn't help with the problem but that she would help find someone who could. Three days later the private agency worker reaches the welfare worker who says she has done all she can and she doesn't know what else can be done. Two days later the worker at the private agency finds out about the service center. The first of the next week, she calls Mrs. Smith and tells her about the center, urging her to go there. By now Mrs. Smith and her children have endured another uncomfortable week, two social workers have said they cannot help, but she has been told that another worker might. How likely is it that Mrs. Smith will again bundle her four children up and trudge out to seek help at this new place?

But suppose that the family worker tells Mrs. Smith that she cannot help directly, but that this does seem to be a very difficult situation for her and her children so she would like to find out who could help. The family worker calls the welfare worker while Mrs. Smith is in the office and learns that the welfare worker cannot help. She asks the welfare worker whether she knows where such help can be sought. She looks up the agencies listed in the agency directory that most communities publish. While Mrs. Smith is still in her office, she finds out about the service center, and calls to see whether it can help and what Mrs. Smith needs to do to get its help. She asks Mrs. Smith whether and when she wants to go there, and arranges an interview time with a worker whose name she gives Mrs. Smith. She shares this information with Mrs. Smith (often writing down names and addresses is helpful), being sure Mrs. Smith understands how to get in touch with the center worker and what the center worker will need to know about her situation. She expresses her interest in seeing that Mrs. Smith gets some help and her understanding that it is hard to be shuffled around from agency to agency before finding anyone who will really listen. She expresses concern that Mrs. Smith get help and urges Mrs. Smith to get in touch with her again if this particular plan does not work out. In this case Mrs. Smith will probably get to the service center. She will also approach the new worker and his demand that she repeat her story once again with some confidence in herself and her judgment in seeking help. Because of the experience she had with the family worker she will expect to be met by a center worker who is concerned. Her quest for help has been met in a way that has furthered her confidence in her capacity to manage her life in a manner more satisfying for her.

We might again examine the experience of driving in a strange city, thoroughly lost, but hoping to work the problem out ourselves rather than stop and ask someone. What happens if we stop and ask someone who reels off complicated, generalized, and vague directions? When we ask him to estimate how far away our destination is, he says "quite a ways" and looks "put off" by our question. How do we feel? Do we decide that we were better off trying it on our own? We have taken the trouble to ask, but we are no further ahead now than before. In fact, we may be worse off because we have now wasted another half hour and feel more confused and less adequate than before.

This example illustrates the problems and principles in referrals. First, we need to recognize that asking for help for ourselves or others is not a simple process. Second, we need to understand that when we decide to talk the situation over with someone else, the time of that decision and the move to implement it is a vulnerable period. It has taken something to get to this point. This short, vulnerable period, in which the client is open to consideration of the work to be done, is all too often followed by despair if something positive and forward moving is not offered.[1] Most people wait until long after they have become aware of a problem before they seek help. They try to solve the problem alone until they become convinced of their inability to do so, so that their sense of capacity to cope has already had enough blows without the worker's telling them that they have again made a mistake by approaching the wrong resource.

The more threatening a problem is to the person asking help, and the more disorganized and confused he is, the less able he is to follow through on complicated directions or to gather up the strength to retell his problem. Any of us who has experienced certain difficulties and been sent to several places before we reached the person who could help (even if our problem was only getting approval to drop one course and add another) can well understand the feeings of frustration or discouragement or anger that come with the demand that we explain our situation over and over again only to be referred somewhere else each time. Maybe our problem was finally straightened out to our satisfaction, but at the cost of considerable time and effort. What would it have meant to us to have had someone pick up the telephone and find out the right place to go and what to do?

Social agencies and the help they offer are complex businesses. It is a testimony to most people's competence that they are able to approach the appropriate agency most of the time. Rather than expect all clients to be able to handle the original request appropriately, we should be surprised that any do so. The worker should treat client confusion and uncertainty as a natural effect of the confusing pattern in which we seem to work.

Our generalized goal for our practice should be that, if we cannot offer active help toward solving a problem, we at least leave the client

---

[1] This principle is the basis of crisis theory and other emergency services which the reader may want to explore but which cannot be developed here.

as well prepared to deal with it as he was when we met him. We should recognize that by holding ourselves out as helping persons and by being in a position that invites or allows the client to approach us, we have engaged in an interaction with him that places a responsibility upon us that is not to be discharged by a simple statement that he has come to the wrong place.

TRANSFER

Transfer is the process by which the client is referred to another worker, usually in the same agency, after the initial worker has been working with the client on the problem. Although the transfer is sometimes made because one worker finds that he has difficulty in working with the problem or the client, usually it occurs because the initial worker is leaving the agency to take a job elsewhere.

In transfer three entities are involved: the present worker, the client, and the new worker. When the client learns that the practitioner is soon to leave the agency, or that for any other reason the worker cannot continue with him, he may feel deserted and resent an ending that is imposed prematurely on him. He may feel that, in leaving, the worker is breaking the contract in which he was offered service and may resent what appears to be the worker's irresponsibility and lack of concern. Many factors may interact to determine the client's reaction. The most important will be the type of client system, the problem, and the type of relationship developed between the worker and the client. For the client whose problem involves internal system changes and who has had life experiences involving painful separations, the worker's departure may evoke all the accumulated pain of the other separations. A task-centered adult group working toward change in the community may also feel a sense of betrayal and desertion but may be more actively concerned about the competence of the new worker who will be involved with them in their work. Unexpected endings are a part of life, and the worker who has made a decision that forces an ending to his association with a client must be aware of his own feelings, the worker who will replace him, and the possible reactions of the client if the experience is to be as positive as possible for the client.

The worker may have difficulty with his own feelings. He may feel that is is indeed betraying the client and violating the contract. He may feel that no other worker can really take his place with the client and may subtly impart this judgment to the client in ways that increase the client's feelings of uncertainty. Leaving the agency can evoke painful feelings of separation in the worker. The worker may also be anxious about the demands of his new job, or so deeply absorbed in these new demands that he does not give the problems of transfer his full attention.

Or all these feelings may churn within him in some complex, interrelated struggle.

The transfer may also pose some problems for the new worker. He may wonder whether he can offer as effective help as did the first worker and may meet the client with a kind of defensiveness and a determination to prove himself rather than continue the work together. He may therefore move out too rapidly with new ideas that the client is not ready for. The client may be angry and hurt about the transfer and because of this, as well as his feelings of loyalty and trust for the first worker, it is often necessary for him to mark some time and do some testing before he is willing to move on. It is to be expected that certain clients will lose much of their trust in the worker and be afraid to risk establishing a new relationship with another person who may also leave. The new worker needs to recognize all these things, especially the right of the client to have his feelings and take the time he needs to deal with them.

A transfer is less hurtful and destructive to the work being done when there is time for both client and worker to deal with it, and for the new worker to get involved in an orderly manner. When a transfer is necessitated by the first worker's leaving the agency, the client often regards it as a desertion. He may feel that if he were important to the worker or, worse yet, if he were a good and satisfying client, the worker would stay with him. Clients need to be told as soon as possible about the worker's leaving, and they need to participate with the worker in the planning for transfer to another worker or, possibly, to terminate their contact with the agency. The feelings clients may have about the change should be recognized by the worker. The worker can invite the client to discuss his feelings. At times, and particularly in group situations, clients can be encouraged to role-play the transfer, from their concern about the first worker's departure through their beginning with a new worker. They can discuss or role-play their fantasies about the new worker.

Clients need opportunities to meet with the new worker. The first time the new worker may just stop in for a minute to be introduced by the old worker and say hello. After he leaves, the worker may discuss with the client what he thinks and feels about the new worker from just this introduction.

The second time, if the client is a group, the new worker may attend a meeting as an observer, or, if the client is an individual or a family, he may sit in on an interview. The old worker remains "in charge," so to speak, and the new worker is just there to get acquainted. At the third encounter the two workers operate as a team, with the new worker gradually assuming the primary professional role. At this encounter the two workers can talk together, trying to assess where they are and how the new worker understands and evaluates the contract, with the client as observer. This helps the client to understand very clearly what the new worker is told about him and what the new worker's commitment is. There might be a fourth, formal session at which the new worker is in charge, but there should be a time at the end of the session for the client and the old worker to meet together (in the absence of the new worker) for good-byes and for assessment both of what has been accomplished by the first worker and of the client's expectations of the second.

If the transfer is being brought about because the client feels that there is a problem between him and the first worker, the situation is different in that it is the client that is leaving the worker. In this situation, the worker needs to carefully examine his own feelings and to be sure that he leaves the client totally free to move on to another relationship.

TERMINATION

Social work intervention is always time-centered. At its best, it is directed toward the realization of goals that are specific enough for progress to be measured in relation to them. In *Social Work with Groups* Helen Northen makes a statement about termination with groups that is applicable to all sizes and types of systems:

> The purposeful nature of social work implies that from time to time it is necessary to assess the desirability of continuing service to the members. The judgment may be that there has been progress toward the achievement of goals and there is potential for further improvement, in which case the service should be continued. Another decision may be that little, if any, progress has been made; if this is combined with little potential for changing the situation, the service should be discontinued. Still another evaluation may be that progress toward the achievement of goals has been sufficient, and the service should be terminated. The social worker has undoubtedly anticipated termination from the beginning of his work with the group and has clarified with the members its possible duration, so that the goals and means toward their achievement have been related to the plans for both individuals and the group. Nevertheless there comes a time when the worker and the members must face the fact of separation from each other and often, also, the end of the group itself.[2]

Evaluation, the appraisal of the progress that worker and client system as a working partnership have achieved, is an ongoing process. The ultimate test of the effectiveness of social work practice is the extent

[2] Helen Northen, *Social Work with Groups* (New York: Columbia University Press, 1969), p. 222.

to which positive movement toward the goals set has been accomplished. Thus the goals as initially developed between client and worker, as periodically evaluated, and as modified periodically by joint agreement become the criteria for evaluating progress. Whenever termination is being considered, a thorough review and evaluation of what has or has not been accomplished and of the processes by which these gains were made or failed to be made, is imperative. In his own, unilateral evaluation, the worker may begin to wonder whether the goals are in sight, and he may be the one to introduce the matter of termination. Or, the client may indicate that he is beginning to believe that he is ready to move on to a new experience and leave the worker behind. This is often communicated to the worker by the client's behavior rather than by verbal discussion. The client begins to miss appointments or indicates with pride that he took some unilateral action toward the goal. These are ways of saying that he can "go it alone."

In talking about the indications for termination in the group, Helen Northen says much the same thing:

> As the group moves toward readiness for termination, there are clues to guide the practitioner in his activities with the group. The goals that members have for themselves and each other have been partially achieved, at least, although movement in the group may have been faster for some than for others. Members come to talk about some of the changes that have taken place in them and in the group. Attendance becomes irregular unless the worker makes special efforts to motivate members to continue until the final meeting. . . . The structure tends to become more flexible; for example, by giving up official roles within the membership or by changes in time, place, and frequency of meetings. . . . Cohesiveness weakens as the members find satisfactions and new relationships outside the group.[3]

The need for termination, whether introduced by the client or the worker, should be discussed well in advance of the termination date to allow sufficient time for this aspect of worker and client experience with each other to be as productive as other parts of work together. To quote Helen Northen once again:

> The time span between the initial information about termination and the final meeting of the group will vary with many factors, including the group's purpose, the length of time the group has been together, the problems and progress of the members, their anticipated reactions to termination, and the press of the environment on them.[4]

These elements should be considered in working with individuals or families. In general the tasks of termination are: (1) working out the conflict

---

[3] Ibid., p. 225.
[4] Ibid., p. 228.

for both worker and client between the acknowledgment of improvement and goal achievement and the movement away from help; (2) working out the fear of loss of the relationship and of the support of a concerned person; (3) examining the experience and recognizing the progress made; (4) considering how this experience can be transferred to other problems as they come along; (5) examining what is involved in stabilizing the gains made; and (6) clarifying the worker's continuing position.

Termination of a relationship has great meaning, and a great investment of emotions and feelings of one person with another entails grief at such a loss. This grief may involve the following typical reactions: (1) the denial of termination (clients refuse to accept the notion of termination and behave as though it were not going to happen); (2) a return to patterns of earlier behavior or a reintroduction as problems of situations and tasks that have been taken care of long ago; (3) explosive behavior in which the client says that the worker was wrong when he thought that the client could go it alone; or (4) a precipitate break in the relationship by the client as though say that he will leave the worker before the worker leaves him.

For the social worker, termination stirs up emotions about both his professional activities and his feeling for his clients. He will undoubtedly feel pleased about the progress which has been made, but, like the client, will feel a sense of loss and grief in the parting. He may find that termination stirs up mixed feelings about the quality of his work: guilt about not having been able to do better; fear of the client's efforts to go ahead on his own.

In the final disengagement, the worker makes clear that the door is open, that he will be available for future problem solving if this falls within his agency's services, and if it does not, that he will help find an agency that is appropriate. He assures his clients of his continued interest in them and of his belief in their ability to move on to other goals and other efforts. It is often well to mark the last contact by some symbol. With a family, group, or organization a party can be helpful. In some instances, a formal letter of accomplishment of goals may be very meaningful.

RECAPITULATION

In this chapter we have discussed three special tasks in social work—referral, transfer, and termination. These are situations in which the worker terminates his relationship with the client. In referral the client's request is considered to be beyond the parameters of the agency's services and the client is referred to others before any significant work on the problem is done. In transfer and termination, the client and the worker have established a relationship over a period of time. We have urged that these three special tasks are important aspects of the social work process and that workers should see them as involving significant skills.

A LOOK FORWARD

In this chapter we have introduced the concept of the limits of the agency's services. In the next we will discuss the agency structure itself, with emphasis on its bearing on the worker's functioning. With the conclusion of this chapter we, too, have been working toward a termination—of the author-reader relationship.

The termination process: A neglected dimension in social work *

Evelyn F. Fox, Marian A. Nelson, and William M. Bolman

The manner in which the therapeutic relationship is brought to a close will heavily influence the degree to which gains are maintained; failure to work through the attitudes and feelings related to the ending of therapy will result in a weakening or undoing of the therapeutic work. The following two examples illustrate this clearly:

A 20-year-old unwed mother had been followed through her pregnancy and delivery by an agency social worker. The mother had great difficulty deciding to give up the baby for adoption so that she could finish college, but she finally did so because of her strong positive relationship with the worker. Soon after she made this decision, the worker told her she would be leaving the agency to get married in several weeks and would not be seeing her anymore; she would transfer her case to another worker. The client appeared to accept this, but that evening attempted suicide by taking an overdose of sleeping pills. The psychiatric resident who saw her after she recovered found a depressed young woman with strong feelings of worthlessness. She said that she had not only lost her baby but had also been abandoned by the person for whom she gave up the baby, the worker. Further discussion revealed that the worker had come to play a part in the patient's life similar to that of the patient's mother in earlier years. After a month's hospitalization and treatment, the patient began to regain interest in school,

* Reprinted with permission of the authors and the National Association of Social Workers from *Social Work,* 14:4, (October 1969), pp. 53–63.

but still refused to return to the agency because of persisting anger and resentment.

. . . . .

A 10-year-old boy had been seen in therapy once a week for a nine-month period by a male clinical psychology trainee because of stealing and disruptive behavior in school. His parents were seen concurrently by a staff social worker at the clinic. These sessions were followed by regular family meetings that involved the boy, his parents, and both therapists. The boy had made remarkable gains by the end of the school term, at which time the trainee was also scheduled to leave the teaching clinic for training elsewhere. During the last family session, the trainee casually announced that this would be his last session because he was leaving the clinic. The boy, who had been actively engaged in the discussion up to this point, withdrew completely upon hearing about the termination. No attempt was made to investigate his feelings or assist him in handling them. The family left the clinic with a silent child and without a return appointment, since treatment was assumed by all to have been successful. As one might predict, the family returned rather disillusioned after several weeks because the boy showed a marked increase in difficult behavior and a renewal of the old symptoms.

Most people would immediately recognize that the reason for treatment failure in the two examples just given was simply improper attention to the termination of treatment. It would be somewhat reassurring to blame this on idiosyncratic reasons such as the worker's insensitivity or failure to apply principles taught in graduate school. However, this defect in practice is a frequent occurrence and is mirrored by a defect in the social work and mental health literature generally.

There are many articles in the social work literature about the importance of initial interviews but virtually none about termination. Unless the subject arises during supervision, it is entirely possible for a social work student to complete training with no exposure to or formal recognition of the importance of this phase of treatment. The result is that there are a large number of social workers practicing in a variety of welfare, adoption, family service, and mental health agencies who lack this awareness. Because the social worker is an especially important key person in the community, a practitioner whose influence for health or disorder is magnified by virtue of his position in relation to needy individuals and families, it can be said that this lack of general awareness of the importance of the termination process presents an important public health problem. The solution must necessarily be intraprofessional and be accomplished both by individual practitioners and by schools of social work.

Because of its sparseness in the literature, the authors have summarized some of the theory about termination. However, the major aim of this paper is to illustrate concretely the various issues and phases of the termination process because this is apt to be more useful for practitioners. Therefore, a clinical example of five therapy sessions will be presented in detail based on observations through a one-way mirror.

Importance of termination

The two examples cited indicate clearly that the manner in which the therapeutic relationship is brought to a close will influence the degree to which gains are maintained. The authors also hope to show that the termination phase may in fact be one of the most significant portions of the whole course of treatment in terms of the work accomplished.

The maintenance of gains achieved during therapy does not need further discussion here. However, the emotional growth accomplished does. A major reason for the importance of termination is the fact that it is a here-and-now experience between client and worker that is affected by earlier experiences related to separation and loss. Mullan and Sangiuliano state:

> Therapeutic termination experience as a transactional event is a unique phenomenon. Its individuality stems from the most basic of all human struggles, the willingness and ability to two or more persons to separate from an intimate and meaningful relationship. Separations are part of the inevitables of existence . . . in any discussion of termination, therefore, it is not only the patient's separating from the therapist which requires attention, but also the therapist's separating from the patient. The therapist's response, experience, and his struggle while terminating are crucial dynamics in the terminal therapeutic process.[1]

Schiff states:

> Of all the phases of the psycho-therapeutic process, the one which can produce the greatest amount of difficulty and create substantial problems for patient and therapist alike, is the phase of termination. It is at this time when the impact of the meaning in affective terms, of the course of therapy and the nature of the therapist-patient relationship is experienced most keenly, not only by the patient but also by the therapist.[2]

In short, it is this reawakening of old losses in the context of a meaningful present relationship that makes the termination phase so useful for the modification of conflicted affects, the development of insights, and other elements of a corrective emotional experience that comprise therapy.

---

[1] Hugh Mullan and Iris Sangiuliano, *The Therapist's Contribution to the Treatment Process* (Springfield, Ill.: Charles C Thomas, 1964), pp. 230–70.

[2] Sheldon K. Schiff, "Termination of Therapy: Problems in a Community Psychiatric Outpatient Clinic," *Archives of General Psychiatry*, Vol. 6, No. 1 (January 1962), pp. 77–82.

There are two major areas that need conceptualization: (1) the major affects involved in separation and (2) the phases in the separation process. Edelson has described three major affective themes in the reaction to termination:

> The theme of narcissism and the response to the narcissistic wound, including panic, rage, and a pervasive sense of worthlessness; the theme of mourning, with accompanying feelings of guilt and grief; and the theme of the struggle toward maturity and independence, including feelings of competitiveness, defiance, envy, jealousy, and the anxiety associated with these.[3]

It is most apt to compare phases in the termination process with phases of "grief work" described first by Freud in 1917 and illustrated by Lindemann's study of persons who lost loved ones in the Coconut Grove fire.[4] The first phase is a period of denial in which the person attempts to ward off either recognition of the loss or important feelings associated with it. The second, a phase that begins when the denial breaks down, is one of considerable emotional expression, usually of grief and sadness but often including anger and expressions of narcissistic hurt. The third phase is a prolonged period in which the reality of loss and the associated feelings of grief and anger are bit by bit worked through in the multitude of current life experiences that bring up memories of the lost person. To the extent that the mourner is able to perform this grief work successfully, he is gradually able to detach or free the emotional ties that are essential for finding new people or interests. There are a number of ways in which the grieving process can be interfered with or arrested. People whose personality structure includes poorly modified ambivalence, narcissism, or the inability to bear strong feelings generally are apt to have special trouble. Because both the worker and client may have these problems, termination can lead to a rich and complex interpersonal challenge for both. Before examining this in connection with a specific case, it is first worth reviewing the usual reasons for termination.

Reasons for termination

This section of the discussion will focus primarily on children because they are most neglected in the literature on termination. Reasons for

---

[3] Marshall Edelson, *The Termination of Intensive Psychotherapy* (Springfield, Ill.: Charles C Thomas, 1963).

[4] Sigmund Freud, "Analysis Terminal and Interminable," *Collected Papers*, Vol. 5 (London, England: Hogarth Press, 1950), pp. 316–57; and Erich Lindemann, "Symptomatology and Management of Acute Grief," in Howard J. Parad, ed., *Crisis Intervention: Selected Readings* (New York: Family Service Association of America, 1965), pp. 7–21.

termination fall into three major categories: those related to treatment itself, those related to the child's family, and those related to the worker.

Treatment-related reasons. Success in treatment is mentioned first only because it is the most desirable reason to terminate therapy. In fact, the authors' experience suggests it is probably the least common reason, at least in training clinics. However, few studies are available, paralleling the scarcity of papers on termination generally, and comparative studies of reasons for termination are urgently needed. The most generally agreed upon point for termination is summarized thus: "Psychotherapists have had to face the question of how "deep" one should go and whether there is ever an end to treatment. The answer Anna Freud proposed was that one need not take a child farther than the position in which all children are at that developmental state."[5] Thus, when a child's personality development shows improvement so that he is functioning at his age and overall organismic endowment level, he may be regarded as "well." There is one major exception to this. If the child's ideal well state is out of focus with the family balance, a compromise will have to be made.

When treatment is terminated because of improvement in the child, one may see modifications in the separation reactions described by Edelson. In the case of an adult, reactions to ending therapy are largely colored by transference. In children, because of their immaturity and dependence, transference elements are less marked and the loss of the worker is perceived more as a real loss. The meaning of this loss then depends on the quality of the relationship. Blanchard has described this well:

> If the therapeutic relationship has had any real meaning for a child, he will naturally have ambivalent feelings in ending it. It is sad to say goodbye to someone who has been loved for a while and to whom one feels grateful, but it is a satisfaction to become independent of help and to be freed from the obligation to keep appointments that sometimes interfere with other interests and activities. Moreover, the child has been brought to the clinic because the parent was dissatisfied with him. If, at the ending, the parent is better satisfied, this adds to the child's happiness in the termination of treatment, which becomes proof that the parent is no longer dissatisfied with him. So, the desirable aspects of ending may well outweigh the regrets.[6]

In older children and teen-agers whose emotional and social development has suffered more serious distortion and for whom the therapeutic process has meant a significant meeting of previously unmet needs, the

---

[5] Alan O. Ross, "Interruptions and Termination of Treatment," in Mary R. Haworth, ed., *Child Psychotherapy* (New York: Basic Books, 1964), pp. 290–92.

[6] Phyllis Blanchard, "Tommy Nolan," in Helen Witmer, ed., *Psychiatric Interviews with Children* (New York: Commonwealth Fund, 1946).

reaction to termination is more like that seen with adults and special knowledge and skill will be required to deal with it. It is worth noting specifically that such children and teen-agers as well as their parents are most heavily represented in clinics and welfare, adoption, and family service agencies, which further highlights the importance of skill in handling termination.

Family-related reasons. Requests that treatment be ended commonly originate from the family. This can be either positive or negative. Often it reflects the fact that the child's functioning now fits with his family and as a result they see him as well, although this has not yet been recognized by the worker. In such a case, it is probably wise for the worker to agree to termination, but to request that the parents permit him to see the child for an additional three or four times to work it through. A second common reason for a family's termination is their leaving the community. Here, too, it is important that the worker have as much time as possible to work on termination with the child. In both situations, however, there are times when the parents' goals for the child are at variance with the goals of the worker and when it appears that the parents' activity is a reflection of parental or family neurosis. The ideal management of this is to shift the focus from individual to family treatment if possible and, if it is not possible, to insist that four to six meetings be left for termination. This is often difficult for workers, particularly if they are new, and is worth stressing because the worker's narcissism can be a complicating factor.

Worker-related reasons. The worker, like the family, may phase out or terminate treatment more because of his own needs than the client's. On a conscious level, he may realize that it is not possible to establish a sound therapeutic relationship and, if the clinic has a long waiting list, he may feel an obligation to treat those clients who seem more amenable to the type of therapy he is able to provide. On a less conscious level, every worker has needs of his own that must be satisfied if he is to provide successful treatment. Ideally, these needs are sufficiently sublimated so that they promote rather than interfere with therapy. However, this is far from being the case with all workers and clients. Therefore, it is ideal if each worker has a clear idea of the kind of clients with whom he cannot work. As mentioned earlier, the worker's narcissistic reaction to termination of therapy is an important issue. When the child does not get well fast enough, when the transference becomes negativistic, or when the family's goals are different from the worker's, the result may be felt as a narcissistic wound and lead to discontinuance of treatment. The concept of the "ideal" patient is familiar to all mental health professionals. While the specific characteristics of such a patient vary with the individual worker, they are derived more from the worker's own needs, for example, the childless therapist who becomes overinvolved with his client, or the frequent occurrences in which the child's conflicts reawaken similar conflicts in the worker. In both cases, treatment will begin to show interference and the child may be terminated prematurely or without adequate attention to the termination. This type of problem occurs frequently enough among workers to be a normal part of professional growth. Therefore, consultative advice can be useful.

There are a number of social factors that estrange the worker and client. When a worker is treating clients of a different social class, he may minimize the impact of certain stresses and be blind to the importance and subtleties of the emotions involved. An especially common form of this is stereotyping the client by assigning him feelings and values believed peculiar to, for example, lower-class persons or Negroes. In doing so, he is engaged in a process that can best be termed "social countertransference."

Another worker-related reason for termination, and probably the one that is most important in terms of statistical frequency, is the worker's leaving the clinic for training or work elsewhere. It is remarkable how universal the tendency is for workers to delay telling the client about this change until a session or two before they leave. In the following case, the social worker knew of the importance of bringing up termination, but found she had great difficulty in doing so. However, her interest and courage were sufficient for her to permit one-way mirror observations of the whole course of termination by two observers.

A process analysis of termination

A 12-year-old girl had been seen once a week by the social worker for four months. She had been referred to the child psychiatry clinic because of symptoms of depression and low self-esteem, overweight, bed-wetting, and recently developed bronchial asthma. During the course of therapy, the symptoms cleared up considerably and the girl felt and acted much improved. However, termination occurred because the worker was leaving the clinic after completing her training. Although treatment might have gone on for several months longer, it was decided that sufficient improvement had occurred to combine the worker's departure with the termination of treatment. The following description of the termination process covers five weekly sessions. It should be noted that the authors have extracted the termination themes from the other material for clarity of presentation. In reality, these themes were intermingled with others, appearing and disappearing during the five hours.

First hour

After ten minutes of discussion about the events of the preceding week (which had been a good week and indicative of the client's improved functioning), Mrs. N (the worker) said that she would be leaving the clinic in June, which gave them five more times to meet together. The client, Amy, asked if she would be seeing someone else. Mrs. N replied by asking whether she thought she needed to continue with another worker. After some hesitation, Amy said she supposed not, if Mrs. N thought it was OK. However, further questions by Mrs. N proved ineffective and Amy became increasingly silent and uncommunicative.

The worker assumed that the silence was the result of thoughts and feelings that were painful for Amy, but she did not know their specific nature. In thinking back to other times in treatment when Amy had reacted this way, she remembered that the meetings at the beginning of treatment has been characterized by many silences. Therefore, she remarked that the silence reminded her of how it had been at the beginning of treatment. Amy nodded and the worker followed up by wondering if it was difficult to talk now like it was then. Amy nodded and said she was feeling kind of shocked. The worker agreed and said: "Yes, in some ways it's hard for me to talk, too, but it's something we both should do." Amy hung her head and began to cry softly. The worker had some trouble with her own wishes to comfort Amy, but confined herself to simply sliding her chair a few inches closer and asking what Amy usually did when she felt sad. Amy replied that she usually just sat and worried instead of getting her feelings out.

Mrs. N wondered if Amy were going to handle her feelings about ending treatment by keeping them inside. With this, Amy talked about feeling "kind of disappointed," but again lapsed into silence. The worker wondered if perhaps Amy felt angry, and Amy again burst into tears after saying, "I wonder why you have to leave now!" However, the worker's further efforts to get Amy to elaborate on this were unsuccessful, and the remaining half hour was spent in rather superficial but friendly talk about a variety of things.

Mrs. N felt this portion of the session was aimless and was not sure she understood what was going on. As Amy left the session, she scrawled a quick sketch of a bomb on the blackboard, which brought the therapist back on target; she said that Amy probably felt like exploding.

Comment.   This interview illustrates many of the issues that arise when termination is first announced. Hiatt states:

> The next interview or two following notice to the patient that termination of treatment is being considered may be as crucial for the long-term results of therapy as are the initial interviews. In the initial interviews, the therapist looks for transference clues in the patient. In the termination process, the patient looks for counter-transference clues in the therapist.[7]

----
[7] Harold Hiatt, "The Problem of Termination of Psychotherapy," *American Journal of Psychotherapy*, Vol. 19, No. 4 (October 1965), pp. 607–15.

The client's question about seeing someone else is, in this context, more a defense against loss than a request for information. Amy's response to the worker's asking her if she needed to see anyone else is also best regarded as defensive instead of being an expression of her insight and recognition of her many gains in therapy. Support for this lies in the many uncomfortable silences that followed her statement that she did not think she needed to see anyone else, but proof was only seen in later visits. Following the worker's linking this silence with a similar defensive state at the beginning of therapy, Amy's denial began to fade, and she recognized that she felt shocked. When the worker then admitted her own feelings, the denial dissolved into tears; at this point the work of termination commenced.

It should be noted that many, if not most, termination processes do not show so rapid and clear a statement of the initial denial, its disillusion, and the expression of grief about loss. In fact, it is suspected that because of the pain and discomfort of the grief about termination, many clients and workers remain in the phase of denial and do not even enter the phase of grieving. The transition in this case may have been facilitated by the worker's frank admission that the idea of leaving was painful for her too.

Second hour

The hour opened with the client playing a trick on the worker. Amy gave Mrs. N a card with a small hole in it and a quarter and asked her if she could push the quarter through the hole. Mrs. N could not do it, whereupon Amy took a pencil, stuck it through the hole, and pushed the quarter with it. The worker laughed and asked if Amy perhaps felt as though her leaving was a trick—a dirty one at that. Amy denied it, but spontaneously mentioned how shocked she had felt at the previous session and told of feeling the same way when a physician who had treated her ended the treatment. "When Doctor S said my treatment was ending, I felt a shock. He saved my life. He really did."

This led to a five-minute digression onto other topics, including a few derogatory remarks Amy made about smoking being bad for a person (Mrs. N had just lit a cigarette). The worker inquired further about Amy's remark because she thought there might be other feelings behind it. It then developed that Amy had never liked Mrs. N to smoke but could not tell her so. This again led to thoughts of Amy's ending therapy, and she decided that they had gotten some work accomplished. One comment was: "Now I take a bath because I'm dirty, not because I wet the bed." She also said that her sprained leg was better. Mrs. N knew this had little to do with Amy's psychotherapy. She suspected there was an implied criticism of her in the remark, that is, that this was another instance of Amy's difficulty in handling and expressing feelings of hurt, anger, and resentment. An opportunity came just before the hour ended, when Amy complained in a hurt manner that in games she was always the last one chosen. The worker suggested that perhaps it would be a good thing to see what they could do to help with these feelings. Amy wondered where they should start, and Mrs. N reminded her of what they had done about her bed-wetting.

Comment. In this interview one can see that the termination work had indeed begun. As was anticipated from the end of the previous hour and from knowledge about Amy's earlier difficulty in handling sadness and anger, she showed more signs of defensive avoidance than of adaptive modification. Sadness over the loss and its importance to Amy can be inferred from her comments about the doctor who saved her life and her shock when he ended treatment. Anger was indirectly expressed by the trick and her remarks about Mrs. N's smoking and about homework. It was, however, encouraging to note that anger and hurt were not simply repressed and denied, but were permitted some expression, which indicated that these feelings were not entirely unacceptable to her. Similarly, both sadness and anger can be seen in Amy's report of what she had gained from therapy and in her comment on being the last one chosen. It seems a short step from this to her feelings of being unlovable (low self-esteem was one of the presenting complaints) and to the fantasy that she was being left by the worker because she was bad, unlovable, and not worth choosing. This may well have underlain Amy's plaintive statement in the first termination hour: "I wonder why you have to leave me now!"

Third hour

Amy came to this hour bringing a camera and said she would like to take a picture of Mrs. N in front of the building. Mrs. N asked if she could take a picture of Amy at the same time. Amy agreed with obvious pleasure and they agreed to take pictures of each other at the end of the hour. The worker remarked: "Sounds like you're preparing for the ending of treatment," and Amy agreed. "How does it feel?" Mrs. N asked. Amy said she was excited by it. "Why?" "Oh, I express myself a lot more now." Amy continued by giving two examples from the past week in which she had been much more assertive with her parents. From the observer's view, she also looked as though she felt more comfortable and self-assured than before.

Mrs. N said it was indeed nice to hear about the good things, but she wondered if there were still some not-so-good things. Amy agreed she still had some of those feelings, but declined to talk about them and instead gave other examples of how well things were going. However, this led to some fifteen minutes of long silences, awkwardness, and talk of school and friends; the worker again felt confused about what was going on. Finally, as Amy was tapping on her knee and looking out the window, Mrs. N said it looked like she felt restless and was ready to stop. Amy agreed, saying she was looking forward to taking pictures.

The worker asked if there were other reasons and, to her surprise, Amy said: "Well, yes, I'm kind of worried about Laurie; she's not eating and is sick." (Laurie was her only sibling, aged 4. Another sister who would have been two years younger than Amy died suddenly of pneumonia when Amy was 5. This tragedy was still incompletely resolved in the family and mention of it still evoked tears. Amy often named dolls and pets after her dead sister.) Although the worker was momentarily at a loss about Amy's concern over a sick sister, she quickly associated it with threat of losing her and asked Amy directly how it would be if Laurie were not here and there were just Amy and her parents. This remark proved to be on target, although Mrs. N had in fact skipped several steps in arriving at the question. Amy said "Terrible!" and instantly became tearful.

When asked if she often thought about Laurie's dying, Amy said, "It's too hard to think about," blew her nose and, in response to being asked how she felt, said: "It makes me kind of mad that you make me talk about it." (After the session Mrs. N said she was feeling rather upset at having provoked such an upset but retained her objectivity enough to continue to be empathically curious about the degree of Amy's tearfulness.) Therefore, she said: "Sure, but I thought you said *you* were thinking about it with Laurie's sickness." Amy rather grudgingly admitted that she used to tell Laurie she wished she would die, but she did not know how awful that was, and went on to tell about a friend of hers who was an only child and who was unhappy. The worker only needed to express her interest and Amy began to talk about when "we first got Laurie, I got to hold her first." This in turn led to how it soon became "icky" because the baby received so much attention. It was then that Amy's daydreaming became noticeable. She and the worker then talked about her use of daydreaming to avoid upsetting feelings before they left to take pictures of each other.

Comment. This interview illustrated graphically the importance of the termination process in therapy. All of the meaningful material about Laurie had never come up before. Its emergence at this time almost certainly occurred because the feelings evoked by Mrs. N's departure reawakened old guilt-ridden death wishes. Amy's talk about wishing Laurie dead, how awful that was, and how unhappy her friend was who was an only child, undoubtedly played a significant role in her low self-esteem and inability to manage feelings of anger. This hour also illustrated how easy it would have been for both the client and worker to avoid this topic altogether. It took considerable persistence by the worker to get through the quarter hour of confusion and restlessness that signaled Amy's inner defensive struggle. Mrs. N was quite surprised at the material that emerged because she thought Amy's restlessness had to do mainly with her impatience to take the pictures. The exchange of pictures seems to be a worthwhile development in termination when it arises in children who are otherwise working well on the termination process. Ideally, it reflects the fact that the child has accepted the impending loss of a real and important relationshp and wishes to have a concrete memento of it. However, this is not intended to mean that all picture-exchanging is "normal" and exempt from the worker's need to evaluate the underlying motives when the picture-taking appears to be serving defensive purposes.

Fourth hour

Amy opened the session by saying that the pictures they took after the previous session were not ready yet. Following this there was a period of sporadic conversation, small talk, and silence. Mrs. N unsuccessfully attempted to get Amy back to the issues of the previous hour. Amy said she had mixed feelings in talking about them. It was just like her feelings about Mrs. N's leaving. At first she felt upset and angry, but then she was not angry, she just felt it was an unpleasant thing to think about. The worker asked how she handled such mixed feelings and Amy replied: "I look at them, take the best, and forget the others. Getting mad only gets you in trouble." She again got restless and fidgety and said: "It's kind of funny, partly I feel like we're finished, and partly I feel like there's things we haven't got to yet." She then went on to tell Mrs. N that she had bought a new troll (a type of doll). The worker asked, "What's he like?" "He's lazy, disgusted, can't be pleased, and doesn't know what to do," Amy replied. She added in a tone of surprise, "Why he's like me!" Mrs. N grinned in approval and asked Amy to tell her more about the doll. Amy talked animatedly about the trouble the doll had with friends. Through talking about the doll, she revealed that she felt caught in a vicious cycle; if she made friends, she got angry when she lost out in conversation or games, and if she expressed this anger, she lost her friends. In short, she lost both ways. This led straight back to the problem she had with the worker. If she told Mrs. N how hurt and angry she felt at her leaving, she was sure the worker would not see her the next time. Mrs. N was moved by this, told Amy that she would continue to be caught in such a vicious cycle if she could not try to express her feelings and asked her to try. Amy stood up with tears in her eyes and walked out of the session.

Comment. This session shows yet another step in the therapeutic process made by this inhibited girl in a response to the frustration and pain she felt about losing the social worker. It seemed as though she improved in her capacity to tolerate disagreeable thoughts and feelings, as evidenced by her admitting she first looked at the feeling and then decided not to act on it. In other words, the inhibition was not at the receptive end (inability to recognize anger because of regression or other defenses), but at the effector or motor output end (choosing to suppress expression of conscious anger). At the effector end, inhibition is more conscious and therefore more available for change. By pointing this out and then asking the client to try expressing her feelings, the worker was showing her own positive countertransference feelings. In effect she was saying, "It's OK to jump, I'll catch you." She should have examined more the client's fear of acting out her anger, that is, the conscious reasons for inhibiting the expression of her feelings. This approach might have led to some discussion of the client's projection of her anger onto others. Thus, her fear of the worker's not seeing her if she got angry is more a statement that if she let herself get that angry, she would not want to come back to see Mrs. N. This in turn could have led back to the whole area of anger and the narcissistic entitlement that maintains it. Mrs. N could only hope that the client's walking out was a healthy sign, since in fact she could not tell until the next and final appointment.

Fifth hour

Amy opened this hour by talking a great deal about her activities and friends. School was ending, and some children were feeling sad about saying gooobye, but she did not mind. "It's not like next fall is forever." Several children were leaving altogether; one was moving out of town. In the midst of the euphoric reportage of how great everything was, Amy said that the pictures they took of each other were "almost ready. I'll have to mail them to you since . . . Dad remembered it took time." Despite the near-mention of this being their last session, she kept talking excitedly and told Mrs. N that many women in her neighborhood were expecting babies. "It's really a mess. Some of them get morning sickness. Laurie got carsick and threw up. That's another mess." Then she returned to talking about school and saying goodbye. Up to this point Mrs. N had only said "Hi" when Amy came in fifteen minutes before. However, at this point she asked: "No more tests, either? You're all done?" Amy's euphoric flight ceased and she said, "Yeah. Here too." Mrs. N asked how she felt about it and Amy replied: "Why did it have to end so soon?" Mrs. N said she felt that way too and Amy began to cry softly. (Both observers felt that the worker should have asked her what it was she hoped to get from the treatment. In discussion following this session, Mrs. N said she had exactly the same thought but did not want to tell Amy the things that had not been done.) The worker let Amy cry a minute and then asked if the changes Amy had noticed (expressing her feelings, being more assertive with her parents, and not wetting the bed) had continued. Amy said they had and that she guessed she was better. Mrs. N asked, "Then why is crying so bad?" and Amy replied, "Because when you cry you have to remember why you're crying." She cried a bit more and when Mrs.

N tried to explore whether Amy remembered walking out of the last hour, she said she did not remember.

Shortly afterward, Amy told Mrs. N she would like to do something other than talk and got out a monster card game. As they played, both surrepitiously looked at the clock. After the game ended, Amy said she would like to leave a few minutes early to pick up a bottle of asthma pills. Mrs. N asked about her asthma attacks and learned that they were much better.

Mrs. N told Amy what had been said in the family conference—that summer is a good time to let things settle into place—to see how things go and how one feels. Should there be the need, she could always come back. Amy sat dejectedly, then got up and both of them left the room. At the hall exit they exchanged addresses, Amy cried again, hugged Mrs. N, and left.

Comment. There were a number of issues that were evident in this final session. The most visible (probably because of the observers' empathic identification with the worker and client) were the many evidences of the affects of separation. Amy's rapid and euphoric monologue was mainly a defense—a denial of the sadness associated with loss. This, however, appeared to be nearly conscious, since she immediately recognized her sadness when the worker spoke about exams being over. The wish to play a game and leave early were partly defensive and partly coping—the latter being her wish not to dissolve (regress) into helpless tears (dependency). Mrs. N correctly respected these feelings because of this element of independence and mastery. Her aim was to steer a middle course between an inhibition of feelings (as the client did early in therapy and termination) and too great an expression of the infantile component of grieving (which would be damaging to the client's newly emerging sense of self-worth and competence).

Although the observers felt that Mrs. N handled this session with her usual competence (other than the obvious failure to ask the client what she had wanted from treatment that she had not got), it was interesting to find that the worker felt she had lost her professional role at times and made a number of mistakes. The authors view this as being exactly the type of feeling that has led professionals generally *not* to report on or study the termination process.

Summary

The termination phase of therapy is, like the beginning phase, singularly important. Whereas the beginning phase often determines the quality of the therapeutic alliance that develops, the termination phase determines the degree to which therapeutic gains are maintained or lost. Also, it often proves to be an extremely productive period for therapeutic work because of the strong feeling stirred up by the forthcoming loss of the worker. A review of the social work and child psychiatry literature revealed a striking absence of attention to this essential phase of treatment. In child psychiatry, the process of termination is taught as a part of case supervision, but this is less apt to happen in social work. This deficiency in the social worker's training is heightened by the fact that social workers will encounter many people whose problems include disturbed human relationships and consequently there is likely to be trouble in ending the relationship.

The major reason for this absence of professional attention seems to be the general sensitivity to loss and separation. The feelings it reawakens in both the worker and client are often strong, painful, and conflict laden. In other words, the authors are suggesting that the gap in the literature is a reflection of the worker's defensive processes against the affects involved in termination—a sort of institutionalized repression. Although defense against affect is common in our culture, in our professional work it is a public health hazard.

From the writings related to other types of loss it is possible to identify the major affects that cause trouble. There are (1) sadness or grief over the loss, (2) anger at the worker for leaving (or at the self for leaving or being able to be left), and (3) narcissistic wounds based on disappointed expectations. Further, it is possible to describe three phases in the management of these affects that constitute the termination processes. They are (1) an initial denial or other defense against the reality of the impending loss, (2) a period of emotional reaction and expression of sadness, hurt, and anger, and (3) a working through of these feelings, so that both the worker and client can go about their respective lives and participate in new relationships with a minimum of unfinished business. Finally, in order to contribute to the scanty descriptions available in the literature, the authors have presented an extended clinical vignette of one case, which showed the process of termination.

Selected annotated references

NORTHEN, HELEN, *Social Work with Groups* (New York: Columbia University Press, 1969).
This group work text is a good addition to the reading list of any social work student, but it is listed here because the chapter on termination is superb.

PANTER, ETHEL, "Ego Building Procedures That Foster Social Functioning," *Social Casework* 47:3 (March 1966), pp. 139–45.
Preparation and accompaniment are useful techniques to help clients confront new situations constructively.

Chapter 12

THE NATURE OF TEAMWORK

In this chapter we are moving from the consideration of the worker-client system of interaction to the consideration of the interaction of the social work practitioner with other professional, or with paraprofessional, practitioners. In working with the client system, a practitioner often becomes aware that members of that system are also being served by other helping institutions of the community. Or it may be that in the role of broker (discussed in Chapter 9) the worker becomes aware of the need to link his clients with various services they may require but which he cannot supply. Or it may be that a service the worker is able to offer, such as the care of children away from their homes, requires him to become part of a team in order to supply that service effectively. (In the care of children away from their homes the social worker will of necessity be involved either with foster parents or with the child care personnel of an institution.)

In any case, *one* important skill of social work practice is the capacity to operate as a productive member of a "service team." The following concepts and methods, which we believe are important to the notion of teamwork, will be discussed in this chapter: the problem of competition, the problem of professional and agency culture, and the problem-solving approach to teamwork and methods of planning and sharing.

THE PROBLEM OF COMPETITION

When helping persons, groups, or organizations attempt to work together on a common problem shared by a common client system, there are both cooperative and competitive elements in the relationship between the helpers. Cooperative work requires that we disclose our relationship with our client to another helping authority who is valuable because he brings a different knowledge, role and function to the helping process. This means we must be willing to cross barriers of difference. This is not so easy. One is constantly amazed at the subtle, and sometimes not so subtle, ways practitioners compete in professional interaction whose stated purpose is cooperation. In most agencies and professional associations there are infinite possibilities of competitive behavior: "I understand the needs of those children better than the foster mother or the teacher"; "My work is more central to the client's welfare than yours"; "My supervisor knows more than your supervisor"; "My agency or my job is where the action really is."

The prevalence of competition in areas in which it is inappropriate, and even destructive to the rational interests of the competing individuals, has been highlighted by experiments in game theory. Game theory is a discipline that seeks to obtain understanding of the problems of human interaction and decision making by studying human exchange from the perspective of strategic games. One game that games theorists use in many different forms is the "non-zero-sum game." Its purpose is to determine under what conditions players will cooperate. In contrast to win-lose games, where there is a winner and a loser, these games are so structured as to make it absurd to play uncooperatively. A player who fails to cooperate has no chance of winning and considerable chance of losing. Nevertheless, researchers in the area of human cooperation are always struck by the frequency with which uncooperative play predominates and, even more surprising, by the frequency with which the play becomes even more competitive as the games go on, and players experience the full negative effects of competition. It is almost as though, once caught in a win-lose situation, the players cannot extricate themselves even though it is demonstrated that it is a destructive situation. And, in social work practice, the most unfortunate aspect of competitive interrelationships of practitioners is that it is the client who is damaged by them. Perhaps social workers are especially vulnerable to competitiveness because it is their status and authority that are involved and the client's welfare that is at stake.

Game theorists have sought to explain this behavior and to isolate variables that will determine how a player will behave. As a result of their efforts players have been classified into these categories: (1) the maximizer, who is interested only in his own payoff; (2) the rivalist, who is interested only in defeating his partner and is not concerned with the result of the game itself; and (3) the cooperator, who is interested in helping both himself and his partner. There have been studies of non-zero-sum games under conditions in which communication between players was impossible and under conditions in which it was encouraged. Improved communication seemed to increase cooperation only in the case of the cooperators, who were already interested in bettering the results for both sides. It failed to change the behavior of the maximizers or the rivalists.[1]

It is possible for a practitioner to work toward changing a "maximizer" (one interested only in his own gain) or a "rivalist" (one only interested in "being one up" or in "putting others down") into a "cooperator" (one interested in helping both himself and his colleagues to aid the client) by the kind of climate he establishes in his professional conferences and associations. For example, the practitioner can actively recognize the importance of each team member in the execution of a task. Child care staff, who often carry the heaviest burden of the daily stress of living with and loving disturbed and deviant children, often find that their efforts go unrewarded by the professional staff, who may assume that they are the only ones who *really know* what the child is like or what he needs. In a conference where a helping person risks proposing a change in a particular way of working, it becomes critical whether he is rewarded for having attempted something worthwhile or whether his suggestion is seen as something for someone else to "top" or "negate." Rivalists often spend a great deal of time developing verbal ability and skill in the use of professional language. They often use this ability and skill to make the point that anyone who risks a new suggestion really doesn't understand the underlying dynamics or he would not be so naive as to make the proposal. This is a cheap way to be "one-up," if that is what is sought. It demonstrates superior knowledge and sophistication at absolutely no cost as the one who is "put down" seldom challenges the negative predictions for fear that they might prove true, thus further revealing his ignorance. Such challenges are especially difficult to contend with when they are presented in elegant professional language and with a knowing air. In such a situation the cost is borne by the person who risks making a proposal and by the client system involved.

THE PROBLEM OF PROFESSIONAL AND AGENCY CULTURE

Effective collaboration requires that helping persons demonstrate respect and trust, expectation and acceptance, in their interactions. The discussion of how respect and trust are demonstrated in the helping relationships also has relevance to professional working relationships. We are all taught the importance of accepting and respecting clients, but we seldom examine what this means when applied to colleagues.

---

[1] Morton D. David, *Game Theory* (New York: Basic Books, 1970).

To work effectively together, to have meaningful exchange, one somehow has to respect the position from which the other acts. The worker who is involved in work across professional agency lines must be perceptive and understanding about the point of view of the other organizations and their professional staff. One mark of a profession is its value system. An important part of all professional education and staff development is the attempt to socialize workers to their agency and their profession (note our chapter on "Values in Social Work Practice"). By this we generally mean working toward the internalization of the values and culture of the profession so that the professional person in whom this process has taken place is constrained to work in certain ways and to take certain positions. This is critically important as protection to the client system, since in the helping process the worker must use himself and his judgment. There is no way another can dictate to the worker exactly how he will use himself to carry out any specific action in any specific situation. Therefore, the only assurance we have that a professional person really can be trusted with his professional tasks is that he acts on the basis of deeply internalized feelings and judgments that stem from his professional values and knowledge. This is the only meaningful protection we have in using a professional's services. However, internalization of our own professional values and culture as the "right" way for us is usually an unconscious process. Internalization can cause tremendous problems in interagency collaboration unless we become aware of our values and culture as our beliefs and our climate and learn to recognize that others have their values and their culture.

In addition to undergoing a process of professional socialization and identification, professional social workers (and members of other professions as well) as a rule work within established institutional settings. The machinery through which they do their work sets boundaries to the ways in which, for practical purposes, they define the problems with which they work. Also, within these institutional settings a professional subculture grows up which, like all cultures, has its own value system and accepted ways of operating. A worker who is engaged in collaborative work with persons outside of his own agency needs to care about his agency and be a part of it and yet to have the capacity to step out of this culture in order to be analytical about it. He needs to be understanding of what is going on in his own agency and yet not be trapped within a particular way of approaching problems. He needs to be able to recognize that other workers have an equal identification with their agencies and an equal need to protect the functioning of those agencies. The social and helping services in the community, their organization and ways of working, must be understood if we are to utilize their services effectively in the service of our clients. Specialized conceptions of how people in need act, or should act, and how they should be helped, guided, or treated can result in bitter rivalry and conflict.

In speaking of "Fragmentation in the Helping Professions," Lawrence Frank writes:

> For example, a family may in its varied contacts receive professional care, advice, and services from a physician, a nurse, a social worker, a nutritionist, a home economist, a probation officer, a lawyer, or judge, a clergyman, a psychologist, a teacher, a guidance counselor, an industrial relations advisor, a banker, a group worker, etc., each of whom may give that family irreconcilable advice and treatment, guidance in how to live, keep health, maintain a home and family, care for and rear children, resolve family discord, and all other aspects of living, especially human relations. The family is expected to resolve these professional conflicts, to reconcile these incongruities, and often mutually contradictory advices into a coherent, consistent pattern of living, a reconciliation which the professionals will not or cannot attain.[2]

In that same article Frank writes:

> Thus students in medical school, nursing, social work, law, engineering, business, architecture, public administration and the graduate departments of the social sciences and humanities are being inculcated each with a different conception of human nature, of human conduct, with different beliefs, assumptions, expectations about people, what and how they act and carry on their human relations. All of these students are going out to practice in our communities, with what Veblen once called the "trained incapacity of specialists" unable to communicate or collaborate in their practice or even to recognize what other specialists see and do. Indeed, we often find bitter rivalry and open conflicts arising not entirely from professional competition but from these very different beliefs and expectations, these specialized conceptions of how people act, or should act and how they should be treated, guided and helped when in need.[3]

THE PROBLEM-SOLVING APPROACH TO TEAMWORK

How does one define the concept of teamwork? The dictionary defines it as the "cooperative effort of an organized group to achieve a common goal."[4] This definition seems to refer us to some of the concepts of problem solving. It seems to require that team members see the payoff

---

[2] Lawrence K. Frank, "The Interdisciplinary Frontiers in Human Relations Studies," *Journal of Human Relations,* Fall, 1954.

[3] Ibid.

[4] *The American Heritage Dictionary of the English Language* (New York: Houghton Mifflin, 1973), p. 1321.

in the honest attempt to identify the most appropriate actions and resources which they can supply to help the client. Thus the purpose of coming together as a team is not to "win" one's way or prove one's "rightness" but to utilize the different capacities brought by the different members of the team in order to expand our knowledge and our range of skills so that we can offer the client the best of service in the direction that the client wishes to go. Teamwork requires that we keep this direction clearly before us as the reason we are together. In teamwork it is essential to recognize that we are trying to build interagency organizations and/or professional teams that function effectively in the interest of the client and the goals he desires to attain. We need to function in the interests of the job to be done. We need to keep a problem-solving focus so that we can communicate around a defined task. Our own problems of communication and relationship must be worked out so that we can offer the client the most effective help possible.

METHODS OF PLANNING AND SHARING

In working with the client system, the worker has come to the conclusion that he cannot offer all the service the client needs or that he may need some help in thinking through what he sees as important factors in service. What does the worker do? The first thing he may want do is to discuss this with his supervisor in order to check out his thinking, and his knowledge of where he might turn for help. The second important step is to talk with the client about how he sees this notion. The worker may present this to the client as something that must be done in light of the nature of the problem, the goals sought, and the limits of service (for example, he may tell a parent who needs to place his child about foster home services and the necessary work with the foster mother), or he may present it as something on which he and the client can come to a decision (for example, the worker may say that his understanding and assessment of the situation might be helped if he could discuss the problem with the psychiatrist on the agency staff).

In beginning a working relationship with other helping persons toward offering his client better service, the worker has the choice of asking the client whether he wants to join the worker in his conferences and planning or whether he assumes that the worker should carry this role alone. Practitioners working jointly with a client seem to have developed a pattern of meeting together privately in order to pool their observations and knowledge of the problem and to come to some understanding of how to proceed. Sometimes clients are told about this meeting, and sometimes they are not. Sometimes the possibility of such a meeting is used as a threat to clients. It is our position that clients should be actively involved in consideration of the way different professionals can   .

be used to help with their problems and that clients must be told about all professional consultations involving them. We would much prefer to offer our clients the opportunity to come with us to meetings with other professionals and to participate in the deliberations so that they may understand what is involved and that they may speak for themselves.

In any case, before approaching another resource, the worker should talk with the client about that resource, about how it may be used, about what it can offer, about why it is suggested at this point, and about what is involved in getting in touch with it and utilizing it. The client should understand what will need to be shared with the other agency. The street gang that the practitioner has been working with as an unattached worker may be very anxious and concerned when the practitioner suggests that an organized agency could offer them a meeting place and opportunities for recreation. What is the worker going to have to tell the agency about them? Will the agency invite them in if it knows about their behavioral history? Is the agency going to try to run them? The parents of an angry, acting-out daughter will have similar questions if foster home placement is suggested as a temporary measure to help both child and parents think things out. Will the foster parents need to be told that the girl steals? What will the foster parents expect of them? Under what conditions will they be able to see their daughter? To take her home? How can foster parents help when they, her own parents, have failed?

The client and the worker will need to discuss how the new service will be contacted and involved in their affairs. The expectations and requirements of the new service vis-à-vis the client will need to be carefully gone into and understood. What will be shared about the client will need to be considered. It is usually helpful to ask the client what he thinks the agency will need to know or should be told about him.

What does one share with another agency about his client? One shares with team members what they need to know in order to work with the client toward solution of the problem in the way the client and you have decided it will need to be worked out. The problem of sharing information with others is not a simple one. When we do this type of sharing we are inevitably confronted with the question of how the other person will use the information in the interests of the client? Social workers who place children in foster homes are often conflicted about what to tell foster parents about the children placed with them. And what information about the natural parents do they share? We have a need to present our clients (parents and children) in a positive light— yet how much information can be kept secret when foster parents and children live intimately as a family? There is no ideal answer to this question. However, one principle that is essential in approaching it is to keep the client system aware of what is being shared and why.

When more than one worker is involved with the same client system, the best device we have for joint planning and joint monitoring of our work is the case conference. The client should be told about these conferences and their outcome. As stated earlier, it is very productive to give some thought to the client's involvement in such conferences. The questions one must ask in deciding this are, Will attending the conference help the client in his analysis of the problem? Will it help give him a sense of being in control of his own destiny? Or is the conference likely to make him feel overwhelmed by professionals and by the problems they see in the situation? Will the decisions being made demand specific behavior of the client, or are they primarily decisions related to agency policies and parameters of service? Is it possible for the client to provide meaningful input into the conference?

In order to work together successfully with a client, the practitioners involved usually need to meet together at least once. There is no substitute for this meeting, and lack of time is not an adequate excuse. Having served as practitioners in large public agencies and carried large case loads, the authors must admit to violations of this principle. However, the fact that something isn't done does not negate its importance. We hope that workers will adopt this as a desirable way of working even if they can't follow through in all cases. Letters and telephone calls are an unsatisfactory substitute for at least one face-to-face planning session around a particular case. In each case conference someone must take the position of chairman. The chairman takes the responsibility for seeing that all agencies and persons involved in the case are included in the conference, for defining the purpose and focus of the conference, for seeing that everyone present is heard, for clarifying the plans of action and who is to do what and when, and for helping to resolve any conflicts. The conference should result in group acceptance of the part each agency is to play. This is facilitated by recording the conclusions of the conference before its termination. Thus everyone has a chance to correct the common plan, and later everyone receives a copy of it. Each agency then carries the responsibility for following through on the plan (which can be seen as a design for coordination) or for pointing out the necessity of changing it. The chairman should also have the responsibility of seeing that the plan is implemented by each agency involved. He, in effect, becomes the "Captain of the Treatment Team." Who is to serve in this role and how he is to be selected should be decided before the team actually begins the action phase of the work with the client. The assignment of this responsibility is an allotment of power and authority. The problems involved in accepting such a position must be considered in this light. There should be a clear focus on the purpose of the conference and drifting away from that focus should be limited. If there are problems of working relationships between the members of the team, these should be approached as problems-to-be-solved and worked through to some acceptable conclusion or they will distort the team's relationship to the client.

RECAPITULATION

In this chapter we have discussed the problems of teamwork in the interests of offering the client system more adequate help in their problem solving. We have discussed the aspects of competition that may be involved and the problem of professional and agency culture, and we have suggested some of the things that go into establishing a team.

A LOOK FORWARD

For further consideration of teamwork in social work practice, we refer you to the readings that follow. In the next chapter we will take up the meaning to the worker of the fact that he works within an agency structure.

Dynamics of teamwork in the agency, community, and neighborhood*

Ralph M. Kramer

Perhaps it is because teamwork—whatever it may connote—is often regarded as "everyone's business" that it frequently becomes nobody's business. While continuous and specialized leadership in this task is indispensable, there seems to be a growing recognition that every direct service agency and its administrative components—executive, staff, and board—all have some responsibility in this sometimes nebulous process of achieving teamwork. This implies that no one group in the agency or community has a monopoly on the responsibility for teamwork, and that no group can consistently evade its own responsibility.[1]

* Reprinted with permission of the author and the National Association of Social Workers from *Social Work*, 10:3, (July 1965), pp. 56–62.

[1] For a development of this point of view, see Ray Johns and David F. De Marche, *Community Organization and Agency Responsibility* (New York: Association Press, 1951), pp. 6–7, 81–83.

Need for interagency teamwork

There are at least four major forces accounting for the greater need for and emphasis on teamwork today: (1) the increasing number of public and private agencies; (2) the continuous development of a wide range of community services; (3) the growth of professional specializations; (4) the emerging awareness of the basic unity of all health, welfare, and recreational agencies. As a result, it has been estimated that a typical youth-serving agency would be involved in various co-operative relationships with at least eighteen different community agencies as they affect more than a dozen different aspects of its program.[2] Nevertheless, it is not easy to overcome the compartmentalization of much of our services today, so often agency-centered instead of community-centered. For this reason, the argument for really effective teamwork must begin with recognition and acceptance of the following six principles which might constitute a creed:

1. We are all members of a single, inclusive profession of social work united by a common philosophy and objective—to help people attain satisfactory personal and social goals.
2. We are all concerned with the same human needs and problems.
3. We all share a common body of specialized knowledge which is applicable to these problems.
4. We all have a common core of basic professional methods, skills, and processes which are applicable in our dealings with individuals, groups, and communities.
5. We all share certain fundamental concepts such as the right of self-determination of individuals and groups; the importance of a non-judgmental attitude; the recognition of causal factors in behavior, and the confidential nature of any material exchanged dealing with our work.
6. We are on common ground in that we serve the same community and the people in it, and therefore we can make a more significant contribution if we work together than if we work independently.

So far, we have been concerned with teamwork between social agencies. This is, however, only one-half of the picture. If such co-operative relationships are to be fully effective, they must not be restricted to agency executives and staff members only but must involve citizens in the community served. There is, therefore, teamwork between agencies of all sorts, and teamwork between these same agencies and representatives of the community they serve. This is represented structurally, for example, in the differences between a council of social agencies,

---

[2] Harleigh B. Trecker, *Group Process in Administration,* 2nd ed. (New York: The Woman's Press, 1950), p. 136.

a community welfare council, and a community or neighborhood co-ordinating council.

A council of social agencies involves only representatives of the health, welfare, and recreation agencies and covers the area of an entire city. A community welfare council has a broader membership base and embraces all operating agencies, governmental and voluntary, and includes many community groups and citizens' organizations which are interested in adequate services. A community or neighborhood co-ordinating council is built upon the interest of citizens in a small locality and is concerned with any problem which arouses concern in the neighborhood.

The concept of teamwork

It may be helpful to conceive of teamwork in terms of a continuum with seven stages: (1) acquaintance, (2) exchange of information (communication), (3) consultation, (4) referrals, (5) planning and co-ordination, (6) concurrent co-operative service, (7) joint operating responsibility.

As can be seen, these co-operative relationships increase in intensity and complexity as we proceed from (1) to (7). Individually and in combination it is suggested, these seven relationships are the referents of the term "teamwork."[3]

Before examining some of the barriers and blocks to teamwork, we should note some of the prerequisites for any one of these seven levels of co-operative relationships. Certainly it is expecting too much of agencies that do not have any teamwork within their own staff to participate meaningfully with other groups. Consequently, *intra-agency teamwork* in the form of adequate communication and recognized channels of authority would seem to be a precondition. In addition, it would be necessary for the agency to have a clear conception of its function and relationship to other community groups, and for its staff to be familiar with this. Hopefully, the agency would also have developed a community strategy in writing, noting the groups with whom it needs to maintain co-operative relationships and the types of representation needed. To implement this, there should be a planned method for staff participation in community relations and an organized procedure for reporting back and involving the agency in a responsible manner.[4]

Six barriers to interagency teamwork

In view of these rather rigorous requirements, it is not surprising to learn that a recent study of co-operation among agencies found no less

---

[3] This analysis of the concept of teamwork and the obstacles to co-operation was suggested by the study of Johns and De Marche, op. cit., pp. 193, 214.

[4] Trecker, op. cit., pp. 144–49.

than twenty-three different blocks to effective teamwork![5] For our purposes, it is possible to reduce them to the following six major obstacles: (1) lack of knowledge of other agencies and the community organization process, (2) "agency-mindedness," (3) intra-agency barriers, such as lack of adequate communication between executive and staff, (4) stereotypes of other professionals and agencies, (5) ineffective machinery and structure for community co-ordination, (6) "too many meetings."

1. *Basic lack of knowledge of function of other agencies and of the principles of community organization.* Perhaps one reason why many staff members are unfamiliar with the precise nature of the services offered by other agencies which impinge on their work is that they are often unacquainted with many of their colleagues. Too often we wait for a crisis or some problem situation to develop before we arrange to meet with other agencies. In addition, some social workers may be unaware of the role of information and referral services, usually under community chest or welfare council auspices, with the result that agency members fail to obtain needed services—either because the worker did not know about their existence, or because it is just assumed that the other agency is overloaded to the extent that there is no use in referring someone.

2. *"Agency-mindedness."* Behind this characteristic are a host of rugged individualistic and isolationist survivals from an earlier period of social work. Agency needs are considered more important than community needs. Out of habit, inertia, or tradition, there is a lack of conviction regarding the need for co-operation with other agencies. Every community seems to have one or more such self-centered agencies. It is often expressed in an unwillingness to reach out and take the initiative in starting discussions regarding a commonly felt need or problem. Instead, such agencies fall back on their limitations and "function" rather than trying to see what can be done about a troublesome situation.

Other manifestations of an agency-centered orientation are the reluctance to share staff and board members for community participation for fear of losing them, jurisdictional disputes, aggressive competition for funds and status, and the belief that one's own program of services is the most important and necessary one for the community. Often behind these vested interests are personality conflicts and professional jealousies, which are frequently the subject of "shoptalk" and gossip.

3. *Intra-agency barriers.* Another block to teamwork on an intra-agency level is the gap between the participation of the executive in community planning and the teamwork responsibilities of the staff. Because of failure in communication, high-sounding expressions of co-operation between agencies made at a committee meeting are not always

---

[5] Johns and De Marche, *op. cit.*, p. 214.

translated into workable arrangements between staffs. Thus it will happen that a group worker may not know what to do when he finds that other agencies are providing services to various members of his group. Frequently there is no organized plan for the participation of the staff in working toward community teamwork, and no systematic passing on of information gained from such participation to all staff members.

4. *Stereotypes of other professionals and agencies.* These are among the most powerful obstacles to teamwork; they are truly barriers which are responsible for much of the lack of understanding and respect which is found in many communities. It is possible to note here only a few of the attitudes and feelings—one could almost call them prejudices—which are behind many of the failures to co-ordinate our community services effectively.

Because there are relatively few fully trained social workers practicing today, there tends to arise a certain snobbishness on the part of those who have completed their professional training, and an equivalent defensiveness by the untrained. Sometimes this is an almost unconscious feeling: that the other agency's workers are not "professional," that they cannot be trusted with "confidential" information, and that they are somehow inadequate for their jobs. All this is reinforced because our profession is so young, and there are still no common standards or even an acceptable terminology which cuts across all fields of service.

We are dealing here with a whole series of tensions and conflicts which spring from *differences* in setting, auspices, practice, and training. These include feelings which workers in public agencies may have about voluntary agency staffs and vice versa; group workers versus recreation workers; caseworkers versus group workers; those who work with "normal" youngsters versus those who work with "problem" children. There is certainly a real need for us to understand and accept differences among ourselves as professional persons to the same extent that we try to do this with our clients or members.

5. *Ineffective machinery and structure for community co-ordination.* While all four of the preceding barriers to teamwork directly involve the agency and its staff, this fifth block to co-operative relationships is rooted in the community. There may not be a community chest, council of social agencies, or a community welfare council in the area—with the result that there is no one organization with a community point of view, one which is "neutral" and which can bring together the separate agencies on mutual problems. Thus, agencies shift for themselves and plan programs with little or no regard for the activities of other organizations. Or there may be a welfare council, but it provides no leadership—it is weak and not respected in the community. As a result, agencies start new programs or change existing ones without clearing with each other

or the council. Why does this happen? Perhaps one explanation is that such a condition may reflect either an inadequate council staff, or more probably that the community itself is not yet convinced of the need for sound social planning since it tolerates this condition.

6. *"Too many meetings."* What is behind this perennial complaint? Going to endless committee meetings is not in itself community planning or teamwork. Evidently many people do not have a creative, satisfying, or meaningful experience at meetings; they are often bored, impatient, or frustrated. One cause of dissatisfaction may be a lack of clarity regarding one's role and function. Responsible participation in meetings is based on knowing why one is present, as well as a commitment to and understanding of the group and community organization process. It is necessary to realize that all groups go through periods of confusion, lack of direction, and resistance to change. Social change is inevitably and annoyingly slow. The fact that productivity may be low at a meeting needs to be analyzed and not be a source of disgust. These and other principles derived from some of the recent findings of group dynamics should be better understood and accepted by all persons participating in committees involving teamwork.

Overcoming these obstacles

First, the individual worker should assume the responsibility of *getting acquainted with other workers in the neighborhood or community* on an informal basis before a crisis or troublesome situation develops. This means that we must make a conscious and planned effort to rise out of our own agencies and their limited programs to become more familiar with our colleagues and the work of their agencies. From this it is but a step to consulting with other agencies on common problems, perhaps arranging a conference and then striving together for a more coherent pattern of services. Such efforts cannot help but improve and sharpen our own effectiveness.

A second responsibility of the worker would be to alert his agency to the importance of *formulating a community relations policy* if the agency does not have one. The preparation of such a policy should involve the participation of both board and staff members if it is to have maximum utility. Among some of the major elements in a community relations policy as suggested by Harleigh Trecker,[6] I would single out the following:

1. Identification with the community and its agencies, which is really a "state of mind" expressing positive and purposeful attitudes.
2. Assignment of representation of the agency to board and staff mem-

---

[6] Op. cit., p. 151.

bers to those community groups where there is a reason for participation.

3. Establishment of channels of communication between those who represent the agency and the rest of the board and staff with reporting back and clearance procedures carefully formulated.

4. Participation widely distributed and of a responsible kind, with agency representatives convinced of the worth of their participation and knowing how to take part in this process.

Third, workers should be concerned that their *agency's inservice training program includes a discussion of the work of other agencies, the community organization process, and how to participate in it effectively.* This needs to be done in a systematic, planned, and continuous way. This assumes that the agency has some responsibility for providing staff members with such information and orientation, and that it will be responsive to the requests of staff regarding the content of inservice training programs.

Probably the most effective, over-all way of overcoming any one or all six obstacles to teamwork is for workers to bring to the attention of their agencies the need to *strengthen the efforts of the central planning and co-ordinating body*, or to organize one if none is in existence. For a community welfare council, which is the primary organization of this type, is by its very nature dedicated to fostering teamwork among agencies and between agencies and the community. It is the unique instrument which has evolved during the last thirty years to combat lack of knowledge of resources, "agency-mindedness," lack of communication, stereotypes, duplication, and outlived usefulness in the health, welfare, and recreation fields. If effective—and it is the responsibility of board, staff, and interested citizens to make it work—it can become a synonym for teamwork.

Community organization considerations

What should be done if there is no such council? The answer is to organize one. The existence of unmet needs is one of the most eloquent arguments for a planned and co-ordinated, community-wide approach through a welfare council structure. In a community without a council, an agency can either ignore unmet needs, complain about them, or do something about them. It can rarely meet the needs itself, nor does it often have the skill, time, and basis for broad support to mobilize the community for such an effort. Consequently, it is suggested that under these circumstances agencies should seek to get together for the purpose of organizing a community welfare council.

We are saying once more that in order to discharge their full professional responsibility, direct-service agencies must not only carry out their programs of service, but must also undertake community organization responsibilities to a certain extent when they are confronted with unmet needs or lack of communication and co-ordination between agencies serving their area. Consequently, it is important for all staff members to know something about the community organization process, the necessary skills involved, and the role they should play. The whole matter of the provision of staff time for participation in community organization is actually an index to the agency's conviction of the relative importance of planning and co-ordinating its services in the community's interest.[7]

Rationale for neighborhood organization

In this concluding section we shall apply our analysis of teamwork and some of its implications for community organization on the level of a neighborhood. What kind of structure and machinery is needed to bring a variety of services to people in a geographic area? Before answering this question, it is important to observe that the philosophy of most youth-serving agencies underscores the importance of neighborhood organization—of being close to the people served. Organizations such as the Scouts and other nonbuilding-centered agencies lay particular emphasis on the centrality of the home, the church, and the neighborhood. Building-centered agencies such as the "Y" are also concerned with the development of extension services so that programs can be brought closer to their constituency. Public recreation departments have been neighborhood-centered for many years.

Because the wide range of governmental and voluntary agency services are not always available in a neighborhood in a co-ordinated way, a variety of forms of neighborhood organization have been devised and used with varying degrees of success.[8] Based on this experience, at least four related efforts are needed today to (1) make more services available; (2) develop integrated patterns of services to meet the varying needs of neighborhoods; (3) co-ordinate services to prevent overlapping and overlooking; (4) provide opportunities at the neighborhood level for people to form groups through which they can act together. "In carrying out these functions, the keynote must be the participation in

---

[7] There are some special problems of participation faced by agencies that are not decentralized, or where excessive work loads prevent release of staff for committee service. Under these conditions, such agencies may have to be very selective by setting priorities and participating in those projects where their services are directly affected.

[8] See Sidney Dillick, *Community Organization for Neighborhood Development— Past and Present* (New York: William Morrow & Company, 1953), for the best exposition of the background and principles of neighborhood organization for social welfare purposes.

these processes of people in their neighborhoods—where families live, shop, go to school and church, and where they vote."[9]

In line with this, there has been a renewed interest in establishing community centers to make available a variety of services under many auspices in the neighborhood. There has been a parallel development as the council of social agencies evolved into a community welfare council with district community councils. These district or neighborhood councils have facilitated citizen participation and have helped make available in the neighborhood the services of city-wide agencies. It is suggested here that the district or neighborhood community welfare council can provide certain values and principles which are necessary and valid not only in urban metropolitan centers, but also for "problem" areas in suburban and rural communities. It is in a key and unique position to meet today's needs for neighborhood organization by: (1) co-ordinating health, welfare, and recreation services at the neighborhood level; (2) helping people become articulate about their needs and enlisting their participation in meeting them; (3) serving as a medium for interchange of ideas among rank and file professionals; (4) serving as a medium for joint planning and action by agencies and civic groups; (5) providing a means for communicating to the city-wide level the neighborhood view or problems.[10]

The district or neighborhood community council, as a co-ordinating, interorganizational body related functionally and staffwise to an over-all community welfare council, is one of the principal means through which direct service agencies and citizen organizations can work together within the larger context of a city or metropolitan area.[11] Indeed, in these days of growing suburban and satellite communities, extensive subdivisions of tract housing, this type of approach to community organization is essential if programs are to get to the people who need them.

Some suggested patterns

For example, these new areas have some special problems involving identity and integration with the larger community, lack of adequate park and recreational space, including meeting places. They tend to contain a large concentration of families with growing children who can utilize and want a wide variety of health, welfare, and recreation

---

[9] Dillick, op. cit., p. 158.

[10] Ibid., p. 161.

[11] Cf. *A Geographical Approach to Community Planning* (New York: Community Chests and Councils of America, Inc.), a symposium based on papers from the 1951 National Conference of Social Work, for a description of current thinking on the role of neighborhood councils.

services. How are we to get to them? The standard reply is in terms of "extension services," which implies a willingness and a capacity to take staff and services to the place where people live. Some agencies have been able to do this more effectively than others, particularly the national youth-serving organizations. There is a real need, though, for a pooling of resources among the agencies having a common interest in serving these subdivisions. Together they can more effectively promote adequate meeting facilities; through joint use of church, school, or home facilities more children can be served—if agencies are willing to share some of their resources. The problem of locating volunteer leadership is often a formidable one and it would seem to make sense for all agencies seeking volunteers to combine their efforts into one recruitment campaign. Similar campaigns for foster mothers or club leaders have been most successful when developed on a joint-agency basis. This approach eliminates competitiveness and, because more people can be reached, results in a better caliber of volunteer leadership.

The same argument would hold for joint training of such leaders. This would require agreement as to the common-core basis for leadership, apart from the special information and knowledge needed in working with specific organizations. But even more important is the awareness of the type of organizational structure which would facilitate this type of co-operative planning and also acquaint the area with the existence of other community services. It is suggested that the organization of a district community welfare council is probably the most appropriate way of meeting these needs of new neighborhoods.

Many agencies have already organized neighborhood councils or advisory committees for their own programs. What is required is a neighborhood council for *all* groups serving the area. Experience has shown that this can best be done under the auspices of a community-wide organization such as a welfare council, rather than by any direct service agency.

Summary

While it has become fashionable to espouse the principles of "teamwork," practice and advocacy have not always been related. Co-operative relationships have become even more necessary as a result of the growing complexity of social work practices. In analyzing the concept of teamwork, certain prerequisites and barriers were noted. Four specific suggestions to overcome such obstacles have been offered; this has implications for community organization, particularly on a neighborhood level. Decentralization of the machinery for planning and co-ordination is proposed as one of the major means of meeting today's need for teamwork in agencies and within the community.

On reducing contention between foster family parents and child-placing agencies[*]

Mary Reistroffer

It is impossible to discuss the foster parent–agency partnership without discussing authority—the central issue. Few people in today's society accept authority for its own sake and many chafe under the restrictions it imposes on personal pursuits. Although all must yield somewhat to ensure a certain orderliness, we do so grudgingly. And are we not dismayed when we see persons—especially our young—confusing freedom with license?

Authority is integral to our lives and society. Some people, however, have profound problems with authority, as shown by their actions and attitudes. Those with pronounced problems with authority may have had bruising life experiences with authority structures and authority personnel; more likely their attitudes stem from a residual of unresolved conflict with the most intimate authority figures they have known—their parents.

We can easily identify these persons who seem to be victims of the authority-negative syndrome. Usually, their negativeness and willingness to do battle with anyone about anything clearly preclude their functioning in a variety of roles. For example, victims of the authority-negative syndrome cannot function as foster family parents and they should not hold positions of power in organizational structures giving them authority in areas involving human services.

Foster parents see the placement agency as an authoritative structure whether or not they or the agency recognizes that perception. They assign to the agency and its personnel the same authority as the police and school. And the placement agency with a mission mandated by statute or enabled by licensure does have authority. That agency can give or withhold foster children, it can hear or not hear foster parent opinions, it can control to a remarkable degree the destinies of the children in its care. True, the agency may be limited by court jurisdiction over children, some external review, and public censure, but usually it seems to mush on with impunity. If the agency does not use its author-

---

[*] Reprinted with permission of the author and the University of Wisconsin—Extension from *Foster Family Care: A Collection of Papers and Abstracts,* University of Wisconsin—Extension, copyright Board of Regents, 1974, pp. 15–24.

ity with wisdom and discretion or becomes too insulated from those on the receiving end of its services, it can easily slide over from being authoritative (having the power to do certain things) to being authoritarian (not being accountable to anyone for anything done or not done).

We must find ways of functioning for the welfare of the foster child despite the high hurdle this authority factor presents in any joined or shared enterprise. I believe there are routes to achieve this, but a firm commitment and hard work from both foster parents and agency workers are required. Administrative planning which enables rather than disables the efforts of foster parents and placement practitioners is also necessary.

Foster parents are, for the most part, *not* victims of the authority-negative syndrome who are seeking to do battle with anyone or anything they construe as authoritative. Indeed, they may be more traditional and supportive of authority, even less contentious, than many of the role-identified groups in society today. They are child-oriented and child-protectionist, but the intimacy of placement relationships prompts emotional reactions. Foster family care is by the nature of the service intimate in style and emotionally laced; how could it be otherwise? If foster parents find personnel in an authoritative structure behaving in an authoritarian way or failing to accord them the privilege of having an opinion or "being heard," they become hopping mad at what they construe as high-handedness, caprice, and irresponsibility. In the placement situation, they often then rationalize their anger by assuming the posture of protecting the child from the agency which placed the child! Whether the anger is directed toward an agency person or toward the agency itself, the situation can rarely be handled without supervisory or administrative intervention. Far too often, without such intervention, the child is replaced, the home falls to closure or nonuse, and bad feelings are rampant.

Where misunderstandings and contentiousness have reached that level, court actions have ensued. Litigation is an extreme course and has been resorted to where agencies have failed to redress grievances and differences. And too often, foster parents who are unhappy with agency performance and planning have become victims of "helpers" from the community who use foster parents and exploit their unhappiness for wholly selfish and self-serving reasons. Consider the aggressive, militant-minded individual (authority-negative syndrome?) anxious to do battle with any established community structure or organization in the human services, or consider a myriad of legal services seeking visibility in the media to justify and expose their services. Both helpers seem to be less interested in the pursuit of justice or the rightness of the cause than in exploiting the situation.

Recently, some court cases have done great damage to the total child welfare effort in a community. Undoubtedly, some have been proper actions but the attendant publicity and sensationalism suggest abuse and self-indulgence rather than pursuit of a just cause. In most instances, this litigation has been prompted by abortive fair-hearing procedures or has been started where review procedures were not available or where agency administration had assumed an authoritarian posture. In the latter instance, the aloof disregard for resolving disagreements and the authoritarian posture have been rationalized by the claim that there must be no breech of confidentiality.

Today's society is clearly redress minded, rights conscious, and accountability oriented. It is likely that a community will identify with and support persons bringing actions against large or impersonal community structures and organizations, whether under voluntary, public, or proprietary auspices. It might be said there will be few places to hide in the seventies!

As to where we are in this third year of this decade, we might take a short side trip and recall our civics class in seventh grade. In that class we heard much of due process, a basic constitutional privilege guaranteed by the Fifth and Fourteenth Amendments. In essence, it guarantees that no individual can be deprived of life, liberty, or property by the government without due process of law. The U.S. Supreme Court has extended this protection to cover a variety of infringements of individual rights only remotely connected with government.

More important, it has defined due process as "fundamental fairness." This concept is as basically American as red, white, and blue or apple pie! It means a person has a right to face his accuser and to receive notice when he is in any way a party to something being heard by the court. Perhaps some of the class-action suits on constitutional questions in federal courts have already made us mindful of the doctrine of fundamental fairness and what it portends in the human services. Within the past year, a federal court in Madison, Wisconsin, ruled on *Lessard V. Wilbur Schmidt et al.* and that ruling has had considerable impact in the mental health field. Had the case *In the Matter Rios* been pursued through appeal to the federal courts, there might have been even greater impact in protective services and child placement. In effect, the Lessard decision holds that a person detained or confined for emotional illness *must* be provided with the needed treatment; if we apply the same principle to the Rios case, it would mean that the child for whom placement is the "treatment of choice" *must* also receive all the help he requires.

These are interesting sidelights on child placement in this decade. The important concept is fundamental fairness. As state courts catch up to federal decisions, the other adjustments will become clear. Consider the impact of juvenile court procedures of *In re Gault* in 1967. Although most current litigation in child placement is not in federal courts and largely relates to local issues in lesser courts, we must realize that this will change. It is time now to move to policy, procedural, and practice changes which recognize fundamental fairness and the right of everyone involved in child placement to be heard.

I believe there are some steps or routes which can and should be taken now, routes which respond to the many societal forces operating today, which give the accountability a supporting public expects, and which follow fundamental fairness in our connections in the child-placement field and other human-resources development fields.

The first group of possibilities is in the area of "paper support" of practice. An agency, for example, should consider using some kind of plan-confirmation letter on each child admitted to the system and placed in the agency's supervision. While the cry of "paper pollution" from the operational level is expectable, this should not be a deterrent. A written plan-confirmation letter is not a great burden and may have many benefits for the child going into foster family placement and for those who serve him.

Many placement agencies, prompted by policy or statutory requirements, process a placement agreement with foster parents. It is usually a general statement of intent and expectations geared to such actions as not traveling out-of-state with the child without notifying the agency or securing permission or not unilaterally filing a petition to adopt. What is needed now is a specific agreement to supplement that general agreement. This is a contract of sorts setting forth the agency's plan for *this* child in *this* placement.

The agreement should be prepared by the caseworker, countersigned by the supervisor, and mailed in duplicate to the foster parents. They sign both copies, return the original to the agency, and retain the duplicate copy. The letter should confirm the plan discussed with the foster parents when the child was proposed to them and specify additional details that were worked out after the meeting with the foster parents.

What are the benefits of such a procedure? The first thing this achieves is the formulation of a plan for *this* child. Too many have paid lip service to the expectation that a child's discharge should be started when he is accepted for care and admitted to the system. This procedure compels an agency and the placement personnel to "go on paper" as to where the agency expects to be with this child six months or a year hence, and commits the agency to some defined plan of action for and with the foster child. Might this reduce the number of children admitted to the placement service system and then seemingly forgotten?

The plan-confirmation letter contains all pertinent elements of the plan—parental visitation and contacts, medical coverage, a date when a court or plan review will be made, etc.

Perhaps one of the major reasons for contention and misunderstanding in the foster parent–agency relationship is the disparity between what foster parents thought they heard or thought they were told and what then happened. The plan-confirmation procedure sets a design for communication, enables a certain administrative control and continuity, especially with new worker assignments, and achieves a more businesslike framework for the agency's mission. When the plan is altered, the procedure repeats itself with a supplementary letter amending the original.

Might this procedure remind placement practitioners and foster parents alike of the temporary nature of foster family care? And again, might it reduce the number of foster children in the limbo of accidental long-duration care? Might the courts which rule on some disputes in this partnership regard this as a more orderly and responsible way of meeting the agency's charge of caring for and planning for a child?

Another procedural route is the completion by the foster parents of a child-progress report for each six months of placement. This form would be filed in the child's record, and would be supplementary to the narrative account of activity for and with the foster child. This procedure would have some obvious and some hidden values.

The obvious benefits are the foster parent input into the information used in subsequent planning, decision making, and recommendations. It would also give some currency to records in following the child developmentally, since experienced and observed behavior is reported. The hidden value is having some support in court cases that question planning. Would not such inclusions convey a sense of the agency and foster parents having knowledge of significant social data on a child in placement?

Many foster parents question, even legally challenge, an agency's replacement planning because of infrequent in-person contact by agency personnel with the home and child. Is it not understandable—pushed by their anxiety over an impending separation from the child—for them to become angry when it seems that agency decisions are based on scant or inaccurate information? Is the foster parents' clamor to "be heard" responded to by this procedural change? Might these views of the foster parents assist the supervising worker in identifying important areas in which the child needs help? In my recent experience with court actions revolving around the question of the agency's plan "being in the best interest of the child," the court has been critical of two or three pages of recording as an inadequate account of several years of a child's life in placement.

And finally, agencies committed to making shoring-up procedural and practice changes may elect to pursue the hard and challenging avenue of a different level of foster parent participation in evaluations. These are the annual reevaluations of the foster home for relicensing or approval for continued use. Foster parents and the agency worker would jointly prepare the written evaluation assessing performance and functioning. Foster parents would be free to append a dissenting view if there were areas of disagreement. This could be a valuable learning experience for foster parents and workers alike. Is it not fundamental fairness to share written assessments with persons whose performance is being assessed? Do our professional assessments have so little integrity or so much bias, or do we have so little skill that this is a hazardous route? Might this route produce less contention and bad feeling than methods currently used?

The second group of possibilities to improve our overall situation in foster family placement includes the redress options and opportunities made available to resolve problems in the foster parent–agency partnership. The foster parents initiating litigation surrender their right to pursue these options and opportunities.

The conference of the foster parents, agency worker, and agency supervisor should be the first step in resolving a problem. All foster parents should have the privilege of requesting this informal conference when there is disagreement or an impasse in the relationship. Some agencies have long made this opportunity available to foster parents, have expected supervising workers to initiate it, and have made it a fair, clearing-the-air session rather than an accusatory procedure. It should be expected that intelligent adults can and do have differing views and that these differing views are not an indictment of either party. Is this conference available in most agencies? Do foster parents know of this availability? In my opinion, about 75 percent of the recent court actions over foster parent–agency differences could have been resolved at this level within a framework of conciliation and reconciliation. When goodwill, fairness and self-control characterize this conference, there can usually be a meeting of the adult minds because of the importance of the child.

Questions not answered or problems not resolved in the informal conference can be sent to an internal review board or panel. A hearing group could be composed of agency personnel, uninvolved foster parents, and emotionally neutral citizens from the community, or it could be composed of specified agency personnel with some or no participation by outsiders. In October 1972, a pilot effort using the latter construction was initiated in one California public agency region. If this is possible in some of the most populous counties of the country, is it not possible in large and small agencies across the nation? Of course, the agency administration enamored of its own power (authoritarianism?) or not aware of what is really happening at the operational level can ill-afford or chance this exposure. Such an administration usually summarily dismisses efforts to establish the internal review board, suggesting that it will breach confidentiality imposed by statute or administrative fiat.

One wonders how such administrations have justified the formation of hearing boards or review panels in public assistance as pushed by the National Welfare Rights Organization demands!

Using confidentiality as a refuge and rationale for not taking affirmative action in making opportunities for redress available is, to even the casual observer, an indication of hard-nosed status-quoism. Cannot foster parents sign a release that will permit discussion of their situation? Cannot a foster child be referred to on a first-name-only basis to protect his identity? Cannot the issues be examined? Cannot responsible community citizens be trusted to honor their pledge to keep information confidential?

Use of the internal review board or panel is based on the agreement that the decision rendered will be binding on both foster parents and the agency. This is much like binding arbitration in the union movement where "both sides live with" the decision. It suggests that foster parents and agency cannot expect the best of all worlds and that "winning" is a self-indulgent side issue. In this mechanism, neither foster parents nor agency should be represented by legal counsel, the session(s) should not be recorded, and the rules of evidence should not apply since this is a fact-finding effort, not a trial. Recording the hearing, including legal counsel, and using rules of evidence might inhibit a full and free discussion of issues, place individual participants in some legal jeopardy, and make it impossible to keep all facets privileged or confidential.

These two levels for redressing wrongs as perceived by foster parents are appropriate for conflicts relating only to judgment and planning decisions. Conflicts relating to licensure should be resolved by fair-hearing procedures under rules and guidelines formulated by the license-granting authority. Hopefully, those rules would provide for legal counsel and for having the hearing fully recorded for judicial review if that step is pursued. The rules of evidence might or might not apply.

Only as foster parents and agency personnel fully comprehend the importance of the foster child who stands between them will they rise to the resolution of problems between them. Recently, a youngster who was made to feel badly because of his reading disability vehemently said, "I'm good 'cause God don't make no junk!" As foster parents and agency remind themselves of the importance of the child for whom both are responsible, they should agree that "God don't make no junk."

Selected annotated references

CHAIKLIN, HARRIS, "A Social Service Team for Public Welfare," *Social Work Practice, 1970* (New York: Columbia University Press, 1970), pp. 103–13.
This is an interesting and enlightening article on an attempt to change and improve the staff service delivery pattern in working with public welfare families. Community organizers and case aides were added to the social casework staff to make a team.

WHITEHOUSE, FREDERICK A., "Professional Teamwork," *Social Welfare Forum, 1957* (New York: Columbia University Press, 1957), pp. 148–57.
This excellent article gives the background of the concept of teamwork and sets forth 18 elements that are found in good teams and teamwork.

Chapter 13

THE SOCIAL WORKER, THE PROFESSION, AND THE BUREAUCRATIC STRUCTURE

Up to this point in the text we have discussed social work primarily as a profession and the social work practitioner primarily as a professional person with the responsibility of working within professional knowledge and values in the interests of the particular client with whom he is involved. We now need to examine other aspects of the social work profession. Most social workers practice their profession within some sort of bureaucratic structure, and this structure inevitably affects the work they do. We alluded to the structure in the last two chapters when we discussed the need for referral of a client because of the limits of an agency's services and when we discussed the fact that one kind of teamwork was teamwork across agency boundaries. As a professional person, the social worker is also a component within a professional system with its own purposes, culture, internal interactions, and external transactions. We now want to examine the meaning of these realities for the social work practitioner.

THE INTERSTITIAL PROFESSION

In the first chapter of this text we spoke of social workers as concerned with the interactions between the individual and society. We now need to return to a consideration of social work as an interstitial profession which serves both the client in need and society at large. This issue is complex in that the individual social worker's function is defined, and his salary paid, by an agency (public or voluntary, traditional or nontraditional) which receives its sanction from and is accountable to the community or to some community group whose members differ from, although they may include, the members of the client system. This point is of fundamental importance since the parameters of the service any particular professional can offer are determined by the parameters of his agency's societal charge. Social workers utilize two types of tools in their work. The first type are the tools of internalized knowledge and skill, which, while they cannot be used up and, in fact, may be increased and sharpened by practice, are costly in that they are what the social worker (or any other professional) sells in order to obtain the money he needs to maintain his physical existence in our society. Most professionals (lawyers, doctors, etc.) sell their services to their clients or patients. In the case of social work, however, services to the client are paid for by the community and may be, at least in theory, available to all members of the community, many of whom cannot afford to pay for them. In addition to knowledge and skill, social workers frequently dispense external resources, such as money. Now, money, whether it is used to pay for the knowledge and skill of the worker or for concrete resources, or is given directly to the client, is usually scarce. And money to support social work efforts is not the social worker's property but belongs to some identified community. The community that allocates its scarce resources to the support of social work services wants to assure itself that these resources are used responsibly.

The client who goes to a lawyer for service, or the patient who goes to a doctor for treatment, may look elsewhere for help if he thinks the service he receives is not adequate. Thus he expresses his evaluation of that professional's competence by depriving the professional of income. If the professional wants to support himself and his dependents, he must practice in a way that satisfies the users of the services by which he supports himself. However, since most client systems do not pay the full cost for social work services, their withdrawal in disappointment and disgust from the inadequate social work practitioner seldom directly penalizes that practitioner. Social workers (and their agencies) are thus well protected from their client's evaluations. However, they are open to the evaluation of their supporting community. The supporting community, however, neither pays nor evaluates workers directly. Rather, it gives its money to an organization, usually called an agency, which hires the professional practitioners. It is usually the agency in interaction with its supporting community through certain representative groups which both sets the parameters of practice within which workers must operate and which evaluates their performance within the parameters.

THE BUREAUCRATIC ORGANIZATION

In the modern world most formal organizations are structured in a particular way. This particular type of administrative organization is known as a bureaucracy and has triumphed in modern society because this form of social organization is thought to operate with an efficiency superior to that of any other form of secondary group social structure thus far devised by man. The classical criteria for a bureaucracy were originally set forth by Max Weber as follows:

1. [The employees] are personally free and subject to authority only with respect to their impersonal official [work] obligations.
2. [The employees] are organized in a clearly defined hierarchy of offices.
3. Each office has a clearly defined sphere of competence.
4. The office is filled by a free contractual relationship. (Thus, in principle, each person makes a free selection, or choice, as to whether he will accept the office and its terms.)
5. Candidates [for offices in the bureaucracy] are selected on the basis of technical qualifications. In the most rational case, this is tested by examination or guaranteed by diplomas certifying technical training, or both. They are appointed, not elected.
6. [The employees] are remunerated by fixed salaries in money, for the most part with a right to pensions . . . The salary scale is primarily graded according to rank in the hierarchy.
7. The [position] is treated as the sole, or at least the primary, occupation of the incumbent.
8. It constitutes a career. There is a system of "promotion" according to seniority or to achievement, or both. Promotion is dependent on the judgment of superiors.
9. The official works entirely separated from ownership of the means of administration and without appropriation of his position.
10. He is subject to strict and systematic discipline and control in the conduct of the office.[1]

Weber says that the Roman Catholic church, the modern army, and large-scale capitalistic enterprise, along with certain "charitable organization, or any number of other types of private enterprises, servicing ideal or material ends are bureaucratic organizations."[2]

Although bureaucracy is usually seen in terms of pragmatic necessity as the most efficient way to organize any large group of people to get any big job done, inherent in its very being are certain dysfunctional characteristics which vitally affect its operations. Social workers are often

[1] Max Weber, *The Theory of Social and Economic Organization* (New York: Oxford University Press, 1947), pp. 333–34.
[2] Ibid., p. 334.

forced to conclude that the relationship between bureaucracy and efficiency is complex, questionable, and perhaps, at its worst, inverse.

To quote from a recent book, *Overcoming Mismanagement in the Human Services,* bearing on some of the problems of bureaucracy:

> A very unhappy social worker, after receiving a poor evaluation from a supervisor, once wrote: "Social welfare like all Gaul is divided into three parts. The first has until recently been inhabited by the Hierarchae, which may account for the fact that the field has been subject to unsteadiness. The second by the Supervisii, which explains why too many of the most able no longer work with those in need of help. They are in conference. And the last by the Reformae, who believe the populace is anxious to substitute social change for sex."
>
> Had he been more dispassionate, this social worker might have pointed out that social welfare is also inhabited by thousands of hardworking, dedicated people who spend their lives under adverse situations with some of the most unhappy and unlucky people in the world and still manage to do a lot more good than bad.[3]

Wilensky and Lebeaux describe the limitations of social work bureaucracy as follows:

> Along with its gains, efficiency, reliability, precision, fairness—come what many students have called its pathologies: timidity, delay, officiousness, red tape, exaggeration of routine, limited adaptability. The agency as a means, a mechanism—the agency—for carrying out welfare policy becomes an end in itself. Between the altruist with his desire to help and the client with his need lies the machine, with its own "needs." These needs can result in an emphasis on technique and method, on organizational routines and records, rather than on people and service.[4]

Barbara Lerner, a psychologist, is concerned with this last limitation of bureaucracy when she writes:

> Bureaucratic means are intrinsically unsuited to the achievement of ultimate mental health ends because they are standardized means—the whole point of breaking up tasks into component parts and component parts into subcomponents is to standardize procedures—and standardized procedures are rational only if one is striving to produce a standard product. . . .
>
> Each human being is a unique entity and wants to remain so. People who voluntarily seek treatment may do so because they want to achieve an ultimate end, such as the realization of something like their full share of the universal human potential for adequate psychosocial func-

[3] Harold H. Weissman, *Overcoming Mismanagement in the Human Services* (San Francisco: Jossey-Bass, 1973), p. vii.

[4] Harold L. Wilensky and Charles N. Lebeaux *Industrial Society and Social Welfare* (New York: Russell Sage Foundation, 1958), p. 243.

tioning, but each person wants to achieve his own unique version of that end in his own unique way. . . .

Thus each client who comes seeking aid comes as a unique individual seeking aid which is individually tailored to the totalty of his needs by a person who is in close enough contact with him to apprehend them and who has the freedom and flexibility to respond to them in unique way.[5]

Lerner goes on to say that the bureaucratically organized agency is organized around "abstract, standard parts: specific programs organized around specific problems that are dealt with by specific procedures," rather than around clients as unique personalities or around the concern of practitioners for their clients. She complains that clients are "then defined in terms of the particular problems around which programs are organized," and are "processed to and through those programs and subjected to the various procedures and techniques which constitute them," rather than seen in terms of their own goals and expectations.[6]

Listening to Lerner, one becomes aware that the problems of professionals in bureaucracies are not restricted to social work. These problems occur in any organization staffed by personnel who spend a considerable number of years in developing a particular expertise. Weissman points out:

Professionals share a desire for and expect a large degree of autonomy from organizational control; they want maximum discretion in carrying out their professional activities, free from organizational interference or confining procedures. In addition, professionals tend to look to other professionals to gain some measure of self-esteem, are not likely to be devoted to any one organization, and accept a value system that puts great emphasis on the client's interest.

The bureaucrat is different from the professional. He performs specialized and routine activities under the supervision of a hierarchy of officials. His loyalty and career are tied up with his organization. Therefore, conflict results when professionals are required to perform like bureaucrats.[7]

CONFLICTS BETWEEN THE BUREAUCRACY AND THE PROFESSIONAL

Every practicing social worker has been confronted with the harsh reality of the conflict between his judgment as to the ideal interventive actions needed to move toward the client's goal and what is possible

---

[5] Barbara Lerner, *Therapy in the Ghetto* (Baltimore: Johns Hopkins Press, 1972), pp. 169–70.

[6] Ibid., p. 171.

[7] Weissman, *Overcoming Mismanagement,* p. viii.

given the resources and parameters of the agency within which both he and the client are operating. Often the most sensitive and concerned workers find themselves discouraged and angered by the many unavoidable compromises they must make between their client's needs and those of their agency in particular and of society in general. Perhaps some of this frustration could be avoided, and the worker could be more effective in bringing about change in agency functioning, if he understood better the bureaucracy within which he of necessity operates. Actually, social work has been a bureaucratic profession from its very beginning, and social workers employed in agencies are not only professionals but bureaucrats. Thus, while social work has struggled to synthesize bureaucratic and professional norms, it has not always recognized that a profession and a bureaucracy possess a number of norms that are opposed in principle.

Weissman points out that one of the crucial problems of professionals who are working to change the bureaucratic structure is their lack of recognition of the difference between nonprofit and profit-making organizations. "Money serves as an alarm system in private enterprise: Ford sooner or later must respond to the tension caused by lack of Edsel sales."[8] In nonprofit organizations the connection between the product produced and the revenues are indirect. Thus the alarm system that would bring change is severely flawed. Both professionals and agency executives may prefer to be judged by effort expended rather than by the success or failure of the effort. Weissman says that without an effective accountability system social agencies cannot solve their problems and administration has little need to seriously consider the views and ideas of lower-level staff since it will not be penalized if it doesn't.[9]

In an earlier chapter we spoke of the importance of evaluation. This has been a long-standing problem in all professions. Who is to evaluate the professional? Against what standard is the professional's work to be judged? The present struggle of the physician against some kind of publicly supported health care is an example of the problem. The physician has successfully maintained up until now that only he (or, in some cases, a jury of his peers that he picks) can be allowed to judge his work. Incidentally, this stance probably explains the growing number of malpractice suits, since patients are no longer content, when the results of treatment are negative, to accept the professional's judgment that the process of treatment was correct. So, too, in the social work bureaucracy the question of who shall evaluate the effectiveness of the work is a difficult one. Is it to be the worker, the supervisor, the executive, the board, or the general public? We have said that con-

---

[8] Ibid., p. vii.
[9] Ibid., p. 3.

tracted goals are the appropriate outcome. It would follow that we hold goal achievement to be a decision of client and worker, not of the agency.

Weber held that what is central to bureaucracy is specialization and the standardization of tasks and the rational allocation or assignment of these tasks in accordance with an overall plan.[10] Collective tasks may thus be broken down into component tasks which are means to a collective end. Two assumptions underlie such a concept. The first is that there is something approaching a clear, consistent, complete, and generally agreed-upon definition of the ultimate end toward which the organization is working, and the second is that the end is achievable through standardized means.[11] When a social agency defines its function it usually states in general terms the ends it intends to pursue. However, these ends are usually expressed in such general terms (for example, "the support of healthy family life") that we cannot measure the extent to which they have been achieved; or the ends are expressed in programmatic terms, such as "crisis intervention," "aftercare program," "family therapy program," or "drug program," which often result in defining the client's problems in terms of programs rather than of the client's goals. And most of us would agree that we do not have standardized means to apply even if the client could fit within a standardized goal. We are simply not able to say in working with individual human beings, "If this, then that." There are too many variables in the situation of the unique human system. A profession works by applying principles and methods to resolve problems determined by unique client input and professional judgment rather than by employing standardized procedures toward some predetermined goal established by a hierarchical authority.

Another conflict between the bureaucratic structure and the professional is found in the orientation toward authority. The professional regards authority as residing in professional competence; the bureaucrat sees authority as residing in the office held. An important difference is found in the orientation toward the client, in that the professional orients himself toward serving the best interests of the client while the bureaucrat seeks to serve the best interests of the organization. The professional usually identifies with his professional colleagues. He should find his identification from his professional association. The bureaucrat identifies with his particular social stratum within the bureaucratic hierarchy. And lastly, there is a different orientation toward the method of exercising power. "The professional norm is to influence clients and peers by modes which are oriented toward the pole of free exchange

---

[10] Weber, *Social and Economic Organization*, pp. 333–34.
[11] Lerner, *Therapy in Ghetto*, p. 167.

while the bureaucratic norm is oriented toward the pole of coercion"[12] supported by the invoking of sanctions.

TYPES OF BUREAUCRATS

In an empirical study of social work performance in large public agencies, Ralph Morgan identified and developed an anchoring description of four ideal types of role conceptions of social workers in a bureaucratic setting. His work is summarized below:

> The *functional bureaucrat* is a professional "who just happens to be working in a social agency." He seeks interaction with and recognition from his professional peers both inside and outside the agency. "Such individuals by their skill, good judgment, and technical efficiency, often provide a type of service" that is recognized by the agency as being highly effective. As a result the agency overlooks certain violations of agency norms as the price it must pay for having such a competent professional on its staff.
>
> The *service bureaucrat* is a social worker who is oriented toward helping his client but who recognizes that he is a part of a bureaucracy. He integrates himself "into the bureaucratic group while maintaining professional peer group ties." While he is still "ambivalent about his identification with his agency, he sees in it the best means of attaining his goal of practicing" his profession, and as a helping resource rather than as an antagonist of his client and himself.
>
> The *specialist bureaucrat* is a classification that Morgan says encompasses the largest group of social workers. This worker is interested in reconciling the "bureaucracy to men and men to the bureaucracy." The social worker specialist bureaucrat uses the rules and regulations of the agency to guide his professional judgment. "While he recognizes that agency directives are in general necessary, he also recognizes the richness of the human situation that can never be fully encompassed by specific rules and regulations." He sees his agency as authorizing him to use his professional discretion to protect the interests both of the agency and of its clients. He realizes that the agency is a bureaucracy and therefore heir to all the dysfunctional characteristics of this form of human organization. He usually has the professional "courage to sacrifice bureaucratic norms when they interfere with his professional function." He has successfully, through understanding and professional judgment, adapted in practice to norms which in theory are essentially irreconcilable. In fact, he may see this constantly shifting adaptation as the very stuff of professional life.
>
> The *executive bureaucrat* likes "to manage men, money, and materials. While the functional bureaucrat is oriented toward his profession, the service bureaucrat toward those he serves, the specialist bureaucrat to-

---

[12] Ralph Morgan, "Role Performance in a Bureaucracy," in *Social Work Practice,* 1962 (New York: Columbia University Press, 1962), p. 115.

ward the profession and the bureaucracy, the executive bureaucrat seems oriented primarily toward the exercise of power. While executive bureaucrats are innovators and do not consider themselves bound by a rigid application of rules and regulations [in fact, they may be daring bureaucratic infighters and risk takers] they tend not to appreciate innovations by their own subordinates." They lean toward enforcement of bureaucratic norms for others and run a disciplined agency.

The *job bureaucrat* is a person, a professional worker, who "has a substantial career investment in the bureaucracy. At the center of his attention is the security of his own career, and he seeks to safeguard and advance it through a meticulous application of regulations and adherence to the norms of the organization." The effective job bureaucrat achieves his greatest success in supervisory or administrative positions. While he holds himself firmly to official policies of the organization, he realizes that the other professionals in his section have a different orientation, and while he tends to supervise closely, he exercises sufficient "selective nonattention" to the less rigid way in which his subordinate professionals operate, that through the proper amount of "social slippage" the social work job gets done. The ineffective job bureaucrat is characterized by a rigid overcompliance with regulations and norms. Directives that originally were issued to accomplish a mission become ends in themselves, and the mission of social work, or even of the agency itself, become secondary considerations.[13]

AGENCY BUREAUCRACY AND THE WORKER

No one ever meets a pure type in real life, so perhaps it is understandable that the authors are not willing to put themselves in any one of the classes listed. But we suppose that we could probably be located somewhere between the service bureaucrat and the specialist bureaucrat. We do not believe that a worker who accepts a position as a member of an agency staff and who utilizes agency resources, no matter how unsatisfactory they may be, can act as though he were a private practitioner or without concern for agency policies and procedures. As a staff member, the worker is bound by the policies of his agency. If these policies are unacceptable, he must either work to change them, while remaining bound by them, or he must leave the agency and work for change outside it.

The first principle for the worker who would give his client maximum service is to understand the organization for which he works and to know how its structure and function were and are determined. If one is going to be actively involved in change, one needs to know what the possible points of intervention are. Three major factors affect the organization of agencies: their source of support, the source of their

---

[13] Ibid., pp. 116–25.

sanction or right to operate, and the areas of their concern. Agencies obviously cannot operate without a source of funds. As a rule an agency's funds come either from public tax funds or from private voluntary contributions, although agencies supported primarily by private contributions may utilize tax funds through various contracts and grants. Any agency's policy and structure, procedures, and flexibility will be determined by the source and adequacy of its funding. As a general rule, the funds are never adequate to the demands that workers wish to meet, so that difficult choices among real needs must usually be made.

The public tax-supported agency will usually operate within legislation and will be dependent on some legislative body (e.g., county commissioners) for its broad policy and for the appropriation of public funds for its support. In some cases the board or commission of a public service may be appointed by an elected executive officer (i.e., governor). Such agencies are usually administered by individuals who may be required to prove their competence by passing various tests. These administrators will determine procedures and more detailed policy issues within the broad legislation that established and maintains the agency.

Private agencies usually operate under the general policy directives of a board of directors. Such a board has three primary functions: it establishes the right of the agency to carry on its program and sanctions the agency's activities; it is responsible for the agency's overall policy; and it is responsible for fund raising. Until very recently almost all boards were composed of an elite group of members with little understanding of the realities of the lives of those for whom they developed programs. Boards almost always operate by consensus. Because the board members of private agencies are volunteers, the members who are constantly on the losing side of an issue soon drop out unless they have a deep commitment. In most situations the board hires the executive of the agency, and it often happens that the executive sees his job as keeping the board happy on the one hand and running the agency his own way on the other. The executive usually controls staff access to the board and the flow of information to the board about the agency's work. So the worker's attempts to represent clients and their interests in policy and program matters are often unheard.

Some social work departments (such as the social service department of a school system, a hospital, a court, etc.) operate as part of a larger host agency. In this situation the financial support and policy-making processes will be determined by those of the host agency, which generally operate under a similar structure.

Agencies have both a function and a program. The program is the ways and means that an agency utilizes to carry out its function as defined by the community. For the practitioner this distinction has some importance in that although an agency's function may remain constant, its program ought to be responsive to the changing needs of the times. Thus an agency whose function is the care and treatment of children may initially have cared largely for orphaned or dependent children but now may be concerned primarily with delinquent children.

Each agency has an organizational (bureaucratic) structure by which it delegates its responsibilities and tasks and stabilizes and systematizes its operations. The executive is the primary administrative officer. He has direct responsibility for the day-to-day functioning of the agency. He is usually responsible for getting the money to run the agency, and this responsibility may occupy most of his time and thought. He is responsible for relationships with the board of directors or a public body. He is usually responsible for working with other agencies toward community social work goals, and for the public relations functions of the agency.

Below the executive on the organization table of a large agency one may find a bewildering array of division directors, unit supervisors, consultants, and line supervisors. A small agency may have only three levels of hierarchy: the executive, the supervisors, and the workers. Line workers are more conscious of their relationship to their direct supervisor—a professional person who is usually held responsible for two functions that at some times and to some people seem contradictory: (1) helping each worker to improve his skills both in the interests of getting the present job done at the best level possible and for the worker's and client's future benefit, and (2) administratively holding each worker responsible for doing the job to certain standards and evaluating his performance relative to those standards.

Many articles in social work literature deal with the supervisory process and its problems. Supervisors, like workers, differ, and some may be more interested in their job security and tenure than in the client's needs for service or the worker's need for both support and learning opportunities. All beginning workers can use considerable help in increasing their awareness of themselves and their way of working, and in adding to their fund of knowledge about people, resources, and helping processes. And in a large agency with considerable work pressure and a constant scarcity of resources, all line workers need considerable support of their supervisors in dealing with the constant frustrations of the day-to-day job.

Harry Wasserman examined the work of professional social workers in a large public agency. He found that structural constraints rather than social work knowledge and skills dictated what the worker was able to offer in the client's life situations. In this instance, eight of the twelve workers studied had left the agency after two years.[14] Wasserman

---

[14] Harry Wasserman, "Early Careers of Professional Workers in a Public Child Welfare Agency," *Social Work* 15:3 (July 1970), pp. 98–101.

concluded that "the two principal feelings expressed by the twelve new professional social workers during the two year period were frustration and fatigue," and that "they were exhausted by having day after day to face critical human situations with insufficient material, intellectual and emotional resources and support."[15] Certainly supervisors cannot wave a magic wand and undo the effects of structural constraints on the worker's capacity to help, but a supervisor who cares about the worker's capacity to help and the worker's mental health can, through support and the offer of intellectual and emotional resources, make a great deal of difference in what the worker is able to do and in how he grows on the job.

Because of the constant strains and problems of the supervisor's job there has been some push in certain agencies to do away with supervision. Perhaps social work could develop a better form than the supervisory process, but one cannot do away with the supervisory function. Doing away with authority relationships does not necessarily change either people or structural constraints or result in more effective work. As long as personal needs, attitudes, and levels of commitment and skill are brought to a job, there is a need for leadership. As Weissman points out:

> The planning and management of an organization requires specific expertise. . . . there is an ongoing need to reconcile the dilemmas and strains of organizational life. . . . as long as there is concern for the effectiveness in an organization, there will be considerable strain between the needs of the individuals for self-actualization and the needs of organizations for achievement and efficiency.[16]

Somehow these strains need to be reconciled and resolved if clients are to be effectively served. The question concerning the supervisor that is of critical importance for the worker is the supervisor's position on the list of roles that Morgan developed.

Perhaps the primary problem with supervision is not that it is not valuable, or not necessary, but that it has been used in such a way that agencies have avoided consideration of their effectiveness by focusing on the effectiveness of their employees. In most agencies, workers receive yearly evaluations on the anniversary of their joining the staff. Perhaps what is needed are set dates on which both the workers and the agency would be evaluated. In other words the agency needs to look at itself at the same time that it is looking at its workers. As Weissman writes:

> The environment in which the agency operates—physical, social, financial—affects the worker's efforts. To tell the worker to refine his skills

---

[15] Ibid., p. 99.

[16] Weissman, *Overcoming Mismanagement,* p. 131.

or work harder in order to be successful is to ignore the impact of environment. The caseload or lack of cooperation from other agencies, not diagnostic or therapeutic skills, may be at fault.

Evaluating individuals at different times during the year solely in terms of their individual therapeutic skills makes it less likely that the agency will have to react as a system to the results of evaluation. The problems of each worker can be viewed idiosyncratically.

. . . Through consultation with experienced workers, agencies should establish the areas of skill needing improvement and the basis upon which to judge improvement—recordings, observations, client queries, and the like. The worker should choose how to get help, whether through conferences with the supervisor, through taking courses, through peer supervision, or through consultation. Letting the worker decide reduces the dependency feelings which develop through forced supervision.

A degree of arbitrariness will always exist unless an agency has some method of appraising success with clients. Without agency standards of success and an evaluation of the worker's record, workers and supervisors are dependent on secondary data. Case presentation becomes more important than the people treated. The way one writes or speaks about a case becomes more important than the results achieved.[17]

Weissman then goes on to discuss the accountability of the agency for evaluation of its job. (This is another side of the earlier argument made by the authors about the need for evaluative research and ways of evaluating services.) He says:

The key to increasing the influence of lower level staff vis-à-vis their superiors lies in a board (or other body) that can hold the agency accountable. Where there is real accountability, the ideas and experience of all levels of staff become valuable, and the incompetence of individuals becomes a matter of serious concern.

If a board discovers that 80% of the agency's clients feel they have not been helped by the agency, the incompetent supervisors have something to worry about.[18]

CLIENT, WORKER, AND BUREAUCRACY

The procedures of bureaucracy as well as the limitations of policy may be frustrating to both the client and the worker. It is well to recognize that "red tape" was and is developed to assure that people with equal troubles receive equal help and resources. But often it really operates to reduce the client's access to services or to make an already complex situation more difficult and confusing. It is the worker's responsibility to act as his client's broker and advocate in dealing with the

---

[17] Ibid., p. 58.
[18] Ibid., p. 59.

policies and procedures of the bureaucracy. These roles have been discussed earlier, but we will add one last word here.

If the worker is to help the client cope with the problems of access to services in the most helpful way possible, it is critically important that he know with accuracy and understanding the policies and procedures of his agency and the way they operate. Workers are not always as careful and disciplined as they might be in getting a really workable grasp of this knowledge. *Paperwork* can become a very naughty word in the worker's language, but the capacity to handle paperwork efficiently, accurately, and with concern for deadlines and the client's time, is an absolute requirement of the worker who would be a skilled advocate and broker. The authors have worked in agencies where certain chief clerks made more important decisions about who got what than some workers because the clerks had mastered the paper flow and the workers were too impatient to do so. While paperwork can be irritating, the worker needs to understand that it is an attempt to establish procedures by which clients are assured equal service.

One of the authors of this book is old enough to have worked in public welfare before the Social Security Act took effect, when it was the responsibility of the local township to aid people in need of money. At that time paperwork was considerably lighter than it became after the agency was able to secure federal funds if it established certain procedures to assure people equal service and the right of appeal if they felt that they had been capriciously denied. However, at that time people were able to secure aid only if they were able to convince the worker and/or his supervisor that they were "worthy of aid." Sometimes this meant that they had supported the proper political candidate with the proper enthusiasm. This decision could not be challenged—there were no procedures to assure this, no paper on which the basis of the decision was recorded. But back to the present.

The worker needs to thoroughly understand the parameters of the policy of the agency and the authority he has for interpretation. A policy is a broad statement. It has to be interpreted by some individual before it can be applied in the interests of another individual. Far too often, a worker will either ask the worker at the next desk what the agency does about such and such, or give his supervisor a quick call.

Our position is that the worker starts with what the client and he have decided is needed as a resource in the problem solution. Next the worker is responsible for finding out exactly what the written statement of the policy says. Then he sits down and thinks long and hard about what that policy actually means and what all the different possible ways to interpret and apply it are. Next he uses the plan made with the client to test the various interpretations, and selects the interpretation that will best enable him to help the client with what is needed for problem solving. The worker then writes down that interpretation of the policy and the way he would apply it to the client situation. If necessary, this statement may be submitted to the supervisor for his approval, but in any case it needs to be made a part of the record of service to the client. Our view is that taking the quick and easy route of asking colleagues or supervisors about policy is not the proper way to perform one's role as an independent professional person; and our experience has been that following that course increases the likelihood of receiving a directive that limits what one can do. Others do not always want to do the hard headwork either, and when one is in doubt about a policy the easier thing is to say no. It is out of this way of functioning—the use of the traditional messages about policy that circulate on the office grapevine—that old patterns get stabilized and become harder and harder to change. By really knowing policy and by utilizing creative interpretations of policy, the worker can help keep the agency active as an ever-changing bureaucracy.

Several years ago one of the authors conducted a study to find out whether clients were receiving aid they needed and why or why not. In the agency under study workers reported great discouragement with the limitations of agency policies and felt that these policies prevented them from really helping their clients. The study revealed that the average client of that agency was receiving less than half of the amount of services and resources to which he was legally entitled under its policies. In other words, it was not the policies of the agency that were limiting client access to services, but rather the narrow and traditional way that workers and supervisors were interpreting the policies. In the year following the study, as workers were helped to assume active responsibility for broadly interpreting policy, the aid to their clients more than doubled in cost, yet no one in the agency or on its board reached out to stop this more expensive way of operating. The point we are seeking to make is that service to the client is not limited to what one does when one sits with the client. Some of the most important work, and sometimes the work that is most difficult and requires the most self-discipline and commitment, is the work involved when the worker takes on the role of broker with his agency's programs and its bureaucracy. Social workers are often the kind of people who prefer to deal with people rather than with paper—yet dealing with paper is a part of everyone's life in today's world. So we can often fail the client in real and hurtful ways if we do not have expert skills in dealing with paper. Operating contrary to traditional grapevine interpretations of policy may often involve the worker in uncomfortable confrontations with his agency colleagues and his supervisor. And it is not easy for an individual worker as part of a system to move contrary to the patterns and relationships in the system. However, if the worker's interpretation conforms to written policy he can usually prevail in the client's interests, which is what social work is all about.

One more word. If policy does not permit adequate service to clients, this needs to be adequately documented. The worker must assume the responsibility of documenting in some detail the problems he sees. It may be difficult to open up board structure and policy so clients can make an impact, but it will never happen if the worker only "gripes." He must present organized evidence of his position.

CHANGING THE BUREAUCRACY

We have reprinted in this chapter an article that deals with ways of changing the agency from within. Therefore we will speak only briefly about some of the strategies and tactics of this type of change. Basically, the following suggestions are a way of problem solving.

1. Be clear about what needs to be changed, about the difficulties that can be anticipated in bringing about the solution, and about the cost of both the problem and its solution.

2. Determine what factors inside and outside the organization are keeping the problem active.

3. Determine where in the organization the responsibility for formal decision making in respect to the problem lies. Who formally makes the decision, and who can influence the decision?

4. Anticipate the difficulties of the solution. Almost any solution to a social problem brings other problems in its implementation. Be sure that the solution is not worse than the problem, and know some ways of dealing with anticipated difficulties of the solution. Find out whether those who have the responsibility of deciding about the problem are simply unaware of it or are strongly invested in present policy or opposed to any movement because a clash of interests and values is involved.

5. Timing one's efforts can be crucial. Agencies are more often open to change (as are individuals) when they are in periods of crisis, for example, when budgets are increasing or decreasing, when there are great decreases or increases in the number of clients served, when their performance reports are being questioned, when new methods of dealing with the problem are being widely acclaimed.

6. The process by which change takes place must be understood, and it must be recognized that the initiation of change often requires a different approach than does the implementation of change. We have often seen workers fight a hard and bruising battle for the initiation of change only to lose the war because they were unwilling or unable

to be an active part of its implementation. It is the changes in the way things are done that are the test of how the client will be served differently.

7. Consider whether change can be achieved more effectively in this situation by advocacy strategy, by collaborative strategy, or by both. Advocacy strategy employs an impressive array of tools, including the use of citizen groups, unions, and professional organizations to engage with the practitioner in litigation, picketing, bargaining, building pressure alliances, contriving for crises to occur, bringing sanctions to bear through external authorities, and encouraging noncompliance with policy by workers and clients. Collaborative strategy may employ some of the techniques outlined by Patti and Resnick. Here the change agent may: provide facts about the nature of the problem; present alternative ways of doing things; try to develop an experimental project that involves different ways of doing things and get permission to implement it; seek to establish a committee to study the situation and make recommendations for change; attempt to improve the working climate of the agency so that individuals feel trusted and safe and thus can look beyond securing their own position to the task to be done; attempt to bring professional values and ethics to bear; use a logical argument to persuade; and point out what is really happening under the present policy. This last approach will require documentation of the results of present policy.

THE PROFESSION AS A SYSTEM

Social work is a profession, and as a profession it resembles other professions in some aspects of its structure and function and differs from them in other aspects, particularly in its purpose and in some of the ways it functions. Bernard Barber, a sociologist, has identified four essential attributes of professional behavior. They are:

> a high degree of generalized and systematic knowledge; primary orientation to the community interest rather than to individual self-interest; a high degree of self-control and of behavior through codes of ethics internalized in the process of work socialization and through voluntary associations organized and operated by the work specialists themselves; and a system of rewards (monetary and honorary) that is primarily a set of symbols of work achievement and thus ends in themselves, not means to some end of individual self-interest.[19]

In writing about the profession most social work authors speak about its youth and its emergent nature. Barber goes on to discuss some of the stresses inherent in an emergent profession. Members of a young

---

[19] Bernard Barber, "Some Problems in the Sociology of the Professions," *Daedalus* (Fall 1963), p. 672.

profession may not be homogeneous with respect to the first two of the four attributes he lists: the amount of professional knowledge they possess and the community orientation they demonstrate. It does cause many problems for social work that its practitioners are often defined as social workers because they are employed in an agency that calls itself a social agency in a job that the agency titles a social work job.

In attempting to deal with this, leaders of the professional association, the National Association of Social Workers, have developed a certification procedure that requires certain qualifying levels of knowledge and skill and the passing of an examination. The association's Code of Ethics, reprinted in Chapter 3, also attempts to set forth the values that social workers must subscribe to. Unfortunately, the code is written in such general terms that it is difficult for the individual worker to apply it in concrete cases. The problems of interpretation also make it very difficult for one worker to censure another through the use of the Code of Ethics.

Lydia Rapoport says that "no other profession is as self-examining and critically self-conscious as social work."[20] While she relates some problems of the profession to its youth, she also attributes much stress to the profession's ambiguous position in society and to its multiple purposes and functions. Social work, concerned with the social functioning of man and the adequacy of the social institutions which affect his functioning, "seeks to embrace and implement some principles and values which may be essentially unpopular and uncongenial to the dominant social order."[21] This particular role of the profession, as has been observed, results in its being seen as a minority group that is both tolerated and feared. From this come outright attacks and depreciation by the society that sanctions social work. In addition, the social views of the profession tend to isolate individual workers from other professional groups.

One problem of social work is that the tasks it is expected to perform are unclear and that the responsibilities for which it is held to account are often contradictory. For example, many people expect the social worker to control every expenditure of the welfare client, but at the same time to further independent behavior on the part of welfare recipients. Both expectations cannot be satisfied—one or the other must be chosen. Social work is supposed to be working to produce social change, but the society of which social work is a part is totally unable to reach agreement as to the kinds of social change it will support.

Rapoport points out other sources of strain for social workers, some

---

[20] Lydia Rapoport, "In Defense of Social Work: An Examination of the Stress of the Profession." Lecture, June 16, 1959, at School of Social Welfare, University of California at Berkeley.

[21] Ibid.

of which we have touched on earlier in this text. Among them are the following:

1. Being constantly confronted with the problems of human need, pain, and injustice.
2. The capacity for self-awareness and self-control required for the purposeful use of the social work relationship, and the need "to harmonize personal capacity and inclination with professional behavior and values."
3. The institutional framework within which the social worker practices.
4. The opposing demands for "the maintenance of nearness and distance, of involvement and detachment, of rapport and objectivity."
5. The requirement for the tolerance of uncertainty, given our limited knowledge about man and his development and our difficulty in attempting to utilize what we do know.[22]

RECAPITULATION

In this chapter we have moved from our focus on the interaction of client and worker for problem solving to what it means for the worker to be a part of the action system of an agency and a profession. It is critically important for a worker's practice that he understand the situation in which he works. We have tried to contribute to this understanding through a look at the nature of bureaucracy and professionalism; the conflicts between bureaucracy and professionalism; the worker and the client as operating within the parameters of agency policy; ways to bring about change in a bureaucracy; and the worker as a professional.

A LOOK FORWARD

As the reader comes to the end of this chapter, we would like to remind him that one of the most complex and necessary skills a worker can develop is the capacity to achieve professional goals through work with the formal organization. The following summary of Robert Pruger's "The Good Bureaucrat" sums up what we have tried to say and should leave the reader with some notions that will be useful in the future.

These, according to Prager, are strategic concerns of the good bureaucrat:

1. "One important property of a good bureaucrat is staying power." This means a recognition that things happen slowly in complex organizations but that whatever changes the worker has in mind, he cannot implement them if he doesn't stay in and with the organization.

---

[22] Ibid.

2. "The good bureaucrat must somehow maintain his vitality of action and independence of thought." Organizational life tends to suppress vitality of action and independence of thought. We must resist such pressure.

3. "There is always room for insights and tactics that help the individual preserve and enlarge the discretionary aspect of his activity and, by extension, his sense of personal responsibility."

And these are tactics the good bureaucrat will employ:

1. "Understand legitimate authority and organizational enforcement." The inescapable degree of generality found in the regulatory policies and codes of the organization allows for considerable autonomy of the individual if he just recognizes it and uses it. The organization's power to control is less than many realize, but if the limits of legitimate authority are recognized, the individual may expand his discretionary limits.

2. "Conserve energy." One should not thrash around and feel discouraged and unappreciated because he does not receive in a large organization the kind of support he receives from his friends. Also, as we said earlier, master the paper flow of the organization. This will not only help the client but will also remove from the worker's shoulders the weight of resentment and emotional turmoil one feels as one looks at the uncompleted statistical forms on his desk. We should describe what can be changed and work on it rather than spend valuable hours bemoaning what can't be dealt with.

3. "Acquire a competence needed by the organization."

4. "Don't yield unnecessarily to the requirements of administrative convenience. Keep in mind the difference between that which serves the organizational mission and that that serves the organization." Rules, standards, and directives as to the way things should be done are meant to be means that serve ends. In organizations means tend to become ends, so that a worker may be more concerned about turning in his mileage report than with the result of his visit to a client. Ends and means should be kept clear.

5. We should remember that "the good bureaucrat is not necessarily the most beloved one."[23]

---

[23] Robert Pruger, "The Good Bureaucrat," *Social Work* 18:4 (July 1973), pp. 26–32.

Casework beyond bureaucracy[*]

Archie Hanlan

In a provocative analysis of urban social problems, Edward Banfield suggests that an alarmist description not warranted by the objective situation may, nevertheless, be acted upon subjectively as a real crisis, thus perpetuating a "reign of error" regarding the problem.[1] In a similar vein, it may be argued that an alarmed emphasis on a crisis in casework has distorted the objective situation. Although that emphasis may be exaggerated, if it is defined as real, then it is real in its consequences for social work.

This article traces the recent emphasis on the bureaucratization of casework practice. Although this emphasis serves to sensitize the practitioner to the agency influences on his practice, it also tends to obscure the options and possible remedies open to both agencies and practitioners. Insofar as the problem is defined in the either-or dilemma of bureaucracy versus professionals, the constricted definition becomes a self-fulfilling prophecy. Such a definition contains an assumption that the conflict is resolvable only outside of the system. Thus, effort to change the existing agency system is diverted or abandoned—costly consequence of such a definition of the casework situation.

Beginning of bureaucratized casework

Casework began, at least in the Mary Richmond era, not in bureaucracies but in voluntary charity organizations where the agency was both the source of knowledge and the place for casework practice. The agency, as the locus for both the theory and its application, followed an apprenticeship model that clearly delineated the fixed roles of apprentice and employer.

It was not until the late 1930s that bureaucracy was identified as problematic for caseworkers. Moreover, it was considered to exist only in the public agencies.

> In the private agency because of the specialized nature of the job, limited case load and selectivity of personnel, the supervisor is able

[*] Reprinted by permission of the author and the Family Service Association of America from *Social Casework*, 52:4 (April 1971), pp. 195–99.

[1] Edward Banfield, *The Unheavenly City: The Nature and the Future of Our Urban Crisis* (Boston: Little, Brown & Co., 1970), p. 259.

to relate himself to the supervisee upon a more deliberate basis. . . . In the public agency, on the other hand, rigidity of structure due to legal and budgetary limitations, hasty changes in policy necessitated by changing conditions, pressure of work and pressure from the community and administration, force the supervisor frequently to assume an executive type of control.[2]

The public agencies—particularly the new public welfare system—exposed some social workers for the first time to the classical features of bureaucracy.[3] A primary characteristic encountered was the hierarchy of positions within the agency, illustrated by the organizational chart showing all positions in the agency in the form of a pyramid with the chief executive at the apex. Within public welfare, the supervisor was expected to assume responsibility for administrative control over performance. This control soon conflicted with the caseworker's demand for some degree of autonomy in his practice.

Another feature of bureaucracy encountered by caseworkers was the set of rules and regulations pervasive in the administration of all governmental agencies. Rules became an anathema of red tape for most social workers. Specialization of duties or division of labor, another bureaucratic characteristic, was still another source of tension for the caseworker. However the caseworker defined his expertise, public welfare demanded a variety of tasks to be performed, and the division of labor was determined by other than casework skills.

Impersonal performance of duty, in Max Weber's sense of objective behavior toward clientele,[4] might have been compatible with casework, but it soon became identified with a non-Weberian notion of indifference and aloofness toward clientele. The fifth characteristic of bureaucracy, tenured office, soon became associated with a rigid civil service system that, instead of preventing inadequate performance, sometimes rewarded it.[5]

Thus, the rational model of bureaucracy that Weber saw as an antidote to political corruption and nepotism became a symbol of the public agency conditions opposed by a new group of caseworkers striving to establish themselves among the professions. The disdain that social workers held for public agencies was reflected in the following pithy comment by Edith Abbott: "Too often our young social workers in the private

---

[2] Case Work Notebook, *Social Work Today*, 5:23 (October 1937).

[3] For a critique of some of the characteristics discussed here, see Archie Hanlan, "Counteracting Problems of Bureaucracy in Public Welfare," *Social Work*, 12:88–94 (July 1967).

[4] Talcott Parsons, *Max Weber: The Theory of Social and Economic Organization* (New York: Free Press, 1964), p. 340.

[5] For a parody on this phenomenon, see Laurence J. Peter and Raymond Hull, *The Peter Principle* (New York: William Morrow and Co., 1969).

agencies have a strangely superior attitude regarding public work—but perhaps this is by way of compensation for their lower salaries."[6]

By the 1950s, especially with influence from the nascent sociology of professions, the characteristics of bureaucracy were increasingly described as constraints upon the professional practice of caseworkers. Now, however, the arguments and analyses were advanced to include the voluntary as well as the public social agencies. In all of social work there was a need for what Robert Vinter calls "an explicit recognition of the effects of organizational structure on service."[7] Reversing the situation in the 1930s, the voluntary agencies were singled out for special criticism in the 1960s. They had fled the urban ghetto areas, and those that remained served only to reinforce the dependency of the people in those areas.[8]

The caseworker versus bureaucracy

Near the end of the past decade, the impact of these and other criticisms was reflected in a collection of papers entitled "Social Casework: Past, Present and Future."[9] The bureaucratization of casework was one of the major factors given central attention. Scott Briar, in the introductory paper, observes:

> In many social agencies certain of the crucial conditions that caseworkers should be able to vary in order to help their clients are normatively prescribed, including the methods of intervention he is to use; where, when, and how often he is to see his clients; and even the very language he is to use to describe his clients and the theory that is to inform his practice. The caseworker who proposes to depart from agency norms in the conduct of his practice is likely to evoke not a dialogue on the relative merits of different practice methods but a reminder that what he proposed would violate agency policy, an almost sure sign that the rules in question exist to benefit the agency and its organizational requirements rather than the needs of its clientele.[10]

---

[6] Edith Abbott, *Social Welfare and Professional Education* (Chicago: University of Chicago Press, 1931), p. 89.

[7] Robert Vinter, "The Social Structure of Service," in *Issues in American Social Work*, ed. Alfred J. Kahn (New York: Columbia University Press, 1959), p. 268. See also Herman D. Stein, "Organizational Theory—Implications for Administration Research," in *Social Science Theory and Social Work Research*, ed. Leonard S. Kogan (New York: National Association of Social Workers, 1960), p. 85.

[8] Kenneth B. Clark, *Dark Ghetto* (New York: Harper & Row, 1965), p. 50. See also Richard A. Cloward and Irwin Epstein, "Private Social Welfare's Disengagement from the Poor: The Case of Family Adjustment Agencies," in *Social Welfare Institutions: A Sociological Reader*, ed. Mayer N. Zald (New York: John Wiley & Sons, 1965), pp. 623–44.

[9] Scott Briar et al., "Social Casework: Past, Present and Future," *Social Work*, 13:5–59 (January 1968).

[10] Scott Briar, "The Casework Predicament," *Social Work*, 13:10 (January 1968).

This analysis of the bureaucratic problems confronting the caseworker was a logical extension of the analysis of displacement of organizational goals that Robert K. Merton had noted long ago.[11] Social agencies exist to serve human beings, clientele; but, as agencies tended to assume lives of their own, the original goal of serving people was replaced by the goal of serving the agency as an end in itself. A major characteristic of the casework predicament, therefore, was the superordinate position of agency needs over client needs.

The last two decades saw the thesis of professionalism advanced in social work. To achieve the antithesis of bureaucratic social agencies was considered an irresolvable problem. Possibilities for synthesis, for moving beyond the dialectical analysis of professionalism versus bureaucracy, were virtually excluded. The few solutions proposed were outside of the existing agency systems, variations on the private entrepreneurial model. Yet these solutions avoided precisely what was considered to be most problematic in other sectors of the society. Bureaucracy was steering society on an inevitable course toward technocratic totalitarianism, and the main hope lay in the possibility that both "technology and bureaucracy can be mastered."[12]

Considering the possibilities for mastering bureaucracy in casework, especially if caseworkers are to act on their declaration of extending professional services to the unserved and the poor, some confrontation is required with the fact that this extension will occur primarily through complex human service organizations. The inadequacy of existing medical and legal services through the private entrepreneurial model in the inner cities is a commentary on the prospects for social services through the private social work practitioner.

A less-than-apocalyptic analysis of the prospect for extending social work, medical, and legal services through complex organizations has been suggested by Everett C. Hughes.

> The people in organizations will be—although in some sense bureaucrats—the innovators, the people who push back the frontiers of theoretical and practical knowledge related to their professions, who will invent new ways of bringing the professional services to everyone, not merely the solvent or sophisticated few. Indeed, I think it likely that the profes-

---

[11] Hanlan, "Counteracting Problems," p. 89.

[12] The quotation is from a statement made by a former president of Students for a Democratic Society in "A Dialogue Between Generations," *Harper's*, October 1967, p. 50.

According to a government publication, "Historically, those on the right have been most anxious about the evils of bureaucracy and most enthusiastic about decentralization. But recently, the 'new left' seems on its way to putting democratic participation in large organizations, including some forms of decentralization, above the left's traditional advocacy of central planning and the nationalization of industry." U.S., Department of Health, Education and Welfare, *Toward A Social Report* (Washington: Government Printing Office, January 11, 1969), p. 83.

sional conscience, the superego, of many professions will be lodged in that segment of the professionals who work in complicated settings, for they must, in order to survive, be sensitive to more problems and to a greater variety of points of view.[13]

Recent literature indicates that some social workers are seeking to invent or borrow new ways for bringing professional services to previously unserved groups through complicated delivery settings other than through private practice. Although the impetus for some of these innovations clearly stems from social work's increased emphasis on professionalism, there is evidence that the civil rights movement, federal funding, and local community interest groups also have played a vital part in the total pressure for change, especially among the voluntary agencies.[14] The efforts of voluntary casework agencies to respond to the needs of black urban clientele appear to be major factors in innovations in both treatment modalities and in organizational structure.[15]

In any event, some alternatives to the classical bureaucratic structure of social agencies are beginning to emerge. These alternatives are presented here in the context of debureaucratizing the existing agency base of casework practice. The emphasis is upon changing or removing some of those bureaucratic features of social agencies that have been dysfunctional for both caseworker and client. These alternatives provide an agency base for casework beyond bureaucracy.

Debureaucratizing the agency

The hierarchical structuring of positions and persons in bureaucracy has had special implications for social workers. For example, supervision of the professional has continued interminably for bureaucratic rather than for professional reasons. One alternative explored in a voluntary agency is the use of a collegial organizational structure for staff to interact with one another as peers rather than as superordinates and subordinates in an agency line of command.[16]

This kind of supervision is not a new "invention," but it is feasible within many types of social agencies. It does not, however, mitigate the need for coordination of staff activities and, especially in larger agencies, for the differential allocation of agency resources within the

---

[13] Everett C. Hughes, "Professions," in *The Professions in America,* ed. Kenneth S. Lynn (Boston: Houghton Mifflin Company, 1965), p. 12.

[14] Richard O. Stock, "Societal Demands on the Voluntary Agency," *Social Casework,* 50:27–31 (January 1969).

[15] Howard Hush et al., "Relevant Agency Programs for the Large Urban Community," *Social Casework,* 51:199–208 (April 1970).

[16] Joseph H. Kahle, "Structuring and Administering a Modern Voluntary Agency," *Social Work,* 14:20–28 (October 1969).

organization. Although staff may participate in these decisions, some ongoing and centralized structure is necessary for both short-range and long-range maintenance and planning of the agency. Thus, collegial structure is not a complete substitute for some hierarchically differentiated structure of staff.[17]

Another debureaucratizing feature would be to legitimize explicitly the professional judgments of the caseworker *in place of* agency rules and regulations that prescribe conditions of the worker-client transaction. This procedure reinforces the supervisor as one of several consultants and trainers rather than as the enforcer of rules and regulations for the professional act. Some rules and regulations remain necessary for effective agency functioning but not as barriers to, or prescriptions for, the actual rendering of service.

The specialization of duties or division of labor should be based not on predetermined agency "slots" or traditions but on the particular skills and interests of the particular caseworker with particular clientele. Professionals have operated too long on the assumption that a caseworker can do casework with everyone. Whatever is thought of generic casework, it does not lessen the need to optimize varying technical skills of staff. Especially as agencies expand the range of clientele served, there is increased need for division of labor by the technical tasks and skills required for particular clientele and not by preconceived agency needs.

Having demonstrated some competence in performance with some clientele, the caseworker should achieve a tenured position in the agency. Although this tenure is not guaranteed employment, it should confirm that the caseworker has met the explicit, minimal expectations of the agency and will not be subject to capricious or sudden dismissal. This bureaucratic characteristic of tenured office should avoid the rigidities of some civil service procedure whereby the flexibility of assignments, promotions, and task performance is unduly restricted.

These brief suggestions for debureaucratizing some aspects of social agencies serve the goal of strengthening the exercise of professional judgment and encouraging the increasingly autonomous performance of the caseworker in the treatment of clients. In themselves, however, they do not change the client's relative position of dependence on the agency and the caseworker. The consumer-client of casework services has a constricted market in which to "purchase" those services. He is often dependent on only one agency and on only one caseworker, and this situation constitutes a monopoly—not a marketplace.

[17] For a thorough discussion of bureaucratic and nonbureaucratic features in public schools, see Eugene Litwak and Henry J. Meyer, "The Administrative Style of the School and Organizational Tasks," in *Strategies of Community Organization,* ed. Fred M. Cox et al. (New York: F. E. Peacock Publishers, 1970), pp. 78–91.

Some studies indicate that efforts to reverse this situation, to increase the dependence of the agency and the caseworker upon the client, in themselves have a debureaucratizing effect.[18] Thus, social work advocacy of new systems for the delivery of social services, such as vouchers and other government subsidization that increases the consumer's independence and choice among agencies, is likely to have considerable impact on both voluntary and public social agencies.[19]

Conclusions

Social work's move toward increased professionalization was accompanied by increased bureaucratization of casework practice. Rather than viewing these developments as mutually exclusive and irresolvable, this writer has suggested ways for adapting and mastering the bureaucracy as the servant of the caseworker and his client. Although this analysis may emphasize a more optimistic view of social agency flexibility, it provides some balance to the dismal view of agencies as unchangeable bureaucracies.

If commitment to clientele is really the primary professional concern, then one way of meeting that commitment is to make the agencies and staffs more responsive to the needs of the client. Unless social workers are to forsake the present for some future social work utopia, they will need to address themselves to some of the mundane, day-to-day, agency-based features of services to clients. This plan will require increased knowledge and awareness of the caseworker's professional self as a source of organizational resistance and a subtle defender of the agency status quo as well as awareness of oneself as an agent of psychological and social change. Thus, casework beyond bureaucracy will require not only debureaucratized agencies but also caseworkers who are beyond becoming bureaucrats.

---

[18] Peter Blau and W. Richard Scott, *Formal Organizations* (San Francisco: Chandler Publishing Co., 1962), pp. 232–34.

[19] See, for example, June Axinn, "The Components of an Optimal Social Service Delivery System," minmeographed (Philadelphia: University of Pennsylvania School of Social Work, 1970).

Changing the agency from within

Rino J. Patti and Herman Resnick

Although the rhetoric of social action in the 1960s sensitized social workers to the negative consequences of agency practices and policies, practitioners have not been particularly active in pressing for change from within their agencies. This is attributable in part to their lack of knowledge and skills in working with large systems. Equally important, however, is the fact that schools and professional associations have been far too timid about challenging inequitable and injurious agency practices. This situation should change as the knowledge and skills needed to undertake organizational change are considered an integral part of the practitioner's training.

As yet efforts to provide an informed and systematic conceptual framework for intraorganizational change are still in the embryonic stage.[1] Intraorganizational change refers to the systematic efforts of practitioners to effect changes in policies or programs from within their agencies, when they have no administrative sanction for these activities. The legitimation for these efforts is derived from the practitioner's ethical obligation to place professional values above organizational allegiance, i.e., he has the responsibility to become actively engaged in promoting an organizational environment that enhances the welfare of the agency's clients and staff.

This article discusses three phases of the intraorganizational change component in social work practice—formulation of goals, mobilization of resources, and intervention. In describing each phase, the authors provide some organizing concepts that will help the practitioner plan his change efforts more systematically. In addition, they illustrate how

Reprinted with permission of the authors and the National Association of Social Workers from *Social Work*, 17:4 (July 1972), pp. 48–57.

[1] A number of important theoretical contributions have helped lay the foundations for the ideas presented here. See Hyman Weiner, "Toward Techniques for Social Change," *Social Work*, Vol. 6, No. 2 (April 1961), pp. 26–35; Weiner, "Social Change and Group Work Practice," *Social Work*, Vol. 9, No. 3 (July 1964), pp. 106–12; George Brager, "Institutional Change: Perimeters of the Possible," *Social Work*, Vol. 12, No. 1 (January 1967), pp. 59–69; Robert Morris and Alfred Binstock, *Feasible Planning for Social Change* (New York: Columbia University Press, 1967); Harry Specht, "Disruptive Tactics," *Social Work*, Vol. 14, No. 2 (April 1969), pp. 5–15; and Roland Warren, "Types of Purposive Change at the Community Level," in Ralph Kramer and Specht, eds., *Readings in Community Organization Practice* (Englewood Cliffs, N.J.: Prentice-Hall, 1969), pp. 205–22.

a careful assessment of goals and resources can help the change agent choose a rational intervention strategy.

Goal formulation

Once the practitioner has identified the organizational problem he wishes to address, he must specify the changes he wants to bring about, i.e., the goal he seeks.[2] Although this task may seem implicit in identifying the problem, the change agent must keep in mind that formulating a goal involves not only a consideration of what should be done to alter or eliminate the undesirable situation, but what can be done under existing circumstances—i.e., he must separate what he would like to achieve from what he can reasonably expect to achieve.

In determining what goal to pursue, the practitioner must consider two important factors. First, he must examine the agency's decision-making process to determine who exercises both formal authority and informal influence on the outcome of his proposal. In other words, how are decisions made in the organization on the specific issue in question, and who is in a position to influence this process? Clearly an administrator does not make his decisions in a vacuum. He is substantially influenced by the information and perceptions provided by subordinates, as well as his own evaluation of how his decision will be received by those who will carry it out. For example, if a change agent's proposal can be distorted discredited, or delayed by someone before it reaches the ultimate decision-maker, that person must be considered central to the decision-making process. In other instances, the decision-maker may reject a proposal, despite his inclination to accept it, to avoid embarrassing or threatening someone whose favor he wishes to retain. The number of persons who may influence the decision-maker on a particular matter will, of course, vary with the nature of the proposal.

Second, the change agent must consider whether those who exercise formal authority or informal influence in the decision-making process are likely to agree or disagree with his proposal. This kind of analysis is important because it enables the change agent to anticipate how much resistance or support his proposal is likely to encounter.

In refining the discussion on agreement and disagreement, Warren's formulation of issue consensus, issue difference, and issue dissensus is

---

[2] Goal formulation rests on identifying the problem and analyzing the factors within and outside the organization that cause it. Force field analysis can be productively employed to help social workers with widely varying knowledge about organizational behavior translate their discomfort about agency situations into explicit, cogent statements of the problem. For a fuller discussion of this instrument and its application in an organizational context, see David H. Jenkins, "Force Field Analysis Applied to a School Situation," in Warren Bennis, Kenneth Benne, and Robert Chin, eds., *The Planning of Change* (New York: Holt, Rinehart & Winston, 1964), pp. 238–44.

useful.[3] Originally, this scheme was proposed in the context of community organization practice, but it seems equally applicable to intraorganizational change. Warren posits an agreement-disagreement continuum between the change agent and the power configuration (those who directly influence or actually make decisions). This continuum is defined by the extent to which these parties have common values and interests with regard to a specific issue. Thus when both parties basically agree on how an issue should be resolved, or are likely to reach an agreement once it has been explored, there is *issue consensus.* When the decision-makers do not recognize the problem or do not understand the substance of the proposal, *issue difference* exists. In this situation the change agent is confronted with either refusal to acknowledge that an issue exists or opposition to his proposal. In either case, however, he believes that through education and persuasion he can tap some mutual values or interests that will serve as a basis for acceptance of his proposal. In situations involving *issue dissensus,* decision-makers also refuse to recognize the issue or oppose the proposal, but the values or interests of those involved are so divergent that mere persuasion or education is unlikely to bring about consensus.

By utilizing this scheme as an analytic aid, the change agent can estimate the resistance, obstacles, or support he is likely to encounter before he attempts to pursue his proposal. This estimate, however rough, will help him to choose the resources and strategies needed to accomplish his goal. Most important, it will help him decide whether he wants to make the personal commitment required.

It has been suggested that the practitioner may not always be able to apply this scheme readily because he lacks direct access to decision-makers, especially in large organizations.[4] Yet he can often determine much about the values and interests of those in authority by carefully assessing how they have reacted to similar proposals in the past. Although administrators do change their views over time, one can expect more continuity than discontinuity on matters that touch their vital interests. In addition, a careful, assessment of the functions an organization serves for groups that legitimate and support it frequently provides important clues as to how a change proposal will be received.

Too many change efforts founder because change agents fail to consider in advance the kind and intensity of opposition their proposals will encounter. Often change agents are so certain that their goal is inherently right that they assume others will agree. Thus an analysis of the sort just described can help the practitioner determine whether his goal is feasible.

---
[3] Warren, op. cit., pp. 207–10.
[4] Conversation with Benson Jaffee, Associate Professor, School of Social Work, University of Washington, Seattle, June 1971.

A goal's feasibility is only partially determined after an analysis of the decision-making process and the extent to which the decision-makers will agree or disagree with the proposal. As Morris and Binstock suggest, the change agent's capacity to overcome the resistance to it is also extremely important.[5] This leads to a discussion of the resources available to the intraorganizational change agent.

Resource mobilization

Assessment and mobilization of resources for intraorganizational change have not been adequately considered by theoreticians or practitioners.[6] In part this may reflect a pervasive tendency to assume that organizational change is solely the responsibility of those officially vested with the authority to effect changes in agency structure and operation. As a result, the focus is usually on how decisions can be implemented rather than how the decision-making process can be influenced.

The concern here is with identifying the sources of power that *may* be available to the change agent who has no legitimate authority for his activities.[7] This is crucial because one of the major obstacles confronting the change agent is his apparent lack of power.[8]

Practitioners frequently complain about some aspect of their agency in one breath and proclaim in the next that there is little or nothing they can do about it because their superiors are resistant to change. This sense of powerlessness is caused in part by their failure to recognize that the legitimation for change efforts is derived from one's professional commitment to client service—a commitment that is independent of a person's position in an agency. Another factor, however, is the general inability of practitioners to assess rationally the resources within an organization that can be marshaled on behalf of change efforts.

Obviously, the change agent must first assess his own qualities and characteristics as they relate to the change being contemplated. For example, if he seeks to reform some aspect of the agency, he will have more

---

[5] Morris and Binstock, op. cit., pp. 25–31.

[6] A major exception is the excellent discussion in ibid., pp. 113–127. See also, Brager, op. cit., pp. 66–68.

[7] The term "power" denotes "a capacity to overcome part or all of the resistance, to introduce changes in the face of opposition (this includes sustaining a course of action or preserving a status quo that would otherwise have been discontinued or altered)." Amitai Etzioni, "Power as a Societal Force," in Marvin Olsen, ed., *Power in Societies* (New York: Macmillan Co., 1970), p. 18.

[8] There is increasing recognition of the power possessed by nonadministrative personnel in organizations. See, for example, David Mechanic, "Sources of Power of Lower Participants in Complex Organizations," *Administrative Science Quarterly*, Vol. 7, No. 3 (December 1962), pp. 349–64; and Jan Howard and Robert Somers, "Resisting Institutional Evil from Within," unpublished paper, undated (mimeographed).

credibility if he is competent in his job. Nothing is quite so damaging to a cause as a leader who is professionally vulnerable. Consequently, the change agent must consider his standing in the agency so that the "action system's" agenda will not be undermined by charges of professional irresponsibility, unethical behavior, substandard performance, and the like.[9]

The change agent should also evaluate his ability to engage in interpersonal conflict. If he is unable to function effectively in such encounters, he should let someone who is skillful in handling situations involving confrontation, disagreement, and negotiation assume primary responsibility. If a practitioner equates his commitment to the change effort with his capacity to engage in confrontation, he may avoid becoming involved. Thus the action system is deprived of talents that could be utilized in other facets of the change effort. For example, some groups adopt a public stance of uncompromising militancy to create conditions in which private negotiations can occur. Since it is difficult for one change agent to carry on both tactics simultaneously, it is most efficient to allocate persons with different skills to these respective areas of activity.

The worker who lacks official authority to change agency policies or procedures must also attempt to identify and mobilize the sources of power that are available to the action system. In most instances, his fellow workers are his greatest source of power. Although they do not represent the only resource he can draw on, they are vitally important if the action system is to be credible.

The following framework, adapted from the work of Raven and French, is useful in relating workers' attributes to potential sources of power.[10] It suggests five types of power and the sources from which they are derived:

1. Coercive power—the capacity to reward and punish.
2. Referent power—the ability of a person or group to attract others, i.e., to serve as a role model with whom others wish to identify.
3. Expert power—the possession of knowledge in some area that the agency considers important.
4. Legitimate power—the capacity to invoke authority that is officially vested by the agency.
5. Value power—the ability to articulate values to which other people are drawn.

---

[9] The term "action system" means those persons or groups that consciously join in planned collective activity to change some aspect of the organization's policy or practice.

[10] See Warren Bennis, *Changing Organizations* (New York: McGraw-Hill Book Co., 1966), p. 168.

Assuming that these sources of power are available to the change agent, then what observable personal characteristics or attributes, found among potential members of the action system, could be translated into the kinds of power just mentioned? The following list of attributes is offered as a point of departure:

Cosmopolitan orientation. Staff members who are committed to professional values and norms and seek affirmation from individuals and groups espousing similar values have a cosmopolitan orientation. This includes practitioners who strongly identify with social causes; have allegiances to outside organizations that seek to protect or advance the interests of exploited, oppressed, or powerless groups; or have made personal or professional sacrifices to meet client needs. Such persons can influence others, including administrators, by pointing out agency practices that diverge from professional principles. They can also serve as liaisons with outside groups (e.g., schools, associations, client groups) that the action system may turn to when seeking support or coalitions.

Informal leadership. Informal leadership is provided by staff members who are sought out by peers and superiors for advice, counsel, and support; influence the tone and direction of informal group interaction; or have linkages with several subgroups in the agency. Such persons are a potential source of power to the extent they can attract others who are ambivalent about engaging in organizational change. Sometimes they can also serve as intermediaries with administrators or bring some legitimacy to the change effort.

Educational or experiential qualifications. Staff members with special educational or experiential qualifications are a potential source of coercive power because they perform specialized or highly skilled tasks in the agency, their professional judgment and knowledge are valued by peers and administrators, or their professional reputation lends prestige to the agency and is likely to attract other talented practitioners. Thus the agency needs them because of the specialized nature of their work or their prestige. Since they are also highly desirable in the employment market, their threats to resign are likely to be believed.

Specialized information or knowledge. Staff members who are knowledgeable about the problem under consideration are a potential source of expert power because they can withhold, selectively utilize, or marshal their knowledge to help the action system make its case.

These attributes do not represent an exhaustive list. Nor is it implied that one person could not possess some or all of them in combination. They are presented to illustrate potential sources of power that may be available within an agency.

The relationship between practitioners' attributes and types of power can be illustrated graphically as follows:

	Workers' attributes			
Types of power	Cosmopolitan orientation	Informal leadership	Education and experience	Specialized knowledge
Coercion	X		X	X
Referent		X		
Expertise			X	X
Legitimacy		X		
Value	X			

This analysis suggests that, other things being equal, an action system is likely to be more powerful in influencing agency policy if it includes workers who possess these attributes.[11] In addition, it appears that an action system's chances of success are increased to the extent that it mobilizes the kinds of power that are salient to its goals and strategies.

Again it must be mentioned that these attributes and their power equivalents are only potential resources. They are of liittle value to the action system unless they are committed to the change effort, and this seldom occurs in the absence of personal energy and willingness to take risks.

Intervention

Selecting and implementing a strategy are, of course, central to the process of intraorganizational change. In this phase the action system chooses a course of action that initially defines the parameters of its efforts to effect the desired change. In situations involving complicated change processes, the action system may use more than one strategy in combination at a specific time or sequentially over a period of time. Seldom, if ever is an action system able to anticipate all the consequences of its interventions or foresee all the forces that will come into play as the scenario unfolds. Consequently, it is artificial to suggest that the strategy an action system chooses and implements is final and irreversible. Indeed, probably the most characteristic activity of the intervention phase is evaluating the effects of the chosen strategy and making necessary adjustments, alterations, and so forth.

Nevertheless, choices must be made, and the change agent is more likely to select an effective strategy if he bases his choice on a deliberate

---

[11] An action system composed of workers with few of these attributes might generate considerable power if its numbers and commitment were high or if it engaged in tactics that were disruptive to the agency. Other sources of power that do not depend on the individual attributes of members of the action system can be mobilized through alliances with other organizations such as funding and standard-setting agencies, professional associations, professional schools, and so forth.

assessment of the goal and the resources available to the action system.[12] The following discussion deals with the relationship between these two variables and strategy.

A number of useful schemes for conceptualizing the range of strategies that are available to the change agent can be found in the literature.[13] Generally, these schemes are based on an underlying continuum, ranging from fundamental agreement to fundamental disagreement between the action system and the "target system" with regard to the substance of the proposed change.[14] The following dichotomy of strategies is useful in discussing the change agent's options.

Collaborative strategies. The adoption of a collaborative strategy is based on the notion that the best way to induce change is to work with the target system. In other words, if the target system is aware of the problem or sees the merits of the action system's proposal, it will voluntarily try to make changes in the organization. A collaborative strategy also rests on the assumption that the target system is rational, open to new ideas, and acting in good faith. Since collaboration implies reciprocity, this stance necessarily implies that the action system is willing to modify its goals to accommodate the needs and interests of the target system.

Operationally, a collaborative strategy may involve the following activities: (1) providing information about the nature of the problem, (2) presenting alternative courses of action (programs, procedures, and the like), (3) requesting support for experimentation with new approaches to the problem (e.g., new forms of service delivery), (4) seeking to establish a committee to study and make recommendations on alternative approaches to the problem, (5) creating new opportunities for interaction between members of the action system and target system to express ideas and feelings, build trust, and learn better ways to communicate with one another, (6)making appeals to conscience, profes-

---

[12] Other relevant variables include the nature and magnitude of the problem that prompted the change activity, whether the change process is considered finite or part of a long-range effort involving several subsequent interventions, the secondary consequences sought by the action system as a result of the change process, the ethical boundaries within which the change agent feels constrained to operate, and the probable effects of a specific strategy on the action system's morale and commitment.

[13] See, for example, Brager, op. cit., pp. 68–69; Warren, op. cit., pp. 210–18; Specht, op. cit., pp. 378–86; Richard Walton, "Two Strategies of Social Change and Their Dilemmas," in Kramer and Specht, eds., op. cit., pp. 337–45; Arthur Blum, Magdalena Miranda, and Maurice Meyer, "Goals and Means for Social Change," in John Turner, ed., *Neighborhood Organization for Community Action* (New York: National Associaiton of Social Workers, 1968), pp. 106–20; and Morris and Binstock, op. cit., pp. 113–27.

[14] The term "target system" refers to those persons who directly influence or are formally responsible for making decisions on the changes proposed by the action system.

sional ethics, and values, (7) persuading by logical argument, selective presentation of data, and (8) pointing out the negative consequences of continuing a specific policy.

Adversary strategies. If the action system adopts an adversary strategy, it believes that to bring about the desired change it must work against the target system. Thus it tries to coerce the adversary into adopting some or all of the changes proposed. It assumes that the target system operates from a relatively fixed position and resists the proposed change because it has an investment in the existing scheme of things, is afraid of unanticipated consequences or financial constraints, or is concerned about losing the support of groups or constituencies that sanction it. In any case, the action system is convinced that it must be made more costly for the target system to adhere to the existing arrangement than to adopt the proposed change and that the organization's failure to respond will be more dysfunctional in the short or long term than any negative consequences that may result from instituting the plan.

Activities

If the action system chooses an adversary strategy, it might be involved in the following activities: (1) submitting to the administration petitions that set forth its demands, (2) confronting the target system openly in agency meetings and public forums, (3) bringing sanctions against the agency through external funding, standard setting, and professional agencies, (4) engaging in public criticism and exposing organizational practices through the communications media, (5) encouraging deliberate noncompliance with agency policy or interference with agency procedures, (6) calling strikes, (7) picketing, (8) engaging in litigation, and (9) bargaining for the purpose of negotiating differences and developing compromise solutions.

In practice it may be difficult to distinguish whether a collaborative or adversary strategy is being used because action systems often utilize elements of both strategies simultaneously or sequentially over time. It is also not uncommon for practitioners to follow a collaborative course of action, although their assumptions about the target system would suggest an adversary strategy. Frequently this occurs because members of the action system recognize that they lack the resources and skills necessary to sustain an adversary approach. In other instances, the choice simply reflects their discomfort about violating organizational norms, fear of losing colleagues' support or approval, or unwillingness to risk their jobs, promotions, and so forth. In any case, the action system is not always able to translate its analysis of the desired strategies into action.

Nevertheless, having set forth the assumptions that underlie collaborative and adversary strategies and some of the activities that tend to be associated with each, it is possible to illustrate how the action system might relate the selection of strategies to goals and resources.

A collaborative strategy is most effective when there is consensus between the action system and target system on the issue in question. Because both systems basically agree on how the issue should be resolved and the major problems are technical in nature, the action system needs the power of expertise. Therefore, it should draw on practitioners who have specialized substantive knowledge about the problem, are able to collect and analyze data in a systematic manner and present it cogently, and have demonstrated some competence in dealing with the problem.

A collaborative strategy is also appropriate, at least initially, in situations that involve issue difference, i.e., when the action system must persuade or educate the target system to recognize the problem's existence or importance and the necessity for action. Although the importance of utilizing change agents who are knowledgeable about the problem cannot be overemphasized, this may not be sufficient. To activate dormant value commitments, the action system may find it advantageous to recruit a change agent with a cosmopolitan orientation, e.g., a person who is identified with social causes or strongly committed to client interests. Because a change agent with these attributes can point out the discrepancy between agency policy and professional values such as racial equality, he often has as much impact on decision-makers as the most carefully executed study. Finally, if the action system wants to promote agreement with the target system by increased communication and attitudinal change, it should recruit change agents who are trusted and respected by the target system, have the skill to facilitate communication and understanding between the interested parties, or are sensitive to the administration's need to maintain agency stability.

When the action system's goals conflict sharply with those of the target system, an adversary strategy is most appropriate. Because there is little possibility of achieving consensus, the action system must pose some credible threat to the agency's operation if compromise and exchange are to occur.

To sustain an adversary strategy, the action system must mobilize members with attributes that can produce coercive power—e.g., workers who are important to the agency because of their experience or educational qualifications, are capable of and willing to engage in disruptive activities, or have links with outside groups that can bring negative sanctions against the agency or support the change effort. In addition to coercive power, the action system engaged in an adversary strategy must be attentive to its own need for stability. This is true to some extent for any group attempting intraorganizational change. But it is particularly crucial when an adversary strategy is used because of the strain and uncertainty involved. Therefore, the system should deliberately try to involve practitioners who are informal leaders—e.g., those who can help group members articulate their fears and frustrations; resolve the internal conflicts that so often occur during intensive change efforts; and provide support, counsel, and encouragement to colleagues who experience feelings of uncertainty or futility.

In general then, the chances of inducing organizational change are maximized when the action system consciously relates its strategy to its goals and the resources available. Conversely, when strategies, goals, and resources are mismatched, the chances of success are considerably reduced.

Whether strategies for intraorganizational change will be properly implemented depends on many factors; some have not been identified, let alone studied systematically. Nevertheless, one specific factor should be considered, that is, how the change agent uses the various contexts of action—the environments within and around the organization that may serve as the locus of change activity. In the general sense, two loci can be identified: those within the organization's boundaries and those in the field of influence or power that surround the organization. It is helpful to relate these loci of action to the types of groups that engage in change activities. Again, in the general sense, there are two kinds of groups: informal groups (those that arise from the unofficial interactions of the persons involved in change activities) and formal groups (those that are officially created and sanctioned by the organization).

In their experience with organizational change, the authors have observed that agency workers usually think of change activities as occurring in formal contexts, both internal and external to the organization. Thus practitioners often believe that the only way to attempt change is to present their plan of action to decision-makers through memos, letters, special meetings and conferences, or the development of formal relationships between the organization and professional associations, educational institutions, and the like. As a result, the plan of action surfaces prematurely, and the change effort languishes for lack of support. Informal contexts are used, but usually in an unsystematic way.

The authors suggest that informal contexts can and should be exploited more carefully. For example, if the agency is not prepared to recognize or act on a problem, the worker may find it necessary to utilize the informal-internal context to develop awareness among his colleagues and recruit members to the action system before he brings the matter into the internal-formal context.

Informal-external activities may involve development of coalitions between members of the action system and selected informal allies outside the agency. These coalitions are often crucial because change agents, especially if they are attempting to bring about major changes in agency structure or purpose, are highly susceptible to being co-opted or isolated by those in authority. Such relationships serve at least two important functions: (1) Informal-external relationships can provide socioemotional support and affirmation to change agents involved in unpopular and perhaps conflict-oriented change efforts. (2) Intraorganizational change agents often benefit from discussing strategies with someone outside the system. An outside peer-consultant frequently gives the change agent a rational innovative perspective that he would otherwise not have because he is caught up in agency norms and procedures and the exigencies of day-to-day operations.

Conclusion

Some critics of American social welfare agencies argue that agency demands conflict with professional values to such a degree that the practitioner who wishes to preserve his ethical commitments must do so outside the context of an agency.[15] The authors believe that the professional can work within an agency and retain his primary commitment to client welfare. Although organizational expectations frequently constrain workers to behave in ways that are deleterious to clients and workers have been victims of dehumanizing organizational practices as often as they have been the perpetrators, the vast majority of social workers will continue to be employed by agencies in the foreseeable future. It is comforting to think of a delivery system in which workers can function as autonomous professionals, unfettered by bureaucratic constraints. But until that occurs, there is an alternative—intraorganizational change.

The development of an intraorganizational change component in social work practice does raise an ethical dilemma. Social workers traditionally seek to counteract an increasingly controlling, manipulative environment by encouraging trust and open communication among people, maximizing the range of choices available to the individual, and promoting rationality in problem-solving. But much of the change that occurs in the world (particularly at the organizational level) results from the exercise of power and from calculated exchanges among parties with selfish interests, rather than through mutual understanding and rationality. Thus the practitioner who wishes to engage in organizational change will in some instances have to decide whether to become involved on these terms. Some will argue that using tactics such as deliberate confu-

---

[15] See, for example, Irving Piliavin, "Restructuring the Provision of Social Services," *Social Work*, Vol. 13, No. 1 (January 1968), pp. 34–41.

sion, threats, unrealistic demands, and disruption—regardless of how worthwhile the goal—seriously compromises the professional's humanizing function and contributes to the very dehumanization he seeks to reduce.

No matter how the practitioner resolves this issue he should be aware of the potential costs involved. If he attempts to effect organizational change through mutual understanding and rational problem-solving, he is likely to be ineffective or irrelevant in some important contexts. If he uses tactics associated with the exercise of power, he runs the risk of being considered unethical by others.

The authors believe that the intraorganizational change agent should use the full range of strategies available to him—selecting those that are likely to be most effective, based on an informed assessment of organizational dynamics. Whether he should use marginally ethical means depends on how grave the problem is. Considering the number of agency policies or practices that do serious harm to the well-being of clients or staff, the authors are inclined to agree with Alinsky that "the most unethical of all means is the non-use of any means."[16]

Selected annotated references

BECK, WALTER E., "Agency Structure Related to the Use of Staff," *Social Casework* 50:6 (June 1969), pp. 341–46.
Greater clarity and flexibility in determining agency goals and setting priorities will affect the attitudes of staff and the agency's usefulness to clients.

BILLINGSLEY, ANDREW, "Bureaucratic and Professional Orientation Patterns in Social Casework," *Social Service Review* 38:4 (December 1964), pp. 400–407.
This study of 100 social workers (predominantly MSWs) in a family agency and a protective agency reviews four patterns of orientation—professionals, bureaucrats, conformists, and innovators—in relation to professionals and bureaucratic norms.

CUMMING, ELAINE, *Systems of Social Regulation* (New York: Atherton Press, 1968).
Cumming describes the complex relationships among social agencies as revealed by movement of clients around the system. She discusses how workers see their roles in the system, how areas of service interact and overlap, and how agencies change over a five-year span. This book will acquaint students at some depth with the organization of the network of "human services" in a middle-sized community.

---

[16] Saul Alinsky, "On Means and Ends," in Fred Cox et al., eds., *Strategies of Community Organization* (Itasca, Ill.: Peacock Publishers, 1970), p. 200.

DAEDALUS, *The Professions* (Fall 1963).

This issue of *Daedalus* contains several interesting and stimulating articles on the development, functioning, and place of the professions. Students will especially want to read Barber's article, "Some Problems in the Sociology of the Professions."

FELDSTEIN, DONALD, "Do We Need Professions in Our Society?" *Social Work* 16:4 (October 1971), pp. 5–12.

The author discusses the conflict between professionalization and consumerism in our society. He feels that this basic conflict is an especially difficult one for social work in that the profession itself espouses a value of democracy and openness. The evolution and nature of the concepts profession and professionalization are well developed.

FREEDMAN, JOEL, "One Social Worker's Fight for Mental Patients Rights," *Social Work* 16:4 (October 1971), pp. 92–95.

This is an account of a social worker who left an agency in order to continue a campaign to improve conditions for clients.

A. D. GREEN, "The Professional Worker in the Bureaucracy," *Social Service Review* 40:1 (March 1966), pp. 71–83.

Green's article is an excellent discussion of social workers' problems and conflicts in attempting to remain professional within a bureaucratic structure. It attempts to delineate some areas of conflict that are distinctive to the social work professional in contrast to other professionals who also operate in such structures. This is an article every student should read and ponder.

GREENWOOD, ERNEST, "The Attributes of a Profession," *Social Work* 2:3 (July 1957), pp. 45–55.

This very basic article on the attributes of a profession is a classic that has been quoted extensively by other authors in writing about the profession of social work. It should be on every student's reading list.

PRUGER, ROBERT, "The Good Bureaucrat," *Social Work* 18:4 (July 1973), pp. 26–32.

Social work is almost entirely an organization-based profession; social workers should develop skills to negotiate the bureaucratic environment rather than attempt to escape from it. Basic to this in an understanding of legitimate authority and organizational enforcement, acquisition of a competence needed by the organization, and a determination not to yield unnecessarily to the requirements of administrative convenience.

SEGAL, BRIAN, "Planning and Power in Hospital Social Service," *Social Casework* 51:7 (July 1970), pp. 399–405.

Segal's article is a case study of the way the social service staff of a hospital went about gaining power in the bureaucratic and professional structure through developing a technical monopoly.

WASSERMAN, HENRY, "The Professional Social Worker in a Bureaucracy," *Social Work* 16:1 (January 1971), pp. 89–96.

Wasserman discusses findings from a study of new employees in a welfare agency. The social worker is powerless and sees the supervisor as incompetent, and administrator is only concerned about financial accountability. In response to the pressures of the bureaucracy, the workers develop defenses that result in their treating clients as objects and in the minimizing of their client contact.

WEISSMAN, HAROLD H., *Overcoming Mismanagement in the Human Services* (San Francisco: Jossey-Bass, 1973).

This slim book is packed with interesting case studies of existing problems in particular service organizations, and offers notions of effective changes that can be brought about in them. The authors feel that it should be on every social worker's reading list.

Chapter 14

CONCLUSIONS

Through these chapters and the selection of readings we have attempted to share our perspective on social work practice. That perspective can be developed and adapted by workers regardless of the setting or relational system in which they choose to practice. In this brief conclusion we reemphasize three recurring themes of the book—themes which are central to this model of practice.

SOCIAL WORK AS A PROBLEM-SOLVING PROCESS

The focus of social work practice is on the relationship between individuals and their environment. A social worker's activities are directed first toward defining and then toward resolving problems that develop in this interaction. This formulation does not specify or limit the social problems which may be subject to social work attention. The problem may be within the individual or the environment, or, as is frequently the case, it may stem from the nature of the person-situation interaction. Also inherent in the problem-solving theme is the notion that the problem has been felt or experienced by some person or group who wish to have it resolved. The experiencing of stress from a problem (either internal or external to the individual) provides the impetus or motivation for the client to become involved with the social worker in a problem-solving endeavor.

SOCIAL WORK AS A CLIENT–WORKER RELATIONSHIP

All aspects of problem solving are undertaken by the worker and client in partnership. The partnership nature of the process extends to decision making as to the nature of the problem and the desired objectives as well as the actual change efforts. This partnership aspect of the work permits operationalization of the concepts of individualization and client self-determination. The worker is not perceived as an expert in what is best for the client but rather as an expert in facilitating a problem-solving process and in mobilizing resources to assist this process. Partnership implies joint input from worker and client—joint decision making and joint intervention. Participation on the part of the worker is as essential as participation on the part of the client.

SOCIAL WORK AS A RATIONAL PROCESS

Problem solving is a rational process in which worker and client jointly define the problem, specify objectives, and work toward the accomplishment of the objectives. Evaluation is the component of this process that provides feedback loops enabling the client-worker partnership to redefine the problem, goals, or intervention plan. The evaluation feedback loops provide a dynamic, systemic quality to the process. The worker, throughout the process, has the responsibility of maintaining a rational stance toward problem solving involving explicit problem definition, specific goals, and a rational plan to accomplish the goals. While all of these components may be changed on the basis of experience and evaluation, whenever activity is being undertaken with a client, the worker is responsible for the clarity of their joint agreement concerning specific problems, goals, and means.

THE BEGINNING

Through this book we have set forth principles in the areas of problem solving, partnership, and rational process which may serve as useful guides to the worker. These principles, however, will be applied in unique, ever-changing client situations. Their application requires the exercise of professional judgment. Such judgment involves the ability to make decisions and engage in actions guided by a set of principles. It is developed from continuous experience and learning.

We hope that the reader's beginning practice will be more exciting, less frustrating, and more positive than the experiences of this worker, who, after two social work jobs, decided to seek other employment:

> I asked when she first became interested in social work. She said that in her senior year in college she decided she would like to be

a social worker. She felt she wanted to go into social work so she could help people help themselves and that helping people was her main reason for wanting to be a social worker.

I asked whether she had expectations about the duties of the social worker. She said that she felt she could remake people's lives. I asked her to elaborate a little more on this and she said that she felt she could help people adjust to their problems in order to have healthy personalities. I asked her what she found when she started work, and she said that when she got her position she found she couldn't remake people's lives because she had a lot of paperwork and reports dealing with her clients. She said she could not change people's patterns of behavior as easily as she thought she could. These behavior patterns are so incorporated into their lives that it is difficult to change their set behaviors. She didn't have enough time to do all that she wanted to help the clients and had to limit her time so that she could interview all her clients, which was a difficult job. Usually AFDC mothers were especially hard to interview because they would change residence about four times a month. She said that only later at the private agency (her second job) was she able to give more time to her clients.

I asked her what kind of people she dealt with at the private agency. She said she took care of adoptions and unwed mothers and that she really liked it better than the public welfare because she had more time with her clients. But she said that this was where she realized something would have to change. I asked her to elaborate, and she said that many times she just didn't have answers for all the problems of her clients. When a client was really open with her, she felt that many times she didn't know quite how to handle the situation. She said she could not go running to a supervisor in the middle of an interview asking what to do now. She said that these certain moments could not be recaptured at any time. She decided that she needed more education, but she didn't know whether she wanted to take two more years of school.

Obviously this worker had little concept of partnership and perceived herself as being responsible for finding the solution to the clients' problems (remaking their lives) and for being the sole change agent. Perceiving herself as the sole expert, she became anxious when she did not have immediate answers to client questions. While it is probably fortunate that this particular person chose to leave social work, we all may at times experience similar dilemmas. To counterbalance the above account we have reprinted a statement submitted by a first-year MSW student as her framework for practice.

As our experience and professional maturity increase, we will find less need to define ourselves as the expert holder-of-solutions-to-the-client-problems and will be increasingly able to acknowledge gaps in knowledge (knowledge on the part of both client and worker) and to engage the client in a joint quest for the necessary information. No worker is expected to know everything; disillusionment and disaster await those who think they do. What is required, is the ability to involve clients, professional colleagues, supervisors and others in comfortably and jointly seeking out the information required for rational problem solving.

If you are seriously pursuing social work you are about to embark on a journey requiring outstanding self-discipline. Earlier we used the analogy of the figure skater and noted that the truly creative use of self in a spontaneous way occurs only after hours and hours of discipline and practice. The ability to engage spontaneously and comfortably in a partnership for problem solving with clients does not come naturally, but develops with self-discipline, with learning, with experience, and with practice. We have found the challenge exciting and rewarding, and we hope that you will enter the profession with both a sureness of what you are doing and a tentativeness which permits change as new information comes to light.

A student's view of social work*

Aviva C. Inberg

I have been thinking about this paper for some time now, and frankly the thought of writing my own theoretical orientation base for practice was quite frightening. As I began to think through my ideas and attitudes and looked at the theoretical base in terms of what I try to do *with* clients when they come into the agency, and why, the paper became considerably less frightening and even more thought-provoking.

I would like to address myself to several major areas which I would consider relevant to my theory base, whether working with individuals or families: my own view of persons and their growth and development (behavioral science foundations), respect and dignity for clients, how persons change (the place for hope), assessment of the client-situation, and relationship. I feel I will also be covering such areas as goal-setting, problem definition, and expectations of client and worker, but hopefully the aforementioned areas will be considered under the major topics to be discussed.

I was born on the Near North Side of our city and have lived there

---

* An original article prepared for a casework class, University of Minnesota, Minneapolis.

all my life. Near North is probably the closest thing that this city has to a ghetto area. I learned many things about responding and relating to people very different from myself. This experience was enormously enriching; out of it grew my desire to become a social worker, and the experience "colored" my ideas about man, his environment, and his growth. When I was in junior high school, one of my friends always came to school late. Many times I asked him why, and then one day he told me. He was late because his older brother worked nights, and he had to wait until his brother came home in the morning so he could wear his shoes; he had none of his own. One of my girlfriends was continually picked up for shoplifting, and the authorities couldn't understand why. I knew it was because she only had two dresses to wear to school and was ashamed. (She had turned to shoplifting as a way to cope.)

How could these teenagers be expected to do well in school and other areas of their lives when their basic physical needs had not been adequately met? I have found Maslow's model[1] for self-actualization useful in my thinking. Maslow's model covers "deficiency motives" which must be met before "being motives" can even be realistically considered. Physical safety, belongingness, and love needs must be reasonably met before self-esteem and, finally, self-actualization can be attained by the individual. I feel that Maslow's model is optimistic and positive and fits in with my basic conception of man, which is that man has a basically positive, growing, developing orientation. Once man's more basic needs are met he is "free" to become all he can hope to be. Until my boy friend had shoes, how could he have self-esteem?

In the book *The Black Ghetto Family in Therapy* by Sager, Brayboy, and Waxenberg,[2] Mr. James, a trained carpenter, needed work to support his family. The man had lost his pride and at one point screamed, "I'm a carpenter. . . . I want to work. . . . I want to be a carpenter." This man had to meet his deficiency needs before he could work on needs higher up on the hierarchy of needs. My ideas on man's growth and development lead me in practice to take important note of the "real," "concrete" physical and emotional needs of the client; only when these are met can man become all he is capable of becoming.

I think that the systems concept of a person-situation fits in well with my basic positive growth orientation. The client's problem is sometimes in the person but also sometimes in the situation (society) and/or in the interaction between the two. The worker "discovers" the place to begin by listening to his client, and together they try to solve the

[1] A. H. Maslow, *Toward a Psychology of Being* (Princeton, N.J.: Van Nostrand, 1962).

[2] Clifford J. Sager, Thomas L. Brayboy, Barbara R. Waxenberg, *The Black Ghetto Family in Therapy* (New York: Grove Press, Inc., 1970).

problem which is keeping the client from reaching his fullest growth potential. I feel that it is important for the client to "solve" problems which are most relevant for him; this allows the ego to grow and leads to positive self-esteem. I don't believe in a client coming to an agency for help and then being given a therapist or worker who restructures the client's problem or position so that it fits his particular agency's function or his personal theoretical bias and formula for conducting "therapy." I see many of the therapists we studied this quarter in class doing just that, providing a "diagnosis for all occasions." This type of service for clients makes me nervous. I feel that all people, regardless of race, religion, cultural background, or socioeconomic status, want to become more than they are, that they are not "satisfied" with self or position in life; they are constantly striving for more, ever reaching for new positive goals.

As I have read the vast amount of literature on the various theories of social casework and family therapy, I am amazed that very few authors give significant meaning and discussion to client dignity and respect. When I first "meet" a client, this is where it all begins for me I express respect for my clients by always being precisely on time (whether it's a home visit or an office appointment), by greeting them in the reception area, by addressing the client by his surname, by walking out with him, and, hopefully, by the warmth in my voice. I truly believe in the *dignity* of every client I see, and I want him to feel it.

I have learned a method of listening, known as active or empathetic listening, which I feel facilitates my expression of respect for the client. When a client presents his problem initially, I do a great deal of active listening. Active listening is a nonjudgmental, here and now reflection to the client of his feeling state as perceived by himself. It is characterized by such words as "You seem to feel . . ." or "You're really feeling. . . ." It appears on the surface to be a simple technique, but in actual practice it is a difficult and literally exhausting experience; however, I feel the technique is well worth the effort of learning and utilizing, since it lets the client know that you are really with him. It also "shows" the respect for the client which I spoke of earlier: it tells the client in essence, "I respect your attitudes, feelings, and values, although they may be different from mine. I can let you *own* your feelings, and I can accept your 'differentness' and your uniqueness." Active listening also helps the client to move from what he says to how he feels, which allows him to take responsibility for his *own* feelings and to become more self-aware. Active listening, I have found, increases the client's willingness to talk with me and does not "shut off" communication. Through active listening, I can often get much data for assessment *without* having to ask numerous questions which I find personally uncomfortable. I think many of my clients have been pleasantly surprised that I really listen and don't "interrogate." I feel the client is worth listening to! Active listening allows me to do so. When I'm with a client, he or she has all of my attention. At that moment, nothing else exists. This to me is the ultimate expression of human dignity and respect.

Since I believe that individuals are positive, goal-oriented beings, I feel change can most definitely come about. If it is true that people are continually striving to be all they can become, change is a natural consequence of that endeavor. For individuals or families to change, I feel they must be really motivated to want to change. They must see the change as beneficial to themselves or their families. This is why I feel the client must be given the chance to decide upon the problem situation and set goals for himself. If the goal is what *he wants,* then change will come about.

I've begun to realize the importance of hope in terms of the client's changing. If the client truly feels that what he wants changed can be changed in some way in the direction of his goals, then he is hopeful, which seems to push him on to even greater strengths in learning to cope with or change his problem situation. I feel that it is the place of the social worker to give "realistic" hope. I may not "know all the answers" to any one problem, but SOMETHING CAN BE DONE! Otherwise, why am I sitting there posing as a helping person?

I have been seeing a mother who has been having some real difficulty in coping with her adolescent sons. After our initial meeting I told her that I was hopeful that some of the things we had been talking about could be worked out. I've now been working with this woman for four months, and just last week she told me how she had always remembered my being "hopeful" and that this alone had given her added strength: "If Aviva can have hope, so can I." I had no idea that such a seemingly simple comment could have so much meaning to this client. I now more fully understand the meaning of hope and its place in the change effort.

In my practice, then, it is the client who decides what goals are to be worked on and also locates where the problem is, as he sees it. I may define the problem elsewhere after data collection and further client interviews, but respect is upheld, since I would always share the information I had gathered with the client and define my position if it differed from that of the client. Sharing of information, to me, is absolutely essential, whether the information shared is test scores (such as the MMPI) or impressions that I have of the client–problem situation.

Social worker–client relationships are partnerships. The sharing of information facilitates the equalitarian partnerships which I strive for in my practice. I feel that my "knowing" alone (test scores, referral notes, impressions) will in no way "solve the problem." Therefore, the information must be shared, discussed, and worked through before it can be helpful to the client. I feel that sharing impressions with a client and letting him know that this is what I think and that I might be right or wrong maintains respect for the client and keeps the partnership intact. If the client can relate to my impression, we can discuss it; if not, he has the *opportunity* to tell me that's *not* how it is. The term used for this process is "dropping the seed and backing away." I feel that at times this technique can be most useful.

I'm also quite willing to share my own here and now feelings with a client. I feel that when I do this the partnership takes on a more "real" quality, that there is more give and take. I've shared feelings with clients, and usually they find this a help—they tell me. "I've been wondering how you feel." It seems to take some of the mystery away from the "person behind the desk." I disclose my feelings by way of "I sentences": "I feel really happy about what you're doing" or "I feel doubtful about what you're saying, as if you really don't want to change." Through "I messages" (as opposed to "you messages": "You don't want to change"; "You make me happy by what you do") the client is once again treated as a respected person. I do not lay my feelings on the client; rather, I take ownership for them. The client is also given the opportunity to decide whether he wants to change. He is allowed to maintain responsibility for the ways in which he will respond to me, without unfair pressure from me. The responsibility for change lies with the client.

When working with clients, I attempt to use the problem-solving model presented by Compton and Galaway. I feel that at this point in my development the model allows for much flexibility and seems to go along very well with my own ideas and attitudes. I feel a definite need for a thorough and timely assessment. I believe it is important to define the problem and its location during the first session and to define short- and possibly long-term goals during the next session. I have found the Goal Attainment Scale particularly useful because it is so specific and concrete. Early problem definition and goals formation are important, I feel, because they alone determine assessment (or data collection). I do not want to know everything about a client or a family, and I don't think I have to in order to help them solve the problem. After data collection, goals may have to be redefined and renegotiated, particularly if data collection, indicates that the client may have over-looked something which I feel is an important aspect of the problem-situation. I then share this "new" information with the client, as mentioned earlier in this paper. I have chosen several areas from the problem-solving outline which I feel have been most valuable to me in doing assessment. These areas are presented in outline form at the end of this paper. I would like to address myself briefly to one particular question from the assessment outline, since I feel that it is most often overlooked by practicing social workers: "What opportunities have been available to learn skills and knowledge that could help the client in coping with thet presenting problem?"

It was discussed in class that there are three "parts" to an individual:

1. The feeling or emotional component;
2. The intellectual or thinking component;
3. The acting or skill-in-acting component.

These parts interact to determine how a person sees and hears, and how he sees and hears can affect the three parts. All three components can be dealt with: intervention can occur in all three aspects of the client system. Feelings are important, but so are the other areas. If a client is feeling anxious because his new job entails transferring on the bus line three times, it may be most useful to collect information about the bus system and to share this with him, or, if necessary, to go on the bus with him for the first time—in other words, to give or teach him new skills and knowledge which would help him cope with the problem. Having the necessary skills could conceivably reduce or alleviate the client's anxiety and help him develop increasingly adequate social skills.

Many times, workers, myself included, take "simple" things for granted: we think that the client *should know* how to make "that" phone call or reward his child. However, such unfounded assumptions can be dangerous. A problem which could have an "easy" answer is over-looked, and so the problem continues to grow (damaging the client's self-esteem in the process) while more complex "fundamental causes" and feelings are sought out.

I feel that a good working relationship is essential in the practice of social work. Such elements as warmth, respect, caring, empathy, active listening, and "I messages" enhance the chances of developing a good relationship with the client. A warm relationship between worker and client can enhance the client's capacity for strength and self-esteem. I enjoy my work more when I feel that I have a positive relationship with my client. However, relationship is NOT ENOUGH! If relationship were all the client desired or needed, he could call the "Welcome Wagon." Relationship comes out of the parternership. It comes by way of working on the problem situation together, through mutual discovering and learning, and, hopefully, through problem solving and enhancement of the client's independent problem-solving skills.

I approach the family situation in much the same way way I do that of the individual client. In working with families, I have found it helpful to have at least a simple framework for considering the differences between a functional and a nonfunctional family. I mentioned earlier my discomfort with a "diagnosis for all occasions." This concept stays in the forefront of my mind when I work with families, and in no way do I try to match the family to the framework.

I see a dysfunctional family as being a closed system with interlocking expectations in which uniqueness and differentness cannot exist. What one member does is determined by how he feels, and the others will respond to him. One member's happiness depends solely on that of other members. Family members do not take responsibility for their own feelings. They complain about others and make frequent use of "you messages" ("If only you would change, I would be happy"; "Other people are destroying me"; "If only you were responsible for me, I would be happy"). Frequently family members have no sense of their own feelings; they are constantly entwined with the feelings of other members. Every problem must be a family problem; the family *owns* the problem; individuals lose ownership of their problems.

I pay special attention to communication patterns (listening for "you messages"), and I try to recognize family rules. I feel that family therapy should help members to be responsible for their own feelings, for themselves, and develop clear lines about what member owns a problem. (Is it an individual's problem, a problem between two members, or a total family problem? In my own limited experience, the problem is usually owned by one or two persons.) Problem-solving techniques can then be used and taught to the members who own the problem. I see a functional family as having members with a strong sense of their own separateness (If I'm happy it is because of what I'm doing). These families are very concerned and caring, but they realize that they will not be destroyed if separated from the rest of the family. The sense of destiny rests with each member as an individual. Each takes responsible ownership of his feelings and lets the others own their feelings also. The members of such families make suggestions and express concern and caring about one another's problems, but they leave the decision to the owners of the problems. My ideas about the family have been influenced by Virginia Satir and Thomas Gordon (Parent Effectiveness Training).

This paper has been an attempt to put my thinking and attitudes into perspective. On rereading it, I feel that my framework is a bit sketchy in parts; hopefully, through further education, knowledge, experience and practice, my ideas will become more fully developed. I also want to leave much room for growth and change. I never want to become a social worker who looks through "heavy lensed" theoretical colored glasses.

Assessment

I. Presenting problem
   A. Where the client places the *location* of the problem
   B. Length of existence of the problem
   C. *Precipitating Factors* of the problem; if the problem has existed previously, those precipitating factors also
   D. Is the problem and/or discomfort *general* or is it thought to be *situational?*
   E. *In what ways has the client attempted to cope with the problem?* Has the client had *success* in previous coping? What *opportunities* have been available for him to learn skills and knowledge that could help in coping with the presenting problem?

II. Client information and functioning
   A. Physical illness, symptoms, physical health
   B. Age, appearance
   C. Intellectual functioning
   D. How the client *"sees" the people and world around him;* the defenses he uses
   E. Ability to reason, to grasp cause and effect relationships
   F. *Affective responses*—too many? too few? Degree of awareness of feelings
   G. *Social roles*—how many? Degree of competence with which they are handled
   H. *Perception of self*—self-worth

III. Socioeconomic status
   A. How this affects the problem
   B. How it is related to self-worth
   C. Job satisfaction

IV. Relationships with others
   A. Important people in client's life
   B. Supportive vs. nonsupportive relationships
   C. Capacity for feelings of closeness and caring
   D. Capacity for openness with others
   E. Balance between dependence vs. independence

INDEX

A

Abbott, Edith, 493–94
Abreaction, history taking for, 266
Acceptance
  basic elements, of, 153–54
  of colleagues, 448–49
  communication of, 154–55
  in cooperative or conflicted relation-
    ship, 157
  defined, 153–54
  development of, 154
  as element of relationship, 143, 153–55,
    148–49
  of provocative behavior, 180
Access to services, 485
Accountability, 484
  reciprocal, 333
  steps toward, 467–70
Action
  alternative courses of, 238
  to implement procedure, 236
  limits on, 28
Action system, 505, 507–8
  agenda of, 503
Active listening, 518
Activism, 133
Activist role, 341
Activity, limitation on worker's, 112
Actualization striving, 130
Adaptation, 124, 272
  to ultimate values, 130

Adaptive
  modification, 440
  responses, 270
  system, 65
Adaptiveness, 271
Addams, Jane, in advocate role, 372
Adequacy of service, 473
Adjustment to adult world, 179
Administration, 350
  techniques borrowed from, 56
Administrative constraints in empirical
  design, 419
Adolescent
  and adult dishonesty, 170
  aggressiveness of, 172
  anxiety of, 174
  areas of professional dishonesty to-
    ward, 171
  background of, 175
  client, 175
  chaotic sexuality of, 172
  disturbed, 176, 180
  disturbed, impact of professional dis-
    honesty, 170–81
  disturbed, professional encouragement
    of, 171
  inertia of, as clients, 178
  institutionalized, 171
  involved with agencies, 171
  open to learning, 180
  rebellion as response to, 170

Adoption, black applicants for, 219
Adult, 181
Advancement, barriers to, 179
Adversary strategy
  activities of, 507
  assumptions underlying, 508
  where appropriate, 508–9
Advice
  unsolicited, 121
  well-intended, 122
Advisory, 198
Advocacy, 349
  in Code of Ethics, 373
  complications of, 373
  defined, 371–72
  knowledge and, 376
  NASW Committee on, 378
  NASW protection of social worker in
    role of, 377
  outside of work role, 374
  in professional education, 372
  school curriculum for, 376
  as social work role, 340, 343–45
  strategy of, 488
  tradition of, 126
Advocate reformer, 372
Affective responses, 523
Agency
  authority, 464, 503
  community, 176
  concerned with social planning and
    action, 25
  critics of, 510
  culture, 448–50
  debureaucraticizing of, 496–98
  decision evoking process, 500
  demands, 510
  direct service, 461
  evaluation as responsibility of worker,
    382
  experiences with welfare, 178
  "extension services," 463
  framework for practice, 2
  functions of, 17–19, 112, 481
  historical divisions of labor in, 17
  identification with, 449
  as instrument of change, 270
  leisure time, 25
  lines, work across, 447
  as object of changes, 270
  organization, factors effecting, 480
  partnership with foster parents, 464
  policies and procedures, 480, 508
  pooling of resources, 463
  procedures as cause of resistance, 199
  program, 481
  selectivity, relating to race, 218
  yearly reports of, 413–14

Agency-mindedness as barrier to intake,
  457
Agency system, 23
Agent of client, practitioner as, 172–74
Agent of community, practitioner as,
  172–73
Aggression, social usefulness of, 172
Agreement
  function of terms, 36
  mutual, 330
  need of specific terms, 36
  requirements of, 35
Agreement-disagreement
  as continuum, 501
  fundamentals of, 506
Aid to Families with Dependent Children, 410
  recipients in California study, 224–25
Alcoholics Anonymous, 218
Alinsky, Saul, 511
Allport, Gordon, 96
Alternatives, 109
  desirable for direction of a person's
    attention, 11
  development of, 170
  quest for, 114
Altruism, 122
Ambiguous words in communication, 196
Amulet, 125
Analysis
  as base of action, 323
  processes and respects of, 324
Analytic method, 62
Anger
  rationalized, 177
  worker attempt to deny, 180
  worker denial of, 177
Answer, effective, 237
Anxiety
  adolescent, 174
  created by environmental conditions,
    303
Application and information forms, 288
Appointments in advance, 106
Apprenticeship model, 492
Approach
  ecological systems, 39–41
  micro-macro, 11–12
  Schwartz's mediating, 7
  setting of practice, 11
Aptekar, Herbert, 263
Art in the helping process, 36–37
Artistry, personal, 26
Ascription(s)
  application of, 207
  as change producing, 213–16
  cultural climate of, 27
  defined, 207

Ascription(s)—*Cont.*
  Hollis's use of, 208
  as interviewing technique, 207
  Konopka's use of, 209
  Northen's use of, 208
  Overton's and Tinker's use of, 209
  Perlman's use of, 208
  Phillip's use of, 209
  place in casework theory, 208
  place in combined practice, 210–11
  place in family treatment, 209
  place in group work theory, 208
  Polansky's use of, 210
  reasons for use, 215
  research design to explore, 211–16
  Satir's use of, 209–10
  Schwartz's use of, 209
  Smalley's use of, 210
  in social work theory, 208–11
  Vinter's use of, 209
  use in increasing sense of relationship, 212–13
Ascriptive episode, defined, 208
Ascriptive statements addressed to family unit, 212
  and change, 210
  classifications of, 214
  client's use of, 215
  as feedback, 213
  as instruments of communication in family theory, 212
  as stimulators of family interaction, 212
  as structure, 213
Assessment, 241, 251, 520
  data for, 518
  deciding action to be taken, 325
  identification of critical factors, 325
  procedures, 108
  role of norms in, 268
  steps of, 324
  in students' outline, 523
  use in various methods, 322
Assistance, specific, 243–44
Assumptions
  of meaning as barrier to communication, 196–97
  of meaning in interview, example of, 197
  about program effort, 414
Assumptive knowledge, 53
Attitude
  while asking for help, 276
  reductionist, 129
Authoritarianism, 465
Authoritative, defined, 465
Authority
  in agency charge, 503

Authority—*Cont.*
  aspects of social work relationships, 158
  characteristics of, 158
  as element of relationship, 141, 143, 148–49, 158–59, 464
  institutional aspects of, 158
  how exercised, 112
  legal, 112
  legitimate, 491
  negative syndrome, 464
  in office held, 478
  orientation toward, 478
  problems with, 464
  in professional competence, 478
  psychological aspects of, 158
  recognized channels in interagency teamwork, 456
  in relationship, defined, 158
  in relationships, 143
  requirements of, 113
  significance of, 158
  source and extent of, 112
Authority figure
  consideration in change process, 500
  legal, 111–14
Autonomous ego, 97
Autonomy, 124
Available resources, 241
Avoidance, defensive, 440

B

"Bad" role, 175
Background
  deprivations in early, 179
  of middle class workers, 175
Backner, Burton L., 227
Bandura, Albert, 344
Bargain, poor, 177
Barrett, Franklin T., 229
Barrier, of class, 217
  communication; *see* Communication, barriers to
  interagency teamwork, 456
  permeability of racial, 218
  racial, 217
Bartlett, Harriet, 7–8, 52, 56–57, 206, 314
  article, 320–26
Beall, Lynette, 330
Beck, Bertram, M., 334
Beginning phase, importance of, 277
Behavior
  antisocial, 178
  change, 350
  dishonest professional, 178
  gains and losses, 178
  human, 134

Behavior—*Cont.*
  maladjusted, 121
  of the parts, 62
  patterned, 109
  problem solving, 234
  relational, 246
  role of antisocial, 179
Behavioral science foundations, 516
Behaviorism, 133
Being motives, 517
"Being Understanding and Understood:
    Or How to Find a Wandered
    Horse," 181–90
Beliefs, 249
  worker's personal, 178
Bergson, Henri, 25
Berkowitz, Sidney J., 54
Biestek, Felix, 140
Bisno, Herbert, 10, 14
Black professional, 221
  anxiety about competence, 168
  black client, communication and inter-
      view with, 221
  black client, relationship with, 221
  establishing identification, 222
  interviewers, middle-class professional,
      221, 227
  psychiatrist, 224
  and race, 168
  traitor to his race, 222
  white client, relationship with, 223
Blanchard, Phyllis, 435
Boehm, Werner, 7
Bogardus Social Distance Scale, measure-
    ment by, 219
Bolman, William M., article, 431–45
Boundaries, 62, 91, 99
  definition of, 63
  of relevant knowledge, 57
  in systems theory, 63–64
Brager, George, 372
Brand, Ethan, 127, 136
Brayboy, Thomas, 219, 517
Brechenser, Donn M., 335
Briar, Scott, 70, 103, 206, 254, 372, 494
  and Henry Miller, 68
Brieland, Donald, 228
Broker, role of, 446, 342–43
Brown, Luna B., 218, 222
Brown, Robert, 193, 205
  article, 206–16
Buber, Martin, 135
Buckley, Walter, 62, 210
Bureaucracy
  casework in, 492
  classical features of, 493
  constraints of, 510
  dysfunctional characteristics, 474

Bureaucracy—*Cont.*
  limitation of, 475
  organization, 474–512
  problems, analysis of, 495
  and professional, conflicts between,
      476
  rational model of, 493
  and strategy of change, 487
  structure, 472, 482
Bureaucrat
  executive type, 479
  functional type, 479
  job type, 480
  service type, 479
  specialist type, 479
  types of, 479–80
Burns, Crawford E., 220
Burns, Mary, and Glasser, Paul, 304

C

"C" street network, 41
Calnek, Maynard, 222
Cannon, Walter B., 95–96
Captain of treatment team, 453
Carkhuff, Robert R., 227
Carr-Saunders, A. M., and Wilson, P. A.,
    321
Carson, R. C., and Heine, R. W., 224
"Cartesian strait jacket," 130
Carter, Genevieve, 18
Case conference, utilization of, 453–54
Casework, 10–11, 117
  crises in, 492
  defined, 139
  group work, community organization
      model, 10
  knowledge borrowed from, 56
  practice of, 98–99
  professional, two parts of, 127
  radical, 8–9
  Richmond's definition of, 98
  task-centered, 335
  services in, 122
  voluntary use of, 123
"Casework Is Dead," 12
Casework Notebook, 492–93
Caseworker, 9–10, 269
  activity of, 98
  and agency monopoly, 497
  versus bureaucracy, 494
  changing role of, 270
  expanding role of, 270
  as helper, 270
Categories
  as abstractions, 185
  as system for organizing facts, prob-
      lems of, 197

Caucasians, 219
Causal factors
  identification of factors, 256, 258
  relationships of knowledge, 61
"Causal Network," 134
Causation, concept of, 97
Cause
  and effect relationships, 62, 131
  and symptoms, 185
Central planning as aid to teamwork, 460
Chairman's responsibility, 453
Change
  activities, types of groups utilized for, 509
  activity, loci of, 509
  costs of, potential, 511
  efforts, prerequisites to, 198
  ethical dilemmas of, 510–11
  formal internal context of, 509
  human, potential for, 70
  informal external context of, 509
  informal external function of, 510
  informal internal context of, 509
  modalities, 341
  possibilities for, 97
  premature effort to produce, 204
  prerequisite to, 519
  processes in social work, 14–15
  processing of, 350
  requirements of efforts toward, 198
Change agent, 501
  attributes of, 508
  social worker as, 198
Charitable impulse, 127
Charity, 120
Checkout, defined, 194
  in communication, 196
Child
  importance of seeing whole, 183
  placement of, 466
  progress reports of, 468
  protection agency, 111
  rearing, 124
  welfare services, 410
Child care staff, 448
Children, 123
Children's Hospital of Philadelphia, 38
Choice, 135
  consumer, 329
  dignity of, 122
  making of, 109
  possibility of, 122, 134
Chronological stage, 247
Citizens as team members, 455
City College of New York, SEEK Program, 227
Civil rights, social worker's commitment, 372

Clarification of problem, 276
Classifications
  as abstraction, 128
  of ascriptive statements, 214
  necessity of, 107–9, 128
  problems of, 197
  procedures as barrier to individualization, 106
  schemes, 94
  use of, 107–9, 115
  and values, 107–9, 115
Client
  aggressive, 200
  and capitalization of hope, 125
  defined, 2, 278
  expectations of, 296
  functioning, 523
  goals of, 237
  hope-discomfort balance of, 287
  hopefulness, 286
  information, 523
  interactions, 243
  involuntary, 115, 126
  locus of control in, 367
  obligations of, 152
  participation, 333
  preference, 227–29
    empirical support, 227
    in selecting professionals, 227
  as primary source of information, 204
  as primary source of intervention, 192
  problem, 517
  projection, 443
  purpose, 239
  responsibility, 334
  role in formulating policy, 326
  self-determination; *see* self-determination, client
  and social class, 437
  status at intake, 394
  stereotyping of, 197, 437
  as subject, 151
  transactional system, 10
  unsolicited treatment of, 126
  unwilling, 126
  view of helping process, 286
  voluntary, defined, 126, 278
Client system, 26, 235, 239–40, 242–45, 252–53, 446, 451
  autonomy of, 241
  awareness of resources, 287
  capacity of, 241, 245
  defined, 207
  expectations of, 241
  goals and expectations of, 240
  intellectual, social, and physical needs of, 245
  interview, 288

Client system—*Cont.*
  and problem solving, 238
  purpose of, 237
  rights of, 241
Client-worker
  agreement, 330
  partnership, 514
  relationship, 23–24, 514; *see also* relationship
Climate
  productive for interview, 199
  workers responsible for, 200
Close watching, 224–26
Closed system, 63
Closeness, negative aspects of, 176
Closure, premature, 165
Clue type social study, 266
Coconut Grove fire, 434
Code of Ethics; *see* National Association of Social Workers (NASW), Code of Ethics
Cognition in psychotherapy, 369
Cognitive elements in relationship, 162
  organization of, 211
Collaboration, 5
  in evaluation research, 411
  in goal operationalization, 415
  interagency, 449
  requirements of, 448
Collaborative strategy
  activities involved in, 506–7
  assumptions underlying, 506
  with colleagues, 448–49
  when effective, 508
  requirements of, 448–49
Colonialism, 123
Commitment to clientele, 498
  to client service, 502
  to client welfare, 143
  defined, 153
  as element of relationship, 143, 148–49, 151, 153
  students' development of, 86
Common ground and interaction, 281
Communication
  of acceptance, 154–55
  ambiguous words in, 196
  anticipation of other as barrier to, 196, 204
  assumption of meaning about, 204
  assumption of meaning as barrier to, 196–97
  of attitude of concern, 151
  barriers to, 193, 196–99, 204
  client created, 198–99
  channels of, 247
  checkout, 197
  contradictory purpose as, 197

Communication—*Cont.*
  defined, 193, 195
  denotative and communicative, 194
  denotative label defined, 194
  double bind, 194
  freedom of, 233
  between foster parents and inter-agency, 468
  in games, 447–48
  inattentiveness as barrier, 198
  inconsistent barriers, 196
  in interagency teamwork, 456
  and interviewing the problems and conclusions of, 229–30
  levels of, 194
  network, 247
  overt and covert, 194
  patterns, 522
  phases of, 193
  process (diagram 2), 193
  resistance to, 198, 205
  respect, 106–7
  stereotyping as barrier to, 197
  style of, 246
  theory, 61, 193
  urge to change as barrier to, 197
  verbal and nonverbal, 194
Community, 239–40, 243, 245, 252
  centers, 462
  chest, 458
  development, organizational forms, 359
  development, self-expression in, 352
  groups, cooperative relationship with, 456
  as organic entity, 251
  planning, 350
  power structure, 251
  problems, 251
  relations policy, elements in, 459
  setting, 177
  as social system, 251
  staff participation in, 456
  study and evaluation of, 251
  systems of support, 38
  work, basis of, 359
Community organization, 10–11
  considerations in teamwork, 460
  functions of district, 462
  knowledge borrowed from, 56
  methodology of, 351
  responsibilities of direct service agencies, 461
  use of contract in, 331
Community organizer, 9–10
Community Welfare Councils, 456, 458, 460, 462
  district, 462
  need of, 460–61

Competence
  anxiety about in black practitioner, 168
  in client preference, 229
  of professional, 113
  requirements of development of, 87
Competing claims, 375
Competition, problems of, 446–48
Competitive behavior in teamwork, 447
Complexities
  organized, 21
  as a part of creativity, 165
Compliance, 122
Components of social work knowledge,
  84, 88
Compton, Beulah Roberts, article, 401
Concentrations
  criteria for, 87–88
  place in social work curriculum, 87
  rationale supporting development of,
    88
  in social work curriculum defined, 87
Conceptualization, 92
Conceptualization ability, 127
Concern for other
  as element of relationship, 143, 149,
    151
  elements of, 150
Concretization, techniques of, 270
Conference, foster parent–agency worker,
  469
Confidentiality
  guarantee of, 174
  issue of, 173–74
  lie of, 173–74
  used as refuge from service demands,
    470
Conflict
  in evaluative research, 412
  power and control, 246
  between practitioner and researcher,
    407–10
Conformity, 122
  burden of, 179
  lie of rewards for, 174–75, 178–79
Congruence
  agency role and position of worker as
    a part of, 160
  agency structure and function in rela-
    tion to, 160
  as element of relationship, 159–62,
    148–49
  elements of, 159
  of practitioner, 160
  qualities of practitioner, 160
Congruent, 163
Connell, Charles, 194
Conspiracy of silence, 221
Consolidation of gains, 405

Consultation, 271, 350
  professional, 452
Contact phase, 275–92
  data collection in, 286–90
  defined, 275–77
  failure in helping process, 285
  goal setting in, 283–85
  preliminary contract in, 285–86
  preparation for, 277–80
  problem definition as part of, 280–85
  requirements of client, 276–77
  requirements of practitioner, 277–80
Content analysis, methods of, 395
Continuing service, selecting for, 218
Continuing care, care giver, 350
Contract, 29
  application to practice, 335
  applied to community organization,
    331
  and community organization, 328
  concept of, 328
  defined, 329–30
  with families, 330
  flexibility, 336
  and goals, 331
  the helping, 152
  implementation, 333
  lack of clarity, 326
  major features, 329
  negotiations, client-worker, 314
  possibilities in social work practice,
    333
  potential, 337
  potential value in implementation, 329
  preliminary contract, 241, 244, 276,
    285
  preliminary uses of, 314
  reformulations or renegotiation, 336
  special modification techniques, 337
  time limited, 328
  theory in literature, 327
  unethical behavior, 318
  verbal, 335
  working, 27
  written, 335
Contract phase, 241–42, 251, 275
  assessment and decision making in,
    314–16
  definition of, 321
  development of an intervention plan,
    317
  diagnosis, 315
  four principles of, 319
  goal setting in, 316–17
  and independent thinking, 315
  intervention, planning for, 317–18
  limits on worker intervention, 317
Contractual alliance with parents, 334

Control, social, 251
Control group, use in experimental research, 418–19
Cooper, Shirley, 167–68
Cooperation
    among agencies, study of, 456
    in evaluative research, 411
    research in, 447–48
Cooperative relationships, 455–56
Cooperative requirements of work, 447
    prerequisites for, 456
Cooperator, game theory, 447–48
Coping activity, 7
Correctional setting, 111
Corrections, 120
Cosmopolitan orientation, 504
Council; *see* Community Welfare Councils
Council on Social Work Education, 69
    curriculum statement of, 57, 84–88
    curriculum study of, 20, 56
Counseling, 206, 243, 344
    aggressive intervention in, 206
    confrontation in, 206
    free association in, 206
    nondirective techniques in, 206
Counselor, marriage, 124
Counterconformity, 164
Courage, as a part of professional self, 143, 166
Courtesy, 106
Cowboys, 189
Coyle, Grace, 141
Creativity, as a quality of professional self, 143, 164–65
Credibility, 503
Crime, 122
Criminal, 122
    viewed as a patient, 174
Crisis, 99
    approach, 264
    inducing as method change, 96
    model, 271
    theory, 95
    theory in institutional change, 95
Critical analysis, students' development of, 85–88
Cross-cultural interviewing, 223
Culture, 114
    American, 127
    background, effects of difference, 226
    complexity of, 104
    identification, 246
    norms as cause of resistance, 199
    of the organization, 250
    professional and agency, 448–50
Cure, notion of, 268
Cybernetics, 61

D

Data, 91
    for assessment, 518
    borrowed, 56
    relevant, 237, 271
    resources, 287
    selection, 286
Data collection, 236–37, 239–40, 271, 275, 520
    collection and ordering, 66
    dehumanizing effects of, 289
    focus, 277
    interview, purpose of, 198
    modes of, 288
    motivation and opportunity, 286
    observation as technique of, 289
    observer sensitivity, 289
    as prerequisite to decision making, 198
    prerequisites to, 277
    principles of, 278
    procedures of, 418
    review of prior to initial contact, 277
    sources and methods of, 287
    use of existing written material, 290
    use of other persons, 289
    use of projective techniques, 289
Death wishes, 441
Decision makers, 509
Decision making
    authority, 110
    base of, 410
    for the client, 111
    client exercise of, 110
    joint, 114
    interviewing as data for, 195
    opportunities for client, 114
Decision, 109
    skill, 233
    timely, 271
De facto ideology, 134
Defense
    avoidance as, 440
    inner struggle, 441
    purpose of, 442
Deficiency motives, 517
Defining the problem, 280
Definition of problem, 235
Dehumanization, 131
Delinquent, 107, 175
    burden on, 174
Delivery system, 510
Démesur (Camus), 131
Democracy, 132
    ideals, 116
    tradition of enlightenment, 133–34
Demonstration project, 409
Demonstrations, concepts of, 270

Denial, 439
first phase of separation process, 434
of limitations, 176
of sadness associated with loss, 444
Dependency
actions that increase, 32
forced, 176
independency, 246
needs, 180
risk of developing, 322–23
Deprivations
in early life, 179
effects of emotional, 175
psychological and economic, 175
Deprived children, 12
Depth psychology, 133
Design
constraints on, 418
development of, 418
Destiny, human, 135
Detachment, 127, 135
Detection, outreach worker, 349
Determinism
biological, 131
psychological, 134–35
Deutsch, Karl, 64
Development of plan, 259
Developmental factors, 246
Developmental stage, 247
Developmental tasks, concern with, 25
Deviance
from a labeling perspective, 107
price for, 122
Deviant, 107, 122, 247
Dewey, John, 234–35
Diagnosis, 125, 128, 131, 518
for all occasions, 518
history taking for, 266
Diagnostic
clues, 296
labels, 128
terms, 92
thinking, 273
Differences
as an aid in helping, 157
barriers of, 447
of individual, 107
literature as testimonial, 223–24
as source of tension, 458
Differential treatment, 267
participation in, 332
Differentiation, 98
Dignity, 125–26
of client, 518
of individual, 104–5, 114
innate, of person, 109
of man, 126, 132–33

Direct service agencies, responsibility for
community organization, 461
Directive approaches, 198
Discomfort, 241, 244
Discrimination in client selection, 218
Dishonesty
with children, 180
of parents and adults, 171
practitioner's reason for, 181
problem for practitioner, 170–81
professional, areas of, 171
"Disliking" in relationships, 150
Distance matching, merits and disadvantages, 224
Division of labor, 493
Divorce, 124
Dix, Dorothea, 372
Documentation, 487
Dogmas, 124
Dollard, John, 268
Double bind, defined, 194
Dropout, 267
problem in practice, 267
Dubey, Sumati, 227
Due process, 466
Dulgaff, Ralph, 58
Dumont, Matthew, 110
Dynamic equilibrium, 65
"Dynamics of Teamwork in the Agency, Community, and Neighborhood," 454–64
Dysfunction, 25

E

Eaton, Joseph, 273
Ecological framework, 38
Ecstatic reason, definition, 133
Edelson, Marshall, 434–35
Education, 120
for advocacy, 376
professional and advocacy, 372
progressive methods borrowed from, 56
Educational qualifications, 504
Effective outcome, 401
Effectiveness
and incomplete knowledge, 71
measurement of, 414
Effector, 443
Efficiency, 474
in achieving program goals, 414
assessment as a purpose of evaluative research, 413–14
Ego autonomy, 97
function, 265
is id energy, 97
psychology, 96, 134
tasks, 271

Emergent qualities, 91
Emotion
  emotional tone, 246
  expression, 434
Empathic
  identification, 444
  listening, 518
  understanding, 223
Empathy, 135, 143, 287
  defined, 155
  as element of relationship, 143, 148–49,
    155–57
  literature as testimonial to differences,
    223–24
  requirements of, 156
  use with nonclient systems, 157
  use in other than helping relationships,
    157
Empiricism, 123
Employment, 246
Enabler role, 340
Encoding, defined, 194
Encounter, 135–36
  handling situations, 503
Ending phase, 422–26
Ends, defined
  in general terms, 478
  in pragmatic terms, 418
Enlightenment, 132–34
  ideas of, 132–34
Enthusiasm, 485
Entitlement, narcissistic, 443
Entrepreneurial model, 495
Entropy, 96
  negative, 63
  principle of, 98–99
Environment, 99, 105, 109, 122, 243–44
  emotional, 98
  physical, 98
  social, 98
Environmental data, 271
  elements of, 269
  manipulation, 97–98, 133
  opportunities, 109
Epstein, Laura, 111
Equifinality, 66
Equipotentiality of diverse interpretation,
  361–62
Equity, 118
Erikson, Erik, 97, 130, 134, 136
Error and uncertainty, 273
Ethical difficulties, 126
  dilemma, 125
  issues in experimental design, 419
  neutrality, 129
Ethics, 133
  Judeo-Christian tradition, 133

Ethics—*Cont.*
  NASW Code; National Association of
    Social Workers *see* (NASW),
    Code of Ethics
  problem, 123
  professional, 257
Ethnic identification, 246
Ethnicity, defined, 216
Ethos of enlightenment, 133
Evaluation, 235, 241–42, 251, 257, 261,
    349, 382–421, 428, 514
  in action phase, 253
  agency worker participation in, 382
  cost saving, 400
  to determine goal achievement effec-
    tiveness, 408
  feedback, 260, 382
  goal, 402
  goal specifications as a prerequisite for,
    383
  for interim changes in planning and
    conducting research, 409
  interrelationship of states, 411
  joint, 406
  justification of, 412
  to measure outcome, requirements of,
    414
  ongoing program modification, 420
  of paraprofessional performance, 225
  perspectives for, 410
  policy formation and program develop-
    ment, 409
  of practitioners programs, 410
  of professionals, 477
  of program administrators, 410
  of program effectiveness, 408
  of service to clients, 382
  by supporting community, 473
  in terms of goals, 407
  two kinds, 404
  what it may indicate, 383
Evaluative research
  administrative concerns about, 412
  assessment of input, 413–14
  assessment of outcomes, 413–14
  assessment of program efficiency,
    413–14
  clarification of purpose, 413
  collaboration process of, 411
  cooperation in, 411
  constraints on, 412
  covert purposes of, 413
  data collection in, 418
  defined, 410
  developing design of, 418–19
  experimental design in, 418
  focus of, 410
  funds, 408

Evaluative research—*Cont.*
 goals, 408
 practitioner concerns about, 411
 procedures of, 410
 process, 411–12
 program monitoring, 419–20
 purposes of, 412–13
 stages in, 411
 utilization of findings, 420–21
Executive, administrative, 482
Expectations
 of client and worker, 516
 of colleagues, 448–49
 contractual, 335
 defined, 154
 as element of relationship, 143, 148–49, 153–55
 of patient, 125
 preconceived, 156
Experimental design
 administrative constraints on, 419
 conflict with service goals, 420
 ethical issues, 419
 evaluative research in, 418
 information yielded by, 418
 preconditions of, 418
Explicitness, 334
Exploitative, 246
Explosive behavior, 430
Exploration, 241, 244
Expression of human dignity and respect, 519

F

Facts, as organized by language, 189
Faculty of schools of social work, 130
Failure, rewards of, 122
Faith healing of patient, 125
Family, 239–40, 243, 245, 247
 agreement, 247
 aspirations of, 248
 boundaries of, 247
 communication, 247
 dysfunctional, 522
 emotional needs of, 248
 formal roles of, 247
 functional and nonfunctional, 522
 informal roles of, 247
 life-style, 247
 physical needs of, 248
 rules, 247, 522
 as a social system, 247
 stability, 247
 system, 252
 values of, 248
Family Service Association, 99
Family treatment (therapy), 94, 264
 use of description in, 209

Feedback, 64, 235, 245, 255–57
 declarative statement as form of, 206
 defined, 206
 description as specialized form of, 207
 lines of social functioning, 83
 loops, 65, 383, 514
 negative, 65
 positive, 65
 research in, 205–6
 as technique for clarifying communications, 203
"Feedback in Family Interviewing," 206–16
Feelings
 component, 521
 countertransference, positive, 443
 mixed, 442
 subjective, 134
 toward worker, importance of knowing, 184
Fidelity, 124
Field concept, 21
Field of influence, 23
Figure skater, analogy of, 205–6, 516
Filters, problem of evaluation, 188
 own evaluational, 182
Findings, utilization of, 420–21
Flexibility, 271
Focus of work, 29
Folk therapies, 125
Follow-up
 date, 384
 information, 393
 interviews, 395–96
Foster care
 administrative planning in, 465
 internal review board in, 469
Foster child
 importance of, 470
 welfare of, 465
Foster family litigation, 465–66
Foster home evaluation, foster parents participation in, 468
Foster parent
 agency conflict, 465
 partnership with agency, 464
Fox, Evelyn E., article, 431–45
"Fragmentation of the Helping Professions," 450
Frank, Lawrence K., 21, 450
Freedom
 to fail, 121
 as illusion, 134
 primary, 121
French, 503
Freud, Sigmund, 96, 119, 129, 189, 434
Freudian psychology, 133
 principles, 134

"Friendly visitors," 139
Function, 91
  concept of, 21
  concept of as prerequisite to team-
    work, 456
  defined by social agency, 478
  interplay of, 23
  professional assignment, 24
Functional statement, 21
Fundamental fairness, 466
  steps toward, 467–70
Funding, relation to policy, 481

G

Gains
  maintenance of, 433
  sources of, in therapeutic relationship,
    363–70
Game
  rules of, 179
  theory, defined, 447
Garvin, Charles, 331
Garwick, Geoffrey, 384
  article, 388–401
Gault case, 466
General semantics, 189
Generalist, social work, 15
Generalization, basis for, 129
Genetic differences, 133
Genuineness, elements of, 159
  as element of relationship, 143, 148–49,
    159–62
Germain, Carel B., article, 263–74, 277
Getting started, 277
Getzel, George, 58
Ghetto
  client, 109
  language of, 221
  problems, ways of conceptualizations,
    39
  speech behavior in, 221
Ginsberg, Mitchell I., 254
Gitterman, Alex, 168–69
Glasser, Paul, 304
Goal, 252, 429
  of action system, 508–9
  caseworkers, 264
  client system, 244
  clients striving for, 518
  conflicting purposes of, 416
  establishing interim, 403
  establishment, 237
  and expectations, 276
  dimensions of, 284
  facilitative, 285
  family, 248
  feasibility, 501

Goal—*Cont.*
  feasibility study of ultimate, 284
  formulation of, 500–502, 520
  generalized, for practice, 425
  identification, 241, 243
  importance of relevance, 416
  individual and personal, 246
  interim, 284
  levels in evaluative research, 416
  long term, 243–44
  measurability of, 316
  modification of, 506
  operationalization in research,
    415
  in social work intervention, 2, 268
  optimal, 284
  original of client, 283
  personal, 246
  personal learning, 386
  possibility of attainment, 316
  predictions of, 400
  problem, relationship of, 416
  problem, separation from, 284
  relationship to theory, 417
  seeking as thrust of problem solving,
    283
  for service contract, 316
  serving agency, 495
  setting of, 283, 516
  short term, 241–44
  of social work, 124
  specification in evaluative research,
    383, 415–16
  of treatment, 336
  value of formulating, 335
Goal accomplishment, criteria for, 417
Goal attainment
  change score, 394
  as comparative measure, 398
  follow-up date, 384
  follow-up grid (Diagram 6), 386
  follow-up guide, systematic basis, 398
Goal Attainment Scale, 520
  and long-term goals, 398–99
Goal Attainment Scaling (Diagram 5),
    384–86
  background, 388
  basic procedures, 389
  collection of information, 389
  concerns of, 384–85
  designation of problem areas, 390
  effectiveness measures, 394
  goal setting, 388
  judgment, 393
  numerical weight, 391
  outcome measurement, 388
  predictions in problem areas, 392
  range of outcomes, 392

Goal Attainment Scaling (Diagram 5)—
  Cont.
  realistic expectation, 394
  reality testing, 400
  therapy, objective setting in, 388
  Sherman specialized formula, 397
  score, 396
  short-term goals in, 398
  single scale, 396
  titles in follow-up, 391
  uses of as feedback, 397
  varieties of, 398
Goal-directed
  behavior, 62
  information collecting, 286
  thinking, 234
Goldstein, Howard, 159
Golding, William, 130–31
Goodman, James, 109
Gordon, William, 7–8, 51, 103, 105–6,
  206
  article, 74–84
"Grapevine," 486
Greenhill, Laurence, 330
Greenwood, Ernest, 206
Grief
  expression of about loss, 439
  feelings of, 434
  grief work, 434
  infantile component of, 444
  about termination, 439
Grosser, Charles F., 332, 341
  article, 351–60
Group, 239–40, 245
  affiliative, friendship and social, 248
  as enterprise in mutual aid, 27
  function of, 33
  functional characteristics of, 244
  meeting, 277
  natural, Nobleteens, example of work
    with, 43–44
  objective, 248
  obstacles to, 29–31
  obstacles to tasks of, 30–32
  as organic whole, 27
  patients, black male, 219
  patients, racial minority, 219
  personal change, 248
  processes, 115, 255
  role enhancement and development,
    33–34
  as system of relationships, 27
  task oriented, 248
  therapy as precondition of parole, 122
  types used in change activities, 509
  work, 10
  worker, 9–11
  worker's contribution of data to, 32–33

Group—*Cont.*
  worker's feeling involvement in, 35
  worker's opinions as data for, 33
  worker's sharing of hopes with, 34
Group work, 10
  knowledge borrowed from, 56
Growth
  positive emotional, 177
  potential, 518
Guidance, 243
Guilt, 136
Guilt in white practitioner, 168

H

Halleck, Seymour, article, 170–81
Halmos, Paul, 103
Hamilton, Gordon, 128, 265, 267, 273–74,
  323
Handicapped person, 181, 185
  child, 182
Handicaps
  meaning of, 183
  symptoms and causes, 185
  understanding of, 183
Hanlan, Archie, article, 492–98
"Hard" data, 417
Harris, Dale, 129
Hartman, Ann, 61
Hawthorne, Nathaniel, 127
Head Start, 99
Healer, authority of, 125
Heine, R. W., 224
Help
  asking for as blow to adequacy, 275
  broadened concept of, 268–71
  as dangerous word, 173
  difficulty of asking for, 276
  as distinguished from treatment,
    268–69
  expressed in action, 28
  factors involved in taking, 276
  object of help, 269–70
  objectives of, 269–71
  reconceptualized, 269–71
  unit of, 269
Helper, 270
Helping acts, 26
Helping function
  components of, 35
  of worker, 111–12
Helping person, 519
  as nonconformist, 164
  qualities of, 163
Helping process, 236, 264, 270–71
  art in, 36
  aspects of, 141
  nature of, 20

Helping process—*Cont.*
science in, 36–37
variations of, 20
Helping relationships, 136, 236; *see also*
Relationship
elements of worker movements within,
24
Helping system, 243
Helplessness in clients, 304
Hersey, John, 223
Hiatt, Harold, 438
Hierarchy, 482
Hippocratic Oath, 134
History
for abreaction, 266
for diagnostic purposes, 266
of knowledge, 56
Hobbs, Nicholas, 344
article, 360–71
Holistic orientation, 62
Hollis, Florence, 208
Home visit, 270
Homeostasis, 65, 95
Homeostatic functions of ego, 96
Homeostatic mechanisms, 99
Homer, 118
Homogamy, defined, 218
Homophyly, defined, 218
Honest approach
methods of developing, 178
prerequisites to, 177–78
Honesty, 124
Hope, 241, 519
capitalization of, 125
discomfort balance, 287
Hopefulness, client, 286
Horse, lost, 189
Hospitalization, experience with, 188
"The House on Sixth Street," 423
Hudson, Joe, 386
article, 407–21
Hughes, Everett C., 495–96
Hughes, Langston, 217
Hull, C. L., 189
Human
behavior and social environment, content pertaining to, 86–87
being as object, 128
change, 70
condition, 119, 134–36
development, universal stages of, 133
interaction, 138
life, 129
motives, oversimplified explanations,
131
nature, mystery of, 133
perfectability, 132–33

Human—*Cont.*
relationship, worth of, 124; *see also*
Relationship
suffering, 119, 128
Humanism, 115
of social work, 108
spirit of, 122
Humanitarian, 116
Humility, 110
Hyman, Stanley, 130

I

Id energy, 97
Ideal patient, concept of, 436
Identification with agency, 449
Identification, sources of, 226
Identifying sources of power, 502
Identity in hierarchical structure in pro-
fessional association, 478
Ideological point of view, 129
Ideology, 102
of the professions, 102
Idios kosmos of Heraclitus, 136
Idiosyncratic patterns, 131
Ignorance in interviews, presumption of,
221
Ill, 122
Image, personal, 246
"Impact of Professional Dishonesty on
Behavior of Adolescents," 170–81
Inattentiveness, barrier to communica-
tion, 198
Inberg, Aviva C., article, 516–23
Incongruence of views of central prob-
lem, 282
Independent variables, operationalizing
of, 415
Indigenous case aides, as paraprofession-
als, 225
Individual, 106, 135, 239–40, 245
change, 11
as human being, 135
inner and outer forces, 135
parts of, 521
psychological approach to, 39
skill-in-acting component of, 521
social interaction impaired, 25
social transaction, 24
Individualism, 155
Individuality, 109
Individualization
concepts of, 514
defined, 265
in social study, 265, 276–78
Individualized treatment, 267–68
Infantile component of grief, 444
Information
collecting, 286

Information—*Cont.*
  establishing need for, 278
  and referral services, 457
  sharing of, 520
  sharing with client, 278
  source of, 279
  for voluntary and involuntary clients, 278
  withholding of, 279
  as yielded by experimental design, 418
Inhibition, 442
Initial contact, preparation for, 227
Initial goal setting, 275
Innate goodness, belief in, 129
Innovation, 264
Inpatient services, 120
Input, 99, 111
  assessment as purpose of evaluative research, 413–14
  in evaluation research, nature of, 247
Insight
  emphasis and direction of, 237
  promotion of, 360
  role of, 362
  as sovereign remedy, 362
Instinct, 122
Institution
  charitable, 120
  of social welfare, 119
Institutionalized
  repression, 445
  setting, 177
Instruction, teacher, 349
Intellectual component, 521
Interaction
  basically dishonest pattern of, 177
  continued, 62
  as focus of social work, 7–9
  honest, 178
  modes of with groups, 250
  nature of, 8
  with professional colleagues, 446
  program of FSA of Nassau County, N.Y., 99
Interactional factors, 249
Interactive complexity, 62
Interactive focus of systems theory, 61
Interagency
  client involvement in, 451
  conferences, 451–52
  cooperation, 456
  coordination, efforts needs for, 461
  principles of, 452
  teamwork, barriers to, 456
Interchange, 99
Interdependence of individuals and society, 6–10, 52
Interfaces between systems, 39

Interim evaluation, 404
Interpersonal relationship; *see also* Relationship
  accuracy dependent upon, 156
  description of, 207
Interpretive therapies, 361
Intervener, role of, 44–46
Intervention, 98, 235, 505, 521
  casework goals of, 268
  casework models of, 98
  defined, 339
  direct, 97
  effective modes of, 264
  limited concept, 340
  limits of worker capability, 317
  methods, of, 257
  methods, factors in selecting, 301
  multiple possibilities for, 93
  new model of, 271
  objectives of and watching roles, 349–50
  procedures of, 260
  procedures, selection of, 261–62
  new techniques, 271
  selection of focus, 304
  strategies and the interview, 192
Interventive actions, 109
  conflicts of judgement, 476
  process, 246
Interventive roles, 340
  activist, 341, 357–59
  advocate, 344–45, 355
  broker, 342–43, 354
  concept of, 339–42
  defined, 340, 345, 350
  enabler, 343–44, 353
  objectives and corresponding roles of, 349–50
Interview, 277
  as central tool of practice, 192
  checkout, 203
  common symbols in, 213
  and communication, 192–230
  as communication, 194
  context of, 194–95
  creating productive climate for, 199
  for data collection, 202, 204
  data collection, purpose of, 198
  establishing purpose, 200
  focus of as worker responsibility, 200
  as funnel, 202
  inexplicit purposes for, 204
  limits of, 195
  as major tool of data collection, 192
  method of focus, 200
  as modality of change, 192
  practitioner's responsibility in, 202
  purpose as element, 195

Interview—*Cont.*
  racial factors in, 206, 216–30
  roles of participants, 195
  sharing worker's input, 203
  social work, characteristics of, 194
  social work, defined, 194
  as specialized communication, 195
  spc~ 'aneity and freedom in, 205
  struc,ure, 288
  structured, completely, 288
  techniques, 204
  as tool of data collection, 288
  use of "why" question, 204
  worker's responsibility in, 199–202
Interviewer-interviewee pairs, effects of
      difference, 228
Interviewing, 115
  as disciplined art, 205
Intimacy, capacity for, 246
Intra-agency barriers to teamwork, 457
Intraorganization
  change, 499, 502, 510
  strategy, 509
Intuition, 156
  moral, 127
Investigation, 241, 244
Involuntary client, defined, 278
Irrational, power of the, 162
Irrationality, of practitioner in relation-
      ships, 161
Issue
  consensus, 501
  difference, 501

J

Janchill, Sr. Mary Paul, 61
Job security, 482
Johnson, Norman, 199
Johnson, Wendell, article, 181–90
Joint participation, 332
Judeo-Christian ethics, 133
Judgment, 2–3, 121
Jung, C. G., 134–35
Justice, 118, 133
Justice system, juvenile, 107

K

Kadushin, Alfred, 50, 55–56
  article, 206, 216
Kahn, Alfred J., 56, 59, 194, 351
Kahn, Marvin, 128
Kammerman, Sheila B., et al., 58
Kaplan, Abraham, 11, 55
Keith-Lucas, Alan, 141, 150, 155, 276
Kelman, Norman, 34
Kidneigh, John C., 14, 75, 81

Kincaid, Marylou, 223
Kiresuk, Thomas, 384
  article, 388–401
Kiresuk-Sherman formula, 396
Klein, Alan F., 328
Knowledge, 118
  ability to predict as test of, 79
  accepted and acted on, 53
  approximate, nature of, 132
  areas of, listed, 74–75
  areas of in social work education, 57
  areas of substantive knowledge, 84–88
  assumptive, 50
  base, changes in, 59
  base for social work, 50, 83
  borrowed, 56
  breaking down, 50
  building, 107
  causal relationships of, 61
  as comprehensive topic, 50
  confirmed, 50
  confusion with values, 77–80
  as control, 156
  criteria
    for borrowing, 71
    for selection, 50, 70
  dealing with ignorance of, 50
  defined, 50, 76–77
  in definition of social work practice,
      51
  development of, 55
  as differentiated from social work val-
      ues, 51
  difficulty of selecting, 57
  and effectiveness, 71
  as element of social work practice, 74
  empirical testing of, 53
  empirically untested, 58
  focus of, 83
  formulation, criteria of, 83
  frame of reference for social work, 58
  functions of, 50, 57
  history of in social work, 56–58
  of human behavior, 57
  importance of, 50
  incomplete, 71
  interventive repertoire dependent on,
      68
  kinds needed in social work, 60
  lack of as barrier to teamwork, 457
  NASW statement of basic, 74–75
  necessity of, 67
  new, 54
  organization of, 14
  of other, 156–57
  problem of identifying, 57
  problems in selection for use, 50

Knowledge—*Cont.*
and purpose, interactive relationship
of, 58
relationship to research, 55
reliance on past, 58
seeking as practitioner responsibility,
72
of social environment, 57
of social welfare policy and services,
57
of social work practice, 57
sources of, 50
systems theory
as framework for organization, 60
as selection tool, 50
terms of, 50
testing of, 50
theory, 53
and theory development, 54, 69
in university curriculum, 72
use in crisis situations, 58
use in planning change, 59
and value
confusion between, 52, 77–79
convergence of, 80–81
defined, 76–77
difference between, 79–80
distinction, 76–78
as guide to action, 78–79
priority over method and technique,
51
problem of separating, 78
roles of, 52
separation of, 81–82
"Knowledge and Value: Their Distinction and Relationship in Clarifying
Social Work Practice," 74–84
Koinonia, 136
Konopka, Gisela, 8, 141, 209
Kramer, Ralph, 454–64
Kropotkin, P., 25

L

Labeling, 108
theorists, 107
Lady Bountiful, 128
Laissez-faire, doctrine of, 122
Language
either-or quality of, 185
forms in our culture, 185
in professional specializations, 188
as thinking, 185–89
as way of organizing facts, 189
Law, knowledge of, 376
Leaders
informal, 507
joint training for, 463

Leadership
casework role in, 270
informal, 504
Lebeaux, Charles N., 318, 475
Lee, Porter, 8
Legal mandate, effects on intervention
procedures, 281
Legislation, dependency on, 481
Lerner, Barbara, 475–76
Lessard v. Wilbur Schmidt, et al., 466
Levy, Charles, 102–3
Lewin, Kurt, 93
Liberty, 118
Licensure, 470
Lie
of adult morality, 172–78
of confidentiality, 173–74, 178
of practitioner anger, 177
of rewards for conformity, 174–75,
178–79
of trust, 176–79
Liebow, Elliot, 223
Lieberman, Dina, 204
Life
crisis of, 271
experience in, 129
model, 271
self-deceptions in adult, 181
tasks, 238
"Liking" and "disliking" in relationships,
150
Limitations
denial of, 175–76
sources of in social work practice, 104
worker's denial of, 176
Lindemann, Erich, 434
Line of command, 496
Litigation, 465–66
Listening, active, 151
Lockean *tabula rasa doctrine,* 133
Loss, 445
Love, 124
Lowell, James Russell, 95
Lowry, Fern, 267
Lying, 171

M

McPheeters, Harold L., article, 348–50
Magic, 125
Magicians, 125
Maladaptive, 122
Maluccio, Anthony N., 312
article, 326–38
Man
ailments of, 123
concept of, 118, 134, 517
dignity of, 118

Man—*Cont.*
 in bear trap, 187
 irrational and instinctual characteristics
  of, 238
 nature of, 103, 133
 as an object, 132
 as subject, 132
Manpo ˙r, shortage of, 264
Marcel, ˛abriel, 135
Marlow, Wilma D., 312
 article, 326–38
Maslow, A. H., 517
Matching
 in communication and interviewing,
  223
 importance of, 229
 racial factors of, 224
In Matter Rios, 466
Maturing, as quality of professional life,
  143, 164
May, Rollo, 133, 136
Mayer, John E., 146, 285, 313
Maximizer in game theory, 447–48
Mead, George Herbert, 25
Measures, specification of in evaluative
  research, 417–18
Meetings, too many as barrier to team-
  work, 459
Menninger, Karl, 108
Mental health
 idealogy of, 134
 services, differential access to, 218
Mentally deficient, 123
Mentally ill, 12, 123
Mercenaries, 126
Merton, Robert K., 22, 310
Messages
 inconsistant, 196
 quality of, 247
Metacommunication, defined, 194
Metapsychology, 98
Methods
 adaptation of, 21
 combined use of, 270
 conceptualizations of, 9–19
 definitions of, 8–10, 21
 primary variables of, 9
 problem solving, 285
 tasks of, 10, 26–27
 and techniques, 54
 typology of, 1, 5–37; *see also* Model
  and Social work
 using client to refine, 184–85
Methodological components, 20, 129
 problems of abstracting common, 19
Meyer, Carol, 57
Micro-macro approach, 11–13
Middle-range theory, 89

Milford Conference, 55
Milieu therapy, 98, 270
Miller, Henry, 102–3, 115, 117
Minahan, Anne, 142
Mobilization, 349
Mobilization for Youth (MFY), 301, 353
Modality of service, 242, 252
Model
 basic assumptions of, 238–39
 conceptual, 99
 crisis, 271
 developmental, 98
 enrichment, 98
 Hamilton's
  conceptual, 266
  of social study, 266
 life, 98, 271
 life-space, 98
 mediating, 5, 17, 37
 medical-clinical, 98
 micro-macro, 11–13
 organic, 23
 problem-focused, 275
 problem-solving, 233–53
 psychotherapeutic, 268, 271
 traditional, 9, 11, 265
Modes of thought, 91
Money, 473
Moral
 concern of casework, 123
 question, 118
 neutrality in, 124
Moralistic attitude, 134
Moralities, professional, 118
Morality, lie of adult, 172, 178
Morris, Robert, 256, 357
Motivation, 241, 513
Motives, underlying, 442
Mullan, Hugh, 433
Multiple causation, 131
Murphy, Gardner, 25

N

Narcissism, 122
Narcissism wounds, 445
National Association of Social Workers
 (NASW)
 certification of competency, 489
 Code of Ethics, 113, 115–17, 373–74,
  489
 Commission on Social Work Practice,
  20
 definition of social work, 6, 51, 74
 limits to worker's self-determination,
  statements on, 113
 priority of obligations, 378
 professional autonomy, 377
 promoting activities, 379

National Welfare Rights Organization, 470
Nature, human, 134
Needs, basic human, 517
  identification of unmet, 261
Neighborhood community development, 351
Neighborhood councils, 462–63
Neighborhood organizations
  functions of, 462
  patterns of, 462
  rationale for, 461–62
Negro social worker, 227; *see also* Black professional
Negroes 123; *see also* Black professional; Race; *and* Racism
Nelson, Marian A., article, 431–35
Neutrality, 127
New York Times, 360
Nisbet, Robert A., 310
Nitzberg, Harold, 128
Nobleteens, 43–44
Noise in communication theory, defined, 194
Non-zero-sum games, 447
Norms, role in assessment of functioning, 268
Northen, Helen, 141, 208, 428

O

Objectives, caseworker and client difference on, 264
Objectives, linkages of long- and short-term (Figure 8), 399
Objectivity in relationships, 161
Objects, of client's reaction, 297
Objects, ourselves as, 132
Obligation
  collateral, 374
  as element in relationship, 143, 148–49, 151–53
  ethical, 374
  inherent, 374
  reciprocal, 334
  in work role, 374
Observations
  necessity of objectivity in, 115
  structured and unstructured, 289
O'Connor, Gerald, 112
"One-up," 448
Operating principles, client-worker understanding of, 313
Opinions, social workers offering of, 11
Oppenheimer, Martin, 359
Opportunity
  adolescents' access to, 301
  factors in assessment, 241, 245

Optimism
  in American culture, 133
  in attitude of social worker, 70
Ordering of needs and resources, 25
Ordering of reality, 95
Oren, Anne, 75, 81
Oreos, defined, 222
Organic whole, Parson's definition of, 21
Organization
  allegiance to, 499
  change, exploitation of formal structure, 509
  change, informal context utilized, 509
  competence, 250
  enforcement, 491
  expectations, 510
  expressions of homophyly and homogamy, 218
  as a factor of community assessment, 251
  mission of, 491
  as necessary for knowledge transmission, 128
  roles, use of, 270
  structure, use of, 270, 482
  technologies, 250
Organizations, difference between profit and nonprofit, 477
Outcome assessment, as purpose of evaluative research, 413–14
Outcome in social work in evaluative research, 413–14
Outcome studies, 408
Overidentification, as result of racial factors, 222
Oversimplification, in explanation of human motives, 131
Overton, Alice, 209

P

Paperwork, as service to client, 485
Paradox, of distance and intimacy, 128
Parameters
  of agency's societal change, 473
  of policy, 485
  of service, 473
Paraprofessionals, 225–27
Parents, contractual alliance with, 334
Parent Effectiveness Training, 522
Parole, dependent on receptivity to counsel, 121
Parsons, Talcott, 21
Partialization, in problem solving, 281
Participant-observation, Sullivan's use of, 135
Participation, joint and differential, 332
Participation, as necessary to change, 135

Particularized treatment, 267
Partisan, workers as, 375
Partnership, 2, 115
    aspect of work, 514
    concept of, 515
    implications of, 514
    nature of client and worker interaction
        in, 312
    nature of process, 514
Paternalism, 168
Pathology, 98
    as cause of resistance, 199
    as outcome of transactions, 39
Patterned-type social study, 266
Patterns of behavior, 515
    of neighborhood organizations, 462
Patti, Rina J., 334
    article, 499
Pavlov, I. P., 189
Pejoratives, substituting new for old, 123
People as objects, 523
Perlman, Helen Harris, 12, 69, 140, 208,
    281
Perlmutter, Felice, 229
Person in environment, as social work
    concern, 92
Person-situation, as unit of help, 7, 9–10,
    269, 573
Personal influence, power of, 139
Personalities, oral dependent, 131
Personality, systems view of 97–98
Personality change, implication of sys-
    tems theory for, 97
Personality dynamics, 266
Phase of treatment, importance of, 432
Phenomena, tendency to oversimplify
    complex, 115
Philadelphia Child Guidance Clinic, 38
Philadelphia Opportunities Industrializa-
    tion Center, 229
Phillips, Doris Campbell, article, 392–401
Phillips, Helen, 209
Philosophy, materialistic, 133
Pincus, Allen, 142
Placement agreement, benefits of, 467
Plan of action, development of, 257
Plan-confirmation letters to foster par-
    ents, 467
Polansky, Norman A., 210
"Populations at risk," 98–99
Positivism as a philosophy, 129
Poverty, 120–22
Power
    in adversary strategy, 508
    alliances of organizations as source of,
        505
    characteristics of, 158
    coercive, 503

Power—*Cont.*
    configuration of, 501
    as element in relationship, 143, 148–49,
        158–59
    exercise of, 478
    expert in use of, 503
    legitimate, 503
    significance of, 158
    sources of, five types, 503
    value of, 503
"Power to the People" movement, 332
Power person, attributes of, 504
Powerlessness, sense of, 39
Practice
    advocacy as a part of, 377–78
    dilemmas, resolution of, 265
    prerequisites for, 255
Practitioner
    behavior as dishonest, 174
    direct service of, 372
    dishonesty of, 170–81
    dual role of, 172–73
    interest in work versus interest in
        client, 184
    limits of ability, 276
    middle-class, 175
    responsibility in data collection, 205
Pragmatic method, 134
Pragmatism, 133
Preconditions of experimental design,
    418–19
Pregnancy, service during, 260
Prejudgements, 106
Preventative actions of worker, 13
Prevention
    example of program for, 261–62
    versus rehabilitation, 12, 14
Principle
    defined, 53
    of self-help, 139
Priorities and feasibility, concept of, 256
Prisons, 122
Privacy
    meaning of, 106
    as right of client, 150
Probation
    office, 121
    orders, 121
Probationer, 112
Probing, as technique of interviewing,
    202
Problem
    assessment of, 198
    clarification of, 276
    definition of, 2, 63, 237, 240–42, 256,
        280, 403, 576
    definition and goals, importance of,
        291

Problem—*Cont.*
  and diagnosis, 297
  of discrimination, 217
  exploitation of, 217
  focused practice, 253–56, 275
  of harassment, 217
  and helping person, 425
  identification, 240–42
  identification as part of preliminary
      contract, 275–76
  of inability to relate successfully, 298
  joint assessment and decision making,
      314
  location outside of the client system,
      282
  negotiation, 280
  as pattern of interactive behavior, 299
  of racial difference, 217
  of rejection, 217
  as seen by client system, 277
  as seen by social worker, 277
  as seen by systems in interaction with
      client, 277
  solution, through group participation,
      306
  solution, through institutional change,
      310
  solution, side effects, 308
  system involved in, defining, 305–6
  viewed as reaction, 297–98
  for work, 277
Problem area
  designation of, 400
  predictors of, 400
Problem-to-be-worked, 285, 404
"A Problem Focused Model of Practice,"
    240
Problem solving
  approach to teamwork, 450–57
  basic assumptions of model, 238–39
  capacity, 251
  and client system, 238
  contact phase of, 275–79
  as cyclical process, 236–37
  and Dewey, 234–35
  ending or termination phase, 275,
      428–30
  framework, 236, 240
  method of, 285
  middle contact phase, 275
  model, diagram, of, 383
  model, discussion of, 206, 233–53, 520
  as mutual undertaking, 13
  outline of, discussed, 239–53
  outline of, long form, 242–53
  outline of, short form, 240–42
  partialization, 281
  as partnership process, 2, 514

Problem solving—*Cont.*
  practitioner's limits of, 276
  and practitioner's responsibility, 234–38
  procedural steps of, 235
  process of, 115, 236, 238, 256
    phases of, 275
    as guide, 402
    individualized, 406
  as rational process, 514
  resources, 251
  stages of, 236
  summary of, 262
  techniques of, 522
  terminal aspects of, 235
  theme of, 513
Process
  defined, 1
  separation, 437–45
  social work, 66, 238–39
  studies of, 387
  of termination, 445
Profession of social work; *see also* Social
    work
  body of knowledge, 251
  commitment, requirements of, 423
  competence, 478
  consultations, 452
  culture, of, 448–50
  function of, 5, 57–58
  historical division of labor in, 17
Professional
  and bureaucracy, 472–90
  dishonesty, impact of, 170–81
  education, 449
  function, 24
  helpfulness, 172–73
  interstitial nature of, 472–74
  judgement, 242, 252, 322, 324, 514
  knowledge, application of, 2, 69
  person
    independence of, 486
    virtues of, 36
  skills, 3
  staff, 448
  values of, 102–16, 508, 510
Professional responsibility, 113–14
Professionalism in relationships, 161; *see
    also* Relationship
Prognosis, 125, 131, 242, 253
Program components
  measurement of in evaluative research,
      417–18
  and relationship of goals, 416
Program efficiency, assessment of as pur-
    pose of evaluative research, 413–14
Program evaluation, criteria for phases
    in, 386–387

Program Evaluation Project, 1969–1973, 338, 398
Program goals
  conflicts in, 416
  operationalizing of, in research, 415
Program input, 413–14
Program outcome, 414
Program priorities in goal development, 416
Progressive forces, 270
Project monitoring in evaluative research, 419–20
Protective functions of social workers, 111–12
Pruger, Robert, 491
Pseudoevaluations, 413
Psychiatrist, 135, 174
Psychiatry, 56, 129, 254
Psychoanalysis, 97
Psychologist
  as agent of school, 173
  social, 106
Psychological factors in social functioning, 269
Psychotherapeutic model, 268, 271
Psychotherapy, 186–87
  of adults, 180
  cognition in, 369
  confidentiality in, 174
  intensive, 97
Pumphrey, Muriel, 76, 130
Purcell, Francis, 282
  article, 301–11
Purpose
  contradictory, as barrier to communication, 197
  covert, of evaluative research, 413
  defined, 145
  in evaluative research, 412–13
  immediate, 145
  knowledge, interaction with, 58
  longtime, 145
  normative, 145
  operational, 145
  in relationship, 143–46, 148–49
  unique, 145
  of work, 111
"Put down," 448

Q

Quality, demeaning, 120
Questionnaires, 288
Questions
  biasing, 202
  open-ended, 202–3

R

Race
  and social work relationships, 167–69
  and society, 168–69
Racial barrier
  to rapport, 218
  to understanding, 218
"Racial Factor in the Interview, The," 216–30
Racial experience, 216
Racial identification, 246
Racism, 167–69
  attitudes, impact of, 167–69
  child of his culture, 220
  society, 163
Rank, Otto, 135
Rapoport, Anatol, 62
Rapoport, Lydia, 489
Rapport
  client-worker, 224
  related to effective interviewing, 224
Rational
  and nonrational processes, 239, 514
  problem solving, 516
  procedure, 234
  thought, 234
Rationality, 238
Raven, Bertram, 503
Reaching out techniques, 264, 270
Reality, 36
  ability to face, 181
  levels of, 132
  objective, 130–31
  of psychic origins, 129
  whole of, 131
Rebound Children and Youth Project, 38
Receiving, defined, 194
Receptor end, 443
Red tape, 484
"On Reducing Contention Between Foster Family Parents and Child-Placing Agencies," 464–70
Reductionism, 269
Referral, 422–26
  case example, 423
  defined, 423
  problems and principles, 425
  as a process, 422
  skills, 423
  transfer and termination, factors in common, 422
Reflective thought, five phases of, 234–35
Regression, 430
Rehabilitation, 12–13
Reid, William, 111, 332, 335
Rein, Martin, 6, 8, 11, 357, 420
Reistroffer, Mary, article, 464–70

Relationship, 135
  acceptance and expectation in, 153–55
  authority in, 143, 158–59
  casework, 128
  charitable impulse, 127
  cognitive elements in, 162
  commitment and obligation in, 151–53
  common elements of, 143
  concept of, 115
  concept operationalized, 200
  concern for other in, 149–51
  congruence in, 159–62
  cooperative, 455–56
  defined, 140–42
  development of, 143–49, 179, 233
  differential use of elements, 143
  elements of, 141–42, 149–63, 521
  elements of power in, 143, 158–59
  emergent characteristics, 143, 147
  empathy as component of, 35, 155–57
  genuineness in, 159–62
  helping, 23, 138, 142–44, 199–200
  human, 138
  irrational elements in, 147–48, 162–63
  loss and quality of, 435
  meaningful, democratic, and collabora-
      tive, 239
  necessity of, 521
  nonrational elements in, 147–48,
      162–63
  nonsymbiotic, 176
  objectivity in, 161
  operationalized, 200
  with others, 523
  as partnership, 519
  practitioner's self-protection in, 161
  precipitate break in, 430
  as prerequisites to teamwork, 456
  professional, 322
  professionalism in, 35, 127, 161
  purpose in, 143–46
  qualities of, 141–42
  quality, depth and nature of, 246–49
  and race, 163–67
  rational elements in, 148, 162–63
  reciprocal rules of, 35
  risks in development of, 179
  roles and relationship, 142–44
  self-discipline in, 143
  self-knowledge in, 143
  sustained, 176
  termination of, 428–45
  therapeutic, 363–436
  as training ground for living, 270
  types of, 142
  use of self in, 143
  variables affecting use of, 144, 147
  worker's affect as component of, 35

Relationship—*Cont.*
  working relationships, 29
Relationships, worker-client
  client's values as factor in, 297
  diagnostic clues in, 292–301
  importance of purpose, 279
  initial reaction, 295
  worker's appearance, 297
  worker's trust in own reactions, 295
Relevance
  of data, 272
  definition of, 267
  in social study, 265–67
Reliability
  defined, 195
  of evaluative measure, 417
Religious identification, 246
Rescue fantasy, 110
Research
  Berkowitz's discussion of, 54
  constraints on, 411–12
  interrelationships of stages of, 411
  and program conflicts, 412
  in social work methods and techniques,
      54
Resistance
  agency procedures as cause of, 199
  as barrier to communication, 198
  cultural norms affecting, 199, 205
  dealing with, 199
  hesitancy to enter strange situation as
      cause, 198, 205
  pathological involvement with problem
      as cause, 199, 205
  techniques of, 178
Resnick, Herman, 334
  article, 499
Resources
  of action systems, 508–9
  concrete, 243
  dispensing external, 473
  equitable distribution of, 352
  mobilization of, 502
  specific, 243–44
Respect
  for clients, 518
  for colleagues, 448–49
  for dignity and uniqueness of individ-
      ual, 105, 516
  examples of overt indications, 220
Response
  affective level defined, 201
  behavioral level of, 200–201
  client's levels of, 200
  cognitive level of, 200–201
  example of perceptual and cognitive
      level, 201
  feeling level of, 200

Response—*Cont.*
  interviewing (Diagram 3), 203
  perceptual level defined, 200
Responsibility
  of chairman, 453
  conception of, 122
  for total community, 109
  of worker in creating climate of inter-
    view, 200
Reynolds, Bertha, 24
Richmond, Mary, 55, 92, 98, 127, 129,
    139, 265–66
Riessman, Frank, 225–26
Ripple, Lilian, 58, 287
Rivalist, 447–48
Rogers, Carl, 155, 189, 196
Roles
  advocate, 344–45
  Bisno's concept of, 341
  caseworker's changing, 270
  of clients and workers, 332
  concept of interventive, 339–42
  defined, 339
  enabler, 343–44
  expectations in groups, 331
  of family members, 247
  functional specialization, 345
  as global concept, 340
  leadership, 270
  misconceptions of, 345–46
  objectives as shaping, 349–50
  performance, 246
  responsibility of, 247
  social, 246
  social broker, 342–43
  in social work practice, 142–44, 252
  tasks, relevant to, 249
  transitions, 271
Rosen, Aaron, 200, 204
Rubin, Gerald, 130, 135
Rules
  as feature of bureaucracy, 493
  of interviewing, 179
  as means, 491
  of work, reciprocal nature of, 35
Rutman, Leonard, article, 407–21
Ryan, Robert, article, 348–50

S

Sachs, Wulf, 224
Sager, Clifford, 219, 517
Salience
  of data, 271
  defined, 267
  of needs, 270
  in social study, 265, 267–68

Salomon, Elizabeth, 102, 108, 115
  article, 127–37
Sangiuliano, Iris, 433
Satir, Virginia, 194, 209, 344
Schaeffer, Alice, 169
Schiff, Sheldon, K., 433
Schizophrenia, diagnosis of, 135
Schubert, Margaret, 331
Schwartz, Charlotte, G., 267–69
Schwartz, Morris S., 267–69
Schwartz, William, 5, 8–10, 14, 16, 104,
    111–12, 199, 209, 318, 328, 344
  article, 17–38
Science, 115
  language of, 123
  needs of, 108
Scientific inquiry, spirit of, 265
Scientific knowledge, 130, 135
  as abstraction, 130–31
  body of, 127–28
Scientific method, 127, 131, 134
  and assessment, 304
Scientific objectivity, dangers of, 127–28
Scientific orientation
  of practitioner, 273–74
  to social study, 266
Scientific precision, 128
SEEK Program, 227
Selective nonattention, 480
Selectivity, relating to race, 218
Self
  actualization of, 517
  awareness, 132, 157, 163, 165
  as basic tool, 2
  capacity to observe, 143, 165–66
  concept of, 211
  creative use of, 162
  of man, 118
  perception of, 523
  professional, 143, 166–67
  use in relationship, 143
  use of for system change, 163
Self-determination, 132
  client, 104–5, 109, 111–14, 514
  is knowledge and value, 52
  principle of, as value, 109–15
  as traditional value, 103
Self-discipline, 143, 156
Self-esteem, 517
Self-fulfilling prophecy, 107
Self-fulfillment, 5
Self-help groups, 332
Self-image
  messages of, 106
  poor, 39
Self-knowledge, 135, 143
Self-perception, 246
Self-protection, 165

Self-protection—*Cont.*
  need for, 165
  in relationship, 165
Self-understanding, 132
Semantics, general, 182
Sensitivity
  in observation, 289
  as part of professional self, 143, 156, 166–67
Separation
  affects involved in, 426–31, 434
  phases in, 434, 445
  problems of, 426–45
  process of, 437–45
  reaction to, 435
Service contract
  arrived at, 313
  defined, 312
  phase of, 312–20
Service goals, conflict with experimental design, 420
Service system, 241, 244
  access to, 485
  compartmentalization of, 455
Service team, 270, 446
Sexual behavior, social usefulness of, 172
Shaman, 125
Sharing and planning in teams, methods of, 451–54
Sherif, Muzafer, 25
"Sick" role, 175
Significant others, 252
Significant systems, 240, 243
Simon, Herbert, 64
Situation, definition of, 269
Skills
  in doing, 14–15, 233
  use by practitioner, 280
Smalley, Ruth, 210
Social action activity, 257
Social agencies; *see* Agency
Social anthropology, knowledge borrowed from, 56
Social change; *see* change
Social conformity, 251
"Social countertransference," 437
Social Diagnosis, 55
Social distance, 270
Social functioning, 7, 83, 269
Social institutions, 122
Social inability, 257
Social investigation, 265
Social network, "C" street as example, 41–43
Social planning, need for, 459
Social policy development, 257
Social problems, 513

Social problems—*Cont.*
  as basis for organizing social work activity, 14
  victims of, 251–54
Social reality, 236
Social resources, 237
Social situations, assessments of, 321
Social skills, 521
Social slippage, 480
Social study, 263–74
  clue type, 266
  patterned type, 266
  scientific orientation of, 266–67
  traditional, 264
"Social Study: Past and Future," 263–74
Social systems, 243–44
Social transactions, as central phenomenon of social science, 83
Social welfare, 119–20
  policies and services, content pertaining to, 85–86
  response system, 255–56; *see also* Agency
Social work
  activities, 9, 11, 13–14, 21, 513
  assignment for profession, 21–24
  central focus of, 6–9
  as client-worker relationship, 514
  clinical orientation of, 8
  conceptual organization of social work activities, traditional, 9–14
  curriculum, 84–88
  defined, 6–7
  development of knowledge and theory in, 54
  education for, 56, 255
  essential characteristics of, 25
  function, 7–8, 22, 24–25
  function, common components of, 24
  function, mediating, of, 16
  as human service profession, 2
  humanitarian tradition of, 132
  intervention, focus of, 5–17
  job assessment of, 5
  knowledge, defining scope of, 57
  knowledge, sources and functions of, 50–74
  knowledge base of, 53
  mediating model of, 5–6, 17–37
  micro-macro model of, 12–13
  organic model of, 21–23
  philosophy of, 105, 127–29
  principles of, 134
  processes of, 66, 238–39
  as rational process, 514
  skill, concepts of, 320
  skill, levels of, 14
  social orientations of, 8

Social work—*Cont.*
  social problem model of, 13–14
  sources of strain in, 490
  students view, 516–19
  target of, 6–9
  theory of, 255
  as a third force, 25
  traditional model of, 9–11
  types of, 142
"Social Work with Groups," 141
Social work practice, 2
  artistic components of, 37
  common elements of, 20
  components, 21
  content pertaining to, 87–88
  defined, 6, 51
  focus of, 513
  framework of, 333
  purposes of, 6
  target of, 7
  values in, 102–16
Social work practitioner, 426
  activity of, 20, 22
  as administrative ombudsman, 332
  as advocate, 371–81
  agency-mindedness of, as barrier to
      teamwork, 457
  as agent of client, 13, 110–11, 172–74
  as agent of community, 172–73
  as agent of society, 13, 111
  as artist, 37
  attributes of, 505
  boundaries of helping ability, 285–86
  central problems for, 37
  as change agent, 8, 198
  and client interaction, 23, 292, 518
  as client partner, 236, 514
  commitment and obligation of, 152
  defensive processes of, 445
  as dogmatic, 182
  ethnocentrism of, 219
  as expert, 514
  field of interaction, 24
  input of, 111
  insensitivity of, 432
  narcissistic reaction of, 436
  personal investment, 34
  as problem solver, 233
  professional responsibility of, 113
  and race, 217–27
  responsibility of, 514
  responsiveness, 334
  as resource, 23
  revaluation of self, 32, 213
  roles of, 209
  self-determination of, 113–14
  as scientific practitioner, 132
  socialization of, 449

Social work practitioner—*Cont.*
  vision of, 35
  as welfare worker, 128
  "The Social Worker as Advocate: Cham-
      pion of Social Victims," 371–81
Socialization, 122, 270
Society, 118
  and race, 167
  racist, 163
Socioeconomic status, 523
  background, 216
  factor of, 245–48
Sociology, knowledge borrowed from, 56
Sociopolitical process in evaluative re-
      search, 411
"Soft" data, 417
Solution
  implementing an already-decided, 283
  as proposed by client, 300–301
Specht, Harry, 282–83
  article, 301–11
Specialization, 478
  in information or knowledge, 504
  as problem in understanding, 188
  as study of language, 188
Speech pathologist, 186
Spitzer, Kurt, 275
  article, 252–63
Staff development, 449
Standardization of tasks, 478
Stanford-Binet tasks, 184
State Board of Education, 185
Steady state, 65, 95, 272; *see also* Sys-
      tems, theory
Stereotypes, 156, 458
Stereotyping as barrier to communica-
      tion, 197
Strategies of change, 115, 505–7
Stress, 95, 513
Structure, 91
  as barrier to teamwork, 458
  constraints of, 482
  in group, 249
  for movement, 66
"A Student's View of Social Work,"
      516–22
Studt, Elliott, 333
Stutter, 182, 186, 189
Subcommittee to Revise the Working
      Definition of Social Work Practice,
      75
Subcultural barriers, difficulty of under-
      standing across, 223
Subsidy, government, 498
Subsystems, 247, 255
Suchman, Edward A., 413–14
Sullivan, Harry Stack, 135
Summation process, 236

Supervisor, 157, 451, 483
Symbiotic model, 24–25
Symbols, 156, 364
Symtomatic behavior, 246
Symptoms
  and cause, 185
  as cause, 186–87
  ignored, 186
  importance of, 186–87
  need to appreciate, 187
  overemphasized, 186
Synanon, 218
Systems, 99
  analysis of, 305
  approach of, 271–272
  approach to service delivery, 38–47
  boundaries of, 63
  change of, 94, 163
  closed, 63
  as conceptual model, 90–91, 99
  in constant change, 62
  consistency with definitions, 90
  definition of, 62, 91
  described, 62
  drawing, 93
  dynamic, 21–23
  dynamic equilibrium of, 65
  ecological approach, 38
  empirical approach, 38
  empirical reality and, 90
  energy of, 94
  and environment, 63
  feedback, as property of, 64–65
  as frame of reference, 91
  as goal directed, 65
  holistic view of, 272
  homestasis of, 65
  inertia of, 64
  input and output of, 63
  interdependence of components of, 272
  language of, 90
  levels of, "layering," 64
  living, 98
  maintenance of, 95
  as models, 92–100
  negative entropy of, 63
  open-properties of, 62–63, 99, 171
  person-situation in concept of, 517
  personalities as, 97
  perspective, 172–73
  predictive value of, 94
  relational, 9–10, 22–23
  semiclosed, 96
  small groups as, 27–28
  of society, 23
  stability of, 508
  static, 65
  steady state of, 65

Systems—*Cont.*
  tension in, 64
  theory, 50, 60–61, 66, 89, 91–94, 99,
    237–40, 265, 269, 271
  time as factor of, 91
  transaction, 10
"A Systems Approach to the Delivery of
  Mental Health Services in Black
  Ghettos," 38
Szasz, Thomas, 170

T

Taber, Merlin A., 8, 16
  article, 38–47
Tally's Corner, 223
Target of change, 282
Target system, 507–9
Task, 10
  accomplishment of, 242
  component of, 478
  collective, 478
  maturational, 97
  of organization, 249
  as organizing concept, 26
  of practitioner, 28–30, 36
  standardization of, 478
Teaching, as aspect of enabler role, 343
Team
  approach, 270
  member of, 448
Teamwork, 454
  barriers to interagency, 456
  central planning as aid to, 460
  community organization considerations
    in, 460
  concept of, 456
  defined, 450
  importance of, 455
  inservice training in support of, 460
  interagency, 456
  methods of sharing and planning,
    451–54
  nature of, 446–54
  overcoming obstacles to, 459
  principles of, 455
  problems of, 446
  problem solving, approach to, 450–51
  purpose of, 451
  requirements of, 451
  sharing with team members, 452
  stages of, 456
Technicians, social work, 128
Techniques
  of concretization and demonstration,
    270
  defined, 207
  discussed, 202–4

Techniques—*Cont.*
  elaboration of, 118
  overemphasis on, 128
  traditional, 376
Tension, 64
Tenure, 482, 493
Termination, 242, 422, 428–30, 435
  in action phase, 253
  as affected by earlier loss, 433
  with children, 442
  denial of, 430
  importance of, 441
  importance of process, 432–34
  indication for, 429
  major area of, 434
  as neglected dimension, 431–36
  phase of therapy, 444
  phases of, 434
  process analyzing, 437–38
  reasons for, 434–36
  tasks of, 429–30
  work of, 440
  worker-related reasons, 436
Theory, 53
  building of, 108
  differentiated from knowledge, 53
  general, of man, 54
  of operational procedures and skills,
    54
  of personality, 68
  of a profession's practice, 54
  relationship to goals, 417
  in social work literature, 52
  three levels of, 54
Therapeutic intervention, 98
  process, nature of, 125, 442
  productive period for work, 444
  regimen of, 125
  termination of relationship, 431
Therapist, 224
  ethnocentricity of, measured, 219
Thorndike, Edward, 189
Tillich, Paul, 105, 135
Time
  as affecting purpose, 145
  individualized limits of, 147
  as variable of relationship, 147
Timms, Noel, 146, 285, 313
Tinker, Katherine, 209
Toch, Hans, 107–8
Towle, Charlotte, 111
Transactional approach, 61
Transfer, 422–28
  and client feeling, 428
  entities in, 426
  new worker and, 427
  process of, 426
  and time of, 427

Transference, 270–71, 366, 435
Transmitting, defined, 194
Treatment
  conventional, 270
  differential, 267
  as distinguished from help, 268–69
  emphasis of, 98
  failures of, 267
  individualized, 267–68
  methods of, 128
  outcome, 125
  as particularized, 267
  plan of, 238
  termination of, 432
Trust
  of colleagues, 448–49
  defined, 154
  lie of, 176–77, 179
  reason for, 177
Truth, 53
  in psychotherapy, 180

U

Uncertainty and error, tolerance of, 273
Understanding, 233
  dogmatism as barrier to, 183
  improved by knowledge of language,
    189
  lack of immediate, 280
  partial, 182
  purpose of, 150
  from similar life experiences, 183
  verbal, 183
United States, 118
U.S. Supreme Court, 466
Untreatability, 128

V

Validity
  defined, 195
  of evaluative measures, 417
  of social relativity, 129
Values, 2, 102, 129, 133, 249
  assertions, criteria of, 82
  basic to social work practice, 74
  concrete, 105
  confusion of, 123
  defined, 51, 76, 103
  dilemmas, of, 102, 115, 117
  as element of social work practice, 74
  focus of, 82–83
  humanistic, and social work practice,
    127–37
  individual, 246
  internalization of, 449
  and knowledge; *see* Knowledge

Values—*Cont.*
  listed, 74
  in literature, 50
  orientation, 129
  paradox of, 118
  personal, 136, 246
  in practice of social work, 102
  premises of, in social work, 104, 114
  professional, 104, 136, 256, 259, 449
  remote, 105
  system of, 129, 246, 253
Vattano, Anthony, 8, 332
Vinter, Robert, 209, 494
Von Bertalanffy, Ludwig, 95–96

W

The Wall, 223
Wasserman, Harry, 482–83
Watson, James, 93

Waxenberg, Barbara, 219, 517
Weber, Max, 474, 493
Weiss, Carol, 224
Weissman, Harold, 475–76, 483–84
Welfare, public, 120–21
Welsh, Betty, 253, 275
Whitehead, Alfred North, 90
Wickenden, Elizabeth, 373
Wilensky, Harold L., 318, 475
Wilson, P. A., 321
Win-lose
  games, 447
  situations, 447
Witchcraft, 125
Worker *see* Social work practitioner

Y–Z

Yamamoto, Joe, 219
Zweig, Franklin, 256, 332

This book is set in 10 and 9 point Caledonia, leaded 2 points. Chapter numbers and titles are 18 point and 14 point Scotch Roman. Reading titles are 16 point Caledonia italic and reading authors are 11 point Caledonia Bold. The size of the type page is 27 × 45½ picas.